THE ISLE
OF MAN

PORTRAIT OF A NATION

THE ISLE OF MAN

PORTRAIT OF A NATION

JOHN GRIMSON

Foreword by

SIR MILES WALKER CBE, LLD (hc)

Chief Minister of the Isle of Man 1986–96

ROBERT HALE · LONDON

© John Grimson 2009
First published in Great Britain 2009
Paperback edition 2010

ISBN 978 0 7090 9002 1

Robert Hale Limited
Clerkenwell House
Clerkenwell Green
London EC1R 0HT

www.halebooks.com

2 4 6 8 10 9 7 5 3 1

Typeset by e-type, Liverpool
Printed in China and arranged by
New Era Printing Co Ltd, Hong Kong

CONTENTS

PICTURE CREDITS

All pictures by the author unless acknowledged otherwise.

LIST OF MAPS AND DIAGRAMS

LIST OF ABBREVIATIONS USED

BT	British Telecom
DAFF	Department of Agriculture, Fisheries and Forestry
DoE	Department of Education
DHSS	Department of Health & Social Security
DHA	Department of Home Affairs
DLGE	Department of Local Government & the Environment
DTL	Department of Tourism and Leisure
DTI	Department of Trade & Industry
DoT	Department of Transport
FSC	Financial Supervision Commission
IPA	Insurance & Pensions Authority
IRIS	Integration & Recycling of the Island's Sewage
MEA	Manx Electricity Authority
MER	Manx Electric Railway
MNH	Manx National Heritage
UK	United Kingdom
US[A]	United States [of America]

FOREWORD

I have great pleasure in writing this Foreword to *The Isle of Man: Portrait of a Nation*, the author of which I first met over thirty years ago.

There are a large number of publications which feature the Isle of Man, the majority of them being single-subject works. The reader will find that this book has a very wide coverage, which includes much historical information that the author has followed through to the present day.

In the last twenty-five years or so, our traditional and sleepy island has been wakened from its slumbers and is now a vibrant and exciting place to be. I am confident that its economic future is bright, that it will retain its natural beauty and that it will continue to provide a wonderfully safe environment in which to live and work.

The island community has skilfully retained its values. *Traa dy lioar*, or 'time enough', is a long-established Manx tradition. To blend that with the modern business requirements of being alert, professional and competitive has been quite difficult. To my relief and great pride, I believe we have embraced that challenge and I believe that the readers of this book will enjoy sharing the experience.

This *Portrait of a Nation* traces the island's development and provides for the reader an enjoyable experience of sharing the transition of which I have so enjoyed being a part.

Read and enjoy.

Sir Miles R. Walker CBE, LLD (hc)
Colby, Isle of Man

To the memory of my beloved wife,
who wandered with me
across the length and breadth of this isle.

PREFACE

I arrived in the Isle of Man in the first week of 1973, have never subsequently considered living anywhere else, and have been gathering material for this book ever since. (One does not like to rush these things.) But, with the passing of the years has come the realization that, if the book were to materialize at all, further procrastination would be tantamount to tempting fate – an open invitation to the grim reaper to intervene before the work was done. So, here it is.

In the early 1970s, the Isle of Man was a very different place from the island of today. The tourist industry – for so long a significant element of the Manx economy – was already in decline, although the island's roads in summer were still thronged with the cars of visitors. The financial sector – such an essential plank in the economy today – was barely into its infancy. In those days, before the establishment of the ministerial system of Manx government, the Finance Board of Tynwald was chaired by John (later Sir John) Bolton, the main architect of the radical changes in taxation policy which eventually led to the island's rise as an international financial centre, which – in the early days – was (and sometimes still is) referred to as a 'tax haven'. In 1976, the reins were taken over by Percy Radcliffe who, for the next five years, ensured that Bolton's foundation was soundly built upon. They were just two of the 'giants' at large in Manx politics at that time. Others were Charles (later Sir Charles) Kerruish, who – in one form or another – was a member of Tynwald from 1946 to 2000, Clifford Irving, Jack Nivison, Howard Simcocks and Victor Kneale. One could not possibly agree with all of them all of the time; their views were so diverse, and often controversial. But, agree with them or not, one could not but recognize them as respected and influential Manx politicians, who matured to become equally respected elder statesmen. They were giants to match those of the earlier twentieth century – Frederick Clucas, Percy Cowley, Ramsey Moore, Samuel Norris, Joseph Qualtrough and the rest, whose campaigns brought the island along the path of reform which has led us to today. They were giants of an ilk which seems strangely absent from the scene today.

Perhaps there is understandable reason for this. In those earlier times, the island laboured under feelings of thwarted ambition for self-determination and resentment towards successive United Kingdom governments at the failure to achieve that aim. Also, the very different economic and social conditions of those times brought pressing need for change and improvement within the isle. Such a climate undoubtedly fostered those political giants to rise to the occasion. Today, when the domestic scene is so improved and self-determination has been achieved – at least to the extent sought by successive Manx governments – perhaps conditions are no longer conducive to a rising of giants.

But this is not intended as a political history, although that is an essential part of the story. In the following pages, I have sought to tell of the changes which have influenced the island and its people, not just over the last half-century or so, but set in the wider context of the story of Man and the Manx from earliest times to the present day. It is a fascinating story, and I hope that I have done it justice. Also, in Part 2, I have set out to guide the reader on a tour of the island, through its historic towns, villages and parishes, and – on the way – have attempted to do justice to the island's natural beauty which, outside the expanded centres of population, remains much the same as it has always been. But, as far as natural beauty is concerned, the written word is no substitute for going out and seeing for oneself, and I hope that I have given a few tips on where to see the best of it.

Anyone writing a book of this nature is inevitably dependent on the work of those who have gone before, and I readily acknowledge my indebtedness to authors and researchers of earlier times, too numerous to list here but all named in the Bibliography. Thirty years ago, there were a handful of books in circulation which gave an all-round view of the Isle of Man for the general reader. Leading the way was A.W. Moore's two-volume classic *History of the Isle of Man*, published in 1900 and reprinted by the Manx Museum and National Trust in 1977. In later times came Robert Kinvig's *The Isle of Man* (first published in 1944 and revised in 1975) and E.H. Stenning's *Portrait of the Isle of Man*, which was an abridgement of his popular earlier volume published in Robert Hale's *County* series. Stenning's *Portrait* was first published in 1958 and revised by me for the last time in 1978. Since then, there has been a dearth of such books for the general, non-specialist reader, although the intervening period has been one of great change for the island. The recent initiative by the Liverpool University Press in embarking on the five-volume *New History of the Isle of Man* (of which two volumes have been published to date) is to be welcomed, although each of its volumes is more attuned to the interests of the specialist than to the lay reader. Hence, I hope that this volume will fill a need on the part of the general reader – whether resident of, or visitor to, the Isle of Man.

I must express my specific gratitude to Sir Miles Walker CBE, LLD (hc), who served the Isle of Man as its first Chief Minister for ten years from 1986, for his willingness to contribute the Foreword to this book. There are also two other people to whom I must express special thanks: Chris Grimson (my son) has been unstinting in his efforts as searcher of the web and reader of drafts and proofs.

Without his help, the gestation of this volume would have been far more traumatic than it was. My friend, Kit Arthurs, has also exercised her considerable talents in reading and error-spotting. And, finally, my thanks go to all those individuals who answered my queries on a wide variety of topics.

In the text, numbers in square brackets relate to works listed in the Bibliography.

John Grimson
Ramsey
2009

N

Point of Ayre

Rue Point   The Ayres

Smeale   A10   A16   Cranstal

A19   A17   Bride

A10   Andreas   A10

Jurby Head   Jurby

A13   Regaby

St Jude's   A9

A14   A17

The   Ramsey

Cronk

A10   The   Sulby   Lezayre

Curraghs   A3

Ballaugh   Gob-y-   Maughold Head

volley   A18   Maughold

Kirk   North   A2

Michael   A14   Barrule

Sulby R.   Corrany

Glen Auldyn   Manx Electric Railway

Snaefell   Port

Gob y Deigan   A4   A3   Cornaa

Sartfell   Beinn-   Dhoon

y-phott   Snaefell   Bulgham

St Patrick's Isle   Glen Helen   Mountain   Bay

R. Neb   Carraghan   Railway

Peel   A20   Colden   Laxey

Contrary Head   A1   Greeba

A27   Patrick   A30   St John's   Baldrine

Greeba   A18   Clay Head

Glen Maye   A1   Crosby   A23

Glen Vine   R. Glass   A2

Dalby   A36   A24   Union Mills   A21   Onchan

Foxdale   Kirk   A22   Port Groudle

Niarbyl Bay   Braddan   Douglas

South   A26   Braaid   A24

Barrule   St Mark's   A37   Douglas Head

Cronk ny   A3   Santon   A5

Arrey Laa   A25   Port Soderick

Fleshwick Bay   Carnanes   Silverburn   Isle of Man Steam Railway

A36   A27   Santon Head

Bradda Head   Colby   A7   Ballabeg

A5   Ballasalla

Port Erin   A3   A12

A31   Ronaldsway Airport

Cregneash   Port   Castletown   Derbyhaven

Calf Sound   St Mary

Spanish Head   Scarlett   Langness

Point

Calf of Man   Dreswick Point

Chicken Rock

TT Course	
Other main roads	
Railways	

0   Miles   4

0   km   6

Map of the Isle of Man

Introduction

THE ISLAND SETTING

It sits in the middle of the Irish Sea, confronted on the one side by 'the adjacent isle to the east' (Great Britain) and, on the other, by 'the adjacent isle to the west' (Ireland). But this does not give the whole picture; the Isle of Man is not merely confronted on two sides, for the island to the east conspires to encircle. The Lakeland hills of England may be strung along the eastern horizon, but it is the Scottish hills beyond Solway that jut out to glower down from the north, while, at somewhat greater distance, the coasts of north Wales and Anglesey present a similar confrontation from the south. Thus, access to the open Atlantic is restricted to two routes: the North Channel between Northern Ireland and south-west Scotland, and St George's Channel between south-east Ireland and south-west Wales.

However, it should not be assumed from this that the presence of those encircling landmasses ensures that the surface of the surrounding sea is enduringly calm and unruffled. Far from it; the adjacent isles may be near enough to be visible (on a clear day) but they are not close enough to provide much in the way of shelter. The western mass of Ireland may prevent the ingress of the long, high swells of the open Atlantic, but the Irish Sea is of sufficient dimensions to allow winter's storms to whip up the shorter, steeper waves which are significantly more discomforting to many a seaborne traveller.

But what of the island itself? Its craggy outline lies with its major axis aligned roughly north-east to south-west, measuring 30 miles in length by 11 at its widest, its bounds set by a coastline the length of which falls somewhat short of attaining its century and encloses a land area of some 221 square miles. Its highest summit, at 2,036 feet (621m), is Snaefell, which stands in the northern half of the spine of hills that slants across the length of the isle from North Barrule in the north-east to Bradda Head in the south-west and is cleft into two distinct portions by the central valley which slices across the island between Douglas and Peel. The nearest point on the surrounding landmasses is Burrow Head, in south-west

Scotland, lying 16 miles north of the Point of Ayre, whilst the nearest shores to west and east are both about 35 miles away.

In an island as small as this, the sea is never far away. Its encircling tides engender an awareness of an intimate presence such as cannot be experienced in the hinterlands of those larger islands that prescribe the bounds of the Irish Sea. Successive Manx generations have grown up with the shore and the hills as equal components of their island heritage. In the words of the island's long-revered national poet, T. E. Brown, their childhoods were 'care-pricked yet healed the while with balm of rock and sea'. And today, islander and visitor alike have come to appreciate that healing balm, seeking to smooth the furrowed brows of a hustling world in an isle where time seems to pass at a more leisurely pace.

In an island such as this, the coast plays a unique and definitive role. An island may lift its mountain peaks to the sky, or it may wallow flatly in the surrounding sea, according to the quirks of a thousand aeons of geological evolution. But, in its horizontal extent, to all points of the compass, it is defined precisely by its coastline and, while admitting to the long-term ravages of storm and tide, it is about as permanent a setting of bounds as it is possible to imagine. It is comfortingly stable in a world of rapid change. Not for islanders the chain of dots dripping from the cartographer's pen across some politically divided landscape. The sea is their frontier; it has always been so and, so far as can be foretold, it will always be so.

The Isle of Man is a child of the Cambrian Period of prehistory, the greater part of its rocky mass originating from sediments deposited on the bed of the primeval sea upwards of 500 million years ago. Subsequent violent convulsions of subterranean upheaval and mountain-folding lifted and twisted its rocks into the daylight, setting them fast in high, contorted strata far above the sea-bed where once they slept, to form that line of hills referred to above.

But, regardless of its earliest beginnings, rooted as it is, deep in its Cambrian bedrock, succeeding misty eras of prehistoric time have left the island with a widely varying geological make-up, and nowhere are those variations more clearly exposed to view than they are along the coast. To be sure, it is the Cambrian rocks – the Manx Slates – which predominate, canting steeply down from that highland spine to the coastal plains on either side, before plunging dizzily over the brinks of its east and western coasts. From Ballure in the north to the mouth of the Santon Burn, the Manx Slates reign supreme along the east coast and, from Spanish Head and the off-lying Calf of Man to St Patrick's Isle, they do the same in the west.

Nevertheless, it was the Carboniferous sediments of 300 million years ago which gave us the limestone ledges of the Castletown area, and the frozen outpourings of a long-dormant volcano stud the shore at Scarlett, on the western outskirts of the town. The sandstone deposits to the north of Peel were once thought to date from the same period, but more recent consensus seems to favour the Devonian, some 60–90 million years earlier. Much later still, the melting back of the glaciers at the end of the last Ice Age stranded vast quantities of sand, clay and gravel against the old pre-glacial coastline to leave the great northern plain above the level of the sea. And along the edges of that plain today, from Glen Mooar in the west and Ramsey in the east, mile after mile of eroded glacial till extend northward into solitude, to the wide and lonely expanses of the Ayres, to the long line of wind-blown dunes flanking their north-west shoulder, and out to the great modern storm-beach of shingle piled high around the northern extremity of the Point of Ayre.

Although the Manx bedrock dates back more than 500 million years, Man has been an island for less than 10,000 years. The earliest species of its post-glacial wildlife arrived by way of the land-bridge from Cumbria before the Irish Sea, swollen by the run-off from the melting icecaps, rose to sever the land-link for ever (or at least until the next glaciation). The first human arrivals of the Mesolithic (Middle Stone Age) came by the same route, and subsequent waves of settlers came over the water from Britain and Ireland, across the deepening shoals of the Irish Sea.

This new island also saw the arrival of ships from the Mediterranean, thrusting out new trade routes along the western seaboard of Europe and through the Irish Sea to Scandinavia and the Baltic. They came to the British Isles to load Irish copper and Cornish tin, and the Isle of Man, a convenient haven for shipping bound further north, had its contact with a civilization which much of mainland Britain never knew.

Over the course of many centuries, the initial Mesolithic settlers were followed by the first Neolithic (New Stone Age) farmers. Then followed further immigrations, of peoples bringing with them the secrets of new technologies: the people of the Bronze Age and the Iron-Age Celts. Strangely, the Romans never came; although they ruled over Britain for 400 years and clearly knew of the island's existence (they even named it), they appear to have passed it by. The Normans did not come either; by the time of the Conquest, the isle was firmly under Norse rule and would remain so until 1265, when suzerainty passed to Scotland for a time, and finally to England in 1333.

As successive waves of immigrants arrived in Man, they were inevitably determined to settle and farm the fertile coastal plains, either forcing the older inhabitants to eke out some kind of existence on the less-productive uplands or, as the Norse settlers of the ninth and tenth centuries appear to have done, establishing themselves among the pre-existing populace and (eventually, at least) achieving a state of peaceful co-existence, no doubt sustained by a fair degree of intermarriage. And, although the Norse immigrants brought with them their own language, it did not replace the existing vernacular; it was the Manx Gaelic (one of the Celtic languages) which survived the incursion. The offspring of a Norse man and a Celtic woman would have been brought up by the Gaelic-speaking woman; hence the language subsumed that of the Norse interloper.

Throughout the course of later centuries, as a consequence of the propensity for successive waves of new arrivals to settle in the prime areas of the coastal plains, all of the island's major centres of population have grown up on or near the coast. The four towns – Douglas (the modern capital), Castletown (the ancient capital), Peel and Ramsey – all developed around their harbours, as did three of the larger villages, Port St Mary, Port Erin and Laxey. Today, the only sizeable concentrations of population situated any significant distance from the coast are those located along the central valley, on or adjacent to the road between Douglas and Peel, and in the northern plain. Thus, some 60,000 of the island's 80,000 people are accommodated within the boundaries of the towns and villages, and extensive tracts of Man's coastal fringes and hinterland remain unsullied by urban development.

In the last two centuries, the island has seen the rise – and in many cases the fall – of industries: the growth of sea-borne trade and the herring fishery and the subsequent decline of the Manx-based fishing fleet; the quarrying of Castletown limestone and Peel sandstone for building – but, of course, all is of brick and concrete and glass today. It has seen the demise of the Manx mining industry, leaving its crumbling remains all but forgotten in some of the most unlikely and inaccessible corners of the island. And it has seen the growth of tourism, which now survives at a level far below those achieved during its heyday of the 1970s, and an increase in immigration which has boosted the expansion of the towns and villages. Light manufacturing industry has flourished, but now faces pressure from lower labour costs in countries elsewhere. Agriculture has seen some amalgamation to form larger farming units, but it produces less than one per cent of the national income. The resounding success story of the past forty years has been the development of the Isle of Man as a banking and financial centre, to the extent that it now accounts for almost forty per cent of national income. It is also a major source of employment and, as a result, the island has enjoyed historically low levels of unemployment.

A unique aspect of the island's political situation is its constitutional relationship with the United Kingdom. The Isle of Man is not, and never has been, a part of the United Kingdom; in formal terms, it is an internally self-governing Crown Dependency with its own parliament, Tynwald (from the Norse *Thingvollr*).

Legislative buildings, Douglas

Tynwald is responsible for enacting all internal legislation, whilst the UK government has responsibility for the island's defence, and for diplomatic representation and other services internationally, in return for which the Manx Treasury pays the UK government an annual multi-million-pound sum. Like the UK parliament, Tynwald is a bicameral assembly, the lower chamber being the House of Keys, and the upper the Legislative Council. Also like the UK parliament, the two chambers sit separately – *but* they also sit together as *Tynwald*. The story behind the name 'Keys' is convoluted and inconclusive and I leave it until later in the book.

   The head of state of the Isle of Man is the British monarch who, within the island, bears the title 'Lord of Man' and appoints a Lieutenant Governor as the Crown's representative. In formal terms, the Crown, via the Lieutenant Governor, is ultimately responsible for the island's good governance, and all Acts of Tynwald require Royal Assent. However, the role of the Lieutenant Governor in the day-today actualities of government has been much reduced in recent years.

The national emblem is the well-known 'Three Legs of Man', surmounting the motto: *Quocunque jeceris stabit* ('Whichever way you throw it, it will stand'). The route by which the three-legs symbol – the triskelion – reached the Isle of Man is unknown, but it made its first appearance here in about the thirteenth century. The Latin motto was a later addition. It is known that, up to 1246, the heraldic symbol of the Norse

The Three Legs of Man incorporated in the national emblem

kings of Man depicted a Viking ship, and so the adoption of the triskelion as the national emblem must have come subsequently. In earlier times, the symbol was known in Sicily (where it was adopted into the national emblem) and in India, where it was known, in Sanskrit, as the *svastika*, a symbol of well-being. In both of these cases, the legs were depicted running clockwise, 'following the sun' (in the northern hemisphere, at least). In contrast, the four legs of the Nazi swastika ran anti-clockwise (heralding the converse of well-being?).

A question which is frequently asked relates to the island's name – the Isle of Man; whence came that? It goes back a long way. Julius Caesar, following his brief forays into Britain in 55 and 54BC, named an island in the middle of the Irish Sea as *Mona*. Confusingly, the isle of Anglesey was also known as Mona and, in Welsh circles, is still known as *Ynys Mon*. In AD74, Pliny the Elder refers to the Isle of Man as *Monapia*, whilst, in about AD125, Ptolemy names it *Monaoida*, Paulus Orosius (*circa* AD400) gives it as *Menavia*, and the Irish monk Nennius (AD858) gives *Eubonia*. Then come the Irish form *Mannan*, the Welsh *Mannaw* and a reference in one of the Icelandic sagas to *Mon*. The earliest written form (or carved, to be precise) to be found in the island itself is on a tenth-century cross-slab (now housed inside the parish church of Kirk Michael) by the prolific Norse sculptor Gaut Bjornson, whose runic inscription makes the dubious claim that 'Gaut made this and all in *Maun*'.

The widely accepted interpretation is that all of these forms stem from the Latin *mons* (*cf* the Scots Gaelic *monadh* and the Welsh *mynydd*), which is suggestive of a mountainous landmass rising from the sea, and which seems to fit the situation. Manx folk today, when not using the island's formal name, will often refer to *Mannin*, *Vannin* or *Ellan Vannin*, the last of which is Manx Gaelic for 'Isle of Man'. Some people, conversely, prefer to think that the island was actually named after the mythological sea-god Manannan, who is the Celtic personification of the Roman Neptune and the Greek Poseidon. Part of the legend surrounding him gives him the appellation Manannan McLir ('Son of the Sea'). As a consequence of this, the island is also sometimes referred to as 'Manannan's Isle'.

Manx Gaelic is taught in some schools and in adult classes but the language has long-since departed from everyday use.

Before bringing this introduction to a close, I feel that I should offer two words of caution to new arrivals in Man: the two words are 'mainland' and 'comeover'. As to the first, Manx folk tend to find references to Great Britain as 'the mainland' more than a little irksome. To islanders, the mainland is continental Europe; hence my reference in the opening paragraph to 'the adjacent isle' – far more acceptable and geographically accurate.

As to the second word, 'comeover' is the term used to identify a person who lives in the island but was not born here. To a limited extent, it is comparable with 'overner', which is encountered in the Isle of Wight. The not-so-subtle difference between the two lies in the fact that an 'overner' in Wight is someone who lives 'over there', whereas a 'comeover' in Man is a person who used to live 'over there' but now lives 'over here'. The term is rarely used in an unkindly way, and is perhaps not heard so much as it once was, but it is still to be heard. At the last census, around 52 per cent of the island's population were not of Manx birth. Some islanders express concern at this situation, and at the overall size of the population but, in a land as small as this, periodic infusions of new blood are essential, both for the good of the modern economy of the island and for the health of its people. It has been going on for thousands of years and, if one thinks back across those years, to the end of the last Ice Age, when no-one was living here, one is forced to the realization that *all* of our ancestors were once comeovers.

Thus we have this island of just over 80,000 inhabitants, occupying a land area of 221 square miles, giving an overall population density of 362 per square mile. This compares with a figure of 181 per square mile for the predominately rural county of Cumbria to the east, and 828 per square mile for the whole of England and Wales. But the island's overall figure gives no impression of the variations in population density in various parts of the isle, since four-fifths of the population is accommodated in the towns and villages. It follows that large tracts of the island's landmass remain gloriously empty. Approximately two-thirds of the island is under cultivation; much of it provides ideal walking country, particularly along the coastal fringes and in the central highlands, and is well served with public rights of way. There are also ample opportunities for the sporting fisherman to follow his bent in the island's well-stocked reservoirs and rivers, provided that he has obtained the necessary licence.

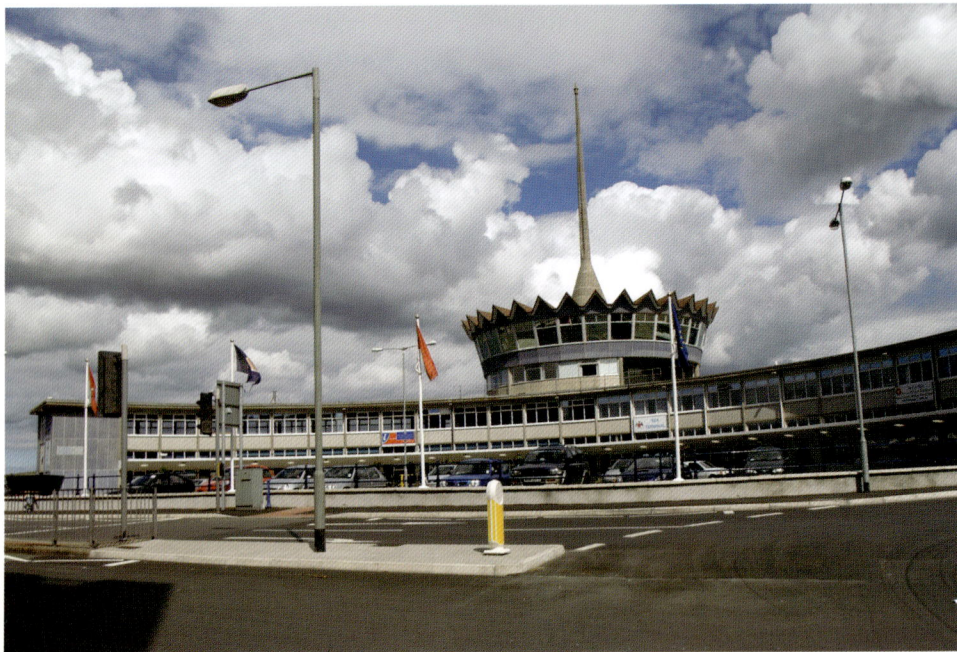

Two ports of entry: (above) Douglas Sea Terminal; (below) Ronaldsway Airport

At the other end of the decibel scale, motorcycling enthusiasts descend on the island in their thousands for the Isle of Man TT races during two weeks of late May/early June, the Southern 100 races in July, and the Manx Grand Prix races in late August/early September. During those periods, the ferries of the Isle of Man Steam Packet Company are kept busy operating shuttle services between Douglas and the ports of Heysham, Liverpool, Belfast and Dublin. For those visitors not bringing vehicles with them, air services are available between Ronaldsway and several UK airports, including Belfast, Birmingham, Liverpool, London Gatwick and Manchester, as well as to Dublin. Motor cycling has a large following in the island but many of those residents who are not enthusiasts elect to go away on holiday during those periods.

Once the leather-clad hordes have departed, the island reverts to its habitual air of peaceful, easy-going calm, and it is easy to be lulled into the unhurried approach to life of the Manx folk of old (which still survives), whose self-employed artisans, when debating whether to start another job today or leave it until tomorrow, would murmur to themselves: 'Traa dy liooar' ('There's time enough') and head for home, not infrequently with a quick call at the pub on the way.

Located at the centre of the British Isles, just north of the fifty-fourth parallel and 4½ degrees west of the Greenwich meridian, the island lies in the same time zone as the United Kingdom and follows the UK practice of advancing the clocks one hour to British Summer Time each year. However, those 4½ degrees of westing result in the sun rising some 18 minutes later than it does on the Greenwich meridian, and so any local event which manages to start within a quarter of an hour of scheduled time is said to be 'over-punctual'.

The distances by sea to the various ferry ports in the adjacent islands are: Heysham 66 miles (107km), Liverpool 82 miles (132km), Belfast 90 miles (145km) and Dublin 96 miles (154km). Distances by air to the Irish destinations are some-what shorter because they do not have to go round the island. Of the other main airline destinations, Manchester is 109 miles (176km) away, Birmingham 167 miles (269km) and London 254 miles (408km).

In our present state of reliance on the motor car, visitors and newcomers to the island are often prone to view as much of it as can be seen from the road and then head for home, believing that they have seen it all; this is a pity, for they are missing much of what the island has to offer. The landscapes of Man present a microcosm of much of what can only be seen in those adjacent isles by travelling far longer distances. We may not possess the high, rugged peaks of the Scottish Highlands, the English Lake District or Snowdonia, or their lochs and lakes, but, reaching down from our lower, more rounded hills, there are broad expanses of highland heather-moor, of curragh wetlands still drying out after the post-glacial melt from the last Ice Age, and dramatic coastal scenes of impregnable rock-cliffs,

of eroding glacial till, with raised beaches and storm beaches and even a few areas
of salt marsh; and all of this in an island extending no more than 30 miles by 11.

Much of this lies (mercifully) beyond the reach of the motor car. In order truly
to 'see it all', it is necessary to make the ultimate sacrifice: to park the car occasionally and take to one's own two feet. And it is only on doing so that one realizes
that it is not such a sacrifice after all, for the returns far outweigh the meagre
debits of energy expended in achieving the goal. It is worth a modicum of healthy
physical effort to experience that healing balm of rock and sea.

PART 1

THE ISLAND AND
ITS PEOPLE

CHAPTER ONE

Geological Origins

As alluded to in the Introduction, the oldest rocks in the geology of Man are the Manx Slates, which form the bulk of the island's mass and originate from sediments deposited on the bed of a young, evolving ocean. Solidifying under the pressures imposed by later, overlying depositions, and subjected to intense deformation during the Caledonian mountain-building phase, much of their mass was thrust high above the level of the sea, thereby ensuring that any later sedimentation would be confined to those areas which remained at or below sea level, that is largely to those areas which today form the island's coastal plains. The only significant later geological events to disturb the peace of the high-lying slates (other than erosion by weather and the much later glaciations) were igneous intrusions – mainly of granite – and, later still, metal-bearing intrusions in numerous locations across the slate massif.

THE MANX SLATES

The Manx Slates are most closely related to the Skiddaw Slates of the Cumbrian Lake District, and were formed from mud and clay-like sediments deposited on the sea-bed at around the same time, in the late Cambrian and early Ordovician periods, from approximately 500 million years ago. The sea-bed in question was that which lay at the bottom of a long oceanic trench which extended from Norway, through north-west Britain and Ireland, and out to the eastern edge of what is now North America, which then lay much closer to the European land-mass than it does today. These deposits had attained thicknesses of many thousands of feet and had become densely consolidated under the resulting pressure by the time the embryonic ocean began to close due to the inward movement of the tectonic plates on either side.

Distorted strata in Manx slate

By the beginning of the Silurian period, some 435 million years ago, the closure was complete and the pressure between the plates built up; the Caledonian mountain-building phase was under way. The Manx Slates, like those of the Skiddaw group and north-west Ireland, and those in eastern North America, were crumpled and deformed and thrust high above the level of the sea, to lie on an alignment from north-east to south-west. (In North America, these movements raised the Appalachian Mountains aloft.) After such severe deformation, the resulting material is more of a shale than what the builder would regard as slate; it does not cleave cleanly enough to be readily usable as roofing slate (unlike Welsh slate).

The slates have been extensively quarried in the past, even though they do not make good building stone, being quite difficult to work down into suitable and uniform block sizes. Consequently, slate-built walls usually take on the appearance of a 'random' structure, rather than that of formal brick or blockwork. However, some impressive examples of the use of Manx slate in building can be found, where long lengths have been used as structural beams and flooring slabs, as, for example, in Castle Rushen, in Castletown. It is also common to find such a beam acting as a lintel in the structure of the most modest traditional Manx cottage, where it will be built in to the front wall of the cottage, passing over the top of the large open fireplace (the *chiollagh*) and on through the building to reach its second resting place in the rear wall – and, in between, carrying the full weight of the structure above it.

One further consequence of the violent folding undergone during the mountain-raising process was that the slate strata became extensively cracked and fractured, opening the way for upward intrusions of molten igneous material from deep inside the Earth. These intrusions would cool and solidify to form the

Period

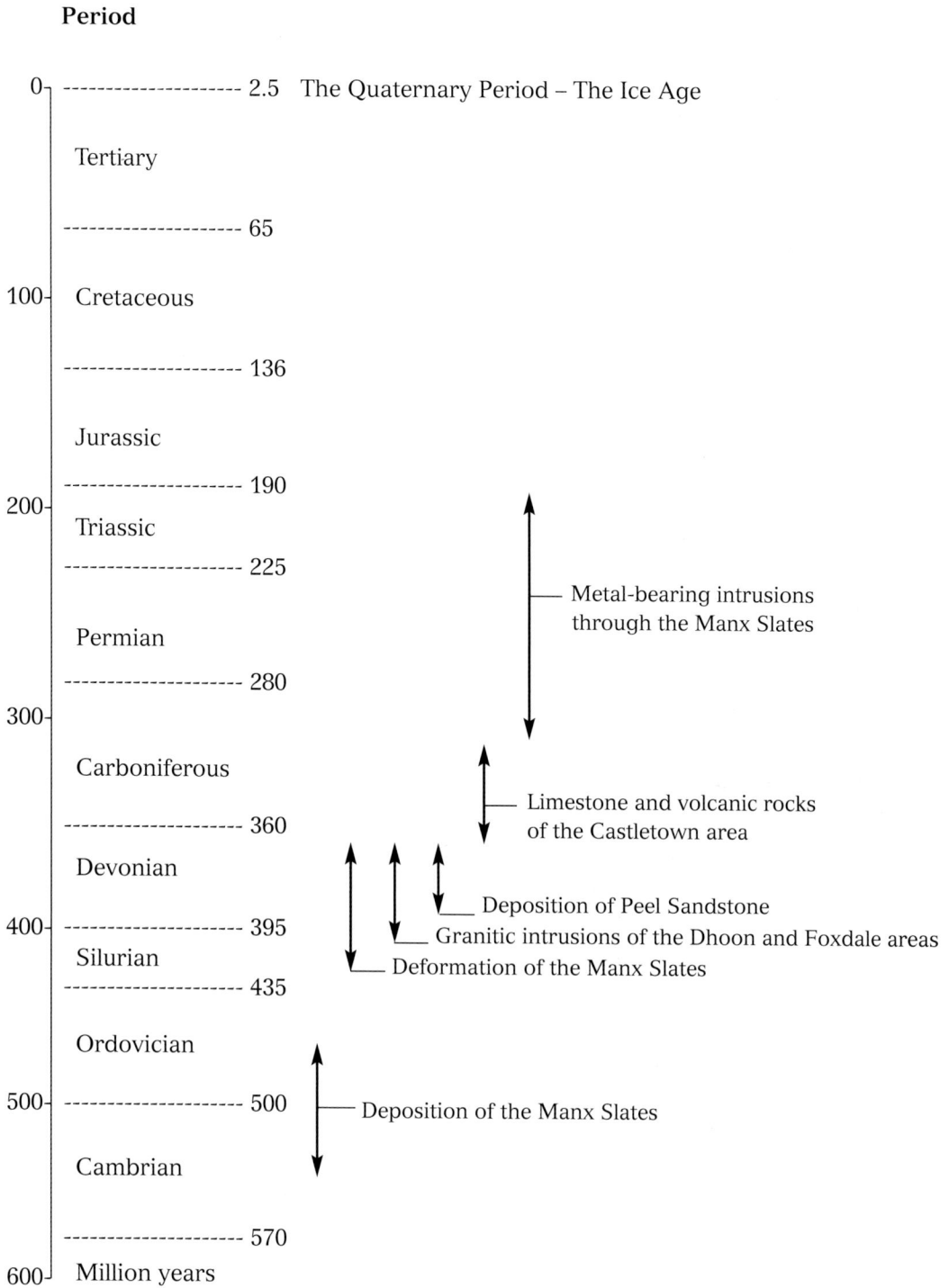

The Sequence of Geological Events

granites of Oatlands (in Santon), Stoney Mountain (Foxdale) and Dhoon (Maughold), as well as the gabbro of Poortown. The original slates in the vicinity of these outpourings were metamorphosed into modified forms by the thermal shock induced by the molten intrusions. The granites have been extensively quarried over the years, and the gabbro of Poortown is now the island's principal source of roadstone.

During the succeeding Devonian Period (360–395 million years ago), the mountains resulting from the Caledonian upheaval were heavily eroded. Under the action of water and frost, the slates readily break down into thin flakes, and subsequently into finer material, which eventually forms a covering of soil. Consequently, the Manx hills are rounded or angular and are undoubtedly lower than they once were. The island has no equivalent of the craggy Borrowdale Volcanics of the Cumbrian Lake District. The Manx uplands provide ideal terrain for the hill-walker but the rock-climber must exercise his skills elsewhere, perhaps on the more testing rocky sea-cliffs that fringe so much of the island's mass; the area around the Sugarloaf and the Chasms, near Cregneash, is a favoured spot.

The occurrence of the igneous metal-bearing intrusions through the slates began much later than the granite outcrops. It was in the mid-Carboniferous period, perhaps 300 million years ago, that metal-bearing issues began to penetrate through the slates. The greatest concentrations were located in the north-east, the south-central highlands and the far south-west. Various of the veins were rich in lead, zinc and silver, whilst others contained significant amounts of copper and iron. These deposits formed the basis of a once-bustling mining industry which has long-since expired.

Geologists detect structural differences between the slates in various parts of the island, and between the various granite outcrops, but, since this is not a textbook on geology, these differences need not concern us here.

THE PEEL SANDSTONE

The red sandstone of Peel is exposed in the cliff-faces extending for about a mile and a half to the north of the town. It undoubtedly extends inland but its extent is obscured by a covering of glacial drift. The sediments from which the sandstone was formed were deposited after the Caledonian upheaval, and so its strata retain a relatively ordered structure. Its age has been the subject of much debate over the years; modern assessment places its origins in the Devonian Period (360–395 million years ago), after the Caledonian mountain-building but before the deposit of Carboniferous limestone in the Castletown area.

Peel sandstone (used to frame these openings) is the island's only freestone but weathers badly

   The old part of Peel today shows much evidence of the use of the local sand-stone as a building material, the most prominent examples being on St Patrick's Isle, where the thirteenth-century cathedral stands roofless within the curtain wall of the castle, overlooking the entrance to the harbour.

THE LIMESTONE AND VOLCANICS OF THE SOUTH-EAST

The Carboniferous Period lasted for 80 million years (280–360 million years ago), and it was during that period that the limestone deposits of the island's south-east corner were laid down. The supra-marine exposures of limestone today are bounded in the south and east by an exceedingly irregularly shaped coastline, and

Point of Ayre

Raised Beach

Lough Cranstal

Lhen

Moraine Deposits

Glacial Till

Killane R
R Dhoo
(Ballaugh R)

Curragh

Alluvial Fan
RAMSEY

Sulby R

Alluvial Fans

Kirk Michael
Glen Wyllin
Glen Mooar

N Barrule

Snaefell

Dhoon
Granite

Peel Sandstone

Poortown
Gabbro

Manx Slates

Foxdale
Granite

S Barrule

DOUGLAS

Castletown
Limestone

Calf of Man

Scarlett
Volcanic Formation

• Chicken rock

0   1   2   3   4   5   6 miles

0   5   10 km

	Raised Beach
	Moraine Deposits
	Glacial Till
	Alluvial Fan
	Carboniferous Limestone
	Devonian Sandstone
	Manx Slates
	Granitic Intrusions
	Mineral Veins

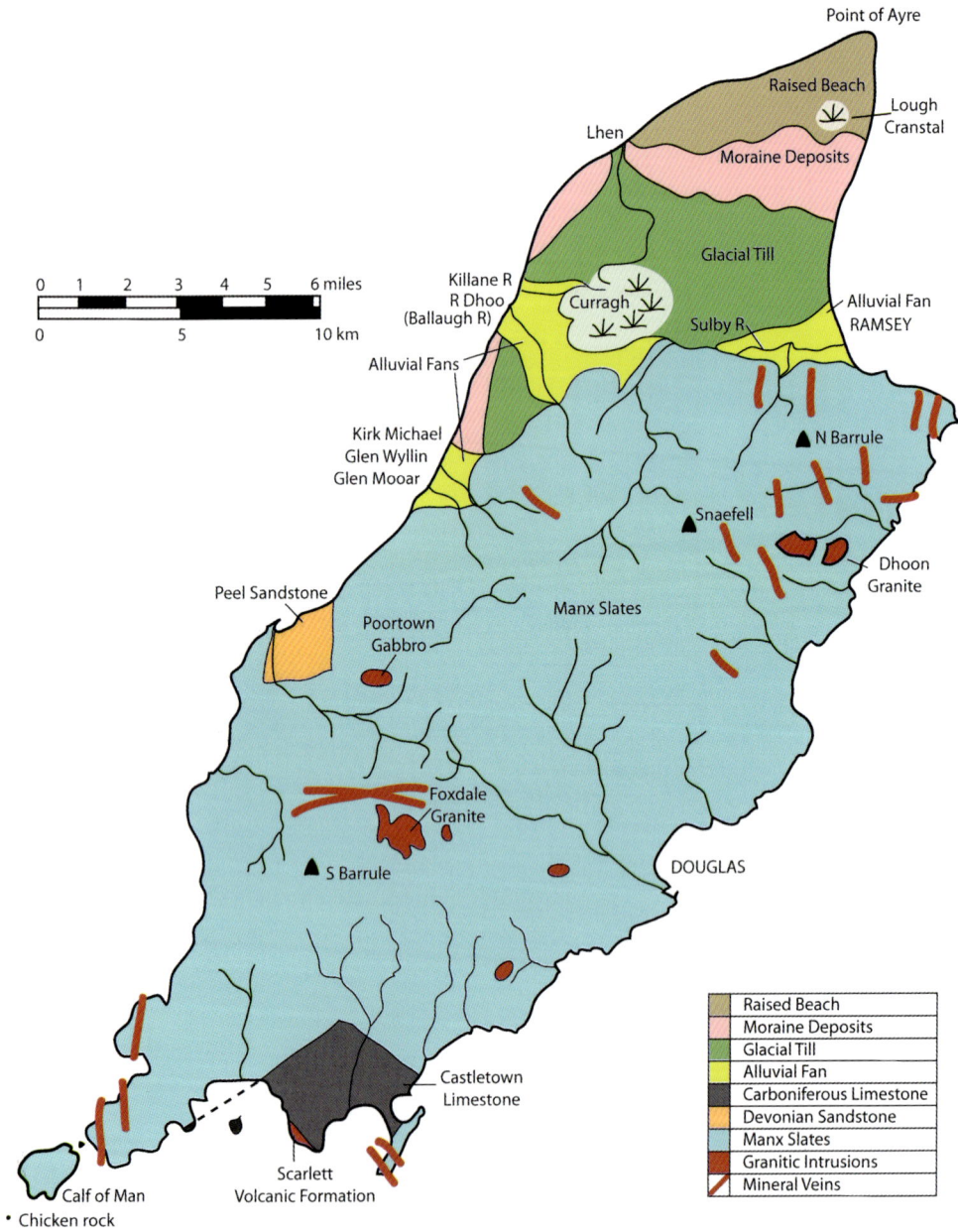

Geology of the Isle of Man

in the north-west and north-east by two contrastingly straight geological faults. The north-western fault-line passes through Kallow Point, at Port St Mary, and strikes north-eastward under Bay ny Carrickey, coming ashore again at the eastern end of Black Rocks and continuing its straight line inland to Ballakewin, where the A3 Castletown–St John's road passes the head of Silverdale Glen. At Ballakewin, it meets the north-eastern fault, which lines out to the south-east to reach the coast at the mouth of the Santon river gorge.

The layout of the fault system, and the fact that the limestone deposits cease abruptly at the fault-lines, suggest that, when the faulting occurred, the land enclosed within the fault-lines subsided, allowing the sea to flood in and the lime-stone sediments to be deposited. The sedimentation almost certainly occurred in a shallow-water environment, as indicated by the presence of wave-generated ripples in the surfaces of the coastal ledges, particularly to the north of Derbyhaven. Numerous fault-lines also cut through the limestone ledges that fringe the shore.

Dividing this limestone coast into two halves, and separating the twin bays of Derbyhaven and Castletown Bay, lies the low, 2-mile peninsula of Langness, an off-lying sliver of slate connected to the 'mainland' by an even lower isthmus of limestone and conglomerate which, were it not for the storm-tossed accumula-tions of shingle and blown sand topping it, would be awash at high tide, making Langness an island. To the north and west of Langness, the limestone resumes its dominance of the coastal scene towards Castletown and beyond to Scarlett Point. Between the town and the Point, evidence of faulting through the limestone ledges becomes more frequent and, at Scarlett Point itself, we see the reason for the intensified faulting; for there, just offshore but connected to it at low tide, stands the dominant form of the Stack. This near-vertical columnar formation of volcanic basalt stands in marked contrast to the horizontal layering of the ledges that lie adjacent; its structure of conjoined columns is similar in form to that of the Giant's Causeway in County Antrim, but less perfect in form. The shore to the west is of volcanic ash cemented by later outpourings of lava from volcanic activity which may have been centred somewhere in the sea to the south, and the surface of the rock today is pitted and pock-marked where bubbles of gas and steam escaped from the pasty magma before it solidified.

Barely half a mile north-west, the limestone returns to the coast, only here, at Poyllvaaish, it is a black limestone shale, which was metamorphosed by the intense heat of the adjacent volcanic activity. Because of its ability to take a fine, polished finish, it is often referred to as 'Poyllvaaish marble'; it is still quarried and has for many years been in demand for ornamental work, such as gravestones and fireplaces but, in outdoor situations, its surface deteriorates badly through weathering. Stone from Poyllvaaish was used for the original steps of St Paul's

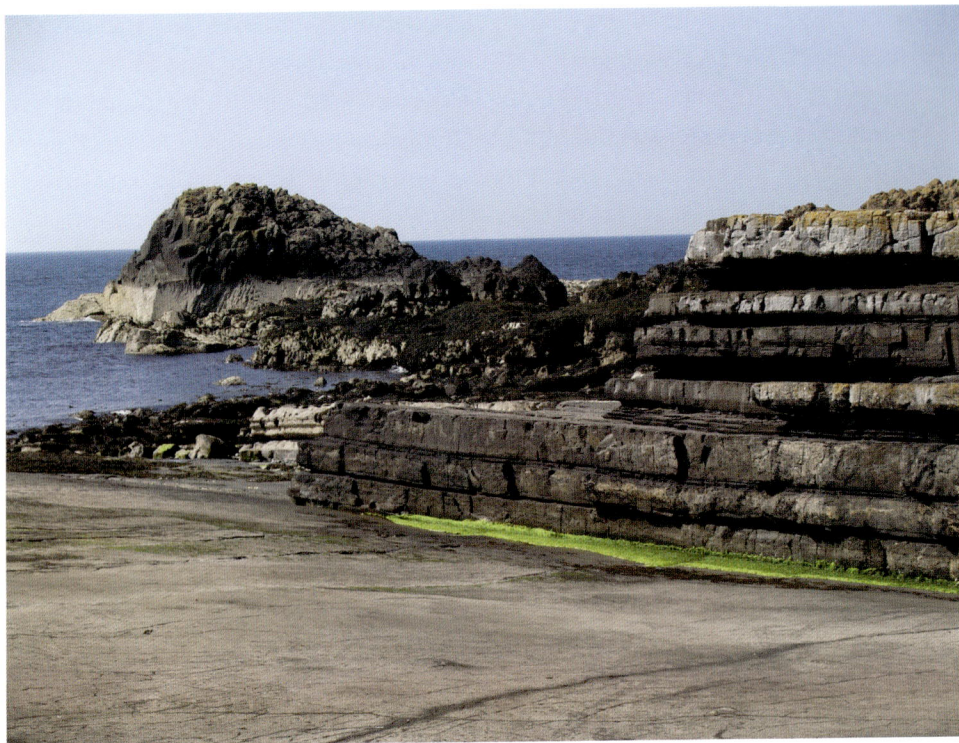

Scarlett: the Stack erupts beyond the limestone ledges

Cathedral but they became weathered and worn to such an extent that they had to be replaced with something more durable.

In addition to the Poyllvaaish working, the limestone formations of the south-east have been quarried extensively over the years. Its use as building stone is plain to see in much of old Castletown and in farm buildings and houses throughout the area; the outstanding example is Castle Rushen, whose stones are as sharp-edged now as they were when they were worked 800 years ago. The stone was also used in all of the island's harbour works. Limestone is still extracted in quarries around Billown and at Turkeylands, mainly for the production of agricultural lime.

Continuing north and west beyond Poyllvaaish, we eventually reach the Black Rocks and the final boundary fault of the limestone area where, apart from the brief resurgence on Kallow Point, the limestones abruptly give way to the ubiquitous Manx Slates. The area we have just left is probably the most fascinating of all in the hard-rock geology of the Isle of Man. The limestone is rich in fossils, many of them whole, others fractured in the volcanic upheavals. Although the supra-marine area containing them extends to barely 3 miles by 2, geologists have identified no fewer than five distinct variations of the limestone formation. The reader wishing for further details of these features will find some useful references in the Bibliography.

THE NORTHERN END IN PRE-GLACIAL TIMES

The events described thus far lead us to a picture of the island's form at the end of the Carboniferous Period, 280 million years ago. In the geology of the present above-water island, no further hard-rock formations are found. Thus, if we draw a line from Ramsey in the east, curving west through Sulby and round to Kirk Michael, that line must approximate closely to the island's northern coastline up to the onset of the Quaternary (glacial) Period, 2.5 million years ago. Along that line, the northern uplands end abruptly in a steep escarpment which sends the Manx Slates canting precipitately down beneath the present thick deposits of glacial drift and below the present sea level.

Boreholes have been sunk through the northern plain at various times, mainly in search of a continuation of the Cumbrian coalfield, but the coal measures appear not to stretch this far. But they did find salt in the Triassic marls underlying the glacial drift; the salt was extracted for a time in the early 1900s but the enterprise was commercially uneconomic and was discontinued. Beneath the saliferous marls lie strata of sandstone from the Permo-Triassic and Carboniferous periods, as well as limestones and shales from the Carboniferous, which rest on the underlying bedrock of Manx Slate. In the south of the northern plain, close to the pre-glacial coastline, the surface of the rock beneath the glacial drift lies some 200 feet (60m) below the present sea level, and slopes down to more than double that beneath the Point of Ayre, suggesting that, before the onset of the glaciations of the Quaternary Period, this was always a sub-marine feature.

THE LEGACY OF THE QUATERNARY

This brings us to the final chapter in the geological evolution of the Isle of Man: the sequence of glaciations that occupied much of the Quaternary Period, which began around 2.5 million years ago. The Quaternary Period is normally divided into two phases: the Pleistocene or Ice Age, which probably lasted two million years or more, and the Holocene or Recent, which runs from the end of the last glaciation to the present day. The number of major glaciations is generally taken as three, interspersed with warmer interglacial periods, each lasting for thousands of years.

The Isle of Man received its ice-sheets from the north, in the form of glaciers flowing down under gravity from the Scottish mountains. The most extensive geographical feature resulting from that period is the great northern plain, formed from the glacial till scraped up in the base layers of the ice-sheets, compacted against the foot of the old pre-glacial cliffs, and the continuing process steadily increasing the extent of deposition ever-further northward. The end result today is a plain which is roughly triangular in plan, its base occupying the full width of the island in the north (8 miles), with its apex (the Point of Ayre) 7 miles north of the original pre-glacial coastline. It is the largest single tract of fertile soil in the isle.

The northern plain is, as one would expect of a plain, essentially flat, apart from one notable feature – the Bride Hills, which completely span the plain from Shellag Point in the east (near the village of Bride) to Blue Point in the west. This formation would appear to mark the line where the final ice-sheet to reach the island (a minor resurgence following the melt of the third and last major glaciation) began to melt back, stranding its cargo of spoil where it lies today as a terminal moraine. According to Stenning [72], the exposures at its two coastal ends are among the grandest drift-cliffs in the British Isles.

The Late-glacial cliff-line at Blue Point

The Bride Hills span the Northern Plain beyond Ramsey

After this final melt-back of the ice, the island's northern coast lay along the northern foot of the Bride Hills; its line can still be seen as the steep escarpment in the glacial till which runs along the foot of the ridge. Later still, as the level of the land rose as it was relieved of the vast overburden of ice, the raised beach of the Ayres emerged from the sea, translating the coastline even further northward. We shall return to the northern plain in the next chapter, to discover how this large, flat expanse of land fared in the long, soggy period that followed the last big melt.

In the meantime, the glacial period left its mark in other parts of the island, both in the form of visible scrape-marks (striations) and in the deposition of 'erratics'. Erratics are rocks and other material that have been transported by the ice from one place to another and, to further understand the island's situation during this period, it is necessary to differentiate between 'local' erratics and 'foreign' erratics. Local erratics are those which have been transported from one part of the island to another, whereas foreign erratics have arrived in the island from elsewhere, invariably from the north.

Foreign erratics are found in the northern plain and the lowland fringes. Along the east coast, they are usually confined to altitudes below 70 feet (20m), whereas in the west the foreigners are found up to 600 feet (180m). These deposits include a range of identifiable types, including one which is unique to the rocky islet of Ailsa Craig, at the entrance to the Firth of Clyde.

Foreign erratics are not found at higher altitudes, although the island must have been overtopped by the major ice-sheets, as indicated by striations on the upland rocks and the drift of *local* erratics at higher levels. This has led to the conclusion that the foreign erratics were brought to Man in the lower, 'dirty' layers of an ice-sheet, to be deposited over the lower reaches of the island. The upper, 'clean' layers of the ice would then divide around and over the higher slopes, and any erratics transported would be local ones. This is particularly evident in the vicinities of the igneous deposits at Dhoon and South Barrule, where local materials were scraped up and trailed downstream for up to 6 miles, to the south and south-west, as the ice ground on its way.

Eventually, once the ice had melted back for the last time and the Ayres had risen from the sea, we were left with an isle whose shape was not too different from that which we see today, although we may conjecture that the northern plain would be somewhat broader (east–west) than today, since an unknown extent of coastal erosion must have occurred in the meantime. But it was a land whose uplands were shedding vast amounts of melt-water onto lowland soils already totally saturated and awash. It was a land recovering, and awaiting the return of life.

CHAPTER TWO

The Shaping of an Island

The latter part of the Quaternary Period, from the end of the last glaciation to the present day, is variously known as the Holocene, the
Flandrian or the Recent. I shall use the first name. Prior to the start of the
Quaternary, the last major glaciation through the Irish Sea (the Devensian)
reached as far south as the coastal regions of Pembrokeshire and County
Wexford. The transitional phase between the melting back of the Devensian
glaciation and the more temperate climatic conditions of the Holocene is often
referred to as the Late-glacial.

The final melt-back of the last ice-sheet from the Isle of Man has been dated
to around 15,000 years ago, a time when the sea level is thought to have been
some 200 feet (60m) below its present level. Since the present depths of water to
the east and north of the island are everywhere less than 90 feet (25m), it seems
certain that the land-link between the island and Cumbria would have remained
for a considerable period. To the west, however, the existence today of a submarine trench exceeding 350 feet (100m) in depth off the Irish coast suggests that
there would have been water separating Man and Ireland from the earliest phases
of the big thaw. The timing of the eventual inundation of the eastern land-link is
not known with any precision but it was probably overtaken by the rising sea level
within the last 10,000 years.

THE LATE-GLACIAL PHASE

As the ice melted and prodigious rates of run-off descended from the hills into the
already saturated lowlands, the routes by which it could negotiate its escape to the
sea depended critically on the location from which it was descending. More
specifically, it depended on whether the run-off was flowing into the northern
plain or elsewhere.

*(above) Laxey Glen, a
typical glacial valley; (left)
a typical water-cut valley
above Sulby Glen*

Let us consider the 'elsewhere' first. There is little doubt that, by the end of the last glaciation, the Manx highlands would have been scraped bare of much of their original soil cover, and the thin soils that remained would soon have been carried down into the lowlands by the run-off, there either to settle on the gentler gradients of the coastal plains or to be swept on into the various watercourses and beyond into the sea. The ability of the upland slopes to regain any appreciable soil cover would rely on the long, slow processes of rainfall, freeze and thaw, and the gradual emergence of primitive forms of flora, to break down the surface slates into some semblance of soil – all over again.

Lower down, the watercourses that are now the rivers Dhoo, Glass, Santon and Silver Burn in the south-east, Greeba, Neb and Rhenass in the west, Dhoo (Ballaugh), Sulby and Auldyn in the north, and Laxey in the east, must all have been conveying tumultuous flows from the hills compared with the meagre trickles they deliver today. Of all of these courses, only the upper section of the Laxey valley exhibits the characteristic U-shaped profile of a glacial valley, albeit with the V-shaped river-cut section in its base. Most of the others display, to varying degrees, the classic V-shaped section, although often disguised by layers of glacial till and alluvial deposits. Over time, erosion of these deposits progressively advanced along the valleys, and many of them display sequences of terraces marking this progression.

In the case of the north-flowing rivers, things were not that simple. In preglacial times, the Sulby and Auldyn Rivers would have made rapid descents along their water-cut courses through the steep escarpment that was the island's northern coast, there to make their unobstructed exits to the sea. Now, however, at the end of the last glaciation, their outfalls could not have been more obstructed, for there lay this great expanse of sand, clay and gravel which had been compacted by the glaciers hard against the east–west run of the old coast-line. This spoil was already saturated by the prodigious amounts of melt-water swept down from the highlands, and so the river-flows which continued to descend from above could do no more than spread out across the surface of the sodden soils that stretched before them. The result was the broad expanse of shallow water which, in later times, was named Lake Andreas and whose remaining vestige today is the Ballaugh *curragh*. The lake would have extended northward from the old coastline of the Manx Slates to the southern base of the Bride Hills.

The outfall of the Auldyn River was probably always sufficiently close to the north-east coast to find its outlet to the sea where Ramsey now stands. The Sulby, on the other hand (then, as now, the island's largest river), was attempting to exit in the middle of the glacial deposits, with no immediate way out. It is probable that, initially, it cut a way through the western end of the Bride Hills, where the

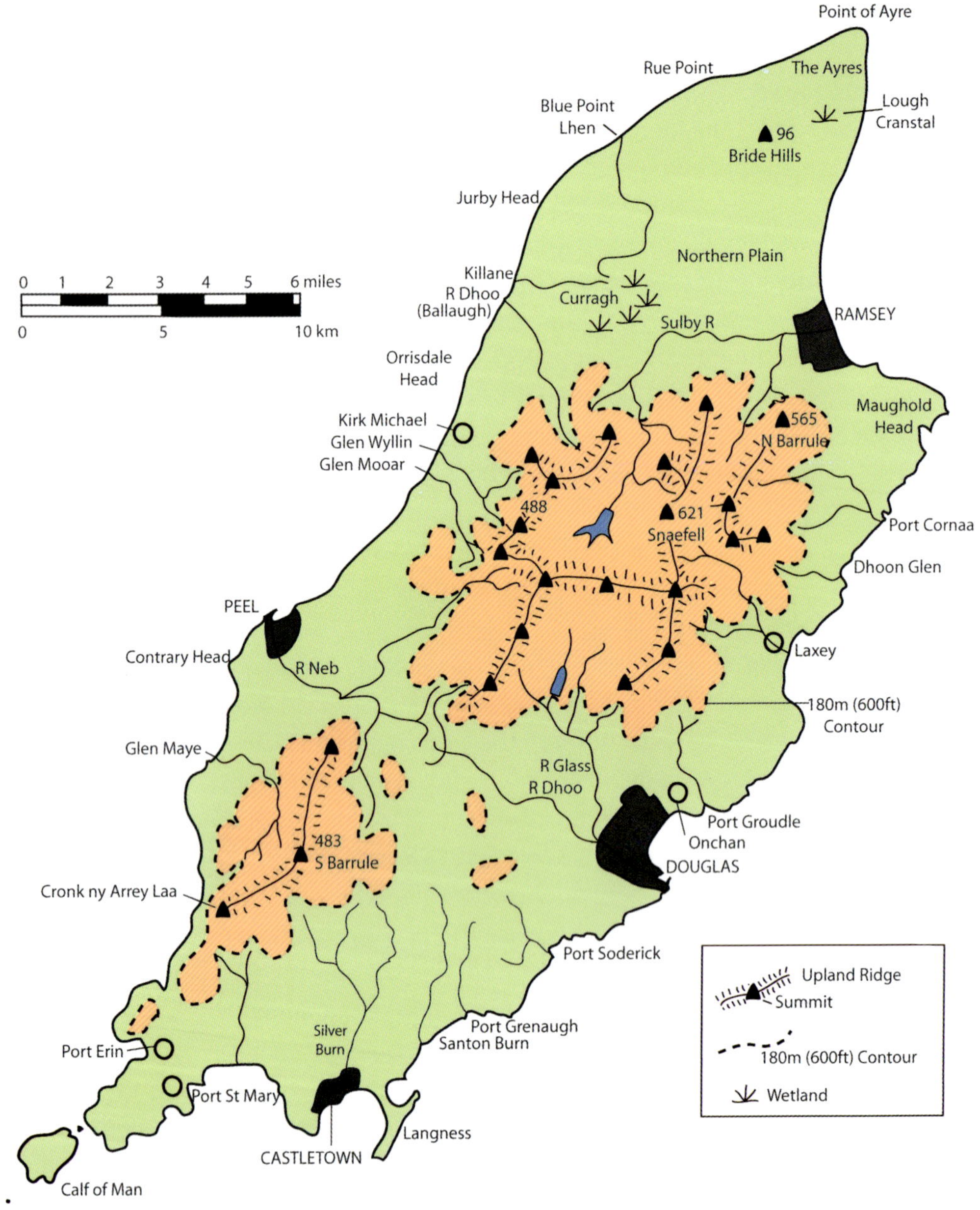

Point of Ayre

Rue Point

The Ayres

Lough Cranstal

Blue Point

Lhen

▲ 96
Bride Hills

Jurby Head

Northern Plain

RAMSEY

Killane
R Dhoo
(Ballaugh)

Curragh

Sulby R

Orrisdale Head

Maughold Head

Kirk Michael
Glen Wyllin
Glen Mooar

▲ 565
N Barrule

▲ 488

▲ 621
Snaefell

Port Cornaa

Dhoon Glen

PEEL

Contrary Head

R Neb

Laxey

180m (600ft)
Contour

Glen Maye

R Glass
R Dhoo

Port Groudle
Onchan

DOUGLAS

▲ 483
S Barrule

Cronk ny Arrey Laa

Port Soderick

Port Erin

Silver
Burn

Port Grenaugh
Santon Burn

Port St Mary

Langness

CASTLETOWN

Calf of Man

Upland Ridge
Summit

180m (600ft) Contour

Wetland

Natural Topography

Lhen now flows. However, it is likely that the great quantities of eroded till carried down by the river would, on arrival in the flatter contours of the plain, be deposited as an alluvial fan that would progressively block its further progress northward. Then, its only way out would be to the east, to link up with the Auldyn River and find its outfall where it does now, at Ramsey.

The drainage flows from Lake Andreas would then find their respective ways in three directions. The Lhen trench, although no longer collecting the flow of the Sulby River directly, was still connected to the lake and would continue to convey its water to the sea near Blue Point. The Killane River would flow westward to enter the sea north of Ballaugh. (Parts of the Killane and the Lhen have been realigned in more recent times and, at one point, lie only 200 yards apart, the former flowing west, the latter east.) And the Sulby, after its abrupt change of direction eastward, would continue to collect water from the south-eastern fringes of Lake Andreas on its way to the sea. The last remnant of the lake today, the Ballaugh curragh, continues to be subject to the 15,000-year drying-out process; photographs of the area taken in the early 1900s show much more water than is apparent today.

A smaller expanse of wetland remains still at the northern foot of the Bride Hills, in the form of Lough Cranstal. Its origin is uncertain but it may have been a lagoon left stranded in an area of poor drainage when the raised beach of the Ayres was elevated up to the north. During his extensive surveys which led to the present Geological Survey map of the Isle of Man, Lamplugh [46], around 1900, described the lough as 'drained to the condition of a waterlogged flat'. As the years have passed, the area has drained further, and the encroachment of vegetation and resulting siltation have undoubtedly reduced the extent of open water in the last century. But, at the time we are now considering, the beginning of the Late-glacial, vegetation had yet to reappear.

SIGNS OF LIFE

When a glacier melts, individual pockets or lenses of ice often become isolated beneath layers of rock debris, shielded from the sun's rays and remaining in the solid state long after the bulk of the glacier ice has gone. When one of these stranded ice-pockets eventually melts, the top-covering of debris subsides into the resulting void, forming a hollow in the ground which may range in size from several feet to several hundred feet across. Hollows formed in this way are known to geologists (for reasons best known to themselves) as 'kettle-holes'. They usually occur in soils offering poor drainage, and so begin their existence as water-filled

hollows. Subsequently, they receive deposits of clay and peat, as developing vegetation encroaches around the edges, and therein lies the importance of
kettle-holes to the palaeontologist, for they retain a record of plant-growth in their
localities.

Kettle-holes are numerous in the Isle of Man; the area that has been particularly productive to researchers has been the coastal region of Michael, Ballaugh
and Jurby. Among the finds retrieved in these locations have been layers of clay
containing bands of moss, organic silts for which radio-carbon analysis has given
a date of around 12,600 years ago, an upper layer of mud containing leaves from
arctic/alpine species such as mountain avens (*Dryas octopetala*) and least willow
(*Salix herbacea*) of 12,100 years ago, and younger organic deposits from 10,500
years ago. All of these plants (even the willows) would have been shrubs only
inches tall; it was still too early for woodland to have developed.

The earliest examples of fauna to be discovered in the island's exploratory
excavations have been those of the order *Coleoptera* (beetles) which, since they
are more mobile than plants, allow more precise determination of the timing of
climate changes. Of the numerous species (almost 200) turned up in Manx
diggings, many are now found only in the south of England and southern Europe,

A kettle-hole: the Bishop's Dub, near Bishopscourt

while others occur north of the Arctic Circle or at sufficiently high altitudes to find their preferred colder climate, giving clear indication of how extreme were the climate changes experienced in Man during the Late-glacial phase.

With the passage of time, as the climate warmed, the pollen record shows that the arctic tundra was taken over by expanding grasslands, interspersed with flowering shrubs and copses of birch, willow and hazel. The forest would later develop as a mix of these species with oak, lime and pine, and alder in the wetter areas. By the time of the first human arrivals, dense woodland covered most of the island, even to the tops. As has been pointed out by Pennington [66], deciduous forest cover in north-west England at that time extended to altitudes of 2,500 feet (750m) and, since Man was still land-linked to north-west England, there is no reason to suppose that the Manx situation was significantly different.

THE HOLOCENE PHASE

The end of the Late-glacial phase and the beginning of the Holocene brings us into the last 10,000 years. It also heralds the arrival of the first wave of human settlers of the Mesolithic (the Middle Stone Age), who had migrated across the still-dry land from what is now Cumbria. These people were hunters and gatherers, and probably exerted minimal environmental disturbance on this densely wooded isle. Their campsites are found in the coastal fringes and in areas where shallow soil deposits supported only sparse overgrowth.

However, humans were not the first mammals to reach Man; that distinction belongs to the so-called 'giant Irish elk', which was not an elk at all but a deer. Its correct Latin name is the magnificent-sounding *Megaloceras giganteous*, and it was in Man as early as the Late-glacial, the only mammal known to have been so. A fully grown specimen stood 6 feet (2m) tall at the shoulder, and the adult male displayed an antler formation fully 12 feet (4m) across. Several skeletons have been recovered and one near-perfect specimen is an exhibit in the Manx Museum in Douglas. *Giganteous* must have been in his element grazing the lush grasslands of Late-glacial Man, before the overgrowth of the forest. Most of the finds have been in the cliffs of Michael and Ballaugh and the coastal lowlands of the southeast, with a few in the northern plain, all areas which were probably still very wet, where the woodland was later in developing. But he must have been extinct before the arrival of the first humans; that huge antler-spread would have been wholly unmanageable in the forest.

The more temperate climate of the Holocene resulted in far more diversity in the range of mammals than thitherto. Red and roe deer were present but neither is here today; likewise the wild cat which was possibly a victim of the later defor-estation. With other mammals – rabbits, hares, hedgehogs, polecats, rats and mice – it is impossible to tell if they were in Man from earliest times or whether they are solely the result of later introductions, either intentional or accidental. Rabbits, for example, were introduced (but were they here earlier?), then polecats were intro-duced to control and harvest the rabbits (but were *they* here earlier?). In the recent past, unless bones were found in well-stratified and dateable deposits, the question remained intractable but, today, radio-carbon dating may provide some answers.

By around 5,000 years ago, people of the Neolithic (New Stone Age) were arriving in Man. It is probable that the land-link to the east had already been inun-dated by a rising sea level; Man *was* then an island and the new arrivals were venturing over the water. The principal difference between the Neolithics and their predecessors was that they were farmers; they needed land – *cleared* land – and they were equipped with stone axes to achieve that goal. The scene was set for the deforestation of Man.

This development is confirmed by a marked reduction in tree pollen around that time and the contemporaneous appearance of pollen from cereal crops, grass and weeds. In early post-glacial times, there would be pressures on upland areas for grazing because of poor drainage in much of the still-saturated lowlands. The clearance of woodland continued through the Bronze Age (c 1800–500BC) and into the Iron Age (c 500BC–AD500), not only to provide land for cropping and grazing, but also to provide timber for building and for the production of charcoal for the smelting of copper and tin, the alloying of bronze, and later for the smelting of iron. Writers in the early historical period are all agreed in their depictions of the island's treeless landscapes. By 1098, quality timber was in such short supply that, on his arrival in Man, Magnus Barefoot, King of Norway, had to import timber from Galloway for the building of fortifications.

THE UPLAND SCENE

The almost total removal of the island's forest cover has resulted in an upland scene today which is predominantly one of open moorland, its ground-cover largely of heathers, dwarf gorse and hill grasses such as the fescues, bents and matgrass. Herbs such as wood sage, heath bedstraw and tormentil are common, and *Sphagnum* and other mosses are widespread. Peat deposits have developed in many locations and exist in formations 10 feet (3m) or more in thickness in the northern hills. Peat was extensively dug for domestic fuel in the past, and some digging continues today (under licence) on the northern slopes of Beinn-y-Phott

('Pen-y-Pott'). Each licensee is allotted a 6-foot by 10-foot plot, on which digging may take place between 1 May and 30 June, and the dug turf must be removed from the site by 30 September.

Up to 150 years ago, grazing herds in the Manx hills would have comprised cattle, pigs, sheep and goats but, in 1860, political changes drastically affected common rights and resulted in marked changes in grazing patterns. The only free-ranging grazers in the island's uplands today are the sheep. For many years past, it has been common practice to burn areas of upland heath supposedly to improve the land for grazing. However, Dr Larch Garrad [28] contends that several researchers have shown the frequent firing of such areas to cause the heathers and gorse to become more dominant at the expense of the grasses and herbs that are the preferred feed for sheep. But the practice goes on; Garrad has questioned the degree of control exerted, and attributes the 'monotony' of the upland vegetation to a combination of prolonged over-grazing and repeated burning.

Official Department of Agriculture, Fisheries and Forestry (DAFF) policy is that regeneration of the heathland flora should be achieved by a combination of mechanical cutting and heath-burning, but, like Garrad, I am dubious as to how much of the former is actually undertaken. There are some 8,000 sheep on the hills at any one time, belonging to the tenant farmers who rent areas of heathland from the department. A hill-sheep subsidy is paid, the stated intention of which is to encourage low stocking levels and avoid overgrazing, but the question arises: does a subsidy achieve that aim? An interesting situation arises when a hill tenancy changes hands: it is customary for the new tenant to purchase the hill stock of the previous one, thus avoiding the tendency of the flock to 'home' back to its original area of moorland if any attempt is made to move it.

Shooting rights are also available in the hills, and some of the holders of these rights operate shooting syndicates, but there are no large-scale commercial shoots such as are found in the adjacent islands.

Although wind speeds over the hills are much higher than those at sea level, they do not greatly affect the plant species now growing there. The heathers and dwarf gorse are all low-growing species; they sit at the bottom of the boundary layer in the flow over the hills and their density of growth provides an environment of mutual shelter.

The 'monotony' of the moorland flora is relieved in places where shelter and soil depth are sufficient. Bracken (if one can think of bracken as a relief) is prominent on some lower slopes; it has spread greatly in recent years and is difficult to eradicate or control. More aesthetically pleasing, perhaps, where slopes are sufficiently steep to deter the sheep, growths of fern may be spread broadly across a hillside, most commonly the sweet mountain fern *Thelypteris oreopteris*. If the soil cover over the slate is fairly shallow, the wood rush *Luzula sylvatica* may crop out in abundance.

The flanks of Sulby Glen are host to a wide variety of flora. Its steep western slopes support a grassland rich in herbs; thyme, catsear, eyebright, harebell and sheepsbit all thrive amid a variety of grasses. The same glen exhibits massed carpets of bluebells in an impressive springtime display.

Elsewhere across the isle, wherever a secluded glen or gully provides sufficient shelter, remnants of ancient woodland are still to be found, some (perhaps) descended from the indigenous post-glacial forest species, others from more recent plantings of two or three centuries ago. Bishops Wilson and Hildesley are recorded as having planted a wide variety of species in the grounds of Bishopscourt, in the Michael lowlands, in the eighteenth century. Several private landowners followed suit. A notable example in the uplands is found along the single-track Druidale road, running between the B10 road at Brandywell, in Michael, and Ballaugh, where we find the ruin of a farmhouse at Montpelier (obviously an imported name), over-looked by a lovely 200-year-old plantation of beech which clothes the slopes that rise to the west. Many of the younger trees have grown as seedlings from the orig-inal stock but, with the area now open to grazing, the survival of newer seedlings is less likely. In the gullies that slice the hillside above the beeches, sheltered from the prevailing south-westerlies, mature rowan and ash flourish.

Sulby Glen in autumn colours

(above) The beechwoods of Montpelier thrive en masse, whilst (below) the beeches above Injebreck struggle in isolation

The beeches of Montpelier, exposed though they be to some fierce upland winds at the 1,000-foot (300m) contour, stand up well with the benefit of mutual shelter. To observe how more isolated trees suffer, we need travel little more than 2 miles from Montpelier, climbing back to the B10 and crossing it to follow the B22 until we come to a sad, solitary line of beeches flanking the roadside. These are the beeches of Injebreck, whose severely wind-pruned and stunted forms lean compliantly to the north-east; and yet, on the opposite side of the road, the massed ranks of a conifer plantation stand firm and true, as do the mixed stock of trees around Injebreck House, demonstrating how trees can thrive when they stand together.

Any major attempts at reafforesting before the First World War and between the wars were largely offset by subsequent felling to satisfy the war-time demand for timber. The first significant development towards reafforestation in recent times came in 1950, with the formation of the Isle of Man Forestry, Mines and Lands Board, now re-formed as the DAFF. In the years following its formation, the original board undertook plantings in many parts of the island, both in the uplands (but generally below the 1,000-foot (300m) contour) and in the lowlands and glens. Plantings have been mainly of conifers: sitka and Norway spruce, Scots and Corsican pine, *Pinus contorta* and Douglas fir. Japanese larch, being a deciduous conifer, brings a welcome variation of colour in winter. Several of the plantations are fringed with hardwoods and other deciduous stock to soften the view.

In the northern hills, the largest plantations are those overlooking Glen Dhoo (above Ballaugh), flanking the upper slopes of Sulby Glen and Glen Auldyn (near Ramsey), on the northern slopes of Beary Mountain (above St John's) and the Colden and Injebreck plantations. In the southern hills, the largest expanses are on the slopes flanking Glen Mooar and Glen Rushen (in Patrick), along the southern and eastern flanks of South Barrule and on Stoney Mountain (Foxdale) and nearby Archallagan.

Overlooking the central valley from the north is the Greeba Plantation, otherwise known as the King's Forest. During the rule of the Stanley family as Lords of Man (of which more in Chapter 5), the rulers claimed possession of the unenclosed uplands as constituting the King's Forest. 'Forest' in this context should not necessarily be assumed to refer to woodland; as in England during the same period, forests were areas outside the enclosures (from the Latin *foris*, meaning 'outside') and reserved mainly for the king's hunting. Tenant farmers regarded the forest as common land, and their rights to use the land for grazing and turf-cutting were recognized in statutes of 1417. Also, a tenant could be granted a licence to enclose part of the forest as an addition to his original holding; the addition was then known as *intack*.

In the years following the passing of the Revestment Act of 1765, under which the ownership of Man reverted to the British Crown (see Chapter 5), the grazing rights of tenant farmers on the upland 'forest' came under increasing pressure, and this became the cause of much unrest, leading to rioting in 1855. After protracted discussions between the Commissioners of Woods and Forests (representing the Crown) and representatives of the House of Keys, it was finally agreed that the commons would be divided equally between the landowners and the Crown. This was formalized by the passing of the Isle of Man Disafforesting Act of 1860. The last remaining areas of Crown land in the island have since become vested in the Isle of Man government, with the DAFF as the custodian of some 28,000 acres (11,000ha) of land, including extensive tracts of upland heath and more than fifty plantations.

When venturing above the 1,000-foot contour in the remoter regions of the island's heather moors, one may readily conclude that mammalian and bird life are thinly spread at these altitudes (apart, of course, from the ubiquitous sheep), and such a conclusion would be accurate. On a calm and windless day, it is possible to stand within these high, expansive tracts and experience the spell of ultimate stillness and total silence. Occasionally, the quiet may be shattered by the cackling of a red grouse as it flaps away into the fastness, or a solitary raven may glide high above, uttering its guttural croak as it goes; then the silence returns.

For the most part, upland mammals go about their business without creating much in the way of noise. Two varieties of hare exist in the island: the mountain hare *Lepus timidus*, descended from the Scottish mountain hare whose coat turns white in winter; and *Lepus hibernicus*, the brown Irish hare. Although there is some overlap of altitude in the habitats of the two varieties, the mountain hare ranges far and wide over the uplands, whereas the Irish species is more common lower down. In the eighteenth and early nineteenth centuries, packs of beagles were kept for hunting the hare. Rabbits, as mentioned earlier, are thought to have been introduced by man, although it is not known when, and they are common below the 1,000-foot line.

The main predator is the polecat-ferret. No evidence has been found of indigenous polecats, but ferrets of the dark polecat variety were brought in to hunt rabbits from the early sixteenth century onwards. Descendants of these, escapees that cross-bred with later introductions of the yellow ferret, are now common, both in the highlands and lower down.

Birds frequenting the higher slopes tend to be of the larger species. Choughs, although mainly birds of the sea-cliffs, may nest wherever they find a ruined building, such as that at Montpelier, and ravens will build on moorland crags or in trees at the heads of some of the remoter glens. The most populous of the crow family are the rooks and jackdaws, which also favour the wooded glens, as well as tree-groups in the lowlands, and jackdaws will also requisition any convenient ruin of a building. Hooded and carrion crows are about in some numbers, the former being the more common, especially in the lowlands. The curlew's questioning call may often be heard across these high acres. Sightings of the short-eared owl are sometimes reported at various elevations; my rare personal sightings have been in the coastal plain of Michael. The barn owl and the long-eared variety reside in smaller numbers.

Examples of sea-birds nesting at inland sites are found in the gull colonies on the slopes of Slieau Dhoo and Slieau Freoaghane, in Michael, where the herring gull and the great and lesser black-backed have been nesting since the 1920s. The most common bird of prey is the kestrel, which seems equally at home over the high moorlands and the lower slopes and meadows. The sparrowhawk is also resident in small numbers. The peregrine falcon appeared to go into terminal decline some years ago, and nesting numbers are now uncertain. The hen harrier is a regular winter visitor.

The resident game-bird population comprises red grouse, partridge and pheasant, with the first-named the most common on the high heaths.

THE LOWLANDS

The lowlands of Man were subject to a clearly defined system of land division long before the rule of the Stanley lords, and even prior to the Norse period. The units of land holdings, and the boundary hedges that delineated them, consolidated and extended through the periods of Norse and Stanley rule, remain largely intact today.

The *mountain hedge,* separating the arable land (generally below the 600-foot (180m) contour) from the rough grazing on the higher slopes, would have been a substantial feature from the earliest of those times, built in what we now accept as the traditional Manx fashion as a sod hedge of turf, soil and stones. By the sixteenth century, permanent boundary hedges were in place to separate adjacent farm holdings in the arable land, and there were strict regulations governing the minimum height and width of these barriers. (For details and for a wider description of early Manx agriculture, see Moore [57].) Where a farmer was granted the lord's permission to extend his holding beyond the mountain hedge, then additional hedging had to be raised to enclose the *intack.*

As will be seen from the description above, these were not live, growing hedges but distinctly solid structures. However, by the eighteenth century, it was becoming common practice to plant gorse and hawthorn along the tops of the sod hedges, both species being imported. At about the same time, some farmers were replacing hedges with dry-stone walls, and both are part of the lowland scene

The mountain wall meanders above Druidale

today. Gorse was also planted in the rough lands and used as winter feed for cattle and horses after being passed through a mill or crushed by hand in a stone trough.

The units of land division that have come down to us from those days are the *treen* and the *quarterland*. 'Treen' is a name of unknown meaning; its possible origin involves links with the Scottish islands which I explore in Chapter 4. The treen represents quite a small holding of land, ranging from 200 to 400 acres (up to 160ha); it was once of some importance as an administrative division but is totally out of use today.

The quarterland, on the other hand, is of Celtic origin and still in use today, particularly in defining the locations of parcels of land. Each treen was divided into four quarterlands, and the quarterland (*kerroo* in Manx Gaelic) was the traditional farm holding, of average size around 90 acres (36ha). Although some amalgamations have occurred in recent years, many a quarterland is still farmed as a single unit. If one has a house on land that was once farmland, one will (on trawling back far enough through the deeds) come to a reference to 'a parcel of land forming part of the Quarterland of ...'.

In times long gone, Manx farmers possessed a range of domesticated livestock breeds that were distinctively Manx, including cattle, pigs, sheep, goats and ponies, probably descended from those reared during the Celtic period or earlier. The cattle were small, dark-brown animals, hardy beasts but slow-growing, and the poor quality of the grazing did not help. By the late seventeenth century, rye-grass seed and clovers were being imported to improve the grazing, followed by the importation of improved livestock to take full advantage of it. This would herald the demise of the old Manx breed. Manx pigs were dark and hairy and roamed, half-feral, over the upper slopes. They, too, have vanished from the scene.

The sole survivor of the old Manx livestock breeds is the *loghtan* sheep, a distinctive creature in terms of both its coat and its headgear. Both sexes are horned, the tup displaying *four* long, curved horns, whilst the ewe possesses two shorter ones. The coat is reddish brown in colour and the meat is said to have a good flavour. The fact that similar sheep are found in other areas of Norse settlement, including the Scottish islands, raises the possibility that today's loghtans are descended from stock brought in by the Norse settlers. However, the quest for more productive modern breeds has resulted in the inevitable decline in the numbers of loghtan, now restricted to the flocks held by Manx National Heritage (MNH), the Ballaugh Curraghs Wildlife Park and a few private stockholders. What a pity it is that there was no MNH two or three centuries ago, so that we might have seen some of those old Manx cattle and pigs in the flesh.

At the same time as the island's grazing lands were being improved, the potato was being introduced and other root-crops were being cultivated. Barley, oats, rye and wheat were cropped; hemp was grown for rope-making, and flax for linen production. Agricultural lands were manured and limed, the lime being produced in kilns initially in the limestone country of the south-east, and later nearer to where the lime was to be used, the stone being shipped around the coast from the quarries of the south-east. Improvements in Manx agricultural practices mirrored those being introduced in England. Crop-rotation schemes were being followed and, after two or three croppings, the land would be allowed to revert to grass to recover (more of these matters in Chapter 7).

One further survivor from the old breeds of Manx animals is the domestic Manx cat – the tailless one. It is uncertain how long the tailless cat has been in Man but it is probably at least 200 years. Similar cats are known in the Far East, and it could be that the first introductions were specimens brought in by a homecoming sailor. The lack of a tail is thought to be due to a defect similar to that which causes spina bifida in humans. Another abnormality in the Manx cat is the length of its back legs, which gives it a rabbit-like gait. A mating of two Manx cats will usually produce a mixed litter of normal tails, short tails ('stumpies') and no tails ('rumpies').

In the years following the Second World War, the increased flow of immigrants (and their cats) to the island led to fears that the increased numbers of

A Manx cat

tailed felines could overwhelm the Manx variety, and so a government-owned
cattery was set up, producing Manx kittens for Manx homes – and for visitors
from across the water. But it was a dismal sort of place and the operation was
terminated some years ago; a few private individuals may still breed them. It has
been claimed that several feral colonies of Manx cats are known, but by whom
they are known, or where, I know not.

Turning to the field of truly wild mammals, rabbits, as mentioned, are widespread below the 1,000-foot (300m) contour. A productive warren was established
on the Calf in the times of the Stanley lords, and rabbits were being collected from
there for the table in the seventeenth century. On the main island, the blown sand
deposits at the Ayres, in the north, and Kentraugh, in the south, also made ideal
warren country. Elsewhere in the island, as the rabbit population grew, the
animals would extend their burrowing activities into the structures of the sod
hedges. Ferrets were employed to retrieve the rabbits from their burrows, having
been fed bowls of meal beforehand to deter them from eating the rabbits themselves. Financial accounts for the Calf show regular entries relating to supplies of
meal for the ferrets. The present polecat-ferret population is descended from
escapees from their number.

The rabbit population in the Isle of Man flourished until the arrival of myxo-
matosis in the 1960s. The disease spread to the Calf soon after reaching the main
island, which raises the question: how? Successive waves of the disease swept the
rabbit population through the 1970s, and still recur sporadically today. In
between, rabbits continue to breed in their well-known fashion and their numbers
seem to recover. Presumably, the disease will vanish when a completely immune

strain of rabbit evolves and becomes the norm. One distinctive feature of the Manx rabbit population is the frequency with which blacks are seen.

Apart from the polecat-ferret, the only other predatory mammal in the island is the stoat, which is far less common and not often seen. The Manx stoat appears to be of the Irish species, and it has been suggested that it arrived in Man when the two islands were joined. However, when one recalls that, even though the Late-glacial sea level may have been some 200 feet (60m) below the present level, the existence of a 350-foot (100m) trench along the Irish east coast today renders it doubtful that the two islands were ever joined in post-glacial times. The great Irish deer was on the prowl early enough to make the transit over the ice but it is doubtful whether the Irish stoat was around at the same time and, even if it was, whether it would have successfully tackled the same crossing. Thus, it is far more likely that it was introduced into Man.

Of the rodents, the wood mouse may have been the first arrival, possibly in the company of Neolithic man. The house mouse was much later in coming (possibly in the nineteenth century) and is very common, as is the long-tailed field mouse. Two rats are common, both probably escapees from ships. The black rat was the earlier arrival, followed by the brown which, when swimming, is often mistaken for a water rat, which is not present in the island. Incidentally, rats are always referred to by Manx folk as 'long-tails', 'long-tail fellas' or 'queer fellas', as it is considered an invitation to ill-fortune to utter the word 'rat'. The pygmy shrew is abundant and may be a remnant of the fauna of the early woodland. The hedgehog would seem to be the commonest wild mammal, judging by the number of flattened corpses on the island's roads.

Three bat species are present: the long-eared, Natterer's and the pipistrelle. A fourth variety, the whiskered bat, also existed in a large colony in Braddan in recent times, until it was exterminated in the 1970s. (The Isle of Man was late in introducing protection for bats.)

As to invertebrates, the woodlouse is everywhere. Snails are not common in natural habitats, not being attracted to the generally lime-deficient Manx soils, but they flock to the walls of houses and other buildings, seeking out the lime in mortar and limewash.

The common lizard is present but not, apparently, in sufficient numbers to justify its name. The sand lizard was sighted by the naturalist Edward Forbes [26] in the early nineteenth century but seems not to have been recorded since. Frogs appear to have been a comparatively recent introduction and are steadily increasing their numbers. Toads and newts are absent, as are snakes.

Notable absentees from the Manx list of mammals are voles, moles, squirrels and foxes. The place-name 'Foxdale' has no association with foxes; it derives from the Norse Forsdalr, the 'dale of the waterfall'.

Plants used for hedging in olden times have been mentioned earlier. Common hedging shrubs today include *Escallonia micrantha, Fuchsia magellanica, Hebe lewisii* and *Hebe salicifolia*. Gorse is still everywhere and montbretia is widespread but, in Manx roadside hedging, the fuchsia is the crowning glory. Incidentally, the Manx national flower is the ragwort, *Senecio jacobaea* (Manx *cushag*). It adds a dash of colour to the upland slopes but, in the lowlands and especially over the water to the east, it is a pernicious weed attracting severe eradication measures. Consequently, it is sometimes irreverently referred to as 'the Manx national weed'.

The expansion of the towns in the nineteenth century, with their fashionable houses and gardens, and the continued development of new housing estates since the 1950s (with their gardens) have undoubtedly extended the range of nesting habitats available to the smaller birds of the lowlands. Apart from some specific absentees, the Manx list of small-bird species is not very different from those relating to the adjacent isles. The thrushes (song and mistle), blackbird, the tits (particularly the great, blue and coal), wren, robin, the finches (chaf, green and gold), linnet, yellowhammer, goldcrest, house sparrow and starling are all common residents. The dunnock (often erroneously referred to as the 'hedge sparrow') is almost as common but its habit of slinking surreptitiously under garden plants renders it much less conspicuous. The tree sparrow is a less common resident and seems to favour certain localities. The treecreeper is also resident in moderate numbers but is more often heard than seen. The bullfinch is a relatively rare visitor.

The pied wagtail is a common resident, as is the grey but in smaller numbers, and the yellow is a visitor passing through in late summer or early autumn. The ring ouzel may be seen in flocks during migratory passage in spring and autumn. The fieldfare and redwing are common winter visitors, frequently seen in large flocks, and the wheatear and spotted flycatcher are summer visitors and passage migrants. The pipits (meadow and rock) are residents and breed in good numbers; the tree pipit is a summer visitor with an uncertain breeding record. Other regular summer visitors are the swift, the swallow, the martins (house and sand) and the cuckoo. The jay and hawfinch are absent, and the woodpecker is an irregular visitor.

Of the larger species, the feral pigeon is widespread in the towns, with substantial populations in Douglas and Ramsey. The wood pigeon is still resident in abundance; it did appear at one time as though its territory was being taken over by that ornithological comeover, the collared dove, but it now seems to be holding its own. The collared dove itself, originating in the Far East, arrived in southern England from continental Europe in 1955, was on the Calf by 1962 and was nesting in the northern plain by 1964. It is now a widespread resident and a common visitor to many a domestic garden.

And, of course, there is the magpie. In his *History of the Isle of Man* (1722), Bishop Wilson records: 'It is not long since a person more fanciful than prudent or kind to his country brought in a breed of magpies which have increased so rapidly as to become a nuisance.' They are here today in ever greater numbers. They favour sites in trees overlooking domestic gardens or parks, where they menace smaller birds and their nests.

On lands outside the urban spread, the lapwing resides in good numbers; a bird with a questioning call – 'peewit?' – its haunts are farmland, the low moors and waterside edges. Some emigrate south for the winter; those that remain flock to estuaries and the coastal flats. The grey heron is also resident in some numbers and may be seen cruising almost anywhere where there is water – which is likely to hold a stock of fish or frogs – a river, a reservoir or even a garden pool. But, large and stately though it is, it does not have things all its own way. It is remarkable to behold a solitary heron, calmly cruising aloft, minding its own business, its long legs trailing out behind, being mobbed on sight by a flock of gulls or crows and being driven off to another location. It always seems to be gulls or crows or both massing together to drive off the intruder.

RIVERS AND GLENS

It must be admitted from the outset that, in the Isle of Man, the word 'river' is often used to enhance the status of a watercourse which is little more than a tumbling stream or a babbling brook. The island's largest river, the Sulby, is a river by any standards. And the Baldwin River and the River Glass, once they have combined and collected the meagre flow of the River Dhoo to reach their outfall in Douglas harbour, may merit the title, as also the River Neb, heading south from Glen Helen, then westward to Peel, and also (possibly) the Laxey River in the east. At least the Silver Burn and the Santon Burn are more accurate in their naming. But what about the trickles of the Ballacottier River (running down to Port Groudle, in Onchan), the Sulby River (a different one, a tributary of the Glass), the Greeba River trickling east through the central valley to meet the Dhoo, the Crogga River in Santon, and the Blaber River (a tributary of the Neb)? Incidentally, 'Port', like 'River', is another oft-used overstatement, a hangover from olden times when many of the island's coves were used as landing places for trade goods, both licit and otherwise.

But, returning to 'rivers', in the north, the Lhen (when in spate) is rather more substantial, forming the main drainage channel through the northern plain and meandering along the Lhen Trench, which appears to have been artificially straightened in places but, overall, runs between the natural contours that were cut through the plain by the much stronger flows of the Late-glacial. Then, at the other extreme, meandering westward out of the plain is the Killane River, which trickles across the shore less than a mile north of Ballaugh Cronk – and less than a stride wide.

It is clear that the flows in all of these watercourses were much greater in the past; that much is obvious when one observes the depths to which their various glens have been cut, and this is further confirmed by geologists' discoveries of alluvial fans of material washed down several of these glens and deposited at their river outfalls. These are found at the mouths of some rivers which are relatively insignificant today, such as those at Glen Mooar and Glen Wyllin, in Michael. The Auldyn River also produced one. But the really significant such feature is the conjoined fan of material brought down by the Glen Dhoo and Sulby rivers and dumped at the foot of the Manx Slate escarpment, there combining to block the Sulby's exit to the north and diverting it permanently eastward.

The flows of most of the Manx rivers were harnessed for power generation in times past. More than 300 waterwheel sites are known, providing power for grain mills, textile and paper mills and for pumping and on the washing floors of the

The Sulby River at the Garey

mines. By the nineteenth century, the rivers had become heavily polluted but most have now recovered.

Seventeen of the island's glens are today designated as Manx National Glens and are well maintained as amenity areas by the DAFF. The same department operates a freshwater fish hatchery at Cornaa, in Maughold, from which various of the island's rivers and reservoirs are restocked, mainly with rainbow trout. Trout and salmon were the main stock of the island's rivers in times past; Laxey received its name from the Norse for 'salmon river', so the species must have been a common sight in those days – but that was before the mining began and its pollution found its way into the river.

Today, several of the Manx rivers hold good stocks of the wild brown trout and receive annual influxes of migratory sea trout and salmon, the former arriving in the major rivers by June and the latter by late September. The main rivers for migratory fish are the Sulby and the Neb, although sea trout may occupy some larger pools in smaller streams. However, the numbers of both species have shown a decline in recent years, and there have been suspicions of poaching and illegal netting. In an attempt to reverse this trend, a total ban on netting for fish along the shores of the northern plain – from the beach outward to 750 metres from the high-water mark – is now in force. It is, in any case, illegal to retain migratory salmon and sea trout caught (by whatever means) in the sea.

Large specimens of the common eel may be observed heading downriver to the sea but the inward run of elvers from the Sargasso Sea may easily pass unnoticed. Occasionally, an observer may be lucky enough to be beside the outfall of one of the smaller streams as it trickles through the beach shingle at a time when the elvers are coming ashore. To watch them wriggling between the pebbles and against the flow as they strive to reach their goal in the quieter waters upstream is a most memorable experience. Once in the river, they remain there for up to ten years, growing to maturity, then return downriver and out to the ocean where they were born, to mate and to spawn, and never to be seen again – a truly fascinating life cycle.

Several of the island's rivers have been dammed to impound water-supply reservoirs. The largest and most recently built is situated in the upper reaches of Sulby Glen; it was completed in 1983 and its crest stands 200 feet (60m) above the valley floor. Before its construction, the largest reservoir (less than 3 miles to the south) was that below Injebreck, in the West Baldwin valley, which impounds the headwaters of the Glass. Its construction was started in 1900 by Douglas Corporation to ensure a supply adequate to meet the future needs of the island's expanding capital.

The smallest reservoir providing water supply today is the Clypse, above Onchan, but there were two smaller ones in the past. Tucked away deep in the tributary valley which slices into the eastern flank of Sulby Glen, the Block Eary reservoir, built in the 1940s, no longer supplies water for human consumption; instead, it supplies a one-megawatt hydroelectric generating plant in the main valley, less than a mile downstream of the Sulby dam. The second, hidden away in the hills above Kirk Michael and concealed from all bar those walking the slopes above it, was an even smaller containment which once supplied water to the village; it is now decommissioned. The two oldest reservoirs are those at Kionslieu and the Eairy Dam, at Foxdale.

All eight of the island's reservoirs, in the custody of the Isle of Man Water Authority (a government body), are open to public access. In the absence of any extensive natural lakes, they generally enhance the landscape and provide opportunities for recreational activities. They also support a wide variety of flora and fauna, and provide habitats for bird-life. The flying insects which breed around the water, including dragonflies, damselflies, mayflies and stoneflies, provide sustenance for the bird-life above and the fish-life below the water's surface. The largest reservoir, the Sulby, impounds 54 acres (22ha) when full; the smallest and lowest-lying, at Ballure, on the southern outskirts of Ramsey, just 3½ acres (1½ha).

It is beyond doubt that the variety of wildlife around, upon and within a reservoir is dependent on its age; it needs time to develop. Garrad [28] pointed out that

The Ballure Reservoir, near Ramsey

the Kionslieu and Eary (the two oldest) were, at the time she was writing (1972), the only large artificial waters regularly to support an appreciable bird population. But time rolls on, although perhaps they are still the most productive reservoirs as the others continue to mature. Tufted duck, pochard, goldeneye, whooper swan and mallard regularly overwinter on the Foxdale reservoirs, and at Kerrowdhoo and Kionslieu, in Onchan, whilst resident coot, moorhen and mallard breed on those waters and at Baldwin, but it may be that the desires of the bird population to winter or to nest there are in conflict with the activities of anglers beside the same waters.

WETLANDS

In the Isle of Man, if we set out to seek 'wetlands' (other than reservoirs), we inevitably head north, and in particular to the northern plain, because that is where most of them are – although, for completeness, we should not forget the curragh at Greeba, in the central valley. The northern plain has many ponds, of varying sizes, some deriving from kettle-holes, others from pits from marl or clay extraction for brick-making, or from sand or gravel extraction, and others of Late-glacial origin which we shall come to shortly.

At Ballacain farm, about a mile west of Sandygate and on the northern edge of the Ballaugh curragh, there is a sequence of ponds (*dubs* in Manx) that seem to have originated from diggings. In them, frogs breed, and whooper swans overwinter. Coots, moorhens, little grebes, teal and mallard breed there. (Mallard are widespread in the north, strutting along the roads and refusing to move over.) Herons feed there, presumably from the heronry at nearby Ballamoar Castle, established in the 1930s. At Ballamoar, another group of dubs is home to nesting curlew, mallard, coot and moorhen, whilst magpies and wood pigeons inhabit the willow scrub. The black-headed gull has been breeding in small numbers in this area since the 1940s but, in the absence of artificial management, the annual die-back of vegetation each autumn deposits humus into the margins. Thus, over time, the dubs become smaller and shallower and can accommodate fewer residents.

On the north side of the A3 road between Kirk Michael and Ballaugh, just north of Bishopscourt, there is a large (but diminishing) kettle-hole known as the Bishop's Dub. It has breeding coots and moorhens, and herons frequent it to feed. It is reputed to be stocked intermittently with fish, and I deduce from the heron's attention that it must be so (unless it makes do with the frogs) but, in a dry summer, it has been known to dry out completely.

There are other dubs, such as those at Nappin, west of the Jurby coast road, which are surrounded by actively worked farmland and thus subject to pollution. The Glascoe Dub, off the east-coast road between Ramsey and Bride, is similarly situated but still serves as a winter feeding site for swans and other species.

In the far north, Lough Cranstal is a very different animal, not originating from diggings but more probably from the post-glacial surface water being tipped back against the northern slopes of the Bride Hills as the raised beach of the Ayres lifted itself out of the sea. However, like the dubs, it is subject to silting, although drains have been dug from time to time. It has been known for frogs to breed abundantly in the drains and for the three-spined stickleback to be resident. Among the birds known to have nested there are the moorhen, coot, little grebe, mallard, lapwing, reed bunting, blackbird, thrush, robin, chiffchaff, whitethroat, wood pigeon, magpie, curlew and the grasshopper and willow warblers. It is suspected that the long-eared owl, which has bred in small numbers on the Ayres, may also take to nesting in the thickets of Lough Cranstal. It is difficult to assess the occupancy of the area and the effects of drainage works or lack of them, since access to the site can be difficult.

Turning south-west now, we direct our attention to the Ballaugh curragh, a truly wet land one mile north-east of the village of Ballaugh. *Curragh* is the Manx word for an area of willow carr; more to the point, it is a wetland, an area where the unwary pedestrian could easily go in over the tops of his boots – well over! As mentioned earlier, this is the last surviving remnant of Lake Andreas, still drying out from the great thaw which followed the last Ice Age, but the drying process was impeded by man's earlier activities.

In the earliest manorial rolls of 1511, the existence of two mills is recorded, one at the mouth of the Killane and the other near the mouth of the Lhen. Although the head of water available would never have been sufficient for large-scale milling operations, the impounding effects of their dams would have retarded the drainage of the area and maintained a consistently high water table. At about the same time, land around the fringes of the curragh was being enclosed as intack. The Lhen mill, the larger of the two, was purchased by the Duke of Atholl in 1809 but was put up for sale forty-seven years later, when the new purchaser was being encouraged to demolish the mill and improve the surrounding land by ceasing to impound water. Both mill buildings survive, although adapted for different purposes, but their dams have long since been breached, and the draining of the curragh continues – slowly.

In 1964, the Isle of Man government acquired 211 acres (85ha) of the Ballaugh curragh as a nature reserve, 26 acres (10½ha) of which were developed into the Curraghs Wildlife Park, which opened the following year. The nature reserve is now under the control of Manx National Heritage (MNH), with the wildlife park

Inmates of the Ballaugh Wildlife Park: (above) Australian wallabies in affectionate mood; (below) a sacred ibis

operated by the Department of Tourism and Leisure (DTL). Already, the park has contributed a new species to Manx wildlife, for Australian wallabies have made their escape and seem to exist quite happily outside the park. Another inmate which *almost* made good its escape was one member of the park's white pelican flock, which has been resident there for many years. This single bird had been allowed to remain free-flying, the rest of the flock having had their flight feathers clipped. The reasoning was that the free-flyer would always return to the park as long as its mates were there and it was fed there. And so it did until the day it decided to seek pastures new. It was eventually recaptured in Scotland and returned to the park, where *its* wings were also clipped. Rather a shame, I thought; to see this large, weird bird winging over the main road outside the park was to witness something straight out of Conan Doyle's *Lost World*.

The curragh as a whole extends eastward into the neighbouring parish of Lezayre, but much of the Lezayre curragh has been drained and is now *garey*. Garey is still wet and may carry pools and soggy areas, but it is drier than curragh and is useful as rough grazing. The next stage in degrees of dryness is *claddagh*, as in Sulby Claddagh, the flat, riverside area at the mouth of Sulby Glen, where the Sulby River turns abruptly east to make its run for the sea. *Claddagh* is trans-lated as water-meadow land, which may be damp most of the time but carries standing water only when the neighbouring river is in spate.

Bordering the northern boundary of the Curraghs Nature Reserve is the Manx Wildlife Trust's reserve at Close Sartfield. This is an area of some 31 acres (12½ha) of curragh, garey and meadow, whose grasses in spring and summer are studded with rampant growths of orchids, mainly the heath spotted, northern marsh and early marsh varieties. The site is also rich in bird-life: tree sparrow, hen harrier, kestrel and sparrowhawk, and in winter, fieldfare, merlin, redwing and snipe. Some hen harriers nest on the site in summer but, after that, this is one of the largest winter roosts of hen harriers in Europe.

In curragh areas, particularly where they are maintained as nature reserves, there is always a fine balance to be struck between allowing nature to take its course and maintaining the site in the condition in which one would wish it to remain. As is the case with all wetlands, if nature is allowed to take its course, the surrounding vegetation encroaches on the margins, and the plant growth in the water, on dying back each autumn, deposits its silt and humus on the bottom; so the pool steadily diminishes. Does one allow that to happen or does one attempt to manage the site?

There are times, especially on sites retained as amenity areas – even semi-wild ones – when nature has to be grappled with a firm hand, as happened at Bishopscourt Glen in the 1990s. The glen's plant growth – and especially the rhodo-dendrons – had overwhelmed everything else, and there was little water to be seen,

A profusion of orchids in the Close Sartfield Nature Reserve, Ballaugh

although it was in there somewhere. The DAFF men moved in and savaged the place, opening up the watercourses and reshaping pools. The immediate result was stark but, after two or three summers, the eventual outcome was superb.

THE COAST

The coastal variations of the Isle of Man may be classified under three main headings, according to their geological origins or subsequent development:

(i) the rock cliffs, predominantly of Manx Slate but including the Carboniferous limestone of the south-east and Peel sandstone in the west;

(ii) the eroding cliffs of glacial till north of Gob ny Creggan Glassey (in Michael) in the west and Ramsey in the east, extending northward to (and including) the exposed faces of the Bride Hills; and

(iii) the raised beach of the Ayres, including the modern storm beach that girds its northernmost extent around the Point of Ayre.

For completeness, a fourth classification (very minor in terms of scale) should be included, and that is saltmarsh. Writing in 1972, Dr Larch Garrad [28] identified a few very restricted areas at Langness, in the lower reaches of the Sulby River and at Port Mooar and Port Cornaa on the east coast. These are places where saltmarsh *plants* grow – saltmarsh rush, sea club rush, sea rush, chestnut rush and ragged robin – but the locations on the east-coast rivers are susceptible to deluge by fresh water when their rivers are in spate. Nowhere in Man will one find anything approaching the great expanses of saltings to be seen in places elsewhere.

The three main classifications of coast, with their differing origins and physical characteristics, greatly influence the range of wildlife – and especially bird life – to be found in each. The hardness of the rock cliffs results in rates of erosion which, in terms of our life-spans, are insignificant; these cliffs are permanent. Their domain is also subdivided by the existence of estuaries and bays which cradle tidal flats and beaches that attract further augmentation of species.

For much of their length, the precipitous nature of the rock cliffs has caused farmers to erect substantial sod hedges running parallel to, and a safe distance from, the edge, to prevent animals from toppling over. This has resulted in the formation of an almost continuous linear reserve of maritime heath, whose plants differ little from those of the uplands. Dwarf gorse, heather and bell heather predominate, together with other species having an affinity with sea-cliffs. English stonecrop, thyme and birdsfoot trefoil are common along this coast, and bluebells and primroses provide colour in spring. This ground cover provides nesting habitats for most of the small birds of the lowlands.

The rock cliffs themselves host many thousands of permanent residents – and that is just the herring gulls, whose numbers are estimated to run well into five figures. They nest on cliffs all round the island (excepting the northern plain), on the Calf and at the two inland colonies on Slieau Dhoo and Slieau Freoaghane. During spells away from their nests and through the winter, many of them flock daily onto the towns' promenades and harbour walls, knowing from long experience that food awaits them there. The food (usually broken bread or cake) is in large bags carried by ill-advised or thoughtless folk who feed it to the creatures. Some even arrive with freshly bought loaves which they proceed to break up and cast abroad. Then, their task complete, the feeders depart for home, leaving the residents and businesses in those areas to endure the screeching noise and biological filth that result throughout the rest of the day, and the days that follow.

The herring gull is an undoubted pest in the urban areas of the coast. It is not uncommon for a gull, tired of waiting to be fed, to swoop down and snatch an ice cream or a sandwich from the hand of an unwary pedestrian on a promenade; Port Erin seems to be a hot-spot for this kind of thieving. The tracking of ringed birds has shown that Manx herring gulls rarely travel more than a hundred miles from the island; when one considers the range of goodies available at home, who can blame them?

The other gull species are fewer in number and much better behaved. The great black-backed gull (its old Manx name is *Juan Mooar* – 'Big John') is resident and breeds in moderate numbers, whilst the lesser black-backed is mainly a

An urban pest

summer visitor in smaller numbers; a few pairs of each are often found in the inland colonies in the Michael hills. The kittiwake has bred in increasing numbers in recent years, its familiar call being heard most commonly around Maughold Head, the cliffs between the Chasms and Spanish Head, on the Calf and around Contrary Head (the seaward shoulder of Peel Hill). Although regarded as a resident, it spends much of the winter at sea.

The above-named sites are also favoured by the auks; not the great one, of course, which is long-since extinct (although its bones have been found here), but the razorbill and guillemot are resident and breed in fair numbers; the black guillemot and puffin are also present, but in smaller numbers. The cormorant and shag are both resident, the latter being the more common of the two. Despite its name, the Manx shearwater now breeds in very small numbers – if at all. Certain members of the crow family seem to favour the sea-cliffs (as well as ruined buildings), notably the chough, jackdaw and raven.

The lower-lying coast of the south-east, around Derbyhaven and Castletown Bay, is popular with wintering flocks of mallard, teal and wigeon, foraging in the wrack cast up along the tideline. Small flocks of storm petrels may often be seen hovering above the floating weed just before it comes ashore, their feet pattering on the surface as they pluck titbits from the floating mass. But although this is the bird ('Mother Carey's chicken') which gave its name to the Chicken Rock to the south of the Calf, it is rarely seen on land in the island.

Along the western shore of Langness in summer, it is not uncommon to spot a family group of shelduck on the water, the young perhaps making their first outing, mother leading the way, with the drake guarding the rear. It is a calm and peaceful scene, but one that is fraught with danger – if the group is spotted by a marauding gull it will make several swooping, hovering passes as it attempts to grab one of the young. This activity attracts the attention of other gulls and they all join in. Despite the best efforts of the parent birds, one gull succeeds in plucking a chick from the water, whereupon all of the gulls fly off, fighting among themselves for possession of the morsel. Down on the water, calm is restored, the family swims on – minus one unfortunate chick.

Up along the fringes of the northern plain, the scene is quite different: for the most part, a line of soft, eroding cliffs with, at their foot, a beach of loose sand or shingle which is swept along the shore by successive tides. The incoming tide approaching the island from the west divides at Contrary Head, one branch flowing south to pass through Calf Sound and around the south-east, the other heading north to flow round the Point of Ayre. The two branches recombine off Maughold Head.

The task of establishing meaningful figures for rates of erosion is a difficult one because the erosion process is complicated by several variable factors. If

*(above) Cliffs under attack at Jurby, whilst (below) dunes continue to build along
the coast of the Ayres*

erosion were due to tidal action alone, with no wind effect, the problem would be relatively simple: the tides – over the long term – are fairly constant, the principal variation in height being the cyclical one during the course of the lunar month. The complicating factor is wind (variable in both strength and direction) and especially storms, in which waves may be driven ashore from any point of the compass. Consequently, a particular stretch of cliff may be cut back severely during one storm and then remain stable for several years.

The only way to present meaningful figures is to make comparisons over a long period of time, and the most reliable period we have is the 107 years between the Ordnance Surveys of 1869 and 1976. The study was undertaken by Jolliffe [40] in 1981, and the figures on the adjacent map are derived from his report to the Isle of Man government.

Most of the island's north-west coast was subject to erosion during that period, the average annual rate being a maximum of 4 feet (1.2m) around Jurby

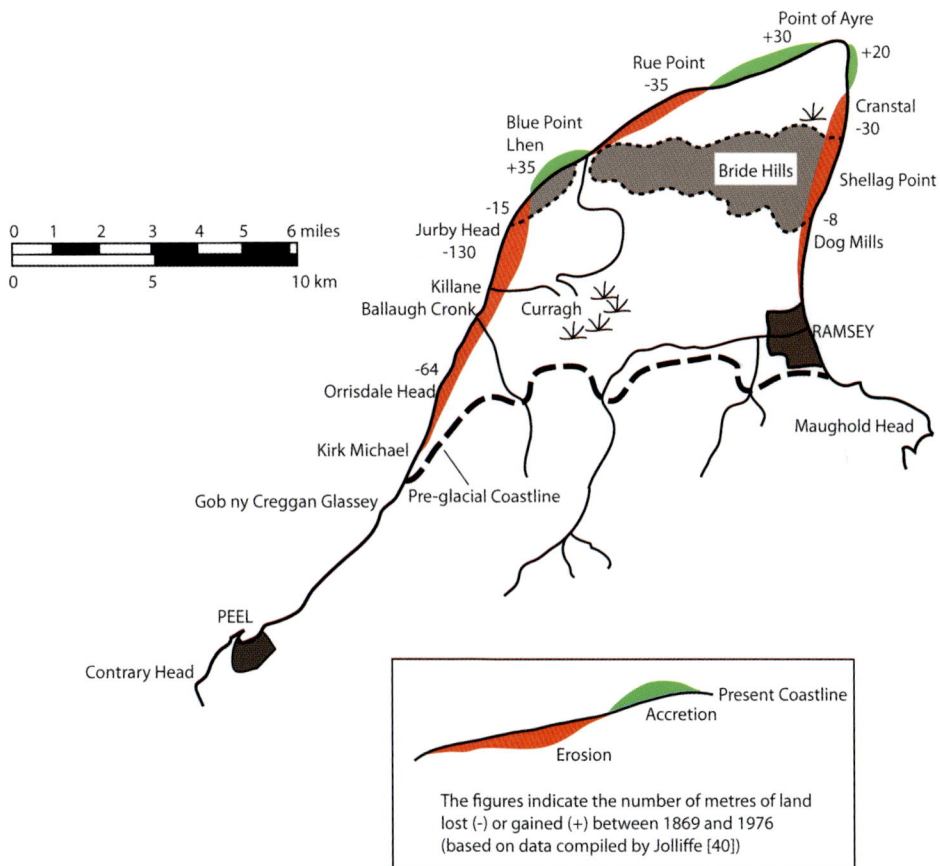

The figures indicate the number of metres of land lost (-) or gained (+) between 1869 and 1976 (based on data compiled by Jolliffe [40])

Coastal Erosion and Accretion on the Northern Plain

The storm beach at the Point of Ayre

Head, but down to 2 feet (60cm) along the Ballaugh and Michael shores. North of Jurby Head, the rate of erosion decreases sharply until, on the south side of the Lhen outfall, *accretion* has been maintained at around 1 foot (30cm) per year and a line of sand dunes has developed. Beyond Rue Point, we are into another zone of accretion, where the sand further south is replaced by the storm beach of shingle which reaches north-eastward to the Point of Ayre. On the east side of the Point and heading south, a further brief zone of accretion occurs until, at Cranstal, erosion is resumed at less than 1 foot (30cm) per year and, by the time we reach the Dog Mills, on the approach to Ramsey, it is down to a mere 3 inches (7.5cm) per year as a long-term average.

The glacial cliffs of northern Man do not attract the abundance of bird life to be found on the rock cliffs to the south, but they do nonetheless have their own attractive features. The graceful fulmar (a member of the petrel family) began breeding here in the 1930s and is now abundant, nesting in colonies on cliff ledges all round the island. They are more easily seen on the northern cliffs, as one is able to walk the shore beneath their nesting sites. They are supposed to disperse seaward at the end of the nesting season but not all of them seem to know this; I have known small groups to remain hanging around their ledges on the Michael cliffs throughout the winter, making forays over the water whenever appetite demanded. The sand martin also burrows into these cliffs, and even the house martin sometimes abandons houses to set up cliff colonies.

Along the shore, black-headed gulls feed, the small numbers that breed on the northern dubs and the flooded gravel-extraction pits on the Ayres being swollen by larger flocks of winter arrivals. The oystercatcher, lapwing, ringed plover and curlew all nest on the plain; the golden plover, turnstone and dunlin are common winter visitors, and all of these – resident and visitor – flock to these northern shores in winter to forage along the tideline. Noteworthy summer visitors are terns (common, Arctic, little and Sandwich), which fly in to nest amid the sand and stony heaths of the Ayres. Any human pedestrian who wanders too close to an unsuspected nest is likely to be dived upon in a most determined manner. Off the Point of Ayre, gannets are seen almost daily, flying their regular fishing patrols from southern Scotland and diving steeply into the water when the quarry is spotted. But they remain aloof from the island; at the end of each day, they return to their colonies in Wigtown Bay and on Ailsa Craig.

CLIMATE

In an island as small as this, it may seem surprising that the weather can vary so much from place to place, the east differing from the west, separated by the hills, or the north from the south, separated by nothing more than the central valley. Why should it be that Ronaldsway airport is sometimes affected by fog whilst the airfield at Jurby hardly ever is? Why *does* the sun (seemingly) shine on Jurby more than elsewhere; surely they are no better than the rest of us? No, as with coastal erosion, so with climate; if it is numbers we seek, then we must deal in averages, and these are collated by the Meteorological Office at Ronaldsway, which is within the ambit of the Department of Transport (DoT).

The Isle of Man benefits from contact with a branch of the Gulf Stream, which enters the Irish Sea by way of St George's Channel and passes out via the North Channel. This brings to the island a temperate climate, with mild winters and warm summers, and with neither (usually) running to extremes. The average monthly hours of sunshine in the winter months range from 42 hours in December to 114 in March. In spring, the figures range from 172 in April to 211 in June, the maximum being 217 in May. Through summer, we have 193 hours in July to 133 in September.

The warmest months are July and August, when the average daily tempera-ture is 14.5° C. The coldest days occur from November to April, the minimum daily average being 4.8° C. The hottest day on record was in July 1983, with 28.9° C (84° F) recorded; the coldest was in 1895, with –11° C (12° F).

Rain falls on approximately half the days of the year, but the amount varies according to locality; with the prevailing wind being from the south-west, rainfall tends to be higher on the east side of the hills than the west, and higher in Douglas than at Ronaldsway or the Point of Ayre. The driest months are from April to July, with a minimum monthly average of 1.83 inches (46.5mm) rainfall in May; the wettest are between September and January, with a maximum monthly average of 3.76 inches (95.5mm) in October.

Thunderstorms are infrequent, as is snow, which must have been more frequent in Norse times; otherwise, how did Snaefell ('snow mountain') come by its name? If snow does fall nowadays, it may linger on the north-facing slopes of the hills but elsewhere it does not lie for long. And if, perchance, an unusually hard winter does come along, it dwells, unfading, in the folk memory, and tales are told of it until the next one turns up.

In this chapter, I have sought to tell the story of the birth and evolution of Man as an island, as a *natural* entity, referring to man and his influence only when that influence has played a significant part in shaping the island's 'natural' scene. In the remaining chapters of Part 1, I set out the story of *man's* developments in Man, of the political, social and cultural advances that have brought the island and its people to where they are today.

CHAPTER THREE

Human Settlement

Ten thousand years ago, or thereabouts, this great hump of rock, soil, sand, clay and gravel stood proud above the still-dry continental shelf on the western fringe of Europe. This 'island', by now densely forested, was already isolated from the land to the west by the steadily rising sea which had occupied the deep trench running parallel with Ireland's east coast. The great Irish deer, *Megaloceras giganteus*, had come and gone, and a relatively limited diversity of fauna had arrived and become established. The most significant arrival was about to materialize.

THE MESOLITHIC ARRIVAL

Palaeolithic (Old Stone Age) man never reached the Isle of Man. When one considers the harshness of the climate in these latitudes at that time, it comes as no surprise that evidence of his existence is found no further north than southern England. Consequently, the first human arrivals in Man were folk of the Mesolithic, or Middle Stone Age, who came by way of the land-link from western Britain, and whose stone artefacts and hunting and gathering lifestyles appear to have been similar to those of the Mesolithic folk of other parts of western Europe at that time. Their conditions of living and techniques of tool-making were probably little different from those of the Palaeolithic; it was the improvement in climatic conditions which allowed them to migrate and occupy lands in higher latitudes.

These early settlers established themselves mainly in coastal locations in the north and north-west of Man, as well as along the low-lying south coast between Port St Mary and Ronaldsway. There would appear to be two clear reasons for this pattern of settlement, the first of which Mesolithic man shares with *Megaloceras giganteus* (unlikely though this may seem, since *Megaloceras* has passed on from Man long before the arrival of the first humans). There is, however, a remarkable correlation between the areas in which the remains of *Megaloceras* are found and those in which concentrations of Mesolithic flint artefacts have been retrieved. The common factor between the two is the lighter soils in those areas, which would have supported a less-dense woodland than elsewhere: the huge antler-spread of the great deer would have been less of an encumbrance in those areas, and early man would have found it easier to form clearings for campsites.

The second reason is that Stone-Age man needed flint from which to fashion his tools, and the only flint in Man is contained in the foreign drift remaining from the last Ice Age. These deposits are more abundant in the north, north-west and south, and markedly less so in the east. Such sites were also well placed for spearing of fish and hunting of mammals and birds frequenting the rivers, streams and wetlands.

Mesolithic folk had no awareness of agriculture; at the appropriate season, they would range forth from their semi-permanent campsites to gather fruits, nuts and fungi from the forest to supplement their basic diet of meat, fowl and fish. It is generally agreed among those who study ancient man that the average hunter-gatherer would roam the country around his base-camp to a radius of perhaps 6 miles. When one considers the various locations of these base-camps – deduced from the high concentrations of flint tools discovered in such places as the south coast from Ronaldsway to Port St Mary, at Peel and St John's, at Glen Wyllin and Orrisdale Head (in Michael), and at Sulby and the Ramsey area – it will be seen that the wanderings of the hunter-gatherers could have covered practically the whole island. The only two such sites that could be described as 'inland' are those at Sulby and St John's, both of which could readily be reached by heading upstream from the coast on their respective rivers.

Considering the nature of their lifestyle, it seems safe to assume that the Mesolithic folk would have exerted a minimal impact on the island environment. Also, bearing in mind their semi-nomadic journeyings, it is impossible to say whether each of the identified base-camps represented a central base for one particular family grouping or tribe, or whether such a group moved back and forth between two or more of these camps. Being so far removed from us by the passage of time, and faced with such a paucity of evidence, it seems pointless even to guess. The evidence, such as it is, tells us that they were here, and no more. It consists of their small, finely chipped flint tools (termed 'microliths') which were doubtless used as spearheads and knife blades.

Beyond the concentrated finds associated with the base-camps, less concentrated distributions of microlithic blades are widespread over the northern plain and along the north-west coast. The fashioning of these artefacts appears to show a style of working unique to these island folk and a complete absence of the

Cumbrian and Irish styles of flint working at that time, suggesting that, once here, the Mesolithic folk kept themselves to themselves. Their worked flints form the only evidence of their being, and it is presumed that their dwellings were constructed from relatively flimsy forest materials that would readily degrade and leave no long-term trace. Certainly, none has ever been found.

Towards the end of the Mesolithic period, around 5,000 years ago, there appears at last to have been an external influence in the production of flintwork in the island, taking the form of larger blades capable of heavier, larger-scale work – axe-heads as opposed to spearheads and knife-blades. It is notable that this change seems to have come from northern Ireland, since the flints were chipped in precisely the same manner as those of the folk inhabiting the banks of the River Bann. Ireland and Man were certainly separated by water at this time, and so these influences and new ideas must have been carried across by boat. Like the earlier Mesolithic settlers, the people of the Bann culture left no lasting remains of either their dwellings or their burials.

THE NEOLITHIC IMPACT

By this time, the land-link eastward to Cumbria had also been inundated by the rising sea level, and so the next wave of arrivals also had to travel by boat. These were the people of the Neolithic, or New Stone Age, and they brought with them knowledge of pottery-making and agriculture. Their stone implements, too, were a cut above the flints of their predecessors and were an obvious prerequisite for the clearance of woodland to provide land for the growing of crops and for the domestication and grazing of animals. These implements were also imported into the island and have been identified as originating in the Great Langdale axe factories in the Cumbrian Lake District. These factories were grouped around a workable vein of rock – a Borrowdale volcanic known as *tuff*, a consolidated form of volcanic ash which is extremely hard and, like flint, can be worked into sharp edges. In what must have been one of the earliest examples of man's *industrialized* working of a natural resource, the vein of tuff was worked as a mine, and the axe-heads were rough-formed in the hillside factories nearby, then transported down to the coast to be polished on sandstone. The nearest parallel to the Borrowdale tuff in Manx geology is the very localized appearance of tuff in the Scarlett volcanic formation, but it seems not to have been worked in a similar way.

The scale of this phase of immigration is unclear. The question remains: was the knowledge of pottery and agriculture brought to Man by a single group of newcomers and then spread among the indigenous population, or was this more of a mass migration? And the same question hangs over the Langdale axes: were they brought in by immigrants or did they arrive as trade goods? They were certainly highly valued as working tools in their time, and were traded across the British Isles. We shall probably never know, but one thing is certain: the development of pottery and agriculture originated in the lands around the eastern Mediterranean and spread across Europe by two routes: first, directly overland through the heart of the continent, and second, coastwise through the Mediterranean and along the seaboards of Iberia and France.

It is thought that the second of these routes is more likely to have been the one which brought the Neolithic culture to the Isle of Man. For one thing (as, for example, A. W. Moore [57] has pointed out), a significant section of the long-term indigenous Manx population today displays distinct physical characteristics (small stature, long heads, dark complexion, black hair and dark eyes) that point to Mediterranean origins. There is evidence that trade routes from the Mediterranean passed through the Irish Sea at this time, and on to the north, towards Scandinavia. Some of the items found in the Neolithic dwelling originate in far-distant places and could have reached Man only by such routes.

Looking at the seas which surround Britain today, one may ask why seaborne traders should route their ships through the Irish Sea, rather than take the direct route northward via the Strait of Dover and the North Sea. The answer may be that those seas were not the same then as they are now. The Dover Strait was probably narrower, and certainly shallower, with tidal streams more rapid and disturbed. The deep-water channel off the Irish east coast would have offered far safer passage. Besides, the coasts bordering the Irish Sea held glittering prizes for the traders of the time; Ireland possessed gold, Wales, Ireland and Scotland had copper, and Cornwall tin – the latter two commodities to become even more important with the later development of Bronze-Age technology. So there were numerous reasons for those seaborne traders to venture to these shores.

Unlike the people of the Mesolithic, who left nothing but a myriad of chipped flints as evidence of their passing, those of the Neolithic left lasting impressions of their occupation of the island, not only in the matter of woodland clearance, but also some sparse remains of dwellings and a number of prominent burial monuments.

The only positively identified site of a Neolithic dwelling was discovered at Ronaldsway in the late 1930s and was excavated before being obliterated by the wartime extension of the airport in 1943. The excavations revealed the outline of a rectangular dwelling, approximately 24 feet by 13 feet (7m x 4m), with a central hearth. The roof had apparently been supported by a number of timber posts, some fourteen post-holes having been identified. Inside the house were appreciable quantities of pottery, tools and animal bones, principally those of cattle, sheep and pigs, suggesting that the family's food supply was maintained by the keeping of livestock. It may have been that the animals were housed in one half of the building, whilst the family occupied the other half, an arrangement that was quite common in parts of western Britain in later times. The implements found at the Ronaldsway site were numerous and varied – flint knives and scrapers for dressing hides, flint arrow-heads, flint adzes, axes and chisels for woodworking, stone axes and hammers – and in their origins were divided between locally chipped flint and polished stone from a Langdale source.

Although the Ronaldsway site is the only known Neolithic dwelling in Man with a positively identified structure, flint concentrations, burial sites and suspected dwelling sites associated with this particular branch of Neolithic culture are found scattered over the south of the island, along the west coast and across the northern plain but, here again, with very few in the east. When I refer above to 'suspected' dwelling sites, I recall archaeologists' laments that they locate sites where there are accumulations of 'accommodation debris' – ashes, pottery fragments, bones – but no structural evidence of a dwelling. Other such sites are described as little more than middens, but surely there must have been dwellings nearby? Nevertheless, finds such as these, together with burial sites identifiable with the Ronaldsway folk form such a distinctive branch of the Neolithic scene that this branch is now known as the 'Ronaldsway culture'.

The most impressive reminders of the Neolithic folk today are their large megalithic burial cairns, mostly multi-chambered communal graves in which the cremated remains of the dead were buried, together with supplies of food and drink in pottery vessels, and arrows and spears for hunting. The whole assembly was then covered over with soil and turf, and often topped off with a large cairn of stones. In succeeding ages, it became common practice for these barrows to be plundered of their stone content for the construction of farm buildings and walls.

One of the most impressive of these barrows, standing in a high, isolated setting about a mile inland from Port Cornaa, in Maughold, is *Cashtal yn Ard* ('Castle of the height'). It was first recorded in the early nineteenth century, when the mound was approximately 100 feet (30m) long and 4 feet (1.2m) high, revetted by post-and-panel walling, but, by the middle of that century, the walling, most of the cairn material and some of the upright stone slabs had been taken for building. The site was excavated in 1932–5 and dated to around 2000BC.

The alignment of the barrow is almost due east–west, with a paved courtyard at its western end, and two portal stones leaning inward to form the triangular

Cashtal yn Ard, Maughold

entrance to the burial chamber, which was originally roofed with slabs. The chamber is divided into five compartments by transverse slabs; inside the compartments were found unburnt human bones, pottery and flints. Close by the eastern end of the chamber is a low mound of earth and stones, reddened and fused by heat, from which it is assumed that the unburnt bones were simply unconsumed residues from the funeral pyre. This is considered to be a typical and outstanding example of the megalithic chambered cairn which formed the burial place of chieftains of the Neolithic age.

Several of the prehistoric monuments of the Isle of Man have been tagged with fanciful and wholly inappropriate names. King Orry's Grave is one such, for it has no association whatever with King Orry, whom we shall meet in the next chapter. King Orry's Grave is another long-barrow, multi-chambered burial site, this one in a residential area on the northern outskirts of Laxey and also dated to around 2000BC. It is unfortunate that this formation has been sliced in two by an old-established roadway – the Ballaragh Road. It is aligned north-east to south-west. The north-eastern portion has a well-formed courtyard similar to that at Cashtal yn Ard, with two standing stones forming a portal, leading to a burial chamber and part of a second before the structure vanishes under a boundary

King Orry's Grave, Laxey:
(above) the north-east portion;
(right) the south-west portion.
The Ballaragh Road cuts
between the two

wall. When excavated, this portion yielded flints, pottery and unburnt bones. The south-western portion was for years situated in a private garden but was acquired by Manx National Heritage in 1999. It has marked similarities to the structure to the north-east. Although the line of sight between the two portions is interrupted by the cutting for the roadway, they seem to lie very closely on the same alignment. If the two portions were, indeed, parts of one long chambered tomb (which is by no means certain), then the total length of the cairn would have been approximately 170 feet (50m).

Down in the far south-west of the island, lies a quite different chambered tomb of the Neolithic age, set out on a pattern unique in the island. This is the Meayll Circle, situated just below the summit of Meayll Hill, which overlooks the hamlet of Cregneash to the south and with a view northward across Port Erin Bay. (A word on pronunciation: 'Meayll' is pronounced in much the same way as a Highland Scot would pronounce it, the vowels and the 'y' being pronounced in rapid succession. The result usually comes out as 'Mull', and the name is increasingly spelt that way today.)

The Meayll Circle is a megalithic chambered tomb with six pairs of burial chambers set out in a circle. Each pair of chambers is approached by a passage leading radially inwards from outside the circle, and the circle is broken to allow entrances into the centre from north and south. It is probable that the chambers, as they became occupied, were progressively capped and covered to form an annular mound, keeping the centre of the circle as the cremation site, although no evidence of burning has been found.

When the site was first excavated in 1897, cremated remains were found in twenty-six urns, and there were smashed remains of others, as well as numerous flint implements. This formation has also been dated to around 2000BC, and the impression of a grain of wheat on a fragment of pottery indicates that crop cultivation was under way by that time. The pottery of the Meayll folk appears as a much finer product than that found in the north, and, although these people produced distinctive pottery and had their own unique ideas on burial cairns, they seem to have existed contemporaneously with the northern folk, since examples of both types of pottery have been found at some sites. Quite close to the circle, lower down the hill to the south-east, some traces were found of the village to which the burial site belonged. Four urns were found there, similar to those in the graves. The traditional name of the place was *Lag-ny-boirray*, 'the hollow of botheration'.

Like all such sites in the island, the Meayll Circle has been much despoiled in the past, with stone being taken for other purposes. Another megalithic chambered tomb, probably from earlier in the Neolithic age and even more despoiled, sits amid farmland on the west side of the old Douglas–Castletown road, at Ballakelly, Santon. It is a smaller burial site than those described earlier but

The Meayll Circle, above Cregneash

its uprights are of considerable size and one of them displays a pattern of 'cup' markings such as are found on stones at one or two other sites in the island. Describing the site in 1956, Stenning [72] opines that many of the stones were just too useful to be left there and could be seen serving as gateposts in a number of fields thereabouts.

There are at least three ancient burial monuments in the island which have been tagged with the name 'the Giant's Grave'. One, at Baldrine, in Lonan, is also known as the Cloven Stones. Since it was surveyed in 1865, it has been hemmed in by housing development, and so we have to rely on the early description and plan of the site. It is a twin-chambered grave with two stone pillars, 6–7 feet (around 2m) high, forming its entrance. The taller of the pillars is split down its full length along a cleavage line in the stone. It would appear that, over the ages, this is the result of weathering, countless successions of rain, freeze and thaw working into the line of weakness and steadily forcing the two halves of the stone apart. But Manx tradition does not readily embrace such mundane conclusions. *This* is undoubtedly the site where the redoubtable King Orry came to test the strength of his sword, and his arm, and succeeded in splitting the stone from tip to base with a single blow – a far more romantic explanation.

THE BRONZE AGE

The Bronze Age in the Isle of Man began around 1800BC. The pollen record confirms that the clearance of woodland and the cultivation of grassland and cereal crops (together with the associated weeds) were well advanced by that time. There has long been conjecture as to whether or not the new trends in crafts and culture that arrived with the Bronze Age in Man were brought in by a fresh wave of immigrants. There were significant new techniques, particularly in the alloying of bronze and in pottery-making, the products of which were finer than those of the artisans of the Neolithic, but these changes could have been introduced into the island by way of the well-established trading links, without necessarily implying a renewal of immigration. Conversely, the marked change in burial customs that appears at the beginning of the Bronze Age suggests at least some significant intrusion of a new human presence.

The climate in the early Bronze Age was warmer and drier than that of today, average temperatures being perhaps 2–3° C higher than today's. Across the British Isles, there is evidence of an extension of agriculture into the uplands at this time. In the Isle of Man, the only evidence of a possible move in that direction lies in the existence of upland burial mounds. It is a plausible assumption that these were associated with upland settlements but their sites have not been located. The nearest anyone has come to locating *any* early Bronze-Age settlements in Man is the discovery of several open-air cooking sites at Clay Head, in Lonan.

Bronze had been in use around the eastern Mediterranean from much earlier times. Once the knowledge of the alloying technique reached the British Isles, Ireland was able to exploit its own resources of copper and readily acquire the necessary supplies of tin by trading across the water in Cornwall. By the late Bronze Age (c 1000 – 500BC), the alloy was probably being produced in Man, using the insular sources of copper at Bradda and Langness and trading for the tin.

In comparison with the earlier phases of its human prehistory, the Isle of Man seems to have been far less isolated from the neighbouring islands during the Bronze Age. There are no longer any uniquely Manx characteristics in the bronze implements, pottery or burial monuments from that time. A continuing connection with Ireland in the mid-to-late Bronze Age is evident, particularly in the matter of burial urns carrying decorations very similar to those found in that isle to the west, and it has been noted that there was near simultaneity between the appearance of new metal-working techniques in Man and southern Britain in the late Bronze Age.

Apart from the replacement of stone with metal and the finer crafting of pottery, the significant change apparent in Man from early in the Bronze Age was the change in burial practices. In place of the large, communal megalithic tombs, came the smaller cairns and mounds marking the individual burials that were a characteristic trait of these people. Furthermore, the *unburnt* body was interred on its side, in a crouching position with the knees drawn up to the chin, in a stone-lined chamber, accompanied by a finely decorated food vessel or, in the odd case, a beaker. This, surely, must indicate the arrival of a new wave of immigration. The practice of cremation, so common throughout the Neolithic period, ceased but would return to favour later in the Bronze Age. Burial mounds of this type litter many parts of the Manx landscape, most still awaiting excavation.

A striking example of the internal structure of a Bronze Age burial is afforded by 'the Giant's Grave' (yes, another one) at St John's, where the minor road passing the west side of Tynwald Hill has been cut through the mound, exposing a cyst of large stone slabs in the roadside banking. It is known that Bronze-Age burial mounds retained a tradition as places of local assembly, and it has been suggested that Tynwald Hill itself (an artificially formed four-tiered mound, rather than a hill) may stand on the site of another burial mound. Tynwald Hill is the venue for the annual open-air assembly of the Manx parliament; it has been so since Norse times, possibly continuing an even earlier custom.

The Giant's Grave, Tynwald Hill

A mixed graveyard of crouched *and* cremated burials occurs on the summit of Chapel Hill, at Balladoole, in Arbory, where the graves lie within the ramparts of a later Iron-Age occupation. This site would receive further burials through the Iron Age and into the Norse period, of which more in the next chapter. Incidentally, much of the excavation of this site was carried out during the Second World War by Dr Gerhard Bersu, one of thousands of 'enemy aliens' interned in the Isle of Man at that time. (And more on that period in Chapter 6.)

Towards the end of the Bronze Age, there seems to have been a growing tendency to site burials in high, prominent locations. Chapel Hill was one such; another was the summit of Cronk ny Arrey Laa, high above the south-west coast in Rushen. The summit cairn marks a large burial mound 1,433 feet (437m) above sea level. In places, it is possible to trace kerb-stones set on edge around the mound. As we shall see, there would soon also be a tendency to site dwellings in such high places.

As in Britain and Ireland, so in Man, there are many monoliths, large, solitary standing stones, out in open country – or at least they were when they were erected. There are two at Port St Mary: one fine example between the railway station and Ballaqueen, standing about 9 feet (3m) tall and weighing several tons, and the other, quite close by at the Four Roads roundabout. Another, above the main Douglas–Castletown road near the Ballalona bridge, in Santon, is massively top-heavy and must be very deeply set into the ground. And in Michael, there are two (at least): one at Berk, above the Peel–Kirk Michael road, is another which shows a pattern of cup markings low down, near its base; the other stands in the middle of a field at Broughjairg, Orrisdale. These may date from either the Stone or the Bronze Age, but how or why they were erected there is anyone's guess.

———————————

THE IRON AGE

Towards the end of the Bronze Age, around 500BC, there appears to have been a marked deterioration in climate over the British Isles and western Europe, and this may have induced mass migrations in search of more favourable conditions. This, in turn, would have applied pressures on existing settled populations into whose areas the immigrants sought to move, resulting in increased demands on resources. Throughout much of the Neolithic and Bronze Ages, the social structure of the island had been that of a widespread, scattered rural population. Now, the rising pressures imposed from outside would necessitate responses involving security, and they would require considerations of 'community' and a 'coming together' to satisfy the need for communal defence.

From the hill fort on South Barrule, the views are extensive – but not guaranteed

The response is marked by a proliferation of hill and coastal promontory forts around the island and an increasing concentration of dwellings within the ramparts of defensive earthworks. Nowhere are these two developments brought together more impressively than on the summit of South Barrule, where traces of more than seventy hut circles can be seen within the inner rampart of a hill fort, whose two concentric ramparts encircle the summit. The huts in the eastern half of the site appear to have been significantly larger than the remainder – an indication of some form of class distinction, perhaps? A radio-carbon date of approximately 520BC was obtained from a sample of one of the hearth contents.

Other hill forts from this period are at Castleward, on a rocky hillock overlooking the River Glass, on the north-western outskirts of Douglas, and at Cronk Sumark, Lezayre, overlooking the northern plain at the point where the Sulby River makes its abrupt turn to the east. In both of these forts, sections of rampart show evidence of vitrification, where the stones have been fused together by the application of intense heat. Similar hill forts appear in various parts of Britain at that time, and many of those also show signs of vitrification.

In addition to the hill forts, more than twenty small promontory forts were built at strategic points around the island's coast in the same period. Most of these are broadly of similar form, occupying a coastal promontory, with cliffs on three sides and guarded on the landward side by a defensive ditch and rampart. Typical of these are the forts at Close ny Chollagh, beside Poyllvaaish Bay; Langness Point, at the entrance to Castletown Bay; Cass-ny-Howin, above the entrance to the Santon Burn; Cronk ny Merriu, overlooking Port Grenaugh; and Gob ny Garvain, on the south side of Port Mooar, in Maughold. Barely a mile to the north of the last-named is one which is best termed a cliff-top fort; it stands at the summit of Maughold Head, on the edge of a rock cliff that drops steeply down to the tight little beach of Traie Curn, whilst the enclosing rampart sweeps in a broad semicircle around the back of the summit cairn of the headland. All of these, it will be seen, were sited in well-chosen, defensive locations, reflecting the underlying air of tension and unrest which seems to have prevailed at that time.

This was the setting for the arrival of the Celts in the Isle of Man around 500BC. The name 'Kelt' derives from the Greek *keltoi*, ascribed to the tall, fair inhabitants of northern Europe, contrasting with the short, dark Mediterranean type already settled here. The Celts and the technology of iron-smelting arrived in Man at around the same time; hence it is probable that the Celts brought the technology with them. If, as seems likely, they came into conflict with the indigenous Bronze-Age folk, with their bronze weapons, these would have been no match against iron.

Nevertheless, the eventual outcome could not have been total annihilation of the small, dark folk for, as mentioned earlier, their descendants are with us today. Whether they were driven off their lands and into the hills, or whether an inter-mingling of the two populations resulted we can never know; perhaps a combination of the two was the most likely outcome. Whatever the result of any conflict at the time, the arrival of the Celts laid the foundation for what was to evolve, over the next two millennia, into the Manx folk culture of the modern era; that foundation was its language. Although the Manx language survived as the vernacular into the early twentieth century, it is no longer in everyday use except by students of the language; as an area of study, it has experienced a resurgence of interest in recent years. We return to the subject in Chapter 9.

The old Celtic language of Man left its heritage in a plethora of place-names and personal names throughout the island. The later Norse arrivals would, to a marked extent, do the same, but their personal names would soon become 'Gaelicized', rendering them of mixed origin.

From the viewpoint of the island's prehistory, the significant feature of the language of the Manx Celts is its similarities – and its contrasts – with the languages in the neighbouring regions in the early Iron Age, since such compar-isons enable us to deduce the direction from which the early Celtic arrivals in Man came. Prior to the mass settlements of the Anglo-Saxon peoples in England in the fifth and sixth centuries, the Celtic language, in one form or another, was dominant throughout the British Isles. The people of Britain could be said, quite legitimately, to have spoken 'British'.

The Celtic languages of the British Isles (and of a wider area extending south into Brittany) divide neatly into two groups, identified as *Brythonic* (or p-Celtic), embracing Welsh, Cornish and Breton, and *Goidelic* (or q-Celtic), comprising Irish, Scottish and Manx. The references to 'p' and 'q' in these designations reflect the frequency with which these two initial letters occur in the two groups of languages. In Manx, the frequency of use of that hard initial 'q' sound is augmented by the additional use of words beginning with a 'k' or hard 'c'; so, whether it be a 'q', a 'k' or a hard 'c', the sound is the same and reinforces this characterization of the Manx Gaelic.

At the time of Julius Caesar's forays into southern Britain in 55 and 54BC, he encountered a people who were speaking the p-Celtic language. This would have come as no surprise, considering the already long-established trading activities between the shores of the Mediterranean and those of the British Isles. In all probability, the people of the rest of the island of Britain, or at least most of it, would have been speaking the same language, or variations of it; this was certainly the case at the time of the Claudian invasion of Britain almost a century later. And a study of British place-names indicates that those of Celtic origin come predominantly from the p-Celtic branch.

In Ireland, the situation is quite different. The Irish language is firmly rooted in the Goidelic (q-Celtic) group, and it is clear that, whichever route was followed by the Goidels in migrating from mainland Europe and into Ireland, they did *not* migrate by way of Britain in any significant numbers; otherwise, they would have left more linguistic evidence of their passing.

The old language of the Isle of Man, sandwiched between these two larger islands, has clear links with that of Ireland; both are Gaelic languages and, although they have evolved into different tongues, the similarities between the two are still remarkable. Examples are the Irish element *bally* for a land division, a village or town name (cf the Manx *balla*), the Irish *kil* for chapel (the Manx *keeill*) and the Irish *sliabh* or *slieve* for mountain (the Manx *slieu* or *slieau*).

All this, of course, does not tell us from which direction the Celts came to Man, but it does tell us from which direction they did not: the east. The Irish Celts reached Ireland by the direct and well-known sea route. The Manx Celts may have reached Man by the same route, or they may have come eastward from Ireland. Once again, we shall never know for certain but a combination of the two movements may well have been the case.

A number of dwelling sites from the Iron Age in Man have been located and excavated. Two outstanding examples were discovered at Ballakeigan, on the north-western outskirts of Castletown; this was another excavation by Bersu in

The archaeological site at the Braaid: (above) the Celtic roundhouse; (below) one of two Norse rectangular buildings

1941–4. The Celtic chieftain's dwelling was typically of circular planform, some 80–90 feet (about 25m) in diameter, and surrounded by ditches. The whole of each house is believed to have been roofed with a covering of turf sods carried on a timber framework to form a dome-shaped covering, supported on concentric circles of timber posts. There was evidence of a lengthy period of occupation during the first three centuries AD. A finely detailed model of the Ballakeigan roundhouse is an exhibit in the Manx Museum.

A mile to the north-west, at Ballanorris, a similar dwelling was unearthed, again by Bersu. Further north, a site at Braaid, in Marown, has yielded evidence of another Celtic roundhouse, this one sharing the site with two rectangular dwellings from the Norse period. And, up in the northern parish of Ballaugh, the low outline of another, 120 feet (36m) in diameter, stands out clearly on the hillside above the village. At a markedly higher elevation than the others, approximately 500 feet (150m) above the sea, it sits close by the mountain wall, overlooking the village from the east.

The dwelling of the humbler Celt was on a smaller scale, around 12 feet (4m) in diameter, with the wall resting on a foundation of sunken stone. There was a central hearth, and the domed roof was left open in the centre to allow the smoke to escape. Just outside the house was a midden, in which animal bones and mollusc shells may still be found. As the family grew in number and influence, there would be a need to enlarge the house, and this would be done by erecting a larger concentric circle of timber posts to support the extended roof. The internal space was partitioned off to provide livestock houses, sheds and stores around the outside, with the inner space being compartmented to provide accommodation for other members or sub-groupings of the same family. By this time, the dwelling would have grown to the proportions of that at Ballakeigan.

The Celtic system of land tenure was a *udal* system, a kind of freehold right based on uninterrupted possession which prevailed in northern Europe prior to the feudal system. The Scandinavians had their *odal* system, and in Orkney and Shetland they still have it. The feudal system was never introduced in Man, despite the attempts of successive lords to force the issue. It was the Celtic custom to amalgamate four quarterlands, or *kerroos*, to form the unit known as a treen. The treen boundaries nearly always followed *natural* divisions in the landscape, whereas the quarterlands, being of later origin, are largely artificial divisions.

In Christian times, each treen was responsible for the upkeep of one small chapel, or keeill. The treens occupied all of the arable land, and the rough land beyond was 'intack', which could be used as grazing by the owners of the quarterlands. To this day, the quarterland farm holdings carry the names of the original holding family; e.g. Ballaclucas, Ballakelly, Ballaquirk. (A. W. Moore [57] gives more detail on the system of land tenure.)

Although the Romans made no attempt to occupy the Isle of Man, the four centuries of Roman occupation of Britain doubtless engendered a period of calm and order around the Irish Sea. Roman galleys would have been a constant presence in these waters as they transported supplies to their outposts along the western coasts of Britain. It is presumed to have been this long period of calm and lack of external threat which encouraged the Manx Celts to abandon their promontory forts and hill forts, and not to reoccupy or renew them until, perhaps, some time after the Roman withdrawal early in the fifth century.

THE CHRISTIAN CONVERSION

It was during this long period of apparent tranquillity that the first Christian influences began to reach the Isle of Man. Christianity had first arrived in south-eastern Britain when Roman power was at its height, and gradually spread north and west into most parts of Roman Britain. St Patrick, who was taken into slavery by Irish raiders when he was sixteen (in or about AD405), was the son of a deacon somewhere in western Britain, possibly Cumbria. Hence it is clear that Christianity was widespread in Britain long before Patrick escaped from slavery and began his missionary travels.

As Roman authority in Britain waned in the early fifth century, the influence of Christianity in the lowlands of the south-east also faded, aided and abetted by the increasing waves of immigration of pagan Anglo-Saxons. As the political scene surrounding the waters of the Channel and North Sea reverted to a less placid state, the western sea routes into the British Isles returned to favour.

Meanwhile, Christian migrants originating in the eastern Mediterranean were steadily extending their presence westward and northward, to the Gironde estuary, the Loire valley and on to Brittany, retracing the steps of the old Stone Age migrations. This wave of Christian expansion initially embodied the principles of eastern monasticism, self-deprivation and reclusive contemplation, but, in the course of its passage through France, the movement came under the influence of one John Cassian, a Scythian who had established two monasteries – one for men and another for women – in the Marseilles area. Although starting out as an ascetic himself, Cassian's philosophy evolved into one which called for monks to deviate from aimless asceticism and instead to adopt a purpose: to convert and educate the people among whom they lived. In this, Cassian may well have been influenced by the teachings of St Martin of Tours, who had died in 397. In any event, this line of thought transformed the movement as it spread its way northward towards Britain and Ireland.

Ireland had retained trade links with Gaul and beyond, and it was probably by this route that the Irish received the monastic idea. It was readily accepted, and what may previously have been a marginal Christian cult became the predominant religious form. The first Irish Monks are identified from about AD540. As Paul Johnson [39] has pointed out, Ireland did not possess any towns by that time, and scarcely any villages; it was still a largely nomadic and tribal society. Contemporary monasticism was also, literally, a *movement*; it moved from place to place among the people, undertaking its twin tasks of conversion and education, and the sea was its chief means of transport. A survey of early Irish monastic settlements has shown that they were small, primitive, scattered and numerous. Irish monasticism was wholly integrated into its local communities; in all but name, it was the Church in Ireland.

Egyptian monasticism, which had been at the heart of the eastern movement, had been a revolt against ecclesiastical hierarchy in general and the episcopate in particular. It is remarkable that the Irish Church, though readily embracing the immigrant philosophy, never openly rebelled against orthodoxy. Bishops remained a part of the system; there were functions for them to perform: ordinations and the blessing of the baptismal chrism, but they were not to consider themselves leaders of society. They were expected to be humble; a cleric should not be seen riding a horse, for, by so doing, he was elevating himself above the common man.

The Celtic Church in the west by this time lay beyond the control of the Church in Rome, and there was one issue between the two that would remain unresolved for another two centuries; that was the method for calculating the date of Easter. The dispute had been rumbling on between various factions for several centuries and would not be resolved until the Synod of Whitby in 664 ruled in favour of the Roman formula.

So how did all of this affect the development of the Celtic Church in the Isle of Man? Did the Manx conversion emanate from Ireland in the west, or by the direct sea route from the south? Or did it come from western Britain? Although we have concluded that the Manx Goidels did not have their origins in Britain, it would not have taken a large body of missionaries from there to spread the Word in an isle the size of Man and leave no trace in the form of place names or peculiar personal names.

In the Celtic religious domain, a useful way of addressing this question is by a study of the names of the clerics to whom the various keeills and parish churches are dedicated. This is particularly pertinent in the Celtic regions because of the early practice of naming a church after its founder or his monastic principal. This contrasts with the Roman practice of dedicating a church to one of the biblical saints or to one of the holy family, which would be of no use whatever in the present context.

A study of Manx dedications reveals four well-known names: St Patrick (*c* 389–461), St Ninian (died *c* 432), St Brigit (born *c* 453) and St Columba (521–97). All four are Celtic saints, and Ninian is the only one not primarily associated with Ireland; his associations lie mainly in south-west Scotland, where he built his church known as *Candida Casa* on the Isle of Whithorn, in Galloway, in the late fourth century. He dedicated it to St Martin of Tours, whose famous monastery at Marmoutier he had previously visited. The remains of Ninian's church stand today on the east side of Burrow Head, the nearest point of land to the Isle of Man. In the island itself, his name is corrupted in the dedication of St Trinian's, the roofless ruin of a church standing beside the Peel–Douglas road in Marown. The Priory of Whithorn once held land hereabouts. St Martin himself had keeills dedicated to him in the parishes of Onchan (Ballakilmartin) and Andreas (Keeill Vartyn), and this could perhaps be through the influence of Ninian.

The remaining three of these saints have strong connections with Ireland. St Brigit enjoyed widespread recognition, with dedications ranging across the southern half of Ireland and southern and eastern Scotland, then down the entire length of western Britain and into Brittany. In Man, she is dedicated in the parish church of Bride. Elsewhere in the isle, her name is rendered in various forms: in

The ruin of St Trinian's Church, Marown

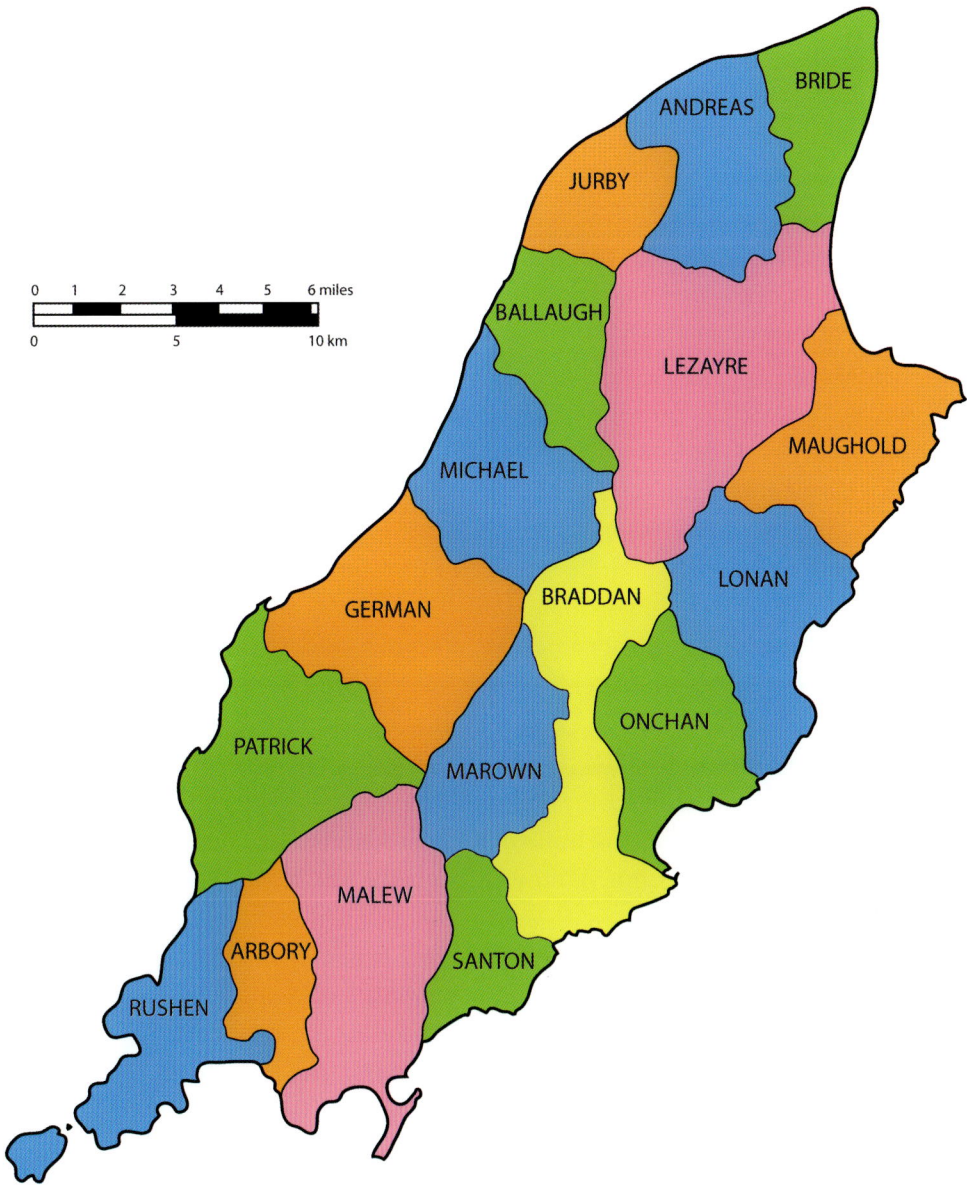

BRIDE

ANDREAS

JURBY

BALLAUGH

LEZAYRE

MICHAEL

MAUGHOLD

GERMAN

BRADDAN

LONAN

PATRICK

ONCHAN

MAROWN

MALEW

ARBORY

SANTON

RUSHEN

0 1 2 3 4 5 6 miles

0   5   10 km

The Ancient Parishes

the same parish, there is the well, *Chibbyr Vreeshey*, and an area of wetland known as *Curragh Breeda*, a form of the name still common in Ireland today. And down in Marown, not far from St Trinian's, an area of land surrounding a ruined keeill is called *Garey keeill Vreeshey*. The *chibbyr*, or well, was a common appendage of the ancient keeill, the well being the source of baptismal water.

St Patrick's influence was broadly spread across Ireland and western Britain. In Man, where his name is often transmuted to *Pheric* or *Pharick*, there is the parish church of Patrick and, on the western edge of Peel, the ruin of St Patrick's church stands within the castle walls on St Patrick's Isle, with the holy well, *Chibbyr Pharick*, close by. Jurby's parish church is also dedicated to Patrick and, spread throughout the isle, there are examples of *Keeill Pharick* and *Chibbyr Pharick* – or *Pheric* – including, in the southern parish of Rushen, *Ballakilpheric* ('the farm of Patrick's church'), this one retaining the Irish element *kil*, in place of the Manx *keeill*.

And so the association with Ireland grows. After Patrick's death in 461, others carried on the work. St Columba, born in Donegal in 521, was related to the royal family of Ulster and to the ruler of Dalriada (now Argyll), and so, in addition to his Christian piety, he doubtless had political influence. After establishing numerous churches in his native Ireland, he set out on the conversion of the Western Isles and the Picts of the Scottish mainland, establishing as his base the famous monastery on the isle of Iona. From there, his monks would spread their influence steadily eastward across northern Britain, then south, down the east coast and into what had become England ('Angle-land' – the Anglo-Saxon kingdoms were established by then). In 634, St Aidan of Iona, at the invitation of the Northumbrian court, founded the monastery at Lindisfarne, and others were to follow, each one spreading the influence further south – to Tynemouth, Jarrow, Wearmouth, Hartlepool and Whitby. Meanwhile, in Kent, St Augustine had landed in 597 to re-establish the Roman version of Christianity, and its influence would spread inexorably northward. The two branches of this great religious movement, with significant differences standing between them, would meet, head-on, at Whitby in 664.

Although there is no evidence that St Columba (or any of the other saints named above) ever set foot in the Isle of Man, nevertheless the power and influence of the Irish-based Ionan movement in the wider region at that time should not be underestimated. The Venerable Bede, writing of Northumbria in the period 634–64, states that 'all the province, and even the bishops, were subject to Iona'.

Within the Isle of Man, dedications to Columba himself are few. In the southern parish of Arbory, the parish church is dedicated to him, whilst the parish takes its name from the lesser-known Celtic Saint Cairbre, and age-old references to 'Kirk Cairbre' have seen the 'C' gradually subsumed into the second 'k' to become today's Kirk Arbory. Within this parish, there is an annual fair day known as *Laa Columb Killey*, 'St Columba's Day'.

Several other Manx parishes and their churches are named after Celtic saints, often using the Irish honorific prefix *ma* or *mo* instead of the Latin *sancti* for 'Saint', as in the parish of Malew, which is named after one of Columba's disciples, St Lua, or Malua. In neighbouring Marown, we have the Irish Saint Ronan (Maronan), and in Santon there is another Irish Saint Sanctan, whose name in a later period was confusingly misrecorded as St Ann. The western parish of German has been the focus of further confusion in the past, when the name of the Irish Saint German became associated with St Germanus, Bishop of Auxerre (no connection).

To complete this round of Celtic dedications, we find St Andrew in Andreas, St Bradarn in Braddan, St Conchan in Onchan, St Lonan in Lonan and St Maughold in Maughold. St Bradarn's name appears (in various spellings) throughout Ireland, Scotland and the Isles. St Conchan is the Irish equivalent of St Christopher but the parish church has been rededicated to St Peter. According to J. J. Kneen [45], there were no fewer than eight Irish saints bearing the name *Lonan* and it is impossible to decide which was the intended dedication. St Maughold was a most significant cleric in Man, and we shall return to him shortly.

This survey of parish dedications now leaves us with four parishes (out of the total of seventeen) whose churches are not dedicated in the Celtic fashion, but in the Roman manner, involving biblical saints or the Divinity. One of those parishes is in the far south-west, the remaining three forming a contiguous block in the north and north-west.

The origin of the name *Rushen* is a mystery. It has been suggested that it stems from *roisin*, which is the diminutive for a promontory. The parish of Rushen does form a coastal promontory, but why then should we have Castle Rushen and Rushen Abbey, both of which are in the parish of Malew and neither of which stands on a promontory? A. W. Moore [57] has pointed to the existence of a St Ruisen, mentioned in the martyrology of Donegal, but it is all very unclear.

However, none of this affects the parish church, which was originally dedicated to the Holy Trinity and later became Kirk Christ Rushen, and this was also the name of the parish. Today, the parish is simply Rushen and its church is referred to as either Rushen parish church or, retaining the old style, Kirk Christ Rushen. It is notable that, following the Norse settlement of the island, all of the Manx parishes and their parish churches would adopt the Norse prefix *kirk*.

In the north, the parish of Lezayre has a similar story, except that there is no confusion over the name. Both parish and church were initially dedicated to the Trinity, later becoming Kirk Christ Lezayre. The church is still usually referred to by that name but the parish is just Lezayre ('the Ayre'), *lez* being the old Norman definite article. Lezayre is the parish of the Ayre. The parish of Michael and its church (Kirk Michael) are dedicated to St Michael the Archangel, and the parish and church of Ballaugh to the Virgin Mary; the church is still known as St Mary de Ballaugh.

So, at the end of this often-puzzling journey back through centuries of misty prehistory, it does seem clear that the early Christian conversion of the Manx was firmly rooted in the west – in Ireland – doubtless reinforced by proselytizing efforts from the north, possibly from Whithorn, almost certainly from Iona which, in any case, could be regarded as an Irish 'out-station'. Whether or not there were other contributions, from the east, from the south (Wales) or along the sea-lanes from western Europe and beyond, in the absence of written record it is too far back in time to know. And the reason why, within the island, just four of the seventeen parishes chose to dedicate their churches in the Roman fashion, when the other twelve did not, remains another enduring question. That period in English history between the withdrawal of the Romans and the Norman Conquest is referred to as the Dark Ages. If you have persevered with me thus far, you will by now be realizing just how extensive, and dark, the Manx Dark Ages were – and they were not over yet.

THE STRUCTURE OF THE EARLY CHURCH IN MAN

The fact that I have included the dedications of the various parishes and parish churches in the above discussion should not be taken to imply that Man had been organized into parishes by this stage of the island's story, for that is far from being the case. It is not known when the parishes were first established, but it may well have been some time after the arrival of the Norse in the ninth century. So, where lies the justification for involving the parish churches in the argument? The justification lies in the old practice of building a parish church on or adjacent to the site of a pre-existing keeill and adopting the dedication of the keeill as that of the church. Also (one must admit, and with a modicum of cynicism), when seeking the answer, or at least a pointer, to a question as clouded as this, one scratches for the evidence as and where one can, whilst always resisting the temptation to fall for the first romantic association that comes along.

When seeking some sign of form or structure to the early Church in Man (say from the fifth to the seventh centuries) and realizing that more than 200 known keeill sites are spread across the isle, with no sign of a more substantial establishment in between, one is tempted to conclude that there *was* no form or structure, that these solitary clerics were sent out from Ireland or Scotland to spread the Word and were left to get on with it. And perhaps that is how it was in the beginning. But there must have been more to it than that, particularly when almost 90 per cent of the known keeill sites seem to have been treen-chapels – one small church serving one treen, and located near the boundaries of its four quarterlands. There must have been some form of insular organization to achieve this distribution.

The earliest keeills were primitive affairs, with walls made entirely of sod, but later versions were faced with dry-stone walling, and later still the stones were bedded in clay or a form of mortar. Their internal dimensions were about 15 feet by 9 feet (less than 5m x 3m), with walls 3–4 feet (1m) high and capped with a steep, thatched roof. The entrance at the western end was often the only source of light but some had a small east window over the stone altar-slab. The foundations of typical keeills can be seen in the churchyard at Kirk Maughold, where there are three, one with an adjoining well, one above the waterfall of Spooyt Vane, in Glen Mooar, Michael, and one at the very remote site of Lag ny Keeilley, on the steep seaward slope of Cronk ny Arrey Laa, in Patrick.

The early keeills were too small to have served as places of congregational assembly; communal worship would have taken place outside, as would baptisms, beside the *chibbyr*. The keeills were often built on sites regarded as sacred in earlier times, thus suggesting a regard for earlier tradition. Some of the later ones were built on artificial mounds that were used as graveyards, and it may be that, following Irish tradition, the hermit-priest did not actually live in the keeill, but in a small adjoining cell. Traces of such features have been found at the Lag ny Keeilly site.

Our search for an organizational centre for the early Church in Man (a monastery, for want of a better term) is hindered by the fact that there is no contemporary ecclesiastical record of events in Man until AD1134. Some writers have compiled lists of Manx bishops in which St German is shown as the first in 447 and St Maughold the third in 498; others have placed St Patrick himself as the first. But there is no hard evidence for any of this, and no justification for naming any individual as 'bishop' prior to the Norse period, which heralded the beginning of the historical record in Man.

However, having noted that the churchyard of Kirk Maughold encloses three visible keeill sites, a known fourth site, and the present church probably covering a fifth, that almost a third of the island's early Celtic cross-slabs have been found there, and that the cliff-top overlooking the nearest landing-beach was guarded by a prominent ramparted fortification, the impression is gained that this was a place of some importance. The majority of the Celtic cross-slabs discovered in the parish have been found in the immediate surrounds of the churchyard and village.

Following a review of all available evidence by B. R. S. Megaw [55] in 1950, it is now generally accepted that whatever occupied the site of the present Kirk

*Kirk Maughold: (above) the churchyard marks the site of an early Christian monastery;
(below) the east keeill with its baptismal well*

Maughold churchyard was the pre-eminent ecclesiastical centre in Man between the seventh and eleventh centuries. In calling it a monastery, we should not expect to see the kind of establishment we would see today. The site, probably the same as the present churchyard (3.5 acres or 1.4ha), would have held a collection of small chapels and dwellings within the defended site. There, student-clerics would undergo their training before being sent forth on their proselytizing labours.

Very little is known of Maughold (the man) but at some time he has become confused with an Irish character named McCuill, who is reputed to have led a dissolute early life in Ireland, been set adrift in the Irish Sea in a one-hide coracle on the orders of St Patrick and ended up coming ashore below the Manx head-land which now bears his name. It was always a fanciful tale and is now largely discredited. (For the full story, refer to W. Cubbon [18].) St Maughold was almost certainly buried in his own monastery, as was Roolwer, the first *authenticated* bishop in Man in the eleventh century.

The present parish church of Kirk Maughold is typical of the traditional Manx parish church: an enlarged version of the early Christian keeill, rectangular in form, lacking transepts and side-aisles, a minimal chancel with no separation between it and the nave. Above the door at the western end stands a rudimentary bell-tower surmounted by an arch, open to east and west, housing a single bell, with the bell-rope descending down the outside to be looped to one side of the entrance door – a wholly unpretentious structure.

The role of St Patrick's Isle in this early phase of the Celtic Church in Man is even less clear. Manx folk-myth has St Patrick landing on the isle that now bears his name in 444, staying for three years, converting the Manx and banishing snakes before appointing his disciple (nephew?) German as bishop in 447. Once again, there is no evidence; the authority for this is one of Patrick's biographers, Jocelyn, Abbot of Rushen Abbey, in 1187 – more than 700 years after the supposed event!

The oldest buildings on St Patrick's Isle today are the Round Tower and the ruin of St Patrick's Church, both dating from the tenth century, the early years of the Viking age. The tower, like similar structures in Ireland, was built as a refuge from raiders. Its entrance door was 7 feet (2m) off the ground. At the first sign of danger, the priests would collect the ecclesiastical valuables from the church, transport them into the tower, haul up the ladder and wait (and hope) for the interlopers to go away.

INSCRIPTIONS IN STONE

The great religious movements in the adjacent islands during this period were characterized by significant developments in learning, literature, the arts and crafts. We often see reference to a Golden Age, of objects of great beauty created on the printed page, in metalwork and in sculpture. The arts on the written page came together to form something which we would term 'scholarship'. Much of this is absent from the Manx scene. The islands to the east and west of us produced such artistic works of learning and beauty as the *Book of Kells,* the *Book of Durrow* and the *Lindisfarne Gospels.* The Isle of Man has nothing to compare with these.

But, in the sphere of sculpture on stone, much has been found. The first inscribed stones in Man were pagan and marked with ogham characters of the fourth or fifth century. The ogham script, using a twenty-character alphabet, was developed in south-west Ireland at that time, each letter being formed by a number of strokes cut into the stone at right angles or inclined to a longitudinal axis. The inscription on a memorial slab usually gives only the name of the deceased and that of his father, but they provide the oldest written record of the early form of Gaelic spoken in Ireland and Man.

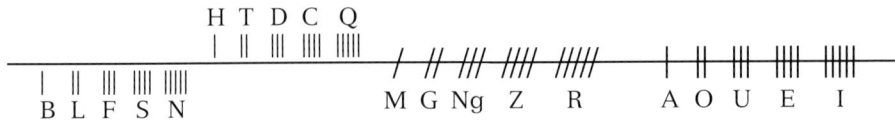

The Ogham Alphabet

Six examples of ogham-inscribed stones have been found in the island, two at Ballaqueeney, in Rushen, two in the Friary area of Arbory, and one each in Andreas and Maughold. The stone from Knock y Doonee, Andreas, is bilingual, carrying an Irish inscription in ogham characters, and a Latin inscription in Roman letters, thus:

Abicatos maqi Rocatos   (in ogham)
Ammecati filius Rocati   (in Roman)

The names are Irish and, writing them in later form, the inscription refers to *Imchadh,* son of *Rochadh.* One of the Arbory stones refers to *Maqleog,* 'Son of Leog', which is thought to be the earliest inscribed example of the use of *maq* to denote 'son of'. If so, Maqleog is the earliest recorded ancestor of the modern-day Claques of Man.

As the Christian influence gained strength in the island, so the practice of engraving representations of the cross on memorial slabs grew, from about the mid-seventh century. The stone used was predominantly the local slate, which was relatively soft and easy to work. During the eighth century, the depiction of the cross began to take on what would become the traditional Celtic form, with a circle circumscribing the arms of the cross.

One of the earliest examples of the form takes us back to Kirk Maughold, where such a slab commemorates one named Irneit, who is thought to have been a cleric within the monastery, but nothing else is known of him. In this case, the circle at the head of the slab encloses a hexafoil cross and the commemoration to Irneit in Latin. Below the circle, the slab displays a pair of *chi-rho* crosses with a second Latin inscription reading: *In Christi Nomine Crucis Christi Imagenem* ('In the name of Christ a figure of the cross of Christ').

Three further Celtic cross-slabs at Maughold are noteworthy. First, an early ninth-century slab is unusual in commemorating the achievement of one Branhui: *branhui huc aqua dirivavit*, indicating that he 'led off water to this place'. Traces of an open stone-lined channel have been found in the churchyard, and it is presumed that this was part of Branhui's work in providing the monastery with a water supply. It is most unusual to find a commemorative slab from this period which tells us more than just the name of the deceased.

Secondly, from around the same period, we have two slabs commemorating Blakman (a Saxon name). It has been suggested that the slabs stood at the head and foot of his grave, although they were not found together. Even more

Celtic scrollwork on early Christian cross-slabs at (left) Kirk Maughold
and (right) Old Kirk Lonan

intriguingly, his name is inscribed in *Anglian* runes. Could this have been an early 'comeover' from the adjacent isle to the east?

And finally at Kirk Maughold (although there are many more standing today in the cross-house outside the church), there is a massive early ninth-century slab bearing the simple inscription *Crux Guriat*, 'the cross of Guriat'. This is thought to refer to the Welsh prince, Gwriad, who sought refuge in the Isle of Man around 825. The slab originally stood beside a keeill near Port e Vullen, one mile north-west of Kirk Maughold. The whole face of this cross has been worked down to leave five hemispherical bosses standing proud, representing the four arms and centre of the cross. The inscription is in Hiberno-British characters. Tradition has it that, whilst in the island, Gwriad fathered a son named Merfyn, known to the Welsh as *Merfyn o dir Manaw* ('Merfyn from the land of Mann'), who returned to north Wales and founded the powerful dynasties of Gwynedd and Deheubarth.

In other parts of the island, there are several impressive wheel-headed cross-slabs, in which the shape of the head of the slab follows the line of the circle enclosing the cross. One sturdy example may be seen, probably still in its original position, outside old Kirk Lonan. A similar example will be found in old Kirk Braddan, and another, more finely decorated slab with two seated dog-headed figures, stands at Kirk Onchan.

The Isle of Man is so rich in exhibits of this type that one cannot possibly do them all justice in a book of this nature. Further information on the Manx crosses is given by A. M. Cubbon [16] and P. M. C. Kermode [43].

But, before moving on, mention must be made of the outstanding example of Manx Celtic stone-based art – the Calf Crucifixion stone, discovered on the Calf of Man in 1773, when the ruin of a Celtic chapel was being demolished. It is a portion of a finely decorated panel on a slab of local slate. Differing from everything discussed thus far, this is not a memorial to the dead; it is thought to be part of an altar-front, or possibly of a decorated reredos. On the fragment, Christ's body is complete, together with right arm and both legs. The figure, still alive and eyes open, is spread upon the cross, the hands are nailed (although the left is missing) and the feet are nailed separately, not together. The Roman soldier, with spear poised, stands at His right side. The central figure is elaborately robed in a fashion found in the art of the eastern Mediterranean in about the sixth century, and markedly different from what became the usual Roman depiction of the scene in north-west Europe.

As Kinvig [44] has observed, this particular Crucifixion theme must have been brought through the Mediterranean to Ireland at an early stage, since it appeared in the *Lindisfarne Gospels* in Northumbria in the late seventh century. The most complete depiction now existing is that of the Athlone Crucifixion, a bronze now in the National Museum of Ireland. The similarities between it and the Calf stone are astonishing and, on viewing the Athlone bronze, the missing figures from the Calf stone fall immediately into place. The figure of the spear-bearer on Christ's right side is balanced by that of the sponge-carrier on His left, and there is a rather sinister gnome-like cherub hovering above each outstretched arm. The similarities between the two versions are so remarkable that one is tempted to assume that the Calf stone was a direct copy of the Athlone bronze, but there are differences of detail, particularly in the depiction of Christ's head. In the Calf scene, the hair is long, with a centre parting, and there is a prominent forked beard, whereas the Athlone head has a straight fringe and the face is hairless.

In the slab collection at Kirk Michael, there is a fragment from the tenth or early eleventh century of a particularly handsome carving of a similar scene. The fragment is the broken-off head portion of the slab, showing the complete figure of Christ with arms outstretched. The hands and arms seem unrestrained, and the feet appear unnailed and almost touching the ground. At the top left-hand corner of the slab is a cock (a symbol of resurrection) and, in the opposite corner, the figure of a winged cherub who seems quite joyful. This has authoritatively been described as a Crucifixion stone, but is that really what the sculptor had in mind? Could it not be a Resurrection scene, with Christ stepping down from the cross, arms extended in triumph? That is how it has always seemed to me.

With the coming of the Norse settlers, the art of the Manx crosses would develop further, and yet, even then, the page of literature would remain unwritten. Manx Gaelic was never a written language until quite recent times. The first written work in Manx was to be Bishop Phillips's translation of the Prayer Book in 1610, a handwritten manuscript of which handwritten copies were laboriously made by many of his clergy. It would be almost 150 years on before it was printed, and another twenty years for the Manx Bible to appear. Apart from those solitary works, the literary canvas remained blank. This cannot be explained away solely by virtue of the Manx language having no written form, for the number of clerics with a knowledge of Latin must have been considerable, and yet there is nothing other than inscribed stones.

In view of the fact that trading and ecclesiastical contacts must have continued, the apparent cultural isolation of Man during this period is puzzling. In the islands to the west and east, the vernacular tongues of the Celtic Irish and the Anglo-Saxon English were already transmuted into written languages. Ninth-century England saw the beginning of the *Anglo-Saxon Chronicle* but no comparable account of Manx history would surface until the fourteenth-century *Chronicon Regum Manniae et Insularum*, the *Chronicle of the Kings of Mann and the Isles*. That was written in Latin and may (or may not) have been composed in the island.

The secular history of Man in the Celtic period up to the end of the eighth century is even more of a blank, which bars us from any knowledge of the lifestyles of ordinary folk. The period seems to have developed into one of relative peace and stability, with contacts with the lands round about being maintained. But the tranquillity was soon to face a threat; it was to come from the north and be rather more than just a chill wind.

THE PEACE IS SHATTERED

By the end of the eighth century, the shores of the Irish Sea had been receiving sea-borne traders from far-off lands for a thousand years or more. The Scandinavians, although later in starting, had nevertheless developed into able shipbuilders, seamen and navigators, venturing afar to Iceland, Greenland and Newfoundland, and so voyages to the Scottish islands and into the Irish Sea had become routine.

The Scandinavians comprised three groups of peoples: the Norwegians (or Norse), the Danes and the Swedes. From their relative geological dispositions, it was logical for the Norse to push their trading routes down through the Western Isles and into the Irish Sea, whilst the Danes concentrated on eastern England, the Low Countries and France. The Swedes, in their turn, directed their trading endeavours – and later settlement – eastward into Russia and beyond.

The Viking ships were long and high-prowed, pointed fore and aft, with long, shallow keels and completely open to the elements. The hull was clinker-built in oak planking, and powered by a single square sail and oars. A pair of T-shaped crutches on the centre-line could receive the unstepped mast and spars and, when the vessel was hove-to, a tent would be draped over the top. The helmsman controlled the ship by means of a large steering board hinged over the right side of the stern; hence, the steering-board side of the ship would later evolve into the *starboard* side and, in order to avoid damage to the steering board while in harbour, the ship would lie with its left side against the quay of the port – the port side. The largest Viking vessel so far discovered is the Gokstad ship, which is now housed in the Viking Ship Museum in Oslo. It is 80 feet (24m) long, 17 feet (5m) in beam, and has positions for 32 oars; it was built in about 850. In all probability, the Irish Sea folk had seen nothing like it before the arrival of the Scandinavians, who came to be known as Vikings after they had transformed themselves from traders into raiders. They were the 'creeklings', who inhabited the *viks* (the creeks, bays and fjords), the numerous natural havens of the Scandinavian coastline.

The first Viking raid on England is recorded in the *Anglo-Saxon Chronicle* for the year 793, when the Lindisfarne monastery was sacked and 'the ravaging of heathen men destroyed God's church at Lindisfarne through brutal robbery and slaughter' [69]. The following year, the monastery at Jarrow was attacked but, on this occasion, some of the raiders seem to have paid the price: 'Some of their war-leaders were killed; also some of their ships were broken up in bad weather, and many were drowned. Some came alive to the shore and were quickly killed at the river's mouth.' [69] They took no prisoners, those monks of Jarrow.

These were the first significant attacks on Britain in 200 years, and none had been expected, so the shock must have been heightened as a consequence. But the Vikings would not return to eastern England for more than four decades. Instead, they turned their attentions to the northern and western isles of Scotland and to the shores around and in the Irish Sea. Iona was attacked in 795, then, three years later, the *Annals of Ulster* record the sacking of the monastery on 'Inis Patraic', which was taken by some earlier historians to be a reference to St Patrick's Isle, on the west coast of Man, but is now generally accepted to refer to Inispatrick, off the coast of Dublin. Nonetheless, that must have been close enough for the message to be received in Man: the Vikings had arrived.

CHAPTER FOUR

The Norse Interlude

What causes a race of fearless seafarers, plying the oceans and trading their wares with peoples of other lands, suddenly to become ruthless raiders of those same lands, plundering, looting and pillaging any transportable wealth that comes to hand? The monasteries would have been prime targets because of the treasures they often contained, but the more mundane human settlements were frequently victims also.

Various students of the period have pointed to unsettled conditions in Scandinavia and other parts of Europe, to the political unification of Norway under King Harald Fairhair towards the end of the ninth century, prompting lesser chieftains to seek land and power elsewhere, to a system of inheritance that diminished the amount of land available to the individual sons of successive generations, and to the pressures of an expanding population on available resources.

One can readily see that such influences would promote a desire to migrate and settle elsewhere, but the Vikings at the *beginning* of the ninth century showed little inclination to settle; most were intent on raiding and running. Did that section of the Norse folk perhaps conclude that raiding presented a more amenable way of living than any alternative available at that time? The plundering of the monasteries would certainly have brought them assets which they could then trade elsewhere to obtain the necessities of life, and this carefree way of life might well have attracted young, strong men who hailed from a pagan culture in which to plunder openly was honourable, whilst to steal covertly brought only shame. In any event, this is an aspect of Scandinavian life on which there is no indigenous historical record to cast a light, for there was one attribute – or lack of it – which the Norse of that time shared with the Celtic Manx: apart from some runic inscriptions on stone and wood, they were illiterate.

Harald Fairhair belonged to the *Ynglinga* dynasty, which had risen to prominence in the region around Oslo Fiord. He succeeded his father, Halfdan the Black, while still a child in the 870s. Some time between 885 and the end of the

(above) The replica Viking ship
Odin's Raven *sailed from*
Norway to the Isle of Man in
1979, and now rests in the House
of Mannanan, Peel, still flaunting
its fearsome figurehead (right)

century, he was victorious in a sea battle at Hafrsfiord, south of Stavanger, against a confederacy of lesser chieftains of the west and south-west of Norway. This was the first significant step forward in his ambition to unite Norway as a single kingdom. It came almost a century after the start of the Viking raids, and so could have played no part in their inception; as an incentive for later overseas settlements, perhaps, but not for the earlier voyages of raid and plunder.

Some Viking bands were known to overwinter among the Scottish islands and then sail away to raid neighbouring coasts, including their own Norwegian homeland, through the summer months. And the *Orkneyinga Saga* contains references to Vikings in winter quarters in Man, who would spend their summers raiding adjacent coasts, returning to Man at the end of the season, before the onset of the next winter's storms.

The Norse interlude in Man was to last for more than 450 years, and its beginning would herald the approach of the island's entry into the historical age – but not just yet. For the two centuries following the first Viking attacks, there is little record of events in Man. The island's Dark Age would drag on for a while yet, but somewhat more is known of happenings in the adjacent isles to east and west and, once the process of Norse settlement was in motion there, it is inconceivable that the same would not be taking place in Man; the island's strategic position between the two would ensure that.

Norse settlement along the coast of north-west England between the Solway and the Dee was well established in the first half of the tenth century, and Danish settlement in eastern England had been in progress during the last quarter of the ninth. Some degree of settlement in those areas had doubtless been developing earlier in that century.

In Ireland, the process would have run to a similar time-scale. The period 920–50 saw attempts to unite the well-established Scandinavian kingdoms of Dublin and York. Just where the Isle of Man would have fitted into this union, if at all, is another unknown but, in the event, any such union was intermittent and short-lived. The king of Dublin, Olaf Sihtricson (otherwise known as Olaf Cuaran), twice established himself as king at York but, in 952, finally relinquished his ambitions in Northumbria to consolidate his rule over Dublin, which he did for almost thirty years. He married an Irish princess – a favoured tactic in such situations – thereby ensuring that the foreign-born ruler and his heirs could call on the loyalties of both their own and the indigenous communities.

However, in 980, Olaf's sons were defeated in battle at Tara by the Irish high king, Mael Sechlainn, whereupon Olaf left the country and, having earlier converted to Christianity, ended his days on Iona. In a turbulent period in Ireland's history, two of Olaf's sons successively held the kingship of Dublin; the second of them, known picturesquely as Sihtric of the Silken Beard, was a contemporary of that great hero of Irish history, Brian Boru. By 984, Brian had established himself as overlord of southern Ireland, whilst Mael Sechlainn retained power in the north, and Sihtric controlled Dublin. A further period of unrest culminated in a fierce battle in 999, in which Brian captured Dublin. Sihtric submitted and came to terms with Brian, who agreed to recognize Dublin's territorial integrity, provided that the Scandinavians pledged military support. Mael Sechlainn also agreed terms and acknowledged Brian's superiority. By the early years of the eleventh century, Brian was being referred to as *Imperator Scottorum*, 'emperor of the Irish'.

The triumph of Brian Boru brought no end to Ireland's internal troubles, and they were not troubles engaging Irish against Norse, or Christian against pagan, for all four of these were well represented on *both* sides of any Irish conflict of the period. They were troubles – as for so long in that island – of tribe against tribe. Brian held the various factions of Ireland more or less together for ten years, until the whole thing erupted again with the battle of Clontarf in 1014. This was essentially a revolt of Leinster against the dominance of Brian Boru.

The battle took place on Good Friday, 23 April, and Brian himself, a devout Christian, would not fight on that day. Sihtric, aware of his sworn allegiance to Brian, had enlisted support from far and wide: Sigurd the Stout, Earl of Orkney, brought reinforcements; there were contingents from Iceland and Normandy, and one named Brodir brought twenty ships from the Isle of Man. Brian Boru lost the battle and his life; Sigurd and Brodir were both slain. Mael Sechlainn regained the high-kingship of Ireland, although Norse kings continued to rule in Dublin which, together with the Irish-Scandinavian trading centres in Cork, Limerick, Waterford and Wexford, were too important to the Irish to be expunged. For the Norse, in addition to the trading activities, these settlements served as bases for the fitting out and provisioning of vessels for raiding trips across the water. The Norse appear never to have sought the conquest of all Ireland; the settlements were sufficient – or perhaps they simply accepted early on that any ambition to rule a unified Ireland was doomed to failure.

At this stage in Man's Norse interlude, into the early years of the eleventh century, we are in the transitional phase between outright Viking piracy and comparatively peaceful Norse settlement, with both activities being pursued simultaneously. As far as conditions in the island itself were concerned, the few external references to Man in the historical record indicate that the main external influence at that time was still that of Ireland. The drastic change in circumstances during the preceding two centuries had been the replacement of the benign influence of the Christian clerics by the more authoritarian power increasingly exerted by the pagan Norse.

THE EARLY SETTLEMENTS

The record (such as it is) of Scandinavian settlement in Ireland, Scotland, England and Wales leads to the fairly safe conclusion that Norse settlements in Man were well established by the middle of the ninth century. In the continuing absence of any insular historical record of the period, we are compelled to rely on the archaeologists' excavations for the evidence. Several sites in the island have revealed the remains of typical Norse-style dwellings – rectangular long-houses. At the Vowlan site in Ramsey (identified on the Ordnance Survey maps as a 'fort'), the foundations of a number of rectangular buildings have been uncovered, each set out on the 'three-aisle' plan of Norse construction (another excavation by Bersu [3]).

The Braaid site, mentioned in the previous chapter, has yielded the stone foundations of two such dwellings, which occupy the site together with the earlier Celtic roundhouse described previously. One of the dwellings is truly rectangular, the two long walls being straight and parallel. The long walls of the second are curved, bulging outwards and giving the appearance of an almost boat-shaped house but with the bow and stern sections missing. In neither case is there any sign of the gable walls, leading to the supposition that these were constructed of timber and turf and have degraded to leave no trace.

Three other sites are to be found in southern coastal promontory locations that were previously occupied during the Celtic Iron Age; they were investigated by P. S. Gelling in the 1950s [31, 32, 33]. The sites are at Cronk ny Merriu in Santon, and Cass ny Hawin and Close ny Chollagh in Malew, and each one has a rectangular house squeezed into a decidedly 'tight' location. Those at Cronk ny Merriu and Cass ny Hawin are laid out on the 'three-aisled' pattern. It is believed that these could only have been used to accommodate the personnel manning the promontory forts, although it has also been suggested that they could have been fortified farmhouses. The promontory location would certainly have provided a convenient layout for defence against assault from the land, with only one of four sides to be defended.

Norse houses were generally about 35 feet by 14 feet (11m x 4m) internally, with walls constructed of soil or turf faced with dry-stone walling. The hearth was usually placed in the centre aisle, on either side of which, extending along the two longer walls, were raised platforms for sitting and sleeping.

The arrival of the Scandinavians as settlers brought a fresh influx of tall, fair strangers into the isle. How warmly, or coldly, they were regarded by the indigenous Celts, how smooth was their integration, to what extent they brought conflict and strife – all of these are questions which can be met only with conjecture. There

The coastal promontory fort at Cronk ny Merriu, Santon

is certainly no clue within the isle to shed the faintest glimmer of light on such themes. Early conflict there almost certainly was; it was still flaring up decades into the eleventh century, but inter-marriage would, in the longer term, smooth the way. Doubtless there would have been a certain proportion of Norse women joining the later migration voyages south from Norway but, overall, there must have been a far larger proportion of Celtic women becoming wives to Norse men.

Experience from elsewhere tells us that the Scandinavians brought with them many of their homeland traditions: systems and procedures for farming, house-building and civil administration, as well as crafts and industries. In Ireland, they took the first step in the long walk to urbanization, building towns through which to funnel their expanding trade; we have already mentioned Limerick, Cork, Waterford and Wexford, as well as their principal centre in Dublin. In England, they did the same, rebuilding and developing the ruinous old Roman fortress town which they called *Jorvik*. In doing so, they formed the basis for towns and cities that we know today. *Jorvik* is today's York, and its Jorvik Centre displays the sights and scents of life in a Scandinavian town of a thousand years ago.

In Man, things were never going to develop to the same scale. The island's population was never large enough to draw in large volumes of trade goods (this is a stricture on island life which still, to a certain degree, persists today), and what population there was was widespread and rural. Most of the Norse settlers, likewise, would have been engaged in rural pursuits. The island's importance would remain strategic, by virtue of its central location, as a port of call on the wider trading routes and in the political to-ings and fro-ings across the Irish Sea. Such urban concentrations as there were would have been relatively small and sited on strategically important coastal locations. The few historical references recording voyages to the Isle of Man in the first half of the Norse period recount landings being made either at *Ramsá* (Ramsey) or at *Holmtun* ('island town', i.e. Peel), and only later at Castletown or *Ragnaldsvath* (Ronaldsway).

The Norse name for Ramsey denoted a 'wild garlic river', referring to the stream later known as the Lickney. As if to emphasize the point, the Gaelic name applied to this stream (as shown on the old Ordnance Survey maps) was *Strooan ny craue*, 'the stream of the wild garlic'. The western settlement of *Holmtun* was named with reference to St Patrick's Isle; it later became Peel after the *pile, peel* or fortress later raised on that isle. The 'wild garlic river' is not the only example of place names in the two languages signifying the same meaning for either a single geographical feature or two neighbouring features. At the southern end of the Michael hills, we find *Sartfell* and, two miles north-east, *Slieau Dhoo*, both meaning 'dark mountain'.

The Scandinavians also left names attached to numerous minor landing places around the Manx coastline – names such as Laxey (*Laxá*, the 'salmon river'), Garwick, Soderick, Soldrick, Perwick, Aldrick and Fleshwick – and there were open landing beaches all along the north-west coast with glen access at *Orrisdale* and *Jurby*. Elsewhere, it is safe to suppose the existence of Norse settlement at places whose names give us the clue: Sulby, Injebreck, Crosby, Foxdale, Colby, Surby and Dalby.

In their burial customs, the Norse brought further change to the Manx scene, for their chieftains and other men of property and influence followed their homeland practice of being buried in their ships. Two such ship-burials have been found and excavated. The first, at Knock-y-Dooney, in Andreas, was excavated in 1927 by the famed Manx archaeologist, P. M. C. Kermode [42]. Knock-y-Dooney is a sandy summit approximately a mile south of Rue Point, standing at the western end of the Bride Hills and close behind the old post-glacial cliff-line. This type of burial may be seen as a relic of the transition from Viking seaborne plunder to Norse rural settlement, with the boat retained for fishing, and finally for burial – the interment of a land-owning farmer-fisherman.

The Knock-y-Dooney boat was about 30 feet (9m) long. The body of its owner had been placed in the centre, and his horse and dog had been sacrificed so that they could accompany their master on his journey. Also in the boat were his sword, spear, shield and battle-axe, together with a smith's hammer, tongs, fishing gear and knives. The whole boat was covered with timber and brushwood, surmounted by a cairn topped with a covering of soil and turf. As the wooden covering rotted away, the whole structure collapsed onto the boat, but retained sufficient bulk to remain as a mound standing some 7 feet (2m) above the surrounding ground. The burial has been dated to around 850.

The second ship-burial was discovered within the rampart of the Iron-Age hill-fort on Chapel Hill, Balladoole, in Arbory, and was excavated by Bersu in 1945 [5]. This boat was slightly longer (35 feet or 11m) than that described above, and the interred body of the man was accompanied by that of a woman. His horse and other livestock had also been sacrificed. The variety of grave goods accompanying the body indicated the wide-ranging trading contacts being maintained at that time, with articles originating in Ireland, England, Scandinavia and central and southern Europe. This pagan burial had been placed directly over some earlier Christian burials in stone-lined graves. The timbers of the boat had long-since rotted away but its outline was clearly marked by the remains and rust-marks of its iron fastenings. The outline of the Balladoole ship is now marked with stones.

The number and distribution of burial mounds thought to date from the same period bears testimony to the thoroughness with which the newcomers settled

Site of the Viking ship burial at Chapel Hill, Arbory

themselves on the most fertile of the island's lands, mainly in the northern plain. More than a score of such mounds are known, most of them yet to be opened up. Two that have been excavated are those at Ballateare and Cronk Mooar, in Jurby, in each of which the body had been interred in a wooden coffin and his weapons deliberately broken before being placed in the grave. In the Ballateare burial, the interred body and grave goods were covered with a mound of turf, near the top of which was a layer of cremated animal bones and the skeleton of a young woman, the back of whose skull had been removed by a blow from a sharp weapon.

These two burials were unearthed in 1945–6 by (whom else but) Bersu [5]. The parish of Jurby is particularly rich in such mounds; in addition to the two referred above, there is one in the parish churchyard, another overlooking the sea from the summit of Cronk ny Arrey Lhaa, and yet another at Knock-y-Dowan, overlooking the Lhen Trench.

MORE INSCRIPTIONS ON STONE

Following the arrival of the first waves of Norse settlers in Man, the inevitable intermarriage between them and indigenous Celtic women resulted in the gradual conversion of the pagan immigrants to Christianity. The time-scale must remain uncertain; Christianity was made compulsory in Norway by Olaf I (Tryggvasson) in 995, but it is known that the religion was alive and well in the Scottish islands before that date, and so the 'home-spun' conversion of the Norse in Man may also have been complete.

Following the initial phase of settlements, the practice of erecting stone memorial slabs to the dead was revived. The slabs initially bore carved figures of human and animal forms in scenes from Scandinavian mythology, and later displayed a mixture of pagan and Christian symbolism. Often, a memorial inscription would be carved along one edge of the slab, using the runic alphabet of the Norse newcomers.

ᚠᚢᚦᚨᚱᚲᚷᠹᚺᚾᛁᛂᛈᛖᚱᛋᛏᛒᛖᛗᛚᛝᛞᛟ

f u þ a r k g w h n i j p e R s t b e m l ng d o

The Norse Runic Alphabet

The oldest runic inscriptions which allow any confidence in dating originate in Denmark around AD300, when a common set of runes was in use throughout Scandinavia and around the lower Danube. The same runes were adopted by the western Germanic peoples about 150 years later. The origins of the runes lie further back in time; they may have sprung partly from the Latin alphabet and partly from the Greek but, equally, they could have had their beginnings in the north Italic alphabet.

The oldest Germanic rune set consisted of twenty-four letters arranged in three groups of eight. It was known as the *futhark*, after the first six characters, the third being pronounced 'th'. Use of the *futhark* spread south into western Europe, where it divided into two distinct sets. In the newer, Anglo-Friesian set, the total number of characters was increased to more than thirty. As a result of some of the changes in characters, this set became known as the *futhorc*, and it was this set which the Anglo-Saxons brought to England. It was the original *futhark* which the Norse introduced into the Scottish islands, Ireland, Man and north-west England. Where the two systems came into contact, any problem would have been relatively slight; these were both Germanic languages, differing little more than two distinct dialects of the same tongue.

The runes represent a significant step forward from the ogham of the Celts. In place of sequences of straight lines, we see characters that are recognizable to us today, admittedly still straight-sided in the main for ease of carving on stone and wood, but they bring us to the threshold of the literary age. And once the scribe embarks onto a written page, straight-sided characters will be rounded-off into even more familiar forms. In the Scandinavian homelands, early literary endeavours would result in heroic poems and sagas relating (however loosely) to historical events, which must be treated with caution before being accepted as gospel.

In Man, the earliest memorial slabs of the Norse period retained the earlier interlaced patterns of the Celtic art, but with the introduction of scenes from Norse pagan mythology, and this would continue for a time following their conversion to Christianity. There are several stone slabs from the pagan period in various of the parish churches, and a favoured scenario is the Sigurd legend. A finely carved slab at Jurby depicts the hero, Sigurd, slaying Fafni, the dragon, with his sword. A carving at Andreas shows Sigurd roasting slices of the dragon's heart on his sword and licking his scalded fingers. A slab at Malew portrays the same scene. On a slab at Maughold, Loki, the mischief-maker of the gods, is shown throwing a stone to kill Otter, the great fisher, who is really a prince under curse and has a fish between his teeth. Sigurd's horse, Grani, is also depicted, laden with treasure which is also part of the legend. Back at Jurby, the Heimdall slab shows Heimdall, the janitor of Valhalla, the abode of the gods, blowing his great Giallar-horn to summon the gods to Ragnarok, the last great battle that would be the end of everything, as foretold in Norse mythology.

If the Heimdall slab heralds the demise of the pagan gods, Thorwald's slab at Andreas illustrates the transition between paganism and Christianity. On one face, Odin, identified by the raven on his right shoulder, is wielding his spear whilst his leg is being devoured by the Fenris wolf. (In the legend, the wolf itself is later slain – together with everything else.) But on the other side of the slab, a human figure carrying a cross in one hand and a book in the other is seen trampling on a serpent. Below the cross is a fish, an early symbol of Christianity. The slab seems to suggest that Odin is dead and Christ lives.

Thorwald's cross-slab has been dated to some time in the tenth century. Through the remainder of that century and onward, Christian symbolism gained the ascendancy in the artwork displayed on the Manx crosses. The parish church of Michael houses the largest collection of Norse cross-slabs in the island (and it will be obvious to the reader by now that there are far more reminders of Norse settlement in the north of Man than elsewhere).

From the mid-tenth century onwards, memorial inscriptions increasingly identified personalities, mainly the names of the interred deceased but, in at least two cases, that of the sculptor. Gaut Björnson was a prolific carver of the Manx Slate in the north of the island. He appears to have been the originator of the distinctive interlaced chain pattern which appears on a series of Norse slabs from that period. His designs were later copied by others. On the slab known as Gaut's Cross (at Kirk Michael) the runic inscription declares: 'Melbrigdi son of Athakan the smith erected this cross for his sin ... [?] soul but Gaut made it and all in Maun.' It is noteworthy that the Norse sculptor was producing slabs commemorating the Celtic dead, suggesting that Norseman and Celt were co-existing in the community at that time. Also, memorials to persons with Celtic names bore inscriptions in Norse because there was still no written form of Manx Gaelic.

On a cross-slab at Kirk Andreas, we find a tantalizing hint to Gaut's own origin: 'Gaut made [this], son of Björnson from Kolli.' Some have identified Kolli with the Hebridean island of Coll, others with the farm at Ballacooley, in Michael, and so the question remains open.

The trend towards more informative inscriptions continued. On another massive slab at Kirk Michael, we find that 'Joalf son of Thorolf the Red erected this cross to the memory of Frida his mother', and at Ballaugh, 'Aleif Liotolfsson erected this cross to the memory of Ulf his son'. At Kirk Andreas, 'Sandulf the Black erected this cross to the memory of Arinbiorg his wife'. Old Kirk Braddan has the lower portion of a cross-slab bearing the incomplete inscription: 'Odd

Gaut's Cross, Kirk Michael

raised this cross to the memory of Frakki his father, but Tho[rbjörn] ...', and what Thorbjörn did we shall never know – unless someone finds the other portion of the slab.

This lower portion of Odd's cross shows that it differed from the normal run of Norse slabs, which were usually rectangular; Odd's cross-slab was tapered towards the top. In the same collection, a full-height slab, complete except for a missing fragment from one side of the cross-head, is similarly tapered. The runic inscription on it is perhaps the most instructive of the lot, for it gives us not only the names of the deceased and his father, but also of his uncle: 'Thorleiff Hnakki erected this cross to the memory of Fiac his son, brother's son to Hafr.' It is note-worthy here that both the deceased's father and uncle bore Norse names, whilst Fiac himself had a Celtic one, probably indicative of a Celtic mother. But Thorleiff's cross also displays a fourth name, a Jewish name; on one edge of the slab, under the ring of the cross-head, is the single word *Ihsus*, 'Jesus'.

At some time in the eleventh century, a further development in style of the Norse crosses appeared, when sculptors began piercing through the slab between the arms of the cross and the encircling ring, leaving the four quadrants completely open. Thorleiff Hnakki's cross has this feature, as does the beautifully carved dragon cross at Kirk Michael.

Of the fifty or so Norse cross-slabs discovered in Man, most have been found in the northern parishes of Michael, Jurby and Andreas. In contrast, of approxi-mately 100 Celtic slabs in the island, almost a third have been found in or around the ancient Celtic monastic site at Maughold, with only seven from the Norse period gathered there.

The art of the Manx crosses continued to evolve into the early years of the twelfth century but, with the establishment of Rushen Abbey in 1134 and the growing influence of Rome, the Norse runes and their associated art forms were increasingly regarded in relation to their pagan origins, and so the age of the great monumental slabs faded away, to be replaced with rather more sophisti-cated craftsmanship and art forms in later times.

STYLES OF LIVING

The archaeological evidence described thus far shows us *where* people lived, and where and how they were buried when they ceased living, but it can tell us little of *how* they lived their lives, and there is little hard evidence and no historical record in Man to enlighten us. There can be no doubt that the indigenous Celtic population continued to speak Gaelic throughout the Norse period, since it survived, largely intact, at the end of the period. The ruling Nordic classes were almost certainly bilingual, as they would remain in contact with the Scandinavian homeland, where suzerainty over Man ultimately lay – even if only nominally at times. The degree of bilingualism among other of the Nordic classes probably depended on their positions on the socio-political scale. The Norse farmer, fisherman or artisan, raising a family with a Celtic wife, would in all probability end up as a largely Gaelic speaker.

Also, it seems to have been a truism that wherever Scandinavians settled – and their areas of settlement extended eastward through Russia to Byzantium and beyond – over time they adapted their lives to blend with those among whom they were dwelling. To put it plainly, they 'turned native'. Their only place of settlement where they did not turn native was Iceland – there were no natives. Even Magnus Barefoot took to wearing a kilt, hence his nickname, which was sometimes rendered as 'Barelegs'. The one possible exception to this generalization is provided by the Northern Isles of Orkney and Shetland, where, by the end of the Norse period, the prevailing language, known as Norn, was almost wholly Scandinavian and very close to Norwegian. But this could have been because the Norse incomers were numerically superior to the islanders among whom they settled. Norn survived as the language of the Northern Isles right through the Middle Ages; it was not until the late eighteenth century in Orkney that the language went into terminal decline, and it remained in use in Shetland until the 1890s. Ultimately, the influence of the English language was too strong and too useful in the modern world for Norn to survive. But in Man, as in most areas of Norse settlement, it was the native language that lasted the course – but the Manx Gaelic suffered the same fate as Norn in the end.

As to living conditions in Man, contrasting with the fortified coastal dwellings described earlier, at least two inland Norse farm sites are known which appear to have had no need for defensive works at all. The first is the Braaid site, referred to earlier in this chapter, which is located on prime agricultural land. The second, excavated by P. S. Gelling in 1970 [30], sits on the 700-foot (210m) contour at Doarlish Cashen, overlooking Glen Mooar, in Patrick. Located on a far more marginal site than the Braaid farm, this upland site indicates that not all Norse farmers grabbed the best lowland locations (perhaps they had already been grabbed).

Although there is nothing to tell us specifically how the Norse lived in Man, there is enough information telling us how they lived elsewhere to enable us to draw conclusions – or at least inferences. In particular, since many of the Norse migrants to Iceland had previously lived in the Sudreys, we may reasonably surmise that styles of Nordic living in Iceland would settle into something similar to those pertaining in the isles (including Man). And in the *Landnamabok* (the Icelandic equivalent of the Domesday Book), there is much information concerning life in Iceland.

In addition, as far as codes of conduct were concerned, these are clearly set out in the sagas. Norse men were expected to act like men, to stand up for their own and to be bold and fearless in all their deeds. Raiding and piracy, if carried out openly and without deceit, were honourable pursuits, but covert stealing, as under cover of darkness or behind the victim's back, was shameful. They were expected to be hard on their enemies but to turn none from the door who sought food and shelter. Therein lay the code of the early Viking seafarers.

Once settled on land, each chieftain or other prominent man resided on his own holding, known as a *byr* (hence so many place-names ending in –*by*), on which would stand his dwelling and other farm buildings, usually arranged round a quadrangle, much like many a farm today. The principal room of the dwelling was built on the 'three-aisle' layout, with seating and bedding arranged length-wise along the walls. The living was mainly agrarian, with the sea and lakes providing variety in food. In the house, the women would milk the cows and goats, make cheese, weave cloth, prepare food and raise children. That was how it was in Iceland, and that was how it would probably have been in Man – but perhaps in a slightly warmer climate.

An improvement in the climate in Man in the eleventh and twelfth centuries allowed cattle to be taken higher onto the upland slopes during the summer months. We know this from the number of shieling sites discovered up towards the 1000-foot (300m) contour. The shieling (Manx *eary*) was a site where upland grazing took place and groups of small huts were built to accommodate those who spent the summer months on the hills with their livestock. Such sites are particularly numerous at Block Eary, on the northern slopes of Snaefell, and in the upper reaches of Druidale, overlooking the Sulby reservoir. Excavations at Block Eary were carried out in the early 1960s by Gelling [34], who uncovered evidence of cheese-making, weaving and a penny from the reign of King Stephen (reigned 1135–54).

Such discoveries suggest a scene of unbroken rural tranquillity but, in those times, the peace could suddenly and unexpectedly be shattered by conflict and strife. And for those harbouring ambitions to rule, life could be particularly fraught.

STRUGGLES FOR POWER

At the start of the eleventh century, the insular record of Manx history remains blank but, away to the north, the sagas were being written and the beginnings of political history emerge from the mist. In the islands to east and west, ecclesiastical scribes were in full flight. In various of these writings, the Isle of Man was given an occasional mention, sufficient to give us some perception of the island's situation in the general scheme of things.

At this time, Scandinavian conquests and settlement were continuing through the islands of Shetland, Orkney and the Hebrides, as well as Ireland (where Dublin remained the hub of Norse influence) and northern England. Throughout this period, the King of Norway would claim sovereignty over all such occupied lands but, in reality, the regional seat of power could shift unpredictably as Norse chieftains vied with each other for supremacy. Thus, at various times, the Manx could find themselves ruled by a king in Dublin, or in the Hebrides, or in the Isle of Man itself. There were times when the Earls of Orkney claimed the island.

In the latter half of the tenth century, the *Annals of Wales* recorded a number of raids on Anglesey and along almost the whole length of the Welsh mainland coast. The Isle of Man and Dublin were often named as the origins of the raiding fleets. Three centuries earlier, Bede had referred to the islands of Man and Anglesey (Mon) as the Menavian islands, apparently perceiving a link between the two. Certainly, any warlord in Man seeking to plunder over the sea might well be drawn to the south. Magnus Haroldson, a Viking leader who settled in Man, led raids on Anglesey in 968 and 971. His brother, Godfrey, who succeeded him in Man in 977, led attacks on Anglesey in 972, 980 and 987, the last of which, recorded in the annals of Ulster and of Wales, resulted in the slaying of a thousand Welshmen and the taking of twice as many as captives into slavery. The religious centres on the Welsh mainland coast were particularly attractive targets, St David's alone being sacked in 982, 988 and 999.

A further reference to the Isle of Man occurs in the *Anglo-Saxon Chronicle* for the year 1000. Through the final two decades of the tenth century, eastern and southern England had suffered renewed raiding by Scandinavian Vikings led by Swein Forkbeard of Denmark (father of Cnut) and Olaf Tryggvasson of Norway. When the latter was converted to Christianity at Andover in the winter of 994/5 and returned home, Swein continued to lead the attacks on his own, harrying the coastal towns westward from Kent to Devon and rounding the south-west peninsula into the Bristol Channel. And once into the Irish Sea, if he ever needed a safe haven, there was an abundance of Scandinavian harbours available to him in Ireland, the Isle of Man, the Scottish islands, or even the estuaries of Danelaw England.

And there, with reference to the Danelaw, we come to the purpose of these attacks, for these were not the almost random, indiscriminate Viking raids of old; they were concerned with the extension and consolidation of the Scandinavian occupation of England. The opposition – if such it could be called – was under the vacillating leadership of Ethelred, 'the Ill-counselled'. At the end of 999, the scribe of the *Anglo-Saxon Chronicle* is openly critical of his monarch's wavering response to the presence of the Danish fleet when he laments: 'at the end it availed nothing ... but was oppression of the people, waste of money, and an encouragement to their enemies'. Then, in the following year, Ethelred took his fleet out to face the attackers, but the Danish ships had turned away to a safe haven in Normandy. In response, Ethelred turned his wrath against Scandinavian-held territories. According to the chronicler: 'The king went into Cumberland and ravaged very nearly all of it ... then they ravaged the Isle of Man.' But it achieved little; the Danelaw remained intact and, in 1016, Cnut was king of all England.

As the first half of the eleventh century progressed, control over the Isle of Man gravitated inexorably to the north. When Sigurd the Stout, Earl of Orkney, was slain at the battle of Clontarf in 1014, he was succeeded by his son, who would come to be known as Thorfinn the Mighty. Sigurd, in his time, had exerted control over Man and had married, as his second wife, a daughter of Malcolm II of Scotland (another strategic marriage). Subsequently – and consequently – Thorfinn's early years as Earl were turbulent, as half-brothers with ambitions of their own vied for influence. (In those days, such situations tended to become turbulent when they involved offspring from one father and two mothers.)

In time, Thorfinn appears to have consolidated his hold over the earldom which, at its height, extended from Shetland in the north to Man in the south, and included mainland Caithness and Galloway and possibly other parts of mainland Scotland. (Much of the 'historical' record is provided by the *Orkneyinga Saga*, which cannot be taken as giving more than a hazy outline of political situations of the period.) By this time, the Scandinavians had come to regard this long string of islands as comprising two distinct groups: the *Nordreyjar* or Nordreys (Orkney and Shetland) and the *Sudreyjar* or Sudreys (the Hebrides and Man). In ruling over this domain, Thorfinn acknowledged his subservience to Harald Hardrada, King of Norway, but doubtless enjoyed considerable freedom of action.

On Thorfinn's death in 1064, control over Man seems to have swung back to the Vikings in Dublin, but things were soon to change once more. The change was trig-

gered in 1066 by the battle of Stamford Bridge, where the last Scandinavian invasion of England was repulsed. By then, Godred Sytricsson, a survivor of the battle,
was recorded as King of Man. Also arriving in Man that year was another survivor,
one Godred Crovan, son of Harald the Black of Iceland. The nickname 'Crovan'
related to fingers, but what was noteworthy about his fingers is unknown. (Both
Godreds had fought on the side of Harald Hardrada, who was killed in the battle.)

It is at this point in the story that we come upon a historical source which *may*
have been written in Man and relates the events to which passing reference was
made towards the end of the previous chapter. It is *Chronicon Regum Manniae et
Insularum*, the *Chronicle of the Kings of Mann and the Isles*; for the sake of brevity,
I shall refer to it henceforth as *Chronicon*. *If* it was written in Man, it would almost
certainly have been the work of monks of Rushen Abbey, which means that it was
written at least a century after the events described. Indeed, its account of
happenings in the eleventh century read like brief summaries of past events,
rather than contemporary records. It may be that the chroniclers were copying
accounts from earlier records kept elsewhere, before Rushen Abbey was established, but there are chronological errors, with dates being fifteen to twenty-three
years too early up to the year 1100, errors becoming smaller (ten years or less)
thereafter. The dates are generally accurate after 1155. In what follows here, the
dates have been corrected to the ones we know to be true.

For the year 1070, *Chronicon* records the death of Godred Sytricsson, King of
Man, with the succession passing to his son, Fingal. The whereabouts of Godred
Crovan during the next nine years are cloaked in mystery, but he must, at some
stage, have moved elsewhere, for, when he next appeared in Man, in 1079, he did
so with a large fleet of ships. He made three attempts to conquer the isle that year.
His first two attempts being repulsed, he returned for a third try, equipped with
an even larger fleet and army.

Chronicon records his night-time landing at the port of Ramsey. Godred took
his force onto the slopes of Scacafell (now known as Sky Hill), but left 300 men
concealed in a wood on the hillside to form an ambush. At daybreak, the Manx
(presumably led by Fingal, but there is no further mention of him) moved onto the
hillside to engage the enemy, and a furious battle ensued, whereupon the 300
emerged from the woodland to attack from the rear and the trap was sprung. The
Manx were compelled to withdraw, but their line of retreat had been cut off by the
tide raising the level of the river at Ramsey. Caught between the enemy and the
river, the Manx surrendered to Godred, who spared the lives of those still standing.

It should be borne in mind that the Manx who were defending their isle were,
by this time, a rich admixture of Norse and Celt, and so there is likely to have been
some underlying feeling of kinship between the two sides once the fighting was
over.

The day after the battle, according to *Chronicon*, Godred offered his men the choice of dividing the island between them and settling down or of plundering and returning home. In true Viking fashion, most of them chose the latter option and departed with their booty. To the few who remained with him, Godred granted the southern part of the island; the northern portion he gave to the surviving Manxmen, on condition that they would never claim hereditary right to any part of it. The island would, in its entirety, be the property of the king, all dues would accrue to him, and this the Manx accepted.

Godred was the man who would become known to the Manx as 'King Gorry', and it would not take long for the second 'g' to be subsumed into the first and for the name to become 'King Orry'. Manx tradition has the story of his arrival on the eve of the battle, of his stepping ashore on a bright, starlit night, to be asked by some local bystander whence he had come. He pointed to the shining band of the Milky Way and declared: 'There is the road which brought me from my country to this place.' Since then, the Milky Way has been known to the Manx as *Raad Mooar Ree Gorry*, 'the Great Road of King Orry'. It is not as fanciful as it may at first sound; the Vikings were skilled navigators, and a knowledge of the stars would be an essential part of that skill.

Thus was taken the first step in re-establishing a kingdom of islands that would be ruled over by Godred and his descendants for the best part of two centuries, and which would leave its defining mark on the Manx nation and its institutions to the present day.

THE KINGDOM OF MAN AND THE ISLES

Chronicon records that Godred subsequently subdued Dublin, a large part of Leinster and the Scots to such an extent that no ship-builder dared to insert more than three bolts into the structure of a newly built vessel. This confusing statement is possibly a reference to a prescribed limit on the size of ship that could be constructed without posing a threat to Godred's maritime supremacy.

In its relationship with Man, little more is heard of Ireland at this time. Godred's not inconsiderable achievement was to meld into one political unit an entity known as the Kingdom of Man and the Isles. 'The Isles' were the Sudreys, the Hebridean islands that had once been part of the much larger earldom of Orkney. Originally, the term 'Sudreys' included Man but, in time, either because this fact had been forgotten or to emphasize the island's status as the political hub of the kingdom, the specific reference to Man was inserted.

For administrative purposes, the Hebrides were split into two groups, divided

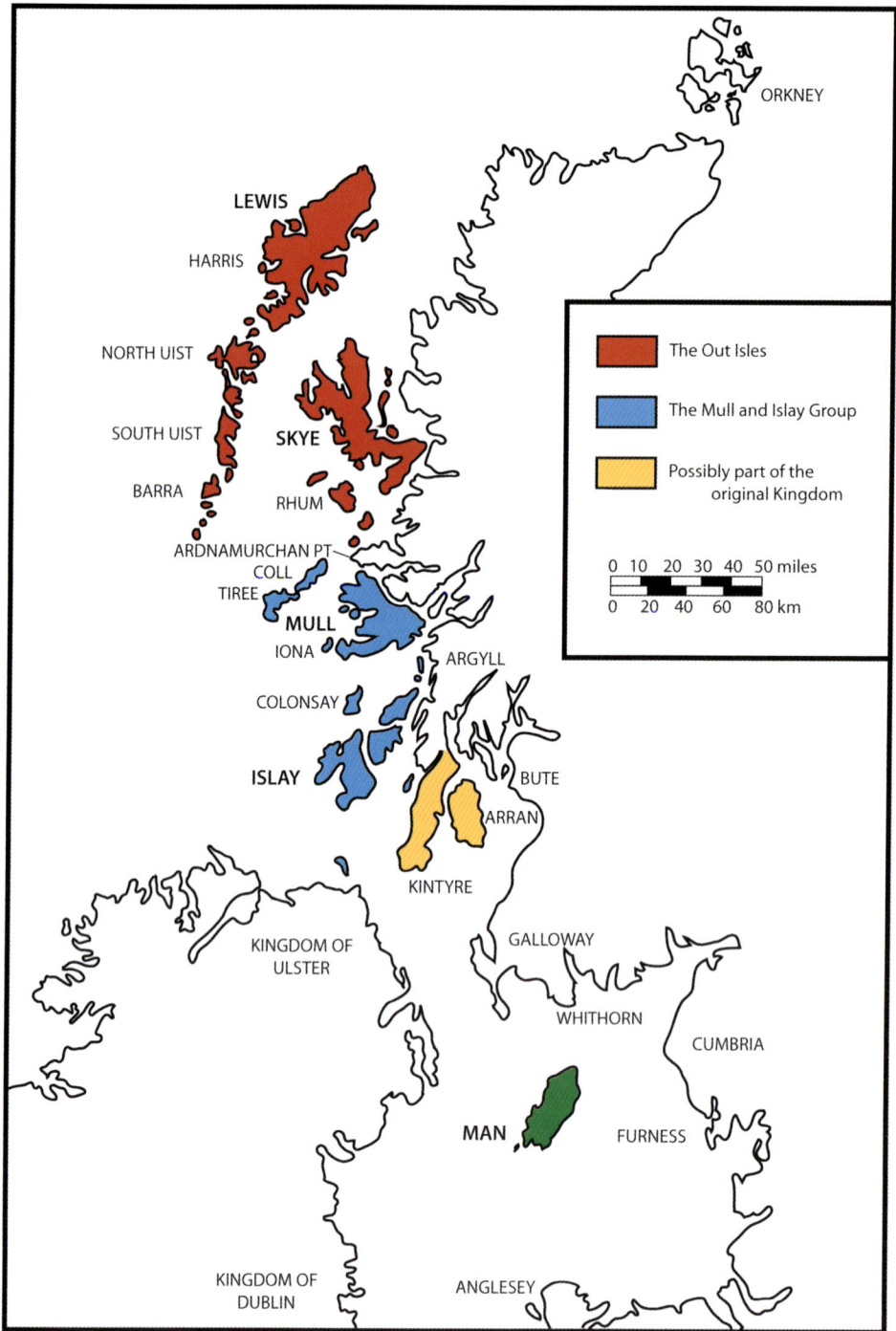

LEWIS

HARRIS

NORTH UIST

SOUTH UIST

BARRA

SKYE

RHUM

ARDNAMURCHAN PT
COLL
TIREE
MULL
IONA

COLONSAY

ISLAY

ARGYLL

BUTE

ARRAN

KINTYRE

GALLOWAY

WHITHORN

CUMBRIA

KINGDOM OF
ULSTER

MAN

FURNESS

KINGDOM OF
DUBLIN

ANGLESEY

ORKNEY

The Out Isles

The Mull and Islay Group

Possibly part of the
original Kingdom

0 10 20 30 40 50 miles

0   20   40   60   80 km

The Kingdom of Man and the Isles

by the Scottish mainland promontory of Ardnamurchan Point. The largest of the isles to the south were Mull and Islay. To the north, the isles of Lewis, Harris, the Uists, Barra and Skye, and many smaller ones, were known (in relation to Man) as the Out Isles. Politically, the Hebridean islands had representation in the Keys, of which more later in this chapter.

Although we are now entering the dawn of Manx recorded history, surprisingly little is known of Godred Crovan. He ruled over the Kingdom of Man and the Isles for sixteen years and died in Islay in 1095. In view of the extent of his domain, he must have spent some considerable time travelling in order to bring it together in a single political unit.

Godred had three sons, Lagman (the eldest), Harald and Olaf. Lagman succeeded to the kingdom and ruled for seven years, but Harald rebelled against him and was captured by Lagman, who blinded and castrated him. (They did not do things by halves in those days.) Subsequently, according to *Chronicon*, Lagman repented of blinding his brother (the castration, apparently, was not so bad as to require penance) and abdicated his kingdom to embark on a pilgrimage to Jerusalem but died on the way.

On Lagman's departure, the nobles of the Isles sent a request to Muircheartach O'Brien, King of Ireland, for some appropriate man of royal stock to act as regent until Olaf Godredsson was of age. The Irish king responded by sending Donald MacTadg, who proved to be wholly unsuitable by virtue of his tyrannical and brutal behaviour and, after three years, he was forced back to Ireland by a collaboration of the chieftains of the Isles.

In 1098, there occurred a battle of Manx against Manx, north against south, at a place called Sandwat, somewhere in the vicinity of Peel. It may be that a degree of animosity lingered between the Hebrideans that Godred had planted in the south and the remainder in the north. The two halves of the island were for long regarded by the Manx as two distinct places – the 'Northside' and the 'Southside' – separated, not by the east–west cleft of the central valley, but by the long spine of hills striding north-east to south-west. Thus, by such division, the parish of Maughold was part of the Southside, the parish of Patrick was in Northside, and the dividing ridge presented a far more formidable barrier to social intercourse than it does today. As Thomas Edward Brown mused in his reverie of *Braddan Vicarage*:

> I wonder if the hills are long and lonely
>   That North from South divide;
> I wonder if he thinks that it is only
>   The hither slope where men abide,
> Unto all mortal homes refused the other side.

However, in 1098, the southerners dared to venture to the other side and lost the day to the northerners, both leaders – named as Ottar and MacMaras – being slain in the process.

In the same year, Magnus Barefoot, king of Norway and grandson of Harald Hardrada, sailed south with a fleet of 160 ships to assert his supremacy over the islands and mainland Galloway. On his arrival at St Patrick's Isle, he found the setting so appealing (despite many bodies from the recent battle still lying unburied) that he chose it as his residence and erected fortifications there. Once established in Man, Magnus sailed south to subjugate the isle of Anglesey. Then, in 1103, he made the fatal mistake of turning his ambition towards Ireland, where he sailed with sixteen vessels. On stepping ashore with his landing party, the group was immediately surrounded by Irishmen; Magnus was killed, along with most of his men. He was buried beside St Patrick's Church in Down.

Magnus's son, Sigurd, succeeded to the Norwegian crown, and to that of the Nordreys and Sudreys, on his father's death. At that point, we enter another obscure period of Manx history that was to last for another ten years.

In 1113, the chieftains of the Isles sent for Olaf Godredsson, who was now of age and had been brought up and educated at the court of Henry I of England. He returned to Man as Olaf I, King of Man and the Isles, to begin a reign that was to last for forty years. He was a devout and peace-loving man who maintained alliances with the rulers of England, Scotland and Ireland, thus ensuring that his reign was one of largely unbroken peace.

In 1134, Olaf made a grant of land to the Abbot of Furness for the foundation of a Cistercian abbey at Rushen (actually in the parish of Malew but the naming of 'Rushen' probably referred to the *sheading* of Rushen, comprising the parishes of Rushen, Arbory and Malew; we return to the question of sheadings later in this chapter). The abbey at Furness had been founded only seven years earlier.

An indication of continuing political relations with Norway is given by a reference to Olaf's son, Godred, journeying to that land in 1152 to pay homage; he seems to have stayed there for some time. Meanwhile, at home in Man, trouble was heading in Olaf's direction, in the form of the three sons of his brother Harald. The trio sailed over from Dublin with a large band of malcontents, demanding a half-share of the kingdom. Before any discussion could ensue, the second of the brothers, Regnald, raised his axe and severed Olaf's head from his body, whereupon they proceeded to divide the Isle of Man between them. A few days later, according to *Chronicon*, they sailed over to Galloway, intent on adding that region to their domain, but the massed ranks of the Galwegians drove them off and they were forced to retreat to Man, where they took their revenge by slaughtering or expelling all the Galwegians then living in Man.

Godred Olafsson, still at the court of the Norwegian king, set out with five ships to return to Man as soon as he received news of his father's death. His first landfall was in Orkney, where he was well received and unanimously elected as their king. He continued south through the Isles and, on arrival in Man, sought out his three nephews and promptly put them to death in revenge for the slaying of his father.

There is little doubt that the reign of Olaf I represented the zenith of the Kingdom of Man and the Isles, a broad, forty-year peak of good, wise and peaceful governance, finally brought to a brutal end. Although the Norse kingdom had a century and more still to run, things would never be the same after Olaf's demise.

During the third year of Godred Olafsson's reign, the people of the Norse kingdom of Dublin invited him to take their throne also. Having assembled a large fleet and a substantial army, he sailed for Dublin, where he was welcomed by the people and, despite fierce opposition from the forces of the Irish king Muircheartach, he took possession of Dublin. Godred returned to Man, where he dismissed the chieftains of the Isles who had sailed in support of him, freeing them to return to their homes.

Now firmly established on the thrones of Man and the Isles and of Dublin, Godred embarked on a phase of tyrannical rule, alienating the chieftains of the Isles who had supported him in Ireland. Eventually, they rebelled and, assisted by Godred's brother-in-law, Somerled, Earl of Orkney, they turned against him with force. In 1156, the two sides engaged in a fierce naval battle off the island of Colonsay. After heavy losses on both sides, the two leaders agreed to divide the kingdom between them.

It would appear that the battle ended with Godred in the weaker position, for Somerled took possession of the islands of Mull and Islay, adjacent to his earldom of Argyll, leaving Godred with what was left of his kingdom in two widely separated remnants – Man in the south, the Out Isles grouped around Lewis and Skye in the north, with the two strategically held apart by Somerled's possessions in the middle. Thus, although successive kings of Man would continue to carry the title King of the Isles, the unity and strength of that kingdom would never again be what it once was.

Two years later, Somerled arrived at Ramsey with a fleet of fifty-three ships and drove Godred from Man; he then ravaged the whole island before departing. The fleeing Godred meanwhile was setting course for Norway to seek assistance, which seems to have taken some six years to arrange. In 1164, Somerled was killed when he arrived at Renfrew with 160 ships and the ambition of ruling the whole of Scotland.

In the same year, according to *Chronicon*, there was a battle at Ramsey between Godred's brother, Reginald, and 'the Manxmen'. The Manxmen were put to flight, and Reginald's reign was to be short-lived, for Godred was already heading back with Norwegian reinforcements to reclaim his kingdom. On arrival, he caught up with Reginald, who was promptly blinded and castrated. After that brutal episode, Godred appears to have ruled relatively peacefully, apart from one abortive attack from Ireland in 1182.

Godred II died on St Patrick's Isle on 10 November 1187 and, the following summer, his body was transferred to Iona. He left three sons, Reginald (another one), Olaf and Ivar. Although the eldest of the three, Reginald was not the true heir to the kingdom, having been born years before his parents' marriage. However, Olaf was only ten years old on his father's death, and so the chieftains of Man and the Isles chose Reginald to succeed. He turned out to be one of the most warlike leaders of the time and seems to have spent much of his reign engaging in the seaborne pursuits of his Viking forebears.

He faced many problems as the years passed and Olaf became older, and disputes arose between them. Reginald granted his brother the island of Lewis, but it was not a prosperous isle and the dissatisfaction remained. At one stage, Olaf was confined to a prison in Scotland but later returned to Man with fresh demands. Their disagreements culminated in another Manx civil war, of north against south. The northsiders embraced the cause of Olaf, whilst the south remained loyal to Reginald. The two sides met on 14 February (St Valentine's Day) 1228 'at the place called Tynwald'. There were heavy losses on both sides, Reginald was killed and his followers were put to flight. The south of the island, which had supported him, was then ravaged and left devastated. Reginald's body was conveyed to St Mary's Abbey, in Furness, to be interred in a plot chosen by him when he was alive.

In addition to his domestic difficulties, Reginald's reign had evolved at a time when England's influence in the Irish Sea was increasing and Norway's was being challenged. In 1205, Reginald had been unwise enough to become involved in events in Ulster. This aroused the ire of King John of England, whose father, Henry II, had assumed the title Lord of Ireland in 1171. Reginald was summoned to appear before the English court in 1206 to pay homage. In doing so, he angered the King of Norway, who summoned him to attend the Norwegian court for the same purpose. Reginald complied and, on his return from Norway, learned that an irritated English king wished him to attend the English court again. Such conflicts of influence were to continue after Reginald's death.

By the end of the twelfth century, the scribes of *Chronicon* were recording current events in increasing detail. They form a long and convoluted story which, out of deference to the reader, I shall summarize in the briefest feasible form.

With the death of Reginald in 1228, Olaf gained possession of the Kingdom of Man and the Isles, which was his lawful birthright, but he would never regain all of the islands that had once been part of the kingdom. He reigned for nine years and, from the start, he was at odds with the two larger kingdoms. In his earlier disagreements with his brother, he had received assistance from Norway. Predictably, Henry III, who was now on the throne of England, summoned Olaf to the English court and extracted an undertaking that he would guard the Irish Sea against invaders and would place fifty ships at Henry's disposal in time of need. Equally predictably, it was the turn of the Norwegian king to be displeased. Olaf was preparing to sail north to Norway in an attempt to mend fences when he died in 1237. He died on St Patrick's Isle and was buried in St Mary's Abbey, Rushen.

Harald Olafsson was fourteen when he inherited the kingdom, and the tension between England and Norway for control of the islands was at its height. In the first year of his reign, he was deposed by King Haakon of Norway for refusing to attend the Norwegian court and recognize its suzerainty. All dues from the kingdom were collected and paid over to Haakon. Harald relented and sailed north, where he stayed for more than two years, working to regain Haakon's favour and eventually achieving the return of his kingdom.

On his return to Man in 1246, Harald was honoured by Henry III of England with a knighthood, but that only served to resurrect Haakon's antagonism. Once more, Harald set out for the north (according to *Chronicon*, journeying through England on the way). He was warmly received and given the hand of Haakon's daughter in marriage. But any marital bliss was short-lived, for, on their return voyage, their ship was overwhelmed by a violent storm off Shetland; Harald, his queen and the whole party were lost.

Harald's brother, Reginald Olafsson, succeeded to the throne as Reginald II in 1249, but his reign was to last just twenty-four days before he was murdered by one Ivar, a knight, and his men near the Church of the Holy Trinity, in Rushen. There followed yet another confused period of conflicting claims to the kingdom which was not resolved until 1252, when Magnus, the youngest son of Olaf II, arrived in Man to be welcomed by the Manx people and be made their king. The following year, he made the by-now customary attendance at Haakon's court, was honourably received and stayed for a year. In 1254, he travelled to the English court, where he was welcomed, knighted and sent home with precious gifts.

By this time, not only were Norway and England vying for Magnus's co-oper-ation in controlling movements in the Irish Sea on their behalf, but Scotland was also displaying increasing influence, strength and ambition in the same area. In particular, Alexander III was intent on gaining possession of the Hebrides, and this was of concern to Haakon.

In 1263, Haakon arrived with a large fleet off the west coast of Scotland but suffered a defeat at the hands of the Scots in a battle off Largs, in the Firth of Clyde. Magnus Olafsson had also taken a fleet north but had sailed into Loch Long to attack the coast there. Haakon retreated to Orkney, where he later died at Kirkwall, and Magnus returned to Man. He subsequently met Alexander, under truce, at Dumfries, where, after paying due homage, he was permitted to retain Man (but not the Isles), on condition that he provide Alexander with ten war-galleys whenever he needed them. Magnus remained King of Man until his death in 1265, and the death of his kingdom would soon follow. A year later, by the Treaty of Perth agreed between Norway and Scotland, the Western Isles *and Man* were ceded to Alexander III of Scotland in return for a payment of 4,000 marks and 100 marks per annum thereafter.

Thus, almost 470 years of Norwegian presence and influence in the Irish Sea was ended, and a kingdom of islands, once stretching from the Isle of Man north to Shetland, was no more. But the Norse influence did not die with the demise of the Nordic kingdom. The Norse interlude in Man left a legacy, significant elements of which remain with us today. The island's Nordic inheritance is more than just a story of long-forgotten kings and dimly remembered battles – far more. In the remainder of this chapter, we review the principal features of that inheritance, which has exerted such a long-lasting influence in Manx affairs.

THE NORDIC INHERITANCE

The main component of the Norse legacy in the Isle of Man was a Scandinavian form of legislative and judicial administration centred on the annual midsummer open-air assembly. This has to be the Norsemen's greatest and most enduring achievement in Man. In the Scandinavian languages, the assembly was (and is) the *thing* or *ting*. In Iceland, the national assembly or parliament is the *Althing*, and in Norway the *Storting*, the great, grand or people's assembly. In the Faroes it is the *Logting* and the lower house of the Danish parliament is the *Folkting*. In Man, both the place of assembly and the assembly itself took on the same name: *Thingvöllr* (now Tynwald), the 'assembly field', and the field in question is at St John's, which is not far from the island's centre. Its location – somewhat closer to Peel than to Douglas – probably reflects the fact that the former was a place of greater importance in Norse times.

The date of the first Tynwald is not known, but it is certain that the Manx Tynwald and the Scandinavian *things* were in being long before Westminster became the 'mother of parliaments'. The island claims to possess the oldest *continuous* parliament in the world; the Icelandic *Althing* first met in or about 930 but there was a long break in its continuity. The Isle of Man commemorated the millennium of its Tynwald in 1979 but it was a date that was plucked out of the air; it was actually the 900th anniversary of Godred Crovan's victory at Sky Hill but not much was made of that in 1979.

The original purpose of the *thing* was judicial, rather than legislative; it was an assembly to which people could take their grievances and where disputes were settled. Over time, it evolved into a gathering where the laws of the land (which were not written down at that time) were spoken to the assembly, so that the people would know the laws under which they were expected to live their lives. The lawman would recite from memory the laws, which were passed down the generations through oral tradition; it was known as 'breast-law'. The lawman himself was known to the Celts as the *briw* (judge), to the Norse as *lagman*, and finally *deemster*, a later Scandinavian title deriving from *domstiorar*, the 'doom-stearer' or judge.

In view of the fact that the Celts had a word for 'judge', it would seem that some system of law-making existed in Man before the arrival of the Norse. In the absence of historical record, it is pointless to speculate on its precise structure, but it is possible to draw parallels with practices in neighbouring Celtic kingdoms, where the system of governance operated through a pyramidal structure, with the king at the apex and the lower orders comprising his nobles, the freemen and, at the bottom of the pile, the serfs. After the arrival of the Scandinavians, nothing much changed in this regard. It is thought that an annual open-air fair was part of the Celtic system, and so the Norsemen, with their *thing*, were merely taking over the ancient tradition, but they would refine it into the Scandinavian model which would survive long after their kingdom in Man had ended.

Successive deemsters were frequently members of the same family, and thereby accumulated a formidable knowledge of the island's 'breast-law' of oral tradition. In this respect, the deemster's influence could have been as great as (if not exceeding) that of the King himself, for it would be part of the deemster's role to ensure that the King was well informed of the growing body of customary law. In later times, it was not unknown for a Lord of Man to express disapproval of the deemsters being privy to laws of which he himself was unaware.

The tradition of the spoken declaration of breast-law at the annual gathering of Tynwald and at court hearings of legal disputes survived for a surprisingly long time. Despite earlier attempts to have the island's laws set down in written form, it was not until 1690 that Deemster Parr produced his *Abstract of the Laws, Customs and Ordinances of the Isle of Man*, and began the process whereby Manx customary law became less reliant on the vagaries of deemsters' memories. The deemsters of earlier times had doubtless been resistant to such a move, seeing it as a diminution of their influence.

From the beginning (it is thought), there were two deemsters, initially one for the northside and one for the south. Later, each deemster could hear cases in the other's court. Today, the First and Second Deemsters both deal with judicial matters island-wide and have the assistance of one or more acting deemsters when the case-load requires.

The annual outdoor gathering of the modern Tynwald is still held on Old Midsummer's Day, 5 July (except when that date falls at a weekend, in which case the gathering is transferred to the nearest weekday), at Tynwald Hill, in St John's. The day is a public holiday. The breast-laws are no longer recited, but the titles and short summaries of all Acts of Tynwald passed since the previous year's gathering are read out by the two deemsters, one in Manx and one in English. As Tynwald Hill is situated in the parish of German, this often leads to the hackneyed old quip which states that the laws are read out in Manx and in English and in German. (It is perhaps fortunate that the parish of Rushen is not in on the act.)

The annual gathering also perpetuates the right of the individual to petition for redress of grievance. Modern petitions frequently (but not exclusively) relate to complaints against officialdom, either government departments or local authorities, concerning actions which have, or have not, been taken. At the appropriate stage of the proceedings, the petitioners are shepherded along the processional way to hand their petitions to the Clerk of Tynwald at the foot of the hill. Petitioners are expected to have explored all other avenues for redress before petitioning Tynwald.

Tynwald Hill and the Royal Chapel of St John

At some stage during the Norse period, the Manx Tynwald *court* (as opposed to the annual gathering) began to take on a legislative and executive role, in addition to the judicial. (The monthly sitting of Tynwald today, where the two branches of the legislature sit together, is referred to as the Tynwald Court.) This additional role would obviously require meetings of the court to be more frequent than the annual gathering, and would involve the king, deemsters and a number of 'the worthiest men in the land', whose original role was to assist Tynwald in defining what the law was, and later in the making of new laws. These 'worthiest men' came to be known as the Keys and to be twenty-four in number, which prompts two questions: whence the name and whence the number?

First, with regard to the name, the worthy men who came to be known as the Keys were probably first appointed in Godred Crovan's time, but we have no record of the name until the fifteenth century. In the earliest document in the Manx Statute Book, dated 1417 and written in Latin, the Keys are referred to as *Claves Manniae et Claves Legis*, 'the Keys of Man and Keys of the Law'. From then until 1585, there is no mention of the Keys, but we find 'the worthiest men', 'the elders', 'the elders of the land', 'the twenty-four' and 'the twenty-four of the land'. From 1585 until 1734, they were 'the twenty-four Keys' and, from then to the present day, they are the Keys. To the Manx, from way back in recorded history, they have been *Yn Kiare-as-Feed*, 'the four-and-twenty'.

For an indication of their creation as a body, we must turn to the year 1422, when the Keys themselves made a declaration to Sir John Stanley, King of Man, that the Keys 'were twenty-four free-holders, namely eight in the Out Isles and sixteen in your land of Mann – and that was in King Orryes Dayes'. It is presumed that 'King Orryes Dayes' referred to those of Godred Crovan's dynasty, 1079–1265, and that the 'Out Isles', as described earlier, referred to the groups around Lewis and Skye. If this be true, then it dates the origin of the twenty-four Keys to some time after 1156, when Somerled of Argyll gained possession of the isles around Mull and Islay.

The derivation of the name 'Keys' has been the subject of much conjecture. Let us dispose of the most unlikely suggestion first. To the Manx, they were always the *Kiare-as-Feed*, and it has been suggested that the name derived from the first two elements of this: *Kiare-as*. Translating into English, this is equivalent to saying that the 'four-and-twenty' should be abbreviated to the 'four-and', which seems highly improbable. The suggestion that the name was derived from the Latin *claves*, as alluded to above, is plausible, and A. W. Moore [57] has postulated that it did not originate with the Manx at all, but with an English clerk of the rolls, who copied the 1417 documents into the Statute Book. The Manx rendering would have been unintelligible to him, but he would be aware from the Latin that the twenty-four were 'the Keys of Man and the Keys of the Law', and so 'the Keys' might be an appropriate title. There is also an analogy (which may be wholly irrelevant) from medieval Welsh law, where revenue officers were known as *Cais*. This term was Anglicized to 'Keys' to describe those who journeyed around collecting cornage, cowgeld and other payments. The practice and terminology spread northward from Wales, through Cheshire, Durham and Northumbria to the Clyde, but there is no record of the Manx Keys performing such duties. They were chosen, as we have seen, from among the chief land-holders and 'the worthiest in the land'. Thus, the English translation of *claves* may well explain it.

At the time of the break-up of the Kingdom of Man and the Isles in 1266, and the loss of the Out Isles to Scotland, the number of Keys was reduced perforce to sixteen, but the Manx refused to accept the loss as permanent. They appointed an additional eight from within Man until such time as the Out Islanders returned to claim their seats – which, of course, they never did. And so the number of Keys in Man has remained at twenty-four to the present day.

Thus, whatever the derivation of their title, there is no doubt that the Keys have numbered twenty-four for more than 800 years, and it is almost certain that, at the time of their first formation, the island was already divided into parishes. If we accept the proposition that the original division was into sixteen parishes (not the present seventeen), then the apportionment of sixteen Keys 'in your land of Mann' falls into place.

There are sound reasons for believing that the parishes of Marown and Santon were originally one. First, Marown today is the only parish without direct access to the sea. In earlier times, such access would have been essential for purposes of transportation and communication, for collecting seaweed to fertilize the fields, and to allow the farmer-fisherman to pursue both callings. Secondly, the present boundary between the two parishes cuts across the treen of Sanrebrek, this being the only case in the island where a treen is split in two by a parish boundary. Thus there is strong circumstantial evidence that these two parishes started out as one, and the original number was sixteen, although there is no clue as to when the change was made.

Another plausible reason for all parishes of the island to have direct access to the sea was in relation to national defence. A common feature of Scandinavian administration was the requirement for all administrative districts to supply a specified number of ships and men in times of need. This may also have been the case in pre-Norse times. At some stage during 'King Orryes Dayes', there was a strategic or administrative amalgamation of the parishes to form six larger units – the *sheadings*. We know that local assemblies (*things*) were held in the sheadings; one is known to have been held at Reneurling (now Cronk Urleigh), in Michael, in 1422, and another at Keeill Abban, near the present St Luke's Church in Braddan a few years later. The local assemblies often served as courts for the settling of disputes and grievances.

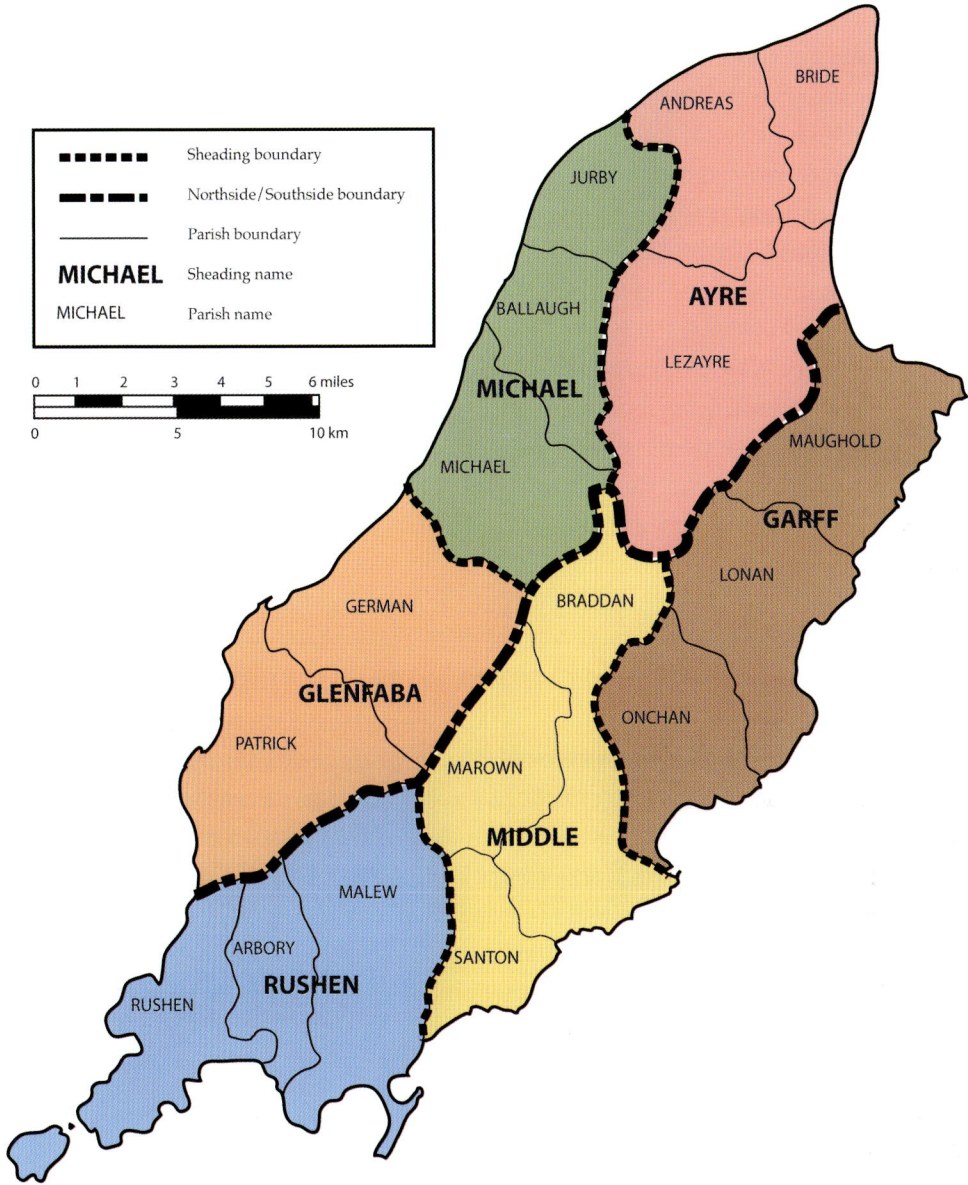

	Sheading boundary
	Northside/Southside boundary
	Parish boundary
MICHAEL	Sheading name
MICHAEL	Parish name

0 1 2 3 4 5 6 miles

0   5   10 km

BRIDE

ANDREAS

JURBY

AYRE

BALLAUGH

LEZAYRE

MICHAEL

MAUGHOLD

MICHAEL

GARFF

LONAN

GERMAN

BRADDAN

GLENFABA

ONCHAN

PATRICK

MAROWN

MIDDLE

MALEW

ARBORY

SANTON

RUSHEN

RUSHEN

The Ancient Sheadings

There has been much speculation concerning the origin of the name 'shead-ing', which is almost certainly Scandinavian. The formation of the sheadings, each consisting of two or three parishes, made for more effective provision of ships and men in times of threat to the nation. The provision of such resources remained the responsibility of the individual parishes but could more readily be co-ordinated through the smaller number of sheadings. The association with ships and local *things* has led to the suggestion that the sheading originated as a ship-*thing* which, in Norse, would have been a *skip-thing*. A far more likely explanation is that it derives from the division of the island into six parts. In the Norwegian tongue today, a sixth is *sjette* and, if an assembly were held in such a district, it would be a *sjette-ting*, which does not require much linguistic slippage over the years to become a sheading.

When the Keys eventually became a democratically elected body, the ancient sheadings were adopted as constituencies, and remained so (with the addition of the four towns) until quite recent times, when the district of Onchan was extracted from the sheading of Garff to form its own constituency, Santon was taken out of Middle and Malew out of Rushen to form the newest constituency of Malew and Santon.

THE SYSTEM OF WATCH AND WARD

In addition to the provision of ships and men in time of war, an island open to assault from the sea needed an effective system of coastal surveillance. As we have seen, the Celts had set up their promontory and hill forts, from which look-out duties were undertaken. The Norse rulers in Man took over this system and devel-oped it into a more formal – almost military – operation. Much later still, when Sir John Stanley came to his new kingdom in 1417 to be inducted by his deemsters and Keys, it was stressed that the custom of 'watch and ward' was a prime requirement for the security of the isle. Four men from each parish were on duty for the day watch and another four through the night. The change-over between the two watches took place at sunset and sunrise. The day watch occupied a watch hill affording extensive views of the surrounding waters; the night watch was positioned lower down, closer to the shore. There are five summits on today's map of the island whose names betray their former use as watch-and-ward hills: North and South Barrule both have derivations from the Norse, illustrating that they were 'ward fells', and no fewer than three hills bearing the same Celtic name, *Cronk ny Arrey Laa*, 'hill of the day watch', in the parishes of Patrick, Jurby and Bride.

As was pointed out to Sir John Stanley during his briefing, penalties for failing to turn out for the watch could be severe: a first failure to appear entailed the forfeiture of a wether (a castrated ram); for a second night's absenteeism, forfeiture of a cow; 'and for ye thrid nighte lyfe and lyme'. The only men exempt from watch duties were the coroner (one in each sheading), his deputies the lockmen (one in each parish), and the moars (collectors of fines and the king's rents, one in each parish). Even the deemsters had to take their turns.

The watch in each parish was under the control of the Captain of the Parish, a title still in existence today but now carrying very few responsibilities; they attend the annual Tynwald gathering and may requisition public meetings for various purposes but, in olden times, the captain commanded the parish militia in this medieval equivalent of the Home Guard of the Second World War. In the event of approaching danger, all fighting men were summoned by sending the *Crosh Vusta*, the 'mustering cross', around the villages and countryside. The cross, about 2 feet (60cm) long, burned at one end and was carried by the lockman or other messenger to raise the alarm and summon the men to muster to receive the captain's orders. Watch and ward continued in operation until 1815. The cross was last used to summon parishioners to a public meeting in Patrick in 1843.

The system of watch and ward appears as an organized and regimented arrangement for the defence of the nation, involving the provision and mainte-nance of ships, the conscription of men and the supply of arms, all of which raises the question: how was it all paid for? And the answer is, of course, by taxation.

We have no detail of a system of taxation in Man during the Norse period, but there is information on such matters in Scandinavia and the Northern and Western Isles, and it reveals some remarkable parallels. Remembering that the Isle of Man at some time fell within the domain of the Earldom of Orkney, it is instructive to study the system of taxation and administrative divisions within the earldom, not forgetting also that Orkney ultimately lay under the suzerainty of Norway.

As H. R. Loyn [47] has pointed out, Orkney was divided into six districts called *husaby* districts, each of which was divided into thirty-six *urislands* which, in turn, were each divided into quarters called *skattlands*. The *skattland* was the basic farm unit and also the basic taxable unit, the 'scot-paying land' (from the Old Norse *skot*, meaning a payment of tax or other assessed levy). The scot would be paid to the *husaby* estate, acting as the collecting agency, which would pass it further up the chain. (Presumably, anyone fortunate enough to be exempt from payment of the scot would get off 'scot-free'.) The Hebridean equivalent of the *urisland* was the *tirung* (cf the Manx treen) and that again was divided into quarters.

The noteworthy parallel in Man lies in the fact that the island was divided into six sheadings (cf Orkney's six *husabys*), each of which was divided into thirty-six treens (Orkney's thirty-six *urislands*), each of which was split into four quarter-lands (Orkney's four *skattlands*). Although we have no knowledge of the tax-paying system in Man at that time, we do know that, in Orkney, the meaning of *urisland* was 'ounce-land'; the *urisland* was responsible for handing over one ounce of silver at the annual levying of tax – a quarter-ounce from each *skattland*. Were the Manx treens and quarterlands subject to the same system? The inference is certainly there.

THE BISHOPRIC OF SODOR AND MAN

As we saw earlier, the arrival of the pagan Norse brought a serious check to the development of Christianity in Man, which only revived after Olaf I (Tryggvasson) of Norway decreed in 995 that Christianity would be compulsory throughout his domains. We have the first authenticated record of a bishop in Man, Roolwer (from the old Norse name *Hrolfr*) in 1070. He was the island's bishop for nine years, up to the arrival of Godred Crovan. Roolwer's base was probably at Kirk Maughold, where he was buried, and his see would have been limited to the single isle.

Chronicon records a succession of bishops after Roolwer but is less than clear on the formation of the diocese of Sodor (a contraction of the Norse *Sudreyjar*, which initially included Man). If the chronicle *was* actually written by monks at Rushen Abbey, it is remarkably lacking in Manx ecclesiastical detail of the period. The picture remains clouded until the return of Olaf Godredsson from the court of Henry I to become Olaf I of Man in 1113. In 1134, he made a grant of land to Ivo, the Cistercian Abbot of Furness, to establish an abbey (according to *Chronicon*) at 'a place called Rushen'. Since the site of the abbey is not in the parish of Rushen but *is* in the sheading of that name, this gives clear indication that the sheadings, and hence the parishes, were in place at that time. (Again, *if* the chronicle was written at Rushen Abbey, it seems strange that the writer should refer to 'a place called Rushen'.)

In 1176, Godred Olafsson made a grant of land to the abbot of another English abbey, Rivaulx. The land was at Mirescogh, a lake in the Lezayre curragh, and a monastery was built on an island there. The building was later abandoned and there is no trace of it today. In the long process of drying-out in the curragh, the island and the lake have also vanished.

The abbey at Rushen enjoyed growing influence during the remainder of the Norse period, and Olaf II, Reginald II and Magnus, the last King of Man and the Isles, were all buried there. The date of the formation of the diocese remains uncertain. A. W. Moore [57] plumps firmly for 1154, whilst acknowledging that it

(above) Rushen Abbey, Ballasalla: that which remains standing is a small fraction of the original. (below) The ruin of St German's Cathedral, on St Patrick's Isle, Peel

might have existed intermittently before that date. But it was under a papal bull of that year that the Sudreys were placed under the archiepiscopate of Nidaros (Trondheim) in Norway. From that date onward, the influence of Rome became increasingly dominant.

The best-known bishop of Sodor in the Norse period was Simon of Argyll, who is credited with the building of the cathedral church of St German on St Patrick's Isle in about 1230. It occupied the isle jointly with the neighbouring parish church of St Patrick, the ruin of which still stands there. The original church of St German is thought to form part of, or to have occupied the site of, the chancel of the larger cathedral of St German, which is also now ruinous. Bishop Simon set up his residence at what is now Bishopscourt, in Michael; the oldest part of the present building is thought to be from his time. According to *Chronicon*, he died in the Church of St Michael and was buried in his own cathedral, which remained in use until the mid-eighteenth century.

Notwithstanding the collapse of the Kingdom of Man and the Isles in 1266 and the transfer of political suzerainty from Norway to Scotland, the bishopric of Sodor remained under the jurisdiction of the archdiocese of Trondheim. When, eventually, the English crown gained possession of Man and the Scots retained

Herringbone stonework in the walling of the ruinous St Patrick's Church, on St Patrick's Isle

the Isles, it was clear that the extended diocese of islands was defunct. But bishops of Man continued to use the old title 'Bishop of Sodor' and, at some stage – probably when it had been forgotten that 'Sodor' included Man – the title became 'Bishop of Sodor and Man', which is how it stands today.

In conclusion, one final element in the Norse legacy relates to how the people of Man came to be called Manx. In universal Scandinavian tradition, a Norwegian was (and is) described as *Norsk*, a Swede is *Svensk*, a Dane is *Dansk* and an Englishman is *Engelsk*, and so it follows that the people of Man were *Mansk*. The transposition of the last two letters to form *Manks* was probably the work of the Manx themselves and, once *Manks* was in place, could *Manx* be far behind? Some 'old-timers' and others steeped in Manx history and language still use the old 'Manks' when writing but they grow fewer in number with the passing years.

CHAPTER FIVE

The British Island

As we have seen, in 1266, two centuries after the Norman invasion of England, sovereignty over the Isle of Man formally passed from Norway to Scotland. A century earlier, the Norman Conquest, like the Roman, had passed the island by as the Anglo-Normans sailed west to extend the Conquest into Ireland. The island's firm allegiance to Norway was, in all probability, its greatest defence. The Normans were, after all, descended from the Norsemen and would have little wish to take them on for such small gain.

But now, in 1266, that protection was gone, and the passing of control to Scotland was no substitute, for a particularly quarrelsome period in Anglo-Scottish relations was already in full flight. In the years that followed, this strategically placed isle would pass from one side to the other and back again, with neither displaying much concern for the plight of its people.

ANGLO-SCOTTISH MANOEUVRES

Nothing is known of Manx history in the first nine years of Scottish rule but there appears to have been an air of unrest in the isle as, in 1275, there was an uprising. The Manx rallied under the leadership of Godred Magnusson (the son of the last King of Man and the Isles) and faced a force under John de Vesci, who had sailed from Scotland to put down the rebellion. The Scots landed at Ronaldsway and engaged the Manx on St Michael's Island, at the northern tip of the Langness peninsula. The Manx were heavily outnumbered and soundly defeated. The battle is recorded in *Chronicon*, but there is no subsequent mention of Godred. If he met his end in the engagement, then that was the end of the male line of descendants of Godred Crovan, the original

'King Orry' of Man and the Isles. 537 Manx died in the battle. The account in *Chronicon* ends with the following couplet:

Ten fifties and three tens plus five and two did fall.
O Manxmen, do beware, lest more horrors shall ye befall!

The Manx screen goes blank once more. Something strange seems to happen to *Chronicon* in the latter years of the thirteenth century and the early years of the fourteenth. There are unexplained gaps of several years between consecutive entries, until the final item in the political record occurs in 1316 and the ecclesiastical account ends in 1376. Is it, perhaps, a related fact, or purely coincidental, that, by the end of the fourteenth century, no monastic chronicles were being written in England either? It may be that the advent of printing technology rendered these great works of history and art redundant. It is certainly true that, in England, the printing press was used to inflame anti-clerical feelings, particularly against the monks and friars, and hastened the processes leading to the demise of the monastic houses, but could the same be said of this isolated island of Man, and at such an early stage of the proceedings? This was the best part of two centuries before the final dissolution of the monasteries. Thus we have another unsolved puzzle concerning this contentious chronicle, which we shall revisit later in this chapter.

Alexander III of Scotland died in 1285, and it is assumed that Man remained under his rule up to that time. Since both his sons and his daughter (the Queen of Norway) had predeceased him, Alexander was succeeded by his only grandchild, the infant Margaret, who was the daughter of King Eric of Norway. The Isle of Man was listed as one of the possessions of the regency that was to rule during her minority, but she was to die only five years later.

There were several claimants to the Scottish throne, and at least two from the distaff side of Godred Crovan's line seeking a revival of the Manx kingdom. However, it was Edward I of England who was in the ascendant at that time. He appears to have taken possession of Man at least seven months before the death of 'the Maid of Norway', for he was then instructing 'the keepers of the land of Mann' that certain merchants were to be given safe conduct to go about their business, and extracting a pledge from 'the People of the Isle of Man' that they would not rebel against his rule.

Meanwhile, across the water, Edward had been invited to Scotland to decide between the numerous aspirants to the Scottish succession. The two strongest claimants were John de Bailleul (or Balliol) and Robert de Brus (or Bruce), both of whom would shortly appear in the Manx historical record. It had been suggested to Edward in advance that Balliol might prove the more amenable neighbour to the English monarch and Edward – ever mindful of his own advantage – concurred with that assessment. He awarded the Scottish crown to Balliol, but reserving to himself absolute rights as overlord and also those 'of any other whomsoever'.

It is probable that this latter puzzling clause may refer to the two claimants to the Manx throne, both of whom were members of the Norwegian royal family in Man. The first, 'the Noble Lady Maria, Queen of Man', paid homage to Edward in Perth in 1291. The second, Aufrica, who claimed to be the heiress of Godred Olafsson, did likewise, and both doubtless pleaded their case for the Manx realm, but it seems to have achieved neither of them any gain. Aufrica, however, signed away all her rights in Man in 1306, in favour of 'the noble and potent man Simon de Montecuto'. It has been suggested that Aufrica was Sir Simon's wife but the issue is clouded. It is not known whether Sir Simon possessed any holdings in Man but it is known that, in 1333, his grandson, Sir William Montecute, would be granted possession of the isle by Edward III. But that still lay in the future.

Balliol, as king of Scotland, was now in possession of the Isle of Man but he seems to have observed insufficient subservience to satisfy Edward. He was deprived of the throne and the island was again English.

In June 1290, Edward had issued a writ to the people of Man, declaring that Walter de Huntrecumbe (otherwise Huntercombe) was appointed custodian of the isle, and that he was to take over that position from Richard de Burgo (or Burgh). And there, with the name of Richard de Burgo, we have the identity of the first known incumbent of the post which, today, we know as 'governor'. He would have been appointed some time in the late 1280s.

The man next appointed to govern Man was Antony de Beck, the ambitious and warmongering Bishop of Durham, who had assisted Edward in his campaigns against the Scots. Once in control of the island, Beck fell out with Edward, but the king died before their differences were settled. Beck was well in with Edward II and so remained as custodian of Man until his death in 1310.

In the following year, Edward II granted the island to his favourite, Piers Gaveston, but his tenure was short-lived; the Manx nobles drove him out and he was beheaded. (You antagonize the Manx at your peril!) The island now entered a pitiful period of bloodshed and strife. Robert Bruce had gained the Scottish crown in 1313 and, in the same year, sailed south to take possession of Man. He landed at Ramsey and proceeded on foot to Douglas and thence to Castle Rushen, which by this time had replaced Peel Castle as the island's principal stronghold. After a month-long siege, the garrison surrendered and Bruce granted the island to Thomas Randolph, Earl of Moray.

Bruce did not return directly to Scotland but made a foray against Ireland *en route*. In 1316, perhaps out for revenge, an Irish force under Richard de Mandeville landed at Ronaldsway and made demands for land, food, cattle and money, which the Manx, under Thomas Randolph, refused. The Irish, enraged by the refusal, confronted the assembled Manx on the slopes of Wardfell (South Barrule). The Manx were routed and, before leaving the isle, the Irish ensured that their ships were well laden with plunder, having denuded the abbey at Rushen of furniture and livestock in the process. The account of this incursion is the last entry in the political record of *Chronicon*.

The twenty-year period from 1313 was such a troubled time for the Isle of Man that it is all but impossible to determine which side was in control at any particular time. But, with the accession of Edward III to the throne of England (one of the ablest kings of that realm) and his grant of full possession of Man to Sir William de Montecute in 1333, a new chapter was opened. The island would, henceforth, be an English possession. Its ruler held the island as King of Man, and was not required to pay homage to the English monarch.

But, no matter how firm and irreversible English control of Man might have seemed, the Scots were in no immediate hurry to abandon their aspirations. In 1343, 'the men of the community of the Isle of Man' (whatever the definition of that phrase might have been) paid 300 marks in 'protection money' to avoid the attentions of Scottish raiders for one year. In 1377, the French stuck their oars into troubled waters; they landed in strength but could not force entry into Castle Rushen, although they extracted payment of 1,000 marks in return for not destroying houses. The final Scottish attack came in 1388, when Robert, Earl of Fife, and Archembald Douglas, Lord of Galloway, landed, raided and returned home.

And yet feelings of nostalgia (or perhaps simply wishful thinking) for Man lingered on in certain Scottish hearts and minds. In 1375, Robert II of Scotland recognized George Dunbar, Count of the Marches, as 'Lord of Annandale and Man'. When Dunbar was preparing to marry the daughter of James Douglas, who was possessed of extensive land-holdings in Scotland, Robert undertook to settle on the couple, as a dowry, 5,000 acres (2,020ha) of land in the Isle of Man when he gained possession of it – which, of course, he never did.

This must have been a dire and dismal period for the Manx people. Their rulers, changing so frequently, could have spent little (if any) time in the place, and took little interest in it – except perhaps to extract such of its resources as were of use for their own purposes. Occasional visitors to the island reported on the miserable plight of the people. In 1290, the isle was described as 'desolate and full of wretchedness'. In 1316, *Chronicon* records that the Irish had 'plundered the land of its more valuable produce' and, in 1400 and 1403, people were having to buy corn in Ireland to supplement local supplies, but how many were in a position to do so is another question.

This sorry situation is underlined by the fact that, in 1343, Edward III granted permission for the Manx to trade with the Scots (a permit that would not have been granted lightly in view of the recent conflicts). Those who actually did the trading would have been the ruling classes, but the civil administration and the secular freeholders had greatly diminished by this time. The power of the ecclesiastical barons had grown to fill the void.

THE GROWTH OF THE CHURCH

The permit of Edward III in 1343, enabling Manx traders to do business outside the island to obtain essential supplies, would have been of little direct benefit to the ordinary folk of Man, for they would have been in no position to trade externally with anyone. The immediate benefit would have been to the governing classes, because they were the only ones capable of such independent action, and they consisted mainly of the ecclesiastical barons, representing the abbeys of Rushen, Furness and others outside the isle. This transfer of power, accompanying the disappearance of the freeholders, was the significant characteristic of this period; any land not devolved to the barons would remain in the demesne of the king, either for his own purposes or for occupation by rent-paying tenants.

Whilst the powers of the civil administration had declined, the strength of the Church, exerted through the religious houses and the influence of Rome, had grown. Even a strong ruler such as Edward III had difficulty in resisting the growth in papal interference; in Man, the increasing power of the Church was uncurbed.

The bishopric of Sodor and Man and the abbey at Rushen had received grants of land and other privileges from the Norse kings. The Abbot of Rushen alone had possession of ninety-nine quarterland farms and seventy-seven cottages at one time, and the abbey was under the control of the Abbot of Furness, who held other land in the isle. There was also a nunnery at Douglas (whose origin is unknown) and other lands were held by the abbeys and priories at Bangor and Sabhal, in northern Ireland, at Whithorn in Galloway, and at St Bede's (or Bee's) in Cumbria. All of the heads of these establishments were ranked as barons and had their own officers and manorial courts. The bishop, too, had his own courts and his own prison on St Patrick's Isle, and his powers were almost on a par with those of the king. The bishop's judges were known as vicars-general; the bishopric today retains a vicar-general but with powers and duties greatly reduced.

The Church in Man had its own written laws – dating back to 1229, when Bishop Simon held a diocesan synod at Kirk Braddan, at which tithes were levied on livestock, grain, beer and cloth. Another synod was held at Kirk Braddan in 1291, under Bishop Mark, at which additional tithes were imposed on merchants, traders, smiths and other artisans, and (for the first time, it appears) there was a tithe on fish.

These measures, unsurprisingly, were the cause of much discontent and, in 1299, Mark was expelled from the island by Edward I. The Pope retaliated by placing the island under interdict, by which all services of the Church were suspended, apart from baptisms and last rites. Bishop Mark returned in 1302 and promptly imposed a tax of a penny a year on every house possessing a fireplace. This could be seen as a spiteful response to his earlier expulsion, but *Chronicon* records that the tax was imposed in order to secure the removal of the papal interdict. The *Chronicon* scribe refers to Mark as a noble governor of the Sodor church, a man of refinement and courtesy. If *Chronicon* was written at Rushen Abbey, and given that a sizeable portion of the bishop's tithes would find their way there, one may perhaps reasonably respond that he would say that, would he not?

The Church tithes would eventually cover all produce, and such tithes as butter, cheese and eggs were taken to the church on Sundays and handed to the priest at the altar. Non-payment of the dues resulted in the defaulter being deprived of receiving the sacrament. In the case of the wider range of tithes, the collections were undertaken by the parish priest or his proctor, and there were payment-enforcement officers called sumners. The most important crop being grain, a farmer was required to give notice to the proctor before stacking the crop. Failure to do so would result in the sumner and two neighbours dismantling the stack and seizing the tithe.

The purpose of the tithes was to cover the costs of the diocese, such as the maintenance of the bishop, the monasteries and the clergy. By the middle of the fourteenth century, of all the tithes paid in Man, almost half went to the bishop, the other half being split between the religious houses (of which the major one was Rushen Abbey) and the parish clergy. The result was that most of the tithes paid by the parish went out of the parish; the incumbent priests came to be known as 'vicars of thirds', since they received (usually less than) a third of the tithes paid in. Most were severely impoverished as a consequence.

A further sign of the increasing influence of Rome on the Church in Man came in 1348, with the consecration of Bishop Russell, not in Trondheim, where his predecessors had been installed, but at Avignon, where the Pope dwelt at that time. The Pope was also to become active in matters relating to the ecclesiastical courts in Man.

In England, various legal restrictions had been introduced to limit the privi-leges of the clergy and the acquisition of property by the Church. It had also been declared that any who sought redress in the papal courts would have no protec-tion under English law and their property would be forfeit to the State. There were no such restrictions in Man.

It was during Bishop Russell's term that the Franciscan friars first arrived in Man in 1373. It may have been the influence of the Cistercians of Rushen Abbey that had kept them out for so long. It may now have been someone's wish to coun-teract the power of the Cistercians that eventually allowed them in. Whatever the motive, the King of Man at that time, William le Scrope, Earl of Salisbury, made a grant of land to the Franciscans in the village of St Columba, the present-day Ballabeg, in the parish of Arbory. Little is known of their activities but one of their buildings remains at Friary Farm. Not surprisingly, the establishment of the friary gets no mention by the Cistercian scribe of *Chronicon*, whose final ecclesiastical entry is for the year 1376.

Bishop Russell was succeeded in 1374 by John Donkan, a Manxman who had previously been Archdeacon of Down. He later seems to have incurred the displeasure of the Pope and was moved to another see in 1392. The passage of the next few years would pave the way for the arrival of a new line of kings and lords of Man that would set the power of the Church into decline and that of the State on the rise.

KINGS AND LORDS OF MAN

Earlier in this chapter, we related the grant of the Isle of Man by Edward III to Sir William de Montacute in 1333. There appears to have been little or no improvement in the plight of the Manx people in de Montacute's reign. He died in 1344 and was succeeded by his son, Sir William de Montacute II, Earl of Salisbury, who sold the island and the kingship in 1392 to William le Scrope, Earl of Wiltshire.

The Montacutes had chosen Castletown as their capital and had erected a Norman-style keep around the old Norse fort of Castle Rushen. This was followed by the construction of a stout curtain wall, all of which transformed the strong-hold into a formidable fortress. Sir William le Scrope, on the other hand, seems to have concentrated his efforts on St Patrick's Isle. Finding the cathedral of St German in an unusable condition, he obtained a papal licence to restore the building to a functional state, before turning his attention to the castle. He strengthened and extended the gatehouse and the curtain wall which encircles

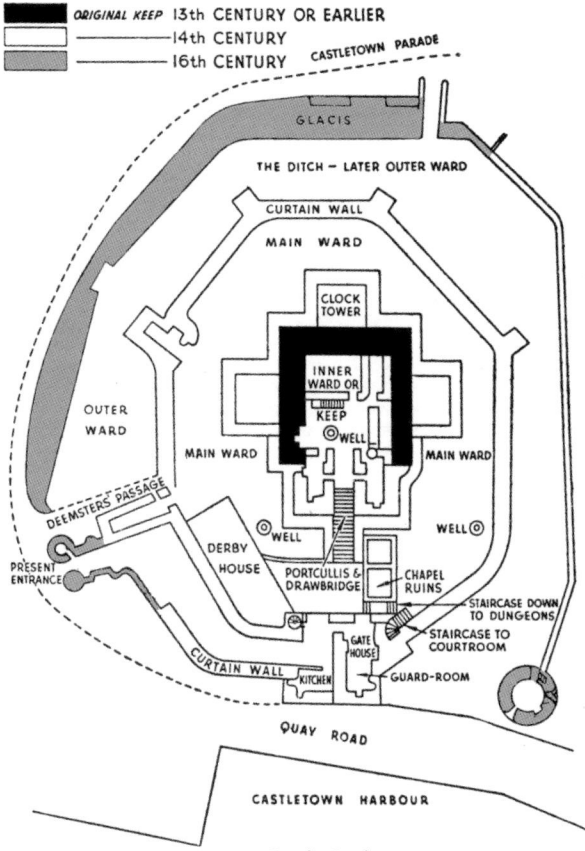

ORIGINAL KEEP 13th CENTURY OR EARLIER
——————14th CENTURY
——————16th CENTURY

THIS PLAN MODIFIED FROM PLANS DRAWN BY THE LATE A. RIGBY F.R.I.B.A.

CASTLETOWN PARADE

GLACIS

THE DITCH — LATER OUTER WARD

CURTAIN WALL

MAIN WARD

CLOCK TOWER

INNER WARD OR KEEP

WELL

OUTER WARD

MAIN WARD   MAIN WARD

DEEMSTERS PASSAGE

WELL   WELL

PRESENT ENTRANCE

DERBY HOUSE

PORTCULLIS & DRAWBRIDGE   CHAPEL RUINS

STAIRCASE DOWN TO DUNGEONS

STAIRCASE TO COURTROOM

CURTAIN WALL   GATE HOUSE

KITCHEN   GUARD-ROOM

QUAY ROAD

CASTLETOWN HARBOUR

Castle Rushen

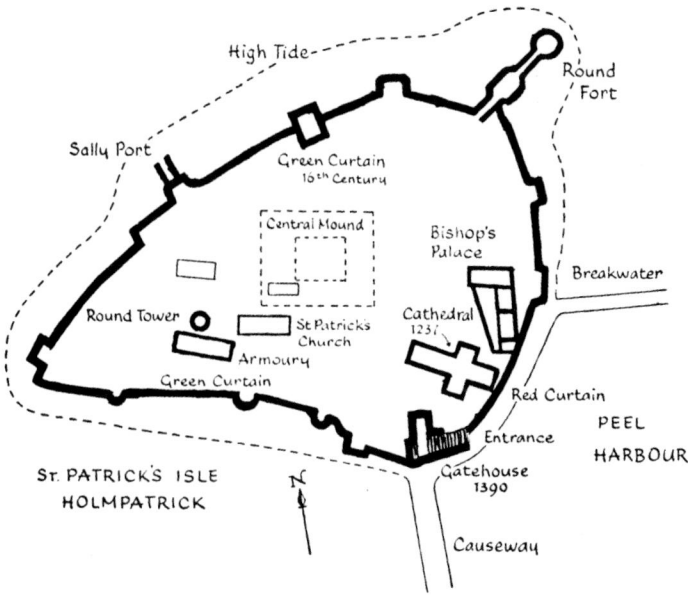

High Tide

Round Fort

Sally Port

Green Curtain
16th Century

Central Mound

Bishop's Palace

Breakwater

Round Tower

St Patrick's Church

Armoury

Cathedral
1231

Green Curtain

Red Curtain

PEEL HARBOUR

Entrance

Gatehouse
1390

St. PATRICK'S ISLE
HOLMPATRICK

N

Causeway

St Patrick's Isle

practically the whole of the islet. But le Scrope's years of kingship were numbered (to no more than seven, in fact). He had been in the pay of Richard II and so, when Henry IV ascended the throne of England, he ensured that le Scrope was parted from his head.

There being no surviving succession to the Manx kingdom, the island was once again in the possession of the English monarch, who gave it to Henry de Percy, Earl of Northumberland. But, after the Percys had rebelled against Henry and been defeated at Shrewsbury in 1403, he was dispossessed of the island, which was finally passed in 1405 to Sir John Stanley. The Stanleys were a most prominent Lancashire family and well placed in court circles. The possession was granted in perpetuity; the island, its castles and royalties, together with patronage of the bishopric, in return for rendering two falcons on paying homage to King Henry, and two falcons to each successive king of England on the day of his coronation in token of homage.

The year 1405 was to mark the start of a long period of relative stability and peace, the latter not wholly unbroken. As kings and lords of Man, the Stanley family were to rule the island, except for two interruptions, for 360 years. Initially, they would retain the title 'King of Man' until, in 1504, they adopted the style 'Lord of Man'. Although the new line of rulers (with a few exceptions) rarely visited Manx shores, they did appoint governors who, in general, handled the island's affairs with a fair degree of wisdom and justice. Through the early years of the fifteenth century, the isle would begin to recover steadily from the dire state of poverty and neglect which had been its lot through almost a century and a half, since the demise of the Nordic kingdom.

The first Stanley king never visited the island but he delegated his son (also John) to confer with the leading men of Man regarding the affairs of the kingdom. He also received their homage as heir apparent. A Lancashire man, Michael Blundell, was appointed governor, one of many from that county to hold this and other posts in the isle.

On the death of his father in 1414, Sir John Stanley II made his second visit to Man and subsequently set out to put the island's internal affairs to rights. He realized early on that, if he wished to be an effective ruler of this isle, he would have to curb the powers of the ecclesiastical barons, chief of whom were the Bishop of Sodor and Man and the Abbot of Rushen. In 1422, he summoned a Tynwald Court to assemble on the hill at Reneurling (Cronk Urleigh), in Michael. The Court was initially to deal with a case involving the attempted murder of Governor Walton whilst he was holding a court of justice in the parish, but Sir John had also summoned the Church barons to attend the assembly. When three of them – the priors of Whithorn and St Bee's and the Abbot of Furness – failed to appear, they paid with the forfeiture of all their land-holdings in Man. The purpose of summoning the senior clerics to the assembly had been to give them the opportunity to swear fealty to the king, which the bishop and other insular barons duly did.

In the spring of the following year, the King summoned his deemsters and twenty-four Keys to attend a Tynwald Court at Castle Rushen, where the laws and constitution of the isle were discussed. Either at this Tynwald or soon after, a code of laws was drawn up by the Deemsters and Keys, defining for the first time the rights and responsibilities of the King, the Church and the people. The King had the power of veto over the appointment of any member of the Keys (for more than four centuries yet, the Keys would continue to be a selected, rather than an elected, body), but he would have the assistance of the council and deemsters when dealing with difficult matters. This early reference to 'the council' tells us nothing of its composition, and it seems to have had no defined constitution. At various times, the council would comprise the Governor, Deputy Governor, the Deemsters, the Clerk of the Rolls, the Bishop, the Archdeacon, the Receiver, the Water Bailiff, the Attorney-General and the Vicar-General.

Also at this time, the Clerk of the Rolls was instructed to keep a written record of all court proceedings in Man. Thus was begun the long, slow process of compiling a written, unequivocal record of case-law in the Isle of Man but, in the meantime, reliance would continue to be placed upon the vast accumulation of 'breast-law' for centuries to come.

The next recorded sitting of a Tynwald Court was held in 1429 and is described in the *Statutes of the Isle of Man* as 'a Court of all the Commons of Mann', presided over by the governor of the day, Henry Byron. At this sitting, four main principles were set out:

(i)   trial by battle was henceforth illegal, all matters of dispute, contention and grievance to be determined 'by God and Country', i.e. by jury;
(ii) no man's goods may be confiscated other than by process of law;
(iii) every man was responsible for debts incurred by his wife; and
(iv) fixed standards of weights and measures were to be established.

Although something of an authoritarian, Sir John Stanley II brought about many changes that were to the benefit of the Manx people and nation. Having divested the Church of much of its power in favour of the State (i.e. the King), he nonetheless maintained a representative form of government, although not, of course, elected. He died in 1432 and, for the best part of a hundred years, the kings of Man were to be conspicuous by their absence. But their interests were looked after by a continuing sequence of governors, several of whom were Stanleys.

Sir John II was succeeded by his son Thomas, who was the first Baron Stanley. At various times, he held prominent positions in Ireland, Cheshire and the English royal household. He represented Lancashire in Parliament until being elevated to the House of Peers; consequently, he could have had little time to spare for Manx affairs.

The next king of the isle was Thomas's son, Thomas Stanley II, who would later become the first Earl of Derby; he was equally busy 'across the water', maintaining his position at the royal court through no fewer than five successive reigns, encompassing the Wars of the Roses. He was present at the battle of Bosworth in 1485, which secured the English throne for the Tudors. After the battle, Thomas adroitly retrieved the crown that had been worn by the slain Richard III and placed it on the head of the victor, proclaiming him Henry VII. In response, Henry created the earldom of Derby for Thomas. An interesting twist to this story lies in the fact that Thomas had married Margaret Beaufort, the widow of Edmund Tudor, Earl of Richmond. Henry VII was the son of Edmund Tudor and Margaret, and thus Thomas Stanley II ended up as step-father to the new king.

Thomas II was succeeded in 1504 by his grandson (his son having died in 1497), who became Thomas Stanley III, second Earl of Derby. It was he who renounced the title 'King' and adopted the style 'Lord of Man(n)', which remains to this day. There is a record of only one visit by Thomas III to Man, when he arrived at Ronaldsway in May 1507 to quell 'a public tumult', but there is no indication of what the tumult was about.

References such as the above serve to remind us that, although there had been undoubted improvements in social and economic conditions in the isle during the first century of Stanley rule, there remained issues, grievances and disputes that caused strong feelings from time to time. Many of the grievances were directed at the lord and – despite the improvements made by John Stanley II – the Church.

The book of *Statutes of the Isle of Man* shows that no new laws were passed between 1430 and 1504. Many of the entries from this period are no more than records of ancient customs of State and Church, or of decrees made by the lord or his officials. They suggest that the island's rulers were more concerned with preserving the lord's privileges and revenues than with the welfare of the people. The Keys were not summoned to gather with any regularity; when they did assemble, it was more often in the role of a high-court jury than a parliament. Such decrees as were set down concerned such matters as the 'Royal fish' – sturgeon, porpoise and whale – which were the lord's by right, as were the most prized species of game, such as deer, hawk and heron. All wrecks and treasure trove were his, and the possessions of all felons condemned to death.

The lord had to be supplied with food – free of charge – for the castles at Rushen and Peel, each quarterland providing one beef-cow per annum, making a total of 864 head of cattle per year. There were also requirements for corn and herring, and taxes were payable for a licence to fish for herring and for importing and exporting goods. A further tax was due for grinding corn at the lord's mills; to avoid this, many people made use of hand-mills, which were confiscated whenever they were found.

The hiring of farm workers and serving maids was subject to strict regulations; hiring was usually undertaken annually in November for men and May for women. A tenant who had difficulty in finding a servant could appeal through the coroner to a deemster. If no vacant labour was available, then tenants paying lower rents were compelled to serve those paying higher. Parents who were infirm, disabled or sick were allowed to keep one of their children at home as a 'choice-child', subject to public notice being given at the parish church one month prior to hiring day.

All of this, of course, came on top of compulsory military service for all men between twenty and sixty years of age, each man being responsible for providing his own bow, arrows, sword and buckler (a small round shield). And, in between times, as we have seen earlier, there were the watch-keeping duties of 'watch and ward'. Furthermore, anyone desirous (and having the means) to get away from all this by leaving the island needed the lord's licence before doing so. Any ship-owner found conveying an unauthorized Manx tenant or servant offshore took the risk of having his vessel confiscated.

Thomas Stanley III was succeeded in 1521 by his son Edward, the third earl, but, since he was only thirteen years old at the time, commissioners were appointed (one of them being Cardinal Wolsey) to manage his affairs during his minority. He, like his forebears, would hold prominent positions in the English royal court, in his case under Henry VIII and Elizabeth I, and there is no record of his ever visiting Man. He did, however, take a great interest in its affairs, and it was during his fifty-year reign that some of the grievances of the people against the Church were redressed. In 1532, the tithes on ale and marriage presents, which had all been paid to the Church, were abolished, and death dues were reduced.

But the most significant development affecting the Church in Man during Edward Stanley's lordship was initiated in England. On 15 January 1535, Henry VIII formally proclaimed himself Supreme Head on earth of the Church in England, and his parliament's Act of 1539 paved the way for the dissolution of the monasteries, although several of the English monastic houses had been forcibly closed in earlier years.

The Act of 1539 did not mention the Isle of Man and did not extend to it. No similar enactment was passed in the island but, nonetheless, the Manx monastic houses were dissolved in 1540 and all the properties belonging to Rushen Abbey, the priory at Douglas and the friary at Bemaken (Ballabeg) passed to the English Crown, together with all tithes accruing from them. The buildings were left to descend into ruin.

Thus came the demise of the abbey at Rushen, the alleged home of the Chronicle of the Kings of Man and the Isles. Rushen was closed three years after the dissolution of Furness but, as mentioned earlier, the final entry in *Chronicon* had been made almost two centuries earlier, following a long period of very spasmodic record-keeping. The earliest indication we have of the *Chronicon*'s subsequent existence is its ownership by a certain Yorkshire scholar and antiquarian, Roger Dodsworth; his inscription in the front of the manuscript is dated 1620. It is not known how the work came into his possession, but he was married to a granddaughter of Sir George Stanley, who was Governor of the Isle of Man from 1536 to 1545, during the lordship of Edward Stanley, the third Earl of Derby, so the manuscript could have come into the Stanley family (of which Dodsworth was now a branch) at the time of the dissolution. It is known that the historian and chronicler William Camden, when gathering material for his *Britannia* (first published 1586), obtained a manuscript (or copy) of the chronicle from Bishop Meyrick and included a transcription in his book. It is thought that Roger Dodsworth passed his manuscript to the library of Sir Robert Cotton in 1620, and it was later transferred to the British Museum, where it resides today. There have been several unsuccessful attempts to have the manuscript 'returned' to Man but there is no solid proof that it was ever here in the first place.

The full effects of the Reformation were slow to take a hold in the Isle of Man. The bishop would have felt the more immediate effect; the loss of papal protection and of the abbeys of Furness and Rushen left him more isolated and subject to the civil power. Among other sectors of the community, the slow pace of the transformation may have been due to Edward Stanley being a staunch Roman Catholic, plus the inherent conservatism of the Manx people. As late as 1576, the Vicar of Kirk Maughold, John Stevenson, is described as 'the last popish priest', and his successor, John Christian, in 1580, as 'the first protestant minister'. It was not until 1610 that the Manx clergy were permitted to marry, an enactment that had been passed in England in 1549.

Edward Stanley was succeeded in 1572 by his son Henry, the fourth Earl, who visited the isle and presided over a Tynwald Court several times. He, too, held high office at the court of Elizabeth I. He died in 1593 and was succeeded by his son Ferdinando, the fifth Earl, but he died only seven months later, at the age of thirty-five.

Ferdinando had married Alice, daughter of Sir John Spencer, of Althorp, in

Northamptonshire, who had presented him with three daughters. (Almost four centuries later, another daughter of the Spencers would come to prominence when she married Prince Charles to become Diana, Princess of Wales.) A question mark now hung over the succession to the lordship of Man. Ferdinando's three daughters were regarded as heirs general, but Henry Stanley's second son, William, was the male heir who became the sixth Earl of Derby.

It appears that resolution of the question was sought conjointly by Alice, widow of the fifth Earl on behalf of her three young daughters, and William, the sixth Earl, on petition to Elizabeth I. On the first day of August 1595, two letters were despatched to the deemsters and other officials in Man, one signed by the two Stanleys, William and Alice, and the other by the Queen. Both were signed at the same place – the royal palace at Greenwich. Though couched in the flowery formal language of the time, the letters are identical in their gist: until such time as the succession in Man was settled, the Queen was appointing one of her own servants, Sir Thomas Garrett, as governor of the isle (as 'Captaine' in the Stanleys' letter, as 'Capten' in the Queen's). Both letters refer to the need for vigilance in the island's defence.

In the fullness of time (fourteen years, no less), the Manx succession was settled in favour of Earl William and his countess, Elizabeth de la Vere, *jointly*, and their descendants. In the meantime, Elizabeth I was dead and James VI of Scotland had succeeded her as James I of England and ruler of Man. Thus, the grant of the island to Earl William and his countess was made by James I in 1609, to be confirmed by a subsequent Act of Parliament, so that their rule actually began in 1612, and the line of the Stanley lords was restored after a break of eighteen years.

Before his succession, Earl William is recorded as being Governor of Man from 1592 to 1594. After that, he appears to have followed in the long-standing tradition of the Stanleys by holding a number of prominent positions in Lancashire and Cheshire and at the royal court. There is no record of his having undertaken any act as Lord of Man; control of Manx affairs seems to have been left entirely to his countess. Their son James, who would succeed as the seventh Earl, later wrote of 'certain agreements between her and my father, and, as I take it, ordered by King James' under which she acted in the Lord's stead, and he mentions her appointment of a governor. There are also records at this time of petitions, which would normally have been addressed to the Lord, invariably being addressed to the countess.

This situation prevailed until the death of the countess in 1627. The son James, who held the title of Lord Strange, then took over the role of Lord of Man, even though his father did not die until 1642. Seacome [70] relates the contents of a deed under which Earl William surrendered all rights in his properties in England, Wales and the Isle of Man to his son, an act which has all the appearance of an abdication.

James Stanley, Lord Strange, was just twenty years old when he acceded as the effective Lord of Man. A year earlier, he had married Charlotte de Tremouille, daughter of the Duke of Thouars, at the Hague, and a formidable lady by all accounts. He must, at some stage, have made a favourable impression on the Manx, for they came to refer to him as *Yn Stanlagh Mooar*, 'the Great Stanley'. One of the first things he did was to appoint a Manxman, Edward Christian, as 'Lieutenant and Capten' (equivalent to Deputy Governor). The Christians were another influential family, with branches long-established in Cumbria and Man. *Yn Stanlagh Mooar* was going to have problems with Christians – two of them.

Edward Christian was the second son of John Christian, who was Vicar of Kirk Maughold between 1580 and 1625. He had led an adventurous life as a sea captain with the East India Company and later as commander of a naval frigate. He returned to the island with a comfortable fortune and came to the attention of Lord Strange, who gave him the appointment referred to above. After a time, the two men fell out and Christian was dismissed in 1639. Their disagreement was over the question of land tenure. Lord Strange was intent on ending the practice which had come to be known as straw tenure, or tenure by straw. All land in the island was owned by the Lord of Man, and all farmers were tenants-at-will of the Lord, i.e. they were holders of their land for as long as the Lord wished it, and no longer. But the system of tenure by straw had become commonplace, probably through the laxity of successive governors or their officers to control such matters, and tenants had come to regard the system as one of fixed tenure, giving them freedom to convey their holdings to others without recourse to the Lord's licence. The system had even gained some degree of official recognition, for the handing-over of a straw from the outgoing tenant to the incomer was witnessed under court proceedings and the transaction was recorded in the court rolls. And the rent, of course, was still paid to the Lord. Lord Strange countered this by introducing a system of leasehold limited to three generations. This was not going to please the tenants, who had grown accustomed to a system which had allowed them to pass their holdings on, without limit, to their children.

James Stanley's approach in such matters was to meet the people, to appear affable and conciliatory and then to go away and do what he had intended to do in the first place. By his own admission (in writings reproduced by the Manx Society [51]), whilst adopting an agreeable demeanour, which 'will cost you nothing; but may gain you much', he placed trusted informers among the people, so that he might be forewarned of impending trouble. And, when meeting with the people, he would employ the tactics of prevarication and 'divide and rule', ultimately letting it be known that, while he could be a fair ruler, he could also be firm – even hard. To some extent, he managed to mollify the opposition by securing reductions in tithes and other payments made to the Church, but that could only serve as a delaying tactic.

In the meantime, Edward Christian had regained the Lord's favour and was appointed sergeant-major (equivalent to major today) in charge of the Manx militia. However, it was not long before he was inciting his men to insurrection. According to evidence given at his later trial, he took over the garrison at Peel Castle and, before a gathering of the Manx militia and parishioners of Patrick and German, called upon the assembly to swear allegiance to him alone. At a court held at Castle Rushen on 13 December 1643 before Governor Greenhalgh, the Deemsters and Keys, Christian was found to have acted 'seditiously and tumultuously ... against ... oure soveraigne lord the king's majestie of England and the lord of the Islande, and the established Government of the same'. He was fined 1,000 marks and imprisoned for life but was released in 1651, when English parliamentary forces entered the island. In 1659, he was involved in a plot against Governor Chaloner; he was committed to Peel Castle and died there two years later.

But further trouble was brewing. In 1642, James Stanley succeeded his father as the seventh Earl of Derby. England was on the brink of a civil war that would bring repercussions for the Isle of Man. It would also bring the earl and his countess into contention with the second troublesome Christian.

THE ENGLISH CIVIL WAR

Having parried, for the time being, his domestic troubles, Earl James proceeded to increase the size of his military forces to be better able to give support to the royalist cause across the water. This, of course, entailed the raising of taxes in Man to meet the cost, which could only serve to reignite popular unrest, for the Manx people must have felt that this was a conflict which was none of their business. There could also have been a hope that, in the event of Parliamentary forces gaining control of the island, the plight of the Manx people might improve. But this was no time for further thoughts of insurrection; with the increased numbers of the Earl's cavalry and infantry on hand, and reinforced garrisons in the castles at Rushen and Peel, any new rebellion would have been doomed from the outset.

In further defence of the island against Parliamentary attack, Earl James caused additional fortifications to be erected. In addition to a fort which Edward Christian had built at the Lhen, a similar one was raised at Ballachurry, in Andreas, the prominent earthwork of which still remains. Other forts in the north were at Ramsey and Port Cranstal. In the Southside, there was a fort at Douglas, of which the only reminder is the name Fort Street, and a stoutly built circular fort of stone on St Michael's Island (also still known as Fort Island), which was built to guard the port of Ronaldsway and still stands there.

*Two Civil War forts: (above) at Ballachurry, Andreas, the figure outside gives a sense of scale;
(below) on St Michael's Island, at the northern tip of Langness*

Apart from two short absences, Earl James remained in Man for seven years from 1644. He assembled a small fleet for the defence of the isle and for the harrying of any Parliamentary ships encountered in the Irish Sea. The actions of this fleet did not get off to a propitious start when, early in 1643, one of his vessels was captured by ships of the Parliament. Later, however, there was more success when the Manx fleet overcame five men-of-war and, on another occasion, successfully defended the Calf of Man against three others. These exploits seem all the more remarkable when one considers that the Manx 'fleet' is thought to have consisted of one frigate, the *Elizabeth*, and a number of longboats, each of sixteen oars and two guns.

During the years of the English Civil War, the Derbys maintained a miniature Royal court at Castle Rushen, which was a haven for Royalists on the run from the Parliamentarians, and where they and invited Manx guests were entertained with masques and feasting. Following the execution of Charles I in 1649, the Earl received a message from Parliament, offering the return of his English estates if he would surrender the Isle of Man. His reply was to the effect that, if he received another such message, he would burn the message and hang the bearer. Parliament made no immediate attempt to take the island, following the earlier repulses by the Manx 'navy'.

In 1650, Charles II (in exile) appointed Earl James to command the Royalist forces in Lancashire and Cheshire in the forthcoming insurrection aimed at restoring the monarchy. The following year, the Earl took 300 Manx foot soldiers to enter the fray, leaving the Countess, aided by Governor Greenhalgh, in charge of the island. The Manx contingent landed at Rossall and made its way to Wigan in time to be severely trounced there. The Manx numbers were decimated, but the Earl and the survivors of his Lancashire/Cheshire force moved to link up with the King at Worcester, where they experienced the decisive Royalist defeat on 3 September. The Earl was captured on the retreat from Worcester, imprisoned in Chester Castle, tried by court martial and executed at Bolton on 15 October 1651. Perhaps the court martial was nothing but a show trial, for Cromwell had written on 29 September that 'Darbie will be tried at Chester, and die at Boulton'.

Despite the less attractive side to his character, there can be little doubt that the seventh Earl of Derby was, in the words of his anonymous biographer (published by the Chetham Society [12]), 'an honourable, brave and high-minded man, sincere in his loyalty, devoted in his patriotism'. He was, indeed, unfaltering in support of his king and prepared to pay the ultimate price in his cause. Some of his policies in Man brought positive benefits to the Manx people; despite being a devout church man, he did secure some relief from the elevated tithes levied on the people by the Church. On a more individual level, he is known to have assisted promising young people in the isle to secure places at English universities and to have made financial contribution towards their maintenance. His letters to his wife and children show him to have been a loving and caring family man. Before his death (of which the Countess remained unaware), he had written from Chester Castle to advise her to surrender to the Parliament and to make the best deal she could for herself, the children and the household. If there was a ruthless side to his use of his power and privilege, that was not unusual for those times. But there must have been something about him that, long after his death, caused him still to be remembered as *Yn Stanlagh Mooar*.

During the Earl's absence from Man, the air of insular discontent had festered on. There was continued resentment over the land-tenure question and the heavy taxation. Feelings over the higher taxes were doubtless heightened by the realization that they were being used to finance a failing cause. One of the leading voices of discontent at this time was another Christian.

William Christian was born on 14 April 1608, the third son of Deemster Ewan Christian, of Milntown, Lezayre. He first comes to prominence in Manx records in 1643, when he was steward of the dissolved abbey lands and a member of the Keys. Also in that year, his father passed on to him the farm at Ronaldsway (today completely covered by the airport) which, perhaps surprisingly, he accepted on the new tenure for three lives, rather than 'by the straw'. This latter act, no doubt, placed him in a favourable light with Earl James and, in 1648, he was appointed Receiver, essentially the lord's land agent. On the Earl's departure to support the royalist cause in England, Christian was left in charge of the Manx militia, with the same rank that had been held earlier by his relative, Edward Christian.

Some time after the Earl's departure, some 800 men convened at Christian's Ronaldsway home, where there was a groundswell of opinion in favour of a petition to the Countess. The assembly took an oath that the people should stand against the Countess until she agreed to redress their grievances. The inducement to take the oath was the disclosure that the Countess had written to Colonel Duckenfield (commanding the force charged with taking the Isle of Man for Parliament), offering to surrender the island in return for the Earl's release (she still being unaware of his execution).

Duckenfield's force to secure the island set sail from Chester on 18 October. It would seem that the leaders of the Ronaldsway meeting were aware of the force and its objective, for, in the course of the following week, the Manx militia rebelled and secured all of the island's forts except for the primary strongholds at Rushen and Peel. All of this had been achieved by the time the English fleet appeared off Ramsey. It does appear, however, that support for the rebellion was not unanimous; some of the Manx were prepared to swear support for the Countess in a stand against the Parliamentary force, but they were a minority.

Having been delayed by storms, the English fleet did not drop anchor in

Ramsey Bay until 25 October, and were further delayed in landing their troops and horses by continuing rough weather. However, Christian and his men sent word to Duckenfield that all of the forts except Rushen and Peel had been taken and there would be no opposition to a Parliamentary landing. The following morning, a Manx delegation ventured aboard Duckenfield's ship and surrendered the island on condition that the laws and liberties enjoyed prior to the changes introduced by Earl James were retained.

Another storm delayed the landing of the force for a further two days but, on 28 October, the landing was accomplished and the force divided into two parties, one proceeding to Peel, the other to Castletown, to lay siege to the two castles. Duckenfield himself led the Castletown contingent and sent a summons to the Countess, calling on her to surrender Castle Rushen. The wording of the summons contained the phrase 'the late Earl of Darby', which was the first intimation that the Countess Charlotte had received of her husband's death. In a distraught state, her initial reaction was one of defiance: she offered to surrender the castle, but on terms that no winning side would have accepted. As Duckenfield drew up his guns outside, some of the garrison inside were already breaking open one of the sally-ports, assisted by Parliamentary troops on the outside. Castle Rushen was taken without a shot being fired, and the fortress at Peel soon followed.

The Isle of Man was now under the control of the English Parliament, and the Countess, her children and household were permitted to leave the island. She has sometimes been credited with being the last person in the three kingdoms and their dependent territories to submit to the Parliament, but this distinction actually seems to reside in Galway, Cromwell's control over Ireland not being complete until 1653.

Parliament appears to have anticipated its success in the Isle of Man, having already granted the island to Thomas, Lord Fairfax in 1649, the year of Charles I's execution. However, the measures put in place by Earl James and maintained in operation by the Countess Charlotte ensured that Fairfax could not physically take on the grant until two years had passed. It was on 23 February 1652 that he was proclaimed at Castle Rushen as 'Lord of Man, and of the Isles', according to James Chalenor, who would later be appointed Fairfax's governor. Colonel Duckenfield had been Parliament's initial appointment as Governor. There is no evidence that Fairfax was actually present at his proclamation as Lord, or that he made any subsequent visits to the isle. As for the Manx, their expectations that the arrival of Cromwell's Commonwealth would bring their hoped-for changes to the system of land-tenure came to naught, for nothing changed. But the Commonwealth did provide men and ships for the island's defence.

James Chalenor is the best known of the island's governors during the years of Cromwell's Commonwealth, mainly for his book, *A Short Treatise of the Isle of Man*, published in 1656 and reprinted by the Manx Society in 1864 [49]. His immediate predecessor as Governor had been none other than William Christian but he was removed from office, and from the offices of receiver and steward of the abbey and bishop's lands because of doubts concerning his financial probity. Thereupon, Christian left the island early in 1659 and went to live on his Lancashire estate, leaving the lord's accounts in a state of some disorder, with uncertainties over payments not covered by receipts. For the time being, these matters rested there, unresolved.

Charles II was restored to the English throne in May 1660. Lord Fairfax led the English delegation to the Hague to invite him to return. Parliament's subsequent Act of Indemnity pardoned all those who had participated in the rebellion or in the subsequent republican governments, with the exception of some fifty named individuals (none connected with the Manx situation). In the Isle of Man, proclamations of Charles as King were made in the four towns on four successive days: in Peel on 28 May, in Castletown on the 29th, Douglas on the 30th and Ramsey on the 31st. By all accounts, the news of the Restoration of the Monarchy was received with rather more enthusiasm than that which had greeted the news of its removal nine years earlier. There was rejoicing in the streets, accompanied by much drinking and the firing of muskets and other weapons. Cromwell's Commonwealth had brought the Manx people none of the improvements for which they had hoped, and now they celebrated its demise. Governor Chalenor described their condition as one of great poverty, and their celebrations for the king would have given them an all-too-brief respite.

With the Restoration of the Monarchy in England, the Isle of Man was restored to Charles Stanley, eighth Earl of Derby. One of his first acts was to place Samuel Rutter at the head of the bishopric which had lain dormant during the years of the Commonwealth. But the Earl's main preoccupation was to bring retribution to the leaders of the rebellion of 1651, of whom the main one was now in London.

William Christian was confined to the Fleet prison at the time, having been arrested over a debt of some £20,000. Being unable to raise bail, he remained in custody for almost a year. On his release, believing that he was covered by the English Parliament's Act of Indemnity, he prepared to return to the Isle of Man. He was about to make the biggest mistake he would ever make.

IN THE MATTER OF WILLIAM CHRISTIAN

The salient feature of the Act of Indemnity passed by the English Parliament was that it pardoned most of those involved in the rebellion *against the English Monarchy*; it made no reference to either the Isle of Man or the Lord of Man.

Christian returned to the isle and, on 13 September 1662, Earl Charles issued a warrant for his arrest on charges of 'illegal actions' and rebellion in 1651 and earlier. He was confined to Castle Rushen and brought to trial, where he compounded his earlier 'biggest mistake' with another – he refused to enter a plea. Under the procedures of those times, such a refusal was taken as an admission of guilt.

The trial at the Court of General Gaol Delivery (the name by which the Manx criminal court is still known today) proceeded before a jury of six men of lowly rank, three of whom were in the direct employ of the lord, and probably all of them so unskilled in the English language (which was the language of the court) as to be wholly unable to follow the proceedings. There is a suggestion in at least one account that they returned their verdict of guilty only after being coerced into producing the result that was expected of them. Christian was sentenced to be hanged, drawn and quartered (the usual penalty for treason) but, out of consideration for his distraught wife, the Deputy Governor ordered that he be 'shot to death, that thereupon his liffe may depart from his bodie'. The sentence was carried out at Hango Hill, overlooking the shore of Castletown Bay on 2 January 1663. It is recorded that he went to his death in a resolute manner, making a fine speech and declining the proffered blindfold. He was buried beneath the chancel of Kirk Malew the following day.

The ruin of the Derbys' summerhouse at Hango Hill, Castletown

During his confinement in Castle Rushen, Christian had sent a petition to the King in Council, pleading that the action taken against him was in breach of the Act of Indemnity, but the document was not received in London until after his execution. The eventual adjudication was that the Act of Indemnity 'did and ought to be understood to extend to the Isle of Man'. This was rather too late for William Christian, but the decision was taxing the minds of legal experts long after his death. In the nineteenth century, an Attorney-General of the Isle of Man, Sir James Gell [29], was pointing out that the Act of Indemnity referred to acts of treason against the authority of 'the existing Government of England, Scotland and Ireland, and the Dominions and Territories thereto belonging'. But the Isle of Man was not a dominion or territory belonging to the Government of England; it was a Dominion *of the Crown* of England, and even if it had belonged to the Government, if Christian was guilty of treason, it was treason against the Lord of Man, not against the King of England, and he could be guilty of the former act quite independently of the Crown. (Even more recently, P. W. Edge [24] has discussed the point.) After considering Christian's petition, the Privy Council ordered that the whole of his estate be restored to his wife and children, and that the deemsters who had passed sentence on him should be confined to the King's Bench to receive 'condign punishment'.

Down the years, much romanticism has been woven into the story of William Christian. During his lifetime, and more so after, he came to be known to the Manx as *Illiam Dhone*, 'Dark' or 'Brown William', referring either to a swarthy complexion or to the colour of his hair. Some time after his execution, a ballad was written, lamenting his death – and other things – under the title *Baase Illiam Dhone*, 'Brown William's Death', from which come the following two stanzas:

> *Gow gys yn Vannister ny Cailleeyn-ghoo,*
> *As eie son clein Cholcad derrey vrisheys dty ghoo;*
> *Ta'n ennym shen caillit v'enish, Vanninee ghooie;*
> *As dty vaase, Illiam Dhone, te brishey nyn gree!*

> Go to the Nunnery of the black-robed nuns,
> And call for clan Calcott until thy voice breaks;
> That name is lost from you, ye native Manxmen;
> And thy death, Illiam Dhone, 'tis that breaks our heart!

> *Gow gys ny Gregganyn, ny gys yn Vallalogh,*
> *Cha vow fer jeh'n ennym shen jir rhyt, 'Cheet stiagh!'*
> *Ec joarreeyn ta nyn dhieyn, nyn dhalloo as nhee;*
> *As dty vaase, Illiam Dhone, te brishey nyn gree!*

Go unto the Creggans, and to the Ballalough,
There is no man of that name will say to thee, 'Come in!'
Strangers have their houses, their land and their all;
And thy death, Illiam Dhone, 'tis that breaks our heart!

The ballad was obviously written some considerable time after Christian's death, for it relates the subsequent fate of some of his contemporaries. The Calcott clan, in particular, resided at the former priory on the outskirts of Douglas (later to become more widely known as the Nunnery), and the Calcott name did not disappear until some time in the eighteenth century, when it became transmuted into the present *Colquitt*. In the second stanza above, the poet seems to lament the arrival of eighteenth-century 'come-overs' (although the name *Calcott* itself originated in Cheshire!). The ballad was not printed until 1781, though probably composed earlier, and was possibly used to arouse feelings at times of political unrest.

William Christian appears as one of the characters in Sir Walter Scott's novel *Peveril of the Peak*, which includes a version of Christian's final speech, but perhaps a more authentic version is that reproduced by the Manx Society [50]. Part of the action in Scott's novel takes place in Peel Castle.

Having followed this summary of William Christian's final twenty years of life, the reader will by now have realized that it is a story with more than its fair share of complications. That there were wrongs on both sides is beyond doubt, and historians have for long been divided (or been unwilling to pronounce) on the question of whether Christian was a patriot or a traitor. There are some in Manx nationalist circles who go so far as to claim him as a martyr who died whilst making a stand for the rights of the Manx people. But 'martyr' is surely too strong a word. He did not die for his belief in the rights of the people; he died for an act of treason against the Lord of Man, who employed him, paid him and entrusted the island and the Countess Charlotte to his care during the lord's absence in time of war. He had taken an oath of allegiance to the lord and had betrayed that oath. If his actions were prompted by feelings for the people's rights, then, in the circumstances of the time, he was working for the lord under a plain conflict of interest. The honourable course would have been for him to resign from the lord's employ and stand unequivocally for the people. But he did not, and he paid the penalty which was the customary one in his day.

So, was he a patriot or a traitor? I suppose that the kindest response that one can make is that he was both, but that he lacked the wisdom – or the forethought – to make the choice between the two, and that was his undoing. Over the years, the name of William Christian or, increasingly, Illiam Dhone, has become embedded in the national psyche, his story being woven in a web of legend and myth down through the ages. Recent years have seen a growing reluctance to use his proper name at all. Increasingly, we see and hear references to 'Illiam Dhone, whose *English* name was William Christian', disregarding the fact that the latter was his real name and that his family name was of Scandinavian origin and not English at all. Those who wish to refer to him by a surname frequently call him Dhone – Brown! And the fashion has spread into the realms of government: we now have a modern government building called Illiam Dhone House – 'Brown William House'.

Today, on 2 January each year, a small gathering of Manx nationalists assembles at Hango Hill to commemorate Christian's death. Two orations are given, one in Manx and one in English, on themes of perceived national concern. This annual ceremony may perhaps be seen as the Manx equivalent (with far smaller numbers and much less noise) of the Orangemen's commemoration of the Battle of the Boyne in that land to the west which seems addicted to grievance. The Orangemen, of course, are commemorating a victory, whereas the Manx nationalists are not. But the Isle of Man, situated geographically between Ulster and Scotland, perhaps lies between the two also in its attitudes to the past, but closer to the latter, the land where the Scots seemed to have consigned their resentments over inter-clan and Anglo-Scottish strife to the deeper recesses of their memory-banks, marked with a label: 'Long time ago – do not disturb'.

The story of William Christian presented here is but a summary of the records that survive. The reader wishing for further detail is referred to A. W. Moore [57, 59] and the account of the 'Manx Rebellion' published by the Manx Society [50].

THE LAST OF THE STANLEYS

At the restoration of the monarchy in 1660, the renewed rule of the Stanleys had more than a hundred years still to run. The Church had been subjugated to the State since 1644, the see of Sodor and Man having been bereft of a bishop during the intervening sixteen years. In 1661, as commented earlier, one of the first acts of Charles Stanley, eighth Earl of Derby, as Lord of Man, was to appoint Samuel Rutter to serve as Bishop. Rutter had been a faithful servant of the seventh Earl, acting as his domestic chaplain and tutor to his children; he had been Earl James's confidant and friend. But he lived barely six months after his installation as Bishop. He was buried in the ruin of the cathedral of St German, where his amusing, self-composed epitaph is still plain to see on his memorial slab today.

Rutter's successor was Isaac Barrow who, after a year, was also appointed Governor, thereby becoming what was known at the time as a 'sword bishop'. The remainder of Earl Charles's rule seems to have been more notable for the actions of Bishop Barrow than those of the Earl himself. On his arrival, Barrow was aghast at the condition of his clergy and the people, both of whom, it seems, were existing in a state of abject poverty. The people, he found, led loose and vicious lives, were rude and barbarous in their behaviour, and showed little evidence of a religious following. The clergy, for their part, were ignorant and underpaid, which provided them with few means to obtain books for the enlightenment of their flocks. Books would, in any case, have been in the English language, which was understood by relatively few – and that was also true of many of the clergy.

Bishop Barrow's dislike of the Manx language led him to conclude that the way out of this situation was to bring the people to an understanding of the English language. It is tempting to think that he might have done better by bringing the liturgy to the people in their own tongue. In the absence of Manx editions of the Bible and the Prayer Book, the clergy had perforce to translate their services ad lib, and many of *them* did not have the grasp of English to tackle the task with any great degree of proficiency.

Barrow's approach to the problem was to raise funds for the establishment of schools. His first achievement in this direction was to retrieve for the Church in Man the tithes which had been diverted from the religious houses at the time of the Reformation and which had ended up with the Lord of Man. The Bishop accumu-lated these tithes and other income with the combined intention of supporting his impoverished clergy and founding schools in all of the parishes. He actually retrieved the tithes from Charles Stanley, eighth Earl of Derby, on a lease of 10,000 years, on down-payment of £1,000 and £130 every thirtieth year, these payments being met by subscriptions raised by the Bishop in England, including a contribu-tion from Charles II. The surplus would accrue interest, which would swell the coffers of what was to become 'Bishop Barrow's Trust'. He also acquired the farms at Hango Hill and Ballgilley, in Malew. A. W. Moore [57] states that he acquired them through his own private charity. Kinvig [44] and Stenning [72] aver that he 'seized' them. Either way, the land at Hango Hill was intended to be the site of a Manx university, which never materialized, but a less ambitious public school (King William's College) would eventually rise on the site, completed in 1833, 163 years after Barrow's death. A major part of the funding of King William's College today still emanates from the Bishop Barrow Trust. During his lifetime, however, he used the trust to support promising young Manx students at English universities.

The bishop's efforts to get Manx children into schools received the backing of Earl Charles who, in 1672, made an order requiring all his tenants to send their children to school or face severe penalties. In 1669, Bishop Barrow was translated to St Asaph but he continued to hold the see of Sodor and Man until 1671, the year before Earl Charles's death.

Charles was succeeded by William Stanley II, ninth Earl of Derby, whose prime memorable act was the appointment of the good Thomas Wilson as Bishop of Sodor and Man in 1698. Earl William would reign for thirty years but Thomas Wilson held the bishopric for no less than fifty-seven. The second Earl William held the same views concerning land tenure that the long line of Stanleys had always held, and feelings of discontent rumbled on, but Thomas Wilson would play a leading role in bringing this long saga to a peaceful conclusion. However, resolution of the issue was not achieved before Earl William's death in 1702. The feelings of the people on the matter were increasingly bitter, and farms were being left unoccupied because of the uncertainties over inherited land tenure, coupled with the effects of poor harvests and poor fishing, which were leading to increased emigration.

The second Earl William was succeeded by James Stanley II, the tenth Earl. By the time of his accession, or shortly after, Bishop Wilson had collaborated with the Keys to draw up proposals to present to the earl for the resolution of this long dispute. At long last, a Lord of Man conceded, and the Isle of Man's Act of Settlement – the Act which has been likened to a Manx Magna Carta – was passed in 1704, and the dispute over which William Christian and his 800 collaborators had rebelled in the Great Stanley's day was finally resolved.

Under the provisions of the Act, the Lord's tenants became the effective owners of their lands, possessing the rights of inheritance and sale of their holdings. The Lord's rent (effectively a ground-rent) was still payable, as was the alienation fine, due to the Lord on the conveyance of a holding from one holder to the next, but apart from these details, the 'tenants' were now owners, free to transfer their holdings whenever, and to whomever, they wished. The old requirement for the tenant to supply food and turf to the castles was abolished. More than two centuries later, on the passing of an Act of 1913, the Lord's rents were bought out by payment of a lump sum.

Without doubt, Thomas Wilson was the greatest Bishop of Sodor and Man of the historical period; saintly and just in his dealings with his clergy and the people, he was held in great affection. Receiving an annual income scarcely more than £400, he gave at least half of it every year in charitable donations. One group who had particular reason to be grateful to him were the Quakers. The Society of Friends had been founded by George Fox in 1647, a particularly unfortunate time for religious deviants in England. A number of them arrived in Man, seeking refuge from persecution, but Lord Fairfax decreed that they were not to be received in any Manx house, nor were they to meet on Sundays 'in any field or outhouse'. Those who did so were persecuted, consigned to the bishop's prison under St German's cathedral or returned to England – where, probably not being re-admitted, they would be sent back to the island to end up in the bishop's prison. Those who refused to pay Church dues were fined, children were baptized against their parents' wishes, and their dead were refused Christian burial. After the Restoration, Bishop Barrow – who did so much good in other ways – maintained the persecution and seized all their property. Bishop Wilson put an end to that, releasing all those detained in prison and forbidding any further persecution of them.

The only one of the Manx Quakers of whom we have much knowledge is William Callow, of Ballafayle, Maughold, who – with others – was banished from the isle for seven years. Separated from his wife and nine children, he was only allowed to return after Charles II issued his Declaration of Indulgence in 1672, which at last brought some relief for this peaceable, harmless and much persecuted group of nonconformists. Today, the bodies of William Callow and his band of fellow-believers rest in their own remote little graveyard, *Rhullick ny Quakeryn*, high above his old home of Ballafayle.

Bishop Wilson died in 1755 at the age of 93 and was the first of five bishops to be buried in the churchyard at Kirk Michael. He had been offered translation to another diocese but declined, with the comment: 'I will not leave my wife [Sodor and Man] in my old age because she is poor'.

By this time, Manx-minted coinage had been legal tender for almost eighty years. In 1668, a Douglas merchant named John Murrey, realizing that trade could

Burials from two ages: in the foreground is the Bronze-Age burial cairn at Ballafayle, Maughold; under the trees beyond is the Quakers' burial ground, Rhullick ny Quakeryn

be better facilitated by a supply of coinage, began producing coins which became known as 'John Murrey pennies'. On the obverse, they carried the legend 'JOHN MURREY 1668' set in a circle around the central 'HIS PENNY I.M.'. The reverse carried the motto: 'QUOCUNQUE GESSERIS STABIT' set around a central three legs (running clockwise). The coins were made legal tender by an order of the Council and confirmed by an Act of Tynwald in 1679, and remained so until 1709, when Earl James II, the tenth Earl, authorized the first official Manx coinage, bearing the Stanley family crest and the three legs (running clockwise). In 1839, the Queen Victoria penny became the first Manx penny to have parity of value with the British coin; once again, the legs were running clockwise. Prior to John Murrey's initiative, the only coinage circulating in Man had been a sundry mix of Scottish, Irish and counterfeit. As a postscript of historical interest, in or about 1720, the same John Murrey bought the Ronaldsway estate from a James Somerville, who had purchased it in 1716 from one William Christian, the grandson of Illiam Dhone.

On the question of the alignment of the triskelion symbol, although there have been some coins and other artefacts showing the three legs running anticlock-wise, it has long been accepted that the correct alignment is clockwise, as depicted on the two earliest examples in the island, those on the Maughold Cross and on the haft of the Manx Sword of State, both thought to date from the fourteenth century. The two most public displays today of the legs running the 'wrong' way are on the supporting structure of the Laxey Wheel and – surprisingly for a government department – on the logo of the Isle of Man Fire and Rescue Service.

The tenth Earl of Derby died in 1736 without issue, and the succession in Man passed through the distaff side of the family to James Murray, second Duke of Atholl. He showed great interest in the island, presiding over the annual Tynwald, and was warmly welcomed. It was during his rule that the statutes of 1737, dubbed the 'Manx Bill of Rights', were passed, imparting the right of trial by jury to all accused persons, and directing that all disputes involving title to land would be decided by common law and sheading jury, and not in Chancery as thitherto.

James Murray died in 1764 and the Manx succession passed to his daughter Charlotte, Baroness Strange, and her husband, John Murray, who, by right of his wife, became Lord of Man. His rule was to be short and would be ended, not by his death, but by political diktat.

'... TILL SOME TRADE BE'

It has sometimes been blamed on James Stanley, seventh Earl of Derby, who proclaimed in 1648 that 'this island will never succeed till some trade be'. Whether or not it was this particular trade (smuggling) that he had in mind is another question. It was all very well for Yn Stanlagh Mooar to lament the lack of trade, but it was he and the earlier Stanleys who had regulated the trading of goods into and out of the island so severely that the situation on which he commented was the inevitable result. But, subsequently, one trade – 'the trade' – developed. It is not clear whether the Lord was the prime mover in relaxing restrictions on trade, or whether the new breed of merchant-trader took the initiative and the Lord did not resist because he saw that he could make something out of it. In the seventh Earl's day, no goods could be imported to or exported from the island without his authority, and his customs duties were levied on all such traffic.

The continuing strategy of watch and ward ensured that the Manx authorities were aware of the approach of all island-bound vessels. On arrival in harbour, a ship's captain was required to appear before the Governor to declare the nature of his cargo and to apprise him of the latest news from beyond Manx shores. After that, if he was a 'merchant-stranger', i.e. one of non-Manx domicile, the captain would be handed over to 'the four merchants', whose task it was to obtain the best bargain possible on the incoming shipment. The garrisons at Castle Rushen and Peel would have first choice of whatever they needed. If the cargo was of wine, the Clerk of Ships was allowed one hogshead, and other allocations went to the Lord, the Governor, Bishop and Archdeacon free of charge. Thereafter, the four merchants were responsible for distributing the remainder for sale around the island.

The export of goods from Man was not permitted until the Governor and Council had ruled that the goods were surplus to insular requirements. The merchant-stranger seeking goods for export was compelled to buy them in public markets; the 'middleman' was outlawed. The island was in dire need of coal, iron, timber and salt but, until the advent of the mining industry, the only wares available for export were agricultural produce and fish. In the face of such restrictions, it is not surprising that conditions for legitimate trading were less than buoyant. In fairness, it should be pointed out that it was not only insular restrictions that were impeding Manx trade abroad, for there were actions by the Imperial parliament which piled impediment on impediment. In 1660, the number of Manx cattle that could be imported annually into England was limited to 600; they could be of the native breed only and they could be shipped only into the port of Chester. And it was not until 1676 that corn, the principal crop of the island, could be imported into England at all.

On top of all this, the amendment of the Imperial parliament's Navigation Act in 1660 required that all goods imported into England be shipped in English vessels, manned by English crews. Yet more strictures on trade with England came after the outbreak of war with France in 1689, when massive increases in the duties on French wine and brandy were introduced, providing a great incentive to smuggling. In 1705, Tynwald Court lodged a petition with Lord Derby (the tenth Earl by this time), complaining that it was impossible to obtain the essential supplies of coal, iron, timber and salt unless such goods as were surplus to insular requirements could be exported to pay for them. This was made difficult by excessive English tariffs. The petition elicited no response.

Until the initiative of John Murrey in minting his pennies, coinage in Man was relatively sparse, and much insular trade was by way of barter, which was of little use in external trading. In the period from the outbreak of the English Civil War to the Restoration, the presence of royalist refugees in the island introduced a supply of external currency, but that would bring no permanent solution.

By the time Bishop Wilson arrived in Man in 1698, 'the trade' was well established and developing strongly. Wines, spirits, tea, tobacco, lace and other goods were purchased in France, Iberia and Scandinavia and shipped into Manx ports, where a comparatively small duty was payable. Furthermore, by landing at one of the secluded inlets such as Dhyrnane, Port Mooar, Port Cornaa, Port Grenaugh, Port Soldrick, et al under cover of darkness, goods could be brought ashore without payment of duty at all. Then, on transferring the cargoes to specially built

Dhyrnane, Maughold, at various times an export harbour for iron ore, a smugglers' cove and a fishermen's landing

smaller, faster craft which stood a fair chance of outrunning the revenue cutters, the goods would be transported to creeks and inlets along the British and Irish coasts. The favoured approach to land would be under the increasing cover of dusk and at a state of tide when larger vessels could not follow them into the shallower inlets.

Bishop Wilson arrived to find the island a flourishing centre for the import and export of French brandy, and he saw the effect it was having on the people of the isle, where drunkenness was rife. He preached against the evils of inebriation, and his vicars-general dealt with drunkards severely. He pleaded with the *nouveaux riches* of the merchant class; they subscribed to his charitable causes, but they were not about to curtail their lucrative business activities. Cellars were constructed under their houses in Douglas, Castletown, Port St Mary and Peel, where stocks of smuggled goods were stored. (It appears that Ramsey was still slowly recovering from being largely destroyed by a storm some time around 1630.) Douglas in particular – until this time an inconsequential fishing village – developed rapidly into a sizeable town and harbour. As the trade developed, so the Lord's dues inevitably increased, but never sufficiently to harm the trade. Many Manx families in later times would owe their wealth and position to their ancestors' business acumen in accruing the rewards of 'the trade'.

The then-flourishing business scene in Man also brought about a marked change in the approach to 'strangers' who, thitherto, had been strongly discouraged from stepping onto Manx shores. Trade was expanding, as were the Lord's receipts from his customs duties, and merchants from the surrounding countries were suddenly welcome; the law was amended so that they could trade legitimately. English and Scottish merchants were particularly prominent arrivals, eager to invest in this new and lucrative business.

There can be no doubt that, in his day, James Murray, second Duke of Atholl, Lord of Man, was more than content to let this burgeoning activity run its course, and that many Manx people were equally happy with it. But it was inevitable that, as the trade continued to grow, the Imperial parliament would, at some point, act to curtail it. The Manx 'trade' had grown out of all proportion to the small territory that had nurtured it. The island had become the centre of an extensive trading network, the Manx hub of which operated entirely legally once the Lord's customs duties had been paid. It was the British end of the system that was illicit, and the Imperial exchequer was being deprived of large sums in customs duty.

A deputation from the Keys had visited London in 1710 for discussions with the Imperial government; Earl James II had paid £100 towards their expenses. Some sort of understanding seems to have been reached, for an Act of Tynwald was passed the following year, under which the smuggling trade would be suppressed (at source, in Man), on the understanding that Great Britain would allow the import of Manx agricultural produce free of duty. However, the British government took no action to implement this undertaking, and so Tynwald felt no compulsion to effect the Manx side of the bargain either. To make matters worse, Lord Derby leased the Manx customs to a partnership formed by two merchants in the business (one from Liverpool and one from Dublin). They paid him 1,000 guineas (£1,050) per annum, and the trade continued to grow. By this step, the Lord moved himself one stage further away from the actual business of smuggling; the two partners were now collecting the customs dues, and he need not know what other business they were up to.

By the time John Murray, third Duke of Atholl, succeeded to the lordship in 1764, the British government had decided that the only way of bringing this situation under control was for the British Crown to purchase the sovereign rights of the Lord of Man. The British prime minister, George Grenville, was instructed to open negotiations with the Duke, aimed at producing that result, and the Duke was, in effect, told to state his price for selling his sovereign rights in Man to the Crown. He was also given a broad hint that, if he did not come to an agreement, possession of the isle would be obtained by other means. Nevertheless, the Duke was in no great haste to respond, saying that he had only lately succeeded to the lordship and needed time to consider the question. To hasten his consideration, Parliament passed an Act on 21 January 1765 which came to be known as the *Mischief Act*. Under its provisions, British customs and excise officers were authorized to search ships in Manx ports and to make seizures where appropriate. Offenders under the Act could be tried in British, Irish or Manx courts. At this stage of the proceedings, such powers were of doubtful legality: British customs officers had no jurisdiction in Manx ports and there had been no illegal goings-on in Manx ports. But Parliament had the Lord of Man in a corner and did not intend to relax the pressure.

The Duke conceded, stating that the lordship was worth £299,773 to him, comprised of the following elements:

Regalities	£42,000
Patronage of bishopric and vicarages	£8,400
Customs dues, lands and manors	£249,373

Parliament replied that they wanted only the regalities and customs and offered £70,000, comprising £46,000 for regalities and £24,000 for customs. Under this arrangement, the Duke would retain the rights to his Manx estates. Probably fearful that Parliament might change its mind, he promptly agreed the terms.

The Keys, however, themselves fearful that the interests of the Manx people would be overlooked in the deal, sent a deputation to London in an attempt to protect the traditional and constitutional rights of the people. But their concerns received short shrift, and a second Act was hurriedly passed through Parliament: this was the Isle of Man Purchase Act of 1765 (though now remembered as the Revesting Act), which was the irrevocable step to the purchase of the island. It was passed on 10 May 1765 and, by proclamation under the great seal of England dated eleven days later, the Isle of Man became a possession of the English Crown, and has remained so to this day.

After the passage of the Act, the Duke and Duchess were granted a joint annuity of Irish £2,000 (English £1,740) and they renounced all rights to the lordship. The Duke died in 1774 and the Duchess continued to receive the annuity until her death in 1805. It was paid out of Irish revenues because Ireland, like England, had benefited from the cessation of the Manx smuggling trade, and it was deemed therefore that Ireland should pay some part of the compensation.

Thus, after no less than 360 years, the long line of Stanleys and Murrays as Lords of Man had come to an end. Despite its long history of discontent over questions of land tenure, taxes and tithes, and the occasional bursts of desperation spilling over into rebellion, the Manx seem to have remained generally loyal to the person of the Lord, expressions of resentment often being directed at the Governor rather than the Lord himself. There would certainly have been little appetite for the isle to be taken under direct rule by the English Crown.

In the run-up to the Revestment, once again we can see wrong on both sides. The Manx end of the 'trading' operation was perfectly licit under Manx law; it was the Imperial government's inability to impose effective control over access to its own shores that lay at the heart of the British problem. As the volume of trade swelled and its lucrative potential became apparent, so the island became increasingly attractive to merchants from neighbouring countries, and Manx laws were relaxed to allow the 'strangers' to operate. And so the trade continued to grow. As remarked earlier, the stationing of British customs officers in Manx ports was of dubious legality, coming as it did *before* the Act of Revestment. Finally, in its determination to curb the activity, the Imperial government took the only step which seemed likely to end it: it was decided (in modern parlance) to clobber the little guy who was causing them so much (expensive) trouble and bring him 'in-house'. Man was a Crown possession.

Those well-known words of James Stanley in 1648 must have been echoing hollowly down the intervening years, opining that there would be no success for this isle 'till some trade be'. Well, by 1765, some very considerable trade had been – and gone.

A CROWN POSSESSION

Revestment was undoubtedly a humiliation for the Manx people and catastrophic for the economy of their island. The smuggling trade, however dubious its ethics and legality, had brought a long-awaited degree of prosperity, although it would have been restricted to those directly engaged in the smuggling and the proprietors of closely allied trades. Since wages and hours of work were still strictly controlled, workers such as farm labourers, maidservants and those employed in many trades would scarcely notice a change in prosperity – except as enjoyed by others. Since most members of the legislature were landowners and employers of labour, it served their interests to maintain strict controls on the working conditions of their employees. To make matters worse for the lower orders, the great influx of 'strangers' at the height of 'the trade' would have raised the demand for everyday commodities, with consequent increases in prices. (A. W. Moore [57] gives a wealth of information on wage rates, conditions of work and commodity prices.)

In the years leading up to Revestment, the Manx gentry and merchant-trader classes had established themselves in well-appointed houses, mainly around

A tholtan, a long-abandoned farmstead

Douglas and Castletown. Ramsey had also recovered from its earlier near-destruction by the sea, and those merchants involved in trade with Ireland might well have favoured Peel. In 1648, the English writer William Blundell had found the island's upper classes residing in 'high, handsome and well-built' dwellings ensconced in their own spacious landed estates. He describes the people of that class as being English-speaking and rather like those to be found in Lancashire and Cheshire. Those lower down the social scale, particularly in the countryside, lived in somewhat humbler style. Blundell described their houses as 'mere hovels'. These were usually low, single-storey dwellings with random-rubble walls formed with stones gathered from the surrounding land and bound together with mud-and-clay mortar. The roof was thatched with straw, secured by ropes of twisted straw (Manx *suggane*), which were tied down to a row of stone spigots projecting from each gable. Often, the roof covering was simply a layer of turf. The floor was of compacted soil or clay, and an open fire burned on a hearth of stone, the smoke from which would leave the dwelling (eventually) through a hole in the roof. Part of the roof-space was frequently used as sleeping accommodation (with less than full headroom), with access by ladder, and the ground floor was often shared with the livestock. As Blundell described the scene: '... in this smoking hut doth the man, his wife and children co-habit and in many cases with the ducks and geese under the bed, the cockes and hennes over his head, the cow and calfe at the bed's foot'. And this situation would change but slowly; in 1881, in his dialect poem *Betsy Lee*, T. E. Brown was still able to observe:

> You know the way them houses is fixed
> With the pigs and the hens and the childer mixed.

Although Castletown was still the island's capital and place of residence of the Lord, Douglas now possessed a superior harbour and had overtaken the capital in terms of trade and population. But the island's population growth was about to receive a check as a result of the Revestment. The acquisition of control of the island by the Imperial government and the abrupt curtailment of the smuggling trade caused immediate concern among the owners of warehouses and other properties whose market values had suddenly plummeted. The 'stranger-merchants' among them made hurried preparations to depart the isle which had provided them with such lucrative livings but would do so no more. Those Manx farmers and fishermen who had neglected their traditional callings for the attractions of 'the trade' had now to re-tame their untended lands and redirect their sea-going activities to the more mundane task of catching fish.

The immediate constitutional consequences of the Revestment were disastrous. The Keys and the Council (which had until then been the Lord's Council) were still in existence but they retained only such powers as did not entail the expenditure of money. All customs duties and taxes were collected by officers of the British government, which met all costs of the administration and retained any surplus. Initially, such surpluses were deposited in an account supposedly to be used for the benefit of the island, but there is little or no evidence of any such expenditure, and it was not long before the Manx surpluses became subsumed into the British government's revenues. The long line of Stanley and Murray lords may have been motivated largely by their own manorial interests, and were undoubtedly authoritarian, even tyrannical at times, but their common policy had been to maintain their concept of self-determination for their island nation. But the Manx ship of state now had a new captain, who was at home in London, and the ship was stopped in the water.

By the time of the Revestment, Bishop Wilson had been dead for ten years and was succeeded by Mark Hildesley, who had embarked on the translation of the Book of Common Prayer and the Bible into the Manx language. In July 1765, he received a letter from the Revd Philip Moore (who had been assisting in the translations), setting out his observations of the island scene at that time. He saw 'nothing now, but anarchy and confusion'. The erstwhile traders had had insufficient time to get their stocks of illicit goods away from the island and had no alternative but to conceal them in remote and secluded places. Others who had knowledge of such caches turned either informer or thief, and those who turned to thieving were frequently the victims of other thieves further down the line. The Revd Moore described bands of armed men ranging over the countryside and entering people's houses in search of stashed contraband: 'a very melancholy situation ... all our people of property are making up their matters as fast as they can and preparing to quit a place governed by martial law and violence of arms'.

To make matters worse, the collapse of trade was accompanied by a slump in agriculture, and at least a thousand people are known to have left the isle at that time. By 1791, Lieutenant Governor Alexander Shaw was observing 'numbers of every description' being compelled to migrate to other countries, and the island 'fast descending into that very miserable state of containing a few great landowners and ... their miserable dependants'. (This was part of Shaw's submission to a commission of enquiry [13] set up by the King in Council to investigate various matters relating to the Isle of Man.)

One of the matters to be enquired into by the King's commissioners was the claim by John Murray (junior), who had become the fourth Duke of Atholl on the death of his father in 1774, seeking an increase in the price paid for the island. This was strongly opposed by the Keys, who knew full well that any further payment would come out of the Manx coffers, and the Manx people had paid a high enough price already in the aftermath of Revestment.

The Commission found generally in favour of the Duke but made no recommendation as to how his claim should be settled, and so King George, in an act of
amelioration, appointed him Governor of Man in 1793. In the early 1800s, he built
himself a fine mansion (Castle Mona) overlooking Douglas Bay; after his departure, it would become a hotel, which it is now. The Duke's appointment granted
him a fair degree of patronage, and he rapidly gained a reputation for nepotism,
leading to the oft-heard exclamation: 'Murrays, Murrays everywhere.' The final
straw came in 1814, when he appointed his nephew, George Murray, as Bishop;
George promptly placed a tithe of 12 shillings per acre on potatoes. This led to a
general riot: the Manx tithe on potatoes had earlier been abolished; the potato
tithe in Ireland was only 3 shillings per acre, and in England just 2 shillings and 6
pence. Angry farmers from all over the isle confronted the Bishop at
Bishopscourt, where, probably fearing for his life, he retracted his claim.

By this time, the Duke, aware of his unpopularity, was ready to leave the isle
but not to relinquish his claim for further compensation. In 1801, he had addressed
a further petition to the King in Council, and the Keys promptly presented a
counter-petition. The proceedings towards a settlement would drag on for another
twenty-four years, by which time George IV would be on the throne. The battle-
lines were drawn not only between the Duke and the Keys, for opinions were
strongly divided in Parliament itself. The Duke certainly had the advantage of a
powerful friend in that high place, none other than William Pitt (the younger). The
complete story makes for a fascinating read, and A. W. Moore [57] gives a very full
account; it is a story of political manoeuvring and mud-slinging back and forth
across the divide. At a sitting of the Tynwald Court in 1822, the Duke informed the
Keys that they were 'a self-elected body, in the choice of which the people of the
Island have not the smallest share' (which was true) and they were 'no more
Representatives of the people of Man than of the people of Peru'. This assessment,
according to a report in the *Isle of Man Gazette*, was given a loud ovation by an
assembly of 'the most respectable natives and other inhabitants'.

The final result was very much in favour of the Duke, and an enabling Act of
Parliament was passed in 1825, under which he would receive the total sum of
£417,144. The purchase was completed in 1828. The price was certainly high,
although it did include all of the Duke's manorial and other rights in Man. The
whole sum had been reimbursed out of Manx revenues by 1866. The year after the
passing of the Act, the Duke departed the isle and never returned.

Looking back on the period between the Revestment of 1765 and the fourth
Duke's final departure in 1826, it must be said, in fairness to him, that his presence
as governor from 1793 was far more beneficial to the island than the period of
Imperial rule immediately preceding it. In the earlier period, agriculture, fishing
and trade were all depressed, and public works, especially on the harbours, were

neglected. In the later period, the island scene became more buoyant in all these sectors. The Manx people might have had mixed feelings about him, but he was a definite improvement over 'the previous lot'.

Following the Duke's departure, English officials were in control once more but they, too, were better than the previous lot. Smuggling, which had lingered on for a while at much reduced levels after 1765, had now all but vanished and Manx revenues from legitimate sources were producing increasing surpluses. Consequently, the Manx populace was looked upon with a less jaundiced eye than before; stringent customs tariffs were eased, and the spasmodic injection of finance for public works brought improvements to the island's infrastructure.

Manx affairs were due to take a further turn for the better in 1863, with the arrival of a new and far-sighted Governor, Henry Brougham Loch, a man not content just to sit back and pass on the Imperial diktat. He could see that the island needed changes to ensure future prosperity, and he could see what the necessary changes were. Under his direction, the Isle of Man would start the long and diffi-cult journey to constitutional modernity, to regain some degree of self-determination.

CHAPTER SIX

This Modern Isle

The early years of Revestment saw the Isle of Man in real danger of losing any prospect of ever regaining any degree of self-government. Under the 'Mischief Act' of 1765, the insular customs establishment was under the control of the Imperial parliament, and its expenses would be met by the levying of taxes on the Manx populace, at rates to be determined by Parliament. This was empowered by an Act of Parliament passed in 1767 and, for the first time, the Manx people were taxed by an external government in whose election they had played no part. In truth, the Manx people never had played a part in the election of Manx governments but at least the Keys were a home-grown unelected body. This was sometimes given as a rebuttal by the British government to Manx requests for the return of Manx revenues to the island: Parliament could not countenance the handing over of Manx revenues to a body which the Manx people had not chosen.

Worse was to come. In 1767, George (later Sir George) Moore, Speaker of the House of Keys, was in London when he became aware of an approach to the Treasury by the Commissioners of Customs in Man, seeking the annexation of the island into the county of Cumberland, and thence into the United Kingdom. Moore's strong representations against this proposal were successful (as he wrote in a letter to Bishop Hildesley) in averting 'the total ruin of the Isle'.

Whilst in London, Moore also voiced the strong disquiet in Man over the high rates of British duty on goods imported into the island. This was a source of discontent that was to rumble on through most of the first half of the nineteenth century, when successive Acts of Parliament raised and consolidated the range of customs duties in the island. Of particular concern were the *ad valorem* duties (duties based on the values of the goods being traded), which ranged from 2½ to 15 per cent. These duties were *additional* to the British duties already paid, since most goods came from or through the United Kingdom. The *ad valorem* duties would remain in being until they were abolished in 1844. At one stage, campaigners for Manx constitutional reform were informed by the British authorities that, if reform were to come about, it would probably take the form of one elected Manx representative sitting in the House of Commons.

That particular threat was not pursued but, at around the same period, there were two attempts to annex the bishopric of Sodor and Man into an English see. In the first, in 1836, an Act of Parliament was actually passed, taking Sodor and Man into the see of Carlisle. This prompted such strong opposition by the Manx people, both clergy and laity, that the Act was repealed. In the second, it was proposed that Sodor and Man should be joined with Liverpool. Again, sustained Manx opposition ensured that the proposal was not followed through.

POPULATION AND NEEDS

Despite recurring outbreaks of disease (smallpox, cholera and typhoid fever) through the eighteenth and nineteenth centuries, the population of the island, in the long term, exhibited a trend of sustained growth. The first official census was taken in 1851, and they followed at ten-yearly intervals thereafter. Before 1851, figures had been collated at irregular intervals by the clergy. The last such figure before the Revestment, taken in 1757, gave a total of 19,144, which, by 1784, had risen to 24,924. Repeated outbreaks of smallpox through the eighteenth century, followed by cholera, typhus and typhoid fever in the nineteenth, must have produced short-term decimations but, overall, the long-term trend remained unstintingly upward. By 1821, the population had passed 40,000.

The census returns up to and including that of 1851 show the rise in population to have been spread throughout the isle – in both town and country – but, thereafter, populations in the countryside were in decline whilst those in the towns continued to climb. The sole exception to the general pattern in the country districts was seen in the sheading of Garff, where population growth continued for a further twenty years, presumably fuelled by the numbers of workers drawn to the mine-workings in and around Laxey. By the 1851 census, the total population of Man stood at 52,387, of which 17,454 lived in the towns, 9,880 of them in Douglas.

A contributory element in the rise in population by this time had been the arrival of a new brand of immigrant – the 'stranger-resident' – the earliest of whom arrived in Man all too frequently with the express aim of avoiding the consequences of debt incurred elsewhere. The incentive for such migrations dated back to an Act of Tynwald of 1737, whereby any person brought before a Manx court for a foreign debt was liable only to the value of his personal effects within the island; any assets he owned elsewhere were out of reach of the court.

Such new arrivals (and others of higher repute) brought money with them, which was injected into the economy, to the benefit of Manx farmers and traders. On the other hand, the increased demand for goods and services would doubtless have imposed an inflationary influence on prices. The legal loophole created by the Act of 1737 was finally closed by a further Act of 1814, by which debtors could be prosecuted for debts incurred elsewhere, and their assets – wherever held – were at risk. Thus, the attraction of the island as a haven for such people was greatly diminished, and this particular form of migration faded away. But another type of migrant was at hand.

When peace broke out in Europe in 1815, there was an imperative in Britain to relax the high levels of taxation that had paid for years of warfare. To achieve that end, the complements of the armed forces were severely cut back. Soldiers and sailors of the ranks were demobilized, many to be reduced to begging in the gutters of the country for which they had fought. Officers (rather better treated) were laid off on half-pay, and many of these, seeking a domicile where they could live modestly and cheaply and free from direct taxation, migrated to the Isle of Man.

This new wave of immigration brought a further impetus to the economy of the isle, and especially to that of Douglas, and in view of their relatively straitened circumstances (by their own standards), it is unlikely that they caused more than a minimal upward pressure on prices. It would doubtless take time for the atmosphere of mutual suspicion between Manx and incomer to attenuate, a suspicion initially aroused back in the days of the 'stranger-resident' of more dubious character. In the meantime, this new breed of 'half-pay officer' would set out to create his own scene of conviviality in Man, with a pattern of social circles and clubs to which well-regarded Manxmen would be invited to dine, to speak and to converse. There were several such clubs in Douglas and at least one in Ramsey. By about 1850, with the presence of the half-pay men and their families throughout the year and increasing numbers of visitors in the summer, there were promising signs for the Manx economy. But there was much still needing to be done.

By this stage, the unique pattern of Manx surnames had become firmly established throughout the island's population. In the years of the early Stanleys, most surnames – whether belonging to the long-term indigenous Manx or to those of Irish, Scottish, Scandinavian or Anglo-Norman descent – had taken on the Celtic prefix *Mac* ('son of'), and such names still predominated in the earliest surviving manorial roll of 1511. Over the following century, the process of transmutation was set in train to evolve the peculiarly Manx pattern of surnames that we see today. In many cases, the prefix *Mac* was simply dropped, as in the following examples:

the original	MacCrystyn	transmuted to	Christian
	MacCorleot		Corlett
	MacCosten		Corteen/Costain
	MacKermott		Kermode
	MacKillip		Killip
	MacQuyn		Quine
	MacQuirk		Quirk
	MacSheman		Shimmin

In other cases, the final letter of *Mac* was incorporated into the personal name, either as 'c' or 'k', or sometimes as 'q', as in:

the original	MacAlisandre	transmuted to	Callister (via MacAlister)
	MacAloe		Callow
	MacLucas		Clucas
	MacReynylt		Crennell
	MacHelly		Kelly
	MacWhaltragh		Qualtrough
	MacFaile		Quayle
	MacWilliam		Quilliam

By the early seventeenth century, all of the above names had assumed their present forms, or close approximations to them. But there were a few cases where it was the *first* letter of *Mac* which became assimilated into the name, and these did not attain their modern form until the middle of the eighteenth century. Examples are:

the original	MacGilcrayne	transmuted to	Mylchraine
	MacGilchrist		Mylchreest
	MacGilrea		Mylrea

The above are but a sample of the large number of uniquely Manx surnames. J. J. Kneen [45], although long dead, remains the definitive source.

An expanding population inevitably brought with it the need for expanding services. The requirement for expenditure on public works, especially in relation to harbours, had been evident throughout the years from 1765 but, with the continued growth of the four towns, the need for works on a wider scale, with particular regard to water supplies, sewerage and highways, became more pressing. But the Imperial control of Manx revenues, and the tardiness with which the British government allocated funds for works in the isle, resulted in scant progress in such matters during the first thirty years after Revestment. This was despite (in the case of harbours) the formation of a harbour board in 1771, the membership of which included four Manx representatives (one for each of the main ports) but, since they were outnumbered on the board by Crown appointees with little interest in the isle or its harbours, the views of the four Manxmen would hold minimal sway over the actions of the board.

In 1791, the fourth Duke of Atholl reported to the Commission appointed to investigate his various claims for compensation that the harbours at Douglas, Peel and Ramsey had descended into states of decay. In Douglas, a large part of the old pier had been destroyed by storms in two successive winters, and the harbour-bed was so littered with stones as to severely restrict the draught of vessels able to enter. The commissioners' report to Parliament prompted the British government to allocate £24,000 in 1793, all of which was spent on the construction of a new pier in Douglas (known as the Red Pier, on account of its construction in sandstone from Annan, in Scotland). Three years later, the causeway linking St Patrick's Isle with the west quay of Peel harbour was raised and surfaced, and the pier was repaired and extended in 1810. In 1815, a pier and lighthouse were constructed in Port St Mary.

It was about this time that the Scots, who had lost all authority in Man in 1333, regained a small part of it almost 500 years later. The Commissioners for Northern Lights, based in Edinburgh, were established in 1786 under an Act of George III, to be responsible for the erection and management of lighthouses, buoys and beacons around the Scottish coasts and islands, and extending as far south as the Isle of Man. The Commissioners' first lights in Man, the lighthouse at the Point of Ayre and the twin lights on the Calf, became operational in 1818, all three designed by the famous Scottish engineer Robert Stevenson, grandfather of novelist Robert Louis Stevenson.

By 1832, the Commissioners of the Isle of Man Harbour Board had them-selves erected a lighthouse on Douglas Head. This would be transferred to the Northern Lights Board in 1859 and they would rebuild it in its present form in 1892. Two further lighthouses were to come in the nineteenth century: that on the Chicken Rock in 1875 and on Langness five years later. The final two would rise in the twentieth century: on Maughold Head in 1914, and on the Calf (between the two old Stevenson towers) in 1968. All are now automatic (apart from that on the Calf, which has been decommissioned) and the old keepers' cottages at the Point of Ayre, Maughold, Douglas, Langness and Port St Mary have been sold off.

By 1838, the Harbour Commissioners had persuaded the British Treasury of their need for enhanced funding to finance harbour works and for port adminis-tration. An Act of Parliament of 1840 provided them with borrowing powers

The lighthouse at the Point of Ayre

enabling the construction of a breakwater at Derbyhaven (the name accorded to the port of Ronaldsway by the end of the Derby period), as well as improvements at Peel and Castletown. In 1844, harbour dues were abolished and the commissioners were funded by an annual amount paid out of customs revenues, an amount eventually fixed at one-ninth of the gross customs revenues which, in 1853, amounted to £3,141. Thus, some improvements were being made but the purse-strings were still in the firm grip of a foreign government.

The question of highways came into a rather different category, for this was the only matter of any significance which lay within the control of the Tynwald administration. In the early nineteenth century, the island's roads were nothing more than narrow, rutted cart-tracks, usually lined on either side by high sod hedges. In 1811, there were only three roads suitable for carriages: those from Douglas to Castletown, from Douglas to Peel, and from Castletown to Ramsey via Ballacraine. They were usually surfaced with broken slate which, under the combined ravages of solid tyres and the weather, was soon broken down to form a sticky clay. In the south, local limestone was used, which was somewhat superior.

Since highways were a purely insular matter, it was for Tynwald to decide how the funding for their improvement and maintenance should be raised. An Act of Tynwald of 1713 was the first relating to highways, and enabled roadworks to be carried out on a parish-by-parish basis, each under the direction of a parochial surveyor. The occupiers of properties abutting the roads were taxed at 3 shillings and 4 pence each and, if the money ran out, the other occupiers in the parish were required to provide carts, horses and men to complete the work. Under a subsequent Act of 1753, 3 shillings and 6 pence was apportioned from each public-house licence and paid into the highways fund, and a committee was appointed to decide its allocation throughout the isle. Ten years later came the first tax on dogs, also for the benefit of the highways fund.

It does appear that these measures brought some marked improvement in the condition of the major roads between the towns but, as the need for wheeled transport grew and the scale of the road-building task increased, so too did the need for more finance. By an Act of 1776, the whole of the public-house licence fee was diverted to the highways fund, and the taxes on dogs were increased. Each holder of a quarterland was required to place four men (a lesser holder in proportion, and a householder one man) for highway labour when required. Fines could be imposed for not providing the labour but increasing numbers of people would choose to pay the fines rather than provide the labour, and so the system would need to be tightened up.

Into the first half of the nineteenth century, a series of Acts of Tynwald brought the following measures to contribute to the highways fund: an Act of 1813 increased public-house licence fees and the taxes on dogs; in 1817, a duty of £20 on a banker's licence was introduced; in 1819, the fines for non-performance of highway labour, and public-house licence fees and dog taxes were again increased; in 1826, a fee of £25 was payable by each advocate admitted to the Manx Bar; and in 1827, a duty of £5 was payable on each brewer's licence. Finally in this run of enactments, in 1830, there were further tax increases, the fines for non-provision of labour were also increased and payment of the fine no longer gave exemption from supplying the labour. In 1843, the total income to the highways fund from taxes was £2,074.

Long before this, it had become apparent that the growth of wheeled traffic would require expenditure, not just on roads *per se*, but also on bridges. Through much of the eighteenth century, when wheeled carriages were few and the transport of goods over land was by pack-horse or horse-drawn sled, the lack of a bridge was no great obstacle in crossing a river, provided that the river was fordable. Apart from the Monks' Bridge, near Rushen Abbey, which probably dates from the fourteenth century, there appear to be no bridges in the island having origins earlier than the eighteenth century.

It was not until 1739 that an Act of Tynwald first recognized the need to repair such old bridges that existed and identified locations where new bridges should

The Monks' Bridge, Ballasalla

be built. For this specific purpose, an annual tax of 1 penny per head was levied on the whole of the population over the age of sixteen. This seems to have been the first occasion on which such a general tax was applied to the whole of the Manx population above a certain age.

During the times when Manx roads had remained in a primitive state, it was a common feature of the insular transport structure that goods, wherever possible, would be conveyed by boat between the nearest convenient harbours. Even after the improvement of the island's road network, the transportation of goods by sea remained a regular feature of the Manx scene until remarkably recent times. (A personal example: in 1973, my wife and I purchased a coffee table in Ramsey; the first stage of its delivery was by the next morning's boat to Douglas.)

With the continuing growth of the towns, the two most pressing needs for their populations were the provision of supplies of potable water and effective systems of foul-water drainage. Prior to such works, the disposal of sanitary waste was by discharge to cesspits, and supplies of drinking water were drawn from wells. As the processes of urbanization continued and the effluent from ever-increasing concentrations of cesspits was seeping into the same body of groundwater from which domestic supplies were being drawn, the growing potential for disease was obvious. Some town districts were served with water brought in by cart from the countryside.

The first Act of Tynwald relating to water supply was the *Douglas Waterworks Act* of 1834, which enabled a company to collect and distribute piped water in the town. The first reservoirs were in Summerhill Glen, on the northern outskirts of the town, followed by the Clypse reservoir (1878) and Kerrowdhoo (1893). By the beginning of the twentieth century, the growth of tourism was imposing further pressures and, between 1900 and 1905, the River Glass was impounded by constructing a dam across the West Baldwin valley, to form by far the largest reservoir in the island at that time. The Douglas water-supply system was by then a wholly public undertaking, having been acquired by the town's commissioners in 1890. But we run ahead of ourselves.

Water-related Acts were passed by Tynwald in 1857 for Castletown, in 1859 for Ramsey, in 1885 for Port Erin and in 1886 for Rushen. But the protracted work of building dams and laying mains and supply pipes to dwellings in the built-up areas would take years to come fully to fruition. Meanwhile, living conditions in the country remained for the most part quite primitive, with the family often sharing their dwelling with their livestock.

In conditions such as these, particularly in the towns, it is not surprising that the population was ravaged by epidemic after epidemic through the course of the nineteenth century. Smallpox, which had been endemic in the second half of the eighteenth century, returned repeatedly in the nineteenth, together with cholera

The West Baldwin reservoir

and typhoid fever. In the three years from 1864 to 1866, the island-wide death-rate per thousand of population ranged from 26.4 to 23.7, of which the towns accounted for 25.8–22.8. And yet, in the longer term, the island's population continued to grow, sustained by a buoyant birth-rate (29.8 per thousand over the decade 1851–60) and continued immigration.

Once the towns were (eventually) provided with fully operational piped water supplies, the problems with public health were greatly alleviated, since the lowland towns were now receiving water from less polluted upland sources. The question of sewage disposal remained to be resolved. The Acts enabling the laying of main sewers in the four towns were passed by Tynwald in 1852, and these were subsequently installed. As all four towns were situated on the coast, their sewage was discharged into the sea untreated – but that was at least an improvement over the former accumulation of pollution in the groundwater under the towns. This method of disposal continued into modern times. In recent years, an island-wide realignment of sewerage systems has commenced, involving treatment prior to discharge to the sea; we return to this subject in the next chapter.

Despite the passing of the Acts of 1852, there were still no local authorities at that time to ensure compliance; the civic affairs of each town were in the charge of an official known as the High Bailiff. (The island still has a single High Bailiff [with a deputy] who acts as the stipendiary magistrate and coroner of inquests.) There is little information on conditions in the towns other than Douglas at this time, but there can be little doubt that they could not have differed greatly from those in Douglas, and certainly could not have been any better.

In Douglas, the streets were unnamed in the early 1800s, and the houses were unnumbered before 1843. In 1829, the streets were illumined (but imperfectly) with oil lamps, and its narrow streets and open gutters were described as dirty and odorous. The principal thoroughfares were Duke Street and Sand Street (later to become Strand Street), extending north from the harbour, close behind the shore of the bay, and these were the first to be paved. Here were to be found the principal shops and some dwellings. An Act of 1836 required a scheme of public lighting by gas; a company was in existence but another twenty-four years were to elapse before any evidence of compliance would emerge.

Years passed by with little sign of improvement but bringing forth repeated complaints from the townsfolk. In 1844, a public meeting was held at which a motion was passed calling for legislation on street lighting, paving, cleansing and policing, but rejecting a proposal for the election of a town council. Popular opposition to the latter proposal continued, the town's inhabitants being reluctant to accept the levying of a compulsory rate. Eventually, a compulsory Act was passed

Strand Street, the main shopping street of Douglas

in 1860 (for Douglas only), by which the High Bailiff's civic powers were transferred to a council of nine commissioners, elected by the people of the town. (It is worthy of note that the Keys themselves were still an unelected body at this time.) Following the election, conditions in Douglas began steadily to improve. Similar developments in the other towns would follow in time, and the situation of the island's ancient capital would be set in ever-deepening irony. By the time of the 1861 census, Castletown was the smallest of the four towns, and its population would actually decline through the remainder of the nineteenth century. The writing was on the wall.

As mentioned above, one of the sources of discontent among the people was the inadequacy of policing. Prior to the Revestment, policing in the towns was undertaken by troops of the garrison, under the command of their captains. After 1765, the role was taken over by a wholly inadequate number of constables (twenty in total, to cover the whole island), controlled by the high bailiffs, and they were employed during the daytime only, so that all manner of nefarious night-time activities could be pursued unhindered. Feelings of discontent persisted, and were voiced (including a petition to the Home Secretary), but nothing was done until 1863, when twelve constables were added to the force, and another twenty-one the following year, headed by a chief inspector who was a military officer. Five constables were then allocated to the country districts, and the principles of law and order began to be applied throughout the isle.

CHURCH AND CHAPEL

By 1830, some 160 years after Bishop Barrow's death, the money invested in his eponymous trust continued to grow, untouched apart from some grants paid to deserving students to attend English universities. Bishop Ward was the current incumbent of Sodor and Man and, encouraged by Governor Cornelius Smelt, he set about seeking a way of founding a public school. The amount then contained in Bishop Barrow's Trust stood at around £5,000, insufficient to build a school, and so Bishop Ward began a fund-raising campaign in England, including an appeal to that eccentric but kindly king, William IV. 'Silly Billy' (the nick-name by which he had become known) responded with his regret at having insufficient funds to contribute but stating that he would allow his name to be attached to the school, and so 'King William's College' it was – and is – a public school on a par with any of the best elsewhere.

Before 1872, there was no direct involvement of the State in the provision of education. The initial establishment of the parochial and town schools had largely

King William's College, Castletown

been due to the influence of the Church, and this situation continued through the first two-thirds of the nineteenth century. It must be said, however, that during the period 1832–68, British parliamentary grants were sometimes forthcoming to offset the costs of school building, extensions and improvements. Bishop Short (1851–7) expressed concern over standards of Manx education, which remained below those obtaining in England.

Before 1851, the standard provision of schools was for there to be one in each parish or town district, but an Act passed in that year made for better provision and regulation of such schools, and committees could be appointed for their management. The chairman of each committee was the incumbent priest of the district, and he was to be responsible for religious instruction in the school. Rates could be levied by the parochial vestries to finance the schools, and there could now be more than one per district. The committees also had borrowing powers through which they could finance school extensions and the building of school-masters' houses.

Education apart, Church matters themselves continued much as before, but they had received a jolt almost a century earlier, when the first wave of Methodism broke on Manx shores. In 1758, John Murlin, known as 'the weeping prophet', spent a week in Ramsey, spreading his fiery message and causing a sensation. Although he aroused great attention, he concluded that no good could come of such 'a nest of smugglers' and, after his departure, no external preacher came near the place for some years.

In the intervening period, the work of translating the Bible and the Book of Common Prayer into the Manx language, started by Bishop Wilson years earlier, was brought to fruition by his successor, Mark Hildesley, and his team of literary clerics. The Book of Common Prayer appeared in print in 1756. The Old Testament to the end of the Book of Job came out in 1771, followed by the remainder of the Old Testament two years later and the New Testament in 1775. This long and arduous literary effort had at last produced the first works to appear in print in the Manx language.

In 1775, the Methodists tried again; John Crook was sent over from Liverpool. He received a mixed reception and left the island towards the end of the year. He returned the following year and was met with renewed opposition, especially in Douglas, where his mission was attacked by a mob incited by the curate of St Matthew's. The Methodists sought the protection of Governor John Wood, who informed the incumbent of St Matthew's that he would tolerate no man being persecuted on account of his religion.

John Wesley himself visited Man in 1777 and was well received by the new Governor, Edward Smith. He found the people to be 'loving and simple-hearted' and was impressed with the island's religious scene, having 'but six papists and no dissenters'. Wesley certainly had no desire to see his Methodism regarded as dissenting from the established Church; he was, after all, an Anglican clergyman seeking to form an extension of the Church, with the aim of putting some zest into the business of worship. Bishop Hildesley once expressed the wish that more of his own clergy were possessed of Wesley's zeal. The Methodist congregations did not regard themselves as members of a separate sect; it was a common practice for parishioners to attend Sunday morning service at the church and then evening service at the chapel.

The Isle of Man was formed as a Methodist circuit in 1778. Wesley made a second visit in 1781, when he found Bishop Mason to be tolerant and friendly towards him, and he reported that Methodists in the island remained 'under the protecting wing of the Establishment'. Methodism continued to gain support in the isle, and Church and Chapel co-existed cordially to a greater extent, and for longer, than was the case in England. In 1781, Wesley was claiming around 2,100 members of Methodist societies in Man out of a total adult population of some 15,000. A Manx hymn book was published for the Methodists in 1795.

For the first sixty years, neighbourly relations were maintained by the Methodists' efforts in ensuring that chapel service times did not clash with those of the churches. The first signs of a separation began to show from 1836 onwards, when chapels started to hold services at times which did overlap those of the churches. Thus, although John Wesley (who died in 1791) had declared that he had no wish to form a separate Church, that – in essence – was what was now emerging. Many Methodists, particularly those who had attended church as well as chapel, considered this to be a great wrong. Nevertheless, the progress of separation was slow and never did attain the degree – even to this day – that divided Church and Chapel in England.

By the early years of the nineteenth century, other religious denominations were beginning to evolve. In 1808, the Congregationalists were sufficiently numerous to require a chapel, which was built in that year. The Presbyterians (mainly immigrants from Scotland and Ulster) did the same in 1813, and the first Roman Catholic chapel was opened the following year. In 1823, John Butcher brought his brand of Primitive Methodism to Man where, for years, the Primitives and Wesleyans regarded each other with mutual suspicion before gradually drifting together under a single banner, which retains strong support in Man today. Baptists also arrived in significant numbers to form a distinct body.

In the early years, there were difficulties and sources of discontent between followers of the established Church on the one hand, who had certain rights under the law, and the Nonconformists, who did not. But, before those differences were resolved, the forces of all denominations felt compelled to unite in opposition to the annexation of the bishopric of Sodor and Man within the diocese of Carlisle, which had been presented as a *fait accompli* by the passing by Parliament of the Act of 1836. As described earlier, the voices of insular opposition were so loudly raised that the Act was repealed.

Once that battle had been won, it was time for the interdenominational difficulties to be resolved. These related principally to the registration of places for the holding of marriage ceremonies and for the registration of births, marriages and deaths. These matters were settled by two Acts of Tynwald passed in 1849. The first was the *Dissenters' Marriage Act*, under which the Governor could cause places of worship, other than those of the established Church, to be registered for the conduct of marriages. The second enactment, the *Civil Registration Act*, enabled births, marriages and deaths to be registered in those same places. Furthermore, those wishing not to be married in a place of worship could have the ceremony performed in the office of a deputy registrar. Thus, the followers of all religious denominations thenceforth had the same rights under the law in these matters.

The total number of Nonconformists in Man at that time is not known with any degree of accuracy but, by 1862, they had a total of ninety-one chapels between them, served by twenty ministers and 200 local preachers. By 1865, Roman Catholic numbers had reached 2,000 and they had a chapel in each of the four towns. In the ensuing years, churches of all denominations seem to have operated in Man in a spirit of friendly and often collaborative co-existence, and certainly with a degree of amity far greater than that sometimes observed elsewhere.

THE REFORMS OF GOVERNOR LOCH

Henry Brougham Loch arrived in the Isle of Man in 1863 and would remain in post as Governor for nineteen years. He would be knighted in 1880 and receive a peerage after his departure from the isle. Loch was a far-sighted and ambitious man with a distinguished earlier career. His correspondence with family and friends shows clearly his desire to use the Isle of Man as a stepping-stone to greater colonial things. And it worked; he would eventually become Governor of Victoria from 1884 to 1889 and Governor of the Cape Colony and High Commissioner for South Africa for the six years following that. To ensure that he and his undoubted abilities were not forgotten during his sojourn in Man, he was frequently in contact with Whitehall concerning matters of importance to the isle. By the end of his term, he had propelled the island through a series of significant stages towards the modern era.

By the time of Loch's arrival, the rivalry between Douglas and Castletown was intensifying. As related in the previous chapter, John Murray, fourth Duke of Atholl, had chosen Douglas as his residence during his term as governor (1793–1808), and it could only be a matter of time before the seat of government was moved to where most of the action was. Governor Ready (1832–45) had arrived to find that there was no official residence for him at Castle Rushen and had taken out a lease on Lorne House, in Castletown. He was, in fact, the first governor of the Isle of Man to be accorded the title 'Lieutenant Governor'. Prior to 1832, the Lieutenant Governor was the Governor's deputy; after that, the post of governor was discontinued and the Lieutenant Governor was the top man – in essence, the chief executive. For brevity, he is still referred to informally as Governor.

Ready's successor, Charles Hope (1845–60), found himself under pressure to make the move to Douglas but, preferring to remain with the seat of government, took over the lease of Lorne House. He remained as governor until the lease on the house expired, then retired and departed the isle.

Hope's successor (and Loch's immediate predecessor) was Francis Stainsby-Conant-Pigott, who promptly decided to take up residence in Douglas, although it cost him considerably more than the British Treasury's meagre rent allowance to take a lease on the Villa Marina, beside the shore of Douglas Bay and but a short distance from the fourth Duke's former residence of Castle Mona.

By the end of his first year in office, Pigott had acquired a firm appreciation of the dominant position of Douglas over Castletown: it was more centrally located and boasted the largest concentration of population in the isle, its harbour was accessible to shipping at all states of the tide and it was in close conjunction with the island's largest concentration of trading activity. To him, Douglas seemed the obvious place to be the island's capital, the seat of its government and of the principal courts of justice. When he eventually voiced his recommendation, the Castletown lobby reacted strongly and the matter was referred to the Home Office, which did not endorse Pigott's recommendation. His sudden death in January 1863 pushed the question of the capital back into the 'pending' tray and opened the door for Henry Loch.

On taking up his appointment, Governor Loch chose as his residence Bemahague, on the northern outskirts of Douglas, and which is today's Government House, the residence of successive lieutenant governors. A man of some astuteness, Loch (like the seventh Earl of Derby more than two centuries earlier) soon realized that, for the island to prosper, there was a need to develop its trading activities and facilities to cater for the traffic in summer visitors, which was then in its embryonic stage and growing. To achieve these aims, it would be necessary to provide Douglas with a pier of sufficient length to facilitate passenger landings at low tide and to improve protection of the harbour.

The construction of a Douglas breakwater had commenced a year before Loch's arrival. The work was to a design by a Mr Abernethy and consisted of a wooden structure standing on a sloping foundation of unbound rubble. (Similar works were undertaken at Ramsey and Peel.) As the work progressed, the structure came to be known as 'Abernethy's birdcage' but, before it could be completed, it was destroyed by storms in the first two months of 1865. The Abernethy design had been forced on Tynwald (which had favoured an alternative design by James Walker), the British government having made it clear that Tynwald could have Abernethy or nothing. By this stage of the proceedings, more than two-thirds of the funds allocated for harbour works had been spent, and there was little solid structure to show for it.

Governor Loch realized that, for there to be any chance of his plans for the island's development coming to fruition, the Manx government must gain autonomy over the raising and allocating of funds for the necessary works on its harbours. He also knew that there was no chance of the insular government achieving that autonomy so long as the Keys remained self-elected.

The Keys had aroused ill-feeling against themselves in 1864, because of their treatment of the proprietors of two Douglas newspapers for their comments after the Keys had refused to grant increased powers to the Douglas Town Commissioners. The two men were called to the bar of the House to answer for their comments, which the Keys regarded as 'a contempt of the House and a breach of its privileges'. At the bar of the House, J. C. Fargher, of the *Mona's Herald*, apologized for his comments and was pardoned. James Brown, of the *Isle of Man Times*, stood by the substance of his observations and was sentenced to six months' imprisonment. He promptly appealed to the Queen's Bench and was freed under a ruling which stated that the Keys had been sitting in their legislative capacity, and not as a judiciary, and so had no power to hand down a sentence. Brown subsequently brought a case against the Keys in the Isle of Man Court of Common Law, on the grounds of unlawful imprisonment, and was awarded substantial compensation.

This affair served to reinforce Governor Loch's conviction that the Keys must be reformed to become an elected assembly. In 1865, during correspondence with the Imperial treasury on the question of raising revenues, he submitted the proposal that the insular government be granted greater powers subject to the Keys becoming an elected body. After protracted negotiations with the British government and the Keys, a bargain was struck. On 18 May 1866, Parliament passed the *Isle of Man Customs, Harbours and Public Purposes Act*, by which Her Majesty's Customs would set aside an increased proportion of the Manx customs revenues to fund such works as Tynwald may determine, but the Governor would have the power of veto. The harbours would remain (ultimately) under Imperial control and Imperial hands would still hold the purse-strings. The Keys grumbled but there was little they could do. Later the same year, Tynwald passed the *House of Keys Election Act* and the deed was done. Under this Act, the Keys also lost their judicial role.

For the Isle of Man's first popular election, held in the same year, the island was divided into ten constituencies, comprising the six sheadings and the four towns. The sheadings and the town of Douglas were allotted three members each, with one each for the towns of Ramsey, Peel and Castletown, thereby retaining the historic total of twenty-four Keys. Of the twenty-four members of the previous House, more than half were returned in that first election.

The qualifications for both members and voters were property-based. Members had to be adult males and owners of real estate of value not less than £100, or of real estate of value not less than £50, together with personal property of £100. Voters were required to be adult males and owners of real estate of annual value not less than £8, or tenants paying an annual rent of not less than £12. Considering that both the voters and the candidates for election were property-qualified, it is perhaps not surprising that there should be feelings of affinity between the voters and the candidates, and that more than half of the members elected were those who had sat in the House before.

In 1881, the electoral franchise was extended to women (but not *all* women), long before the corresponding measure in the United Kingdom. The Act of 1881 extended the franchise in Man to women (being spinsters or widows) who were owners of real estate subject to the same qualifications as men. But, unlike the men, women *tenants* of property remained outside the franchise, as did married women totally. In 1892, the franchise was extended to women tenants of property, and the property qualifications for members of the Keys were abolished, so that any adult male (other than a clergyman) could stand for election. Finally, under the *House of Keys (Election) Act* of 1919, the franchise was extended to all adult men and women who had lived in the isle for the whole of the preceding twelve months, and all (other than clergymen and the holders of offices of profit under the Crown) were eligible to stand for the Keys. By this time, of course, Governor Loch had long-since departed, so let us back-track a little.

Throughout the years of Loch's governorship, the Isle of Man steadily grew in prosperity. There was increasing trade, both in goods and in the traffic of visitors, and public works proceeded at a steady pace. Loch was disappointed not to have regained full insular control of the harbours, yet improvements were made nonetheless. At Douglas, work was started on the construction of the Battery Pier, on the site of the collapsed 'Abernethy's birdcage', and on the Victoria Pier, on the north side of the harbour, which was completed in 1873. With these two works, the structure of Douglas harbour was beginning to take on something approaching its

Douglas outer harbour and the bay

present form. Work to extend the Victoria Pier would occupy the years 1886–91, and 1930 would see the start of an extension to the old Red Pier, lying midway between the Victoria Pier and the South Quay, and which would become the Edward VIII Pier, one of the few structures commemorating that brief-reigning monarch.

Port Erin had also received funds for harbour works; it had been one of Governor Loch's first initiatives to provide the village's harbour with the break-water for which Manx fishermen had been pressing for some years. Loch encouraged its construction but it suffered repeated storm damage during the course of the work. It was completed in 1876, at great expense, but was again damaged, beyond repair, in 1884. Its ragged remains still provide limited protection to Port Erin's harbour today.

Despite the failure of the breakwater, the development of the railway between Douglas and Port Erin acted as a stimulus to the growth of the village as a holiday resort. A string of modern hotels and boarding-houses rapidly developed along an upper promenade fronting the northern half of the bay. But, although the railway also served Castletown and Port St Mary, that town and village never developed in the same way, probably due to the disinclination of the citizens of those two places to see them transformed into holiday resorts. It is a view which seems to have persisted to the present day.

Remnants of the old breakwater stud the waters of the Port Erin Bay

A tram of the Manx Electric Railway departs Laxey station

Through the 1870s, the steam railways of Man had spread as far as they were going to spread: from Douglas south to Port Erin, west to Peel, and north from St John's to Ramsey. But, in the 1890s, steam was to face the challenge of electricity, which would propel rail traction directly north from Douglas to Laxey, then onward to Ramsey, to rival the much longer steam-hauled route via St John's. And from Laxey, a further line would eventually reach the summit of Snaefell.

Douglas, of course, continued to prosper. Its harbour had been developed to form the only capacious, deep-water, 24-hour port in the island. As a consequence, the town blossomed as a holiday resort. New hotels and boarding-houses sprang up along the existing promenade, which was extended southward to the harbour to form Loch Promenade, at the southern end of which a grand new hotel, the Villiers, was built and named after Governor Loch's wife, Elizabeth Villiers. In front of the Villiers, the newly constructed Victoria Street descended to the promenade and provided a major route to what would become Upper Douglas. The architect for the Villiers project was W. J. Rennison, who was responsible for a string of hotels on Loch Promenade, several of which still stand, although the Villiers has been demolished to make way for a modern office block.

Improvements were also in hand at Ramsey, the south pier being built in 1876, but the landing of boat passengers at low tide had to wait another ten years, until

Loch Promenade, Douglas

the Queen's Pier was completed, 600 yards south of the harbour entrance. With the town now accessible by rail and sea, the place became ripe for further development and, over the thirty years from 1861, the town's population rose from 2,891 to 4,866, and a string of hotels sprang up along the newly built Mooragh Promenade.

Henry Loch was knighted in 1880 and departed the island two years later. He had presided over the most significant phase in the island's development since the sorry day of Revestment. He had overseen many valued programmes of public works, and brought about the gradual transfer, between 1866 and 1874, of the various branches of government and administration from Castletown to Douglas. He had directed the Isle of Man to what we can now recognize as the threshold of the modern era. In their dealings with the British government during his governorship, the Manx people may not have gained all that they had wished for, but the island's political and commercial situation had greatly improved, and that success would not have come (as A. W. Moore [57] put it more than a century ago) 'if it had not been for the influence and assiduity of Governor Loch – a fact which should never be forgotten by Manxmen'. Before leaving Britain for high office in the Australian state of Victoria, Loch would spend two years as Her Majesty's Commissioner of Woods and Forests, with responsibility for Crown lands in (among other places) the Isle of Man. His successor as

Lieutenant Governor was Spencer Walpole, son of the British Home Secretary of the same name.

Douglas and Ramsey continued to grow and prosper, and a system of local government was in process of evolving. By 1882, the Douglas Town Commissioners were levying a town rate which was limited to 1 shilling in the pound; the limit would be raised to 1 shilling and 3 pence two years later. In 1886, the upper limit was abolished and the town's commissioners were granted unlimited borrowing powers, subject to Tynwald approval. In the same year, they gained ownership of the town's foreshore which, up to that time, had been vested in the Crown. In 1895, the town was incorporated as a municipal borough, with eighteen councillors, six aldermen and a mayor, the latter being elected from among the eighteen. (The position of alderman was abolished in 1989.)

The local administration of the other towns and villages followed a similar pattern, although Douglas remains the only town incorporated as a borough. Ramsey acquired town commissioners under an Act of 1865, Peel and Castletown in 1883, and the four largest villages followed later: Port Erin in 1884, Port St Mary in 1890 and Laxey and Onchan in 1896.

In the rural parishes, developments were somewhat less rapid. The establishment of local administrations in the towns and larger villages had been led primarily out of concerns for public health. In the more widespread communities of the parishes, such concerns were less urgent. However, a fifth village district (Michael) was formed as a separate entity from the parish of Michael in 1905 because of concerns over public health, and we deal with this story later in this chapter. (The two districts have since been recombined. The village district of Onchan was also constituted originally in isolation from the parish of Onchan; these two districts have also been amalgamated in recent years.)

The Local Government (Amendment) Act of 1894 had as its primary intention the provision of a public health authority for the rural areas, in the form of a Local Government Board, a board of Tynwald responsible for public health throughout the island apart from the four towns and four villages. The Act's secondary provision was for a board of commissioners for each parish, with few responsibilities, the principal of which would be refuse collection and (where necessary) street lighting.

These developments were proceeding long after the departure of Governor Loch but they continued along the path set out by him during his term of office. The numbers of summer visitors continued to grow. The first British-owned boats had begun operating passenger services before 1820. The island's own ferry company, the Isle of Man Steam Packet Company, began operations ten years later, and still operates today under its original name, even though the age of steam is long past, as is the era of conveying postal packets by sea.

Spencer Walpole was Governor for eleven years. During his term, there were again difficulties over customs duties, insofar as it was difficult to ascertain that commodities consumed in the Isle of Man had been subject to duty paid in the island and not in the United Kingdom. The situation was exacerbated when the British government reduced its duty on tea, thereby providing an inducement to merchants to pay the duty in the United Kingdom before transporting the merchandise to the Isle of Man, the island's exchequer being the loser. To rectify the situation, Walpole negotiated an agreement with the British government, under which Manx duties were initially paid over to the British Treasury, which would then pay back an amount based on the estimated consumption in the island. The calculation would be based on population, taking into account the number of summer visitors. The agreement initially related to tea only, but was later extended to other commodities and, by 1910, was accounting for 41 per cent of the island's total customs revenue. This initiative was the first step towards the 'Common Purse' agreement between the Isle of Man and the United Kingdom, which has remained in operation to the present day.

Before following developments into the twentieth century, we should not overlook two aspects of social policy in which the insular government was active in the latter years of the nineteenth century; these were in the fields of education and the relief of poverty. By the Education Act of 1872, the State assumed direct responsibility for the education of its children. Attendance at school was compulsory for children aged between 7 and 13. The starting age was later lowered to 5. Each town and parish was constituted as a school district, under the control of a school board which was responsible for overseeing standards at its school and for enforcing attendance. Revenue costs were met by a combination of school fees, the levying of a school rate and grant aid from the insular government, the latter being subject to strict Whitehall control. The school board was also empowered to waive the school fees for children of the poor. Part of the Whitehall system of control was an insistence that subjects taught and standards set should be the same as those for schools in England and Wales, and the same inspectors would visit to assess performance. A. W. Moore [57] attributes these requirements to the wisdom of Governor Loch (the author of the 1872 Act, following the pattern of the 1870 Act for England and Wales), thereby ensuring that Manx education did not become too insular (in the worst sense of that word) and that standards were maintained at an appropriate level. In the event, by the turn of the century, standards were on a par with those across the water and attendance records were somewhat better. Under an Act of 1892, elementary education became freely available to all.

The question of social poverty was one that exercised the mind of Governor Loch's successor, Spencer Walpole. In 1887, he proposed a number of measures to alleviate the problem. The following year, his proposals became law, under which poor relief could be granted; Tynwald Court could, on the recommendation of the Governor, resolve that a town or parish was not making adequate provision for the relief of its poor, and the ratepayers of such district could elect a committee (later known as a board of guardians) to decide on the sum necessary for the relief of the poor. The towns of Douglas and Ramsey promptly acted on the provisions of the 1888 Act, followed by Castletown in 1895, and by several of the parishes later. By 1895, 974 people were in receipt of poor relief, almost two-thirds of them in Douglas.

AN ISLAND AT WAR

During the final years of the nineteenth century, the island's economy was bene-fiting greatly from the growth in the numbers of summer visitors, with the number of arrivals reaching 418,142 in 1899 (a record up to then) and rising further to 634,512 in 1913. But such influxes did not come without leaving an effect on the ethnic Manx who came into contact with the (mainly) English visitors. The Manx novelist, Sir Thomas Henry Hall Caine [10], was complaining in 1891 that the island had suddenly become too English. He did not begrudge the northern factory worker his annual break on Manx beaches, but he could see the effect it was having on the 'Manxness' of the Manx. On the other side of the coin, he recognized the sadly depleted state that would be the island's lot in the absence of the visitor's contribution. Suddenly, the Manx reaction to contact with the English seemed to have reversed, compared with earlier times when the Manx elite had adopted the standards of the incoming gentry of Lancashire and Cheshire. Now, the English influence had become more basic, working-class, and the Manx elite detached themselves in an attempt to re-establish their Manx roots, or at least to protect their status. And this was just part of a wider reaction to the new breed of visitor. Those Manx folk who were concerned for their cultural, Celtic heritage (among whom Hall Caine was prominent) sought to redirect the visiting industry to attract the more discerning patron, who would wish to seek out the differences, the antiquities and mysteries of this Celtic isle.

Among the aims of this new-found cultural movement was an attempt to reverse the decline of the Manx Gaelic language. The Manx Language Society was formed in 1899, but its name – somewhat ironically – was only later translated to its present form, *Yn Cheshaght Ghailckagh*. But it was a futile aim; the future course of the island into the modern world was already emerging, although perhaps rather indistinctly at that time. The higher orders in society had already abandoned the language in favour of English, and the rest would follow. What had once been the national everyday language was in terminal decline, and the vernacular of the isle would evolve into a Manx dialect of English, of which the prime literary exponent would be the poet T. E. Brown. (We return to this subject in Chapter 9.)

In the second year of the twentieth century, the island received two notable arrivals. The first brought the two most distinguished summer visitors up to that time: King Edward VII and Queen Alexandra, who arrived in the royal yacht in August 1902, landing at Ramsey and travelling on by road to Douglas, to record the first arrival on Manx soil of a reigning British monarch. (When Queen Victoria and Prince Albert anchored in Ramsey Bay in 1847, only the Prince ventured ashore.) They departed two days later.

The next notable arrival in 1902 was to stay rather longer: Lord Raglan, grandson of the British commander in the Crimean War, arrived to take up his appointment as Lieutenant Governor and would stay until 1919. His term of office, coupled with the outbreak of the First World War, was not to be a happy period for the Isle of Man. The Lieutenant Governor at that time was still, in effect, the island's chief executive (indeed, its sole executive) and chancellor of the exchequer, which suited Raglan's character and temperament admirably. A confirmed traditionalist of the colonial school and an unwavering conservative, he would brook no hint of liberal reform that would reduce the powers of the Governor or control of the island by the Imperial power.

A leading light in the reform movement at that time was one Samuel Norris, journalist and printer, who was involved in the formation of the Manx National Reform League, which concentrated attention on constitutional and social reform as issues in the 1903 general election. The programme gained such support that a majority of the successful candidates had declared in favour of it. By that stage, the Governor's implacable opposition to any such moves was well known.

In February 1907, the Keys decided to bypass the Governor and petition the Home Secretary, seeking greater control of Manx affairs and (among other things) a fixed term of office for the Governor and a Legislative Council having a majority of its members elected, with only a minority of Crown appointees. When forwarding the petition to the Home Office, Raglan expressed his firm opposition to its contents. Referring to the question of a part-elected Council, he made the extraordinary (but telling) statement that 'there is not a man in the House of Keys, and hardly one outside it in the Island, who would strengthen the Council if summoned to its deliberations'.

The Manx general election of 1908 took place whilst the Keys awaited the response of the Home Office to their petition. A clear majority of the newly returned members had expressed support for its aims. When the reply came, it did not go far enough to satisfy the Keys. The Home Office was agreeable to a fixed term of office for future lieutenant governors and to the introduction of a minority of indirectly elected members to the Legislative Council. (At this time, the Council was still composed entirely of unelected officials, most of whom were appointed by the Imperial government.) But, with regard to fiscal matters, the Home Office was implacable in its opposition to any diminution of Imperial control over the Manx exchequer. Thus, the matter remained unresolved, but the dispute would erupt again two years later, when a proposal to increase the funding for advertising the island as a holiday destination was accepted by the Keys without first consulting the Governor. When the proposal went before Tynwald (i.e. the Keys and Council sitting as a single chamber), it was promptly ruled out of order. Equally promptly, the Keys resolved not to participate in any further business until the question was settled.

After a delay to test the Keys' resolve, which was unyielding, the Home Secretary (Winston Churchill) appointed a departmental committee in March 1911, under the chairmanship of Lord MacDonnell, to inquire into the constitutional position of the Isle of Man. The committee reported in August of the same year, and the Home Office revealed the extent to which it was prepared to accept its recommendations the following year. The principle of limiting the term of future governors to seven years was accepted, as was a limited reform of the Legislative Council, which would now comprise the Bishop, two deemsters, the Attorney General, four members elected by the Keys and two appointed by the Governor. This would require an enabling Act of Tynwald which, as events transpired, would be delayed until after the end of the forthcoming war.

On the question of fiscal control, the MacDonnell Committee had proposed limited increases in the powers of Tynwald, but the Home Office, taking cognisance of the unwavering opposition of Lord Raglan and unease on the part of the Treasury, grudgingly granted powers that were even more limited. The real seat of power remained with the Governor who, with his inbuilt control of the Council, could thwart the wishes of the Keys, even if the latter were unanimous. The passage of any item of business required the approval of both branches of the legislature and, as a last resort, the Governor still had his veto.

Another bone of contention arising at that time was the question of social reforms for the alleviation of poverty, which were already under way in the United Kingdom. But the immovable object standing in the way of reforms in Man was (as always) the Governor. Raglan had made it abundantly clear that he was not a social reformer – indeed, he was not a reformer of any shade – and discontent over this matter would rumble on through the years of the war. Thus, by the time that Britain and her dominions declared war against Germany on 4 August 1914, the Isle of Man had already been engaged in two phases of unarmed conflict of its own: the first cultural, with the island divided on itself, the second political, against its Imperial ruler.

'It'll all be over by Christmas.' Such was the optimism alive in much of the populace in August 1914. (They would say the same in September 1939.) The optimism in Man was largely born of hope that the bustling tourist season that was already in full swing would exceed the record level of the previous year. But the season was cut off in its prime, and the summer arrivals in Douglas just managed to clear the 400,000 mark. Confidence was hardly boosted by the pronouncements of the Governor, who advised all visitors to return home as soon as possible (which was sensible and understandable in the circumstances) and the proprietors of holiday accommodation to sell their properties and establish themselves elsewhere (which was probably less helpful). It is hard to think of a less appropriate time to try to sell property than at the outbreak of a war, especially if hordes of others were following Raglan's advice and joining a stampede to leave the island.

From 1866, the Isle of Man had paid an annual contribution of £10,000 to the British government in return for defence and common services but, on the outbreak of hostilities, this was no longer considered sufficient, and so, in September 1914, Tynwald voted an additional £10,000 towards the cost of the war. Recruiting offices were opened in Douglas and, during the four years of the conflict, 82 per cent of the island's male population of military age (8,261) went to war, of whom a total of 1,165 did not return, being killed in action, suffering fatal wounds or reported missing in action.

The Isle of Man Steam Packet Company, faced with a sudden and severe loss of trade, found nine of its vessels requisitioned by the Admiralty. This left the company with six ships, three of which it placed in dock for the duration, leaving three to operate the single remaining route between Douglas and Liverpool.

From the start, the Manx were never left in any doubt as to who was in charge of Man in wartime. Throughout the conflict, decisions concerning the island were made with little or no consultation with Tynwald. In the second month of the war, the first consignment of 200 'enemy aliens' arrived for internment at the former Cunningham's Holiday Camp in Douglas. 'Enemy aliens' were German nationals living in Britain, and citizens of other countries on the opposite side of the conflict, who were deemed to be a threat to the nation if they were allowed to remain at large. Among them was Carl Bernard Bertels, German-born creator of the two giant cormorants, the Liver Birds, which in 1911 had been hoisted to the tops of the twin towers of the newly completed Royal Liver Building, overlooking the Liverpool waterfront. The Cunningham's site had been used to provide holidays for young men under canvas during the ten years from 1904. By the end of September 1914, it had been encircled with barbed wire, and within two months was accommodating 3,000 internees, initially in tents but later in huts providing sleeping accommodation, recreation, entertainment and workshop facilities.

It soon became clear that Cunningham's alone would not be sufficient to house the growing numbers of internees, particularly following the sinking of the liner *Lusitania* by a German U-boat in May 1915, which prompted retaliation by rounding up many more of the aliens in Britain who had initially been allowed to remain at large. Attention fell on the farm at Knockaloe, 1 mile south of Peel, which had been used before the war as a camping ground for the Territorial Army. By the following year, Knockaloe was holding 20,563 men, of whom 16,936 were German and 3,382 Austrian. In addition, the camp was staffed by some 250 Manx people who were employed in a wide range of capacities, including clerks, storekeepers and medical staff. The camp was guarded by 2,000 military personnel. Indeed, with a population greater than that of Douglas, the place was more akin to a town than a camp. Samuel Norris [61] estimated that the camp's stores held stocks worth more than £100,000 and had a turnover in the region of £12,000 a month. Wherever practicable, goods were purchased within the island. Thus, while most of the island's hoteliers and boarding-house keepers were in dire financial straits, many Manx traders and farmers were enjoying prosperous trading conditions brought on by the presence of the camps. And the staff of the camps had secure employment for the duration. As for the inmates, they had recreational and educational facilities to relieve the boredom of camp life, they were well cared for and remained in generally good health.

Another sector of the island's financial scene that was doing better than ever before was the Manx government itself, whose revenues for the fiscal year 1914–15 came in at a record £93,000, yielding a surplus of income over expenditure of £10,900 which, when transferred to the Government's reserve account, swelled its total to £74,665. In the following financial year, the revenue surplus was up to £18,000. (Raglan had predicted a deficit.) Such healthy surpluses were due largely to the taxes on imported foodstuffs and other consumables brought in to satisfy the needs of 26,000 internees, as well as the resident population of some 52,000. (The sum of those two figures would remain well in excess of any resident population recorded in a Manx census up to and including 2001.)

The existence of such financial surpluses caused growing unrest among those sections of the community (mainly hoteliers and boarding-house keepers) whose livelihoods had relied on the holiday trade. Their incomes had become vanishingly small, many were reduced to the brink of penury, whilst other sections of the community were thriving as never before – and there was still no income tax. Even the editor of the *Manchester Guardian* reported sympathetically on the Manx situation (which is rather more than one could expect of *The Guardian* of today).

One of the leaders of the renewed movement for redress was none other than Samuel Norris, one of the founders of the Manx National Reform League in 1903. Now, in December 1915, he founded the War Rights Union, with the intention of pressing the Manx government for a reduction in business rates. Lord Raglan had already made it clear that he would never countenance a reduction in rates as long as he remained Governor, and so the Union petitioned the Home Secretary, whose only positive response was to suggest that relief for the impoverished should be paid out of the reserve account, which should then be replenished by the imposition of taxation.

The campaign for reform became more militant, with the formation of the RRR Party (standing for Redress, Retrenchment and Reform), which declared that Raglan should be replaced with a governor 'of financial ability and sympathy with representative government'. Furthermore, the campaigners asserted that Raglan should repay some of his salary, having been away from the island for nine months, allegedly on sick leave. He returned in time to preside over the annual Tynwald assembly at St John's on 5 July 1916. The RRR presented him with a petition for redress of grievances, and the crowd produced a forest of placards demanding a new governor, taxation on wealth and the abolition of taxes on food. As Raglan led the procession down from the hill at the close of the proceedings, a sod of turf was thrown from the crowd, hitting him harmlessly on the hand, but perhaps making him even less inclined towards consultation than he had been before.

That same year saw a number of the campaigners, including Samuel Norris, taken to task for withholding the payment of rates. The coroner was authorized to seize items of furniture that would be put up for auction to cover the payments outstanding. Norris and the RRR urged the public not to enter bids for the items, whereupon he was charged with wilfully impeding the work of the coroner and languished in gaol for the next twenty-eight days. All of this was of great interest to the British press, with one newspaper referring to the 'Gilbert and Sullivan' nature of Manx governance which, at that time, was not an unrealistic analogy.

In 1917, feelings of unrest were augmented by public concerns over the price of bread. Similar concerns in Britain had led Parliament to place a subsidy on the cost of flour, sufficient to reduce the price of a large loaf to 9 pence. Under public pressure in Man, the insular government pursued the same course, funding the subsidy by withdrawing £20,000 from the surplus account, whereupon the Imperial Treasury directed that any such subsidy in future should be funded from revenue and not from the surplus. With this in mind, Lord Raglan put forward a Bill to introduce a single, basic rate of income tax but the Keys would not accept it and the matter was not (immediately) progressed.

The following year, with drawings from the surplus account forbidden and with no income tax to boost the revenues, the bread subsidy came to a halt, as a consequence of which the price of a loaf soared once more. On 3 July 1918, Manx trade-union leaders called a general strike for the following day; most shops and businesses remained closed, electricity supplies were switched off and all transport (including steamer traffic) was at a standstill. The day following the first of the strike was Tynwald Day. In desperation, Raglan postponed the ceremony and then, of his own volition, promptly restored the 9-penny loaf.

Tynwald Day fell on a Friday in 1918; by the following Monday, Raglan was in London for discussions with the Home Office. The new Home Secretary, Sir George Cave, sent him back with a firm brief to inform the Keys that, if they failed within one week to pass a Bill imposing an income tax of 2 shillings (10p) in the pound on annual incomes of more than £500, then Parliament would pass one for them. On 18 July 1918, only minutes before the passing of the deadline, Tynwald passed the required Bill and, for the first time in its history, income tax had arrived in the Isle of Man. In its first year, 1918–19, the tax revenue exceeded £66,000, which was more than triple the amount needed to cover the bread subsidy. The rate of tax was subsequently lowered. Four months later, the war was over.

BETWEEN THE WARS

As described earlier, the war had brought benefits to some in the civilian population but had produced only hardship for others. For the poor and unskilled workers, little had changed by 1918, except that food prices at the end of the war were, on average, 60 per cent higher than they had been at the beginning. There were demands for wage increases which could not, in all conscience, be ignored. Farm labourers were granted an increased weekly wage of 16 shillings (80p). Highway and Harbour Board wages were raised to 23 shillings and 4 pence for a 56-hour week, and many unskilled labourers worked seventy hours a week for between 22 and 25 shillings (£1.10 – £1.25). By the war's end, more than 300 people were in receipt of poor relief, but that was less than a third of the number who had been receiving it in the 1890s.

The Isle of Man Steam Packet Company also found itself in straitened circumstances at the end of the war. Of the nine ships requisitioned by the Admiralty, only three survived, and the company was left with less than half the passenger-carrying capacity that it had before. However, compensation for the wartime loss of six vessels would be forthcoming, and this would be used to return the company's fleet to its full strength, but it would take time.

Lord Raglan resigned as Governor in the last month of 1918. Few can doubt that his sixteen-year tenure coincided with the blackest period in Manx history since the sorry day of Revestment in 1765. It would certainly have been over-optimistic to predict that his departure would result in the lifting of the cloud which had loomed over this aspiring nation for so long, but it would, perhaps, have been excusable to hope that it would herald the beginnings of a glimmering of a silver lining.

During the war, successive Home Secretaries had given undertakings that the constitutional reforms recommended by the MacDonnell Committee in 1911 would be progressed once the hostilities were over. Indeed, one of them had already been accepted by the British government before war broke out, i.e. the recommendation that future lieutenant governors should serve a fixed term of seven years, and that would be the term for Raglan's successor. He was Major-General Sir William Fry, an Irish-born career soldier who, during an earlier posting to the Isle of Man, had married the eldest daughter of Sir John Goldie-Taubman, of the Nunnery, in Douglas. He arrived in the island with a brief to initiate reforms and he was clearly sympathetic to that brief. One development that would assist that process was the result of the 1919 general election, in which seventeen new members were returned to the House of Keys, one of whom was Samuel Norris. One of his first actions as a member of the Keys was to propose the provision of state pensions for all those over the age of seventy; it was approved unanimously. (Although Norris died in 1948, his printing firm, Norris Modern Press, was still operating in the 1970s but seems to have disappeared since.)

The last of the wartime internees departed Cunningham's Holiday Camp in March 1919, and the first of the new stream of young male campers arrived two months later, to be housed in a mixture of tents, chalets and dormitories. The camp now had capacity for up to 4,000 campers, and its new dining hall was capable of accommodating 3,000 at a single sitting. In the twenty-one years from 1919 to 1939, a flow of almost a million young men must have holidayed there.

The flow of mainstream visitors also began to recover; in 1920, the total number of arrivals was up to 561,124, but the record season of 1913 was destined never to be exceeded. The visitors continued to be drawn primarily from the working classes of north-west England, and the onset of the interwar depression would cause marked reductions in their numbers. The situation was worsened still further by the general strike in Britain in 1926, which produced a record low in visitor numbers during the interwar period. From a total of 540,628 visitors in 1925, the number plummeted to 384,705 in the year of the general strike. But the visiting phenomenon recovered strongly in subsequent years, with the record for the interwar period being set in 1937, with 593,037 visitors.

In the meantime, the town of Douglas had continued to improve and extend its facilities as the island's main holiday resort. The principal development involved the widening of Loch Promenade and the formation of a line of sunken gardens which commenced in 1929 and occupied the next six years, providing some much-valued winter employment in the process. Two new cinemas were opened and two existing theatres were converted to provide two more picture houses; a *palais de danse* also opened.

The revival of the holiday trade prompted the British government to seek an additional contribution towards the cost of the war. The Isle of Man, Jersey and Guernsey were all in the sights of Whitehall as targets for contributions. The magnitudes of the sums being sought aroused strong feelings in all three islands. Negotiations dragged on over eight years from the end of the war until, having witnessed the susceptibility of the Isle of Man's economy to the effects of the depression and the general strike in Britain, the British government downgraded its demands and settled for a down-payment of £100,000 and a further £400,000 payable over twenty-five years. Overall, this was equivalent to an increase from the £10,000 which had been paid annually ever since 1866 to an annual £60,000. This was the settlement agreed upon, but it had raised, once again, the question of the extent to which the island's finances should be under the control of Whitehall.

The visiting industry may have enjoyed a revival of fortunes during the post-war period, but problems of housing and poverty remained. The clearance of slums between Douglas harbour and the railway station was authorized by Tynwald in 1922, street-widening works were instituted, new housing was developed on the Pulrose estate, and apartment blocks on Lord Street in the 1930s. But, among the poorest and the unemployed, there were many who could not afford the rents for council housing, and saw emigration as their only recourse. The island's population, which had been 60,284 in the 1921 census, had fallen to 49,308 ten years later. Recovery thereafter would be slow.

And the island's traditional industries were not experiencing good times either. Farming had benefited greatly from the influx of internees, and their departure forced a retrenchment. By 1939, the acreage of land under cultivation had decreased by a quarter and the acreage under cereals by almost a third, but the consequent increase in rough grazing supported a marked expansion in the number of sheep.

Fishing, too, suffered a contraction but this seems to have been in the face of competition from 'foreign'-registered boats (mainly East Anglian and Scottish), rather than a shortage of fish or the loss of the alien market. The tonnage of herring landed in the British Isles generally had reached its peak in the years immediately prior to the First World War and, although there had been a subsequent reduction in landings, it had not reached the level of an acute shortage. But, by 1937, 80 per cent of the herring landed in the island were being brought in by boats registered elsewhere. The reduction in the number of operational Manx fishing vessels seems to have been a matter of choice. Increasingly through the course of the twentieth century, both farming and fishing developed into activities demanding to be taken seriously, each as a full-time occupation, and, whenever the modern descendant of the old-time Manx crofter-fisherman has been compelled to make the choice between working the land and working the sea, he has almost invariably chosen the former.

With the exception of agriculture and fishing, there was little industrial activity in the Isle of Man. The last of the Laxey mines closed in 1929. The island-wide lack of power supplies had restricted other industrial and manufacturing activities, but the development by Douglas Corporation of its power station at Pulrose and the establishment of the Isle of Man Electricity Board to cater for the rest of the island would together fill that need and provide the impetus for new developments in future years.

Transport – by road, rail, sea and air – would also develop rapidly, and we deal with those in the next chapter.

<hr />

WAR AGAIN

'I have to tell you now that no such undertaking has been received, and that, consequently, this country is at war with Germany.' At 11.15 on the morning of Sunday, 3 September 1939, the voice of Prime Minister Neville Chamberlain emerged mournfully from a million wireless sets across the British Isles. 'The war to end all wars' had not lived up to its promise, and the quickly resurrected prediction that 'it'll all be over by Christmas' would be even wider of the mark than it had been the first time.

The first casualty in the Isle of Man was the annual Manx Grand Prix motor-cycle race meeting, which had been due to run from 12 to 14 September. With the threat of war looming, advance bookings had been slow; then the cancellations made things worse. Preparations for the meeting had been completed; the first practices were due to be held on Monday the 4th but, in the light of Chamberlain's broadcast the previous day, of course they never happened.

Meanwhile, in Britain, arrangements were hurriedly made to deal with the 75,000 people of German and Austrian origin who were in the country at that time, around 60,000 of whom were refugees from the Nazi threat, most of them Jewish. All such persons were classified as 'enemy aliens', and all were required to appear before 'enemy-alien tribunals' which were set up across the country. Aliens were classified in three categories: a class A was deemed to pose a positive security threat, to be interned for the duration of the war; a class B was one of suspect loyalty who could remain at liberty but subject to restrictions; and class C was for those who satisfied a tribunal that they posed no threat to national security.

In view of the numbers to be processed and the perceived urgency of the situation, this was inevitably a very hurried exercise and, with so many local tribunals scattered across the land, nationwide consistency was all but impossible. Nevertheless, by the end of February 1940, some 73,000 cases had been examined, of which 569 had been classified into category A, 6,782 in category B and approximately 66,000 in category C. In the spring of that year, the rapid German advance across the Low Countries prompted further inflows of refugees to add to the confusion. Then, to make matters even worse, when Italy entered the war on 10 June, thousands of Italians living in Britain suddenly became enemy aliens. All Italians between the ages of sixteen and seventy who had lived in Britain for less than twenty years were rounded up and interned. In London alone, some 4,100 were taken into custody, among them managers, chefs and waiters from some of the city's most prestigious hotels and restaurants. Furthermore, it was also decided to intern all of those aliens who had previously been classified as category B. With such numbers to process, if the situation had not been chaotic before, it was now.

In the Isle of Man, once again, it would be the holiday trade that would be dealt a body-blow but, this time round, at least some of the hoteliers and boarding-house keepers would benefit from a new influx of internees. The British government had decided not to repeat the strategy which had led to the large camp at Knockaloe in the First World War, but to requisition selected groupings of hotels and boarding-houses in various parts of the island. The first was sited on the Mooragh Promenade, in Ramsey, where a string of thirty properties was requisitioned; the occupants were ordered to evacuate the premises, taking their personal possessions with them, but furniture had to remain *in situ*. Those ejected from their properties would find accommodation either with family or friends or in those tourist premises that had not been requisitioned, and they would receive compensation for the occupation of their own premises – on a scale to be decided later. The Mooragh camp was cordoned off with barbed wire which extended across the road and promenade to the back of the shore. The camp opened in May 1940 and was occupied throughout the war, guarded by men of the Royal Welch Fusiliers.

There would be six camps in Douglas, not all operational for the complete duration. On the seafront, there were Granville, Sefton, Central, Palace and Metropole, each taking its name from the hotel which formed its centre, and, behind and above the promenade, Hutchinson was set up in the cordoned-off Hutchinson Square. Granville, together with the adjacent Regent Hotel, was eventually taken over by the Royal Navy as a shore training establishment.

The first camp to open in the Douglas area was actually the Onchan camp, which occupied sixty houses in a prominent position overlooking the northern end of the Douglas promenade with views across the bay. The houses ranged in size from four bedrooms to thirty-two, and the barbed wire enclosed four roads around Royal Avenue, together with a football pitch and tennis courts, probably making it the most agreeable of all the camps in which to be confined. There was one camp in the west of the isle; this was Peveril Camp, based on the hotel of that name (now demolished) in Peel. All of these camps were for male internees, and all had access to their own dedicated hospital facilities; that for Peveril Camp was at Ballaquane, a pre-war guest-house directly behind the hotel. Hospital facilities for the camps on the east side of the island were centralized on the requisitioned Falcon Cliff Hotel, just behind and above Douglas promenade.

The first women destined for internment in the island began arriving at the end of May 1940. A mixed lot, some were category A Nazi sympathizers who had been on the War Office's 'wanted' lists from the beginning, but the majority were category B, some with children, others alone, and some pregnant. For them, the Isle of Man lay at the end of a long and difficult journey, many having been jeered as they passed through Liverpool on their way to the docks. On arrival in Douglas, they were transferred by train to Port Erin.

The women's camp in the south of the isle was called Rushen. Its inmates were accommodated in the seafront hotels and guest-houses of Port Erin and in the

The Mooragh Promenade, Ramsey

much smaller collection of similar establishments fronting Chapel Bay, Port St Mary, centred on the *Ballaqueeney Hotel*. Others were billeted with local families, who were paid 1 guinea (£1.05) per head per week. The Chapel Bay complex also housed some British military personnel, including a contingent of the women's Auxiliary Territorial Service (the ATS). The *Ballaqueeney* was later adapted to house married couples from among the internees.

Because of the spread of accommodation areas forming Rushen Camp, the close confinement of the inmates behind barbed wire was less practicable than in the other camps, and so the simple (if rather drastic) expedient of placing a single barrier of barbed wire between Fleshwick and Gansey was adopted, thereby cutting off the whole of the Rushen peninsula. With strict control of road access into and out of the area, this arrangement was less than popular with the locals, but it gave internees greater freedom to move about than existed in the men's camps, although a strict night-time curfew was imposed.

The total number of internees held in the Isle of Man during the Second World War never attained the levels in the previous conflict. By the first week of August 1940, the total number held in the men's camps had reached its peak of 10,024. Thus, with the numbers held in Rushen Camp approaching 4,000, the total complement of the ten camps never exceeded 14,000. But, among them, were a surprising number of men of varied gifts and talents who would rise to prominence after the war – and a few who already had. An outstanding example of the latter was a man whom we have met earlier in these pages.

Dr Gerhard Bersu, a German-born professor of archaeology, had had a distinguished academic career in his native land before and after the First World War, until being sacked by Hitler. In 1938, he was excavating an Iron-Age site in Wiltshire but, in the following year, he suddenly became an 'enemy alien', whereupon he and his wife were interned. When the *Ballaqueeney Hotel* came to be used to house married couples, the Bersus were moved there together. Dr Bersu was granted permission to undertake excavations on some of the island's archaeological sites, which he did with great distinction, directing the work of volunteer internees while his wife surveyed and catalogued the sites.

Musicians turned up in the camps in fair numbers, among them the well-known piano duo, Rawicz and Landauer, who were in Hutchinson Camp. Onchan Camp saw the formation of three-quarters of the famous Amadeus String Quartet: Norbert Brainin and Siegmund Nissel (violins) and Peter Schidlof (viola). They would meet the fourth member, cellist Martin Lovett, after their release. The man largely responsible for melding the four talents together was pianist Ferdinand Rauter (also at Onchan Camp), who had first met Schidlof in a London police station after the two had been rounded up for internment.

There were numerous other names from the camps that would become well-known after the war: Charles (later Sir Charles) Forte, (Sir) Nikolaus Pevsner, R. W. 'Tiny' Rowland (of *Lonrho* fame) and George (later Lord) Weidenfeld, who would later link up with Harold Nicolson to form their eponymous publishing firm. The wide range of activities carried on in the camps makes a fascinating story; the definitive account by Connery Chappell [11] is as complete a version as we are likely to get.

By the end of 1944, the run-down of the internment camps was well advanced. After the D-Day invasion, increasing numbers of German prisoners were being taken, and the camps were being cleared of internees to make way for the expected influx of prisoners of war. As in the First World War, farmers and traders had found a welcome and stable market for their wares in supplying the needs of the camps and the military. Also, in contrast with the First World War, many hoteliers and boarding-house keepers (as well as ordinary householders) had been receiving income.

Many farmers, having seen their regular workers depart for war service, also had reason to be grateful to those internees who turned out to serve as farm workers. The Italians were favoured above the Germans for their cheerfulness and willingness to work. The Germans would work but were more dour and unresponsive to those around them. Later in the war, after Italy had surrendered, the Italian internees were released into civilian life, and farmers had to place more reliance on the Germans. Some of the Italians chose to stay in Man, and there remains a scattering of Italian surnames across the isle today.

Regarding matters more military, we need to backtrack to the immediate pre-war years. Reacting to the threat posed by German rearmament in the late 1930s, the Air Ministry had recognized the wisdom of moving training units well away from the English east coast. In 1937, an approach was made to the Manx government with a proposal to establish a flying training unit in the island. The favoured location was at Jurby, attractive because of its location in the flat, lightly populated northern plain. There had, in earlier years, been civil flying operations from two grass airfields in the island, one known as Hall Caine Airport, near Ramsey, and the other at Ronaldsway, in the south. Both were considered too small for the proposed use, although Ronaldsway would continue in operation in another role. On the outbreak of war, Hall Caine and other likely landing areas were obstructed with old buses, lorries and other suitable objects to thwart any such attempts. (We return to the earlier, civilian operations in the next chapter.)

The proposals for Jurby prompted opposition from local farmers but, when the new Lieutenant Governor, Vice-Admiral Leveson-Gower (later Earl Granville), brought forward an enabling Defence Bill, it was passed by Tynwald and the work of construction went ahead, with two intersecting concrete runways and perimeter track being laid down. The Manx government agreed to pay £100,000

*Jurby airfield today: (above) the control tower surveys the distant hills;
(below) a Second World War mess-hut*

per year towards the cost of rearmament, and the Air Ministry would finance the construction of the airfield, which was predicted to bring a population of up to 400 into the area, with attendant benefits to the farming, construction and service industries.

The airfield opened on 18 September 1939, in the occupation of No. 5 Air Observer School with a rag-bag collection of obsolescent aircraft: Westland Wallaces, Bristol Blenheims and Fairey Battles. On 1 November, the unit became No. 5 Bombing and Gunnery School. Then, in July 1941, it reverted to its original name when it was decided that there should be a single combined course on navigation and weaponry. The only aspect of the operation which had not seen much change in that time was the unit's collection of ageing aircraft. (This was understandable for a training unit at that time, the overriding need being to strengthen the front-line squadrons.)

In the meantime, the Air Ministry had been on the look-out for a suitable site for a fighter base to supplement the training school at Jurby. As the German occupation spread across continental Europe, it had gained control of airfields in northern France and brought its bombers within range of Liverpool, Glasgow and Belfast, hence the perceived need for a defensive airfield in the Isle of Man. Air Ministry eyes alighted on another area of the northern plain, around Ballaghaue Farm, Andreas, only 4 miles north-east of the Jurby field. Some 500 acres (200ha) of land were the subject of requisition orders, and work proceeded to form a triangle of three runways and taxi-ways. Much waste material from the defunct Laxey mine workings was trucked in for use in the groundworks and, when that was running low, more was transported in from the Foxdale 'deads'. The Andreas airfield was securely fenced, in contrast to Jurby, where fencing was minimal and roads remained open to the public.

The first operational fighter unit, comprising Spitfires of 457 Squadron, was detached from Jurby to Andreas in early October 1941. Many shipping patrols were flown over the Irish Sea but no enemy aircraft were engaged over the island. The runways at Andreas were somewhat longer than necessary for the fighters of the time, and the station was used as an emergency landing ground for aircraft flying the North Atlantic ferry route, whose aircrews brought newly built American B17 Flying Fortresses and B24 Liberators over the ocean to Britain to engage in the European sector of the war. One further item of work necessary in relation to the Andreas airfield was the lowering of the church tower to little more than half its original height, since it stood close to the flight-path from the main runway. The rectory was requisitioned as the officers' mess.

Jurby and Andreas airfields remained operational throughout the war. Jurby, at various times, saw the passage of a variety of aircraft types, from Hurricanes and Spitfires to Blenheims, Wellingtons, Ansons, Lysanders – and one *flying boat*

Kirk Andreas, with its truncated tower

which landed there. On 20 May 1945, a Sunderland of 423 Squadron had been on convoy escort duty when it experienced an engine fire. The best course was deemed to be an emergency landing at the nearest shore base (it had been done before). The crew made a successful landing but, by this time, the fire had spread into the structure of the wing. The crew evacuated the craft and ran like hell – the Sunderland contained a full load of depth charges which there had been no time to jettison. There were no casualties but the resulting explosion caused great damage to hangars and practically every window on the site – the only damage suffered by Jurby throughout the course of the war.

But, in the ordinary course of events at Jurby and Andreas, death came all too frequently, both in training and operational sorties. It is no coincidence that the largest concentrations of war-graves in Man are in the churchyards of St Patrick's at Jurby and at Kirk Andreas. The headstones commemorate flyers of the Royal Air Force, the Dominions of the Commonwealth, the United States and Poland. They range from eighteen-year-olds to those of an age where they would not have been compelled to serve at all – except by self-compulsion.

From the beginning of the war, the small existing airfield at Ronaldsway was developed into an air gunnery school, equipped with Lysanders and Wallaces for target-towing and some Gloster Gauntlet biplanes fitted out for cine-gun practice.

However, early in 1943, the Manx government was informed by the Admiralty that it intended to develop the Ronaldsway site into a Royal Navy air station for the training of torpedo, bomber and reconnaissance aircrew. For this, it had to acquire an additional 480 acres (195ha) of land, bringing the total area up to 850 acres (350ha), with King William's College losing some of its playing fields and the old Ronaldsway farmhouse (once the home of the infamous William Christian) being demolished in the process. The Governor, Earl Granville, authorized the necessary land requisition under Parliament's *Defence of the Realm* legislation. Four runways, with lighting, were put down and a three-storey control tower erected on the west side of the field.

Royal Naval Air Station Ronaldsway was commissioned on 21 June 1944 and named HMS *Urley* (Manx for 'eagle'). Three training squadrons operated from the station thereafter, all flying the Fairey Barracuda, the aircraft which had been so successful in crippling the battleship *Tirpitz* in its Norwegian fiord in April 1944. Part of the training of the Ronaldsway squadrons entailed practice attacks on targets in the bay at Derbyhaven, and two Barracudas came to grief in its waters while doing so.

The Royal Naval also had a presence in Douglas, turning Cunningham's Camp into HMS *St George*, a shore training establishment for boy-seamen, transferred to the island from three more vulnerable locations in England. More than 8,500 passed through its gates during the course of the war. The Douglas Head Hotel became HMS *Valkyrie*, the radar training school which produced some 30,000 fully trained operators during the same period.

The Army had a presence also. The Villiers and nearby hotels became an officer-cadet training unit, processing around 4,000 men for commissioning as officers. Up on Onchan Head, the Majestic Hotel was transformed into a hospital by the Royal Army Medical Corps, and the Empress Hotel, on Central Promenade, became the headquarters of the RAF Regiment. There could have been few hotels that were not in use for one purpose or another, and this, coupled with the presence of so many off-duty servicemen in search of night life – be it cinema, dance hall or public-house – ensured that the atmosphere in Douglas never took on the air of gloom which had prevailed in the First World War. Ramsey benefited similarly from the presence of the two airfields in the north.

The Isle of Man Steam Packet Company was, of course, affected by the war in a similar way to that of the previous one. The company had been operating sixteen vessels in 1939, of which the Admiralty requisitioned ten. Of the remaining six, three were small passenger vessels, with the remainder carrying freight. Passenger numbers had contracted markedly, most arrivals now being new internees, prisoners of war or servicemen and their families. Once the Liverpool docks came within range of German bombers, the passenger sailings there faced increasing hazards and, towards the end of 1940, the passenger vessel *Victoria* suffered damage from a mine. Sailings were switched to the safer Fleetwood route and services continued without interruption.

Of the ten Steam Packet vessels taken over for war service, eight participated in the evacuation from Dunkirk in May/June 1940, ferrying well over 24,000 troops across the English Channel to safety, more than 7 per cent of the total rescued to fight another day. By the war's end, four of the ten vessels had been lost, three of them at Dunkirk, including the *King Orry*, which had been a survivor of the first war.

As the war progressed and Liverpool increasingly became the target of enemy bombing raids, their pyrotechnics could readily be seen and heard along the island's east coast, visual displays being especially vivid on the night-time horizon. In the island itself, the air-raid sirens were sounded on forty-three occasions but no raids actually materialized. A small number of bombs fell on the island but, for the most part, they appeared to have been jettisoned by aircraft which had either failed to locate their targets or were fleeing from fighter pursuit.

After the war's end, Andreas was the first Manx airfield to close. It was open to the public for Battle of Britain Day in September 1946, then, days later, the last group in residence, No. 11 Air Gunnery School, flew its Wellingtons over to Jurby, and that was the end of Andreas's service career. Jurby would remain in RAF occupation – in various guises – until 1963, and it was bought from the Air Ministry by the Isle of Man government the following year for £133,000. Ronaldsway, of course, remains operational in a modern role. The Royal Navy departed the field in 1946, and it was bought from the Admiralty by the Manx government two years later for £200,000. It is now the Isle of Man's airport and, lest it be thought that the price paid was excessive, it should not be forgotten that the construction cost laid out by the British government was in excess of £1 million.

In retrospect, the Second World War was not the economic disaster for the island that the First had been. It is true that large contributions were paid to finance the war, but three airfields had been constructed, two of which were retained by the Manx government, and the sustained presence of large numbers of internees and military personnel had enabled the island's hoteliers, farmers and traders to survive, even to prosper. But there had been a cost: of the thousands of Manx men who went away to fight the war, 490 did not return.

AFTER THE WAR

The end of hostilities in 1945 brought a year of great activity and hope for the future. VE Day (Victory in Europe Day) was celebrated on 8 May, and VJ Day (commemorating victory over Japan) on 15 August. In between, King George VI presided over the annual Tynwald assembly at St John's, with Queen Elizabeth at his side. In the towns, on the airfields and across the Rushen peninsula, the barbed wire was taken down. Hoteliers retrieved their furniture from storage and proceeded to reclaim their premises for the purposes for which they had been built, looking forward to a resurgence in visitor numbers in the first post-war season. The Steam Packet Company was anticipating the same phenomenon; with Admiralty compensation for its lost ships and a revival of passenger revenues, the company would embark on restoring its fleet to full complement. And with the Isle of Man government in possession of its newly acquired airport at Ronaldsway, the way was now open for an additional source of passenger traffic and, although its volume would never challenge the numbers travelling by sea, air traffic would show a sustained growth over the years.

At the end of August 1945, Lord Granville departed to become Governor of Northern Ireland and was succeeded by Air Vice-Marshal Sir Geoffrey Bromet, the first RAF officer to hold the post. Throughout the latter years of the war, the Keys had made renewed demands for the formation of an executive council, under the presidency of the Governor, to discuss the question of constitutional reform with the United Kingdom. In October 1946, the first Executive Council was appointed by Tynwald, consisting of seven members drawn mainly from the chairmen of the various boards of Tynwald and appointed by the Governor on the recommendation of Tynwald. Any further constitutional reform would require legislation by Parliament but the British government intimated that it was prepared to transfer powers to the insular government and to remove Treasury control of the Manx exchequer. Nothing much happened, however, until the late 1950s.

In the meantime, visitor arrivals had recovered well in the immediate post-war years. In the three years 1947–9, the annual number of arrivals remained above 600,000 and not far below the all-time record of 1913. Such levels were probably maintained through a folk-determination to holiday well and relax after six years of wartime restrictions, and this could be done despite the continuance of food rationing, to which people had grown accustomed. Also, the cost of foreign holidays remained beyond the pockets of most working-class people; the era of cheap foreign travel was yet to arrive. However, the initial post-war revival was not to last and, through the 1950s, visitor numbers showed a steady decline.

Another feature of 1950s Man was rising unemployment. An extensive house-building programme had been in progress through the late 1940s and into the early 1950s, but its end saw increasing numbers claiming benefit. The situation was compounded by a reduction in the Manx fishing fleet, which had faced little competition from boats from elsewhere during the war years but, as the British fishing industry experienced its post-war recovery, the Manx fleet did the reverse.

And it was not due to a shortage of fish, as the landings of the British and Irish boats continued to prove; it was as if the Manx fisherman had lost the will to compete. (As noted earlier, a similar trend had been apparent between the wars.)

The only positive features of the island's employment scene at that time came from the manufacturing sector. Operations for clothing manufacture were established in the premises of the old woollen mills at Laxey and St John's, together with carpet-making in Douglas and textiles in Ramsey. The largest manufacturing enterprise was (and is) the Ronaldsway Aircraft Company, still popularly known as 'Martin-Baker', established in 1951 to produce aircraft ejection seats. By the end of the decade, such factories were employing over 1,000 workers.

Nevertheless, in an island so heavily reliant on the summer holiday trade, it was inevitable that there would be a considerable pool of unemployment each winter. The creation of winter-work schemes by the Manx government provided some relief, but many resorted to seasonal emigration, taking up labouring jobs on the farms of Lincolnshire and East Anglia and returning in time for the next summer's influx of visitors. Many others took the more extreme course of permanent emigration, with the result that the island's population fell from 55,253 in 1951 to 48,133 in 1961, the lowest total since 1841.

Two most significant Acts of Tynwald passed in the immediate post-war years followed similar Acts of the Westminster parliament. In the sphere of education, Parliament's *Education Act* of 1944 paved the way for a comprehensive system of secondary education, and Tynwald followed suit with its Act of 1949. As a consequence of the formation of a single education authority in Man in 1920 (in place of the previous twenty-five), the implementation of the 1949 Act was more straightforward than might otherwise have been the case. In fact, the system of secondary education in Man had been essentially comprehensive since before the war, and was the first to operate anywhere in the British Isles. The 1949 Act notwithstanding, Manx schools would remain subject to Ministry of Education regulations and to inspection by His Majesty's Inspectors.

The second significant innovation (and undoubtedly *the* most significant in terms of expenditure) was the introduction of the Manx National Health Service. Again, Tynwald's Act of 1948 followed that of Parliament of 1946. The insular government's Health Services Board became responsible for providing a public health service which was free 'at the point of delivery'. The board assumed responsibility for the three existing public hospitals, those being the Ballamona mental hospital, the White Hoe isolation hospital and the Cronk Ruagh sanatorium. The three voluntary hospitals, Noble's Hospital, Ramsey and District Cottage Hospital, and the Jane Crookhall Maternity Home, would remain independent but with public funding, subject to their full co-operation with the board. But that arrangement proved problematical and an Act of 1963 provided for the last three hospitals to be transferred to the board. The National Health Service quickly became (and remains) the most expensive service on the Manx exchequer.

In 1957, constitutional matters at last appeared on the agenda for discussions between the Manx and United Kingdom governments. Under 'the 1957 agreements', the two governments agreed to the repeal of two Acts of Parliament of 1866 and 1867, resulting in the cessation of United Kingdom control over Manx customs revenues, although the Governor retained the power of 'initiating and regulating expenditure ... for the maintenance of good government in the Island'. It was further agreed that Manx customs duties would be kept in line with those of the UK, as required for the continuance of the Common Purse Agreement. The Manx government also agreed to pay an annual contribution in return for defence and common services (i.e. consular and other representation abroad), this contribution to be 5 per cent of the Isle of Man's receipts from the Common Purse. These agreements paved the way for the far-reaching reforms of 1958, when Parliament's *Isle of Man Act* of that year repealed all earlier legislation on the control of Manx finances. In the same year, Tynwald's *Finance Act* and *Customs (Isle of Man) Act* enabled Tynwald to regulate its own finances and customs duties. Things were on the move, but there was much still to be achieved, especially with regard to the Governor's influence in financial matters.

The discussions that led to the 1957 agreements had highlighted the fact that there remained much dissatisfaction among members of Tynwald concerning the island's constitutional position. To lay these matters open for further discussion in 1958, the Governor of the day, Sir Ambrose Dundas, appointed a commission under Lord MacDermott, a former Attorney-General and Lord Chief Justice of Northern Ireland, who reported a year later. Acting on the recommendation of the commission, four Acts of Tynwald were passed in the next few years. These were: (i) the *Isle of Man Constitution Act 1961*; (ii) the *Finance Board Act 1961*, creating a board of that name and the new post of Government Treasurer; (iii) the *Police (Isle of Man) Act 1962*, enabling the creation of a Police Board; and (iv) the *Isle of Man Civil Service Act 1962*, leading to the creation of the Civil Service Commission.

The common objective of the four Acts was the transfer of executive powers previously exercised by the Lieutenant Governor in these areas to appropriate bodies responsible to Tynwald, although the Governor still remained ultimately responsible for the execution of those powers. The principal feature of the *Constitution Act* was to bring about a revision in the formation of the Executive Council. The council, which had existed since 1946, had proved less successful as a 'cabinet' of government than had been intended. Its membership of seven contained a majority who were chairmen of boards of Tynwald and, as MacDermott had identified, 'board loyalties' often impeded the need for 'collective responsibility'. The reformed Executive Council of seven members comprised the chairman of the Finance Board, the chairmen of four other boards (elected by Tynwald), and two members of Tynwald appointed by the Governor, the latter presiding at its meetings. MacDermott was unequivocal in urging that, if the Isle of Man wished to progress towards responsible government, a sense of collective responsibility must be engendered in Executive Council but, as the Commission acknowledged, this could be a difficult task in a small community where local differences are strongly felt (and that remains true today).

During its deliberations, the MacDermott Commission received a submission from the Home Office, setting out the island's relationship with the United Kingdom, the essential features being that the Isle of Man was a dependency of the Crown, the UK government retained ultimate responsibility for good governance of the island and controlled its international relations and external defence. Furthermore, the Westminster parliament was empowered to legislate for the island, whilst all insular legislation required the assent of Her Majesty the Queen in Council. That was the position in 1959 and, although the Crown's representative has had most of his executive powers transferred to Tynwald in the intervening years, that, ultimately, is an accurate statement of the island's constitutional position today.

NEW RESIDENTS

The year of the MacDermott report was also the year for a new Lieutenant Governor. Aware of Tynwald's newly gained freedom to control the island's finances, Sir Ronald Garvey was convinced of the need to revive the Manx economy and, with his encouragement, Tynwald enacted legislation in 1960 and 1962, abolishing surtax on personal incomes and reducing the standard rate of income tax from 22.5 to 21.25 per cent; it would remain at that level through the 1960s and into the 1970s. With British governments of the day levying a top rate of income tax of 98 per cent and introducing capital gains tax in 1964, the Isle of Man became a very attractive place to which to relocate, and the Manx government began an active campaign to attract new residents.

The policy brought positive results in a number of respects. During the 1960s, the island received more than 9,000 new arrivals, and the total population was lifted from its low point of 48,133 in 1961 to 54,581 ten years later. The influx of so many newcomers prompted a perception on the part of opponents of the policy – especially followers of the Manx nationalist party, *Mec Vannin* – that most new residents were of retirement age, contributed nothing to the working population and created an imbalance in the age structure of the population. They were accused of causing increased demands on the health services and posing a threat to the island's culture and heritage. Many newly arrived incomers of the time could have been excused for thinking that the painting of slogans ('Tax dodgers go home') on walls and road surfaces *was* part of the island's culture.

In reality, as the results of the 1971 census showed, although there were many retired folk among the new arrivals, the largest percentage of new residents were aged between twenty and twenty-four, they were active in the workforce and their arrival did much to correct the existing imbalance in the age structure of the population caused by the emigrations of the 1950s, most of those emigrants being of working age and taking their children away with them. Many new residents, when settling down among new-found Manx friends, would soon have been assured that the painted slogans did not represent the sentiments of most Manx people.

The success of the new residents policy in the 1960s brought undoubted benefits to the construction and service industries and to the Manx economy generally, at a time when the holiday trade continued to lag in the doldrums. The new residents policy was maintained through the 1970s and, by the census of 1981, the population had reached 66,101, the first time it had risen above the previous record of sixty years earlier. It is also worthy of note that, of the 19,359 new residents arriving in Man during the twenty years to 1981, 2,092 of them were Manx people returning to settle.

Surprisingly, the island's tourist industry regained some of its old buoyancy in the 1970s, with visitor numbers being boosted to a peak of 634,616 in 1979 (very close to the record year of 1913) by the Manx government's promotion of that year as Millennium Year, commemorating the thousand years of Tynwald. This growth in numbers was undoubtedly assisted by the sudden and rapid rise in oil prices in those years (being the period of reduced supplies by the OPEC cartel), leading to sharp increases in the costs of foreign travel. But, with the advent of the 1980s, the Manx holiday trade went into a sustained decline from which it has never recovered. A study of total passenger arrivals (by sea and air) over recent years would – at first sight – suggest a quite different situation, with annual totals well above 650,000 and arrivals by air now exceeding those by sea. But, when account is taken of the numbers of Isle of Man residents and business travellers (well over 400,000 between them), the true picture of the decline in Manx tourism becomes apparent. The age of cheap mass-travel to destinations in the sun was one in which the island could not compete at anything like the same levels as before. Hoteliers and boarding-house proprietors responded to the decline in custom either by closing down or by selling up to enable amalgamations with neighbouring premises. To make matters worse, the disastrous fire at the Summerland indoor leisure centre in 1973 was followed by the *Fire*

Precautions Act of 1975, which required the retrospective compliance of all places of tourist accommodation and public assembly, often at great expense which was too much for some smaller businesses to survive. During the 1970s, the number of hotels and guest-houses fell by more than 45 per cent, and the number of bedrooms by 26 per cent. The Douglas Bay Hotel, on Douglas Head, and the Majestic, on Onchan Head, were both demolished and replaced with apartment blocks, and (saddest of all) the historic Villiers was flattened to make way for an office block.

THE OFFSHORE FINANCIAL CENTRE

If the year 1866 is identified as the threshold of modernity in the Isle of Man, then 1970 (or thereabouts) must surely have been the threshold of today. In 1970, the Isle of Man government commissioned PA International Management Consultants to investigate the structure of the Manx economy and make recommendations for future action. The report [62] was published the following year and identified tourism as still the largest contributor to the national income, but now bringing in just 31 per cent of the total, as compared with 75 per cent in its heyday. Manufacturing produced almost 27 per cent of total income (of which engineering was a growth sector), income from abroad 20 per cent and the construction industry 17 per cent. Agriculture, fishing and forestry between them yielded less than 5 per cent. There were three main recommendations:

(i)   steps should be taken to arrest further decline in the tourist industry;

(ii) growth in the manufacturing sector should be encouraged; and

(iii) (recognizing its importance to the construction industry) the government's new residents policy should continue.

But the consultants seem not to have spotted the potential of the phenomenon which was just appearing on the horizon.

As noted earlier, the Manx government's prime intention in maintaining low rates of income tax through the 1960s had been to attract new residents, and a significant proportion of those who responded were working people. But, increasingly, the island came to the attention of United Kingdom residents who had accrued personal wealth and wished to protect it from the UK's regime of punitive taxation. Hence, the Isle of Man came to be recognized as a 'haven', together with Jersey and Guernsey and certain other jurisdictions in continental Europe, Bermuda and the Bahamas. In addition to having stable governmental systems (a necessary prerequisite for 'tax-haven' status), the three British islands had the advantage of being closer to home.

The next phase of the process resulted largely from actions taken outside the island. In 1972, the British government's redrawing of the boundaries of the sterling area (the area within which sterling could be moved freely) left the Isle of Man and the Channel Islands (plus Gibraltar from 1973) as the only places outside the United Kingdom remaining within the sterling area. At a stroke, this removed competition from other low-tax areas and resulted in an expansion of financial business in the British islands. The process was further accelerated by the British government's abolition of exchange controls in 1979, leaving UK residents and corporations free to invest anywhere in the world.

In the Isle of Man, there remained one problem – the *Usury Act*, an ancient piece of legislation under which the government could (and did) stipulate the maximum rate of interest that could lawfully be charged. Its only effect in modern times was to act as an unintended brake on investment in the island. At times when interest rates elsewhere were higher than the maximum usury limit in the island, then – of course – bank deposits would be moved elsewhere. To avoid this outflow of funds, the government of the day had no choice but to raise the limit. Successive Manx governments clung on to the *Usury Act* long after it had ceased to serve any useful purpose (if, indeed, it ever did). The Act was repealed in 1979 and sterling deposits surged by 51 per cent in the first year thereafter.

These developments paved the way for the transformation of the Isle of Man from its initially unintended role as a tax haven (largely benefiting the wealthy individual) into an offshore financial centre conducive to corporate businesses, such as banks, building societies and insurance companies. In the financial year 2002–3, the financial sector accounted for 44 per cent of the island's gross domestic product.

The 1970s saw a happy coincidence in the growth of the financial sector and the (temporary) resurgence in the tourist industry. Consequently, the decade was a prosperous one for the island. Of course, this did nothing to soothe the sensitivities of the nationalist community. By the mid 1970s, slogans were again appearing on walls, this time the work of a new, secretive organization known as *Fo Halloo* ('the underground'). The 1976 Tynwald assembly at St John's was briefly disrupted by demonstrators waving placards demanding that the government 'Close this tax haven'. Later slogans on walls and roads appeared in code: 'FSFO', which was taken to imply that the financial sector should 'go away'. ('FS' did not heed the message, any more than I and many others had done in the 1970s.) Finally, in the 1980s, the campaign descended into arson, with attacks on two houses nearing completion on the outskirts of Douglas, for which the perpetrators were gaoled in 1989.

CONSTITUTION AND GOVERNANCE TODAY

The process of devolution of power from Parliament to Tynwald which began in 1958 continued to make steady progress through the remainder of the twentieth century. Successive British governments, from the early 1970s onwards, let it be known that they would not impede Manx aspirations towards further degrees of self-determination (although I do not recall hearing of any such intimations during the years of the Blair/Brown Labour Governments; perhaps the Scots never did relinquish their ambitions to rule the Isle of Man). Successive Manx governments have responded positively but with caution. Despite the Lieutenant Governor having been divested of the last of his everyday executive roles (he no longer presides over sittings of Tynwald or of the Legislative Council), the constitutional position of the island *vis-à-vis* the United Kingdom remains as stated earlier in this chapter.

The island's legislature, or parliament, is Tynwald (or Tynwald Court) and, apart from the annual outdoor assembly at St John's, it meets at monthly intervals in the Tynwald Chamber of the Legislative Buildings in Douglas, when the two branches of the legislature, the Legislative Council and the House of Keys, sit together. The Tynwald Court has the general role of scrutinizing government administration and public expenditure. In the words of the MacDermott Commission's report in 1959, the legislative function of Tynwald, apart from making minor amendments, 'is confined to consenting or rejecting Bills passed by the Council and the Keys in their legislative capacities' (although the rejection by Tynwald of a Bill which has already passed through the Keys and the Council is almost unheard of, and would require a very unusual set of circumstances for it to arise). Once a Bill has completed three readings in both the Keys and the Council, it must be signed by the President of Tynwald and at least a quorum of each branch (i.e. five members of the Council and thirteen of the Keys) before being submitted for the Royal Assent, which may, in certain circumstances, be granted by the Lieutenant Governor. Following the Royal Assent, the title and short summary of the Act are read out at the next following annual Tynwald assembly at St John's; the Act is then constituted into Manx law. Tynwald also has the role of approving, amending or rejecting subordinate legislation, such as orders, regulations and European Community instruments. Tynwald may criticize ministers, or even the Council of Ministers, but cannot interfere with the statutory powers of executive government.

The President of Tynwald is elected by the members of Tynwald Court from among their number. The President of Tynwald also sits as the President of the Legislative Council; therefore, if the person elected has, up to that point, been a

The annual Tynwald assembly on and around the hill

member of the Keys, he or she transfers to the Council, causing a by-election for the vacant seat in the Keys. Two regular events in Tynwald's year (in addition to the St John's assembly) are the debates on the Government's Policy Report and on the Budget. The former is delivered at the October sitting by the Chief Minister, and sets out the Government's policies, proposals and legislative programme for the ensuing three years. The Budget statement is presented by the Minister for the Treasury at the February sitting.

The House of Keys, the publicly elected chamber of Tynwald, still comprises the historic total of twenty-four members, representing a mixture of fifteen one-, two- and three-seat constituencies. Elections are held every five years, and members (MHKs) are elected by the 'first-past-the-post' system. A preferential voting system was employed for the 1986 and 1991 elections, but the system was unpopular and was discontinued in time for a return to the old system in 1996. This means that the voter in a single-seat constituency has one vote, whereas a voter in a multi-seat constituency has the same number of votes as there are seats, which itself raises the question as to whether a basic tenet of democracy is being achieved. The distribution and representation of constituencies are as follows (proceeding clockwise from Douglas):

Douglas North			2 members
Douglas East		25,347 voters	2
Douglas South		at 2001 census	2
Douglas West			2
Middle	(the Parishes of Braddan and Marown	4,544	1
Malew and Santon (those two Parishes)		2,842	1
Castletown		3,100	1
Rushen	(the Parishes of Rushen and Arbory, including the Villages of Port Erin and Port St Mary)	8,528	3
Glenfaba	(the Parishes of Patrick and German)	2,315	1
Peel		3,785	1
Michael	(the Parishes of Michael, Ballaugh and Jurby)	2,976	1
Ayre	(the Parishes of Andreas, Bride and Lezayre)	2,694	1
Ramsey		7,322	2
Garff	(the Parishes of Maughold and Lonan, including the Village of Laxey)	4,928	1
Onchan		8,803	3

It is notable that Onchan, which, in official terminology, is a 'Local Government District' (i.e. it is neither a Town nor a Village), boasts a population second only to that of Douglas.

At its first sitting, a newly elected House of Keys chooses its Speaker from among its number. The Keys sit in their own chamber on most Tuesdays, except on the monthly occasion when they sit as part of Tynwald. There are no party politics in Tynwald proceedings, most members presenting themselves as independents. There exists a Manx Labour Party which usually has a minority representation in the Keys, but party activism is rarely evident in proceedings. With a largely 'independent' House, Manx government tends to proceed on a 'consensual' basis, rather than by party confrontation.

The nationalist party *Mec Vannin* was formed in 1964 but did not make a serious attempt to get members into the Keys until the election of 1976, when it fielded ten candidates, one of whom was successful. This was to be Mec Vannin's one and only success in House of Keys elections, but it was to last for less than a year; in 1977, a split in the party led to the formation of the Manx National Party (MNP), and the Mec Vannin member switched to the MNP. He lost his seat in the 1981 election, and that marked the end of the MNP. Since then, Mec Vannin has seemed content to exist as nothing more than a pressure group.

Ultimate nationalism, in the form of campaigning for complete independence, has not won the support of a significant part of the Manx electorate, and most members of the Keys in recent years have, to varying degrees, sought to gain as great a degree of self-determination as practicable, whilst retaining those features of the relationship with the United Kingdom which are amenable and convenient. There are two such features which are overwhelmingly convenient: firstly the presence of a larger neighbour which is able to stand guarantor for the island's defence and external relations, and secondly, the Customs and Excise Agreement which, although tying the Manx rates of indirect taxation to those of the UK, does provide a convenient method of collecting the Manx duties without the need to set up an expensive insular bureaucracy to do so. The island pays for such services, and that is as it should be. PA International Management Consultants prepared a further report [64] for the Isle of Man Government in 1976, recommending the abrogation of the agreement, the abolition of value added tax and its replacement with a sales tax, but the government of the day chose not to follow that path. An updated version of the agreement was signed in 1979, and was modified again in 2007. The arguments for and against the agreement are long and detailed; Mark Solly [71] gives a good account.

No account of the Manx political scene would be complete without mention of a more recent phenomenon – the Alternative Policy Group. The APG was formed after the election of 1991 and later changed its name to the Alliance for Progressive Government. Seemingly responding to the earlier adoption of the ministerial system, the APG set out to act as a parliamentary opposition, initially refusing to accept any office within the established government. However, its expressed aims being to achieve increased autonomy for the island, greater accountability in government, more emphasis on economic development and abrogation of the Customs and Excise Agreement, there were a number of issues (but not the last-named) on which the group's aims differed little from those of the Government. Initially, the group seemed more intent on changing procedures within Tynwald than in promoting external policies. Then, from 1993, its members began accepting posts within government departments, and external observers began to wonder where the 'opposition' had gone. The APG still exists as an alliance of members within Tynwald, but lacking any apparent party structure outside. An even more recent arrival on the political scene is the Liberal Vannin Party which, at the time of writing, is still in its infancy, with one member in the House of Keys. Consequently, Tynwald continues largely as an assembly of independents and, although there are things to be said in favour of a party system, few people seem to lament its absence.

On 12 July 2006, Tynwald made the quite surprising decision to lower the minimum age for voting in general elections to 16. In what appeared to some to be a move of unseemly haste, Chief Minister Donald Gelling presented the proposal to Tynwald on a Supplementary Order Paper under the *Representation of the People (Amendment) Act 2006,* which had only received the Royal Assent just prior to the sitting (and the Bill had contained no reference to the measure). Arrangements were then hurriedly made to ensure that the names of all sixteen- and seventeen-year-olds were on the register of electors in time for the November general election. Such haste! Why do other pieces of legislation have such long gestation periods?

The Legislative Council is regarded as the 'upper house' of Tynwald; it is the modern form of the ancient Lord's Council, from the days of the Stanley lords. The Council of today comprises eleven members, three of whom are *ex-officio*: the Lord Bishop (who has a vote), the Attorney General (who does not) and the President of Tynwald, who presides over meetings of the Council, at which he has a casting vote (only) in the event of a tied division. The remaining eight members are elected by the Keys from among their own number or (quite rarely) from outside. The election of a member to the Legislative Council must be supported by a majority (i.e. at least thirteen) of the members of the Keys. Members of the Council (MLCs) serve until the last day of February following the fourth anniversary of their election (i.e. they serve for between four and five years). They are elected in two groups of four, in different years, thus providing a degree of continuity. There have been repeated attempts to have members of the Council publicly elected but no-one has yet produced a formula to gain sufficient legislative support.

The Second Deemster ceased to be a member of the Council in 1965, and the First Deemster in 1975. The Lieutenant Governor ceased to preside over meetings of the Council in 1980, being succeeded by the President of the Council, this office itself being superseded by that of President of Tynwald in 1990.

The principal role of the Legislative Council is that of a revising chamber, analogous to that of the House of Lords in the United Kingdom. The passage of a Bill through the legislative process requires that it receives three readings in the House of Keys and three in the Legislative Council, although not necessarily in that order. Bills are usually initiated by the Keys but may occasionally originate in the Council. The Council may delay the passage of a Bill which does not gain its approval but, if the Bill is again passed by the Keys in the next legislative session, it may proceed without the approval of the Council.

The amount of legislation being enacted today to govern our lives (and not just in the Isle of Man) is increasingly the subject of comment, and often of complaint. It is of interest to note that A. W. Moore [57] was remarking on the same phenomenon (although certainly on a smaller scale) more than a century ago. He points out that, during the period from 1417 to 1824, all of the laws enacted were contained in 425 pages; between 1824 and 1863, they occupied 568 pages; 1863 to 1882 saw 1,180 pages; and 1882 to 1893 produced 1,046 pages. In this modern age, when the statutes are recorded and filed in a very different manner, it would require a most laborious process to continue Moore's page-count into the present day, but the following chart shows the number of Acts passed in the years of the twentieth century (and up to 2002) and which remained in force at the end of 2002. It should be stressed that the chart exaggerates the trend, since it does not include the laws passed in the earlier years of the century and which have since been repealed. The trend, nonetheless, is clear.

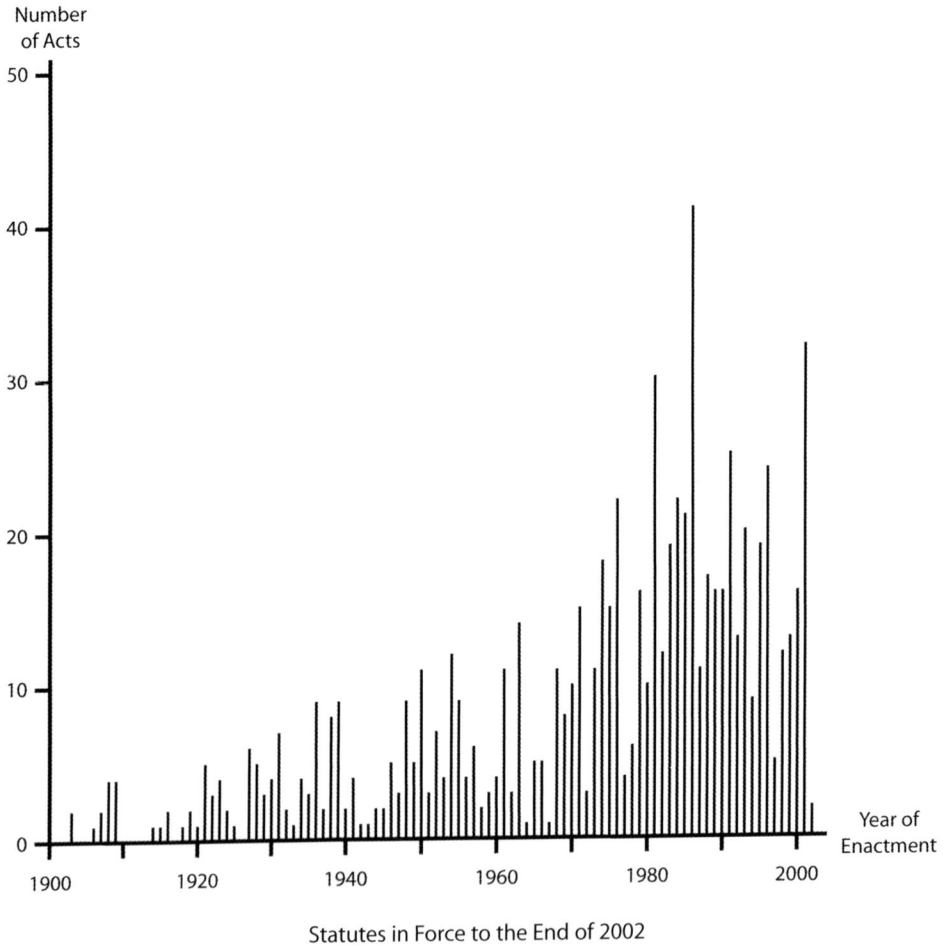

Statutes in Force to the End of 2002

It is also fascinating to find that a section of one of the earliest recorded Manx laws is still in force. It is Section 11 of the *Customary Laws Act* of 1417, which deals with the powers of the Coroner and reads as follows:

11 Coroner's Arrest

Also it is our law, that no Coron[er] arrest any Man for Debt owinge, unless he have a speciall Warrant from the Lord or his Lieutenant; but in Points of Fellony, or delivering of Servants, or for Surety of the Peace, with many other Points that belong unto his Office, he ought to do these by vertue of his Office without Warrant.

This is the earliest surviving example of the writing down of a law which had previously been passed down the generations by word of mouth. It was formally confirmed as remaining in force as recently as 1978, under the *Pre-Revestment Written Laws Act* of that year.

Two pieces of contentious Manx legislation have been repealed in recent years, both largely as a result of the European Convention on Human Rights. The first, by an Act of 1992, resulted in the decriminalization of homosexual acts between consenting adults in private. (How the old legislation could ever have been enforced without the aid of an 'SS'-style police force was never clear.) The second repeal, in 1993, ended judicial corporal punishment by whipping (more commonly known as birching). This was a most divisive issue among the Manx population of the day and, had it not been for the facility for recipients of the birch to petition the European Court of Human Rights, this particular repeal would doubtless have been much later in arriving. It was also in 1993 that the death penalty for murder was removed from the Manx statute book, although no execution had been carried out for more than twenty years. In the years before the repeal, a Manx deemster had no choice but to sentence a convicted murderer to death (it being the mandatory sentence); the sentence would subsequently be commuted to one of life imprisonment on appeal to the Home Office.

Executive government in the Isle of Man is centred on the Council of Ministers, whose membership comprises the Chief Minister and the nine ministers heading the various departments of government. The ministerial system was introduced in stages between 1985 and 1991, with the aim of rationalizing and streamlining the structure and operations of government, the nine departments replacing the previous twenty-six boards of Tynwald, each headed by a Chairman. The island's first Chief Minister was Miles (later Sir Miles) Walker (1986–96). The present Council of Ministers (broadly equivalent to a cabinet) replaced the former Executive Council. The present departments are: the Treasury; Home Affairs (DHA); Agriculture, Fisheries and Forestry (DAFF); Health and Social Security (DHSS); Trade and Industry (DTI); Tourism and Leisure (DTL); Local Government and the Environment (DLGE); Education (DoE); and Transport (DoT). The department which places the heaviest demand (by far) on the public purse is the DHSS (£168.4 million in 2003–4), which takes more than double the funding of Education (£79.9 million). The DTL also has responsibility for public transport, both road and rail. The DoT is the highways and drainage authority, with additional responsibilities for the island's harbours and Ronaldsway airport.

The welfare state in the Isle of Man, especially in regard to the National Health Service, social security and education, has developed along broadly similar lines to that in the United Kingdom. In the provision of public-sector housing, some local authorities are functioning housing authorities, with central government (via the DLGE) funding 100 per cent of the deficiency. In other parts of the island, the Department acts directly as the housing authority.

The resident population of the isle, after declining to its low-point in the 1961 census, showed a steady recovery in subsequent years, attaining a record level of 76,315 in the census of 2001, engendering (sometimes heated) discussion over the question of a possible upper limit to be imposed by Government by means of immigration controls. After years of debate, the *Residence Act 2001* was passed by Tynwald, but it is an enabling Act only, with measures to be brought into effect when circumstances arise that may be prejudicial to the island's quality of life, and there the matter rests. Since as long ago as 1966, the Isle of Man has held a mid-term 'mini-census', so as to provide population statistics every five years, instead of the previous ten. In the meantime, there is no definitive figure for the island's maximum sustainable or 'desirable' population.

The Isle of Man's relationship with the European Union is set out in Protocol 3 to the United Kingdom's Treaty of Accession, under which the island, although acknowledged not to be a member state of the Union, is recognized as part of the customs territory of the Union. There is, therefore, freedom of movement of manufactured and agricultural goods in trade (but not of services) between the island and the Union. Under the arrangement, the island makes no fiscal contribution to the Union and receives no funding from it. This arrangement was seen in the island as being the best compromise between two extreme alternatives: full membership of the Union (under the umbrella of United Kingdom membership) would have thwarted any Manx aspirations towards a greater degree of self-determination, and complete independence from the Union would have left the island facing tariff barriers on its trade goods, which would have meant its virtual exclusion from the markets of the United Kingdom and the wider Union.

As the Isle of Man is part of the common travel area of the British Isles, any persons lawfully present in the United Kingdom, Ireland or the Channel Islands have freedom of travel to the island and to take up residence. Equally, there is freedom of travel in the opposite direction. Conversely, a person who is excluded from the United Kingdom under the terms of its Immigration Acts is also excluded from the Isle of Man. However, all persons entering lawfully into the Isle of Man must comply with the island's domestic legislation, especially with regard to employment: before taking up employment or self-employment, any such person (unless an 'Isle of Man worker' or an exempted person) must hold a work permit issued by the Department of Trade and Industry.

The facility for freedom of travel between the island and much of continental Europe may seem, at first sight, to leave the island open to an influx of illegal immigrants and asylum-seekers, such as have been so problematical in the United Kingdom. Two factors militate against such an influx: firstly, it is almost impossible for strangers to 'disappear' into communities as small as those in the Isle of Man; secondly, any such immigrants are ineligible for social security or any other benefits and, hitherto, the impact of illegal immigration has been very small.

Immigration matters are handled by the Isle of Man government's Immigration Office. In 2002, the number of legal immigrants processed by the Office amounted to 1,382, and eleven illegal immigrants were deported from the isle. In the same year, there were no asylum-seekers and just one the year before. Persons seeking asylum in the UK are not permitted entry into the island; any found here are returned to the UK to await a decision. The three largest contingents of legal immigrants in 2002, in terms of their countries of origin, were: South Africa 446, India 410 and the Philippines 219.

THE LEGAL SYSTEM

The Manx legal system has developed over the centuries and, while subject to successive external influences, has maintained a unique independence of structure. Its Scandinavian origins are evident in the titles of its High-Court judges, the Deemsters, and yet, after such a long history of association with (not to mention subjugation by) England, and then Great Britain, it is not surprising that several aspects of the Manx legal system have developed along lines similar to those in England and Wales, but with adaptations where necessary to suit insular requirements. As the Clothier Commission, set up to inquire into Manx legal services, reported in 1990, 'The freedom to review legislation of other countries and to select and extract only those parts considered appropriate to the Island's needs, after noting the success or otherwise of that legislation elsewhere, is obviously of great advantage.' The commission concluded that it was in the best interests of the Isle of Man 'to preserve the distinctive character of its legal system'. The titles of some of that system's courts and law officers present (to the outsider) the most immediate display of that distinctive character.

The principal courts in Man are the High Court of Justice, the Court of General Gaol Delivery and the Courts of Summary Jurisdiction. The judges of the High Court are the First and Second Deemsters and the Judge of Appeal, all three being appointed by the Crown. The two deemsters are members of the Manx bar; the Judge of Appeal must be a member of the English bar and a Queen's Counsel. Acting deemsters may also be appointed by the Lieutenant Governor from time to time, according to need. On taking the oath of office, a deemster swears that he will 'without respect of favour or friendship, love or gain, consanguinity or affinity, envy or malice, execute the laws of this Isle justly between our Sovereign Lady the Queen and her subjects within this Isle, and betwixt party and party, as indifferently as the herring back-bone doth lie in the midst of the fish'. The deemsters may act in any division of the High Court but the Judge of Appeal sits only in the Appeal Division, now named the Staff of Government Division. The High Court has four divisions:

(i)   The Staff of Government Division hears appeals from the other courts under any two judges of the High Court, although a judge may not, of course, sit on an appeal against his own initial judgment. Any appeals against judgments of the Staff of Government Division are heard by the Judicial Committee of the Privy Council in London.

(ii) The Chancery Division deals with disputes over land, the estates of deceased persons, trusts, charities, the property of children and the mentally infirm, and related matters.

(iii) The Family Division deals with divorce, domestic disputes, adoption and other matters relating to children.

(iv) The Common Law Division deals with all other civil disputes.

The Court of General Gaol Delivery is the island's highest criminal court, equivalent to the Crown Court in England, and its trials are heard by a deemster

The Isle of Man Courts of Justice

and a jury of seven (or twelve in cases of homicide). Most criminal prosecutions, other than the most serious cases, are dealt with in a Court of Summary Jurisdiction, where trials are held before the High Bailiff or his deputy sitting alone, or by two or three justices of the peace (lay magistrates) sitting with the legally qualified Clerk to the Justices. A Juvenile Court deals with cases of offences by children.

LOCAL GOVERNMENT

It comes as a surprise to many, both within and without the isle, that a country of a mere 221 square miles (572 sq km) should be served by no less than twenty-four local authorities, but such is the case. The various bodies are:

(i)   the Corporation of the Borough of Douglas;
(ii) the Town Commissioners of Ramsey, Castletown and Peel;
(iii) the District Commissioners of Onchan and Michael;
(iv) the Village Commissioners of Laxey, Port St Mary and Port Erin; and
(v)   the Parish Commissioners of Andreas, Bride, Lezayre, Maughold, Lonan, Braddan, Marown, Santon, Malew, Arbory, Rushen, Patrick, German, Ballaugh and Jurby.

Each authority employs a Clerk (part-time in most of the parishes, Braddan and Malew being the exceptions) and such supporting staff as are required for the range of services provided, which varies appreciably between the towns and the parishes. Nine of the authorities function as public-sector housing authorities: those serving the four towns, the Onchan district, the villages of Port St Mary and Port Erin, and the parishes of Braddan and Malew. In most of the parishes, the largest single item of expenditure is refuse collection, followed by a comparatively restricted range of other local services.

The reasons for Onchan and Michael being designated as 'Districts', rather than Parishes, are historical. The Village District of Onchan was created in 1895 as a separate entity from the parish of that name. In 1905, the Village District of Michael was established in the same way. In Onchan, there was a pressing need for drainage work in the village and, in Michael, an outbreak of enteric fever had highlighted the need for a public supply of potable water and for mains drainage. (The village of Laxey was created out of the parish of Lonan in 1895 for similar reasons, and that village is still established.) In each case, the Village District was established because of a perceived unfairness in funding the required works by raising a rate on the whole parish. In the case of Michael, this thinking proved counter-productive, for the new district now had even fewer residents to bear the cost via their rates. In 1924 (nineteen years after the formation of the Village District), a public inquiry was convened to ascertain why nothing had been done. The commissioners of the day did not come out of it in a very good light, but a scheme was evolved in which a rate of 2 shillings (10p) in the pound was to be levied; this would meet less than half of the cost of the drainage works but central government would meet the rest, and the water supply would follow.

With the passage of time came a gradual realization (not universally held) of the artificiality of such small and arbitrary divisions. The two Onchan districts were recombined in 1986, and Michael followed suit in 1989. To protect sensibilities in each case, and to avoid the impression that any one authority was taking over the other, but also to recognize the mixed urban/rural nature of the amalgamated area, it was termed a 'District'.

There have been repeated attempts in recent times to bring about further reorganization of local government in Man, by the formation of four or five regional authorities, but all such initiatives have sought to progress matters through a consensus of the twenty-four existing authorities, and have come to naught. For the foreseeable future, it seems almost inconceivable that such fundamental change will be achieved by consensus. An old adage concerning turkeys and Christmas springs to mind.

CHAPTER SEVEN

Trade, Industry and Commerce

T he industries with the longest histories in Man are undoubtedly agriculture, fishing and forestry. In the earliest times of human activity, endeavours in forestry would have been entirely negative in character, involving the clearance of woodland to provide land for the growing of crops and the grazing of animals, and also to provide timber for fuel and building. The much later developments of renewed woodland plantations and amenity plantings in the island's glens have been covered in Chapter 2. Although agriculture and fishing have always been considered to be traditional components of Manx life and the Manx economy, the two of them together now contribute a very small proportion (less than 1 per cent) of the island's national income and employ an equally small proportion of the workforce. Other industries and enterprises have come and gone; yet more have come and survive – some even to prosper. We start this survey with the oldest.

AGRICULTURE

Little of any detail is known of the 4,000-year development of agriculture in Man before the beginning of the nineteenth century. We have tantalizing glimpses from historical sources of the improved farming practices introduced by the Cistercian monks of Rushen Abbey in the twelfth century, and of the reforms wrought by Bishop Wilson on his own farm at Bishopscourt in the eighteenth century, and then of his persuading other farmers of the benefits to be obtained by following his example. But we know precious little until 1812, when Thomas Quayle produced the first systematic survey of Manx agriculture.

Quayle depicts a quite primitive scene, and describes Manx farming as 'a recent art'. Little attempt appears to have been made to practise crop rotation; the routine seems to have been to grow cereal crops (mainly oats and barley) continuously on the same ground until it became unproductive, and then to allow it to revive under grass and grazing. Methods for the movement of farm produce were primitive indeed, consisting of either horse-mounted creels or horse-drawn, wheel-less sleds which caused untold damage to the surfaces of roads and tracks. Livestock populations in the island at that time are generally unknown but the sheep population in 1806 was estimated to be around 18,600 (there are more than 175,000 today).

A large number of small farms has always been a characteristic of the Manx agricultural scene. Thomas Quayle commented on this feature of the industry in 1812; the picture was little changed a century later and, although amalgamations have occurred in more recent times, the spread of small holdings is still extensive.

Trends in number and size of farm holdings

		1940	1945	1970	1980	1990	1995	2000	2004
<20 acres	(<8ha)	339	263	210	210	218	250	252	227
20–50	(8–20)	222	162	113	107	114	111	120	118
50–100	(20–40)	320	280	224	147	152	116	99	90
100–150	(40–60)	161	177	154	116	107	89	67	57
150–200	(60–80)			109	84	87	72	74	65
		97	101						
200–300	(80–120)			76	77	67	71	68	62
>300 acres	(>120ha)	10	128	73	80	77	75	83	90
Total		1,149	1,111	959	821	822	784	763	709

Source: DAFF, *Reports on Agricultural Returns*

The most abrupt change in the sizes of holdings is seen at the end of the Second World War, when the number of large farms is increased more than tenfold, with most of the smaller categories decreasing in number, resulting in a reduction in the total number of holdings which has continued to the present day.

Accompanying the consolidation of farm holdings has been a sustained reduction in the agricultural workforce, reflecting the increasing mechanization of Manx farming. Furthermore, a comparison of the manpower figures with the number of farms (220 workers on 709 holdings in 2004) leads to the firm conclusion that the farmer with the smaller holding is working his land either single-handedly or with reliance solely on his family.

Trends in agricultural workforce

	1945	1970	1980	1990	1995	2000	2004
Regular workers	1,202	441	381	307	236	178	145
Casual workers	394	84	126	85	88	100	75
Total	1,596	525	507	392	324	278	220

Source: DAFF, *Reports on Agricultural Returns*

At the end of the First World War, the former internment camp at Knockaloe was retained by the insular government and reinstated as a farm. Its 346 acres (140ha) were acquired from its former owners for £7,800, and most of its prefabricated huts were dismantled and cleared away (some may be seen around the isle to this day). The project was funded by a legacy left by the island's great benefactor, Henry Bloom Noble, who willed £20,000 for further education in agriculture. By the time the land had been restored to farming condition, the remainder of the legacy had been spent.

Knockaloe opened as an experimental farm in 1924, initially as a livestock

A hut from Knockaloe, still in use at Kirk Michael

breeding station, under the auspices of the then Board of Agriculture, and later the DAFF. The station steadily diversified to research new advances in crop and animal husbandry. Its director doubled as the Government's agricultural advisor, and Knockaloe became a valued dispenser of advice and assistance to Manx farmers. The products of its breeding programmes (cattle, sheep, pigs and poultry) were sold to farmers to assist in improving their stock. Research was carried out into crops best suited to the Manx climate, an artificial insemination service was set up and demonstrations of farm machinery held. However, from the early 1990s onwards, the extent of Knockaloe's operations was scaled down and, in 2005, it was announced that the station would close; the future use of the site is unclear.

Over the years since the Second World War, the area of land under cereal crops has decreased markedly, down from 17,747 acres (718ha) in 1945 to 10,365 acres (419ha) in 2000, of which wheat was occupying some 17 per cent (in 2000) and Laxey Glen Mills, which produces flour for all the island's bakers, was importing wheat to make up the shortfall. Potatoes and other root crops have also declined greatly over this period, possibly in the face of unrestricted imports.

One sector of Manx agriculture which is protected against foreign imports (for the moment) is the meat market. Recognizing the delicate balance of the farming industry of such a small nation operating in a much larger free-market area, the European Union has granted the Isle of Man a derogation of the require-ment for the free movement of goods in the sector. Under the terms of the derogation, the importation of beef and sheep-meat into the island is strictly controlled by the Manx government at a level below 20 per cent of domestic consumption. But this is not a permanent arrangement, and it is uncertain how long the EU will continue to extend the concession. In the meantime, it has certainly been beneficial to the island's meatstock sector. Both beef and dairy herds have continued to grow in number, although not yet sufficiently to keep the government-run abattoir at Tromode operating to its full capacity.

Dairy farming in Man has been particularly successful, being outside the realm of EU milk quotas. The collection of milk from farms and deliveries to shops and doorsteps have been undertaken by the Isle of Man Milk Marketing Association (the MMA) since 1960. It moved to its present creamery at Tromode in 1974, where, at full capacity, it processes 60,000 litres of milk into 6 tonnes of cheese per day. The MMA's annual production of cheese approaches 1,300 tonnes, 85 per cent of which is exported. Its output includes the Cheddar and Cheshire varieties and other speciality cheeses, and the Association has won awards for several of these.

As noted earlier, the total sheep population in Man now exceeds 175,000, most of which are farmed in the lowlands, but with a sizeable proportion of the hardier breeds left to range free on the hills. The Manx *loaghtan* sheep is kept in some numbers (6,784 in 2005); Manx National Heritage has small flocks on some of its sites but the largest flock by far is to be found at Ronague, in Arbory, where their owner (reputed to be the world's largest breeder of them) produces *loaghtan* meat for those of a more discerning palate.

Pig and poultry production have both declined sharply over the years, the latter surviving mainly as a much-reduced egg-laying flock, barely 10 per cent of its size in 1970.

In the financial year 1999–2000, the Government injected £6.43 million into Manx agriculture through its support schemes. In the same year, exports of milk and cheese earned £6.25 million, with meat exports bringing in a further £3 million. And yet there is no sign of recovery from the long-term decline. Despite the amalgamations that have brought about some larger farm units over the years, the average Manx farm is still small compared with those to be found elsewhere. Unless this situation is addressed, it seems likely that Manx farming will remain confronted by the realities of global economics in this age of free passage of goods across state boundaries.

FISHING

The long-term decline in the Manx fishing industry has been alluded to in the previous chapter. In the early years of the twentieth century, Peel was the home port of 80 per cent of the Manx fishing fleet; their landings were predominantly of herring, and this formed the basis of the Manx kippering industry. The herring fishery occupied only four months of the year, from July to October; it would start off the west coast of the isle and work south towards the principal herring ground, south-west of the Calf. In the early years, the fleet would continue round to the east coast for the 'back fishing' but this was soon discontinued.

From the earliest days of the fishery, Manx waters were not fished only by Manx fishermen. Even in the days of sail, throughout the nineteenth century, Cornish fishermen were regular visitors to Manx waters and were instrumental in bringing about a change of rig in the Manx fleet. The Manx boats were originally square-rigged but were later changed to the fore-and-aft yawl, or 'dandy', arrangement. When the Cornishmen arrived displaying their lugger rigs, the Manxmen adopted them and called them 'nickeys', supposedly because Nicholas was a common name among the Cornishmen. Later in the century, the Manx reverted to a fore-and-aft rig and called it a 'nobby'. (The fishermen of the Scottish west coast at that time had similar vessels called 'nabbies'.)

As fishing vessels became larger, and especially after the advent of steam, the Irish Sea became the hunting ground for fleets from even further afield. Larger drifter fleets from East Anglia and eastern Scottish ports fished the North Sea grounds from September to December. But the boats could not then be laid up until the following season; their building costs still had to be paid off and they must be kept working in areas where there were still fish to be had. The differing herring seasons around the British coasts made this feasible. A typical year's round for the East Anglian fleet would see the boats departing their home waters early in the new year, sailing south and west for some fishing off Cornwall (possibly finding some mackerel), then into the Irish Sea for the Manx season, before continuing north to work Scottish waters, turning south into the North Sea in time for the next 'home fishing'. And the driftermen were not the only ones to make this circuit of Britain, for the boats were followed from port to port by hordes of Scottish 'fisher-lassies', who would gut, salt and box the fish as they were landed. Wherever they went, they presented a scene of lively, cheerful, noisy activity, but one that concealed a silent portent of disaster to come. When the North Sea herring fishery collapsed into extinction in the late 1950s, more pressure would be diverted onto those remaining fishing grounds, including the waters of Man.

The effects of the increased pressure on the Irish Sea fishing grounds were not long in showing. In 1955, the total herring catch landed in Manx ports was 3,815 tonnes; ten years later it was down to 1,135 tonnes. Through the 1970s and 1980s, strict catch quotas were applied as a conservation measure. In 1986, the total herring catch was a mere 798 tonnes. Today, Manx kippers are still produced in the season, but almost exclusively using herring which have been caught else-where. The white-fish catch has also faded away: just 20 tonnes in 2004, none at all the year before, and a mere 6 tonnes in 2002.

The Isle of Man's territorial waters were extended from 3 to 12 miles in 1991. The extension included the rights to all minerals (except coal) under the seabed (previously belonging to the Crown in the form of the Crown Estate Commissioners), in consideration of which the Isle of Man government paid £800,000. However, the extension did not give the island the right to control fishing within its 12-mile limit; it still controls fishing activities within the former 3-mile jurisdiction, but it may impose controls within the wider zone only with the agreement of the four fisheries ministers of the United Kingdom, i.e. those for England, Wales, Scotland and Northern Ireland. Of course, the UK can impose controls within its 12-mile limit without the agreement of the relevant Manx minister. The most recent approach to the UK government on this matter was rejected in January 2006.

A relatively recent innovation in the Manx fishing scene is the harvesting of shellfish. The scallop *Pecten maximus* and the queeny *Chlamys opercularis* were first dredged off the south of the island just before the Second World War. Since 1970, the expansion of the shellfish sector has been useful in offsetting the decline in herring and white-fish landings. Conservation measures have been instituted in recent years to prevent over-exploitation of the beds. A valuable export market has opened up for frozen shellfish meat, with output going to the United States and continental Europe. It has been estimated that, of all the shellfish stocks in the north Irish Sea, 65 per cent of scallops and 40 per cent of queenies are to be found within the Manx 12-mile limit.

Much research into the marine biology of the area has been carried out since the early twentieth century at the Port Erin Marine Biological Station, an outstation of Liverpool University standing on the south side of Port Erin Bay. Besides its teaching and research activities, the station has, with funding from the DAFF, done much to maintain stocks of fish and crustacea in Manx waters but, unfortunately, the establishment has now closed and the university has vacated the site.

MINING AND QUARRYING

The first recorded reference to mining in the Isle of Man appears in the year 1246, when Harald Olafsson, King of Man and the Isles, granted a charter to the Abbot of Furness, permitting the use of all mines that may be found within the kingdom, together with 3 acres (1.2ha) of land at Rakenaldwath (Ronaldsway?) for the building of houses and the storage of ore. During the wartime extension of Ronaldsway airfield, much evidence of lead-smelting was uncovered. Incidentally, this charter of 1246 bears Harald's seal displaying the Scandinavian ship emblem; thus, the adoption of the three legs as the national emblem must stem from some later date.

The widespread intrusions of metalliferous veins in the Manx Slates have been commented on in Chapter 1, and it is unsurprising that, once the extent of their existence was known, they would receive the attention of those with mining interests. In 1292, Edward I granted John Comyn, Earl of Buchan, a licence to dig for lead on the Calf to cover the eight turrets of his castle at Crigleton, in Galloway. The title deed given to Sir John Stanley as King of Man by Henry IV in 1406 includes reference to 'mines of lead and iron'. But although it is clear by inference that mining operations were going on in those times, there is no actual record until the mid-seventeenth century, when Sir James Stanley (*Yn Stanlagh Mooar*) received a report from his Deputy Governor, Captain Edward Christian, that the veins of lead in the cliffs of Bradda Head contained much silver. Private individuals began obtaining mining leases from the Lord of Man, in return for one-fifth of the output.

When the lordship of Man was restored to the Stanleys after the Restoration of the Monarchy, Charles II's renewal of the grant made specific reference to 'Mynes Royall of Gould and Silver', a mine royal of silver being one which yielded more than 60 ounces of silver (1.7kg) from one ton of lead. Mining operations at that time were on a relatively small scale, compared with later times. In 1669, the Lord's share of all output from the mines amounted to 32.65 tons. In 1700, a total of 227.5 tons of iron ore was shipped out from the Dhyrnane mine, in Maughold. Copper mines were also operated on the Lord's lease in the south of the isle. In those places where smelting of the ore was carried out on site, imported coal was the fuel. Trial borings for insular coal were made in the late seventeenth century, and again in the nineteenth, but hopes that the Cumberland coal measures might extend this far west were never fulfilled.

The distribution of the Manx mine workings (all now defunct) lie broadly in two groupings, to the north and south of the central valley, on or to the east of the central spine of hills. The northern group lies to the east of the central ridge: in the Laxey valley, from the top end of Laxey village to the head of the valley on the eastern flank of Snaefell; to the north, in the upper reaches of the Cornaa valley, where lie the remains of the East Snaefell and North Laxey workings; and on the north-east coast were the haematite mines of Maughold, the most productive of which was Dhyrnane, which possessed its own snug little cove from which the ore could be shipped out.

The main area of the southern group lies astride the mountain ridge, running almost due east–west under the Foxdale area and resurfacing westward in the upper reaches of Glen Rushen. In the extreme south, there were workings for copper at several sites, including Langness and Bradda Head – in addition, in the latter case, to the lead and silver extraction previously mentioned. At South Bradda, the engine house and chimney still stand low down on the cliff-face, with visible traces of workings higher up. Similar remains are visible on the north side of Bradda Head. In the early eighteenth century, John Murrey's smelt-house at Derbyhaven was processing 30–40 tons of lead ore per year, on which a duty of £3 a ton was paid to the Lord. The derelict remains of the smelt-house still stand; it may (or may not) be the same building in which Murrey, some forty years earlier, had minted his 'John Murrey pennies'.

Mining operations at Laxey began (so far as we know) around 1780. The workings were entered by adits from the river bank, and yielded ores of silver-bearing lead, zinc blende and some copper. Water was always a problem in the mine workings and, in 1854, the great Laxey waterwheel was built and named the *Lady Isabella*, after the wife of Governor Hope; it is more widely known today simply as the Laxey Wheel, and remains one of *the* sites for visitors to see. It is a back-shot wheel, supplied with water from a cistern higher up the valley, and can

(above) The 'Lady Isabella', or the Great Laxey Wheel. (below) The rotary motion of the wheel was converted into horizontal oscillatory motion of a push-rod running on rollers along the viaduct to power the pumps higher up the valley

be stopped by diverting the water into a by-pass channel. Power was transmitted from the wheel to the pumps by a long, oscillating beam running on rollers atop a stone-built viaduct, at the far end of which the horizontal motion of the beam was translated into the vertical motion of the pump-rods by a rocker mechanism. The wheel has a diameter of 72.5 feet and a width of 6 feet (22 x 1.8m), and has been reputed to be the largest wheel in the world. It normally operated at 2½ revolutions per minute and could lift 250 gallons (1,140 litres) of water out of the mine workings per minute. At the time of its opening, the workings were already at a depth of 200 fathoms (1,200 feet or 365m) and would go deeper as the years passed. The wheel was built to the design of a Manxman, Robert Casement, who was assisted by a visiting expert on beam-engines (named Bowden) who spent a year on site. Various components of the wheel were made by the Mersey Iron Works, the Vauxhall Foundry in Liverpool, and Gelling's Foundry in Douglas, the latter being responsible for the massive rim. Today, the *Lady Isabella* turns simply as an exhibition piece and does no useful work.

The Laxey Mining Company was formed in 1848 (later renaming itself Great Laxey Limited) and ran the mining operation through its boom years of the next half-century. In 1854, the company was producing more zinc blende than the combined outputs of all other mines in the British Isles, and the company's £80 shares were trading at £1,200. As operations expanded, shafts were sunk along the flanks of the Agneash valley, linking up with an adit running along the line of the vein. Waterwheels were installed to provide the power, but coal-fired steam power was also being introduced. The company built the road to Agneash and established its office there. Its operations also extended along the main Laxey valley, culminating in the Snaefell mines, at the head of the valley. The main adit led to a shaft descending to 171 fathoms (1,026 feet or 313m). In 1897, this was the scene of the island's worst mining disaster, when 19 (some say 20) miners died from carbon monoxide poisoning after they entered the mine for the morning shift. The remains of the wheelcase and other buildings, as well as the spoil heaps (the 'deads'), are still there, just below the Ramsey–Douglas mountain road.

Meanwhile, in the south, the main concentration of commercial mining interests lay along the clutch of veins extending almost due east and west of Foxdale. At the western extremity lies Beckwith's mine, overlooking Glen Rushen. Then, working eastward, we have Cross's and Dixon's mines and, beyond the main St John's–Castletown road, the Upper and Lower Old Foxdales, Old Flappie, Maghie's, Louisa and the East Foxdale group which sits on the eastern end of the lode, just downstream of the Eairy dam.

Throughout their years of production, the Foxdale mines were generally more productive of lead/silver ores than those of the Laxey group, reaching a maximum lead output of 4,800 tons in 1894, from which 85,522 ounces of silver were produced. But the silver-bearing ores could be very variable in their yields: in 1875, Great Laxey produced 107,420 ounces from 2,400 tons of lead; the following year, only 57,460 ounces emerged from 2,500 tons. As noted above, Great Laxey was more prolific in zinc blende, its maximum yield being 11,753 tons in 1875.

By the start of the twentieth century, the outputs from all of the Manx mines were in decline. The last of the Foxdale mines closed in 1911. The Great Laxey operation was halted by a strike in 1919, and that company never resumed working, but the mining lease was acquired by Williamson's of Laxey (a grocery firm, among other interests) in 1922. But the resumption was short-lived and the last mine closed in 1929. Many of the redundant miners emigrated, to utilize their hard-won skills as 'hard-rock men' in the mines of the Commonwealth Dominions and the United States, where many of their descendants may be found today.

Old mine workings above Glen Rushen

Thus ended the long history of the Manx mining industry. It had seen great times in its heyday but was finally worked out and in its wake left scenes of utter despoliation wherever it had operated. The spoil heaps (the 'deads') at Laxey blighted the village for years, until they were cleared for use as hardcore in the Second World War airfield-building programme. The Foxdale 'deads' are still visible today, on the edge of the village, bordering the road that leads eastward to Douglas. The area to the east of Glen Rushen retains many visible reminders of the mining operations.

It seems worthy of note that, when the mining companies of old had need to resort to 'renewable' sources of energy (to use today's jargon), they invariably opted for water rather than wind, apparently realizing the two salient features pertinent to that choice: (a) that water is more reliable and less variable than wind, and (b) that the density of water is 800 times that of air, a very relevant factor in the fluid-dynamic generation of power. Perhaps those mine-owners of two and three centuries ago were more *au fait* with these basics than are the protagonists of wind-farms today.

SALT AND STONE

During the course of the unsuccessful drillings to locate coal in the nineteenth century, salt was discovered in the Triassic marls beneath the northern plain, about 100 fathoms (600 feet or 180m) below sea level. The Manx Salt and Alkali Company set up an extraction plant at the Point of Ayre and evaporation pans in the old Ramsey shipyard. The salt was extracted by pumping sea water down into the marl to dissolve the salt. The resulting brine was conveyed to Ramsey through an iron pipeline which was laid along the shore. Production started in about 1901 and, in the early years, output was running at around 7,000 tons a year. But the operation was always under pressure from cheaper imports; the extraction of salt by evaporation could never compete with the large-scale mining of the deposits lying beneath the Cheshire plain. The Manx operation closed down in 1956, and the old shipyard is again a shipyard. Sections of the pipeline are exposed occasionally along the shore.

In days long past, all stone for building was quarried locally; today, none is. The most abundant insular stone is, of course, the Manx slate, but its use for building was always limited by its unpredictability in splitting and cleaving while being quarried and worked. It was rarely used for roofing (Welsh slate being far superior) but was sometimes used in 'random-rubble' walling (as in the old St German's Cathedral on St Patrick's Isle), and those quarryings which fortuitously split into long 'planks' were often used as lintels, gateposts or even flooring slabs (as in Castle Rushen).

In the west, the red sandstone of Peel can be seen in the buildings in the old parts of the town and on St Patrick's Isle, where it is evident in the tenth-century Round Tower and in the gatehouse and parts of the curtain wall of the castle, to where it was ferried across from the Creg Malin quarry, on the far side of the bay. The limestone of the south was used on a much wider scale. The quarry at Scarlett (long out of use and flooded) provided stone for the building of Castle Rushen (the earliest parts of which date from the thirteenth century) and King William's College, as well as in harbour works all round the isle. To the west of Scarlett Point, the Poyllvaaish quarry, source of the so-called 'Poyllvaaish marble', is worked only occasionally to provide the odd slab for a headstone, mantelpiece or other decorative piece. Building stone is still quarried for such purposes as stone walling and the stone facing of house and other building walls.

The southern limestone is still worked in the quarries at Billown and Turkeyland, Malew, and is used mainly in the production of agricultural lime. In the early 1800s, because of the sparsity of fuel for large-scale lime-burning, the stone was taken from the quarries in blocks and shipped around the island to

*Relics of the limestone industry: (above) the flooded quarry at Scarlett; (below) in
earlier times, the foreshore ledges were quarried*

landing points closer to where the lime was required. There, if the site was an out-of-town location, the boats would approach the shore at high tide and drop their cargoes into the shallows. As the tide receded, the kiln operators would retrieve the stone and cart it away to the local kiln for burning. Two such sites were at Glen Trunk, in Michael, and Port Mooar, Maughold, where remains of the kilns may still be seen. Today, with adequate island-wide power supplies, the lime is produced at the quarry and transported in bags.

For road-building purposes in the past, the island's three main granitic exposures, at Dhoon, in Maughold, Granite Mountain, Foxdale, and at Oatlands, in Santon, have all been exploited. Nowadays, the gabbro extracted at the government-owned quarry at Poortown, in German, provides for most of the island's requirements.

TOURISM AND SEA LINKS

The development of the Isle of Man as a tourist centre has been discussed in the preceding chapter, and the subject will inevitably rise again later in this and subsequent chapters. But the growth of Manx tourism and the development of the island's shipping services are inseparable; the two have always been intrinsically linked. Without the potential for large flocks of incoming visitors, the numbers of Manx passenger vessels would never have attained the levels they did.

When the late E. H. Stenning produced the 1965 revised edition of his *Portrait of the Isle of Man* [72], he could still truthfully write: 'The main source of the Island's wealth today is the visiting industry ... The way the possibilities of reaching the Island gradually grew to supply this vast industry is worthy of consideration.' The second statement remains relevant in a historical context but, by the time I came to produce the 1975 revision of Stenning's work, the scene had changed so radically that I felt compelled to rewrite much of his chapter on *Trade and Industries*. The financial sector was already king, and tourism was then having to vie with manufacture for second place. How things had changed in one brief decade.

In the latter half of the eighteenth century, the only way for the ordinary traveller to reach the Isle of Man was to turn up at one of the ports of north-west England and make enquiries regarding any vessel about to sail with cargo for the isle. As early as 1767, the imperial government had instituted a 'regular' shipping service between Whitehaven and Douglas. This, of course, was still in the days of sail and, although 'regular' may have been the intention, 'regular' was not always apparent in the reality. The outward journey from Whitehaven was scheduled for a Monday, with the return trip on the following Thursday, but it was all dependent on the wind and the weather.

The first steamship to enter Manx waters did so in June 1815; there is some doubt as to whether she was the *Elizabeth* or the *Henry Bell* but she called in at Ramsey *en route* from the Clyde to Liverpool. The first regular steamship service to the island was opened in 1819 by the *Robert Bruce*, owned by James Little and Company, of Liverpool, operating a weekly service between Greenock and Liverpool via Portpatrick and Douglas. The following year, two additional vessels were added to the route, giving a thrice-weekly service.

In 1822, another Liverpool firm, the St George Company, began a Liverpool–Douglas service with the *St George*. She was a marked improvement on previous vessels but, as soon as she had seen off all the opposition from the Douglas route, she was switched to the company's Irish service, being replaced with the *Sophia Jane*, a much inferior little ship. This caused considerable resentment in the isle and, at a meeting of Douglas merchants, Mark Cosnahan, member of a well-known Santon family, was encouraged to undertake the construction of a steamship, the *Victoria*. He ran her for two months as a private venture, then offered her to the Douglas merchants in £50 shares. The offer was not taken up, and so Cosnahan sold her to Captain John (later Sir John) Ross for his expedition to probe the North-west Passage.

Under Ross's command, the *Victoria* seems to have undergone a slight name-change, for the ship in which he departed for the Arctic in 1829 bore the name *Victory*. Ross had intentionally sought out a steamship for his expedition, which was innovative in polar exploration at that time, but he was to regret it, recording in his journal that the large, noisy steam engine 'was not merely useless; it was a serious encumbrance since it occupied with its fuel two-thirds of our tonnage'. (The paddle wheels might also have been an encumbrance in the ice.) The engine was eventually taken out of the ship and dumped on the ice, and the *Victory* proceeded under sail alone. A suitable anchorage was found for the first winter and the ship was bedded down in the ice from which she was never to escape. After its fourth winter in the Arctic, the expedition travelled over land and ice to be picked up by a passing whaler. The *Victory/Victoria* was never seen again.

Meanwhile, in the Isle of Man at the back-end of 1829, a further meeting was held in Douglas to explore the cost of building a locally owned vessel. Subsequently, 290 shares of £25 were subscribed; thus, with capital of £7,250, the Mona's Isle Company (named after the company's first vessel) was formed, and the name was changed to the Isle of Man Steam Packet Company two years later.

The *Mona's Isle* was built on the Clyde by John Wood, with engines by Robert Napier, and was launched on 30 June 1830, with the Three Legs of Man resplendent on each paddle casing. She was 116 feet (35m) long, displaced 200 gross tons, and could make the Douglas–Liverpool crossing in eight hours at 8½ knots. Her summer schedule provided thrice-weekly sailings: Mondays, Wednesdays and Fridays to Liverpool, and Tuesdays, Thursdays and Saturdays return. In 1831, fares were 10 shillings (50p) cabin class, and 5 shillings steerage, with children under twelve half-price. Fares were later reduced to meet the competition from the St George Company, which had returned its flagship *St George* to the Douglas–Liverpool route. But fate was to take a hand with the competition.

One November evening, faced with the approach of a south-easterly gale, Captain Gill of the *Mona's Isle*, having landed his passengers and cargo in Douglas, decided to leave the port and ride out the storm at sea. (At that time, Douglas harbour lay completely exposed in that direction.) The *St George* was at anchor in the bay but, as the weather worsened, she parted her cable and was wrecked on the Conister Rock. Her crew scrambled onto the rock, exposed and surrounded by storm-driven seas. It was largely due to the organizational abilities of Sir William Hillary, a prominent Douglas resident whose house (Fort Anne, now demolished) overlooked the harbour, that the seamen were brought safely ashore. Hillary was subsequently influential in raising funds for the construction of the Tower of Refuge on the rock, so that mariners wrecked in the future could

The Tower of Refuge stands on the Conister Rock, beside Douglas harbour

seek shelter from the elements until rescuers could reach them. He also became a founder of the Royal National Lifeboat Institution.

The St George Company persevered on the Douglas–Liverpool route until July 1831 and then left the scene, leaving the field open for the Steam Packet Company. As the years passed and the growth in the holiday trade continued, the company's fleet expanded to meet the demand, and the island's resort towns expanded their accommodation, entertainment and leisure facilities to follow suit. In 1844, the Steam Packet Company operated three vessels, all of less than 500 tons; by 1899, the fleet was up to eleven ships, one of them over 2,000 tons, and in the late 1930s the company was operating fifteen vessels, the largest more than 3,000 tons. As older ships were sold or scrapped, to be replaced either by newly built vessels or second-hand purchases, a number of characteristically Manx names were reused time and again, and the practice continues to this day. Over the history of the company, twenty-eight different names have been applied to its vessels, those most frequently used being: *Ben-my-Chree* six times; *Mona's Isle, King Orry, Tynwald, Mona's Queen* and *Snaefell* five times; *Mona* four; *Douglas, Fenella* and *Peveril* three; and *Manxman, Manx Maid, Lady of Mann* and *Conister* twice.

The company's vessels went through the full range of construction and power plant, the first four being wooden paddle steamers; the change to iron construction came with the first *Ben-my-Chree* in 1845, and then to steel with the *Mona's Isle 3* in 1882. The old coal-fired steamers gave way to oil-fired steam turbines (the smoothest of all) and finally to diesel-powered vessels. Numerous routes have been served over the years but, today, they have been whittled down to four: Heysham, Liverpool, Belfast and Dublin.

After the Second World War, the two growth areas in seaborne traffic were in containerized freight and in the numbers of passengers travelling with their cars which, in earlier years, had to be loaded and unloaded by crane. The company's first purpose-built car ferry was the *Manx Maid 2*, launched in 1962. Five more have followed. The cargo carrier *Peveril 3* (launched in 1963) was returned to the builder for conversion to container traffic but the growth in demand in that sector was such that a second vessel had to be chartered; this was later purchased and renamed *Conister 2*. By 1976, the company's fleet was down to nine ships.

The Steam Packet Company entered troubled commercial waters in the late 1970s. At that time, the company possessed roll on/roll off facilities for its freight services but its four car ferries were all side-loaders. In 1978, a rival company, Manx Line, appeared on the scene and secured approval to operate a roll on/roll off freight and passenger service between Douglas and Heysham. Very soon, both companies were struggling, and it became obvious that there was insufficient custom to keep the two firms running profitably. Manx Line was the first to be bought out of trouble when it was taken over by Sealink, which itself was later acquired by Sea Containers Ltd. Sheltered under the umbrella of a much larger operator, Manx Line continued operating from Douglas and attracting business from the Steam Packet Company. Eventually, the two companies began operating a joint service to Heysham, the Manx Line vessel was sold and the Steam Packet Company ended up in the ownership of Sea Containers. In 2003, when Sea Containers itself was in difficulties, the Steam Packet Company was sold first to Montague Private Equity for £142 million and then to Macquarie Bank of Australia; it still operates under its old name, with a single conventional multi-purpose vessel, *Ben-my-Chree 6*, of 12,500 tons (by far the largest ship the company has ever owned), giving a twice-daily service to Heysham, and two fast craft on services to Liverpool, Belfast and Dublin. Since 1995, the Manx government has operated a 'sole user agreement' with the Steam Packet Company, guaranteeing the company sole use of the Douglas harbour linkspan, subject to its compliance with certain public-service requirements.

In more than 175 years of operations, the Steam Packet Company only ever lost one vessel in peacetime; this was the *Ellan Vannin* (342 tons) in 1909. At 1.13 a.m. on 3 December in that year, she departed Ramsey for Liverpool with fourteen passengers and 60 tons of cargo. In severe storm conditions, she crossed

Superseacat Two *leaves Douglas for Liverpool*

the Mersey Bar at around 6.45 a.m. and foundered shortly thereafter, taking all on board with her. The event remains a vivid folk memory among the Manx, and the story was revived by Hugh Jones, of the popular 1970s singing group, The Spinners, in his moving rendition of *The Ellan Vannin Tragedy*, which is still heard from time to time. Understandably, the name *Ellan Vannin* has never been reused on any of the company's later vessels.

It has to be said that modern ferry crossings of the Irish Sea are not always what they were even thirty years ago. I still recall a winter's crossing in the late 1970s. Having departed Heysham promptly at 2.15 p.m. and made the crossing in a rising Force 10 storm from the south-east, the ferry (Manx Line's *Manx Viking*, if memory serves) was refused permission to approach Douglas because of the dangerous conditions. The night was spent cruising off the island's east coast, waiting for the storm to subside, as sounds of smashing crockery accompanied each plunge of the bow into a trough and each climb out on the other side. At daybreak, with little sign of abatement, the decision was made to sail round the Calf to Peel, where the vessel berthed more than ten hours after leaving Heysham. But that was not the end of it: the passengers could disembark but they could not take their vehicles with them, for Peel has no roll-off facility. No ferry would sail

Fishing and commercial shipping in Ramsey harbour

in such conditions today; the modern health-and-safety culture and the dreaded risk assessment have put paid to such adventures.

Two smaller shipping companies remain active in the freight business, both based in Ramsey. The Ramsey Steamship Company, formed in 1913, carries bulk cargoes such as grain, cement, fertilizers and coal to the island from various UK ports, and in recent years was still providing a coastal service between the island's harbours. (It was this firm which delivered our coffee table from Ramsey to Douglas in 1973.) Mezeron Ltd, a more recent arrival, brings general cargoes into Ramsey in containerized and palletized units on regular sailings from Belfast and Glasson Dock, at the mouth of the River Lune, all of which serves to maintain the port of Ramsey as a hive of activity in the freight-moving scene.

AIR LINKS

The first heavier-than-air craft to operate from Manx soil belonged to the celebrated aviation pioneer, Claude Grahame-White, who, in July 1911, flew demonstration flights from Douglas to commemorate the coronation of King George V. Pleasure flights and irregular passenger and freight services followed, using the Douglas foreshore and the original, undeveloped airfield at Ronaldsway as landing grounds. These activities continued into the 1930s and, in 1935, the so-called 'Hall Caine Airport', named after the Manx novelist and located at Closelake, 3 miles west of Ramsey, also came into use, and services were operated from there to Manchester and Glasgow. This northern airfield remained in use for less than four years, possibly because of its inconvenient distance from Douglas.

By this time, Tynwald had consistently declined to develop the Ronaldsway site as a national airport, and so it was left to its private operator, Captain Gordon Olley, to carry out improvements, levelling the field, extending the runway and building a hangar, workshops and booking office. By the approach of the Second World War, Olley's Isle of Man Air Services were flying routes from Ronaldsway to Manchester, Liverpool, Blackpool, Carlisle, Glasgow and Belfast. The development of the airfield during the war and its subsequent purchase by the insular government have been described in the previous chapter.

The Isle of Man Airports Board (a board of Tynwald) was established in 1948 to operate the airport as a commercial venture, although it was soon apparent that it would require an annual subsidy. Post-war services were flown by British European Airways (BEA, later merging with BOAC to become British Airways (BA)) and such bygone names as Cambrian Airways, Dan-Air, Derby Aviation and

Silver City Airways. The types of aircraft arriving followed developments else-where, from the piston-engined Douglas DC3, through the ubiquitous Vickers *Viscount* turbo-prop to the BAC111 turbo-jet. A new terminal building was completed in 1953 to handle the increasing traffic.

The aforementioned Derby Aviation eventually became British Midland Airways and, in 1982, an offshoot of British Midland became Manx Airlines, an island-based company better able to respond to island needs. The company continued to serve the island for almost two decades; when it was eventually sold to British Airways, and services continued under the BA label, those who had complained of Manx Airlines' performance began to wonder what they had been complaining about. But things did get better – for a time. BA oper-ated a restricted pattern of routes, to Gatwick, Luton, Manchester and Glasgow, before withdrawing altogether. Other, smaller companies flew serv-ices to Belfast, Birmingham, Bristol, Dublin, Jersey, Liverpool, London City, Newcastle and Southampton, the most commonly seen aircraft being the British Aerospace ATP (advanced turbo-prop), the BAe146 (4-jet) and the Boeing 737 (twin-jet).

There followed something of a scramble by smaller airlines to fill the void left by Manx's demise and BA's subsequent departure. In contrast with its policy on sea ferries, the Manx government adheres to an 'open-skies policy' with regard to airlines, not wishing to restrict the competition. The initial rush in the early 2000s resulted in some airlines beating an early retreat from some routes when it was realized that the levels of available custom were insufficient to sustain all of the companies trying to service them (shades of the Steam Packet/Manx Line situa-tion). But the growth in air travel in recent years, especially by island residents and business folk, should ensure that at least two (and probably more) airlines will remain in the longer term.

In addition to the scheduled airline services, there are a number of firms established at Ronaldsway specializing in air-taxi and charter operations. The airport is now under the control of the Department of Transport. The terminal building has been further extended in recent years, and the establishment of the adjoining freeport in 1989 has provided a duty-free zone where commodi-ties may be imported, processed and exported, and are not subject to value-added tax or customs duties until they are withdrawn to enter the intended market. In the case of goods imported and processed within the freeport and then exported elsewhere, taxes and duties are not payable in Man at all. This is an attractive feature for certain types of business; one of the earliest occupants of premises on the Ronaldsway freeport was the diamond firm De Beers, the product being industrial diamonds which are exported all over the world.

INSULAR TRANSPORT: ROAD AND RAIL

As noted in the previous chapter, Manx roads were relatively late in being brought up to acceptable standards, in modern terms, firstly because the wheel was comparatively late in discovering the Isle of Man (or vice versa), and secondly because of the ready availability of coastal shipping services between the Manx ports. The greatest improvement in the condition of the Manx roads was seen in the interval between the two world wars, when funding for road improvements took the largest slice from the Manx exchequer (this was in the days before the National Health Service). Responsibility for the island's roads was spread between the then Highway and Transport Board and six local authorities (the four towns, Port Erin and Port St Mary), with Government meeting most of the costs. Thus, in fiscal effect, Government had the responsibility, and an Act of 1981 enabled the formal transfer of that responsibility to the board island-wide.

But, more than a century earlier, the poor state of the island's roads had given the railways a head start in the insular transport stakes. The Isle of Man Railway (IMR) was formed in 1870, with the intention of linking Douglas with Peel, Port Erin and Ramsey. Shortage of funds caused the abandonment of the Ramsey project. The line to Peel was opened in 1873, and that to Port Erin a year later, at the same time bringing Castletown and Port St Mary into rail contact with the capital. Both lines were laid to a narrow gauge of 3 feet (915mm). Some wealthy British investors had been involved in the formation of the IMR, including the Duke of Sutherland, and it was he who opened the line to Peel in 1873. The steam locomotives were built by Beyer Peacock, of Gorton, Manchester; all had four coupled driving wheels with a 2-4-0 wheel arrangement, and No. 1, which hauled the inaugural train, was named *Sutherland*. In later years, after a period in storage, *Sutherland* was restored to traffic in time to haul the 125th anniversary train in 1998. Several of the other original locomotives remain in traffic.

Ramsey was left isolated from the Manx rail network until a group of northern investors formed the Manx Northern Railway Company (the MNR) to construct a line from Ramsey, via Sulby, Ballaugh and Kirk Michael, to connect with the IMR system at St John's. Laid to the same 3-foot gauge, the line was opened in 1879 and, with the two companies collaborating, the northern undertaking was able to operate a through service between Douglas and Ramsey (albeit of 26 miles) without passengers having to change trains at St John's.

The extension of the railway system thus far opened the way for places other than Douglas to develop and reap the rewards of the holiday trade. In the south, Port Erin grasped the opportunity enthusiastically, Port St Mary to a markedly lesser extent, and Castletown hardly at all. In the west, Peel soon had a string of

The Queen's Pier, Ramsey, strides out towards England

hotels and boarding-houses springing up along the new promenade at the east end of town. And in the north, similar developments began on Ramsey's Mooragh, a strip of coastal wasteland to the north of the harbour mouth, although construction of the promenade itself did not begin until 1886. The northern town was to receive a further boost to its holiday trade in that year, with the completion of the Queen's Pier, a quarter of a mile south of the harbour. Striding out almost half a mile into the sea, the iron pier provided (for the first time at Ramsey) the facility for steamers to berth and discharge their passengers at all states of the tide. The population of the town almost doubled in the thirty years to 1891. The last passenger-landing on the Queen's Pier was in 1970 and, eventually being deemed unsafe, the government-owned structure was closed to the public in 1991.

An additional branch of the island's steam railway system was the line from St John's to Foxdale, opened in 1886 by the Foxdale Railway Company, which had an operating agreement with MNR. It must have seemed like a good idea at the time: the Foxdale mines were turning out prodigious quantities of ore to be shipped out, and needed imported coal to power their pumps; the MNR would have freight to carry in both directions between their Ramsey terminal and Foxdale. But, towards the end of the century, the Foxdale mines were in competition with cheaper sources of ore elsewhere. As the demand for the Foxdale ores declined, so did the need for coal. The Foxdale branch became a continual drain on the MNR's finances.

A further source of financial embarrassment arose in 1898, with the arrival in Ramsey of a more direct form of competition, in the form of the Manx Electric Railway (MER). This line had been built in stages from the company's terminus at Derby Castle, at the northern end of Douglas promenade; first the 2½ miles to Groudle Glen in 1893, then to Laxey in 1894, and later on to Ramsey. Having reached Laxey, the branch line of the Snaefell Mountain Railway was constructed in 1895, reaching its summit station 1,990 feet (606m) above sea level, just 46 feet (14m) below the island's highest point. Whereas the low-level MER line was laid to the 'standard' Manx gauge of 3 feet, the Snaefell branch was designed to a gauge of 3ft 6in (1,067mm), the extra width accommodating a central rail for emergency friction braking. The Snaefell branch was always intended to be for summer operation only, and so it remains today.

The MER was always going to have the upper hand over the Manx Northern; its new electrical technology would yield propulsive power that would keep a train moving on gradients which would bring a steam locomotive to a stand, and its 17-mile route to Ramsey contrasted starkly with the MNR's 26 miles. In 1903, the

A tram of the Snaefell Mountain Railway stands at Laxey station

MNR made a plea to Tynwald for financial assistance, which was refused, where-upon agreement was reached between the two steam railway companies for the IMR to take over the whole of the Northern's system, thereby bringing all of the island's steam-hauled operations under one management.

As the years progressed, both of the remaining systems began to feel the effects of competition from the emerging bus services. The IMR responded by introducing bus services of its own. The Foxdale branch line was closed early in the Second World War and never reopened. From the early post-war years onward, there were repeated threats of closure to one or both of the rail systems. A principal disadvantage of the MER was always its lack of a central terminus in Douglas, despite the fact that Douglas Corporation's horse-drawn tramway, opened in 1876 and employing the same gauge, is just yards away from the MER terminus and traverses the full length of the promenade to the sea terminal. But the connection and extension of the electrification were never made.

In 1956, a committee of Tynwald recommended the complete closure of the MER. Instead, Tynwald resolved to nationalize the system and keep it in operation as a tourist amenity. A new board of Tynwald was created to control it. Nonetheless, the Laxey–Ramsey section was recommended for closure in 1966, and again in 1973. In 1975, Tynwald approved the closure of the northern section; within two years, it was open again. And so it went on.

The future of the steam railway in those years seemed no brighter. Early in 1965, the Isle of Man Railway Company announced that its network, which had been closed for the winter, would not reopen, as it had proved uneconomic to operate. Two years later, the Marquis of Ailsa and a group of fellow enthusiasts were granted a 21-year lease to operate the system as a summer tourist attraction. The network opened for the summer of 1967, when services were run over all three routes, but the St John's–Ramsey line did not reopen for the 1968 season, and would never open again. In 1972, the Marquis made known his intention to surrender the lease, and Tynwald responded by offering a subsidy to maintain operations over the Port Erin line. The Peel and Ramsey lines remained closed and the tracks were put up for sale as scrap. The last of the track was lifted in 1976; even the horizontals of the viaducts over Glen Mooar and Glen Wyllin were taken down, leaving their stone piers pointing aimlessly to the sky.

The Port Erin line was finally bought by the Manx government from the Isle of Man Railway Company in 1978 and vested it in the existing MER Board of Tynwald. Both lines now operate as tourist attractions, the steam railway in the summer season only, and the MER maintaining a year-round service to Ramsey but with a reduced service through the winter months. Both operations are now vested in the DTL.

It was in the 1920s that the railways began to experience the emergence of competition from modes of transport using the ever-improving roads. Initially, the railways would face the challenge of the bus operators; later, both would suffer from the increased numbers of motor cars. Douglas Corporation began operating buses in 1914, concentrating on services within the town and the westward route to Peel. In 1927, an English bus company, based in Cumberland, established a subsidiary Manx operation under the name Manxland Bus Services. That was when the IMR responded by setting up its own bus operation. The subsequent competition for passengers resulted in an early example of the Steam Packet/Manx Line syndrome which was to follow fifty years later: there were insufficient passengers to go round. Eventually, the IMR bought out the opposition to form Isle of Man Road Services, through which it sought to provide an integrated railway/road-bus system.

Almost fifty years later, the influence of the motor car was being powerfully felt. Both Douglas Corporation and Road Services were receiving government subsidies in order to keep their bus operations running. In 1976, Tynwald accepted the principle that there should be a single publicly owned bus undertaking, and that it should be formed by the purchase and amalgamation of the two existing undertakings. Thus was born Isle of Man National Transport (now Isle of Man Transport), managed today, like the railways, under the auspices of the DTL.

As in so many other parts of the British Isles, bus services in many rural areas of Man are remarkably sparsely used, and yet any suggestion that a particular service should be reduced is met with vociferous opposition. Accepting that fact, there has for years been a body of opinion which believes that, if near-empty buses are to be driven around the island's roads, it is preferable to drive a near-empty small bus, rather than a near-empty large one, but, although this innovation has been in use for years in parts of rural Scotland (for example), it has not yet found favour in Man.

Throughout the years of bus operations in the island, from the mid-1920s onwards, a number of independent coach operators have existed side-by-side with the larger scheduled service undertakings, principally to transport holiday-makers to the island's resorts and tourist attractions, but also to cater for local parties wishing to be conveyed to events or functions. Such carriers still operate but their numbers are very much smaller than was once the case.

PUBLIC-SERVICE UNDERTAKINGS

WATER SUPPLY in the Isle of Man began as a fragmented patchwork of district undertakings, the development of which has been touched upon in Chapters 2

and 6. Legislation passed by Tynwald in the nineteenth century enabled the regulation of water companies in six districts, these being the four towns, the village
of Port Erin, and the parish of Rushen. Later legislation enabled the local authorities to purchase and operate these undertakings as public utilities. By the end of
that century, Douglas Corporation was operating a public water utility, whilst Port
Erin and Rushen were being served by a joint undertaking of the Village
Commissioners and the Rushen Water Company. In the other towns, private
companies operated but they were later absorbed into regional boards.

The difficulties in the rural parishes were harder to resolve. The districts were
small, as were their populations, and co-operation between boards of commissioners not always readily achieved. Their rate-borne revenues were limited and
most parish boards were reluctant to impose significant rate increases on their
parishioners, no matter how noble the cause. In his annual report to the Local
Government Board in 1907, the Board's inspector lamented the lack of action on
the part of parish authorities and stated that 'the majority of the Boards of Parish
Commissioners are inert and, in some cases, dead'. The situation concerning the
parish and village of Michael, described in the preceding chapter, well illustrates
his point. It was not until 1936 that the Northern Water Board was formed,
covering the parishes of Ballaugh, Jurby, Andreas, Bride and Lezayre, which were
without public supplies at that time. To overcome a similar problem in the south,
Tynwald established the Southern Water Board in 1939, buying out the existing
undertakings in Castletown, Port Erin, Port St Mary, Malew and Rushen, and
incorporating the parish of Arbory.

Following the Second World War, a further step in the consolidation of water
supplies was taken in 1946, when Tynwald agreed the formation of the Isle of Man
Water Board, to be responsible for all public water supplies outside Douglas.
Thus, the new board would absorb the undertakings of the Northern and
Southern Boards, and of local authorities other than Douglas Corporation, as well
as buying out the private undertakings then operating in Ramsey and Peel. The
final stage in the consolidation process came with the passing of the *Water Act
1972*, under which the Isle of Man Water Authority became responsible for the
public utility throughout the isle, thereby bringing to an end Douglas
Corporation's independent operation after a run of eighty-two years. Also in 1972,
the Isle of Man Gas Authority was formed and, two years later, the two authorities were combined to become the Isle of Man Water and Gas Authority. Finally,
in 1983, for reasons to be explained later in this chapter, Tynwald agreed the
privatization of its gas undertaking and the Authority reverted to its former name.

During the lifetime of the Water Authority, its largest and most prestigious
infrastructure project has been the construction of the Sulby dam and its associated works. Seventy years after the completion of Douglas Corporation's dam in

the West Baldwin valley, the balance between the demand for water and the available supply was beginning to look precarious, particularly after the drought of
1976. Subsequent events have confirmed the Authority's astuteness in proceeding
with the Sulby project after being accused of profligacy with public funds at the
time. The dam was completed in 1984. It rises 200 feet (60m) above the valley floor
and impounds a surface area of 54.4 acres (22ha) when full. The 'associated works'
include a pumping station at the foot of the dam, from which a rising main
conveys water up to the broad ridge on the west side of Beinn-y-Phott, from
whence it is piped under gravity down to West Baldwin at times when that reservoir needs replenishing.

Lower down in Sulby Glen, on the southern edge of Sulby village, a new water
treatment station was completed in 2005. It supplies treated water to the whole of
the 'old' Northside (i.e. north of the highland ridge) plus the parish of Maughold
and the northern part of Lonan. A similar but larger treatment plant in Douglas,
replacing the old, obsolescent works, was completed in 2008. The two plants
together serve the whole of lowland Man.

The Water Authority is funded mainly (93.4 per cent in 2005) by rate-borne
revenue, the remainder coming from the proceeds of a government bond. In
order to pay for infrastructure improvements (mainly the treatment works and
replacement mains), the Authority instituted a fifteen-year sequence of annual
rate increases, beginning in 1999: these being 15 per cent for the first three years,
10 per cent for the next seven, followed by annual increases of 8, 7, 6, 5 and 4 per
cent. Thus, compounded over the fifteen years, the water rate ends up almost four
times (actually 3.96) what it was at the beginning. The plan was none too popular
when it was announced but it went ahead anyway. The Water Authority became
a statutory board of Tynwald in 1988; although government-owned, it is virtually
free to operate as a commercial enterprise.

SEWERAGE developments in the Isle of Man followed broadly the same
sequence, and over the same period as the provision of public water supplies. The
various Town Acts and related legislation ensured that, by 1919, sewerage
systems in the four towns, Port Erin and Port St Mary were complete. Once again,
there was little progress in the rural parishes until a new board of Tynwald, the
Local Government Board (LGB), was formed under an Act of 1894. The LGB
became, to a large extent, the public health authority for the whole island. In more
recent times, it has been transformed into the DLGE, and responsibility for mains
drainage has been transferred to the DoT.

Up to the end of the twentieth century, sewage from all of the island's towns
and villages was being discharged, untreated, into the sea. There were also
twenty-five small-scale treatment works at inland sites. Through the 1980s,
concerns were being expressed that sea water on the island's beaches was not

meeting EU standards on bathing-water quality. In 1991, Tynwald adopted the principle of an all-island sewage-treatment plant, with sewage from local collection stations being conveyed to it through pumped mains. The scheme was given the name IRIS (Integration and Recycling of the Island's Sewage), the 'recycling' element being the intended use of the waste, when processed into pellet form, as a fertilizer. Part of the concept of the IRIS strategy was to enable the small maintenance force employed at that time to concentrate their efforts on one modern plant instead of the numerous old works.

At the time of writing, Douglas, Onchan and the south of the island are connected to the treatment works at Meary Veg, in Santon, although commissioning defects are still to be resolved. Apart from Onchan, the whole of the island north of the central valley still awaits connection to the system, and there remains a body of opinion which suggests that it might have been less costly to build – and certainly to operate – perhaps three or four smaller regional treatment plants as an alternative to pumping sewage all across the island.

GAS supplies in the Isle of Man evolved along analogous lines to those which first supplied the water. The Tynwald legislation of the nineteenth century, which enabled the town authorities to regulate the operations of water companies, permitted similar controls over private gas undertakings. There were initially five companies, serving Douglas from 1836, Castletown, Peel and Ramsey in 1857, and Port St Mary in 1898, all producing coal gas.

By the 1960s, some of these companies were facing financial difficulty and on the point of ceasing operation. In order to ensure continuity of supplies throughout the island, Tynwald, between 1965 and 1967, agreed to purchase the three undertakings serving Peel, Port Erin and Port St Mary, and Castletown. From that point on, the island's needs for gas were met by two distinctly different commercial sectors, Peel and the south now being served by a publicly owned, subsidized undertaking, with the rest of the isle still served by private companies. The state undertaking was initially controlled by a committee of Tynwald, then by the newly formed Isle of Man Gas Authority from 1972, and later still by the combined Water and Gas Authority from 1974.

In 1983, the Calor Gas company, which had already acquired the business of the former Ramsey Gas Company, approached the Isle of Man government with a proposal to purchase the publicly owned gas undertakings. Faced with the opportunity to off-load the loss-making enterprise to a well-established company, the decision by Tynwald to sell was uncontentious. By that stage, the gas undertakings in Man no longer involved the production of gas in the island; it was now imported by coastal tanker in the form of liquid petroleum gas (LPG). The availability of bottled gas then facilitated the extension of gas services into rural areas where mains services had never existed. The expanded Calor undertaking traded under the name of Calor Manx Gas until it became a subsidiary of a Channel Islands company under the name Manx Gas, which now serves the whole island.

Natural gas arrived in the island in 2003 as a result of the construction of the latest power station at Pulrose, in Douglas. Gas from this source is sold to Manx Gas, which has converted the appliances of its consumers in the Douglas/Onchan area, Union Mills and Glen Vine. The remainder of the island remains on LPG. Once the Government had sold its gas undertaking, the Water and Gas Authority reverted to the Water Authority, the last reference to a gas authority vanished, and control of the privatized undertaking was left to self-regulation within the industry.

POWER GENERATION must rate as one of the oldest service industries, alongside smithing, milling, haulage and other ancient service trades. In its earliest forms, power outputs from generating systems were mechanical rather than electrical, the principles of which would remain unknown for centuries, of course. The earliest examples of power generation are seen to have been specifically for the mechanical milling of grain, and the power generated was, of necessity, for specific local use, in the absence of any means of power distribution. Where a thermal output was required, as in the smithy or lime kiln, then it was generated by the burning of peat or imported coal.

Windmills were never numerous in the Isle of Man. Restricted by useless calms at one end of the spectrum and damaging gales at the other, the range of conditions in between would have been – as now – erratic and unreliable. There are a few truncated towers still to be seen in various parts of the isle, the best-known being the so-called 'Witches Mill' in Castletown. Other 'stumps', some incorporated into adjoining dwellings, exist near Ballacoraige (on the western edge of the Ballaugh Curragh), at Jurby East, Ballawhane in Andreas, Baldromma in Maughold and at the Beaconsfield Towers residential home in Ramsey. The only hint of the mill which once stood in the centre of Kirk Michael village is given by the name of the terrace of 'Windmill Cottages'.

Watermills were far more numerous all around the island. The earliest complete manorial roll, covering the years 1511–15, lists thirty on which rents were being paid, and their number would increase in later times. There is evidence that the Norse side-shot mill, in which the wheel and top stone rotated in a horizontal plane, was in use in Man in the sixteenth century, and probably later. The mills ranged in size from the small installation associated with an individual farm, and used to power such operations as the threshing and grinding of corn, to the much larger town mill, which worked as more of an industrial operation. Later on, as we have seen, watermills would be used to provide power in the mines. Garrad et al [1] give a comprehensive survey of such operations.

The first electricity-generating station in Man was completed in 1893 by the Isle of Man Tramways and Electric Power Company, the company which was

Beaconsfield Towers residential home, Ramsey, displays the stump of the old corn mill

initially responsible for the Manx Electric Railway. The station was oil-fired and was built specifically to provide an electrical supply for the MER. As the line was extended northward, additional generating stations were built at Laxey, Snaefell, and Ballaglas in Maughold. In addition to energizing the railway, electricity was supplied to premises located sufficiently close to the line. Unlike the modern mains supply of 240 volts AC, the company's output was at 500 volts DC.

The first electricity-generating station in the island built solely to provide a public supply was completed by Douglas Corporation in 1923. It was located in a building on North Quay, employing diesel-driven generators, and producing an output (seeming minute to us today) of 615 kilowatts. Six years later, a second station was built at Pulrose, at the south-west corner of the town. This was a coal-fired station, using fuel imported through the nearby harbour, and eventually supplied consumers not only of Douglas Corporation, but also of the Isle of Man Electricity Board, which was formed under an enabling Act of 1832 to supply consumers in the remainder of the isle, even though it then possessed no power station of its own. The Pulrose plant was extended in 1948, and this enabled the old North Quay generators to be decommissioned.

The Isle of Man board became a fully fledged electricity undertaking (instead of merely retailing a supply from Douglas Corporation) with the completion of its power station at Peel in 1950, followed by a subsidiary station at Ramsey. The ready availability of relatively inexpensive oil at that time led to both stations being diesel-powered. In 1954, the two boards reached agreement on power trading at times of peak demand and, over subsequent years, the question of a merger was repeatedly mooted. The principal difficulty lay in the disparate geographical natures of the two areas being served: the Douglas undertaking served a compact, densely concentrated community, whereas the Isle of Man board catered for a population which was spread across the rest of the island, and its distribution costs were therefore much higher.

However, by 1984, agreement had been reached and the Manx Electricity Authority (MEA) was in being. As with the Water Authority, the MEA became a government-owned undertaking; the Government being the ultimate financial guarantor, but the Authority would be virtually free to operate as a commercial undertaking. In 1990, the Pulrose D generating station was completed on the Douglas site; Pulrose B (from 1966) and C (1972) were still running, and the Ramsey station (1960, extended 1982) was being used in a stand-by capacity.

The 1990s were a decade of activity and planning for the MEA. An approach by Scottish Power plc to purchase the Authority and install an undersea inter-connector cable was referred by the Manx government to independent consultants, who recommended acceptance of the offer. But that was a step too far for Government. An earlier proposal for the island to have its own undersea cable had been rejected on the grounds of cost and the principle that the island should retain direct control of its own electricity supplies. A new 38-megawatt generating station was opened at Peel in 1995, bringing the total effective capacity of the MEA's installed plant to 95 megawatts, all of it diesel-powered apart from the one megawatt of the Sulby hydro-electric station.

But the island's demand for electricity was growing beyond all estimates. In 1991, the total load on the generating system amounted to 56 megawatts, and was forecast to reach 82 megawatts by 2014. In fact, that figure was reached in 2002, and it had already become obvious that more capacity would be needed. The dreaded undersea inter-connector cable between Douglas Head and Bispham, near Blackpool, a co-operative venture between the MEA and National Grid plc, became a reality in 2000. This would not only enable the importation of 'top-up' supplies at times of peak insular demand, but also benefit the MEA's trading position by allowing the Authority to export power at times when trading prices were high and import when they were low.

In 2001, Tynwald approved the MEA's proposal to bring natural gas to the island via a connection to the Scotland–Ireland pipeline belonging to Bord Gas Eireann, the gas being used to fuel a new power station at Pulrose and to provide

Pulrose power station, Douglas

a mains supply to consumers via the Manx Gas network. The new station, Pulrose D, was built on the site of the old A, B and C stations and rated at 75 megawatts. The station became operational in 2003. Through the 1990s, the MEA produced impressive results in terms of cost savings and forward planning, and consumers appreciated successive reductions in tariff. But trouble was in store.

The MEA's initial entry into the natural gas operation was funded by a £185 million Treasury loan, approved by Tynwald in July 2001. In 2004, it became known to the Government that the MEA, in the name of a subsidiary company, had taken out two bank loans, totalling £120 million, without Tynwald's approval. Part of the increased capital was used to buy out National Grid's share in the undersea cable. Differences arose between the MEA's board and government circles over the legality of the additional loans; it is a complicated question and one which has never been resolved. Relations between the two sides became so strained that the MEA board resigned *en masse* in 2005, whereupon the Government assembled a replacement board, chaired by a member of the Keys.

There can be no doubt that the earlier board of the MEA fulfilled its prime statutory requirement of providing the island with a generating system capable of meeting forecast demands for electricity into the foreseeable future. The system allows a balance to be struck between two fuels (gas and oil), depending on future price fluctuations, together with a third source via the undersea cable. At the time of the cable's installation, the Authority had also installed a fibre-optic cable as a provision for future upgrading of the island's telecommunications. One cannot help wondering whether the previous board had a better plan in mind for dealing with its borrowings than the replacement board, hastily cobbled together by the Government, which promptly cast £50 million of public money into the pot to repay one of the loans, the legality of which had still not been established. After initially resolving to test the legality of the dealings through the courts, concerns over the cost of doing so led the Government to abandon the proposed action; hence the lack of resolution of the question.

WASTE DISPOSAL methods in the Isle of Man have been a subject of intense debate and contention over the past thirty years. For many more years past, the adopted strategy had been one of disposal to landfill sites, these most recently being the worked-out sand and gravel pits in the vicinity of the Point of Ayre. By the late 1970s, however, a realization was dawning that the island was running short of holes in the ground and that some other method of waste disposal must be found.

In 1979, Tynwald voted in favour of incineration but little of substance followed. In 1982, Tynwald confirmed this policy but, only two years later, turned towards medium-density baling. In 1988, we came full circle, back to incineration. After that came a full review of all possible methods of dealing with waste, fuelled by concerns over the cost of incineration and the rising volume of objection from the environmental lobby, which repeatedly pointed out that incinerators elsewhere (the obsolescent ones) were being decommissioned, but never relating that others (modern ones) were being built. Following the review, Tynwald confirmed its policy on incineration in 1990, and did so again in 1994, but by this time the proposed plant had ceased to be an incinerator and had become an 'energy-from-waste plant'. The change in terminology

The island's refuse incinerator (incorporating energy recovery) at Richmond Hill, south of Douglas

could be seen as a vain attempt to appease the environmentalists, but it also recognized that the design would incorporate waste-heat recovery to generate an electrical output which would be 'exported' to the MEA. A site at Richmond Hill, in Braddan, was approved by Tynwald in 1998, and a sum slightly in excess of £43.5 million was voted through two years later. The incinerator was operational in 2004, twenty-five years after Tynwald's first vote in favour, and in the nine months to the end of that year, 15,821 megawatt-hours of electricity were sold to the MEA. Although the solid residue from the incineration process still goes to landfill, the quantity of such material is greatly reduced.

In addition to the 'mainstream' of waste disposal to the incinerator, residents are able to deposit appropriate types of waste materials at a number of 'civic amenity sites' throughout the isle, where the materials are sorted according to their suitability for recycling, reuse or composting, any remaining being directed to the incinerator or to landfill.

POST AND TELECOMMUNICATIONS

An insular post office (albeit under the control of the Imperial government) was established in 1767. A packet vessel was chartered to provide a weekly service transporting mail between Whitehaven and Douglas. In 1822, the service was transferred from the Cumberland port to Liverpool and, eleven years later, the contract was awarded to the Isle of Man Steam Packet Company to provide a twice-weekly service. Residents had to collect their mail from their town's post office until 1842, when postmen were employed.

The Isle of Man's postal service did not become separated from that of the United Kingdom until a surprisingly late date – 1973. In 1966, when the UK government was in process of transforming its Post Office into a public corporation, the Isle of Man was offered the opportunity of taking over its own postal and telecommunications, the two being offered as a single undertaking. Tynwald refused the offer; whilst recognizing the undoubted potential of controlling the insular postal service – both in relation to the financial advantage and with regard to the associated publicity – telecommunications at that time were in the early stages of tremendous technological advance which continues to this day. Tynwald's consensus, therefore, was that insular responsibility for the telecommunications sector would place an intolerable burden on the public finances.

The UK government left the door open by way of its *Post Office Act 1969*, which enabled the islands of Man, Jersey and Guernsey to assume responsibility for their postal and telecommunications systems at some future date if they so wished. By this time, the Manx government was having second thoughts – but only in relation to the postal service. After prolonged negotiations, the UK authorities agreed to treat the two services separately. On 5 July 1973 (Tynwald Day), the Isle of Man Postal Authority came into being, at a cost to the Manx exchequer of £148,624; the Authority's surplus at the end of its first year was more than enough to pay it off. Since then, the Authority's activities have brought in revenues by way of postal charges, and its philatelic bureau has maintained interest in, and publicity for, the island world-wide through its long succession of stamp issues.

The first electrical communications link between the Isle of Man and England was made in 1864, by way of the undersea telegraph cable between St Bee's, in Cumberland, and Port Cornaa, Maughold, but external telephone communication would come much later. The first insular telephone service was operated under licence from an exchange in Athol Street, Douglas, by one George Gilmore, from 1889. He later sold out to the National Telephone Company, which was later absorbed into the UK Post Office, and it was under the Post Office that the first telephone call was made between Douglas and Liverpool in 1929. Later still, when the UK's postal and telecommunications undertakings were divided, the latter became British Telecom (BT).

Until 1984, telecommunications services in the Isle of Man were still provided by BT, a publicly owned undertaking regulated by UK legislation. By this time, negotiations had been ongoing between the Manx and UK authorities concerning the possible transfer of control of the island's service to Tynwald. However, in 1984, BT was privatized and, at a stroke, Tynwald was relieved of having to consider further the thorny question of whether or not to take over the running of the island's telecommunications undertaking; the incumbent operator was now a private company, Manx Telecom, a Manx-based, wholly owned subsidiary of BT. Under the provisions of the *Telecommunications Act 1984*, Tynwald became the regulatory and licensing authority for the island's telecommunications services, and its first task was to decide who was to provide the service. In 1985, the Manx government invited tenders for the licence, to run for a period of twenty years. The result was a keenly fought competition between Manx Telecom and Cable and Wireless plc; the decision went in favour of the incumbent.

Manx Telecom had already embarked on a major programme of renewal and upgrading of its systems and, following the granting of the licence, this continued. Old copper cables were replaced with fibre-optics, and all exchanges were upgraded from analogue to digital technology. A new satellite communications station was built at Port-e-Chee, on the western outskirts of Douglas, and a new undersea cable laid between Groudle and Millom, in Cumbria. In the meantime, Manx Telecom had ceased to be a subsidiary of BT and now operates under the umbrella of the communications company O_2.

In addition to all of this, thanks to the foresight of the much-maligned former board of the MEA, we still have the Authority's undersea fibre-optic connector which, at the time of writing, is about to be brought into use. All of these developments, enabling ever-greater quantities of data to be processed at ever-increasing speeds and transmitted to virtually anywhere on Earth, offer great benefits in terms of time and cost to business users, and have been among the prime factors in attracting a wide spectrum of commercial enterprise to the island. Continued development in this field is essential if the island is to maintain its position as a stable and dependable centre for commerce in an age when commercial players are acting on an increasingly global stage.

MANUFACTURE

Historically, the prospects for manufacturing activity in the Isle of Man were always constrained by the island's restricted range of natural resources, these being limited to agricultural produce, fish and wool, from which stemmed the principal activities of the brewing of ale from grain and the manufacture of cloth and clothing from wool. The manufacture of rope and nets was a thriving activity in former times, using imported hemp, as was the making of sailcloth. The last of the rope yards (Quiggin's of Douglas) closed in the late 1950s. The immediate post-war years were, in general, a period of recession, exemplified by the decline in the holiday trade and high levels of winter unemployment. This was a time when manufacturing activity elsewhere was reorganizing to achieve the benefits of large-scale production, placing any smaller undertakings in the island (and elsewhere) at a competitive disadvantage.

The Government attempted to address the problems of the Manx economy by increasing support for the farming and fishing industries, but soon realized that policies were needed to attract new industries to the island, rather than propping up the old ones. In 1949, the *Development of Industry Act* empowered the Governor to provide grants to those wishing to establish or develop suitable industries. An early success came in 1951, with the arrival of the Ronaldsway Aircraft Company in a purpose-built factory opposite the airport terminal building. This was the first of a new type of island-based industry, one which imported all of its raw materials and component parts, and exported the whole of its output of aircraft ejection seats. For the first time, a company's management had recognized the Isle of Man as an attractive place in which to base its activities, even though the island offered no market whatever for the company's products. In return, the company's presence for more than half a century has been a great boon to the island: with well over 500 workers, it remains the island's largest private employer.

Other companies followed, some of which have faded from view, while others have been longer-lasting. A shoe-manufacturing company was set up on the Ronaldsway site in the early 1960s and thrived for forty years before finally succumbing to the hard economic realities of Far-Eastern competition. The Dowty company, assembling aircraft components, was established in Onchan in 1965 and became the island's third-largest employer, now trading as Smith's Aerospace. By the end of 1970, winter unemployment was lower than it had been throughout the previous decade. Indeed, there came a time when the thriving engineering sector seemed in danger of running short of labour, but the Government's New Residents Policy was successful in keeping things moving. New companies continued to arrive, and new jobs continued to be filled. By 1975, manufacturing accounted for 15.6 per cent of the island's national income; by contrast, in the financial year 1972–3, the Treasury's estimate of tourism's total contribution had already fallen to 14 per cent (having been nearer 50 per cent in 1967–8).

In more recent years, the Manx government has maintained its programme of incentives for new arrivals in the manufacturing sector. Official policy has been to concentrate new manufacturing undertakings in industrial and trading estates established for the purpose, these being in and adjacent to Douglas at the Hill's Meadow, White Hoe, Spring Valley and Snugborough trading estates, at the northern airfield site at Jurby, and in the south at the Balthane (Ballasalla) and Ronaldsway industrial estates. A newer development is the Isle of Man Business Park, close by the Spring Valley estate.

The manufacturing sector's proportion of the national income actually declined through the 1990s and has been static at around 7 per cent during the 2000s, although its actual income product, at more than £108 million in 2003–4, was greater than it had ever been. (Tourism's share was 5 per cent in that year.) In fact, all sectors of the Manx economy – even tourism and (in most years) agriculture and fishing – have shown increases in absolute income during that period, contributing to a marked and sustained increase in the island's total income, year on year. Thus a concentration on percentages alone does not tell the whole story.

CONSTRUCTION

The primary activity of the Manx construction industry in the years following the end of the Second World War was concentrated on housing. The unsatisfactory condition of much of the island's housing stock had been evident before the war, but the intrusion of six years of war had precluded much in the way of works to correct the situation.

The post-war need for house-building and improvement works was evenly spread over both the public and the private sectors. The formation of the several public housing authorities at that time, with the LGB having overall responsibility, has been covered in the previous chapter. In 1946, the LGB obtained Tynwald's approval for a wide-ranging programme to tackle the housing problem, after the newly elected Labour government in Britain had intimated that it would not be averse to a higher level of Tynwald funding than had at first been planned.

The LGB's programme included a scheme for new public-sector housing, financial incentives for private-sector building, and a scheme for the temporary housing of those without satisfactory accommodation. For the latter purpose, Tynwald approved the Government's plan to purchase the wartime camps left by the armed services at Castletown, Ballasalla, Glen Maye and Andreas, and adapt their hutted accommodation to form temporary housing units. The programme provided a total of 329 family units; by 1958, twenty-two were still occupied.

Up to the end of the financial year 1958–9, more than 2,000 new public-sector houses had been built and existing housing stock improved, including more than sixty flats built by Douglas Corporation prior to the First World War. In the same period, 1,484 private-sector houses were built, 41 per cent of the total. The post-war government initiatives were, of course, a boon to the Manx construction industry, whose component firms ranged in size from jobbing builders to medium-sized companies developing housing estates. The Isle of Man would never see – indeed, could never expect to see – the Manx equivalent of a Wimpey or a Barratt; the place was just too small.

By 1959, it appeared that the island's needs for new and improved housing had been met. Then there arose the aspirations of those still living in pre-war accommodation who wished for – and, with government assistance, could afford – something better. Housing for the elderly was also recognized as a new requirement. On top of this, the Government's newly introduced New Residents Policy added further to the demand for housing, and so the market took off once more. In the twenty years to the end of 1981, more than 9,000 new houses were built, almost a quarter of them in the public sector.

By this time, the mortgage industry in the UK had been deregulated, and things were changed for ever. When I obtained a mortgage to buy my first house in the 1960s, the borrowing was limited to 2½ times my salary, and my wife's earnings were ignored. In a very short time, wives' earnings were being included and the factor had increased to four or even five times their combined salaries. When that sort of money is injected into *any* market, prices invariably rise, and it is practically impossible to return them to their former levels. Hence we have arrived at the problems confronting first-time buyers in recent years, in the Isle of Man as elsewhere. The Manx government has raised a number of schemes to assist first-timers into home ownership, but the problem persists.

The thrust of private-sector house-building continued through the 1990s but, inevitably with the rise and consolidation of the business sector, a need arose for the construction of commercial and other larger-scale projects. The majority of office developments took place in and around Douglas, in many cases replacing or improving buildings which had taken on a rather down-at-heel appearance. In addition, a series of prestigious government projects maintained the activity: the power stations at Peel and Douglas, the replacement Noble's Hospital in Braddan, the refuse incinerator at Richmond Hill, the IRIS all-island sewerage scheme, and the construction of a new prison at the Jurby airfield site, replacing the old Victorian institution in Douglas. Naturally, such large-scale projects were beyond the scope of insular construction firms, and the contracts were awarded to off-island companies, but with some Manx firms participating as subcontractors.

THE FINANCIAL SECTOR

The financial sector of the island's economy comprises banking, insurance and a wide range of other commercial business activities. When Stenning produced the second edition of his *Portrait of the Isle of Man* in 1965, he made no mention of a financial sector, and yet ten years later it was the largest single contributor to the isle's economy. Its origins and early development have been described in the previous chapter.

The history of banking in the Isle of Man goes back to the very early years of the nineteenth century. In those days, such banks as existed provided services almost exclusively for island residents and Manx companies, and that remained substantially true into the 1960s. At the beginning of the nineteenth century, the island seems to have been awash with promissory notes and counterfeit Bank of England notes, to such an extent as to cast doubts on the legitimacy of genuine currency. The first legitimate Manx notes were issued by the bank of Taubman, Quayle and Kelly, in Castletown, which traded between 1802 and 1817. In the latter year, Tynwald passed an Act prohibiting all notes under the value of £1 and requiring all banks issuing notes to be in possession of a licence from the Lieutenant Governor, for which the fee was £20. Also, the bankers' real and personal estates were to act as surety against redemption of the notes. One of the first banks to be licensed was that of the brothers John, Henry and James Holmes, which had opened for business in 1815. It continued trading until 1853, when it closed with debts of almost £100,000. Among the depositors facing ruin was Sir William Hillary, who had to part with his mansion at Fort Anne and live out the rest of his life in much-reduced circumstances.

In 1840, Tynwald decided to bring Manx coinage into line with that of Great Britain by adopting the formula of 12 pence to the shilling, instead of the previous 14. In a further Act of 1865, the principle of limited liability was recognized. In 1851, the Bank of Mona, a subsidiary of the Bank of Glasgow, became established in the four towns. Two years later, following the closure of the Holmeses' bank, the Douglas and Isle of Man Bank was founded by George Dumbell, a prominent businessman, attorney and member of the House of Keys. Despite its official name, the bank was known throughout its life, and long after its demise, as Dumbell's Bank. It started life as a private bank but became a public company in 1874. In 1878, the Bank of Mona and its parent bank in Scotland failed, amid charges of theft and fraud. The Mona's imposing building on Prospect Hill, Douglas, was later to become Government Office.

The Bank of Mona's collapse left Dumbell's Bank facing its main rival, the Isle of Man Banking Company Ltd, founded in 1865 and numbering the island's great benefactor, Henry Bloom Noble, among its founders. Dumbell's Bank fared well under the sound and businesslike stewardship of George Dumbell but, following his death in 1887, things were never the same; due to inept management and outright fraud (for which some were later gaoled), the bank closed for business on 3 February 1900 – 'Black Saturday'. Many of the bank's depositors faced ruin, and a number of Manx companies collapsed with the bank. Its failure came as a deep shock to the whole island, which now faced the end of the nineteenth century with an air of doom and gloom. (The collapse of Dumbell's Bank remains an oft-recalled event in the folk-memory of the isle.) But the island as a whole recovered as it headed into the boom years of its holiday trade, and Dumbell's main rival was a survivor: the Isle of Man Banking Company is now the Isle of Man Bank, listed as No. 1 in the Isle of Man Companies Register, and still in business alongside numerous others.

As noted earlier, the Isle of Man government's initiative in reducing the rate of income tax in 1961 was intended to attract new residents and new industry to the isle, rather than set it up as a tax haven for wealthy individuals and non-residents. It was the 1972 decision of the UK government to scale down the sterling area to encompass only the UK, the Isle of Man, the Channel Islands and the Republic of Ireland (plus Gibraltar a year later) which accentuated the potential of British islands as tax havens by removing many of their erstwhile competitors from the field. Some wealthy individuals moved into the isle and – more importantly – new industries followed. The development of the construction industry encouraged an increase in the number of engineering consultancies, and the expansion of all manner of commercial activities was accompanied by a proliferation of firms providing accountancy services. Many of the UK's well-known accountancy firms and consulting engineers became established in the island, and the number of law practices also increased. Today, those professional and scientific services together provide 16 per cent of the national income.

Back in the early years of the growth of modern Manx banking (the 1960s), a number of companies that purported to be banks were registered in the island. Some of them offered no services to insular interests; others appeared not to trade at all, and it was realized that stronger regulation was needed in order to protect the island's reputation as a developing commercial centre. The *Banking Act 1975* was an attempt to provide adequate control over banking operations, enabling the licensing and inspection of banks, and exerting control over the use of the word 'bank'. Those banks already established in the island, which included most of the large British institutions, were not overly enthusiastic at the prospect of external regulation, being of the view that reputable banks were quite capable of regulating themselves. Perhaps *reputable* banks were, but a regulatory system, to be effective, had to be capable of dealing with (or preferably preventing) the emergence of the other sort. Events in the early 1980s were to prove the validity of that thesis, and illustrate the shortcomings of the controls then in place.

The abolition in 1979 of the island's Usury Act – a largely ineffective means of maintaining Manx interest rates at artificially low levels – abruptly increased the island's attractiveness as a financial centre, and set in train a sequence of deposit growth which has continued to this day. In the year immediately prior to the Act's abolition, total deposits (sterling and non-sterling) in the Isle of Man stood at £352 million. By the end of 1980, they had more than doubled to £743 million and, after the first ten years from abolition, had reached £4,629 million. By the end of 2004, the figure was £30,700 million. But, back in the 1970s and 1980s, the new deposits were not only being placed with the large established institutions, but also with a number of smaller private banks which the Manx government had initially been reluctant to license, but which it had done under pressure from local interests.

In June 1982, the Manx-based Savings and Investment Bank (SIB) collapsed with debts of £42 million. The resulting publicity was a serious blow to the island's reputation as a financial centre, and raised questions over the concept of 'offshore' banking. The Government's response was prompt: the Isle of Man Financial Supervision Commission (FSC) was established by Order in January 1983 and formalized by the *Financial Supervision Commission Act* of the following year. This reflected the Government's determination to prevent any repeat of the SIB affair by strengthening regulatory powers over banks, building societies and other deposit-takers, and for the prevention of financial crime. Establishment of the Isle of Man Insurance Authority followed, later to become the Insurance and

Pensions Authority (IPA), to regulate the activities of insurance and life companies operating in the island. Despite the shock of the SIB's collapse, it appeared to have no discernible effect on the inward flow of deposits.

In subsequent years, the Isle of Man's operations as a financial centre (together with those of the other Crown dependencies) were put under the microscope from three different quarters in succession. The first, in 1998, was at the behest of the UK's Home Secretary, Jack Straw, who initiated a review of financial regulation in the Crown dependencies, to be undertaken by a retired Home Office official, Andrew Edwards. One suspects that he was expected to uncover a financial cess-pit of corruption and crime, but that he departed surprised, if not actually disappointed. In his report, Edwards concluded that the three islands (Man, Jersey and Guernsey) were 'clearly in the top division of offshore financial centres'. Any criticisms he raised of the Manx system were responded to positively by the Manx government, intent on maintaining the island's reputation as a centre of the highest probity. Edwards had confirmed, in very specific terms, that the island's regulatory standards already complied with those of the international community, especially of the European Union, and it was a member of various international groupings of nations concerned with standards and the prevention of money-laundering, tax-evasion and other financial crime.

But Edwards's commendation was not sufficient for the EU or for the Organisation for Economic Co-operation and Development (OECD), both of which, in 2000, directed their threatening glares in the island's direction, referring to its 'harmful tax practices'. (Simplistically, for 'harmful', read 'low', but there is far more to it than that, although it is beyond the scope of this book to go into detail. Anyone wanting to know more should consult David Kermode's work [41].) In defending the island's status, the Manx government was able to fall back on Edwards's findings but also recognized the need for some degree of compromise if the isle's reputation were not to be needlessly damaged. The compromises were offered on the proviso that all other member states of the OECD operated to the same standards; i.e. the smaller jurisdictions were not to be regulated more harshly than the larger ones. The combination of robust defence and well-judged compromise appeared to serve the purpose; in 2001 the Government was informed by the OECD that the Isle of Man would not be named in a list of 'unco-operative tax havens' to be published later that year. Since then, the island has gone quietly about the various facets of its business. Its economy continues to grow at a very satisfactory rate and, in the financial sphere, it retains its AAA credit rating and has no national debt.

The latest tax initiative by the Manx government to attract more business to the island has been the introduction of reduced rates of corporate income tax: as from April 2006, approximately fifty registered banks and those companies receiving income from land or property in the Isle of Man are charged a flat 10 per cent rate of corporate tax on earnings, whilst all other companies are zero-rated. There is facility in the legislation for a 'cap' to be set on a company's liability to the 10 per cent rate and, although at the time of writing the level of the cap has not been finalized, the Government's Income Tax Division has stated that the 'corporate tax cap would likely be at a level of £6 million or higher'. Thus, assuming £6 million to be the figure, a company's chargeable profits beyond £60 million would not be liable to tax.

This initiative appeared to cause some consternation in the two competing financial centres in the Channel Islands, and doubters in the Isle of Man – recognizing that a large number of companies would be relieved of tax liability altogether – questioned how the shortfall in revenue would be met. The proffered reply was that more business activity would result in more workers paying more income and value-added taxes, but time alone will tell.

MISCELLANEOUS SPHERES

There are a number of other strings to the Isle of Man's bow which contribute to its economic growth; I mention just two of them here. The first is the Isle of Man Marine Administration and its shipping register. The Manx government has possessed regulatory powers over merchant ships using Manx ports and plying Manx territorial waters since the late 1970s, when, after discussions with the UK government, a whole raft of legislation was passed by Tynwald, covering such matters as the surveying of passenger ships, the detention of unsafe vessels, conditions of employment, and wrecks and salvage. The long-term aim was to develop the island as a centre of excellence in the regulation of shipping – and not only within Manx territorial waters.

The Isle of Man's ship register today covers merchant shipping operating world-wide. The Manx register is an integral part of the British register, and a Manx-registered vessel is a British vessel and flies the red ensign. Nevertheless, the Manx administration operates independently of the British and is able to apply the same standards of regulation, or higher (but not lower) than those of the British administration. This foundation has enabled the Manx register to assemble a fleet of 384 merchant vessels and charter yachts (as at 31 January 2005), totalling more than 7.5 million gross tonnes. The Manx register is divided into four sections: the main merchant vessel register, a small-ships register, a fishing vessels register and a charter register. The administration provides a 24-hour service to deal with matters arising across the various time-zones of the world, and employs a team of professionally qualified marine surveyors to undertake the initial and subsequent inspections in accordance with international regulations. In 1996, the Manx register was listed in the top rank of flag states, alongside the UK, France and Finland, by the Paris Memorandum of Port State Control, which grades the performance of flag states whose ships have been inspected in European ports. The Manx government now operates an aircraft registry in parallel with the ship register.

In a totally different sphere, the Isle of Man Film Commission was set up in 1995 to attract the makers of feature films and television productions to the island. The Commission operates within the Department of Trade and Industry, which can provide 25 per cent of a film's budget in the form of equity investment, which means that 25 per cent of any profit made by the film is reclaimed by the DTI. To qualify for financial support, the film company must spend at least 50 per cent of its total shooting days in the island and spend at least 20 per cent of its budget (excluding the fees of actors, writers, director and producer) in the island.

Since its formation, the Commission has co-financed more than fifty feature films and a dozen television productions, each production company spending, on average, around £500,000 in the island. The films have included such well-known titles as *Waking Ned, The Libertine* and *Stormbreaker*, and have brought such stars as Johnny Depp, Madonna, her then husband and film director Guy Ritchie, Helena Bonham Carter, Ewan McGregor and Bill Nighy to Manx shores. One well-known Douglas restaurateur takes great delight in relating how, such being the popularity of his establishment, he had to turn Johnny Depp and party away one evening when they turned up without booking in advance. The only aspect of the filming activity which causes discontent in some quarters is the seemingly inordinate number of road closures in various parts of the island while filming takes place. On the outskirts of Ramsey, privately owned studios provide facilities where companies may film indoor scenes requiring the use of purpose-built sets.

CONTROL OF EMPLOYMENT

As the Manx economy has continued to grow over the years, and immigration has kept pace in order to satisfy the expanding labour market, fears have been expressed that immigrant labour might take jobs that could have been filled by Manx job-seekers. The original *Employment Act* of 1954 provided protection for resident male workers. The present situation is controlled by the *Control of Employment Act 1975*, as later amended, which is administered by the Work Permits Committee of the DTI. The 1975 Act extended the protection to resident female workers, and now requires any person who is not an Isle of Man worker to obtain a work permit before taking up employment or self-employment in the island. An Isle of Man worker is a person who was born in the island, or has been resident in the island for not less than ten consecutive years, or satisfies one of several other criteria. There are certain exemptions, including the Chief Constable and other members of the Isle of Man Constabulary, Crown appointments made by the UK government, ministers of religion, doctors and dentists, and certain temporary employments subject to specified time limits.

Any employer wishing to engage a person who is not an Isle of Man worker must have advertised the position in the island and must show that there was no response from an Isle of Man worker capable of filling the post. There have been cases in recent years in which the Government's own attempts to fill senior positions have fallen foul of the system, and where appointments (such as those of Chief Fire Officer and Director of Education) have been awarded to external candidates subject, in each case, to the receipt of a work permit. In each case, the Work Permits Committee refused the application on the grounds that one of the other applicants was an Isle of Man worker who was capable of filling the post. One presumes that, in each of these cases, the interviewing panel chose the candidate who was adjudged to be the best able to fill the vacancy, which raises the question: in making appointments at such senior levels, should the panel not be free to select the *best* candidate, rather than one who is merely *adequate*? If the Chief Constable is exempt, why not other chief officers?

THE MEDIA

In the Isle of Man, 'the media' comprise just two elements: the newspapers and radio broadcasting, the island's size and population not being adequate to support its own television station. Television items of Manx news sometimes find their way into BBC North-West bulletins or those of the ITV Granada region.

The first newspaper to appear in the Isle of Man was the *Manks Mercury*, whose inaugural issue was published on 27 November 1792; it was succeeded nine years later by the *Manks Advertiser*. Both were written by English journalists and printed in English, at a time when relatively few Manx people spoke English. The newspaper publishers' clientele was thus restricted to the small numbers of 'stranger-residents' and the elite few among the Manx who did 'have the English'. Consequently, there was much touting for government support, in the form of public notices and advertising, in order to supplement the limited sales revenues.

Reporting techniques during those early years were often quite aggressive and confrontational and, by 1817, Tynwald felt compelled to pass legislation rendering false and libellous reporting a criminal offence. The *Manks Advertiser* waded into the war of words between the Manx and the stranger-residents, and later supported the unpopular fourth Duke of Atholl, whilst the *Rising Sun* (later becoming the *Manx Sun*) lined up with the self-elected Keys against the Duke. Later still, the *Sun* continued to support the Keys against the reformers, such as Samuel Norris and his ilk. Around 1850, most of the newspaper barons of Man became either insolvent or dispirited and departed the isle. Two who persevered were James Brown, of the *Isle of Man Times*, and Robert Fargher, of the *Mona's Herald*. Both campaigned in favour of public elections to the House of Keys, and we have touched on their confrontation with the Keys in Chapter 6.

Through much of the nineteenth century, newspaper production in Man entailed a laborious sequence of manual processes, the Manx press being slow to adapt to mechanization. The first press capable of printing a newspaper in one pass was installed by the *Isle of Man Times* in 1892, and was later used to launch the island's first all-year daily, the *Daily Times*. (There had been previous attempts at summer-season dailies.) Although the *Times* was the first to introduce mechanized typesetting, by the early 1930s its photographic blocks were still being produced in Blackpool, and it lost much of its circulation to the *Isle of Man Examiner*, which was the first to set up its own photographic department in 1934. To make matters worse for the *Times*, its daily edition, which had enjoyed a distinct time advantage as long as the UK papers arrived by sea, lost that advantage when they began to be flown in during the 1930s.

The *Examiner* continued to thrive at the expense of the *Times*, which was bought into the same ownership in 1958. The daily edition of the *Times* ceased publication in 1966. Further competition arose in 1972, with the appearance of the *Ramsey Courier*, later to become the *Isle of Man Courier*, which was in the same ownership as the old-established *Mona's Herald*. When I arrived in the Isle of Man at the start of 1973, there were no fewer than five weekly Manx newspapers still in production: the *Mona's Herald*, the *Weekly Times*, the *Examiner*, the *Courier* and the *Manx Star*. Through the late 1970s and early 1980s, Hill Street (the old Douglas equivalent of London's Fleet Street) was having its own share of industrial disputes over new technology. Old hacks of that time could be heard complaining that they were suffering from the 'Hill Street blues'. (You have to be of a certain age to recall the American television series.) As a result, the *Mona's Herald* met its demise in 1975, to be followed later by the *Star* and the *Examiner/Times* group. Staff from the latter group banded together to launch the *Manx Independent*. The owner of the *Courier*, which became a free-sheet in 1982, acquired the assets of the *Examiner* group and relaunched that title in the same year, later acquiring the *Independent* also.

Thus we come to the present situation, in which three weekly newspapers survive: the *Isle of Man Examiner*, the *Manx Independent* and the *Isle of Man Courier*. All three are operated by a Manx-registered company, Isle of Man Newspapers Ltd, but owned by an English parent-company. Consequently, as far as Manx news coverage is concerned, the only competition to the island's sole newspaper proprietor is that provided by radio.

RADIO BROADCASTING

Radio broadcasting first reached the Isle of Man in 1922, in the form of transmissions from the BBC in Manchester. Radio receivers were soon being marketed in the island, and some were even being assembled by early Manx-based entrepreneurs. By the mid-1930s, some Manx thoughts were already turning towards the prospect of a Manx commercial station which, by transmitting into the UK and beyond into Europe, could be used to advertise the island as a holiday resort. But successive UK governments maintained an implacable opposition to the very concept of commercial broadcasting and, furthermore, were adamant that such aspirations transcended the range of matters on which the island was empowered to legislate for itself. Broadcasting beyond the bounds of the Isle of Man was a subject for the UK's determination and did not accord with its obligations as a member of the International Telecommunications Union (ITU).

The scene for confrontation was set in 1962, when the *Wireless Telegraphy (Isle of Man) Bill* of that year (a Bill passed by a Tynwald only too well aware that it was unlikely to receive the Royal Assent) was indeed refused the Royal Assent. The Bill would have enabled the island to establish a radio station capable of broadcasting well beyond Manx shores. On the British side, the Bill was probably viewed as a futile gesture of protest (which undoubtedly it was); on the Manx side, its rejection only heightened Tynwald's ambition to achieve a greater degree of self-determination.

However, only two years later, the UK government had at least overcome its aversion to commercial radio and agreed that the island could set up its own station, provided that its transmissions did not reach the United Kingdom. Tynwald accepted the licence from the UK's Postmaster-General, viewing it as a starting point, and granted the concession to a private operator. And so Manx Radio was born, operating initially from a caravan and using a low-powered transmitter; the operation began by covering the TT races from 7 June 1964.

Less than one month later, on 5 July (Tynwald Day again), the high-powered transmissions of the pirate station, Radio Caroline North, began blasting out from a ship anchored off Ramsey Bay, just outside the 3-mile limit, in direct contravention of ITU regulations. Because of the Manx ambitions for their own high-powered station, there were Manx sympathies for Radio Caroline. But, early the following year, the UK Home Office sought the Manx government's co-operation in legislating against pirate radio stations, and with the request came a warning that, if Tynwald did not process its own legislation in the matter, then Parliament would legislate for it. The scene was set for the most serious constitutional confrontation between the Isle of Man and the United Kingdom in modern times.

Although a Manx Bill was prepared for passage through the legislature, the Keys were not prepared to pass it until they received assurances that Manx Radio would be granted increased transmitting power. Such assurances were not forthcoming, and so, on 7 March 1967, the Bill was overwhelmingly rejected in the House of Keys. On 1 September, the UK's *Marine etc Broadcasting (Offences) Act 1967* was extended to the Isle of Man, an action which effectively cut off the pirate radio ships from all their sources of supply. On 19 March 1968, a chartered Dutch tug arrived in Ramsey Bay and Radio Caroline was ignominiously towed away later that day.

Shortly after the imposition of UK legislation on the island, a joint standing committee was formed to deal with matters of common interest between the two jurisdictions. The committee continued to meet for several years and, although it did nothing to further the transmitting power of Manx Radio, it did appear to bring about an improvement in mutual understanding. But the Manx Radio affair had brought about a firmly expressed resolve on the part of Tynwald that the island should seek a greater degree of independence from the UK.

Manx Radio was nationalized by Tynwald in January 1968 and has remained in public ownership ever since. Its restricted transmitting power had limited its listener base and hence its commercial viability. The main component of its income today is still from advertising as a commercial station, but it has always been recognized that it would need an annual subsidy in order to maintain the element of public-service broadcasting. Manx Radio's transmissions from its modern premises on Douglas Head are received in the nearer reaches of the adjacent isles, and today, of course, the contents of its news and other programmes can be downloaded world-wide via the internet. In recent years, licences have been granted to two additional Manx-based broadcasters; both operate primarily as commercial music stations and receive no government subsidy.

Manx aspirations for greater self-determination in the field of communications have materialized over the years. The regulation of broadcasting and telecommunications in the isle today is in the hands of the Isle of Man Communications Commission, which was formed in 1985 as the Telecommunications Commission and took on its present name when it also became the broadcasting regulator in 1989. The Isle of Man government's published guide to its departments and statutory boards (of which the Commission is one) describes the Commission's main role in relation to broadcasting as: 'To ensure the provision and maintenance of a broadcasting service as a means of information, education and entertainment and to further the interests of the Isle of Man in the whole field of radio and television' and to 'keep under review the reception in the Island of programme services provided from places within the Island *and elsewhere* [my italics], and the quality and content of those services'.

It is clear from this that the Commission has a duty to review services provided by external broadcasters, such as the BBC and ITV. But it has no regulatory powers over them and can only pass comment. There has been resentment for some years on the part of Manx payers of the BBC's licence fee, particularly in those parts of the island where the only regional programmes receivable from that broadcaster are from the North-East region (i.e. from Newcastle) or Ulster, despite the fact that the North-West region (centred on Manchester) is closer and is the channel carrying news and other programmes of Manx interest. The Commission has been aware of the situation for several years – as has the BBC.

CHAPTER EIGHT

Sport and Recreation

W hen those without first-hand knowledge or experience of the Isle of Man hear the island's name mentioned in association with the word 'sport', minds will almost invariably turn to thoughts of motor-cycle racing. The association between the two has become so deeply ingrained over so many years that occasional successes by Manx sports men and women in other spheres, even when resulting in world championship or Commonwealth Games successes, make little *lasting* impression outside the isle when it is that noise-making other sport which grabs a large slice of the public's attention, year on year. And so, in setting out on this survey of the island's sporting scene, I suppose that we should begin with the obvious one.

MOTOR SPORT

The Tourist Trophy races began as a competition for cars, rather than motor cycles. The initiative for the first meeting, held in 1904, came from the Royal Automobile Club of Great Britain (the RAC), which wanted to hold trials to select the British team to compete in the following year's Gordon Bennett race, to be held in France. James Gordon Bennett had arrived in Paris in 1887 to establish a European edition of his father's *New York Herald* and went on to sponsor a variety of events in motor-boat racing and ballooning, as well as in motor racing – and it was he who sent Stanley to Africa in search of Livingstone.

The inaugural Gordon Bennett race was run in 1900 from Paris to Lyons. The early races were marred by crashes and organizational failures. The 1903 race was run over a road course at Ballyshannon, in Ireland, after the Imperial government had refused to allow the closure of public roads in mainland Britain; hence the RAC's approach to the Isle of Man government in 1904, and the subsequent special sitting of Tynwald which gave its approval, with the encouragement of the

Governor, Lord Raglan (one of his more liberal and helpful initiatives, possibly influenced by his own interest in motor sport).

The course chosen for the 1904 trial took in most of the island and amounted to something over 50 miles, heading south from Douglas to Castletown, then north via Foxdale and Ballacraine to Kirk Michael, and onward through Ballaugh, Ballamoar and St Jude's to Ramsey, thence returning southward to Douglas via the mountain road. Five laps of the course had to be completed within a strict time limit, and many of the island's roads at that time were not even surfaced. Early film of those events, and of the early motor-cycle races, shows the mountain road in particular to be little more than an unmade cart-track.

In 1905, the trial became a race, which was run in September. Morning practices were allowed, commencing at 4 a.m., and the race was reduced to four laps, totalling 209 miles. There were fourteen starters, and the winner was J. P. Napier in an 18hp Arrol Johnston at an average speed of 33.8 mph. Ironically, it was in this same year that the Gordon Bennett race – the event which had prompted the RAC to come to the Isle of Man only a year earlier – was run for the last time. Amid much inter-nation bickering over the rules, James Gordon Bennett lost heart in the event and departed to follow his other interests. But the RAC Tourist Trophy races continued in the Isle of Man for a time.

For the 1906 race, a shorter course was chosen. Running from Douglas to Peel, then via Kirk Michael to Ramsey and the mountain road to Douglas, this one measured just over 40 miles, giving a total distance of 161 miles for the four-lap race. It was won by the Hon. Charles Rolls at an average speed of 39.29 mph.

In 1909, the course was shortened; by leaving the old course at Ballacraine and heading direct to Kirk Michael, the distance became the now-familiar 37¾ miles, and this has been known as 'the TT course' ever since. This was the year which also saw changes in the regulations, restricting engine power to a maximum of 25.6hp, the number of cylinders to not less than four, and specifying a minimum tare weight of 1,600 pounds (725kg). These changes prompted great efforts in designing motor vehicles for enhanced performance. Those were the days when such competitions really did bring about marked improvements in automotive design.

After 1909, the Tourist Trophy was not raced again until 1914, after which the First World War intervened. After the war, there followed a further gap until 1922, when the race was revived again and was run for the last time in the Isle of Man. The RAC Tourist Trophy was revived for a third time in 1928, when it was run over the Ards circuit, in Northern Ireland, and, after the Second World War, it survived in Northern Ireland into the 1950s, when most of the classic road races for cars were succumbing to the rising death-toll from crashes.

ISLE OF MAN NEWSPAPERS

*Vintage Rolls-Royces gather for the centenary of the Hon. Charles Rolls's victory
in the 1906 Tourist Trophy*

Back in 1907, the Auto-Cycle Union (the RAC's counterpart for motor cycling)
had approached the Manx government and received Tynwald's approval for a
motor-cycle race to be run that year. The chosen course was much shorter than
that used for the cars, starting from St John's and running east to Ballacraine
before turning north to Kirk Michael, then south to Peel and returning to St
John's, giving a circuit of approximately 16 miles. The inaugural race was won by
C. R. Collier, on a Matchless, at an average speed of 38.23 mph, and the speeds
would steadily increase from there. In 1908, it was J. Marshall on a Triumph at
40.49 mph, then H. A. Collier on a Matchless at 49 mph in 1909, and C. R. Collier
again on a Matchless at 56.63 mph in 1910. In 1911, the event was switched to the
TT mountain course, as used for the car races, and has remained there ever since.
As the years passed, the other famous names in British motor-cycle manufacture
would appear in the island: AJS, BSA and Norton; all would be prominent at the
annual TT meeting until the Germans and Italians, and then the Japanese, muscled
in on the act. And famous names also lined up as riders: Stanley Woods (still
revered today from the inter-war period), Geoff Duke, John Surtees, Mike
Hailwood, the Italian Giacomo Agostini and the Ulsterman Joey Dunlop.

By the time the motor-cycle TT had reached its half-century, the week-long
meeting had settled into a pattern of races for five classes of machine: the Senior
(for machines up to 500cc engine capacity), Junior (up to 350cc), Lightweight (up

to 250cc), Ultra-lightweight (up to 125cc) and a class for side-car combinations. The fiftieth anniversary event was also the occasion on which the circuit was first lapped at over 100 mph. The Ultra-lightweight class has since disappeared, and the largest machines now have double the engine capacity of the largest quoted above. Apart from the Senior and side-car classes, the other categories are now identified by 'modern' names: the TT Superbike, the TT Superstock and the Supersport Junior TT. The Senior race is always held on the final day (Friday) of race-week and is one of the island's 'extra' public holidays (the other being Tynwald Day). At the centenary meeting in 2007, the Lancashire rider, John McGuinness, became the first to take the official lap record beyond 130 mph, with a lap time of 17 minutes 21.99 seconds (130.35 mph).

The roads making up the TT course are closed for practice sessions during the week prior to race week. Thus, the actual period allowed for the meeting is the TT fortnight of late May/early June. For many years, practising for the races was apportioned over a number of early-morning, evening and Thursday afternoon sessions. The morning sessions commenced at 5 a.m. but these have been discontinued in recent years and those time allocations reapportioned to other sessions.

By 1923, the TT races had become so well established and popular among the motor-cycling fraternity that a group of island enthusiasts formed the Manx Motor Cycle Club and submitted a proposal for an additional race meeting on the TT course, intended for amateur riders. The task of defining an amateur became so intractable, however, that that part of the idea was dropped, but the event was intended to provide opportunities for those enthusiasts who had never ridden for a manufacturer's team to tackle the intricacies of the course before – perhaps – graduating to the TT itself. Thus was born the Manx Grand Prix (known simply as 'the Manx' or the MGP) and it was an immediate success. Enthusiastic club riders came from all over the British Isles, the Commonwealth and elsewhere, and were made welcome by fellow-enthusiasts in the isle. The event continues to run each September, on similar lines to the TT but without a side-car class.

The circuit begins in Glencrutchery Road, Douglas, where the start/finish line straddles the road between the grandstand on the east side and the scoreboard on the west. The original grandstand was built in 1926 by Douglas Corporation for £2,000. The first mile of the circuit descends steeply down Bray Hill to Quarterbridge, where a sharp right-angled turn takes the rider west, out of the capital, along the Peel Road. There follow 7 miles of undulating, sometimes twisting, sometimes straight road leading to the crossroads at Ballacraine, where a second right turn takes the rider north, through the twists and turns and steep little climb of the section through Laurel Bank, Glen Helen and Creg Willy's Hill (originally *Creg Willy Syl*, or Willy Syl[vester]'s Crag), and up onto the high, undulating Cronk-y-Voddy straight. After the Cronk-y-Voddy crossroads, where the

TT action at Windy Corner

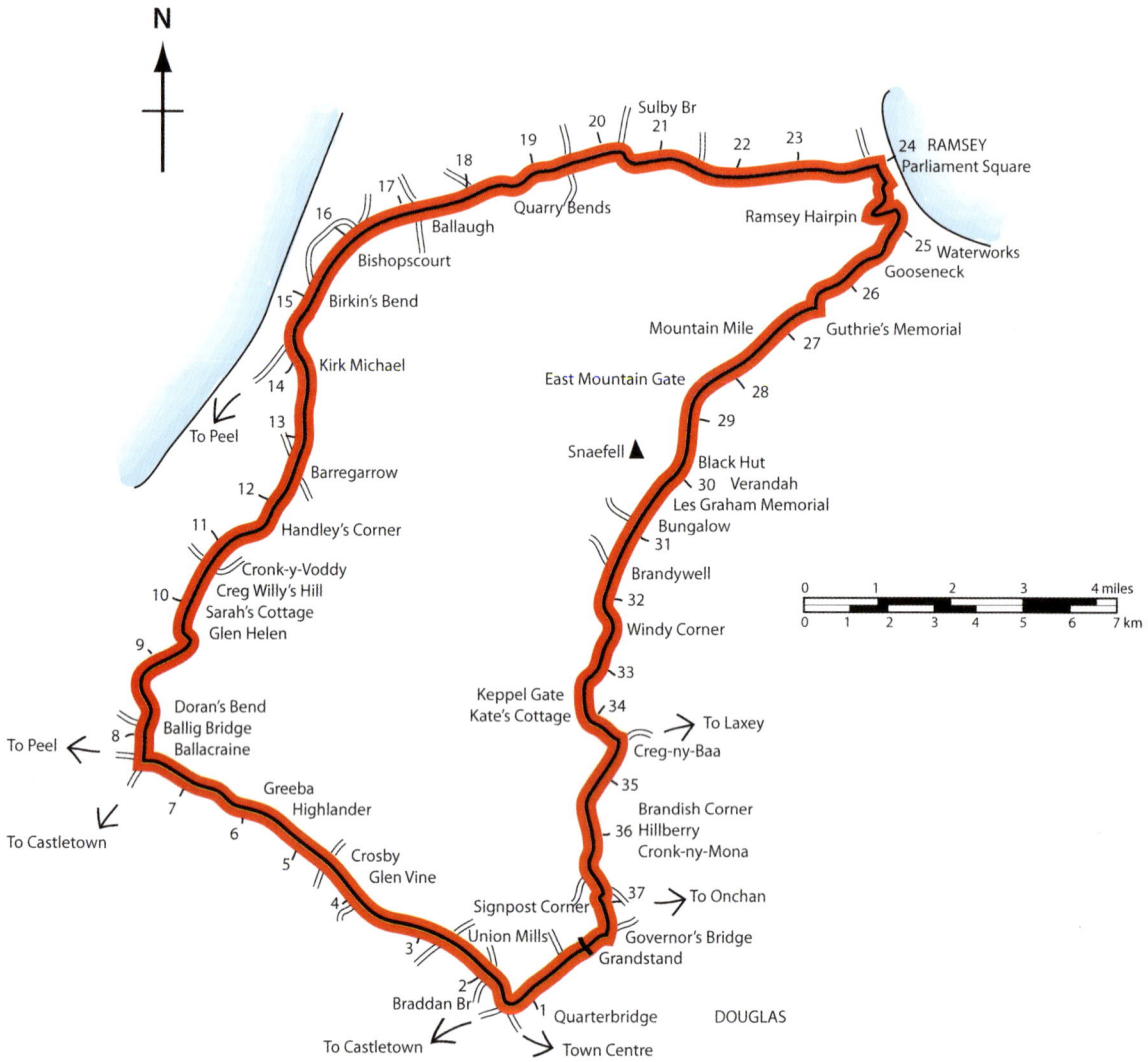

N

RAMSEY
Parliament Square

Sulby Br
Quarry Bends
Ramsey Hairpin
Waterworks
Gooseneck
Guthrie's Memorial
Mountain Mile
East Mountain Gate
Snaefell ▲
Black Hut
Verandah
Les Graham Memorial
Bungalow
Brandywell
Windy Corner
Keppel Gate
Kate's Cottage
Creg-ny-Baa
To Laxey
Brandish Corner
Hillberry
Cronk-ny-Mona
Signpost Corner
To Onchan
Governor's Bridge
Grandstand
Union Mills
DOUGLAS
Braddan Br
Quarterbridge
To Castletown
Town Centre

Ballaugh
Bishopscourt
Birkin's Bend
Kirk Michael
To Peel
Barregarrow
Handley's Corner
Cronk-y-Voddy
Creg Willy's Hill
Sarah's Cottage
Glen Helen
Doran's Bend
Ballig Bridge
Ballacraine
To Peel
To Castletown
Greeba
Highlander
Crosby
Glen Vine

0   1   2   3   4 miles
0   1   2   3   4   5   6   7 km

The TT Course

rider continues straight ahead, there is a twisting, downhill section of 3 miles to Kirk Michael, where a broad, sweeping right-hander (leaving the Peel Road on the left) brings the rider into the village, which he transits at around 150 mph. On leaving the village northward, he negotiates Birkin's Bend. (Many of the landmarks thus named either recognize riders who rode here for many years or commemorate those who came to grief at the identified spot.) The next landmark on the course is Ballaugh Bridge, a hump-backed bridge coinciding with a left/right squiggle at the entry to the village. The experienced rider takes off from the crest of the bridge and (usually) lands safely on the far side. (*Caution*: the reader is strongly advised not to try this at home – and definitely not at Ballaugh Bridge.)

At this point, the rider is approaching the halfway mark on the circuit. He is on the flattest section of the course and negotiates the Quarry Bends, with the Curraghs Wildlife Park on his left, and is then on the Sulby Straight, where he may well be clocked at over 200 mph. He continues east into Ramsey. In the town centre, another sharp right turn takes him out of Parliament Square, and he is heading south towards the mountain climb. Beyond the top of May Hill, he encounters the Ramsey Hairpin, an extreme left-hander which takes him out of the town. After that, there is a right-hand bend at the Waterworks and another at

A side-car unit accelerates out of Parliament Square, Ramsey

the Gooseneck, climbing all the while. A mile further on, there is a left/right squiggle at Guthrie's Memorial (with fine views over the northern plain if he has time to look), and then he is into the Mountain Mile, a straight, slowly climbing section on which intermediate speeds are often clocked. The end of the Mile brings a right and a left past East Mountain Gate (the gate across the road has long-since gone, so he does not have to stop to open it), then on to the Black Hut (the original of which is also long gone), and the rider is onto the Verandah, a long, sweeping right-hander with the steep shoulder of Snaefell rising on the right and a long view down the length of the Laxey Valley on the left. The right-hander eases into a left and the small stone building of the Les Graham Memorial flashes past on the right. A few more rights and lefts bring the rider to the Bungalow (which has also long gone) and he negotiates the level crossing over the Snaefell Mountain Railway.

He is now heading to the highest point of the course, at Brandywell, having climbed 1,384 feet (422m) above the sea at Ramsey. As he leans into the left-hander, passing the junction with the B10 Brandywell road on his right, the rider will certainly not notice – as indeed the reader who ventures this way may not notice – a small item of historic commemoration a few yards into the minor road. So, while the TT rider continues on his way back to Douglas, let us pause for a brief digression.

View over the northern plain from Guthrie's Memorial

Just inside the B10 road is a cattle grid and, on the crest of the parapet flanking the outside of the grid, there is a commemorative plaque which reads: 'This by-pass was opened by His Excellency the Lieutenant Governor and Lady Butler on the 24th April 1935.' 'By-pass' was the original Manx term for a cattle grid, and related to the gated section beside the grid, which enabled herded livestock to by-pass the grid when the gate was opened. Before the hill lands bordering the mountain road were fully fenced off, the mountain road itself was gated to restrict the wanderings of sheep, causing some inconvenience to early Manx motorists. And the TT riders of that era had to be prepared to be confronted by animals on the road and also to rely on the goodwill of farmers and volunteers to open the gates; hence the increased activity in the early 1930s to fence off the mountain road and install 'by-passes' on the side roads. They are all called cattle grids today.

By now, our TT rider is well on his way on the long downhill stretch towards Douglas, negotiating the moderately fast right-hander at Windy Corner, through a series of long, easy curves before throttling back to take the left-hand bend past Keppel Gate and Kate's Cottage, which opens up a high-level view across Douglas and the bay. From Kate's, he surveys the steep, rod-straight descent to where the public house at Creg-ny-Baa seemingly stands at the end of a long cul-de-sac. But our rider knows better; cutting back on his speed, he takes the 90-degree right-hand corner in front of the pub (a popular vantage point for spectators) and sees another long, straight descent to the left-hander at Brandish Corner, followed by yet another straight descent to Hillberry. A right-hander at Hillberry, followed by a left at Cronk-ny-Mona, and he is suddenly in among the estates of north Douglas and Onchan. Ninety degrees to the right at Signpost Corner and a short series of curves brings him past the entrance to the Governor's residence at Government House, then – abruptly – he comes to the main road from Onchan, which he imme-diately deserts to negotiate the tight little hairpin in the dip over the old Governor's Bridge, which must be taken at low speed. Emerging from the dip, our rider rejoins the main road, which has by-passed the old bridge, and he has just three-quarters of a mile of straight before crossing the line from whence he started.

Motor cycling as a sport has always been associated with risks of accident, injury and death, and this is particularly so where races are held on public roads, where much of the course is hemmed in by buildings, boundary walls, lamp-posts and other solid obstacles waiting to catch the unwary (or simply unlucky) rider. By the time it celebrated its centenary in 2007, the Isle of Man TT had amassed a significant tally of rider deaths. During the 1970s, several international riders crit-icized the dangers of the course, and a few decided to stay away. In 1989, the event was demoted from the World Championship series but its attraction among race-goers has shown little sign of decline. The difficulty in recent years has been in finding sufficient accommodation for the annual influxes during TT and MGP fortnights. The decline in the 'mainstream' tourist industry has produced a marked reduction in the number of visitor-beds available; a boarding-house does not survive on a mere four weeks' custom a year. The Manx government's response has been to encourage the island's householders to register under its 'Homestay' scheme, whereby, subject to a satisfactory inspection of the premises, a private dwelling may be accepted as a lodging-house for visitors during race periods.

And it is not only race competitors who risk injury or death at such times, for too many race-followers also place their lives on the line and all too frequently lose them. Local road-users also get caught up in these incidents. The Sunday between TT practice week and race week is known as 'Mad Sunday', when thousands of visiting race-goers take to the course, many of whom – in view of the volume of traffic on the road – ride at higher speeds than is prudent. Coupled with the fact that many of the visitors are from continental Europe and accustomed to driving on the right, the old question-and-answer quip – Question: Why do the British drive on the left? Answer: To avoid the traffic coming the other way – is not always relevant at this time of the year. In an attempt to minimize the risk, the mountain section of the course is restricted to one-way traffic on Mad Sunday, but the casualty figures would seem to indicate that there is no perfect solution to this problem.

Living in the vicinity of the TT course brings its own inconveniences. Anyone living inside the course cannot get anywhere outside the course while the roads are closed for practising or racing. And those living north of a line between Kirk Michael and Ramsey must travel a roundabout route via Ramsey and Laxey to reach any southern destination. There are other aspects of the TT scene which some residents throughout the isle find irksome, one being the extent to which public funds are used to support the event, in the form of advertising, promotion, prize money and expenses. From 1929, an annual amount of £5,000 was set aside to support the event; by 1996 this had grown to more than £500,000, and that did not include expenditure on road maintenance. Many motorists tend to be resentful when they see a stretch of the TT course being resurfaced, when it was resurfaced only a year previously and which, for ordinary road traffic, was perfectly serviceable. Their irritation is enhanced when there are roads in other parts of the isle that would – if they could – be crying out for attention.

There are other circuits in the island which are used for motor-cycle racing. The main one of these is the Billown circuit (otherwise known as the Southern 100 course), which is used for the Southern 100 races in July and also for supporting races during the TT period. The circuit is an irregular square, its starting grid being on the Castletown by-pass, from which the riders make four left turns in succession, the first taking them north over the railway, the second at Billown, then again at Ballabeg, and finally at Ballakaighen to return to the grid. The length of the circuit is 4¼ miles.

*Motor sport: (above) on the road with
the Manx International Rally; (right)
off road with the Manx 2-Day Trial*

ISLE OF MAN NEWSPAPERS

ISLE OF MAN NEWSPAPERS

lavished on the TT) but, in the late 1990s and early 2000s, the numbers of visiting cyclists were showing a decline and, following the 2003 meeting, it was decided to end it. As one of the well-over-forties who competed in the latter years of the event, I am inclined to the view that, had these cycles been petrol-driven, DTL support might have continued for longer, rather than allowing the series to die so precipitately.

Nevertheless, cycling continues to thrive within the isle, across all the age groups, supported by a lively and competitive club structure. There is still an annual time-trial over the TT course. But nowhere is the depth of enthusiasm so apparent as in the junior and younger age-groups, the starting point for which came in 1991, with the completion of Phase 1 of the National Sports Centre (NSC) on the site of the former King George V Park, in Douglas. This comprises a 400-metre running track with a stadium and an all-weather hockey pitch, the whole of which is encircled by a tarmacadam perimeter road which, conveniently, is an almost exact 800 metres.

At an inaugural evening to attract the younger element into the sport (or just into a fitness activity), just fourteen riders turned up but, today, an average of well over 200 – some so young that they still have stabilizers fitted to their bikes – congregate at the NSC every Tuesday evening through the season, where they are sorted into age groups and set off on their circuits of the perimeter road. The person doing the sorting and the setting-off is likely to be a well-known Manx woman who has been there from the beginning, Dot Tilbury MBE, who has worked tirelessly to develop support for the junior ranks. Financial support has been won from a number of corporate bodies, enabling trips to the UK and Ireland to be subsidized and allowing young Manx riders to compete at a higher level. And it has brought results.

In 1995, a nine-year-old cyclist turned up for his first Tuesday evening session at the NSC; eleven years later, at the 2006 Commonwealth Games, Mark Cavendish won the Isle of Man's first gold medal at the Games for twenty years, and went on to achieve gold at European and world level. Others are following, and showing distinct promise in international competition. In the Commonwealth Games, the Isle of Man competes as a distinct nation (as do England, Scotland and Wales) but, in the wider international context, a Manx athlete has to secure a place in a British team.

Towards the end of 2006, the Isle of Man Cycling Association submitted a plan to the Onchan District Commissioners to redevelop the Nivison Stadium, the centrepiece of Onchan Park, when the lease for the stadium came up for renewal. The stadium was built in the early 1950s, when its banked circuit was used for cycle racing. Visiting stars such as the British international Reg Harris raced there. However, in the mid-1960s, the track was adapted to accommodate stock-

Cyclists mass at the Point of Ayre for the start of the End-to-End Challenge

car racing, involving modifications which made the circuit unusable for cycle racing. Over the years, the surface of the track deteriorated and the stadium increasingly became in need of refurbishment, which was at the heart of the Cycling Association's proposal. The banked circuit was to be reinstated to provide a 250-metre track (the international standard size) and Manx cyclists would have a facility for training and competition at a time when events on the open road were either being abandoned or switched to alternative venues through fears for competitors' safety. The financial commitments were in place, with no expense to the local authority. When tenders for the lease were submitted, it was a straight fight between the Cycling Association and the existing stock-car promoter. It was perhaps predictable that, in the Isle of Man, the motor-sport lobby would prevail in the end.

ATHLETICS

As a participatory sport, athletics in the Isle of Man is on a par with cycling, with three mainstream athletic clubs, plus the Manx Fell Runners (whose specific purpose is self-evident in the name) and the Isle of Man Veteran Athletes' Club, which caters exclusively for male athletes over forty and women over thirty-five, whilst also promoting open events. Manx clubs are affiliated, through the North of England Athletic Association, to the British Athletic Federation, under which, for sporting purposes, the Isle of Man is included as part of the county structure of Great Britain. (The island's cycling clubs are affiliated to the British Cycling Federation in a similar way.) This may not accord with the purist sentiments of Manx nationalism but those who participate in the sport generally appreciate the opportunities this gives them to compete within that structure. Travel expenses to and from the UK are offset by corporate sponsorship of the clubs and by way of grant-aid from the Isle of Man Sports Council.

In addition to the usual range of track and field events, road-running and race-walking have a long tradition in the island. The event with the longest history is the Peel–Douglas road race, which was first run in the late 1800s but does not appear to have been held every year in those times. From a start-line outside the Peel town hall to a finish by the war memorial on Douglas promenade, the length of this classic course is just under 11½ miles. It is still run today, as are numerous other point-to-point and road-circuit races, including the Isle of Man Marathon in August. The marathon starts and finishes in Ramsey and takes in two laps of a circuit in the northern plain, by way of Bride, Andreas and St Jude's. The course is flat, apart from the 160-foot (50m) climb of the Bride hill, 4 miles from the start (but which somehow seems twice as high on the second lap). The marathon is run in conjunction with a one-lap half-marathon, with staggered start-times, and the two races are extremely popular and attract numerous visiting athletes each year. The NSC perimeter road also provides a secure, traffic-free venue for road races.

ATTRIBUTION UNKNOWN

A vanished race: runners on the TT course

Of course, once the motor racers, motor cyclists and cyclists had shown their mettle over the TT course, it was only to be expected that the runners would wish to follow suit. The first foot-race was staged in 1955; it became an annual event and was soon attracting an international field. The first three races in succession were won by Tom Richards, of South London Harriers, who had won a silver medal for Britain in the 1948 Olympic marathon. After a few years, the course was extended at the Douglas end, with the intention of making the race a full 40-miler. It was later found to be half a mile short of the 40 but it was, nonetheless, an endurance test for any athlete (writing as one who struggled over it on six occasions).

The extended course started and finished at the Douglas war memorial and joined the TT course at Quarterbridge, thereafter following the classic course to Ramsey and beyond. The standard marathon distance (26.2 miles) was reached midway through the mountain climb. At Governor's Bridge, the runners were diverted down Blackberry Lane (in Onchan) and Summer Hill and on to the Douglas promenade to the finish. The record for this course was set in 1978 by Cavin Woodward, of Leamington Athletic Club, who completed the circuit in 3 hours 52 minutes 19 seconds, which was only 1 minute 39 seconds slower than the record for the original course.

After the completion of the first phase of the National Sports Centre (which is close beside Quarterbridge), the start and finish of the race were moved there and the course length was adjusted to give an accurate 40 miles. But the event's days were numbered; rising fears for the competitors' safety on the increasingly busy course meant that the 'Isle of Man 40' did not survive the 1990s, and Woodward's course record will probably stand for all time.

A more recent initiative in international sport was the establishment in 1985 of the Inter-Island Games (later to be known as the Island Games). The underlying philosophy was for competition between the sports men and women of small island communities (whether they be nation-states or not), without their being overwhelmed by the might of larger countries. The range of activities encompasses fourteen different sports and, as at 2006, there were twenty-five competing members of the Island Games Association, these being:

Åland	Gotland	Prince Edward Island
Alderney	Greenland	Rhodes
Bermuda	Guernsey	Saaremaa
Cayman Islands	Hitra	Sark
Falkland Islands	Isle of Man	Shetland Islands
Faroe Islands	Isle of Wight	St Helena
Froya	Jersey	Western Isles
Gibraltar	Minorca	Ynys Mon (Anglesey)
	Orkney	

The Games are held biennially in one of the member-islands. The 1985 inaugural meeting took place in the Isle of Man, and recent gatherings have been in Shetland in 2005, Rhodes in 2007, with Åland scheduled for 2009.

The race-walkers also have an extensive calendar of events at various venues around the isle, including their own version of the Peel–Douglas race and – inevitably – they were for years attacking the TT course, both as an individual race and as a team relay, but both have also succumbed to fears for road safety.

But the biggest event by far (in terms of competitor numbers) in the Manx athletics calendar is the Parish Walk, an 85-mile circuit of the isle, during which the competitor is required to touch a gate-post of each of the seventeen parish churches *en route*. The event is said to have originated as a challenge between two men in the late 1800s but it was not revived as an open race until 1960. Nowadays it is held in June and starts at 8 a.m. on a Saturday from the National Sports Centre. Thus, anyone intent on completing the course on the same day must do so in less than sixteen hours, which is rare. There is a time limit of twenty-four hours.

From the NSC, the course encircles the island in a clockwise direction, calling at the church gates of Braddan (2 miles), Marown (4½), Santon (11½), Malew (15), Arbory (17), Rushen (19½), Patrick (30½) and St German's, in Peel, after 32½ miles. This marks the finish of the junior men's race (under twenty-one), the women's race and the veteran men's race, although any of these competitors may continue if they wish. From Peel, the walker is into the loneliest part of the race; the field is by now well strung out and heading towards the hours of darkness, and each successive stage seems far longer than it actually is. Kirk Michael is passed at 39 miles, Ballaugh at 42, Jurby at 45½, Bride at 52½, Andreas at 55½, Lezayre at 62, Maughold at 67, Lonan at 78½, Onchan at 83 and finally the Douglas war memorial at the end of 85 gruelling miles.

Although the event does attract visiting walkers, the entry list each year is overwhelmingly local, as is the list of past winners. The numbers have, also, increased dramatically. In 1995, there were 266 entrants, of whom eleven completed the 85 miles. The entry of 500 was exceeded for the first time in 1998, when there were thirty-five finishers. In 2003, there were 1,050 entrants and sixty-four finishers, and only three years later, more than 1,500 entered, of whom 162 (forty-six of them women) completed the course within the time limit. This growth in numbers has caused traffic problems in the early stages of the race, where the field is still a concentrated mass of striding humanity, and some sections of road are now closed to vehicular traffic, and others made one-way, until the field has passed through.

In 1979, the Manx walker Derek Harrison (then holder of the British 100-mile record) set a best time for the Parish Walk of 15 hours 20 minutes 51 seconds and, for many years, it seemed as though that standard was here to stay. However, in 2006, it was well and truly shattered by another Manx walker, Sean Hands (at the time, British 100-mile champion), with a time of 14 hours 47 minutes 36 seconds, which may well stand for a long time to come. The women's record for the race is 16 hours 16 minutes 36 seconds, set in 1998 by the English walker Sandra Brown.

Another very popular classic in the Manx race-walking calendar is the End-to-End Walk, held in September, and following a course of 39½ miles from the Point of Ayre, through the west of the island and finishing at the café at Calf Sound. This event originally followed a more direct route down the east side of the island but, once again, fears arose over road safety and prompted a switch to the quieter west in 2002. The record for the present course is 6 hours 57 minutes 2 seconds, set by Robbie Callister in 2003. The women's record of 7 hours 23 minutes 3 seconds was set in 2005 by Sue Biggart.

THE NATIONAL SPORTS CENTRE

The first phase of the National Sports Centre, completed in 1991, has been referred to earlier. Phase 2 was opened in 1999 and completed a range of sporting and recreational facilities which are the envy of many a visitor from the United Kingdom and elsewhere. It is perhaps unfortunate that its name refers only to 'sports' and makes no mention of 'leisure', because it engenders a belief among too many people (residents included) that its facilities are intended for serious sports people only, and nothing could be further from the truth; its facilities are open to all.

Whereas the main feature of Phase 1 is centred on the athletics arena, the principal activity to catch the eye on entering Phase 2 is in the water-sports area, comprising an eight-lane, 25-metre competition pool, with adjacent leisure pools and children's play features. The same building also accommodates gymnasium facilities, indoor games courts, including squash, badminton and basketball, and a licensed café. The island in general is well provided with facilities for swimmers, with pools also at Ramsey, Peel and Castletown.

The NSC is also the main venue for the Manx Youth Games, inaugurated in 2002 and organized as an annual event by Manx Sport and Recreation to encourage schoolchildren to try out various sports and to advance to higher standards in the activities of their choice. It is a one-day assembly, encompassing twelve different sports, most of them using the facilities of the NSC. Some island sports clubs have found it advantageous to select promising youngsters from the Games and direct their progress towards the competitive ranks.

The National Sports Centre, Douglas: (above) Phase 1 provided running track, grandstand and all-weather hockey pitches; (below) Phase 2 provides swimming pool and indoor court facilities

As noted earlier, the perimeter road of the NSC hosts a variety of running, walking and cycling events. In 2006, it was the scene of a particularly prestigious meeting, and one which comes round to any specific venue very infrequently. It was the Centurions' 24-hour walk, incorporating the British 100-mile championship, which is held at a different venue each year. On this occasion, Manxman Sean Hands retained his British championship in 19 hours 16 minutes 3 seconds, only eight weeks after setting the new Parish Walk record, followed by the English holder of the women's Parish Walk record, Sandra Brown, in 19 hours 28 minutes 38 seconds, with the aforementioned Sue Biggart in third place.

HORSE-RACING, BOWLS AND BALL GAMES

If the reader is under the impression that there is no horse-racing in the Isle of Man, then the reader is correct, but it was not always thus. It is a sport that was indulged in long ago; although the date of its inception is uncertain, it was somewhere in the time of the Derbys and may well have been the precursor of the Epsom Derby. A. W. Moore [57] notes that James, Lord Strange, offered a prize of £5 in a race for Manx horses in 1628, apparently in an attempt to improve the insular breed which, even towards the end of the 1600s, was being described in Camden's *Britannia* as 'poor and small, and very unsightly ... and their hair long and straggling'. This is hardly the description of a racing thoroughbred – or even of a sturdy working horse.

Stenning [72] seems to have been the first writer in modern times to unearth evidence, still held in the Rolls Office, suggesting that the race was being run in the time of *Yn Stanlagh Mooar*, the seventh Earl (1627–51), and that it was resurrected by his son Charles, the eighth Earl, after the Restoration of the Monarchy. The document indicating Charles's intention to revive the race reads:

> It is my good will and pleasure yt ye 2 prizes formerly granted for hors runing and shouting [sic] shall continue as they did be run or shot for and so to continue during my good will and pleasure.
>
> Given under my hand at Lathom ye 12 of July 1669 ... Derby, 8th Earl.

The course is described in some detail, which is not altogether clear today:

> Every rider shall leave the first two powles in Macbrae's close, one on his right hand, the other on his left; the two powles by the rocks on his left hand, the fifth powle in the coney warren also on his left hand and so turning next to Wm

Looyre's hose on his left, the next two powles, one on either hand and the
distant distance powle on either hand.

It is thought that the start and finish were at the Derbyhaven end of the
Langness peninsula, with the turn near the old Langness farmhouse (now a ruin).
How long the sport continued is also unknown. Much of the course of the
'Langness Derby' is now occupied by the Castletown golf links but, down into
modern times, the area was still referred to as 'the racecourse'. Although the 'hors
runing' may be long gone from Man, the 'shouting' (shooting – I think) remains in
good health, both clay-pigeon and rifle.

Golfers are well catered for in the Isle of Man, with eighteen-hole courses at
Pulrose (the Douglas municipal course), Howstrake in Onchan, Mount Murray
in Santon, and in Castletown, Port Erin, Peel and Ramsey, plus a nine-hole
course at Port St Mary. Those at Onchan, Castletown and Port St Mary lie in
particularly scenic coastal settings, and the clubhouse at the latter course is a
popular eating-place for non-members, and even non-golfers. Golf in the island
has a lively and competitive club structure, and the Manx championship is
played for annually.

Archery has a strong following, and green bowling is well provided for, with
crown greens at Noble's Park in Douglas, Onchan Park (also flat green), Mooragh
Park in Ramsey, and in Castletown, Port St Mary and Port Erin. The indoor centre
at the NSC also has facilities for indoor flat-green and short-mat bowling.

Tennis courts are also present in good number, with municipal facilities at
Noble's Park, Onchan Park, Ramsey's Mooragh Park, and at Peel and Castletown.
The club scene is similarly healthy, and the game, including veterans' tennis, has
a strong following. Insular competition is structured into league divisions: three
for the men, two for the women, and three for the mixed. Manx teams, under the
aegis of the Isle of Man Lawn Tennis Association, compete in the Inter-Counties
Championships in the UK. As far as club facilities are concerned, pride of place
must surely be given to the Albany Lawn Tennis Club, with headquarters
bordering Douglas Corporation's nurseries at Ballaughton Meadows. Those facilities, which have been developed over the past forty years, now feature three
outdoor hard courts (with floodlighting for evening play), an indoor court and a
two-storey clubhouse. The club's big moment came in 2001, when the Island
Games returned to their birthplace. The Games were opened at the NSC by Prince
Edward, and the Albany club went on to host the tennis tournament, interested
spectators at the finals being Prince Edward and Sophie, Countess of Wessex. The
club has a strong coaching element, particularly for its junior members, and
exemplifies how a sport can be run (as in cycling) to nurture its younger participants towards the main stream of competition.

TEAM SPORTS

Under this heading, I include football, rugby, hockey and cricket. Football has a strong following in the island, with club and league structures for both men and women, and an annual Cup Final. Manx teams often compete against English clubs, both at home and away. One notable success for an Isle of Man team in England came in a league competition which may not be familiar to those who do not follow the sport (and possibly to many of those who do): the English Football Association's National League System Cup, a rather confusing title since it is a knock-out competition unconnected with the FA's well-known league set-up. However, in July 2006, at the end of a countrywide competition, an Isle of Man team won its way through to the final and defeated a Cambridgeshire side 4–0 to take the cup, to great island jubilation. This success earned the Isle of Man the right to represent the English FA in a round of the UEFA Regions Cup the following year. The Isle of Man FA runs development squads each year aimed at the advancement of promising young players.

Rugby Union football also has a vigorous following in the island, perhaps on a smaller scale than the Association version, but it also has a women's league. The same could be said of hockey but this sport has the rather unusual feature

A classic stroke in the Youth Cricket Festival

of operating three leagues: one for men, one for women and the third for mixed teams.

Cricket also flourishes in its season. In addition to a knock-out cup competition, there are three senior league divisions, as well as leagues for the under-fifteens, under-thirteens and under-elevens. Thanks to the growth of corporate sponsorship, Manx teams are able to travel abroad for international matches, and younger players can be sent across the water to experience competition at different levels in England. A recent innovation is the Standard Bank Youth Cricket Festival, staged in the island in August for teams of players aged between eleven and fifteen. The week-long festival in 2006 saw two Manx teams competing against two from India and one from West Yorkshire. Cricket, like other sports in Man, has benefited enormously from the growth in the financial sector. Many of the commercial undertakings, and other firms also, have given generous sponsorship to clubs, to individual events or to both.

RECREATIONAL ACTIVITIES

The Isle of Man abounds with opportunities for all manner of activities for leisure and recreation, ranging through diving, kayaking, sailing, fishing, riding and pony trekking, abseiling, rock-climbing, leisure cycling (as opposed to the competitive kind) and walking. There are a few private diving schools in the island and, needless to say, only experienced divers or those under expert guidance should attempt to plumb the depths of Manx waters. Instruction in such activities as abseiling, rock-climbing and kayaking is provided at the Ard Whallin Outdoor Pursuits Centre (near the Baldwin reservoir) and the Maughold Venture Centre. The rounded, ice-sculpted hills of Man present few locations to attract the rock-climber and, consequently, this activity is mainly confined to certain areas of the sea-cliffs. For the horse-rider and pony-trekker, a few equestrian centres provide tuition and guidance along the island's byways and on to the open moorlands and hill-tracks.

Perhaps not surprisingly for an island community, sailing is a popular pursuit among cruisers, racers and dinghy sailors. For the racing yachtsman, the classic event of the year is the Round the Island race, starting and finishing at Ramsey and requiring an anti-clockwise circumnavigation of the isle. There are six yacht clubs, and the inner harbour at Douglas now has pontoon facilities for yachts and a water-retention scheme to ensure that they remain afloat at the lower states of the tide. But, after pontoon berths have been allocated to resident yachts, are there sufficient remaining to serve the needs of visiting yachtsmen who would wish to come? It is an oft-debated question. Proposals for marina developments at Ramsey and Port St Mary have fallen to objectors at the planning stage – predictably. In the meantime, many of the numerous British and Irish yachtsmen who visit each other's shores every summer may continue to by-pass the Isle of Man because of its traditional lack of facilities for them. To be fair, it should be said that there are places in various of the island's harbours where the visiting sailor may find a sheltered berth but those desiring a formal marina setting – with its fuelling, watering and other facilities – must try their luck in Douglas.

For those for whom yachting seems too quiet and lacking in action, the annual Honda power-boat meeting may be more appealing. The Honda Formula 4-Stroke Power-Boat Series is a national series held at various venues around the UK, the first round of which is staged in Douglas Bay in late June. The races are in two classes, one for boats powered by 150hp engines, and the other for those of 225hp. The boats in each of the classes are identical and all of the engines are by Honda. Thus, the competition is a test of the skills of driver and navigator.

Fishing – both freshwater and sea – is popular as a pastime and as a competitive sport. For fishing in fresh water, anglers are required to hold a licence issued by the DAFF, and separate licences are required for reservoir and river fishing. All eight of the island's reservoirs contain brown trout, whilst six of them (Ballure, Clypse, Kerrowdhoo, Sulby, Baldwin and Cringle) are stocked with rainbow trout reared at the DAFF's fish hatchery at Cornaa. The reservoirs vary greatly in size, from the deep, broad, exposed 54 acres (22ha) of the Sulby, down to the sheltered 3½ acres (1.4ha) of the Ballure, on the southern outskirts of Ramsey.

The island's clear, fast-flowing streams offer enticing opportunities to fish for wild brown trout, using the fly, spinner or worm (live bait is banned from the island's reservoirs). Migratory salmon and sea-trout are usually to be found at the appropriate times of year in the main Manx rivers (the Sulby, Santon and Neb), sea-trout normally arriving by June and salmon by late September. Sea-trout may also be found in some of the larger pools on the smaller streams.

There are strict regulations regarding the season and limits on catches. The seasons for reservoir and river fishing differ: extending from March to the end of October for reservoir fishing, and in the rivers from April to the end of September for brown trout, but to the end of October for migratory fish. On the reservoirs, no more than four trout may be caught and retained on any one day, and the angler must not continue fishing after the fourth fish has been killed. On the rivers, a day's catch may comprise up to six fish, of which no more than two can be salmon or sea-trout, and the angler must cease fishing after the capture of the sixth fish.

Sea fishing is popular, both from the beaches of the northern plain and from the piers and breakwaters of the island's harbours. In times past, a favoured spot for leisure fishing and competitions was Ramsey's Queen's Pier but its sadly dilapidated state now rules it out as a venue for such pleasures. This government-owned structure is a listed building; any private owner would have been compelled to take restorative measures long ago, but the only 'maintenance' this structure has seen in years has been the permanent closure of its gates because the timber decking has become too hazardous to walk on.

Leisure cycling is an ideal way in which to see the Manx countryside. The DTL's information centre at the Douglas Sea Terminal has an information sheet giving details of suggested cycling routes, which are waymarked on roadside signs. Cycle-hire facilities are available at various places in the island.

The Manx coast, moorlands and hill country provide ideal environments for the leisure walker. The island is well served with public footpaths, which are shown on the Ordnance Survey's Landranger series sheet 95 at 1:50,000 scale and, on the larger scale of 1:25,000, on the Isle of Man Government's two-sheet map of public rights of way. There are four established long-distance footpaths: the *Raad ny Foillan* (the 'Road of the Gull'), which follows the coast in a 95-mile circumambulation of the isle; the *Bayr ny Skeddan* (the 'Road of the Herring'), extending roughly north–south between Peel and Castletown; the Millennium Way, which was established in 1979 to commemorate the millennium of Tynwald and strikes down the middle of the isle between Ramsey and Castletown; and the Heritage Trail, which follows the route of the old railway line between Peel and Douglas. We shall return to these long-distance routes in Chapter 10.

For those visitors (and others) who prefer to walk in company and with a knowledgeable guide, the Isle of Man Walking Festival was first held in 2004 and gained in popularity to such an extent that two events were staged in 2006. The walks are graded according to distance and effort required, and each is led by a person with knowledge of the area to be covered.

As hinted earlier, shooting – in the form of clay-pigeon and rifle-shooting – is still followed as a sport. And it is not unusual for the wanderer in the Manx lowlands to come across a countryman with his 'broken' gun over one arm and a bag of rabbits on the other. Also, according to the DAFF website, the Department lets tenancies on its hill lands to individuals who operate shooting syndicates. I can only comment that, in more than thirty years of roaming the island's hills and moors, I have never seen or heard any sign of one. Maybe I have just been lucky.

CHAPTER NINE

People, Culture and Tradition

I t has been claimed in the past that the Manx people were never divided into the various strata of a class system, implying that Manx society was a homo-geneous, egalitarian whole. The degree to which there is truth in that claim depends critically on one's definition of 'class'. It is certainly true that successive Lords of Man never succeeded in imposing a system of feudalism on the Manx people, and there was never any formal insular structure of noble aristocracy. Any individuals holding such rank were those – usually from England – who were appointed to perform specific roles in the governance and administration of the isle, and, when their terms of duty expired, either returned whence they had come or moved on to new appointments elsewhere.

Nevertheless, from the early seventeenth century – and probably far earlier – there was undoubtedly a distinct stratification in Manx society. Those Manxmen who held official appointments as deemsters, attorneys-general and captains of parishes usually came from land-owning families and, although there were no great landed estates to compare in size with those to be found in the adjacent isles, their holdings were normally a cut above those of the plebeian norm. The Christians of Milntown provide a prime example. And later, as the smuggling trade developed, other families advanced their fortunes, either directly from 'the trade' or by secondary trading of the goods smuggled in. Legitimate trading also brought accumulated wealth, and the sizes of dwellings and their locations in extended lands gave clear indication of the acquired status of their owners. Thus developed a Manx elite.

Such transformations of status inevitably fuelled the drift of population from the remoter rural areas, as the newly self-elevated elite sought more appropriate locations for themselves closer to the towns. After 1815, with the arrival of the half-pay officers and stranger-residents in their midst, the Manx elite began to model themselves on the educated, cultured, English-speaking folk with whom they came into contact. But this had been going on for at least two centuries earlier. Speed, writing in 1611, describes the more prosperous elements in Manx society as imitating the gentry of Lancashire, whilst most of the rest of the population existed as the typical rural peasantry of the time.

Further evidence from the early 1600s of the conflicting priorities of class arose from the corn shortages resulting from a succession of poor harvests. A number of export prohibitions had been imposed in order to protect grain supplies at home. The farmers were generally discontented with the prohibitions; the presence of exporters at the corn markets helped to maintain higher prices. The Keys in particular (being mainly land-owners and farmers) were intent on maintaining grain prices. On at least one occasion, the Douglas dockside was the scene of a riot which prevented the loading of grain for export. If the evidence from that period is not sufficient to illustrate class divisions among the Manx, then it is difficult to think of any that would.

From those early beginnings, the divisions between the upper and lower orders would become more clearly marked by the language issue: between those who could speak English and those (the majority) who could not. The Manx elite must, of necessity, have remained bilingual in order to conduct business in the town and to deal with staff on the farm or in the home. It is ironic that, by the time the first books were being printed in the Manx language (the Book of Common Prayer, the two Testaments and the Methodists' hymn book) in the latter half of the eighteenth century, the decline of the language was already in train. At about the same time, a collection of *carvals* (religious songs) was being gathered together by A. W. Moore, who published them in 1891 under the title *Carvallyn Gailckagh*, the first example of original literature in the language.

There was a second irony arising out of this situation (already noted in Chapter 6). The Manx elite, of whom the novelist Hall Caine was a leading light, had been happy to adopt Anglicization, as long as it was the educated, cultured English that provided the model. But, by the end of the nineteenth century, the Steam Packet boats were bringing in hordes of holidaymakers from the factories of north-west England – mass-invasions of the lower orders – and there ensued a frantic scramble among the Manx elite to distance themselves and to regain their Manx roots, including their language. They formed the Manx Language Society and (another irony) only later translated its name to *Yn Cheshaght Ghailckagh*. But it was too late; the decline was destined to be terminal.

The continuing drift from the country and the Anglicization of the elite left the rural peasantry as the true guardians of Manx culture, tradition and (for the remainder of its reign as the vernacular) the Manx language. And, although the description 'peasantry' is no longer relevant and the everyday language is now English, it is the country folk of Man who remain the living custodians of the old Manx customs and traditions. And it is those rural folk of today who still match most closely the descriptions of the Manx given by writers of thirty or more years ago.

PEOPLE

As the processes of urbanization and immigration have continued, the progressive contact between Manx and incomer has tended to diminish the uniquely Manx traits of the indigenous population in the towns, where the greatest mix occurs. It is in the outlying country districts that the distinctive Manx characteristics are preserved. There is a temptation to assume that, since the Manx-born population accounts for a fraction under 48 per cent of the total (2001 census), more than half of the total must be English, but this is far from being the case. In fact, just over 38 per cent of the population of Man are English-born, the remainder being Scottish, Irish (almost equally from the two sides of the border) and Welsh, with small proportions from a range of other countries.

Stenning [72] gave a studied description of the Manxman of fifty years ago, a description which probably remains broadly true of the Manx countryman today. And there are a fair number still fitting that description in the towns also. Stenning found a people who were cautious, careful and thrifty; in company, they were attentive listeners but reluctant to speak out among strangers. A direct question – even from someone known to the recipient – would often elicit a stony silence in reply. The Manx sense of humour, quite distinct from that encountered in the adjacent isles, is gentle rather than boisterous, ill at ease with innuendo. A friendly nudge of the elbow, which would not raise an eyebrow in an English pub, may produce quite a different reaction in the Isle of Man. Stenning's final piece of advice to the incomer on his dealings with Manx folk was never to joke with a Manxman until you have known him for thirty years – and then only gently. This description could be taken to imply a certain aloofness on the part of your average Manxman and, if that was an accurate allusion in Stenning's time, it would seem that Manx folk have softened somewhat over the intervening years (such has certainly been my experience). But various strands of this make-up can still readily be identified without too much seeking.

One unchanging feature of Manx country folk is their unfailing hospitality; they are all too ready to welcome the wanderer descending from the hills at the end of a long day's tramp, and to extend an invitation to rest and take some refreshment. The generosity of the Manx people to charitable causes is also legendary, exemplified each year in the results of the Royal British Legion's Poppy

Appeal, in which – almost invariably – the Isle of Man district heads the list of amounts raised per capita.

Another undimmed component of the Manx make-up is the desire for 'skeet': information, stories of other folk's affairs – just plain gossip, really. Until recent years, there were four regular features in the Manx newspapers which served to satiate this lust; these were 'Other People's Money' (the list of proven wills), the divorce-court lists, the property transactions and the planning applications. The latter two are still published, but the first two have quietly disappeared. There was no prior announcement, no explanation. They both, after all, go through due public process but, mysteriously, they ceased appearing in the pages of the press. It seems to have been the result of a rethink of editorial policy, a search for balance between public interest and privacy of the individual. But what next? The property transactions?

The sense of national identity felt by most Manx people is not confined solely to those who live in the isle, or even to those who have personally migrated elsewhere. In many parts of the world, especially in the United States and Commonwealth countries, there are large numbers of people of Manx descent, many of whom have never set eyes on the place. Yet they, too, feel that same sense of identity which compels many of them, if only once in their lives, to make the long journey to see the land of their ancestors' birth. Such visits are frequently timed to coincide with Tynwald Day, so that they may take in the atmosphere of the island's national day. The organizing committee makes arrangements each year to welcome such 'home-comers'.

LANGUAGE AND LITERATURE

We have noted the decline in usage of Manx Gaelic and the attempts that were made to stem that decline. Nevertheless, the vernacular of the island today is English, and that is the situation because, over a period of more than two centuries, successive strata of Manx society – influenced by the social, economic and trading conditions in which they lived and worked – *chose* to adopt English as their working tongue. But did they, in the long run, have any choice in the matter? In seeking to stem the tide of decline, *Yn Cheshaght Ghailckagh* adopted the motto: *Gyn chengey, gyn cheer,* 'Without tongue, without country'. I may offend some by saying so, but what a gloomy prognosis! And how wide of the mark. Is the Isle of Man any less of a nation because, long ago, its people chose to speak another tongue? Is the Republic of Ireland any less of a nation because of its embrace of English as its first language?

Looking back over those years, and scanning forward to the situation today, it is difficult to imagine how the Isle of Man could function in its present role in today's world had it not adopted English as its first language. It is equally difficult to avoid the conclusion that, given the island's location in the midst of those larger islands to east and west, Man's linguistic evolution was inevitable – almost predetermined. The alternative, surely, would have been social and economic isolation.

The demise of Manx Gaelic as the vernacular led to the rise of two brands of English in island use: standard English as spoken by the higher orders, and the Manx English of the remainder. In the field of literature, the Manx poet, T. E. Brown, was the leading island exponent of both forms. The following extract from his narrative poem *Betsy Lee* illustrates his use of the dialect:

> Now the beauty of the thing when childher plays is
> The terrible wonderful length the days is.
> Up you jumps, and out in the sun,
> And you fancy the day will never be done;
> And you're chasin' the bumbees hummin' so cross
> In the hot sweet air among the goss,
> Or gath'rin' blue-bells, or lookin' for eggs,
> Or peltin' the ducks with their yalla legs,
> Or a climbin' and nearly breakin' your skulls,
> Or a shoutin' for divilment after the gulls,
> Or a thinkin' of nothin', but down at the tide
> Singin' out for the happy you feel inside.
> That's the way with the kids, you know,
> And the years do come and the years do go,
> And when you look back it's all like a puff,
> Happy and over and short enough.

Thomas Edward Brown was born in Douglas in 1830, the son of Robert Brown, chaplain of St Matthew's and later vicar of Braddan. He began his education at the Braddan parochial school, taught by his father, before being sent to King William's College, although his father had vehemently opposed the spending of Bishop Barrow's Trust Fund on founding the establishment. From 'King Bill's', Brown went up to Christ Church, Oxford, where he was given a rough time by his fellow-students, who appeared to look down on this rough colonial boy. That notwithstanding, he took a first in Classics and another in History and Law. In 1853, he was made a Fellow of Oriel College, Oxford, where he remained until returning to the island to become Vice-Principal of King William's College from 1855 until 1861. He was ordained in 1856. He left the island again to take on the headship of the Crypt School, Gloucester, before moving once more in 1864 to become second master at Clifton College, Bristol. That would be his last teaching move and he would remain at Clifton for almost thirty years.

Although Brown's dialect poems are the most prized of his works in the island, his poems in standard English are equally worthy of attention. It is clear from much of his output that, during his long sojourn in England, he often hankered after the pastoral calm of his native isle, or mused and mourned over old friends departed, as in *Old John* and *Chalse a Killey*. Nowhere is his yearning for the isle, and nostalgia for past youth, more clearly stated than in *Braddan Vicarage*:

> I wonder if in that far isle,
>   Some child is growing now, like me
> When I was child: care-pricked, yet healed the while
>   With balm of rock and sea.
>
> I wonder if the purple ring
>   That rises on a belt of blue
> Provokes the little bashful thing
>   To guess what may ensue,
> When he has pierced the screen, and holds the further clue.
>
> I wonder if beyond the verge
>   He dim conjectures England's coast:
> The land of Edwards and of Henries, scourge
>   Of insolent foemen, at the most
> Faint caught where Cumbria looms a geographic ghost.

… and so on for another thirteen stanzas. And those opening lines from *Clifton* –

> I'm here at Clifton, grinding at the mill
>   My feet for thrice nine barren years have trod;
> But there are rocks and waves at Scarlett still,
>   And gorse runs riot in Glen Chass – thank God!

prompt the question, why did he stay away so long?

The best of Brown's poems have been compared with those of Wordsworth and Blake, and his dialect poems certainly make him the Manx equivalent of Burns. He retired from Clifton and returned to the island in 1893. He died in 1897 while on a return visit to Clifton; he is buried there, together with his wife and son Braddan.

Although born a generation and more earlier than the much-revered E. H. Stenning (died 1964), their careers produced one interesting parallel and one revealing near-parallel. Both men held the post of Vice-Principal of King William's College (Stenning from 1945 to 1953). The near-parallel arises from Stenning's holding the Archdeaconry of Man, an appointment which Brown had turned down in 1894, explaining his reasons in a letter to A. W. Moore [59]: 'I must be free … to do what I like, say what I like, write what I like, within the limits prescribed for me by my own sense of what is seemly and fitting. Literature is my calling. To hold up a mirror to my countrymen comes natural to me …' And in a further letter: 'Every man should follow the bent of his nature in art and letters, always provided that he does not offend against the rules of morality and good taste.' All of which says much about the man, and indicates – perhaps – how far we have travelled since then.

A Manx writer of much wider popularity than T. E. Brown during his lifetime was the novelist Thomas Henry Hall Caine (always known as Hall Caine). A generation later than Brown, Caine (1853–1931) was well connected outside the island, and his activities abroad served to enhance his reputation and the popularity of his novels, a string of which – including *The Deemster, The Bondman, The Manxman, The Christian, The Master of Man* and *The Woman of Knockaloe* – were mostly, but not exclusively, woven into a Manx setting and were translated into many European and other languages.

In 1891, Caine delivered a programme of lectures on the Isle of Man to the Royal Institution, in London, and these were later published as *The Little Manx Nation* [10]. In one passage, he alludes to the annual spectacle of the island's national day and to how the more cynical outsider might react to the scene:

'Our little nation is the only nation now on earth that can shake hands with the days of the Sagas, and the Sea-Kings. Then let him who will laugh at our primitive ceremonial. It is the bade of our ancient liberty, and we need not envy the man who can look on it unmoved.'

It is a pity about that first sentence, which is demonstrably lacking in accuracy (what about Iceland?) but the remainder identifies a sentiment residing in many a Manx breast today.

Hall Caine was elected Member of the House of Keys (MHK) for Ramsey in 1901 but his commitments outside the isle seem to have had a deleterious effect on his attendance at sittings, to the dismay of his supporters. But a string of honours followed from outside the island: he was knighted in 1918 for his literary contributions to the Allied cause in the First World War, he was made an Officer of the Order of Leopold for his humanitarian assistance to Belgian refugees, and he became a Companion of Honour in 1922 for his contribution to English literature. In view of his great popularity in the isle at the time of his election to the

Keys, it is ironic that his star should have been eclipsed so radically in later years. Today, it is T. E. Brown who is the literary custodian of Manx tradition, and Caine is little read. He is buried at Kirk Maughold.

Manx Gaelic today is kept alive by teachers of the language and enthusiasts who wish to gain or retain fluency, and there has been a distinct revival of interest in the language in recent years. One of the island's primary schools (St John's) has gone so far as to undertake most of its teaching in Manx Gaelic, in which tongue the school is now styled as *Bunscoill Ghaelgagh*, the 'Gaelic Primary School'. But it must be beyond doubt that Gaelic will ever regain its former status as the island's first language.

In everyday life, there are words and phrases which are frequently used, some heard daily, such as '*Moghrey mie*' ('Good morning'), '*Fastyr mie*' ('Good afternoon' or 'evening'), '*Shoh Radio Vannin*' ('This is Manx Radio'), and the smallest room in the house – and especially if it is located at the bottom of the garden – is the *Thie veg*, 'the little house'. Towards the end of each year, the greeting is '*Ollick ghennal erriu as blein feer vie*', 'A merry Christmas on you and a very good year'. On the doors of dwellings, house numbers are sometimes spelled out instead of applying the numerals, the numbers one to ten being: *nane* (or *un*), *jees* (or *daa*), *tree, kiare, queig, shey, shiaght, hoght, jeih*. The days of the week are (beginning with Sunday): *Jedoonee, Jehune, Jenayrt, Jecrean, Jerdein, Jeheiney* and *Jesarn*. And in the days when church services were conducted in Manx, the Lord's Prayer would be rendered as:

Ayr ain t'ayns Niau,	Father at us who is in Heaven,
casherick dy row Dt ennym,	holy be Thy name,
Dy jig Dty reeriaght,	May Thy kingdom come,
Dt'aigney dy row jeant er y	Thy will be done on earth as it
thalloo myr te ayns Niau.	is in Heaven.
Cur dooin nyn arran jin as	Give us our bread today and
gagh laa,	each day,
As leih dooin nyn loghtyn myr	And forgive to us our sins as we
ta shin leih dauesyn ta jannoo	are forgiving to those who do
loghtyn nyn'oi.	wrongs against us.
As ny leeid shin ayns miolagh,	And lead us not into temptation,
Agh livrey shin veih olk,	But deliver us from evil,
Son Lhiats y reeriaght, as y	For with Thee [is] the kingdom,
Phooar as y Ghloyr,	and the power, and the glory,
Son dy bragh as dy bragh.	For ever and ever.
Amen.	Amen.

We have noted the emergence of two forms of English in the Isle of Man, coinciding with the decline in the use of Manx Gaelic. There is a third form which is still encountered in the spoken language; it has been commented on by Manx (and other) writers, especially those engaged in journalism, and has been identified as 'Manxlish'. This often takes the form of the insertion of a superfluous letter into the intended word, as in *grievious, mischievious,* or the omission or substitution of a letter, as in *expeck, suspeck, ek cetera.* In some cases, the substitution of a letter may result in a quite different word with a quite different meaning; the following sentence contains one such example: 'I had such a *tremendious* amount of *refuge* to get rid of that I was *frikened* to *aks* the binmen to hump it out to the wagon, but I had to do *sump'n'* to get shut of it.' Such aberrations as these may be expected during a period when one vernacular is giving way to another, but these examples seem to have become firmly engrained over the centuries, like fossilized remnants of that far-off age of transition. Sometimes, whole words are substituted, with quite confusing results, as in the run-up to the 2006 general election, when one sitting MHK who was seeking re-election proclaimed during a radio interview that the criminal justice system gave too much consideration to the criminal and not enough to the *perpetrator.*

This, conveniently, brings us to the question of the pronunciation of Manx place-names, which is a veritable minefield for the visitor or newcomer to the island. Rather than delve into all the intricacies of semantics, I shall confine myself here to the most commonly met pitfalls. The most frequently raised question is how to deal with the pairing 'gh', and there is no single answer. Sometimes it is pronounced as 'f', as in *Ballaugh,* sometimes as an aspirated 'gh', as in *Ballalough* (occurring in several places), sounding almost like the Scottish *loch.* In other situations, it is pronounced as a hard 'g', as in *Ballaragh* (Lonan), *Ballaghennie* (Bride) and *Glen Darragh* (Marown), and even as a 'k' in *Curragh* (Ballaugh) and *Claddagh* (Sulby).

Other difficulties attend the appearance of place-names ending in 'y'. The oft-met *Ballakelly* is pronounced just as it is written but, if the ending is 'ey', the 'y' sound is frequently advanced by one character, so that *Ballakilley* becomes 'Ballakillya', and the family name *Killey* is treated in the same way. At the southern end of Ramsey, one finds *Lheaney* ['Meadow'] Road which, similarly, is pronounced 'Lhenya'.

Similar effects occur when the 'y' is embedded within the word – and even when 'y' is absent from the written form. On the coast of German is a place identified on the map as *Lynague* but spoken of as 'Linyugue'. *Cronk Grianagh* occurs in Braddan and German, where the second element becomes 'Grinyugh'. On the Santon coast, we have *Port Grenaugh,* which is voiced as 'Grenyugh' or even 'Grenyuck'. At first sight – and sound – one is tempted to assume that this pronunciation has arisen in similar fashion to that occurring in the Scottish highlands, i.e. by splitting the name into its three elements – Gren-ai-ugh – and then running the three rapidly together – until one is reminded that the old name of the place was *Port Grennick*! Incidentally, the Manx family name of *Kennaugh* is treated in the same way, i.e. 'Kenyuck'.

The soundest advice to be given to the newcomer in this land of linguistic mystery is to listen and learn – and see also Appendix A.

CUSTOMS THROUGH THE YEAR

We have noted the caution of the old-time Manx in the presence of strangers, and of their reluctance to answer direct questions. Such reticence severely obstructed the early efforts of would-be investigators and recorders of the old Manx customs and superstitions. A Scottish visitor by name of Campbell, editor of *Popular Tales of the West Highlands,* arrived in 1860 but found his enquiries impeded by that same strand of reserve on the part of the Manx peasantry. He described his diffi-culties in a letter to A. W. Moore [59]:

> I found them willing to talk, eager to question, kindly, homely folk, with whom it was easy to begin an acquaintance ... but any attempt to extract a story, or search out a queer old custom, or a half-forgotten belief, seemed to act as a pinch of snuff does on a snail. The Manxman would not trust the foreigner with his secrets; his eyes twinkled suspiciously, and his hand seemed unconsciously to grasp his mouth, as if to keep all fast.

Moore himself, being Manx and well known (for many years Speaker of the House of Keys, as well as writer and scholar), was in a far stronger position to garner such confidences from his fellow countrymen but, as he readily pointed out, by the time he came to compile his *Folklore of the Isle of Man*, much had already been forgotten and lost. A century after Campbell, we find Stenning describing the same trait of reserve among the Manx folk and cautioning against jokes before thirty years of acquaintance are under the belt. Having arrived in the island in the early 1970s, I can recall old-timers (most now departed) who were the very epitome of Stenning's description. But, a generation on (a generation which has seen great changes in Manx life and society), there has surely been a discernible softening, a character less austere, less reserved, and perhaps I *may* interject a joke now and then – if only gently. Change may seem inevitable, given the island's situation in today's world, and if some of the changes in society are not welcome to all, it is no longer enough to blame it *all* on immigration; there are other influences. Television can transmit changing attitudes through the airwaves far more rapidly than the Steam Packet Company can transport them over the sea-waves.

However, much of the old tradition has been recorded, and some of the old customs and superstitions are still observed. Many of the ancient customs were associated with the seasons. Both the Celts and the Norse celebrated the start of summer and winter, and also held mid-season festivals. One of the main of these was New Year's Day, known to the Manx as *Laa Nollick Beg*, 'Little Christmas Day'. As elsewhere in the British Isles, the body of superstition bound up in the occasion was largely associated with the 'first foot' (Manx *qualtagh*) to step across the threshold. The degree to which good or ill fortune would attend the household during the coming year depended critically on the characteristics of the *qualtagh*. A dark-haired man was definitely preferable, and his desirability decreased with increasing shades of fairness; a red-haired man was almost worthless. The cat had to be kept indoors all night on New Year's Eve, for, allowing it to be first across the threshold could prove disastrous. A woman *qualtagh* was generally not quite as bad as the cat but an old woman was far worse. It was customary for the *qualtagh* to bring some small gift to the house, in the hope that some good fortune would attach to it. On the day itself, the Manx housewife swept the floor away from the doorway and towards the hearth, to avoid sweeping any good fortune out of the house.

Of course, the festivities associated with New Year began on the previous evening. Thirty and more years ago, it was customary for some Manx families to keep 'open house' on New Year's Eve, and for friends to drop in – even to 'do the rounds' and call in on two or more such gatherings during the evening. The recollection of a 'come-over's' first Manx New Year's Eve, of being collected by a couple of Manx friends and being conducted around the local open houses, of proffering a small gift at each and making more Manx friends, is one which remains firmly engrained in my memory.

When Britain belatedly adopted the Gregorian calendar in 1752, there was one festival date-change which the Manx resisted long and hard – and that was Christmas. When 3 September 1752 suddenly became 14 September, there were protests across the British Isles by many who felt that they had been robbed of eleven days of their lives. In the Isle of Man, the main festival at Christmastide was *Yn Oie'l Voirrey*, 'the Eve of the Feast of Mary'. The Manx refused to budge over the commemoration of Christmas, and continued to celebrate it on the traditional day which, on the new calendar, became 5 January and was known thenceforth as 'Old Christmas Eve'. And, by coincidence, Old Christmas Eve is the Twelfth Night of Christmas on the modern calendar.

The celebration of *Yn Oie'l Voirrey* took place in the parish church. The priest would take Evensong and then depart to let the rest of the proceedings run their course, but delegating the parish clerk to ensure that things did not get out of hand. *Carvals* were sung, frequently not of a religious content but of a dubious nature concerning bishops, vicars, wardens and tithes.

The phenomenon eventually infiltrated into the chapels, and John Wesley and his preachers were ill at ease, both with the form of the celebration itself and with the Manx language in which it was performed. Where the *carvals* did have a religious content, they often dealt with sinning and repentance, and this did not make the Methodist preachers any happier, for, having little understanding of the language, they could not follow what was being sung – particularly about the sinning.

The Methodists never did manage to suppress *Yn Oie'l Voirrey*, and it was eventually accepted into their calendar, albeit in somewhat refined form. The tradition of *carval*-singing died out, to be replaced with hymn-singing. The date is still commemorated, although no longer as a service. In Kirk Michael, there is an annual concert comprising plays, recitations and musical offerings.

In Stenning's day, the parish feast on Shrove Tuesday, *Yn Oie Ynnyd*, 'the Eve of the Fast', was still held in every parish but it seems far less widely observed today. Good Friday, *Jy-heiney chaist,* was a day of superstitions. No iron object of any kind was to be inserted into the fire. The poker and tongs were set aside and a stick of mountain-ash was used in their stead. To avoid using an iron griddle on the fire, a large, thick cake (Manx *soddag*), comprising a kneaded mix of flour, eggs (shells included), salt and soot was baked directly on the hearth, and that was the sustenance for the day. On Easter Sunday morning, folk would ascend to a local high summit to watch the sunrise and hope to see the sun dip two or three times on the horizon in supplication to the risen Christ.

The traditional May-day Eve, *Oie Voaldyn,* fell on 11 May on the Gregorian calendar, and again the change of day was resisted. This was an occasion for much activity aimed at appeasing the fairies and warding off the influences of evil spirits and witches, all of whom were exceedingly active at that time of year. Fires were lit on the hill-tops and in the fields to keep the evil ones at bay. A bundle of gorse would be ignited in each field, so positioned that the wind would drift the protecting smoke over crops, livestock and dwelling.

The following day, 12 May, was May Day, *Laa-Boaldyn.* Rising early, young girls ventured forth to bathe their faces in the morning dew, which ensured a good complexion and protection against the witches. In each parish, a Queen of the May was chosen, a young maid arrayed in fine attire representing the flowering of womanhood and the blossoming of summer. She was attended by a number of maids of honour and by a young man, her captain, who commanded a troop of officers for her defence. The May Queen's assembly would meet opposition from the Queen of Winter, who was a man dressed as a woman, also with 'her' captain and defending troop. The whole of Winter's company was dressed thickly and heavily to suggest the gloom and degeneration of the darkest season. The two companies set out from their respective headquarters and proceeded towards each other, the May Queen's party preceded by a band of flutes and violins, whilst Winter's advance was accompanied by the clanking of cleavers on tongs. The two parties would meet on a chosen area of common or other land, where the two forces engaged in mock-battle. If Winter's forces managed to capture the May Queen, she was ransomed for as much as it would take to pay the expenses of the day's activities. According to a description by George Waldron [74], writing in 1731 and quoted by Moore [60], after payment of the ransom, Winter and 'her' company retired to 'divert themselves in a barn', while the May Queen's assembly remained on the green, dancing into the evening, which ended with a feast.

In all probability, the origins of this custom lay in Scandinavia. Moore quotes one Olaus Magnus, writing in the sixteenth century of a very similar observance in southern Sweden. No maidens appear to have been involved there; it was a straight conflict between 'two Norse troops appointed of young and lusty men' representing, respectively, Winter and Summer. And if, perchance, it seemed that Winter was gaining the upper hand in the battle, the bystanders would intervene to restore the balance. Having just endured one long, dark northern winter, they were not yet ready, at the beginning of May, to stand by and watch Summer give way to Winter so soon.

In Moore's day, 12 May in the Isle of Man was still the date for the letting of houses, paying house rents and the hiring of farm girls, although the letting of lands, payment of land rents and the hiring of men-servants were done at Hollantide. All of the erstwhile activities of May Day have long-since faded from the scene. Shame!

During the week running up to Ascension Day, the ancient custom of peram-bulating the parish boundaries was observed. In the reign of Elizabeth I, it was required that the people undertake an annual circuit of their parish, accompanied by the curate, who would ensure that they gave thanks to God for the gifts of the earth which they saw around them. It was also deemed important that the people should know where the boundaries of their parish lay, especially in the times when so many civic duties were apportioned on a parish-by-parish basis. Nowadays, it would be almost impossible to 'beat the bounds' of a parish precisely and completely, because of the difficulties imposed by fences, hedges, walls and the need to gain access to private lands. Occasionally, a partial beating of bounds may be organized in some parish or other but, as a regular feature, the custom has long since disappeared. Incidentally, the complete circuit of a parish would have been no mean feat of pedestrianism. The circuit of Michael, for example, would have totalled some 18 (often hilly) miles.

The old-time Celts are not known to have had any particular affinity for the celebration of midsummer (although they could have done so without telling us). And yet we have Old Midsummer Day – 24 June on the old calendar, 5 July on today's – which is Tynwald Day, lending further credence to the belief that an assembly held on this day was of Scandinavian origin. It is likely that the Nordic folk in their homelands, having endured the long darkness of the northern winter, would relish celebrating in the warmth of summer's sun at its zenith.

Having been repulsed by the smoke clouds generated for that purpose on May-Day Eve, the fairies, hobgoblins and witches were known to regroup on the eve of Midsummer Day to renew their acts of playfulness, mischief or downright evil. And the Manx Celts and Manx-Norse in their island – like the Scandinavians in their homelands – rekindled the flames to generate their smoke-screens of defence.

The differences between fairies and hobgoblins lie mainly in their behaviour and temperament. Incidentally, they have an intense dislike of being called fairies; they are correctly referred to as 'the little people', or 'the li'l folk'. The 'fairies' are the 'good little people', or *mooinjer-ny-gione-veggey*, and are generally playful and benign, except when aroused – as when they are called 'fairies'. They generally live outdoors, around the farm or homestead, but will shelter indoors on cold and stormy nights. Scraps of food and a saucer of milk or water must be left for them overnight. They will not touch it but it must be there. If it is not there in the morning, it must have been taken by the family dog or cat, and the li'l folk will not be best pleased.

The Manx hobgoblin, or *phynnodderree*, is a quite different character, malicious, malevolent and a trouble-maker. A. W. Moore described him as a 'fallen fairy', a small, harsh-looking devil with a hairy face and bright, evil-glistening eyes. The *glashten*, or *glashen*, is a particularly nasty cousin of the *phynnodderree*, capable of all manner of evil around the house and farm. He is well known also throughout the Scottish highlands. Several stages further up the scale comes the *buggane*, the malevolent Manx giant. His voice may often be heard booming out through the darkness of a stormy night. He delights in uprooting trees and causing great damage to buildings. The roofless ruin of the church of St Ninian (now called St Trinian's), standing beside the Peel–Douglas road in Marown, that was one of his jobs.

But I have digressed (again); back to Old Midsummer Day. This pagan festival – almost impossible to eradicate – was adopted by the Church as the feast-day of St John the Baptist. At the eastern end of the processional way leading to Tynwald Hill stands the Chapel of St John. In 1636, Bishop Parr reported to his archbishop that he had found the people assembled in a chapel of that dedication, engaged in the practice of 'gross superstitions', which he immediately stopped and replaced with divine service and a sermon. He gave no account of the 'gross superstitions'.

Although the open-air assembly on Midsummer Day appears to have been mainly of Norse origin, it may be significant that the old Celtic sea-god, *Manannan Mac Lir*, has at some time wheedled his way into the act. *Manannan* (possibly 'the Mankish man') *Mac Lir* ('son of the sea') is well-known in Irish and Welsh folk-legend, and the earliest references to him come from the west. Through the long ages of Celtic mythology, he seems to have descended from the throne of the sea-god to assume human form as merchant, navigator and necromancer. In the ninth-century *Glossary of Cormac*, his wide-ranging activities are related. He was able to 'roll on three legs like a wheel through the mist' and, according to the four-teenth/fifteenth-century *Book of Fermoy*, he could conjure up a mist to envelop himself and others so as to conceal them from their enemies. But the feature which is particularly relevant in the present context is the matter of the rushes. Wherever he was on Midsummer Eve, the people would bring to Manannan quantities of green rushes as a mark of homage. And today, at the annual outdoor assembly on Old Midsummer Day, the processional way between the Chapel of St John and Tynwald Hill is strewn with rushes. In Moore's day, a neighbouring farm was held on tenure subject to the supplying of this service. Moore [60] gives a far more detailed account of these matters than we have space for here.

The first day of August was called *Laa Luanys*, or *Laa Lunys*, 'Luanys's Day', which was probably associated with the Celtic god *Lug*, known to the Welsh as *Lleu*, who was reputed to have been brought up at the court of Manannan. In Ireland, his day was celebrated with a fair, at which games and sports took place. In Man, a great fair was held in Santon on that day, which was said to be *the* event of the summer half of the year. The fair had disappeared in Moore's time (writing in 1891) but he records that the practices of ascending the highest hills and visiting the sacred wells on that day were not totally extinct.

These practices, and the superstitions associated with them, were clearly not agreeable to the Church, which attempted to put an end to them, failed to do so, and then endeavoured to attach a religious significance to them by changing the date to the first Sunday in August which, after the change of calendar (and acknowledging the reluctance of the Manx to recognize the new calendar), became the first Sunday after 12 August. It did not work.

In 1732 (before the calendar change), the curate and wardens of the parish of Lonan complained to the Ecclesiastical Court of 'a superstitious and wicked custom' practised in several parishes by many young people 'and some of riper years' who climbed to the summit of Snaefell on the first Sunday in August and there behaved themselves 'very rudely and indecently for the greater part of that day'. But these practices declined more by process of natural attrition than by ecclesiastical suppression. Moore reports that, towards the end of the nineteenth century, it was still possible to see a few persons ascending to the hill-tops on the first Sunday after 12 August, ostensibly in search of bilberries, and others lurking furtively in the vicinity of the wells.

The completion of the harvest is still commemorated in Manx churches and in the community, in the latter by functions which are now much changed in form. In the old-style Harvest Festival, known as *yn mheillia*, the completion of the harvest on each farm was marked by the making of a doll from the last sheaf of corn to be cut. The doll, *babban ny mheillia* ('doll of the harvest'), was decked out with ribbons and wild flowers and then paraded round the field before being carried to the farmhouse, where it was placed on the kitchen chimney breast, there to remain until the following harvest. The farmer would usually provide supper for his workers that evening to celebrate the 'harvest home'. Some farmers may still do this but today's *Mheillia* usually takes the form of a social gathering in the local public house or parish hall, where a range of produce is auctioned off, and items other than farm produce are also taken along to be auctioned for charity.

The eve of the Church festival known as All Hallows', or All Saints', falls on 31 October, but those still refusing to accept the 'loss' of their eleven days from 1752 would be commemorating All Hallows' Eve (or 'Hallowe'en-tide', or 'Hollantide') on 11 November. And A. W. Moore tells us that, in 1891, the Manx were still clinging on to the latter date, thus indicating that the Manx Hallowe'en only reverted to 31 October within the last hundred years or so.

Among both the Celts and the Norse settlers of Man, there was a tradition that the end of October marked the end of the year and a belief (in pre-Christian times) that the sun-god was approaching the nadir of his power and influence. It followed from this that the powers of darkness – the fairies, hobgoblins and witches – would be encouraged to come out and make their mischief, and so the bonfires were lit and smoke clouds generated, just as on May-Day Eve. Christmas, New Year and Easter apart, the tradition of All Hallow's Eve, or *Hop-tu'naa*, is the custom most widely followed in the isle today, although the bonfires and smoke clouds are no longer part of it. In its earlier form, the procedure was far more comprehensive than that followed now, probably because so much has been forgotten, but it involved groups of children and young people going from door to door and performing a certain ritual. Each group carried a hollowed-out turnip, with holes cut in one side to represent eyes, nose and mouth, the interior illumined by a candle, and with one of their number carrying a tin in which to receive the donations from enthralled householders. The group would knock on a door and sing, rather like a preview of what was to come at carol-singing time – except that there was only ever one song, and it was more of a chant than a song.

It is interesting to note that, when Moore was compiling his *Folklore of the Isle of Man* in 1891, he made no mention of *Hop-tu'naa*; in his day it was still the old-style *Hog-annaa*, 'New Year's Night', another indication that this was regarded as the eve of another year. The ditty that was shouted out on the doorstep varied slightly in different parts of the island and from time to time through the ages, but one early version was something like the following:

Hog-annaa	–	It's New Year's Night,
Trolla-laa	–	The moon shines bright.
Hog-annaa	–	I went to the well,
Trolla-laa	–	And drank my fill;
Hog-annaa	–	On my way back
Trolla-laa	–	I met a witch-cat;
Hog-annaa	–	The cat began to grin,
Trolla-laa	–	And I began to run.
Hog-annaa	–	Where did you run to?
Trolla-laa	–	I ran to Scotland.

Then there was more concerning what was happening in Scotland, and ending with: '*Hog-annaa – Trolla-laa!*'

In earlier versions, the lines in English would, of course, have been sung in Manx and, in a later form, the reference to 'New Year's Night' was changed to 'Hollantide Night'.

As a further pointer to the 'New Year' association, the similarity between *Hog-annaa* and the Scottish *Hogmanay* is too close to ignore, especially when the chorus '*Hog-annaa, Trolla-laa*' is almost identical with that of a Scottish song whose chorus is '*Hogmanay – trollalay*' and which was sung on New Year's Eve. Moore suggests that the Norse influence is present in the second word of the Scots' chorus, which may have derived from *troll-a-la* 'trolls [driven] into the surf'. Today, the groups of children with their candle-lit turnips exuding a distinctly troll-like countenance sing out the chant which has now been reduced to:

> *Hop-tu'naa, Trolla-laa*
> It's Hollantide night
> The moon shines bright
> *Hop-tu'naa, Trolla-laa*

because hardly anyone remembers the rest of it. An alternative version, of unclear meaning, is also frequently trotted out:

> Jinny the witch [or 'squinney'] went over the house
> To get a stick to lather the mouse.
> *Hop-tu'naa, Hop-tu'naa.*

of its dedicated saint. All save one have now vanished from the scene, the exception being *Laa Columb Killey*, St Columba's Day, in the parish of Arbory. But this, too, seems to have fallen by the wayside at some time, since A. W. Moore (writing in 1891) makes no mention of it and J. J. Kneen (1925) refers to it in the past tense. But, by Stenning's time (writing in 1958), it had become firmly re-established as an annual fixture, and appears in good health today, when it is staged in June.

The last survivor of the old parish fairs was actually that held at Kirk Michael at Michaelmas, 29 September, the feast-day of the Archangel Michael. The scale of the Michaelmas fair was said to be on a par with that of the Midsummer fair at St John's, and was the occasion for hiring farm workers for the coming year. Here again, there was a reluctance to accept the 'new' calendar, and the date was moved back to 10 October. The fair survived until 1940. The St John's fair, of course, never did die out, but that is almost certainly attributable to the fact that it never was *just* a parish fair; it commemorated the island's National Day and was bound to survive.

WITCHCRAFT AND SUPERSTITION

A deep-rooted belief in the power of magic, and in the crafts of the necro-mancers, witches and wizards who practised it, was characteristic of the Celtic peoples of the British Isles and continental Europe. Their pagan religions provided fertile ground for the cultivation of such beliefs. The sun, in particular, was seen as an all-powerful being, responsible for the seasons which nurtured the very subsistence of the people, and had, therefore, to be appeased with offerings of prayer and sacrifice. To facilitate this need, a priestly class – the Celtic *Druadh* – evolved to act as intermediaries between the people and their gods, analogous to the priestly class which arose with the coming of Christianity.

The *Druadh* of Ireland and Man were the parallel of the Druids of Britain and Gaul, and it was in Gaul that Julius Caesar first encountered them. Writing of his experiences in the region in the 50s of the first century BC, he expressed his belief that Druidism had originated in Britain and then spread into Gaul. This version is doubted today, and it is likely that the druids exerted far more political influence in Gaul than they ever did in Britain. Nonetheless, more than a century later, the Roman governor in Britain, Suetonius Paulinus, having fought his way across north Wales to occupy Anglesey, was confronted (according to the Roman historian Tacitus) by an intimidating sight:

The enemy was arrayed along the shore in a massive, dense and heavily armed line of battle, but it was a strangely mixed one. Women, dressed in black like Furies, were thrusting their way about in it, their hair let down and streaming, and they were brandishing flaming torches. Around the enemy host were Druids, uttering prayers and curses, flinging their arms towards the sky. The Roman troops stopped short in their tracks as if their limbs were paralysed. Wounds were received while they stood frozen to the spot by this extraordinary and novel sight.

Recovering from the shock, the Romans pulled themselves together and overcame their opponents.

Although the *Druadh* of Man never had to face a Roman invasion, Tacitus's account of the engagement on Anglesey suggests that the hardened troops of the Roman legions were brought to a halt as much by the sounds of the curses and incantations directed at them as by the wild and savage vision that confronted them. Curses suggestive of black magic were not taken lightly in those times. Pliny the Elder noted that the British were obsessed with magic and ritual. If the same ideas held sway in Man (though there is no historical record to tell us), this would help to explain how such rituals and customs became so deeply engrained in the lives of the old pre-Christian Celts, and how they remained so long after their conversion to Christianity.

By virtue of their claims to be the communicators between the people and their deities, the *Druadh* assumed positions of power over the former, who were in awe of the influence the *Druadh* were supposed to hold with the latter. With the growth of Christianity, the influence of the *Druadh* declined, and they progressively faded from the scene, but the beliefs and superstitions which they had fostered lingered on. The rise of Christianity brought with it the concept of the devil, in whom all powers of evil were concentrated. And the belief that humans who gave their souls to him could receive delegated powers in return was not all that great an extension of their former belief in the powers of the *Druadh*. Almost inevitably, a new class of person arose to fill the role, known variously as the magician, enchantress, sorcerer or witch. By their spells and charms, they were able to induce all manner of ill-fortune on people, and others could use similar powers to counteract such evils, even to curing ills and sickness.

A particularly feared power of the sorcerer was that of the 'evil eye', which had only to be turned on a person, or on someone's livestock or crops with evil intent for ill-fortune to follow. There were two ways of countering such a curse. If the identity of the witch casting the evil gaze was known or suspected, a quantity of dust was gathered from where she had stood, or from the threshold of her abode. The dust was then applied to the victim. In cases where the witch could not be identified, there was yet another brand of practitioner, the 'charmer', who could be engaged. The *fer-obbee* (men-charmers) and *ben-obbee* (women-charmers) were the Manx equivalent of the witch-doctor. Their rituals involved charms, incantations and (where appropriate) medicinal herbs. Their methods were little different from those of the witches themselves, but they were accepted as acting with good intentions.

T. E. Brown described the full range of the witch's powers in his dialect poem *The Manx Witch*. In the following extracts (which are but a small part of a very long narrative poem), he begins by warning against buying rings or charms from strangers, and then goes through the full range of consequences that could befall the wearer, before pronouncing the desired fate of the practitioner of the black art.

> A wutch? Of coorse she was a wutch,
> And a black wutch, the wuss that's goin' –
> The white is – well, I'm hardly knowin'
> [If they exist,] but these ould things
> That's sellin' charms to sailors, rings,
>
> ....
>
> I s'pose the most of ye's got the lek
> Somewhere hung about your neck.
> But there's odds of charms; for some is just
> A surt of a blessin'; but some is a cuss,
> Most bitther, brewed in the very gall
> Of spite and hate, and'll creep and crawl
> Over your body and over your sowl,
> Aye, man! Aye! At laste so I'm tould –
> And through and through, and makin' you sick,
> And makin' you mad – aw, they know the trick!
> Cussin' your fingers and cussin' your toes,
> Cussin' your mouth and cussin' your nose,
> Every odd jint, and every limb,
> And all your inside – that's the thrim –
> Cussin' your horse and cussin' your cow,
> Cussin' the boar and cussin' the sow –
> Everything that's got a tail;
> Aye, and your spade, and your cart, and your flail,
> Plough and harras, stock and crop,
> Nets and lines – they'll navar stop –
>
> ....

And not a word, but the evil eye –
There ye are! You're struck, they've done ye!
They've got ye – you're tuk! They've put it upon ye –
Aw, [ter'ble] shockin'! And harbs! They picks them
The right time of the moon, and they'll take and mix them –
I've seen this woman myself goin' pryin'
Under the hedges, and stoopin' and spyin';
And if she seen me, she'd give a gurn
Most horrid at me. Yis, and they'll burn,
And they'll fry and they'll stew, and makin' faces –
What is it they won't do? – Brutes o' bases!
I know their par and I know their mar –
Divils! divils! that's what they are!
And should be tuk and burnt the way
They used to be – by gough, I'll lay
You'd smell the brimstone – you would so –
But no justice now, nor nothin' – no!

So what *was* the fate of those found guilty of practising the black art? The best-known tradition (but with no historical record to confirm it) is that which has become associated with Slieau Whallian, the hill overlooking St John's and the Tynwald fairground. Popularly known as 'the witches' hill' (although that is not the translation of its Manx name), tradition has it that a person suspected of witchcraft was taken to the summit of the hill and sealed inside a barrel, through the sides of which metal spikes had been driven into the interior. The barrel was then released to roll down the hill. If, on reaching the bottom, the occupant of the barrel was found to be dead, then it was considered that the judgment of the Almighty had been handed down. If, on the other hand, the accused survived the journey alive, then it was clearly a sign of sorcery and the witch was consigned to the stake. However, as I say, there is no documentary evidence of this practice.

There is record of only two executions for witchcraft, involving a mother and son who were burned at the stake in the market place at Castletown in the early seventeenth century. The secrets and rituals of witchcraft were often kept in the family and passed down the generations. Apart from the two known executions, convicted practitioners of the black art were treated far less brutally. Church records contain numerous accounts of trials, which were heard by the Ecclesiastical Court, presided over by the Vicar-General. The penalty on conviction was either a fine or an act of penance, which usually entailed the convicted person standing at the door of one or more of the parish churches on Sunday mornings, enveloped in a white sheet and carrying a candle. In another case from the seventeenth century, the Vicar-General had before him a woman with a long history as a practitioner of the art. She was charged with making the claim that, if she were supplied with a pair of pewter dishes – new and having been put to no previous use – she would convert them into wings and fly over the sea to Scotland. The Vicar-General dismissed the case, declaring that it was not unlawful for a woman to fly from the Isle of Man to Scotland. It is not recorded whether the ambitious aviatrix ever achieved her goal, but my guess is that the Vicar-General was being most astute in calling her bluff and leaving her to prove her claim.

In later times, when the powers of sorcery and witchcraft were on the wane, traditional customs and superstitions which had been employed to protect against the influences of the black art continued to exert a hold on the imagination of many in the Manx population. Even among those who acknowledged that the dark influences of occultism had gone (or had never been), there remained a belief (for example) that the power of the elder tree (Manx *tramman*) – even if no longer repelling the evil intentions of the witch, then at least as a guardian of good fortune – should not lightly be discarded. And if – just if – there happened to be the odd witch or two still lurking behind the *thie veg* – well, better to be safe. It has to be admitted that the *tramman* was a particularly effective defence; the bottom of our old garden at Kirk Michael was a mass of it, and we were never bothered by witches – or elephants, for that matter.

On a somewhat smaller scale, sprays of herbs were (and are on occasion) worn as defence against evil spirits or simply as good-luck adornments. At Midsummer, two plants have been resorted to at various times in the past. *Hypericum perforatum*, St John's wort, or *Bollan-feall-Eoin* in Manx (the 'herb of John's feast'), was worn all over Christendom on Midsummer Day, 24 June, which is also St John's Day. In Man after 1752, still ignoring this new-fangled calendar, it was worn on 5 July, Tynwald Day, when it adorned the lapels of those partici-pating in the ceremonial activities, and of many of those in the crowd.

Stenning, writing in 1958 [72], complains that in the early nineteenth century, members of the House of Keys began wearing the mugwort (*Artemisia vulgaris*), which invoked the name of Artemis, or Diana, and had connotations of paganism. He refers to wild frolics and dances in the heather on South Barrule, 'revels too shocking to be told'. (Why am I never invited to any of these?) He observes that the attempts of the Church to subsume the pagan festivals within the Christian ethos appeared to have suffered a reversal on St John's Day. It was doubtless the intention of the Church that the feast of St John should fall on the same day as Diana's, but it is still the mugwort that is worn today, having acquired the Manx name of *Bollan-vane* or *Bollan bane* ('white herb').

Other herbs were valued for their medicinal or other properties. The primrose (Manx *sumark*) was supposed to bring good luck. They were loved by the li'l folk, and were picked on Mayday Eve and scattered over the farmyard and in front of the houses. The water violet *Pinguicula vulgaris* (Manx *Lus-y-steep*, the rennet flower), in addition to its cheese-making properties, was good for poor eyesight and toothache. The shamrock (*Luss-ny-tree-duillag*, 'the plant of three leaves') was also good for toothache. The four-leaved clover, *Luss-ny-kiare-duillag*, was efficacious against any loitering evil spirits. The Manx national flower, the ragwort, *Senecio Jacobaea* (Manx *cushag*) was effective against infection, and the *Luss-yn-aacheoid*, 'the plant of the sickness', or purple meadow-button, was valued for deflecting the evil eye.

But the notions of witches and their crafts were 'a lang time a-dyin'', as were their reputed connections with the animals of the field, especially the hare and hedgehog. Numerous stories are told of sorcerers and witches transforming themselves into hares and back again. A. W. Moore recounts the tale of a pack of farm dogs chasing a hare out of sight behind some hedges. On catching up with his pursuers, the farm workers found them at a standstill, barking and whining around a man who was well known as a suspected witch. Being hard-pressed, he had been forced to return to human form, to the puzzlement of the dogs.

In other cases of dogs chasing hares, where the hare was run to a standstill and turned to face them, they would not approach it, but stood whining around it. And again, when a farmer had shot a hare and followed his dogs to retrieve the kill, he would find them howling in front of an old woman sitting on a rock, nursing a broken leg and uttering curses at man and dogs. I can only repeat the stories as they were told.

There are numerous wells (Manx *chibbyr*) throughout the isle, many of which had church connections and were reputed to possess medicinal properties. Most of them were not deep, but shallow springs or hollows which nonetheless contained water throughout the year. Several were thought to be effective against eye infections, such as *Chibbyr Catreeney* (Catherine), in Arbory, *Chibbyr Pherick* (Patrick), above the sea-cliffs of Peel Hill, and another of the same name near Social Cottage, in Lonan, where a Mayday fair was held until 1834. *Chibbyr Vaghal* (Maughold) had similar powers, and its water was also resorted to by infertile women. And water from the well at Glencrutchery was taken by farmers' wives from Onchan (rather than using their own wells) because it was known that a few drops added to the churn caused the butter to form much more rapidly.

Tales of ghosts and hauntings were legion in times gone by. The one which is most widely remembered nowadays is that involving the *Moddey dhoo*, the black dog, which was reputed to haunt Peel Castle. This black, shaggy-haired canine (the first element is pronounced 'mauthe', with a short 'e' on the end) frequented the chambers of the castle, particularly the guardroom, eventually (it is said) causing the death of a soldier of the garrison in about 1660, after which, according to the official guide to the castle, it was never seen again. Nevertheless, there are still those today who will tell you that they knew a person who knew a person who knew another person who claimed to have seen the *Moddey dhoo* and who died shortly thereafter.

But let us turn from superstitions of the land to superstitions of the sea. Fishermen were always a superstitious bunch. A herring must not be turned over on the plate, regardless of whether it is being consumed on land or sea. When the first side has been eaten, the backbone is lifted clear, so that the remainder may be consumed. To turn the fish on the plate would be to invite the overturning of the boat which hauled it from the sea.

Manx fishermen themselves had many an odd custom of their own. John Dyson [23] recounts that, until the middle of the nineteenth century, fishing in the Isle of Man was 'a curious mixture of drink, superstition and religion'. The boats, which had lain, keel up, all winter, were launched into the water in April. Each skipper hired his crew at the 'boat's supper', which was held around Christmas time, with plentiful supplies of pies, puddings, rum and *jough* (beer). The skipper passed a shilling (5p) to his first choice as crewman and named his terms. If the terms were agreed, the coin was passed on, and on, until the crew was complete. Before the boats left harbour to fish, the parson would visit the quayside each morning and evening to read divine service, and any crewman who missed this proceeding was barred from sailing that trip. If the boat's ballast had been replaced, it would be checked carefully for white stones, which were bringers of bad luck and must be removed.

On leaving harbour, another superstition was observed – that the third boat to set out would have no luck in the fishing. To avoid this misfortune, the second and third boats were lashed beam-to-beam and departed together. Once clear of the harbour, all hands doffed their hats, a prayer was said, and a measure of rum was served. At the end of the trip, as they approached port, the fishing boats were met by 'bimming' yawls, carrying fish-buyers, who would board the fishing boats and strike a bargain for the catch, after which, a shilling deposit – known as the 'earlys' or 'earnest' – was paid over and a bottle of rum passed round. The buyers' smacks would be waiting in the harbour to run the fish to the English markets, or they would be salted and barrelled for export to the sugar plantations of the West Indies. On stepping ashore, the crew would repair to their chosen pub and divide the proceeds of the catch between them. Any odd shillings left over were called 'God's portion' and the future good fortune of the boat depended on its being given to the poor. Of course, not all of the fish caught went for export, for fish was a staple part of the Manx diet, the other being the potato; hence the well-worn reference to the traditional Manx diet as 'spuds'n'herrin''.

In the early 1800s, there were more than 250 boats in the Manx fishing fleet, with up to ten men per boat. Manx fishermen never worked on a Saturday evening or on a Sunday. Towards the end of that century, with drifters flocking in to the Irish Sea from Scotland, East Anglia and Cornwall, there were many hundreds of boats fishing from the Manx ports during the herring season, and the peculiarly Manx customs began to fade from use. Today, the numbers of Manx boats and Manx fishermen are greatly reduced – as are the remnants of the old customs.

MUSIC AND THE ARTS

There was always a firm musical strand running through the Manx character, initially embodied principally in vocal and dance forms, but extending also into the instrumental. In historical times, the love of singing was nurtured in the churches and chapels, and then spread into the secular life beyond. The growth of external trade, the visiting industry and immigration were influences which would inevitably bring changes to the spectrum of secular music; in later times, radio, television and the music industry would accelerate the process. The choral tradition today is maintained through the efforts of the Manx Festival Chorus, the Douglas Choral Union (founded 1892), the Lon Dhoo Male Voice Choir and the Lon Vane Ladies' Choir.

The main event displaying the island's vocal tradition is the annual Manx Music Festival, otherwise known as 'the Guild', which is held in the newly refurbished Royal Hall of the Villa Marina, in Douglas. Founded in 1892, this is the event of the year for Manx singers, although non-Manx participants are not excluded. The highlight of the week-long festival is the competition for solo singers, the winner of which is awarded the Cleveland Medal, donated by the Cleveland Manx Society in the United States.

The other venue for regular musical competition and performance is the Erin Arts Centre, in Port Erin, which hosts the annual Lionel Tertis international viola competition. The competition was first held in 1980; it is the only such competition for the instrument and, in 2006, attracted players from thirty-four countries. The centre also hosts the Manannan International Festival of Music and the Arts, an opera festival, the Young Musician of Mann and Young Singer of Mann competitions, as well as a number of other stage and musical performances during the year.

Traditional music and dance at Yn Cruinnaght

Much of the old traditional Manx music has doubtless been lost over the years, yet much – both music and dance – still remains and is performed at the annual national festival, *Yn Cruinnaght*. This week-long gathering in July is centred on Ramsey but takes in other venues around the island, and visiting groups from other Celtic regions – Ireland, Scotland, Wales, Cornwall and Brittany – give the gathering an international flavour. The *cruinnaght* is the Manx equivalent of the Welsh *eisteddfod*, and local *cruinnaghts* and *eisteddfods* were held in the island in years past; indeed the Cronk-y-Voddy *Eisteddfod* has been staged in recent years. The original national festival, *Yn Cruinnaght Ashoonagh Vannin*, died out in the 1930s but the present gathering was revived in 1977.

The Manx folk music performed today is remembered largely due to the collective efforts of A. W. Moore (*Manx Ballads and Music*, 1896) and W. H. Gill (*The Manx National Song Book*, 1896). One of the collected items was a plaintive ballad concerning a reclusive old character named Mylecharaine. George Borrow translated the ballad into English and tells us:

> In the turf bogs of Jurby, from history we learn
> There lived an old miser called Mollycharaine.

The melody to this song became so popular that it was revised and adapted to be performed as a ballad, dance-tune or hymn, and one form of it became known as the 'Manx National Air'. W. H. Gill took this version and revised it further, and this was adopted as the Manx National Anthem:

> O land of our birth,
> O gem of God's earth,
> O Island so strong and so fair;
> Built firm as Barrule,
> Thy throne of Home Rule
> Makes us free as thy sweet mountain air.

Like the British National Anthem, there is more than one verse but relatively few people remember the rest of it.

The instrumental tradition in Manx music – particularly the orchestral – has shown growth in the past thirty years, with the Manx Sinfonia (now renamed the Isle of Man Symphony Orchestra) and the Manx Youth Orchestra both flourishing. Orchestral concerts by visiting British symphony orchestras are occasionally staged at the Villa Marina. The brass-band tradition has been strong in the island for decades, with the long-established bands of Douglas, Crosby, Castletown, Rushen and Ramsey, together with the Manx Youth Band and that of the Salvation Army. The Isle of Man Arts Council sponsors a season of summer concerts at the Villa Marina each year, in which most of the bands participate.

The opera scene in Man is sustained by the Manx Operatic Society and the Manx Gilbert and Sullivan Society. It appears that the non-musical form of drama was slow to achieve a level of popularity comparable with that of the musical theatre. Some sort of balance was struck in 1932, with the formation of the Legion Players (extant today), and yet the impression persists that Manx audiences are still more receptive of the musical form. Perhaps this merely reflects the age-old proclivity of the Manx to sing; certainly it should not be taken as a reflection on the qualities of Manx players of straight drama.

An unusual theatre production which has remained popular since its inception in 1986 (possibly in part due to its unusual venue) is the open-air 'Shakespeare in Peel Castle'. In a run of five evenings at the end of July, the Theatre Set-Up company performs one of Shakespeare's works within the curtain wall of the castle. Patrons bring their own chairs or blankets or cushions, and those seated on chairs are kept apart from those on the ground so that all can see. The only possible disruptions come from the screaming of the gulls and the sighing of the wind. The promoting company is headed by John Shakespeare – whom else?

In the range of fine arts, there are seven names which (to my mind) are remembered above the rest, four of them Manx, of whom two are still living. In the field of architecture, three names stand out, and they are the three who were

*The Gaiety Theatre: (above) a horse-drawn tram passes the theatre; (below) the
ornately decorated interior*

not Manx-born, but came to the island to do specific (and outstanding) work and then departed.

Frank Matcham (1854–1920) was the leading theatre designer of his day (perhaps of any day). He was engaged by the Palace and Derby Castle Company to convert the old Marina Pavilion dance hall into the brand-new Gaiety Theatre. And what a job he made of it. The interior has been described by some as 'ornately vulgar'. Ornate certainly, but vulgar? – never! To be seated in the body of that magnificent auditorium, surrounded by those swirling, seductive mouldings to ceiling and box-fronts, bathed in their softly lit pastel shades, is to dream of being enfolded within the welcoming embrace of a large, enticing, voluptuous woman – and wishing never to be released. (I regret leaving my female reader to dream up her own fantasy.)

The Gaiety was opened in 1900, and Matcham followed it with the (now-vanished) Palace Ballroom in 1902, two facilities well timed to meet the peak years of the island's visiting industry. Seventy years later (1971), in a rather run-down state, the Gaiety was purchased by the Manx government and received some much-needed repairs. In the 1990s, it was given a thorough make-over and restored to its original glory.

The Gaiety Theatre is one of the two prime venues left to us today for the performing arts. The other is the neighbouring Villa Marina. This was the work of Douglas Corporation, which purchased the Villa Marina estate – successively the residence of Governor Pigott (1860–3) and Henry Bloom Noble – and, with funding from the trustees of Noble's estate, built the Royal Hall. It was opened in 1913, and its ancillary appendages, including the art deco Arcade, followed in later years. In the late 1990s, the Villa Marina was purchased by the Manx government from the Corporation (which was an unwilling seller) and given a £12 million refurbishment, reopening in 2004. Henry Bloom Noble – in bronze – stands guard at the entrance.

Another visiting architect to work in Man was Baillie Scott (1865–1945), who arrived in 1889 and stayed until 1901. His work in the island was mainly concerned with houses and their interiors, and he also produced designs for furniture. It was his work on prestigious buildings in Europe that brought him to prominence. His well-known namesake, Sir Giles Gilbert Scott (1880–1960), architect of the Anglican Cathedral in Liverpool and Waterloo Bridge in London, also came to the island. His design for the present Roman Catholic church in Ramsey (the Church of Our Lady Star of the Sea and St Maughold) in 1910 replaced the much smaller church which stood on the site. He was also responsible for internal additions to St Mary's, in Douglas, and the original St Anthony's in Onchan.

An artist and sculptor who worked with Baillie Scott at some time was Manx-born Archibald Knox (1864–1933), who trained at the Douglas School of Art. His paintings of Manx landscapes are still popular in the island but, in the wider field,

The Church of Our Lady Star of the Sea and St Maughold, Ramsey

he was known for the quality of his artwork in pewter and silver, which he undertook for Liberty's of London, incorporating designs based on the interlaced patterns of the Manx Celtic and Norse cross-slabs. His collaboration with Baillie Scott involved the design of decorative features on and in houses, and he later produced designs for Manx war memorials. He also produced fine illustrations for books but is probably best known among the general public today for having a public house in Onchan named after him.

There are two modern Manx-born sculptors with international reputations. The bronze of Henry Bloom Noble at the entrance to the Villa Marina is the work of Bryan Kneale, holder of a professorial chair at the Royal College of Art, who received his initial training at the Douglas School of Art. He is responsible for the bronze of Hall Caine which stands in Summerhill Gardens, at the north end of the Douglas promenade. His other prominent work in the island is his modern interpretation of the Three Legs of Man, which greets travellers as they emerge from the air terminal building at Ronaldsway and aroused mixed feelings when it was first erected. (For what it is worth – I like it. I can just imagine Manannan Mac Lir, having transformed himself into this sleek triskelion form, poised to rotate away at dizzying speed into the mist.)

The second Manx-born sculptor, Michael Sandle, another holder of a professorial chair (but in Germany), also trained at the Douglas School of Art (and the Slade). Much of his work takes the theme of war and its brutality, and yet it covers a wide variety of subjects, ranging from the Siege Bell, in Malta, to the memorial to the Royal National Lifeboat Institution, in Douglas, and *The Viking*, a sculpture which adorns a door at the Erin Arts Centre.

Over the years, there have been numerous painters of the Manx scene (both Manx-born and incomers) but, in the absence of a class of landed gentry – which else-where would have provided the nuclei for private art collections – the

The bust of Sir Hall Caine in Summerhill Gardens, Douglas

island lacked any focal point to which such works could be drawn. The artist whose reputation stands above the rest (and whose story is the most inter-esting) is John Miller Nicholson (1840–1913). Born into a family which ran its own painting and decorating business, Nicholson felt drawn to painting of a more artistic bent. Entirely self-taught, he received encouragement in his artistic ambitions from the wife of Governor Loch (the former Elizabeth Villiers) and John Ruskin. After a visit to Italy, his work won acclaim when shown outside the island. In 1880, he and Lady Loch promoted the island's first art exhibition, and the interest thus aroused led to the foundation of the Douglas School of Art in 1884. Following his death, a large quantity of Nicholson's works was purchased by a charitable trust, and this would later form the beginnings of the Manx Museum's art collection.

MANX NATIONAL HERITAGE

It used to be known as the Manx Museum and National Trust, the former branch being responsible for the main museum in Douglas and its out-station sites in various parts of the island, whilst the Manx National Trust was custodian of lands and ancient monuments. Today, following what seems to be a universal urge to have 'heritage' somewhere in all such titles, it is Manx National Heritage, or MNH, and it is the guardian of comprehensive collections of artefacts and archives which illustrate the history and prehistory of the island and its people. MNH is responsible for all the functions previously undertaken by the Manx Museum and National Trust. Its headquarters is in Douglas, at the Manx Museum, *Yn Thie Tashtee Vannin*, literally 'the Treasure House of Man'. It is interesting to note that *tashtee* is also used for 'bank' (the financial sort, not the river bank). Besides the main museum, there are a dozen other museum or similar sites around the

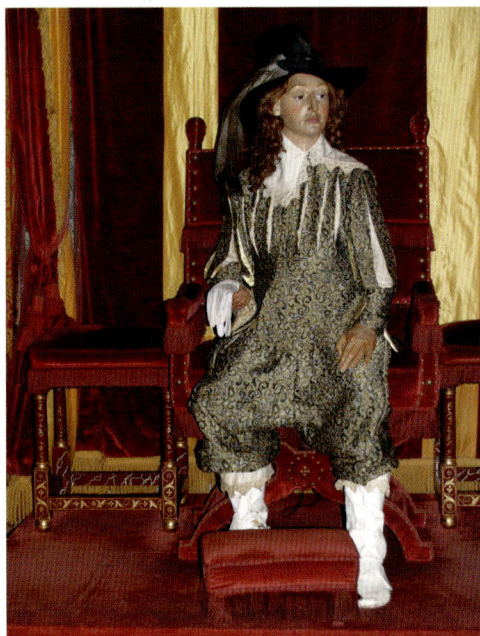

A seventeenth-century Lord of Man sits in regal splendour in Castle Rushen

island, which together are marketed under the brand-name 'The Story of Mann' and have won a number of major awards.

The Manx Museum, opened in 1922, occupies the building that was the original Noble's Hospital, and has galleries depicting the island's geology, archaeology, natural history and human and social history. The National Art Gallery contains works by John Miller Nicholson, Archibald Knox, Bryan Kneale and William Hoggatt, who, though Lancaster-born, spent much of his life in the island. The oak-panelled walls of the T. E. Brown Memorial Room contain furniture and personal effects belonging to the poet, together with a marble bust of him by Charles Swinnerton. The bay window previously displayed three stained-glass panels depicting characters and scenes from Brown's poems, but these have been moved to a less exposed location inside the building. The MNH Library is the principal location of Manx archives, with extensive collections of public and private papers and printed Manx books and articles. Its reading room is open to all who wish to delve into its archives.

In Peel, on the site of the old railway station, the House of Manannan takes up the Story of Mann. Opened in 1997, this is the newest of the MNH out-stations. Some impressive and imaginative displays depict life in a Celtic roundhouse and a Nordic longhouse, complete with sound effects. The largest single object on display is the replica Viking longship *Odin's Raven*, which was sailed from Norway to Peel in 1979 to commemorate the Millennium of Tynwald. Other displays show aspects from later periods of the island's nautical heritage, including the smoking of Manx kippers. Glowering across from the other side of the harbour, stand the ruins of Peel Castle and the old cathedral of St German, among which the visitor may wander, with audio-guidance from the recorded voice of Manannan.

Down in the old Manx capital of Castletown, the limestone fortress of Castle Rushen – seat of the resident kings and lords of Man – stands perfectly formed and perfectly preserved. Here again, there are static displays of life inside the fortress, with sound effects including conversation in the banqueting hall – right down to the grunting of an old codger seated on the loo.

There are three other museum sites in Castletown. Bridge House, the tall, gaunt-looking building standing beside the harbour, was the home of the Quayle family. The Nautical Museum was the boat-house belonging to the property and was donated to the nation by the Quayle family. It was used to house Captain George Quayle's armed yacht *Peggy*, which still sits at the head of the slipway down which she used to slide into the harbour. After George Quayle's death, the exit from the slipway was bricked up, and so the *Peggy* has nowhere to go today. The upper storey of the boat-house was fashioned into the stern quarter of a ship, with a small stern window overlooking the harbour, and a promenade deck (more

The armed yacht Peggy *sits in her tight little boat-house at the Castletown Nautical Museum*

of a balcony) outside. Inside were a ship's galley and wine-bins, and all sorts of merry japes went on there. (More of this in Chapter 12.)

Hemmed in on the south side of Castletown harbour is the old House of Keys. Here, one may listen in on recorded debates and even vote on such contentious issues as – should women have the vote? Nearby, the old Grammar School was built initially as the church of St Mary and became the Grammar School in 1570. It was closed in 1930.

In Ballasalla, Rushen Abbey is not the earliest, but is considered the most significant, religious site in Man. Founded in 1134, it is still believed by some that *Chronicon Regum Manniae et Insularum*, the Chronicle of the Kings of Man and the Isles, was written by the monks of the abbey, but it is far from certain where it was written. There is a visitors' centre which tells the story of the site, and archaeological excavations continue each summer.

Also in the south is the Cregneash Folk Museum, which was the first open-air folk museum to be established in the British Isles, based on an idea from Scandinavia, where such things had long been popular. The MNH holding at Cregneash comprises a group of traditional thatched cottages, furnished to show the domestic arrangements and rural trade activities in the nineteenth and early twentieth centuries. Harry Kelly's cottage is the very epitome of the basic (very

Harry Kelly's cottage and the turner's shop, Cregneash

basic) crofter-fisherman's dwelling of the time, with the wide, open hearth and fireplace, the *chiollagh*, and the *slouree*, the large iron cooking-pot suspended above the hearth. The other buildings are equipped as a weaver's cottage, a turner's shop and a smithy, all with their roofing thatch lashed down securely with ropes attached to stone pegs projecting from the gables. The site includes a farm holding which, including rough grazing, extends to some 430 acres (174ha) and is worked extensively with horse-drawn equipment. MNH's main flock of *loghtan* sheep is also kept there.

A mile to the south-west, the road comes to a dead-end beside the Sound Restaurant and Visitor Centre, which looks out across the often-turbulent waters of Calf Sound to the Calf of Man, also owned by MNH and operated as a bird observatory. Some people assume (and it even appears in MNH literature) that the Sound Visitor Centre stands on the Isle of Man's southern extremity. A glance at the map shows the error of the claim; the southernmost tip of the isle is actually Dreswick Point, which is the southern extremity of the Langness peninsula.

Up along the west coast, halfway between the Sound and Peel, a similar (but smaller) café and visitor centre stands above the coast where the rocky promontory of Niarbyl, 'the Tail', juts out into the sea beyond a pair of traditional Manx cottages, also owned by MNH and a favoured location for filming.

Calf Sound: the Thusla Cross looks out to the Calf of Man

Fishermen's cottages at Niarbyl

The Grove Museum stands in the northern outskirts of Ramsey. It consists of a Victorian villa with associated outbuildings. The house contains the furnishings and effects of the wealthy family – the Gibbs – who lived there, whilst the outbuildings house the vehicles and equipment used on the adjoining farmland. The conservatory provides a convenient eating-place for visitors. The house is of no more than modest size for its type, but those who believe that there were no social divisions in old Manx society should visit the Grove and then compare what they see there with what they have seen at Cregneash.

There are other sites and ancient monuments in the ownership of Manx National Heritage, together with extensive holdings of land, much of it of high landscape value, and we shall come to these as we travel round the island in Part 2.

TYNWALD DAY

And so we come to the day which – historically, culturally, socially, and with the persistent underlying awareness of national identity – sees the principal gathering of the year. Stemming from its ancient Scandinavian roots, and only lightly modi-

PEOPLE, CULTURE AND TRADITION

fied by centuries of post-Nordic history, the open-air gathering of Tynwald at St John's proceeds in unchanging form on 5 July. If 5 July falls at a weekend, then the assembly and the national holiday are transferred to the Friday or Monday, whichever is the nearer to the fifth of the month. In Man, the name 'Tynwald' has come to be used for both the assembly and the place of assembly, whereas, in its Scandinavian birthplace, the *thing* or *ting* was the parliamentary assembly, and the *völlr* the field in which the assembly gathered.

At St John's, the early morning of Tynwald Day is a scene of bustling activity. The surface of the processional way leading from the church to the hill is overlain with the traditional covering of rushes, whilst a multitude of stands and stalls are given their final touches on the adjacent fair-field, in readiness for the riot of fairground trading and frolicking that will follow the formal proceedings. The seating arrangements on the hill itself will have been set out in good time, beneath the large conical canopy which surmounts it. The canopy and the spectators' grandstand will have been erected during the preceding week. In the days before modern transport, Manx people would leave home at some unearthly hours in order to be at the field in time – it was that important.

The proceedings today begin for the dignitaries at 11 a.m., with a service in the Royal Chapel of St John the Baptist, and it is so timed that the outdoor procedures may begin at around midday – which is when the old pagan festivities would have reached their height. The service inside the chapel is broadcast through loudspeakers to the crowd outside. There is no record of a dedication to St John on this site before 1577. It was clearly the intention of the early Churchmen to subsume the former pagan midsummer festival within a Christian feast on the same day, and it was surely no coincidence that St John's feast-day was scheduled for 24 June – Midsummer Day. But, as hinted earlier, and as we shall see again, there is one item of pagan symbolism which has regained its hold on Tynwald Day.

The present church – granted the special status of a chapel royal – was completed in 1849, on the site of an earlier one erected centuries before. In the entrance porch stands the broken fragment of a Norse cross discovered on the site. Its carving is in the same style as that of Gaut's cross in Kirk Michael, but the runic inscription on this one reads: 'But Osruth carved these runes'. The first function of the chapel was that of a court-house and, at the same time as its construction, a 4-foot (1.2m) wall was erected to support the ancient banking which encloses the hill, the processional way and the chapel-court. On the north side of the processional way stands the elegant National War Memorial designed by the famous Manx archaeologist P. M. C. Kermode, commemorating the outstanding contribution by Manx men and women to the British armed services in the Napoleonic and two world wars. It may seem something of a paradox that this small nation, which struggled so long and so hard to wrest increasing measures of self-determination from the grip of successive British governments, should nonetheless continue to display unerring loyalty to the Crown, and yet that impression still persists.

After the service in the Chapel of St John, the dignitaries emerge to begin their procession along the rush-covered way to the hill. And it is then that we see the lapels of our Manx legislators adorned with sprays of mugwort, *Artemisia vulgaris*, the herb of the festival of the pagan goddess Diana, and now known in Manx as *Bollan vane* (white herb). This is the practice of which Archdeacon Stenning complained in 1958. He does not mention the Manx name *Bollan vane* (Moore does not mention it either) and thus it appears to be a more recent appellation. A later collector of Manx folklore, W. W. Gill (1879–1963), in his *Third Manx Scrapbook* (1963), does apply the name to mugwort, but also gives *Bollan-feaill-Eoin* as an alternative name, although this obviously translates to St John's wort. And Moore himself [60] is not blameless in this confusion: having stated that practices with herbs and fire on May-Day Eve and Midsummer Eve were the same, he identifies *Bollan-feaill-Eoin* (correctly) as St John's wort on May-Day Eve, and then as 'John's Feast-day wort (mugwort)' on Midsummer Eve, thereby applying the Manx name to two different plants. Even the committee of Tynwald which produced the official guide booklet, *Tynwald: Symbol of an Ancient Kingdom* (last known edition 1976, now out of print), referred to '*Bollan-vane or Bollan-feailleoin*, herb of John's feast', when it was not the herb of John's feast that was being worn. It would appear that the only authority to get it right was Stenning. In summary:

(a) St John's wort, *Hypericum perforatum*, Manx *Bollan-feaill-Eoin, was* worn in the Christian midsummer festival of St John.

(b) Mugwort, *Artemisia vulgaris*, Manx *Bollan vane, was* worn in the old pagan midsummer festival, and *is* worn today at St John's on Tynwald Day.

According to Stenning's account, members of the House of Keys began the reversion from Christian to pagan symbolism in the early nineteenth century, and the practice persists to this day.

But, back to the ceremony, as the procession approaches the hill. At the head of the moving line is the sword-bearer, carrying the Manx Sword of State vertically point upwards, followed by the Lieutenant Governor and the rest in prescribed order. If the Queen, as Lord of Man, or another member of the royal family is present, then Her Majesty or that other member takes precedence behind the sword-bearer and presides on the hill; otherwise (and usually), it is the Governor's role.

Tynwald Hill is not a natural hill at all, but an artificially constructed circular mound formed in four tiers. Tradition has it that the soil for its construction was brought from all seventeen of the island's parishes, thereby reinforcing the notion that the purpose of this day's proceedings was to symbolize the unity of this island-nation. The lowest of the four tiers is 82 feet (25m) in diameter, the second 52 feet (16m), the third 32 feet (10m) and the topmost 19 feet (6m), the tiers all being about three feet (0.9m) in height.

As they process onto the hill, the Governor takes his place on the topmost tier, facing east along the processional way, accompanied by the President of Tynwald and members of the Legislative Council. The Keys occupy the second tier. The third level is taken by the High Bailiff, the Archdeacon, the Vicar-General, the Mayor of Douglas, the chairmen of the town and village commissioners and the clergy. The Captains of the Parishes, fulfilling their only formal role nowadays, occupy the fourth tier. At the foot of the hill are the two Deemsters, the four Coroners and *Yn Lhaihder* (literally 'The Reader', who is proficient in Manx Gaelic). The First Deemster stands on the south side of the entrance to the hill, facing the Second Deemster on the north. The assembly is completed at ground level by a massed choir and a military band from a visiting contingent of one of the armed services.

After the singing of the British and Manx National Anthems, the Lieutenant Governor opens the proceedings with the instruction:

Learned Deemster, direct the Court to be fenced.

The first Deemster then passes on the instruction with the words:

Coroner of Glenfaba Sheading and *Yn Lhaider*, fence the court.

The coroner thereupon fences the court by proclaiming:

I fence this Court of Tynwald in the name of our most Gracious Sovereign Lady the Queen. I charge that no person do quarrel, brawl or make any disturbance and that all persons do answer their names when called. I charge this audience to witness this Court is fenced. I charge this audience to witness this Court is fenced. I charge this whole audience to bear witness this Court is now fenced.

(At this stage it is probably safe to assume that the Court has been fenced.) *Yn Lhaihder* then repeats the fencing pronouncement in Manx.

There then follows a short ceremony in which the four Coroners-elect (for Glenfaba and Michael, Ayre and Garff, Middle, and Rushen) ascend the hill to receive their staves of office from the Lieutenant Governor, and to take the oath of office, administered by the First Deemster. Except in cases of death, retirement or incapacity, it is usually the outgoing Coroners who are re-appointed.

The Governor then instructs the deemsters:

Learned Deemsters, I exhort you to proclaim to the people in ancient form such
laws as have been enacted during the past year and which have received Her
Gracious Majesty's Royal Assent.

In ancient times, the laws would have been read out in full, to ensure that all
the people were informed of their contents. Today, only the title and short
summary are read out. The First Deemster, if he is proficient in the Manx
language, announces the first new law in Manx, and is followed by the Second
Deemster, who repeats it in English. If neither Deemster is proficient in Manx,
then a suitable person will have been appointed to perform the Manx orations –
most probably *Yn Lhaihder*. The process continues until all the new laws have
been promulgated.

Towards the end of the formal proceedings, the opportunity is given for individuals to present petitions for redress of grievances. Such petitions must relate
to matters in which the petitioners have exhausted all other lawful means of
redress – i.e. the petition to Tynwald must be the petitioner's last resort. The petitioners are ushered along the processional way to the foot of the hill, where the
Clerk of Tynwald receives their petitions. In the weeks that follow, each will be
checked to ensure that it relates to a valid complaint and complies with the relevant standing orders of Tynwald. It will then be left to 'lie on the table' of Tynwald
until such time as a member decides to pick it up and propose some action to
redress the grievance. The system is thus reliant on the recognition by the
member that the complaint is one which is worthy of remedial action.

The ability to present a petition to Tynwald on Tynwald Day is often referred
to as an 'ancient right', and there doubtless were occasions in times long past
when such petitions were presented, but how regular the practice was is another
question. It was certainly not a regular procedure in the last century. When an
attempt was made to present a petition to the unpopular Lord Raglan at St John's
in 1916, the would-be petitioner was informed that standing orders did not permit
it. Nothing more was heard of the practice for another forty years. When another
petitioner presented himself at the foot of the hill in 1956 and declared: 'Your
Excellency, I have a petition to present', a silence of uncertainty descended on the
proceedings; no-one had heard of such a thing for years. But he, too, was told that
it was contrary to standing orders. However, the incident prompted a debate at
the next meeting in the Tynwald chamber, which eventually led to the drafting of
standing orders permitting the submission of petitions at the foot of Tynwald Hill.
Thus, our present 'ancient' right of petition dates from 1956.

But, with the passing of the years, there comes a growing impression that an increasing number of people are trying to 'play the system', culminating in one recent occasion when no less than eighteen identical petitions were submitted, all relating to the same subject. In these litigious times, when there are multiple routes whereby most grievances may be redressed, is the petition to Tynwald being used as a means of redress on the cheap? I do not know the answer, but I am increasingly aware of the question.

At the end of the formal proceedings on the hill, the First Deemster calls on the:

> Freemen of Man in your ancient Tynwald assembled, I call upon you as an expression of your loyalty to give three cheers for Her Majesty the Queen.

Following this, the procession retraces its steps down the hill, along the processional way and into the church, where a meeting of Tynwald Court is convened to conclude any formal business. The remainder of the day is for the public, and the fun and frolics of the fair-field.

Cynics may gaze on these proceedings and smile, and call them 'archaic', 'outdated', 'pointless' – even 'comical'. In confronting such epithets, and in bringing this account of the Isle of Man's national day to a close, I can do no better than reiterate the lines of Hall Caine which I quoted earlier in this chapter:

> Then let him who will laugh at our primitive ceremonial. It is the bade of our ancient liberty, and we need not envy the man who can look on it unmoved.

PART 2

OUT AND ABOUT

CHAPTER TEN

The Leisure Island

The wide range of more formal, 'organized' leisure activities available in the Isle of Man has been illustrated in Chapter 8. My main purpose in Part 2 of this book, particularly in Chapters 11–16, is to conduct the reader on a perambulation of the island, starting in Douglas and its surrounds, and working progressively clockwise around the isle so that, by the end of it, we shall have visited all of Man's towns, villages and parishes. As in other islands and other countries, there are places in Man where only the walker may go, being completely inaccessible to the motor vehicle, and so, in this opening chapter of Part 2, we begin by exploring the island's network of public rights of way, with which the island is very well endowed. In addition, there are rights of public ramblage over most of the Isle of Man government's holdings of hill-lands.

The island's public rights of way are shown on Sheet 95 of the Ordnance Survey's *Landranger* series at a scale of 1:50,000, and at the larger scale of 1:25,000 on the Manx government's two-sheet *Public Rights of Way and Outdoor Leisure Map*. Possession of one of these is an essential prerequisite for anyone intending to undertake any serious walking in the island, and especially before venturing onto the hills. The island possesses four designated long-distance paths, and we begin with these, starting with the oldest.

THE MILLENNIUM WAY

The first of the long-distance paths to be established was the Millennium Way, opened in 1979 as a permanent commemoration of the thousand years of Tynwald. But its origins would appear to go back much further than that. Approximately 25 miles in length, it is supposed to follow the line of an ancient trackway known as the Royal Way (Manx *Raad ny Ree*, Latin *Via Regia*) from Ramsey, over the heights of the northern hills, and south to the ancient seat of kings at Castle Rushen. The route is referred to in the medieval writings of *Chronicon*, but why any Nordic sea-king, on returning from Norway or the Western Isles, should choose to land at Ramsey and then march the length of the island to reach his home at Rushen, when there was always a perfectly good landing at Ronaldsway, has always been beyond me. However, ours is not to reason why ...

The walk can be made in a single day or split into two by taking a break at Crosby. The start of the Way is signed at the entrance to the farm track which ascends the northern flank of Sky Hill from the A3 Ramsey–Kirk Michael road, about 1 mile west of Ramsey. The walker setting out from the town leaves Parliament Square by the Lezayre Road (along the TT course in reverse) and turns off on reaching the waymark. The route climbs steeply through the Sky Hill plantation, above the site of the battle in which Godred Crovan won the kingship of Man in 1079. Sky Hill was the Norsemen's *Skogarfjall* ('wooded hill'), and its crest was the site of the day watch for the parish of Lezayre under the old 'watch and ward' system.

On attaining the crest of the hill, the walker is faced with easier gradients and open views over most points of the compass. At Park-ne-Earkan ('pasture of the lapwing'), the country opens out onto a broad expanse of wild, exposed moorland. The trees are left behind, save for a line of sparsely clad, almost skeletal pines which stand along this lofty ridge and can be seen on the skyline from all over the northern plain. To the east, the contours fall away – gradually at first, then more steeply – into the secluded, water-worn cleft of Glen Auldyn, with the long ridge of North Barrule standing sentinel beyond. There are ruined buildings up here, betraying the former presence of farmers who once lived on these slopes with their flocks. Today, the sheep are on their own, except for the rooks and crows and other birds that have taken over the ruins, and the occasional mountain hare scampering away at the first hint of an alien approach.

The way continues south, directly towards the brooding summit of Snaefell, incongruously adorned with radio antennae and the summit 'hotel'. The railway terminus is just below the summit and concealed from the northern viewpoint. One's first impression of this landscape is influenced greatly by the weather. In the gloom and the wet, it can seem a most desolate spot – at other times, totally different. The last of the trees have been left behind, the only vegetation now the heather and dwarf gorse, intermingled with the occasional outcrops of bilberry, and the whole underlain with the spongy springiness of the peat. This section of the way becomes quite boggy and indistinct in places, and one must keep a sharp look-out for the waymarks. In recent years, board-walks have been laid over the wetter sections. The walker was never so cosseted when I first walked this route in its inaugural year – no board-walks and most of the waymarks had been 'nicked' as souvenirs. It became a strict compass course.

The hills of Michael rise to the west of the Sulby Reservoir

As the route comes onto the broad saddle between Slieau Managh and Clagh Ouyr, we come within half a mile – and earshot – of the mountain section of the TT course. (Incidentally, *Slieau Managh* is the 'mountain of the monks'; much of the land to the north was owned by the monks of *Mirescogh*, the 'forest of the mire', whose monastery stood somewhere in the wetlands of the Lezayre curragh.) The old Royal Way swung south-east at this point (and this may still be done) to meet the present road at East Mountain Gate. To avoid the traffic, today's Millennium Way deviates south-west to traverse the western flank of Snaefell. On the way, a broad new vista opens up to the west, across the upper reaches of Sulby Glen and its reservoir, to the Michael hills and the sea beyond. On a clear day, the Mountains of Mourne line the western horizon.

After crossing the saddle, we drop down into the steep-sided little valley which collects the tributary streams that feed the Block Eary reservoir, whose only role today is to supply the hydro-electric generating plant in the main valley below. *Block Eary* translates as 'black shieling', and, at the point where we cross the stream, we are in the midst of a group of small mounds which mark the sites of shieling huts where medieval farmers spent their summers with their flocks in the uplands. The mounds were excavated in 1958–9, when pottery and a twelfth-century coin were uncovered. These are the best examples of such shielings in Man.

Climbing out on the south side of the valley, the route traverses the north-west flank of Snaefell and skirts the top end of Tholt-e-Will Glen and its plantation, before descending to the road which traverses the whole length of Sulby Glen from the Bungalow down to the Sulby crossroads. A short distance below our crossing point, the road slices through the remains of an ancient cross-dyke known as *Cleigh yn Arragh*. This earthwork of rampart and ditch stands at right angles to the ridge on which the road is built, and probably extended originally down to the stream on either side. Its date of origin is unknown but it probably dates from the Iron Age. But who built it, and against whom it was built – who knows? The only clue: we stand, at this point, close to the old dividing line between Northside and Southside, so was this a defence work by the north against the south, or vice versa? The name it bears today probably developed over a long period of time. *Arragh* may derive from the Old Irish, meaning 'rampart'. The Manx *cleigh*, which has the same meaning, may have been added after the meaning of *arragh* had been forgotten. Thus we have 'the rampart of the rampart'. Other Manx place-names have evolved through similar loss of folk-memory; Little London, in Michael, is another.

The slopes lower down are dotted with *tholtans*, the roofless ruins of the dwellings of hill-farmers and their families who, long ago, gave up the struggle of upland life and moved down into the lowlands. One such dwelling, Sherragh Vane, now hidden from view within the trunks of the Tholt-e-Will Plantation, was immortalized by T. E. Brown in his narrative poem, *Kitty of the Sherragh Vane*. If you fancy trying to track it down from where we now stand, just drop down the mile or so through Tholt-e-Will Glen to the point where the Sulby road crosses the river, and follow the instructions – if you can:

> The Sherragh Vane
> Is up Sulby glen,
> High up, my men –
> High up – you'll not see a sight of it
> From the road at all,
> By raison of the height of it –
> Terbil high; and a little skute
> Of a waterfall,
> Slip-sloppin' from the root
> Of an ould kern –
> You know the turn
> At the Bridge, and the Chapel?
> Well, in on the gate,
> Behind there, that's the road, like straight

For Druid-a-whapple;
And just you're passin'
The School, and up you go –
A track – a track, you know,
On the side of the brew, criss-crassin',
Till you come out on the top like a landin',
And the house standin'
Two fields back –
And all that steep
You can't see the river, not the smallest peep,
Nor the gill, nor nothin'; but lookin' right over
At Snaefell …

On second thoughts, better to leave it for another day. Let us continue.

Crossing directly over the Sulby Glen road, our way drops steeply into the valley on the south side of the ridge, beyond which the summit of Beinn-y-Phott ('Penny Pot') rises directly ahead of us. Beside the stream cradled in the valley-bottom, there are visible remains of early mining operations which never amounted to anything productive and were curtailed some time in the 1860s. But a more pleasing relic of quite simple beauty and workmanship is the old pack-horse bridge which straddles the stream in a single hump-backed stride, formed of a single course of interlocking stones – and no mortar. Quite exquisite!

From the bridge, we climb out steeply on the other side, veering to the west of Beinn-y-Phott, heading for the col between it and Carraghan. Already, the line of the B10 road is visible above us as it contours the slopes on its way between Brandywell and Barregarrow. Half a mile down the road from our crossing point is where the pumped water main linking the Sulby and Baldwin reservoirs passes under the road and begins its descent into the West Baldwin valley.

Once beyond the road, the route of the Millennium Way becomes more discernible on the ground, as we continue south and pass below the summit ridge of Carraghan. We are now in the parish of Braddan, and panoramic views open up to the south, along the two Baldwin valleys, out over Douglas, and round to the long sliver of the Langness peninsula in the distance. Our well-defined track now runs beside the mountain wall and eventually meets the minor road which descends the ridge that stands between the two Baldwins. On the way down, we pass Cronk Keeill Abban, where a Tynwald was held in 1429. Similar gatherings had been held at Kirk Michael a few years earlier, but it is not clear whether these were local or national assemblies. It is interesting to note that Cronk Keeill Abban was part of the estate of *Algare*, a name of Irish origin and meaning 'place of justice'.

A pack-horse bridge on the Millennium Way

A short distance down the road, stands the small, plain church of St Luke and, a few strides further down, we pass Algare itself, which was the birthplace of the Manx lexicographer and grammarian, John Kelly, in 1750. Kelly was a pupil of the Rev. Philip Moore, headmaster of Douglas Grammar School, and was himself later ordained. He assisted Moore in the very considerable role that he played in the translation of the Bible into Manx. Kelly produced the first book of Manx grammar, published in 1804, and also a multilingual dictionary in Manx, Irish and Scots Gaelic, the Manx content of which later formed the basis for the first Manx dictionary.

Our long descent from the uplands is arrested in the hamlet of West Baldwin, approximately 1 mile below the dam, where the track levels out to cross the bridge over the Glass and then the road, to begin the final ascent on the way to Crosby. But this ascent is nothing in comparison with what has gone before. We are now in the parish of Marown, the only parish in Man lacking a coastline, and the country through which we pass highlights the fact that we have left the high-lands behind us. As we follow field paths and climb over stiles, we recognize that we are suddenly part of a scene of typical lowland farming. But the uplands still crowd in on our right: the long ridge of Lharghee Ruy, Slieau Ruy and Greeba Mountain, terminating in that great, sloping shoulder of the King's Forest which plunges down to the central valley, popularly known in earlier times as the 'Plains of Heaven'.

As we top the crest of Cronk ny Moghlane, a broad panorama opens up over the whole of the south and east. The favoured translation of this name is 'hill of the sows' but, as J. J. Kneen [45] pointed out all those years ago, the holder of this land in 1511 was one Donald MacAleyn, and so the name is more likely to represent the 'hill of MacAleyn'. 'MacAleyn' has since become transmuted to the present Manx surname *Callin*.

We are now on a well-defined track, continuing downward and, in a field on the right, are the fenced-off remains of an early Christian site, *Keeill Vreeshey*, '[St] Bridget's Church'. Almost immediately, we step onto the A23 road from Strang, which makes a 90-degree turn down the hill and into Crosby, to the crossroads which probably gave the place its Scandinavian name, the 'village of the cross' – unless an actual cross once stood here. As we stand there at the crossroads, we have covered approximately 13 miles, and anyone seeking a convenient point at which to break this walk into two stages has now reached it.

It must be admitted that the southern section of the Millennium Way has little to offer that is in any way comparable with the route to the north. From the ascent of Sky Hill to the descent into Baldwin, the northern section is 100 per cent hill-walking, and if, *en route*, you have been soaked by a sudden change in the weather and your walk has been reduced to a compass course, if your boots have been overtopped by boggy groundwater or filled with stream-water through slipping while stepping across the narrowest of watercourses – well, that is all part of the adventure. The south, by great contrast, offers a combination of metalled roads and field-paths, leading to a pleasant enough glen-traverse and riverside walk in the final 3 miles.

However, I acknowledge that the long highland slog is not to everyone's taste, and the gentle lowland stroll may be more acceptable, so let us proceed. Having descended to the crossroads at Crosby, we stride over the A1 Peel–Douglas road and immediately begin to regain height by tackling the stiff little ascent of the B35 road to St Mark's, 5 miles distant. On the way, we pass the old parochial church school that once stood at the heart of Marown's rural population, until most of it migrated down into the central valley; the modern school is in Glen Vine. At the top of the climb, we reach Old Kirk Marown, dedicated to St Runius, the latinized rendering of the Irish *Ma Ronan* (*ma* meaning 'saint'). The modern church (1853) is also down in Glen Vine but the old building is still used for occasional services.

The road ahead passes beneath an avenue of oak, and off to the right is the site of St Patrick's Chair, a small group of standing stones, one of a number of sites in the isle bearing the name of the patron saint of Ireland. A further ascent opens up broad views over the southern lowlands, and our final destination is in sight – but

Old Kirk Marown

still 9 miles away by our destined route. The road begins its descent into the south, crosses the A24 Douglas–Foxdale road and continues downhill to Campbell's Bridge, which bears an inscription stating that it stands equidistant (6¼ miles) from Douglas, Castletown and Peel. The bridge takes us over the Santon Burn and into the parish of Malew.

The B35 eventually conducts us down to the hamlet of St Mark's, which is where we are to leave it. In the centre of the hamlet, the church is of the typical plain, rectangular, Manx pattern; its construction in 1772 was initiated by Bishop Hildesley to meet the needs of a growing population. There followed the adjacent school building (1843) and almshouses (1846).

The way out of St Mark's is by a welcome return to field paths, but it is all too brief, for, in little more than a mile, we step out onto a major highway with no footpath, the A3 St John's–Castletown road at Ballamodha. This was never part of the ancient Royal Way; the Millennium Way of 1979 was routed this way to give the walker the opportunity – after a further mile or so – to traverse the length of Silverdale Glen, which is a congenial enough way to enter the final stage of the walk. At the lower end of the glen, the disused mill-pond – one of two constructed by the monks of Rushen Abbey – is now a boating lake, accompanied by a café, shop and children's amusements. The old mill building stands adjacent.

Further along the river bank, the Monks' Bridge spans the Silver Burn in two arches, to bring the old Royal Way across to rejoin our own. The bridge (it was sketched in Camden's *Britannia*), the old Manx name for which is the *Crossag*, the 'little crossing', is just 3 feet and 3 inches wide – precisely 1 metre; were those medieval monks working in the metric system so early? The bridge was built by the monks of the abbey, probably in the early fourteenth century, and is the only bridge of medieval date in Man. A few strides on, to where the ford spans under the river, a glance to the other side shows the mill building (in recent years converted into apartments) standing on the site of the second of the monks' mills. The dam and mill-race were swept away in a flood in 1830. And then we come to the abbey itself, which is open to the public, and where archaeological excavations continue each summer, but we leave that until later.

In Ballasalla, we cross the main road, following the waymarks, and walk along the right bank of the Silver Burn as far as the footbridge, where we cross and continue with the river on our right and the railway on our left. We enter the old capital of Man where the railway does – at the station. The official end of the Millennium Way is at Castle Rushen. Estimates of the length vary. My figure is 25 miles, which is lower than most others. It is almost impossible to get an accurate figure. Even a precise measure on the flat of the map does not allow for all the ups

The Abbey Ford, Ballasalla

and downs along the way, which remain imponderable. Quoted figures range between 25 and 28 miles.

Regardless of my reservations concerning the southern section of the Millennium Way, the traverse of the complete route remains a worthy accomplishment for the dedicated pedestrian. Even before 1979, it was a dearly held ambition of many who were that way inclined to walk the length of the isle at least once in their lifetimes.

RAAD NY FOILLAN

The year 1986 was designated Manx Heritage Year. The Manx Heritage Foundation had come into being in 1983, under an Act of Tynwald of the previous year. Its objectives included the promotion of the cultural heritage of the island and the provision of facilities for public enjoyment of that heritage. As its contribution to 1986, the then Isle of Man Highway and Transport Board designated two new long-distance footpaths. The first recognized the long-held desire on the part of many to see a continuous right of way established around the island's coastline. This ambition was realized, *almost* in its totality, with the designation of the *Raad ny Foillan*, the 'road of the gull', a route of some 90 miles (145km) which follows most of the coastline, but with a few deviations due to a continued lack of a coastal right of way.

Raad ny Foillan is pronounced as 'raed na foal-yun'. Since the route passes through all of the island's towns and larger villages, the walk can be split into a number of easy stages. In this description of the route, I have chosen Douglas as the start and finishing point, following a clockwise path around the isle, and have divided the journey into four manageable stages. The waymarks along the route bear the silhouette of a gull.

DOUGLAS TO PORT ERIN

The first stage, to Port Erin by way of the island's south-west extremity at Calf Sound, entails some 24 miles of coastal walking. An intermediate stop could be made at Castletown or Port St Mary but most of the hotel and guest-house accommodation in the south-west is in Port Erin.

The beginning is easy enough, along the paved way of the Marine Drive, 3 miles of scenic byway following the route of the long-vanished Southern Electric Tramway which, in 1895, was hacked out of the face of the cliff to provide a spectacular ride from Douglas Head to the popular glen at Port Soderick. Its track was the only one in the isle to be laid to the British standard gauge of 4 feet 8½ inches (1,435mm). The tramway closed in 1939 and never reopened. The route was adopted as a road but was later cut by a rock-fall at Wallberry and was never reinstated as a through-route for motor traffic, but it retains sufficient width through the affected section for a pedestrian way.

Since passing under the stone-built arches of the old toll gate on Douglas Head, we have been in the parish of Braddan. This is a rugged stretch of coast, with cliffs rising steeply to 400 feet (120m) above an untrodden shore, and the contorted strata of their Manx Slates providing ample evidence of the immense forces to which they were subjected millions of years ago, as the structure of the island pulsed and folded to deep subterranean and crustal pressures.

Beyond Little Ness, the mile-wide bay of Port Soderick opens up, with Santon Head rising from the water on the far side and the long, low peninsula of Langness jutting into the sea further south. Port Soderick lies at the mouth of an attractive wooded glen which is substantially undeveloped apart from a short promenade beside the shore, with a hotel and refreshment room which – popular in their day – have stood empty and deserted for many years. The name of the place probably stems from the Norse *Sudr vik*, meaning 'southern creek'.

The country to the south is typical of the island's agricultural coast. The arable

The east coast from the Marine Drive

and grazing lands of the coastal plain have been extended as far as is practicable towards the cliff-edge, but the steepness of the broogh has deterred the harrow and the plough and the grazing of animals which are held back by a turf-covered hedge – the coastal equivalent of the mountain wall found in the uplands. This has preserved inviolate an almost continuous strip of natural vegetation. These rough, uncultivated margins gird the island in a veritable unplanned nature reserve, where bracken, heathers and dwarf gorse run rampant, and birds flock to these unmolested sanctuaries in great numbers. The chorus of gull, fulmar and kitti-wake is ever-present, echoing from a thousand facets of unassailable cliff. On the lower waterside rocks, shags congregate like pins on a pincushion. Their larger cousin, the cormorant, is less numerous but, with a cheery disregard of the ornithological niceties, they are both referred to in Man as 'cormorants' or – particularly by the older folk – as 'Jinney Divers'. The guillemot population has shown some recovery since the pollution incidents around the Irish Sea in the late 1960s and 1970s. Many birds which are normally regarded as land species also haunt the island's cliffs. Martins and swallows return each spring to join residents like the jackdaw, raven and the scarlet-legged chough, and the kestrel – the island's commonest hawk – hovers above the brooghs in search of its next meal. Even the curlew, that haunting bird of the uplands, descends in flocks to feed by

Port Soderick Halt, on the Isle of Man Steam Railway

the shore, then wings up to the pastures of the cliff-top, where they sit and quietly nod off as the digestive juices start to flow.

There is a coastal way south from Soderick, along a cliff-edge path outside the farmers' walls and fences, out towards Santon Head, where cliffs fall sheer for 300 feet (90m) to an inaccessible shore, and debris of smashed driftwood and plastic squeezy bottles lie stranded in tight little rock-girt coves. But that path is not public, which is a great pity. The official route of the *Raad ny Foillan* follows the line of Port Soderick Glen, passes beneath the railway bridge by Port Soderick Halt, and rises to join the A25 road at Ballaveare. There follow 2 miles of tarmac, the first along the main road beyond the Crogga River (where we enter the parish of Santon), then heading seaward once more by a single-track byway, re-crossing the line of the steam railway, eventually to rejoin the coast on the north side of Santon Head. This brings us past the modern sewage treatment plant of the IRIS scheme at Meary Veg, which was intended to serve the whole of the island but may never achieve that aim.

The way ahead lies by the sheltered inlets of Port Grenaugh, lonely little Port Soldrick and down to Cass-ny-Hawin, where the Santon Burn tumbles to the sea along the line of the fault which marks the temporary end of the slate and the beginning of the limestone. Beyond, the twin back-to-back crescents of Derbyhaven and Castletown Bay lie separated only by the low isthmus which anchors Langness to the Ronaldsway shore.

It is while following this coastline south that we realize how effectively the old Celtic islanders of the Iron Age utilized the most strategic points as look-out posts and coastal defence forts. They had at least three forts on the cliffs of Santon Head and two more guarding the mouth of the Santon Burn. They preferred natural promontories, with cliffs on three sides, and defended the fourth with a rampart and ditch. The sites at Cronk ny Merriu, overlooking Port Grenaugh, and the southern fort at Cass-ny-Hawin each contains the outline of the characteristic rectangular Norse-style house, indicating that the Norsemen took over these sites in their turn. The Norse also left their place-names scattered about the place: Grenaugh was their *Graen-vik*, 'green creek', and Soldrick was their 'sun creek'. In the northern cliff of the latter creek, there is a huge cavern where, in the later times of the smuggling trade, the 'free-traders' could conceal their merchandise safe from the prying eyes of the Lord's men.

These apparently minor inlets of the Manx coast were far more intensively used in times past than they are today, both by the old-time crofter-fishermen and by the free-traders. Thus, places like *Port* Soderick, *Port* Grenaugh and *Port* Soldrick were probably deserving of their prefixes. The word 'port' did not necessarily imply a harbour with wharves, jetties and warehouses; any sheltered inlet with a landing beach would qualify, which accounts for the frequency of the word on maps of the Isle of Man.

Beyond the mouth of the Santon Gorge, we are in the parish of Malew, and the cliffs decline, canting down to meet the cracked limestone table of a shore which extends to the mouth of Derbyhaven. The coastal path skirts the eastern edge of Ronaldsway Airport and joins the road which brings us to Derbyhaven, which is the name given to both the sheltered natural harbour cradled behind the northern end of Langness and the quiet hamlet which sits beside its shore. The original name of the place was Ronaldsway, after one of the early Norse kings, Ragnald, and his practice of dragging his boats over the narrow neck of land separating the two bays. The boat-dragging path became *Ragnaldsvath*, 'Ragnald's way', until the Derbys came and changed it to Derbyhaven. But William Christian's farm – and hence the later airport on the same site – remained Ronaldsway.

In later times, Derbyhaven served as a fishing harbour. The breakwater which provides shelter from the east was built of local limestone in 1842–3, but there was little subsequent development and the hamlet has declined into the sleepy little place that it is today. Some of the old herring houses still stand beside the road to Langness.

This is a convenient point at which (if the walker so desires) to make a diversion to Langness, although it is not an official part of the *Raad ny Foillan*, and the out-and-back diversion, taking in the full length of the peninsula, entails an additional 4 miles. It could, alternatively, be left to another day, but let us press on. Beyond the old herring houses, the road divides into two surfaced single tracks, one eventually turning north, the other south. Alongside the branching of the ways stands the diminishing ruin of John Murrey's smelthouse, where, from the early eighteenth century onwards, considerable quantities of lead ore were brought for smelting, on the site where the 'John Murrey pennies' had been minted in 1668. On the shore opposite is the ruin of a nineteenth-century kiln in which local limestone was burned to produce lime.

Langness is a bit of a geological anachronism. It sits there, long and low in the water, in full view of the high coast to the north and the high coast to the south, with low-lying ledges of limestone close by to the north and the same close by to the south; an off-lying sliver of slate linked to the 'mainland' by a low isthmus of limestone and conglomerate which, were it not for the storm-tossed accumulations of shingle and blown sand which surmount it, would itself be awash. Without the topping of sand and shingle, the bays of Castletown and Derbyhaven would be one, Langness would be an island, and Ragnald would not have had to drag his boats across the isthmus.

Out on the long ness itself, the Norsemen fortified each extremity (as the Celts had done before them) to guard the approaches to their havens, and built the plain rectangular chapel which stands a roofless ruin on St Michael's Island, connected

Langness: (above) one of the arches at Langness Point; (below) intruding greenstone dykes have been eroded by the sea

to the main peninsula today by a single-track causeway. Later came the English, and their contribution also stands on St Michael's Island: a circular, stone-built fort which was part of Henry VIII's scheme for defence in the sixteenth century. It was built by Edward Stanley, third Earl of Derby, repaired and rearmed by James, the seventh Earl (whose initials are carved over the entrance), and was named Derby Fort in 1645. It is similar to the one which has long since disappeared from the end of Fort Street, in Douglas.

Langness today slumbers peacefully, unruffled by reflections of a ruffled history that called for defensive forts and look-out posts. Its only human presence today is divided between the patrons of the golf course and its hotel in the north and the occupants of the former light-keepers' cottages in the south. The land in between is let for grazing. Down towards the south stands a plain, untapered tower of limestone, built as a seamark by the British government in 1811. Around the inside of its circular wall, a tight little spiral of stone steps (with no guard-rail to prevent you from falling off) winds to the top, whence the views are long and wide: back along the east coast as far as Douglas Head, north-west to the 'Watch-and-Ward' peaks of South Barrule and Cronk ny Arrey Laa, westward to the Calf and the graceful form of the lighthouse on the Chicken Rock, with the tower on Bradda Head rising beyond the saddle in the hills behind Port St Mary.

The slates of Langness dip from east to west, forming a line of low cliffs along the seaward side but becoming overlain to the west by a coarse conglomerate containing such an abundance of iron oxide as to permeate its rusty stain deep into the slates beneath. In places, the conglomerate lies unconformable across exposed ledges of slate, leaving open arches in between. The lighthouse stands on Dreswick Point, which is the Isle of Man's southern extremity, where also stands a prominent 'mushroom' rock, sprouting a bulbous head of conglomerate perched on a stem of slate which has been weathered and slimmed by the elements of centuries. Over on the south-western tip of the peninsula, Langness Point lies severed from the rest due to erosion by the sea along intruding dykes of volcanic basalt, which is softer than the surrounding slate.

It was the presence of the dykes and outcrops of copper along the shore that lured the old-time prospectors here. They came in search of a workable vein of copper, and they found it. The Langness mine went down 240 feet (70m) and extended horizontally for 1,800 feet (550m), but conditions were such as miners would not tolerate today. There was no cage to transport them to and from the working levels; they climbed up and down a laddered shaft, now sealed with a slab of concrete. When charges were laid for blasting (for which *dynamite* was used), the men withdrew some distance along the gallery, stuffed their fingers in their ears and waited for the wind to clutch at their clothing as the blast-wave swept past them. The ore was trucked to the bottom of the shaft and hoisted to the surface, and the waste from the crushing machines was disposed of in the time-honoured fashion of coastal mining – by dumping it over the cliff. The Langness mine continued working until about 1930, which was later than most of the Manx mines.

Although Langness is a quieter place today, there have been disputes over public rights of way in recent times. The only legally established right of way to the south is along the single-track through the golf course, terminating at the car park approximately two-thirds of the way down. Beyond that, the way south has traditionally been open to walkers by courtesy of the landowner, and that still seems to be the situation today.

It is in the winter that Langness bustles with life again. The summer visitors (both humans and birds) have departed, and the winter visitors have arrived: winging skeins of wigeon, mallard and teal, of golden plover and the curlew down from the hills, all of them flocking to the shore to feed. And food is there in abundance, cast up by winter's storms from the twilight depths of the laminarian forests, dense submarine jungles of weed that fringe much of the island's coastline. Great quantities of the stuff are cast up, with much marine invertebrate life caught up in it, and the birds descend *en masse* to forage on this richly stocked larder. Ducks and waders are joined by gulls and jackdaws, starlings and sparrows, raven and chough, to form one screeching, twittering ribbon of gorging birdlife strung out along the shore. And if there is weed drifting in the shallows, they start on that also, the gulls grazing the mass as they ride the swell, and flocks of tiny, fluttering storm petrels pecking from the air, their feet pattering lightly on the waves that rise beneath them. In the weeks that follow, the cast-up wrack begins to rot and stink. My, how it stinks! It must always have been thus, because, on the western shore of Langness, there is a marshy depression where the wrack accumulates in large quantities and, beyond living memory, it has borne the Manx name *Poyll Breinn*, the 'stinking pool'.

We return to Derbyhaven to resume our journey along the *Raad ny Foillan*, following the road towards Castletown, skirting the southern edge of the airport, with the grey, austere but elegant buildings of King William's College on our right and the ragged, propped-up remnant of the Derbys' summerhouse on Hango Hill on the left, the site of William Christian's execution in 1663. Following the promenade, we walk into the town centre, cross the footbridge over the harbour and find the formidable grey stone fortress of Castle Rushen on our right and the old House of Keys standing back on the left. And straight ahead, at the centre of the Parade (a reminder of the town's former garrison status), stands the tall Doric column raised to commemorate General Cornelius Smelt, Lieutenant Governor (1805–32). We shall return to Castletown in Chapter 12; in the meantime, we must press on if we are to reach Port Erin before nightfall.

Along the western shore of Castletown Bay, the Scarlett coast displays the remains of the old limestone industry. The quarry was worked until the early twentieth century but is now flooded. To the south are the kilns in which the stone was burned and slaked to produce lime, and to the north lie the remains of the jetty from which the stone was loaded into boats for transportation to kilns in other parts of the isle after local sources of fuel had been depleted.

All along the shore, the limestone abounds in its natural state; broad, undulating ledges of it, laden with the fossilized corpses of creatures which inhabited the seas of the Carboniferous period, and criss-crossed with cracks which have been there since deep subterranean forces caused its surface to ripple and fracture 250 million years ago. But the dominant feature of the Scarlett shore is not sedimentary at all, but volcanic, for it is on Scarlett Point that the great hump of basalt known as the Stack erupts beyond the limestone ledges, its columnar structure similar to that of the well-known Giant's Causeway in County Antrim, but less perfect in form. The shore to the west is of volcanic ash cemented with lava from the volcano which must have been somewhere in the sea to the south of the island. Much of the shore rock is pitted and pockmarked by escaping bubbles of gas and steam which emerged from the pasty lava before it set solid for ever.

The coastal path from Scarlett runs a delightful course along a low, turf-capped cliff and conducts us into the broad curve of Bay ny Carrickey, the 'bay of the rock', the rock in question being the Carrick, a low knoll of limestone surmounted by a navigation beacon which sits in the middle of the bay. On the far side lie the close-knit houses of Port St Mary and, beyond the village, a high-stepping coast strides out to where Spanish Head glowers across the Sound towards the Calf.

At Close ny Chollagh, we find another of the Celts' promontory forts, enclosing the sites of three circular dwellings from around the first century BC to the first century AD. Also crammed into the enclosure was a later Norse-type rectangular house, probably from the medieval period. This is the only Manx coastal fort known to have defensive works on all sides, with a solidly constructed stone wall on its seaward elevation, probably because the cliff is so low. After excavation in 1953–6, the house sites were filled in and only the rampart and ditch are now visible.

Continuing north into the bay, we cross a minor watercourse known as the Dumb River, which separates the parishes of Malew and Arbory. And there we arrive at Poyllvaaish (Manx 'bay of death'), where the limestone regains its supremacy of the coast, only here it is the almost black limestone shale which, because of its ability to take a fine polished finish, is often referred to as 'Poyllvaaish marble'. It is still quarried on a small scale and used for the production of gravestones, mantelpieces and other decorative features.

Beyond Poyllvaaish Farm, Chapel Hill rises insignificantly behind the coast, a location which the Celts fortified by erecting a stone rampart around the whole of the flattish summit. Near the western end of the enclosure is the low outline of *Keeill Vael*, [St] Michael's Chapel, which gives the hill its name. But the most exciting find on Chapel Hill was made at the eastern end of the enclosure, where, in 1945, excavations revealed the remains of a Viking ship burial, one of only two such burials known in Man. The Viking chieftain had been laid to rest in his ship (of which only the iron clinch-bolts remained) in company with a woman (wife or sacrificed servant?), his horse and other livestock which had been slaughtered to accompany him on the voyage to Valhalla, on which he set out in the late ninth or early tenth century. This pagan burial had been placed directly over some stone-lined Christian burials from earlier in the same period. The outline of the ship, about 35 feet (11m) long, is now marked with stones.

The coastal path brings us out on the Port St Mary road at Strandhall, another location where – at the appropriate time of year – hordes of sea birds and land birds quarrel over the rotting heaps of wrack thrown up along the tideline. We walk on, into the parish of Rushen, and, at the eastern end of the Black Rocks, we come to the line of the fault which marks the western limit of the limestone. From the shore, the fault runs out south-west beneath the bay and grazes the tip of the Port St Mary promontory at Kallow Point, producing there the most westerly outcropping of limestone in Man. Beyond the fault-line, we are back in the domain of the rampant slates.

The *Raad ny Foillan* enters Port St Mary by the sleepy northern suburb of Gansey. Of all the Manx ports, the one which is most deserving of the description 'quaint' is undoubtedly Port St Mary. Its grey stone houses, set along narrow streets and byways, climb one above another in a delightfully random fashion behind the harbour. The village derived its name from the ancient church of St Mary which once stood above the shore of Chapel Bay. It is a popular but quiet place, possessing none of the more raucous attractions of the traditional seaside resort, but sporting the basic necessities of a fine sandy beach flanked by a prom-enade and a modicum of accommodation to provide for those who have not lost the knack of enjoying themselves without the aid of artificial stimuli.

The clubhouse of the Isle of Man Yacht Club stands beside the harbour and, out along the quay, there is still some evidence of a fishing industry, but much reduced from earlier times. To the west, modern residential development has spread to threaten the outlying hamlet of Fistard, which stands high on the flank of Glen Chass, looking out over the small inlet of Perwick Bay. The bay was prob-ably where the Norsemen had their *fiskagardr*, or 'fish garth' or enclosure, from which the hamlet took its name. In the cliffs above the bay, the strata of the slates twist and contort in weird fashion, and in places one can see traces of the wave-cut platform notched in the cliffs when sea levels were higher than today's.

Fistard is the starting point for one of the most spectacular coastal walks in Man (or anywhere else, for that matter), following high cliffs for 4 miles to the west, climbing 400 feet (120m) above the shore of Bay Stacka and beyond Spanish Head, before dropping steeply back to near sea level beside the waters of Calf Sound. On the way, we pass below the 538-foot (164m) crest of Cronk ny Arrey. Although the name gives no clue, this was obviously a hill of the *day* watch; night watchmen would have neither seen nor heard any sign of approaching danger from up there. On the crest of the hill today, the Civil Aviation Authority operates a radio-navigation beacon. On the landward side of the hill lies Cregneash, the last of the old-style Manx villages.

Below the radio beacon, we pass above the Sugarloaf, a tall cone of rock which has become detached from the main cliff-line by erosion. Immediately to the west of this lie the Chasms, a heavily faulted area in which deep fissures slice vertically down through the 300-foot (90m) wall of Cambrian grit to the shore, and where the placing of an incautious foot may send its owner hurtling to the bottom or leave him jammed deep down in a narrowing cleft. The extent of the faulting raises another possibility for the original separation of the Sugarloaf: did it initially become isolated as a result of the faulting?

A few strides further to the west, we find a low stone circle, marking a Neolithic burial site known locally as Cronk Karran, lying slap in the middle of a faulted area, which makes one wonder whether the faulting occurred before or after Stone-Age man was here. Such tumuli were built as circular mounds, bounded by a wall of stones 3–4 feet (about 1 metre) high and roofed over with wood, wattles and earth. In time, as the roofing materials rotted and collapsed, the stones were raided by farmers for wall-building and for use as gate-posts, leaving only the lowest ring of stones to mark the spot today.

Much of the coastal land to the west of Perwick Bay is in the custody of Manx National Heritage. A well-trodden path twists, plunges, then rises again through the bracken and heather. It takes us up above Bay Stacka, where tall cliffs ring to the cries of gull, kittiwake and fulmar, the grunts of shag, cormorant and razor-bill, a cacophony so noisesome as to drown the croaks and clacks of jackdaw, raven and chough. It takes us up onto Spanish Head, its shadow cast darkly on the water at its foot, where a galleon of the Armada is fancied to have been wrecked but almost certainly never was. And over the brow ablaze with gorse, there is an unfolding scene of the Calf of Man, with daylight showing clear through the wave-cut eye of the Burroo rock at its southern tip, the slates of Kitterland parting the tide-race through the Sound, and the distant tower of the Chicken Rock light tapering with graceful symmetry above the most southerly, and also the most westerly, rock in the Manx group.

As we make the final approach to the visitors' centre above Calf Sound, we

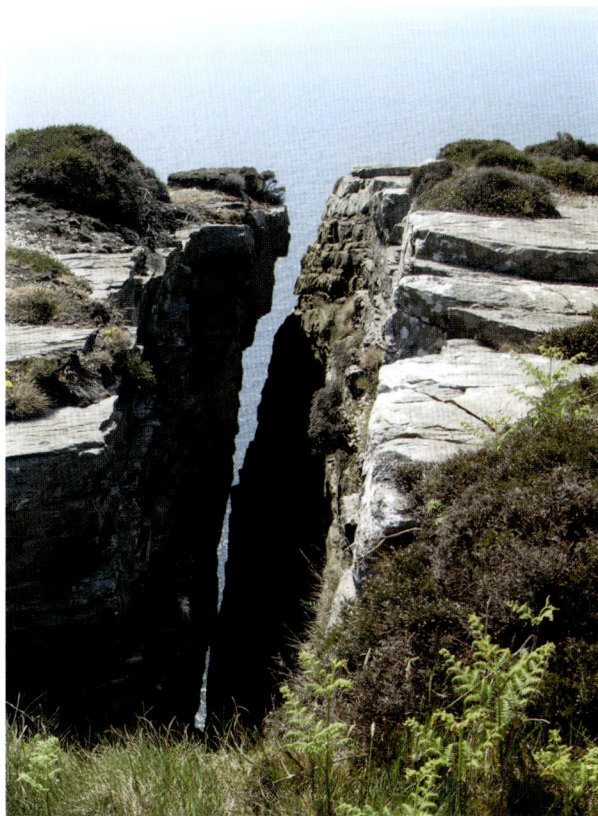

The Chasms: (left) fissures slice down from cliff-top to shore; (below) the Sugarloaf stack stands detached in the water

*View south from the Chasms: Black Head is in the distance; the stone circle in the
foreground marks the burial cairn known as Cronk Karran*

traverse the minor headland of Burroo Ned, which has a rampart across its landward side, enclosing house foundations and indicating a fortification probably
from the Celtic Iron Age. The name of the headland is an interesting mix of Norse
and Gaelic, *Burroo* being the gaelicized form of the Norse *borg*, a dome-shaped
hill, and the second element stemming from the Manx *edd*, meaning 'nest'. The
original Manx version of the present name may well have been *Burroo ny edd*, 'hill
of the nests'.

The modern visitors' centre is certainly an improvement over the rudimentary
wooden shack which was there before, and it provides a comfortable venue for a
refreshment break. There are just 2 miles remaining to Port Erin, north-eastward
above the coastal indentations of Aldrick and Bay Fine, with long views across
Port Erin Bay, Bradda Head and beyond. The broad but shallow curve of Aldrick
got its name from the Norse *Aldarvik*, 'old creek', the 'old' referring to aged people
or (more probably) to old (i.e. previous) inhabitants, suggesting that this may be a
reference to the pre-Celtic people of southern Man, where the small, dark, wiry
type is still to be found in the indigenous population. In later times, as J. J. Kneen
pointed out almost a century ago, attention was drawn to the small, dark, wiry
types to be found in Spain, and this supplied further fuel for the fanciful tales of a

Spanish wreck off Spanish Head. Of one thing we can be sure: the name Aldrick goes back much further than 1588.

The steep descent into Port Erin, past the buildings of the former Marine Biological Station, brings us down to the western extremity of the promenade, facing north across the bay to Bradda Head. A tumbled line of blocks projecting into the water is all that remains of the ill-fated breakwater project that was intended to transform the bay into a secure haven, sheltered from the fury of winter's westerlies. But it was just such a westerly that reduced the structure to its present state in 1884. Turning towards the centre of the village, we pass the present small harbour, sheltered by a short pier of limestone.

PORT ERIN TO PEEL

The derivation of Port Erin's name remains uncertain. Some have linked it with the Manx *Purt Chiarn*, 'Lord's Port', or *Purt Yiarn*, 'iron port'. Others again have tried an association with *Eireann*, Ireland, but none of these is entirely satisfactory. In 1595, it was *Port Earn*; its origin may have been pre-Celtic and now lost to us.

Close behind the promenade, in the centre of the village, the redbrick railway station stands at the southern terminus of the only surviving line of the Isle of Man Steam Railway. The line was originally conceived with high hopes of freight and passenger traffic deriving from the projected harbour facilities, but those hopes were dashed with the destruction of the breakwater.

It is the tall northern promontory of Bradda Head which dominates the whole vista of Port Erin Bay. Its cliffs rise almost sheer for 400 feet (120m) and it is surmounted by the tower erected in 1871 to the memory of William Milner, a Liverpool safe-maker who was a great benefactor to the village and a backer of the doomed breakwater project. Directly beneath the tower, the derelict engine house of the South Bradda mine stands on a ledge only 15 feet (4.5m) above the sea, and there are other remains on the north side of the headland. Several hundred tons of lead and copper were extracted from the Bradda mines in the late 1800s, but they appear never to have made a profit.

It is by way of Bradda Head and Milner's Tower that the next stage of our coastal journey begins; this is a stage of some 14 miles. From Bradda Glen, at the north end of the village, our route climbs the headland, passing the tower and continuing onward to the 766-foot (233m) summit of Bradda Hill, before descending steeply to the narrow, stony beach at Fleshwick Bay. These are just the first of several severe ascents and descents to be encountered on this section of our journey. This was the Norsemen's *Flesvik*, 'green spot creek', a narrow, north-facing inlet, hemmed in on the west by the steep flank of Bradda Hill and to the east by the equally steep slopes of the Carnanes, and which seems ideally aligned to accumulate quite disproportionate quantities of seaborne refuse on its confined shore.

Our onward way lies up the steep eastern shoulder above Fleshwick and along the heather-clad lofty ridge of Lhiattee ny Beinnee (Manx 'side of the peak'). It would be hard to better the walk along this ridge in the soft light of morning, to watch the fishing boats bucking through the swell almost 1,000 feet (300m) below, and to see the high western coast of Man rearing and plunging its way northward to the wicked-looking rhino's horn of the Niarbyl reef. (I know that *Niarbyl* is Manx for 'the tail' but, to me, it has always looked like a horn.) This untamed wilderness of heather and gorse is the complete antithesis of the pampered greens and browns of the coastal plateau spread out below us to south and east.

We descend the steep northern flank of Lhiattee ny Beinnee with the cairned summit of Cronk ny Arrey Laa (another 'hill of the day watch') looming ahead of us and, in the col between the two hills (the Sloc), we have a brief encounter with the west-coast road which ventures within a quarter-mile of the cliffs here before veering away to the landward side of the hill.

Ignoring the road, we continue north, and another stiff climb brings us to the summit of Cronk ny Arrey Laa, at 1,433 feet (437m) above the sea, the highest point on the Raad ny Foillan. Two miles to the north-east, the Southside's highest

The Niarbyl reef, from the summit of Cronk ny Arrey Laa

peak, South Barrule, rises just 153 feet (47m) higher than the point on which we stand. These slopes are the preserve of the ubiquitous sheep, of birds at nesting time and bees grazing the heather. As for the sheep, if they have recently been rounded up for dipping, they wander back onto the slopes smelling just like freshly disinfected public toilets.

Perhaps the heights of Cronk ny Arrey Laa are also haunted by the ghosts of Stone-Age men who were buried on its summit 4,000 years ago. Two thousand years later, low down on its steep western flank, a solitary hermit-priest lived in a tiny cell beside his remote little chapel at Lag ny Keilley ('hollow of the chapel'). Unless you are something of a rock-scrambling gymnast, you will not attempt to reach it by a direct descent from the summit, but will prefer instead to continue north to where our path intersects the old pack-horse trail which crosses the MNH property at Eary Cushlin. The keeill site may then be reached by cutting back along that trail which slants down the seaward flank of Cronk ny Arrey Laa at a much more comfortable gradient. This keeill would have been typical of those built in many parts of the island between the eighth and tenth centuries. Its walls were of sods of earth, roughly faced with stone on the inside, but only a low ruin now remains, together with the outline of the priest's cell. Some 250 yards to the north, a baptismal well lies amid the heather and bracken above the path.

Back on the official route of the *Raad*, we are now in the parish of Patrick, and the path descends to a point close above the shore at the mouth of Glion Mooar, where its stream – having tumbled down the steep cleft of the glen – spills down the face of the cliff at a point called Gob ny Ushtey, 'point of the water'. There are several 'gobs' around the coast of the Isle of Man; it is a Gaelic word meaning point, beak or mouth. So if you are less than enchanted to hear your children telling their rowdy friends to 'shut their gobs', don't be too hard on them, for they are only practising their Gaelic.

Our way continues ever northward and eventually descends to the shore of Niarbyl Bay, at the northern extremity of which that treacherous flagstone reef juts out into the sea. The name comes from the Manx *yn arbyl*, meaning 'the tail'. Beside the shore, straight from the pages of a magazine, a brace of fishermen's thatched cottages gaze south along the coast, a perfect spot for a romantic liaison. This is a favoured location for filming.

The rugged coast of Niarbyl flags extends north to St Patrick's Isle but remains inaccessible to us for the next 2 miles, as we are diverted onto the road and must follow it until we see the waymark pointing past farm buildings and down the southern flank of Glen Maye to the shore. The stream here falls and cascades through its final mile before making its exit across a stony beach. From here, our way lies along the final 3 miles of cliff-top to Peel. We pass Contrary Head on the way, so named because the flood tide divides here, one branch flowing south

(above) Peel sits at the start of the north-west coast, whilst the castle (below) guards the harbour entrance

through Calf Sound, and the other north round the Point of Ayre. The two branches recombine off Maughold Head. There are some interesting caves at the base of Contrary Head, and a very steep path down the cliff-face to them.

The mile-long ridge of Corrin's Hill rises beyond Contrary Head, and Corrin's Tower stands on its summit. Thomas Corrin built his tower on the hill above Peel in 1806, on land which was part of his holding at Knockaloe Beg. He was a staunch Nonconformist who wished to demonstrate to like-minded souls that it was possible to be buried in unconsecrated ground. After initial opposition from the Church, he had the remains of his wife and children transferred from Patrick churchyard and reinterred in his own small burial ground beside the tower and, on his own death in 1845, he was buried there beside them. They lie there still. His tower is often called 'Corrin's Folly', but that seems rather unkind. He proved what he wanted to prove, and was buried where he wanted to be buried, surrounded by views extending from the Calf of Man to the northern plain, and on clear days to the Mull of Galloway and the Mountains of Mourne. And his tower serves a useful purpose as a seamark.

Corrin's Hill is undoubtedly the best place from which to see Peel for the first time, although relatively few people ever discover it from that location. It appears beyond the brow of the hill, spread out like a map below, and separated from the ancient fortifications and monastic remains on St Patrick's Isle by the harbour which conveys the muddy outfall of the River Neb to the sea, whilst the coast beyond curves long and low into the north.

The Vikings called it *Holmtun*, 'island town', and the name was probably used concurrently with its Gaelic equivalent, *Purt ny Hinshey*, 'port of the island', both names alluding, not to the Isle of Man itself, but to St Patrick's Isle. The name *Pile*, denoting a fortress, was first applied to St Patrick's Isle in 1231 and, by the late seventeenth century, the town itself had become *Peeletowne*, which was later shortened to *Peel*. The rather fanciful title of the 'Sunset City' has been awarded by later generations who have come to admire its fine western evenings, when the sea sparkles darkly, ready for sleep, and the sandstone walls of the town glow with a russet hue in the rays of a falling sun. And the commonly held belief that any place with a cathedral – albeit a ruinous one – was automatically a city led to its claims to the title. But it is not so; a city needs a royal charter, and Peel does not have one.

PEEL TO RAMSEY

Setting out from Peel to walk northabout to Ramsey involves a stage of 27 miles, although, if you are carrying camping gear, an easy first stage could involve stopping off at the campsite in Glen Wyllin after the first 6 miles. The first mile of the coastal path from Peel takes us above the sandstone cliffs but then returns us to the A4 coast road, which must be followed until we arrive at the site of the level crossing of the old Manx Northern Railway at St German's, where we veer left to follow the disused track northward, past the station house which has long since been converted into a dwelling. By the time we pass Ballanayre Strand, the sandstone is behind us and the Manx Slates are back with us, finely brecciated to form areas of crush conglomerate intersected by dykes of greenstone. On the shore below Lynague (reached by a public path from the adjacent coast road), there is an interesting system of caves, accessible only at low tide, and many of the standing rocks have been worn into top-heavy mushroom shapes by centuries of wave-powered sand-blasting. But there is no onward route for us along the shore; to both north and south, the way is blocked by sea-washed rock, even at low tide.

The resurgence of the slate is a brief one. We are still a mile short of Glen Mooar when we find the edge of the rocks slanting away inland, to leave us at the start of a long line of cliffs carved out of the glacial deposits of the northern plain, and a long beach of sand and shingle which stretches along the west coast to the Point of Ayre and down the east as far as Ramsey. Along most of this coast, there are no cliff-top paths, and so the shore must suffice, although the official route deviates from it now and again to provide some variation.

The isolated shore at Lynague, German

Following the disused railway track north, we are brought up short at Glen Mooar (the 'great glen') by the absence of the old viaduct which carried the railway across to the other side. We are forced down the embankment and into the glen. Its upper section is a Manx National Glen, maintained by the forestry division of the DAFF, and cradles the remains of an early Christian keeill, *Cabbal Pherick*, '[St] Patrick's Chapel'. But our way is downward, across the A4 road, to follow the minor road to the shore.

Much of this shore cannot be walked at times around high water, especially at high spring tides, and so it is well to check the tide tables before setting out. For the most part, these cliffs rise on a deep base-layer of boulder clay, with strata of glacial sand and gravel above, and on top of it all lies a varying depth of blown sand which has been whipped up from the shore by the prevailing south-westerlies and deposited on the land behind the cliff-top.

Following the shore northward, we find the glens becoming less significant features of the coast, as the hills are left behind. Glen Wyllin ('glen of the mill') slices down to the shore on the southern outskirts of Kirk Michael. Like Glen Mooar, it has a broad alluvial fan of post-glacial flood gravels and silt spread across its lower reaches, indicating how much wider these watercourses were during the post-glacial melt. Coastal protection in the form of rock armour has been placed along the cliff-foot on either side of the glen's river outfall but, inevitably, the sea continues to gnaw away at the cliffs to north and south of the protected zone. The lower portion of the glen (below the A4 Peel–Kirk Michael road) was once owned by the railway company and was popular for its leisure attractions – whose patrons used to travel in by train, of course. Today, it is maintained as another Manx National Glen, approximately half of which is leased by the Michael District Commissioners, who operate it as a camp site.

Kirk Michael is the only sizeable village along the whole of the 27 miles of coast between Peel and Ramsey. The *Raad ny Foillan* leaves the shore at Glen Wyllin, climbs the northern escarpment and follows the former railway track into the village. Just beyond the site of the level crossing in Station Road, the old station buildings now serve as the fire station. At the centre of the village, the *Mitre Hotel* is reputedly the island's oldest inn, catering for the needs of Michael folk and wayfarers since 1786. The parish church contains the largest collection of Norse crosses in Man, and its churchyard holds the graves of five bishops of Sodor and Man.

Our way continues along the line of the former railway, running closely parallel with the A3 road to Ramsey, until the waymark at Rhencullen directs us westward to regain the shore at Glen Trunk. A short distance up from the shore stands one of the island's best-preserved lime kilns, in which limestone was burned to produce agricultural lime. With no nearby harbour facilities, the boats

The Mitre Hotel, *Kirk Michael*

conveying the stone from the south would simply bring up to the shore at high tide and dump their cargoes over the side, leaving the stone to be hauled up to the kiln when the tide fell.

Our way now lies along the shore, and the next 2 miles are frequently impassable at high water. The cliff-line here has receded approximately 200 feet (60m) in the past hundred years, and we are now passing beneath the island's most extensive exposure of glacial deposit. At Ballakinnag Cronk, the Ballaugh stream tumbles across the shore and is usually fordable with ease. A quarter of a mile back from the coast stands another old church whose population has migrated. St Mary de Ballaugh (also known as Ballaugh Old Church) is another example of the traditional plain, rectangular Manx church. It contains the only Norse cross to be found in the parish and, outside, two tall stone gateposts lean secretively towards each other like a couple of old crones sharing a piece of juicy gossip after morning service. The larger, modern church stands with the modern village, beside the A3 Ramsey road, which is now 2 miles inland. And the 'gh' in *Ballaugh* is pronounced as an 'f'.

The cliffs march on to the north, with a tidemark of milk cartons and plastic sundries from a score of ships' galleys cast up along their feet. Tumbled walls of sand and clay echo to the piping of oystercatchers and the bubbling call of the curlew, while small colonies of fulmar occupy any convenient ledges and burrows on precarious-seeming cliff-faces. The Killane stream discharges its trickle of drainage water from the curragh onto the shore, below the old mill building and adjacent modern dwelling which stand perilously close to the edge, protected – for the moment – by sundry deposits of concrete rubble at the cliff-foot. Close by to the north, below Ballateare, protection was placed in the form of stone-filled gabion baskets some years ago, but the sand on which they stood was soon undermined, and baskets and contents tumbled.

On the north side of Jurby Head, the summit of Cronk ny Arrey Lhaa, another 'hill of the day watch' (this one for the parish of Jurby) stands closer to the sea each year. The next access between shore and land is at Sartfield, where the Jurby sewer pipe strides across the shore and into the sea. The parish church of St Patrick stands back from the cliff-top and has a good collection of Norse and Celtic crosses. But there is no direct access from the shore, and the only way to include it in this journey would be to leave the shore at the Killane and return to it at Sartfield.

Beyond Jurby Head, the coastline curves into the north-east and is less exposed to the full force of the prevailing south-westerlies. Ranks of marram-covered dunes line the base of the cliffs, and we now have the choice between striding along the tide-line and strolling through the dunes. On the north side of Cronk y Cliwe ('hill of the sword'), at the back of the dunes and the foot of the cliff, stands the gaunt structure of a Second World War concrete-making plant, used in the construction of military emplacements. And in the same area – at low tide – can be seen the wreck of the Fleetwood trawler *Passages*, which ran aground here in 1929. Much of it has rusted away but the engine block and some of the frames still show at low water.

The road to Bride generally hangs back from the coast, and a few by-roads provide intermittent access to the shore. At the Lhen, we encounter the outfall of the principal stream still draining the ancient post-glacial swamp of the curraghs, and the only one on this stretch of coast which *may* present an obstacle to the pedestrian. In summer, there is usually no problem but, if the river is in spate, be prepared to remove footwear, roll up trouser-legs, and wade across – and a stick may be helpful to maintain balance.

At Blue Point, another significant change occurs: the cliffs turn abruptly away and head *inland*, whilst a low, dune-backed shoreline continues resolutely into the north-east. Those inland cliffs mark the line of the ancient coast, cut into the edge of the northern glacial deposits some 6,000 years ago, before the land had completed its post-glacial rise on being relieved of its vast over-burden of ice. The land between the ancient cliff-line and the present shore is today a flat expanse of raised shingle beach, with a patchy covering of blown sand supporting a low vegetation of heath and dwarf gorse. It was known to the Norsemen as the *eyrr*, a gravel bank, and today we call it the Ayres. Its broad triangular tract stretches across the top of the isle, and its apex forms the Point of Ayre, which now lies 1½ miles beyond the old cliff-line.

Despite threats of development in the past, the Ayres remain a splendidly empty tract, disturbed only by the whistle of the wind through its tussocky acres and the hum of the bees through the course of its summer days. The curlew trills, the oystercatcher pipes, hovering larks twitter and the lapwing repeats its monot-onous questioning call. Nesting terns rise from the pebbles to wheel and dip aggressively over the heads of human intruders. To seaward, the inquisitive head of a grey seal may be seen, roving far from its breeding colonies on the rockier coasts to the south. And gannets patrol offshore, frequently diving into the sea in pursuit of fish before turning back to their nesting colonies in Scotland.

This is the youngest of all the island's shores. Along its western section, the dunes are still building, as sand is blown up by the wind and retained among the spreading growths of spiky marram. And now that the marram (known as *bent* in Man) is no longer cut for thatching, the dunes are more stable than in the past. In the midst of the marram, one finds growths of sea holly and sea bindweed, as well as spurges of the genus *Euphorbia* and the occasional Isle of Man cabbage, *Rhynchosinapis monensis*. There are even orchids here, including the rare, dense-flowered *Neotinea intacta*.

Out along the eastern section, where shingle replaces the sand, high banks of it are thrown up by winter's gales to form the great modern storm-beach which forms the island's northern extremity. Even here, on this uncompromising stony shore, plants like the yellow-horned poppy, English stonecrop, sheepsbit and thyme thrust out from between the pebbles and, as their leaves fall and rot into humus, the grass, heather and gorse will eventually follow, all reaching out to colonize that which the sea has thrown up. This is life in the making.

But the Ayres have not entirely escaped the attentions of *Homo industriosus*. The extensive deposits of gravel are worked to provide aggregate for the construction industry. Such workings are never pretty, but it is a sensible use of indigenous resources when the alternative is costly importation. And when the excavators move on to a new location, the worked-out pits become flooded and overgrown to form new habitats, unplanned nature reserves half-forgotten in this wilderness of sand and scrub.

At the Point of Ayre, Robert Stevenson's red-banded lighthouse stands in splendid isolation at the end of the road from Bride. Even on the calmest day, when the tidal stream flows – which it does four times a day (two floods and two ebbs) – the current rushes past this rasping shingle bank like some great river in spate. On a clear day, the coast and hills of Galloway are visible in the north, and over to the east 'Cumbria looms a geographic ghost'.

The low light at the Point of Ayre surveys a passing ferry

Turning our backs on the Point of Ayre to follow the coast south, we are able to walk the crest of a low cliff as far as Cranstal (identified on the map as Phurt), which was the site of the night watch for the parish of Bride. In the seventeenth and eighteenth centuries, this place was known as Cranstall Port and Cranstyl Harbour, but there is no trace of a harbour today – just a few cottages sitting behind the low cliff.

Down the coast a way, the cliffs rise again and we must resort to walking the shore. We pass beneath a 250-foot (75m) wall of sand and clay which marks the eastern termination of the Bride Hills; its crest is yet another Cronk ny Arrey Laa (sometimes it is *lhaa*, sometimes *laa* – remember that most of these names were set before the Manx language was ever written down). This one was the hill of the day watch for the parish of Bride. It rises above a point on the coast identi-fied as Shellag Point. The old name was just Shellag, from the Scandinavian *selvig*, meaning 'seal creek'. There is no vestige of a creek here now but, thirty years ago, there was a cleft in the upper portion of the cliff-face which could have been its last surviving remnant. The cliffs are heavily eroded by the sea and scored by rivulets of escaping groundwater tumbling to a shore which becomes progressively less stony as we continue into the smooth curve of Ramsey Bay. Periodically, sections of the old iron pipeline which conveyed the brine from the extraction plant at the Point of Ayre to the Ramsey saltworks are uncovered by wave action.

The cliffs decline in height to the south, and the A10 road from Bride draws in close. The first access point between shore and road since Cranstall appears at the Dog Mills, barely a mile from the Ramsey town boundary. The old name was *Mwyllin ny moddey*, 'mill of the dogs'. As we enter Ramsey, we are almost at the end of the long beach. To the south of the town, the rocks rise again to form the solid, out-thrusting promontory of Maughold Head, re-asserting their dominance on the coastline beyond.

RAMSEY TO DOUGLAS

The coastal route south from Ramsey presents a striking contrast to the long beach we have just traversed. As we have seen in the earlier stages of our journey, the rock cliffs of Man provide some of the most dramatic coastal scenery to be found anywhere in the British Isles. The principal difference between this and the coast we have just left behind is that we can no longer follow the base of the cliff (unless we travel by boat) and take in every detail of their precipitous faces and the wildlife inhabiting them. Much of the detail is hidden from above, but the scenery more than compensates.

Between Ramsey and Douglas lie some 22 miles of rugged coast. We leave Ramsey by the A2 Laxey road, but the amount of road-walking may be minimized (if the tide is not high) by crossing the last mile of the long beach, passing beneath the east-striding legs of the Queen's Pier and returning to the road by way of Ballure Walk, which is really a glen. We soon deviate onto the A15 towards Maughold (the 'ugh' is pronounced 'ck') but soon leave it to circle the rocky promontory of Gob ny rona ('point of the seal'). Here, MNH has a 9-acre (3.6ha) holding where lie the remains of the coastal fort built by James Stanley in 1643 as part of the island's defences against Cromwell's Parliamentary forces.

At Port e Vullen ('port of the mill'), we return briefly to the road and then take the path south-eastward through the Maughold Brooghs. On the north side of Maughold Head, the path to St Maughold's Well branches off and descends a steep grassy slope to where a trickle of spring water falls into a rocky basin at the cliff-edge. The summit cairn on the headland stands 385 feet (117m) above the sea and is surrounded by the remains of the promontory fort which has been described earlier. The day watch for the parish of Maughold was kept here. A whole new vista opens up in the south, along a rock-girt coastline, undulating and much indented, reaching down across a handful of lonely coves, beyond the steep, 600-foot (180m) cliffs of Bulgham Bay and across the broad sweep of Laxey Bay to the out-thrusting mass of Clay Head which shuts the rest of it from view.

Before leaving the summit, advance *carefully* to the edge and direct your gaze down the precipitous face to the seemingly inaccessible little beach of *Traie Curn* ('shore of the cairns'). Its old Manx name was *Purt ny Giare as Feed*, 'Port of the Four-and-Twenty' (i.e. the Keys). Tradition has it that, in the old Kingdom of Man and the Isles, when the eight members of the Keys representing the 'Out Isles' (the Hebrides) arrived to attend the annual Tynwald gathering, they would come ashore at this isolated landing, make the perilous ascent of the cliff, and begin their overland journey to the Tynwald. Their zigzag path up the face of the cliff became known as the *Raad ny Kiare as Feed*, the 'Road of the Four-and-Twenty'. But why would any rational being choose to make a landing at such a potentially hazardous spot when – as *Chronicon* records – the Norse kings of Man and the Isles themselves routinely landed at Ramsey, Ronaldsway or St Patrick's Isle? And if there were eight members representing the Out Isles, why was it the Road of the Four-and-Twenty – unless the sixteen members for Man gathered to meet them on arrival? Yet again, who will ever know?

The Maughold lighthouse stands halfway down the cliff on the south-east corner of the headland which forms the eastern extremity of Man. The light is now automated and the former keepers' houses – up on the cliff-top – have been sold off. Maughold church and the few dwellings of the adjacent hamlet nestle in the dip on the landward side of the headland. The church, probably dating from the eleventh or twelfth century, stands on a site which was the centre of early Celtic Christianity in Man. The churchyard contains three visible keeill sites – one with an adjoining well – and the known site of a fourth; the present church may cover the site of a fifth. The fourteenth-century Maughold Cross, carved from a block of St Bee's sandstone, was moved inside the church in 1989; it had stood in the church-yard since 1937, and outside on the green for centuries before that. The parish's collection of Celtic and Norse crosses is housed in the open-fronted cross-house beside the church. The churchyard contains the graves of some eminent island characters: Edward Christian, one of the leaders of the 1643 rebellion against 'the Great Stanley', seventh Earl of Derby; General Sir Mark Cubbon, Commissioner of Mysore 1834–61; Robert Faragher, founder of the *Mona's Herald* and one of the campaigners for a popularly elected House of Keys; Sir Hall Caine, novelist; and P. M. C. Kermode, historian, naturalist and first curator of the Manx Museum.

The coastal footpath resumes by the gate at the seaward side of the church-yard and descends through the fields to the secluded little cove at Dhyrnane. An old lime kiln is passed on the way, and there are remains of past iron-ore work-ings round about. At the head of the cove stand the crumbling ruin of a fishermen's store and a red-rusty winch, from which an equally rusty cable reaches to seaward but slants beyond sight into the shingle before reaching it. The night watch for the parish of Maughold was kept here, and here also was the harbour (though small) for shipping out the iron ore, and for the handling of smuggled goods.

Port Mooar is the largest of the eastern coves. A solitary cottage sits behind a shore of sand, shingle and rocks, and a small group of sea-view dwellings lines the southern cliff. There is no coastal route south from here, and so we must take to the road. Walking up from the shore, we soon return to the A15, which has descended the hill from Maughold church. Following it south, over the level crossing of the MER at Ballajora, we soon take to the narrow minor road which climbs steeply to the peaceful hill-top location of the Quakers' burial ground, *Rhullick-ny-Quakeryn*, described in an earlier chapter. On the opposite side of the road is a chambered burial cairn from the Neolithic age. Continuing, our minor road crosses the A14 and the MER tracks again and descends into Cornaa, where we leave it to follow the left bank of the river down to the shore.

The mouth of the Cornaa River is solidly plugged with a storm-beach of shingle. Nothing daunted, its mountain waters simply back up behind the stony bank and percolate through to the seaward side. The impounded water behind the storm-beach cradles a patch of saltmarsh, but its salinity varies according to the amount of fresh water coming down the river. Port Cornaa was another inlet used for off-loading limestone in the nineteenth century, when the shortage of fuel in

Port Cornaa cradles a patch of saltmarsh behind its shingle bar

the Castletown area necessitated the building of kilns elsewhere. There was no shortage of fuel at Cornaa; there was peat up on the Barony Hill to the south, and timber grew well in the shelter of the valley. The ruin of the kiln still stands behind the shore.

From Port Cornaa, our route heads inland again along the minor road which initially follows the right bank of the river and then takes to a tributary glen around the back of the Barony Hill. We continue to Laxey by a combination of byway and B-road. If time permits, it is worth making the detour into Dhoon Glen. This is a Manx National Glen, maintained by the DAFF, and the brooghs that loom high on its southern flank are in the custody of Manx National Heritage. Although short, it is the steepest of the Manx glens. Its stream plunges and tumbles more than 500 feet (150m) in half a mile, and a footpath follows it down to a tight little beach of sand and pebbles, where great raking slabs of Lonan flagstone rise steeply from the shore. Part-way down, we pass the stone-built casing of the large waterwheel which pumped water and lifted spoil from the adjacent Rhennie Laxey mine, where men grovelled in the depths for ten years from 1859 in quest of lead and zinc – and came up with precious little. The footpath out through the southern brooghs gives impressive views of the towering cliffs above Bulgham Bay.

Dhoon beach, with its sloping slabs of Lonan flagstone

From the head of the glen, our way lies along the old pack-horse road which is now designated as the B11, and we are now in the parish of Lonan. Set in the roadside hedge at Ballaragh is the Spiral Stone, a granite boulder with spiral markings thought to date from the Bronze Age. From here, the road takes us steadily downhill, with the view ahead across Laxey Bay to Clay Head. The B11 cuts through the chambered cairn known as King Orry's Grave, but this lies half a mile off our present route. Where the road swings right towards Laxey village, we keep straight ahead, down a plunging slope towards the harbour. Crossing the A2 Ramsey road, the final descent of the steep northern brogh brings us down to the harbour bridge.

Laxey provides the opportunity for a refreshment break, or a longer stop in our journey, for there is much to see here and another 9 miles lie ahead before reaching the sea terminal at Douglas.

These 9 miles form probably the least satisfying section of the whole of this circuit of Man, because of the lack of a truly coastal route and the amount of roadwork involved. It begins well enough; Laxey's short promenade points the way south and, if the tide is low, we may double that distance by continuing along the shore until the rocky out-thrust of Gob y Rheynn bars further progress. A short ascent takes us up to the main road at Fairy Cottage, and we follow the tarmac to the northern outskirts of Baldrine (rhymes with 'line'), where a minor way descends to the mouth of Garwick Glen. The glen itself is private but the beach is not. (There are no private beaches in the Isle of Man, although some isolated strands lack public rights of way to access them.) A path ascends the southern brogh of the glen and joins the minor road to Clay Head. A blend of field-path and by-road brings us south to Old Kirk Lonan, the ancient parish church, standing in a field behind the coast with scarcely a dwelling in sight.

Old Kirk Lonan served as the parish church until 1733, when a new one was built closer to Laxey. Although in a seemingly remote situation today, the church stood beside a main travel route, for the present byway which brought us here, and which continues south to Groudle, was part of the old bridleway along the east coast. The church is thought to date from the twelfth century but the foundation of an earlier one is known to lie beneath. Most of the parish's collection of ancient crosses (all of them Celtic) are grouped in the roofless western portion of the building, but its most impressive monument stands outside in the churchyard. It is a stout, wheel-headed cross-slab, 5 feet (1.5m) high, more than 3 feet (90cm) broad, and decorated with tightly interlaced Celtic designs. It has probably stood in the same spot since its sculpting in the ninth or tenth century.

As we cross the footbridge over the Groudle River, we enter the parish of Onchan, known in the old days as Kirk Conchan (after the Celtic saint), then Kirk

The harbour at Laxey

Onchan, and now Onchan. Groudle Glen curves westward in a lazy 'S', under the bridge that carries the coast-road south, and up along the northern edge of the village, where it becomes Molly Quirk's Glen. The name 'Groudle' derives from the Norse *krappdalr*, meaning 'narrow glen', and part of it is known as *Glion Coon*, which has the same meaning in Manx. Its upper reaches are pleasantly wooded and undeveloped. Lower down, in the heyday of the tourist industry, its trees were hung with fairy lights and the old waterwheel turned beneath the floodlights on summer evenings. There were sea lions in a pool just above the shore, and a mile of miniature railway ran out along the northern cliff. It was a popular place in the season, only a couple of miles out of Douglas and with the electric railway halt right opposite the main entrance. Now, the sea lions have gone, but the miniature railway – after being abandoned for some years – has been restored by a group of enthusiasts and is back in seasonal operation. The glen's southern broogh now sprouts a conspicuous settlement of holiday bungalows. Meanwhile, just round the corner on the high southern cliff, some buildings still stand on the site of the old Howstrake Holiday Camp – a reminder of an earlier age.

And so we are almost back at the point from which we started. The remainder of our route lies along road and promenade – the final 3 miles to the sea terminal.

The east coast from above Groudle

The most satisfying end to such a journey is to arrive on Onchan Head late on a fine summer's evening, when the last fringes of the sun have retreated before the advancing darkness of the night, to see the lights on the Douglas promenades arching from end to end along the bay, and the circling beam on Douglas Head flashing its message to the sea.

BAYR NY SKEDDAN

The second long-distance path to be established in 1986 was the *Bayr ny Skeddan*, the 'road of the herring'. It is based on the route said to have been taken in the past by Manx fishermen when travelling between Peel and Castletown. In terms of distance, it is not in the same league as the two paths we have already followed, being a mere 14 miles (23km) in length.

If setting out from Peel, the starting point is beside the old anchor in Mill Road, close by the House of Manannan. The route follows the first mile of the former railway line to Douglas, past the power station and the smoke houses where the Manx kippers are still produced, following the right bank of the River

Neb. The waymarks bear the silhouette of a herring. At Glenfaba Bridge, we leave the railway track, cross the A27 Patrick road and take to a track which conducts us past Knockaloe Beg (Thomas Corrin's old property) and climbs to join the coastal footpath behind Contrary Head. We then follow the coastal path south as far as Glen Maye.

I must admit to harbouring long-felt doubts concerning this part of the route. Why would fishermen travelling between Peel and Castletown choose to climb up to the high coast above Patrick, only to descend and leave the coast on reaching Glen Maye, barely 2 miles on? However, on arriving in Glen Maye village, we return to a more 'believable' route to the south.

The long, curving glen which we now follow sports no fewer than three different names throughout its 3-mile length. The lowest stretch, between the village and the shore, was named *Glen Maye*, 'yellow glen', probably because of the clay often suspended in its stream. The middle section has the name *Glen Mooar*, 'great glen', before becoming *Glen Rushen* in its topmost section. So how did one glen come to have three different parts bearing three different names? *Glen Rushen* has always been a mystery. According to J. J. Kneen, the glen was once known as *Glen Maye* (or ancient renderings of it) along its entire length. In 1515, it was being referred to as *Glen Moy*, so was the later *Glen Mooar* really

The south-west coast, seen from Niarbyl

meant to indicate a 'great glen', or was it simply a corruption of *Glen Moy*? This land is brimming over with unanswered questions.

From Glen Maye village, we follow the narrow Glen Rushen road, which has no through route for vehicular traffic, following a partial collapse some years ago. It follows the line of the glen, with the Arrasey Plantation on the left, then the Lhargan Plantation on the right, and the mass of South Barrule looming straight ahead. We pass abandoned slate quarries and arrive at a small reservoir, at the lower end of which there is a choice of two paths. The official route takes the right-hand fork and slants through the Carn y Chrock Plantation ('cairn of the urn'), which adjoins the southern end of the Lhargan. This path reacquaints us with the A27, which we must then follow for a mile to the Round Table crossroads. The mile of roadwork may be avoided by selecting the left-hand fork at the reservoir and following the track which slants up the south-eastern flank of Glen Rushen, through the Glen Rushen Plantation, to arrive directly at the crossroads.

The A27 crosses the A36 on the col below the steep western shoulder of South Barrule. The area is said to take its name from a large, low mound (which may cover the site of a Celtic round-house) just to the east of the crossroads, and the appearance of which was thought to resemble a large round table. (A round-house site in Arbory is also known by that name.)

By whichever route we arrive at the crossroads, we follow the A27 across and, almost immediately, the path to the summit of South Barrule branches off to the left. It is less than a mile to its cairn but involves a climb of close on 600 feet (180m). But our way lies a few yards further down the road, where a track veers off to the left, heading south-east and downhill, through the Cringle Plantation to meet the B39 Corlea road. The road is followed north-eastward for a quarter of a mile, before taking to the track through Glenmoar Farm, descending all the while, eventually to join the A3 Castletown road below Ballamodha. At this point, we have joined the route of the Millennium Way, described earlier, and we follow that route for the remainder of our journey, by way of Silverdale Glen, Ballasalla and the banks of the Silver Burn, to our finishing point in the shadow of Castle Rushen.

THE HERITAGE TRAIL

The Isle of Man's fourth long-distance footpath (if 11 miles can be classified as long-distance) utilizes the track of the former steam railway line between Douglas and Peel – or at least as much of it as has not been built over. Since the first mile out from Douglas railway station is no longer accessible as a walking route, the official terminus at the Douglas end of the trail is at Quarterbridge, a distance of

Locomotive No 4, Loch, *arrives at Douglas with its train from Port Erin*

10½ miles (17km) from Peel, but if the walker is intent on starting (or finishing) at the Douglas station, then a further mile can be added. This is the only one of the island's long-distance paths on which the gradients are quite minimal.

If starting from the Douglas railway station, we must initially turn our backs on the railway and head for a brief excursion onto the streets, up Bank Hill and left along Peel Road, past the terrace of shops built by the railway company and still known as the 'Railway Shops'. We pass the Hill's Meadow industrial estate, partly built over the track of the Peel line. On approaching the traffic lights at Pulrose Road, a glance over and down to our left shows where the line passed under the two-arch bridge on its way out of town. The line never was doubled, and so the second arch remained unused. The Port Erin line has already turned south by this point.

To leave the main-road traffic behind at the earliest opportunity, turn left at the lights and, almost immediately, cross Pulrose Road to enter the car park beside the power station. Continuing through, we cross the footbridge over the River Glass ('green') and enter the National Sports Centre. Over to our left, the Rivers Dhoo ('black') and Glass combine to form the Douglas River on its final 1½-mile run to the sea. Bearing right, we follow the tarmac perimeter road which parallels the right bank of the Glass, passing the running track and grandstand.

Approaching the NSC office building, we can at last tread the line of the former railway – it passes *behind* the building.

On crossing the busy New Castletown Road at Quarterbridge, we are now at the official start of the Heritage Trail. The first half-mile has been surfaced to provide an access road between the inside and outside of the TT course when the course itself is closed for racing. At all other times, this section is closed to vehicular traffic.

Passing under the A1 Peel–Douglas road at Braddan Bridge, we are now on the inside of the TT course. There was a halt on the line hereabouts, where, once upon a time, up to 20,000 visitors would flock to attend the open-air Sunday services in the field behind the parish church – a sight which is seen no more. Leaving the tarmac behind us, we follow the left bank of the Dhoo. On the approach to Union Mills, we pass the Snugborough trading estate and then cross the river to enter the station, where the single platform still survives. The surrounding scene is heavily wooded, and – straight ahead – the road-bridge carries the A1 further on its way. There was a passing-loop here, and an access roadway still slopes down from the main road.

Beyond the A1, we are back on the left bank of the river and on the outside of the TT course, where we shall remain for the duration. We pass the small industrial

The deserted station at Union Mills, a vintage crane preserved on a short section of track

estate which occupies the site of the mills which gave the place its name. William Kelly's woollen mills operated here through most of the nineteenth century. There was also a corn mill and both drew their water from the same pond. Some of the old buildings survive and are occupied for more modern industrial purposes.

After Union Mills, the housing and industrial estates are left behind and we are in open country. Between the track and the river can be seen some of the last vestiges of the central valley's curragh, with growths of willow carr which thrives in such wetlands. The route of the railway was chosen with the aim of skirting the most boggy areas, but parts of the track can be quite wet and muddy nonetheless. We pass Glenlough ('glen of the lake', but there is just curragh and *garey* today), where the farm camp-site is popular with visitors. The trail crosses the A26 road at Glen Vine, and a section of the way ahead has been surfaced to permit tanker access to the local sewage works. We pass behind Marown parish church, then cross the B36 at Crosby. The gatehouse still stands at each road crossing, but there is no surviving trace of Crosby station, nor of the passing-loop that was there; there are playing-fields now.

Further on, we are back on the right bank of the river which, from here on, takes the name of the Greeba. We leave it at the village of that name, where its course swings abruptly to the north and gathers its headwaters from the great horseshoe between the Beary and Greeba mountains. But we are soon beside another (relatively minor) watercourse which has descended from the Archallagan Plantation, through wild Glion Darragh ('oak glen'), before turning along the central valley. However, whereas the Greeba and Dhoo were flowing eastward, this one is heading west, to link up with the Neb at St John's, for we are now at the highest point of the trail, 185 feet (56m) above the sea.

With no natural fall to east or west in this part of the central valley, but with water being shed from the hills to north and south, drainage is consequently poor, except where ditches have been cut in attempts to improve matters, and there remain areas of natural curragh to be seen hereabouts. One such is an area known as Curragh Glass, 'green marsh', where there is much marsh vegetation with a dense overgrowth of willow carr, which runs rampant in the wet. In places where the drainage has been improved, breaks may develop in the willow scrub, allowing coarse grasses to intrude, and the land may transmute into *garey*, suitable for rough grazing. It was undeniably an outstanding engineering achievement to construct a stable track-bed through country such as this.

The curragh is terminated in the west by the Curragh Road, which is the name given to that stretch of the A3 between Ballacraine and the Hope crossroads. We cross the road, where the gate-house still stands, and continue into St John's, alongside the access road to the local amenity site, and with the 1,094-foot (333m) peak of Slieau Whallian rising close on our left. On the way in, we pass under the bridge which carried the Foxdale branch over the Peel line, and then we arrive at the site of the station, with precious little of it remaining to view. Unlike the railway company's station buildings on the Port Erin line, those on the Peel line (with the exception of Peel itself) were simple wooden structures and were never replaced or improved. Even here at St John's, which – once the Isle of Man Railway, the Manx Northern and the Foxdale companies were fully operational – was a hive of activity, the simple wooden station building served the Isle of Man Railway Company to the end of its days. By contrast, the red-brick building of the Foxdale company still stands and may be seen a little further along our route.

St John's was the point at which the Manx Northern line began its divergence to the north, but initially continued in parallel with the Peel line. Thus, there were two sets of tracks on the level crossing over the A40 road in the centre of the village. In attempting to follow them today, we must make a short detour round the site of the agricultural mart and the local sewage works. On regaining the route, both tracks remain visible; both are now public rights of way, both bridged – side-by-side – over the River Neb as it flows down from the north and turns abruptly westward. On the opposite side of the central valley, the Foxdale river presents an almost mirror-image, descending from the south before it, too, heads west to join the Neb.

As we follow the Peel line, the Ramsey branch rises alongside and begins its swing to the north to the point where it was bridged over the A1 Peel–Douglas road at Ballaleece. The bridge has gone; anyone following that route today must descend the southern embankment to cross the A1 and then ascend the other side. But that is for another day. Straight ahead now, the valley opens out to the west, and the long ridge of Corrin's Hill stands across the valley's mouth, apparently barring our way.

Pressing on beyond Ballawyllin Farm, there may be seen traces of the branch-line which curved back in the reverse direction to our own, crossing the river on a wooden trestle bridge to serve the internment camp at Knockaloe during the First World War. We enter an area known as Congarey ('the rabbit warren'), where the river was impounded by a weir to supply water to the Glenfaba Mill, built about 1850, and whose buildings still stand on the right of the track, with much of the machinery intact. The mill-race passed under the railway. The pond behind the weir was known as the Red Dub ('the red pond'). Incidentally, *Glenfaba* is pronounced variously as 'Glenfarba', 'Glenfairba' or 'Glenfaeba': take your pick.

When we pass under the A27 Patrick road at Glenfaba Bridge, we join the route of the Bayr ny Skeddan for the final mile into Peel. Passing the power station and the kippering houses, we make the crossing of Mill Road and stand beside the old anchor which reclines at the entrance to the station yard, which is now the car park of the House of Manannan. The water tank still stands in the yard, and the station building is incorporated into the House of Manannan, across the road from which stands the Creek Inn, which was originally the Railway Hotel.

THE CALL OF – AND PRESSURES ON – THE WILD

In addition to the four formally established long-distance footpaths, the island abounds in areas in which the walker may select his own route in search of the wilderness, which will often involve a circuitous course beginning and ending at a convenient car park. The most extensive such area is provided by the northern hills, bounded in the south by the central valley, to the west and north by the A3 portion of the TT course, and in the east by the A2 Laxey coast road. The most promising area in the south of the island lies in the line of hills running south-west from Slieau Whallian and narrowing down to the coastal ridge which terminates at Bradda Head. Armed with the Ordnance Survey's Landranger sheet 95 or the Isle of Man government's map of public rights of way, the walker should be able to select a route to suit individual requirements regarding distance and effort.

These areas are well provided with off-road public rights of way, which may be either footpaths or 'byways open to all traffic'. The latter (which I shall hereafter refer to as 'byways') are usually the remnants of thoroughfares which were the 'highways' of the horse age. They were not – and are not – surfaced or maintained to any significant degree; they were formed in an era which had never heard of the internal combustion engine, and they have never been adapted to meet its requirements. And thereby arises conflict. The unsurfaced byways are used (quite legally) by walkers, trail-riders and users of four-wheel drive vehicles, and the pedestrians resent the accelerated erosion resulting from the vehicular traffic. They also resent the intrusion of motor vehicles into areas to which the walkers resort in search of the peace and tranquillity of the wilderness.

The problem is made worse by the questionable classification of some of the byways. A typical example lies in the parish of Lonan, where a byway leaves the northern outskirts of Laxey and climbs north towards Slieau Ruy. After 1½ miles, the byway comes to an abrupt end on the hill at the point where it intersects a circuit of footpaths which encircles a trio of summits; there is no onward route for the motor vehicle. The question arises: what is the purpose of such a byway? Is it not an open invitation to rider or driver to press on (illegally) along the public footpaths? And who is there, in that desolate spot, to police the law? Even on the

*Pressures on the wild: byways that are open to all traffic (and many that are not)
are frequently reduced to this state*

byways where all may go legally, the erosion in many places becomes so extreme
that walkers and horse-riders have great difficulty in negotiating the deeply
rutted tracks.

In recent years, some of the island's byways have been closed to vehicular
traffic during the winter months in an attempt to minimize the problem, but the
situation has been exacerbated further by increasing numbers of visiting motor
cyclists, in winter as well as summer. As more hill tracks in Britain are closed
to off-road vehicles, groups of trail-riders are seen arriving on the ferry; they
spend a weekend on the island's tracks and are gone before anyone is aware of
any damage. The DoT has not the resources either to enforce the present partial
closures or to undertake maintenance to make good the damage. It would
surely be simpler to institute a total ban on motor vehicles from the island's hill-
tracks, but the motor-cycle lobby is strong in the Isle of Man. In 2002, the DoT
gave notice of its intention to make an order prohibiting the use of mechani-
cally propelled vehicles on certain rural highways not maintained for use by
motor vehicles. Predictably, the department backed down in the face of the
opposition. Meanwhile, the mutual resentment between the two groups of
users simmers on.

CAMPING

Visitors to the island who come for the walking are frequently also interested in the camping facilities, and so I end this chapter with a brief survey. 'Wild' camping is not permitted on government-owned land. The four principal camp-sites are all either in or not far from the central valley. The site nearest to Douglas is at Glendhoo, just off the TT course at Hillberry. On the course to the west of Douglas is the Glenlough farm site, midway between Union Mills and Glen Vine. Also close to the course, in the west of the isle, is the municipal site at Glen Wyllin, Kirk Michael, which is just a few strides from a favoured spectating point – the fast right-hand bend known as the Douglas Road Corner. And further west, but off the course, is another municipal site at Peel.

Caravans have always been a thorny issue in Man. Motor-caravans and folding caravans are permitted, but non-folding touring caravans are not. To be totally accurate, the caravans themselves are not specifically banned, but anyone bringing one to the island will find that there are no sites with planning permission to accept it. That being so, it is unlikely that the Steam Packet Company would agree to transport it.

The argument against caravans has always centred on the unsuitability of Manx roads for such vehicles, and that objection is – in general – probably valid. But it might have been feasible to designate (and waymark) certain direct routes between the sea terminal and specifically approved camping sites, and impose a ban on all other roads. That is undeniably a minority view; caravans are even more unpopular than marinas.

CHAPTER ELEVEN

Douglas and the East

The growth of Douglas, with its beginnings in the small medieval fishing village clustered around the mouth of the Douglas River, is a continuing phenomenon. The increases in population and commercial activity in the town which has been the island's capital since 1869 have imposed pressures for corresponding growth in the surrounding parishes of Braddan, Marown and Onchan. These four districts – the capital and the three neighbouring parishes – can be considered to be the accommodation hub for those with employment in Douglas, although – in truth – people now commute daily into the town from all parts of the island. This has brought the additional problems of traffic congestion and an unsatiated demand for parking space on the streets of the capital. Unsurprisingly, traffic streams into and out of Douglas are at their most intense during the two peak periods of the working day, and the introduction of flexible working hours by government departments and some private employers has done little to alleviate the situation. A brief experiment with a park-and-ride scheme was not a success, and public transport provides little relief when commuters so value the convenience of their own vehicles, regardless of the delays encountered *en route*.

Consequently parking facilities are at a premium throughout the working day. Despite the availability of multi-storey and other off-street parking, these either offer inadequate capacity or do not attract sufficient patrons who are prepared to pay for their use. And, as more on-street parking areas are restricted to short-term use for the convenience of shoppers, the competition for day-long parking becomes more intense and, in some parts of the town, the discontinued park-and-ride scheme has been replaced by an informal park-and-walk culture. It is all a far cry from the Douglas of yore.

DOUGLAS

As noted earlier, the marked expansion of Douglas in the eighteenth and nineteenth centuries, and its acquisition of capital status, were intrinsically linked with

The Battery Pier, Douglas (above), with its protecting stabits along the outside, and (below) a close-up of the stabits

the development of its harbour. And those developments occurred at Douglas, rather than any of the island's other ports, because (a) it was on the right side of the island for convenient trading links with Britain, and (b) it possessed the only harbour (initially tidal, like the rest) reasonably capable of seaward extension to form a deep-water port accessible to shipping at all states of the tide.

At the beginning of the Victorian era, the harbour consisted of the inner, tidal portion only, bounded by the North and South Quays, and extending to seaward as far as the Red Pier, built of red sandstone and completed in 1801. A stone jetty to protect the harbour mouth was built out from the south side, below Fort Anne, the imposing residence (now demolished) on Douglas Head. The development of the deep-water port followed, with the construction of the Battery Pier, running out north-eastward from Douglas Head, with the Victoria Pier enclosing the north side of the harbour, and the entrance from the open sea lying between the two. Both piers were completed in 1872, the former being built on the site of the earlier, collapsed breakwater ('Abernethy's bird-cage'), and the latter being lengthened in 1887.

In the twentieth century, the old Red Pier was extended by the building of the present King Edward VIII Pier along the middle of the outer harbour, opened in 1936 and leaving very little visible reminder of the old sandstone structure. In 1983, the Battery Pier was strengthened by the placing of a breakwater of interlocking concrete 'stabits' along its seaward side, each stabit being a massive tripodal casting of concrete. The present sea terminal building was opened by Princess Margaret in 1965; its distinctive upper storey (nicknamed the 'lemon-squeezer') was originally a restaurant, with fine views across the bay. Today, it is in far more mundane occupation as the headquarters of two government departments, the DoT and the DTL.

More recent changes in the inner harbour have involved its transformation into a yacht marina. At its seaward end, the old swing-bridge (which was originally a tollbridge for carriages but later a footbridge only) has been replaced with a lifting road-bridge, in conjunction with a rising sill (or flap-gate) which rotates upwards from the harbour bed to retain water and allow the yachts to remain afloat at low tide. The marina could have been an attraction for visiting yachtsmen but, by all accounts, all available berths have been snapped up by residents, and so the need for marina facilities for visitors (if we are still interested in attracting visitors) remains. But any proposal for a marina in any of the other Manx ports attracts the inevitable objections. The Douglas facility itself was not without its detractors. The neighbouring thoroughfare along North Quay has been the subject of a multi-million-pound improvement scheme, involving pedestrianization and the creation of a continental atmosphere with outside eating areas fronting the cafés and pubs.

The biggest single hazard confronting ships approaching Douglas harbour in earlier times was the islet known today as the Conister Rock, which lies close

Douglas inner harbour and North Quay

by the approach to the port entrance from the north-east. The old name of the rock was *Kione y sker,* a quaint amalgam of Manx and Norse meaning 'end of the reef'. The reef was formerly known as the Pollack Rocks, and its landward end is now covered by the base of the Victoria Pier. The frequent wrecks occurring on the Conister in the early nineteenth century could not fail to be noticed by Sir William Hillary, whose residence, Fort Anne, overlooked the harbour from the south. He was personally involved in a number of rescues of shipwrecked mariners, and launched an appeal for the founding of the organization which became the Royal National Lifeboat Institution. He was also instrumental in raising funds for the building of the Tower of Refuge on the Conister Rock in 1832. Hillary was later ruined by the collapse of the Holmes Bank in 1853 and had to dispose of his fine house. He is buried in St George's churchyard.

Hillary's predecessor at Fort Anne was the profligate Irishman, Buck Whaley, who was responsible for its building. His nefarious activities led to his being driven from his native land, and he arrived in Man complete with a wealthy wife whose inheritance was conditional upon her continuing to live on Irish soil. Accordingly, before building his house, Whaley acquired a boat-load of Irish soil and spread it across the site. Thus, Fort Anne arose to stand on Irish soil on

The old Douglas Head Hotel is now an apartment block

Douglas Head. After Hillary's time at Fort Anne, the place was eventually turned into a hotel. It thrived for as long as Manx tourism survived but was struggling commercially by the early 1970s. It was later demolished. The office building which currently graces the site is not dissimilar to the original.

The growth of the town of Douglas went hand-in-hand with the growth of its harbour and trade. The completion of the Victoria Pier in 1872 posed the question of access to the town behind it, which, at that time, lay via a network of narrow, cobbled streets. In the previous decade, Samuel Harris, a prominent Douglas lawyer and land-owner, had raised funds by public subscription for the construction of a promenade fronting the centre of Douglas Bay, and which bears his name. There were now proposals for Harris's promenade to be linked to the Victoria Pier by reclaiming land from the sea and building a new promenade. The result was Loch Promenade, opened in 1877. A portion of the old sea wall can still be seen, incorporated into the boundary walling on the west side of Strand Lane, one of the back lanes that run between, and parallel with, Strand/Castle Street and the promenade. This work, together with the broad new thoroughfare of Victoria Street, opened up access into the old town.

At the other end of the bay, Queen's Promenade was completed in 1890, and the horse tramway was soon extended to run from end to end of the bay. By the turn of

Reminders of old Douglas: (above) a preserved section of the old sea wall in Strand Lane; (below) the Jubilee Clock stands at the end of Victoria Street, the modern building on the right replacing the historic Villiers Hotel

the century, the horse trams were conveying more than half a million passengers a year, beside which today's figures look insignificant, due to both the decline in tourism and the growth in personal transport. With the northern end of the horse tramway just yards from the southern terminus of the MER, it does appear that an opportunity has been missed in not linking the two systems. Both are laid to the same gauge; if the overhead lines of the MER were extended to the sea terminal, the electrified system would then be far more amenable as an *insular* transport link (in addition to its tourism potential) than it is when terminating at the north end of town.

Throughout the course of this nineteenth-century work, the town began to spread northward and westward from the harbour. The narrow thoroughfares of Duke Street, Sand (now Strand) Street and Castle Street retained – and still retain – the town's main concentration of shops, but others sprang up along the new Victoria Street and beyond, as this modern thoroughfare was extended through the town, swinging northward to form Prospect Hill, Buck's Road and Woodbourne Road. New streets branched out to right and left from this new highway which had brought the town's development onto the higher ground behind the promenades, leading to the demarcations – still in common use today

The sunken gardens on Loch Promenade; in the week leading up to Tynwald Day, the Manx and Norwegian flags fly on alternate flagpoles

– of 'Lower Douglas' and 'Upper Douglas'. Buck's Road was so named (according to Brown's *Guide of the Isle of Man*, 1880) because:

> A short distance beyond Christian Road, and on the other side of the way, stands a slate-covered house not remarkable for anything, but here dwelt Mr Buck, the builder of this the first house erected in Buck's Road, which was named from that circumstance.

T. E. Brown gazes down Prospect Hill

The expansion of the town continued through the twentieth century. Some of the road and street names in various parts of the town give clear indications of former land usage:

Anagh Coar	'Marsh of the herons'
Ballabrooie	'Farm of the river banks'
Ballakermeen	'Kermeen's farm'
Ballanard	'Farm of the height'
Ballaquayle	'Quayle's farm'
Farm Hill	(which would be 'Ballachrink' if expressed in Manx, although in 1580 it appears to have been Ballaquirk)

Down on the promenades in the latter decades of the nineteenth century, hotels and guest-houses were being built apace to cater for the growing numbers of visitors. At the southern end stood two imposing buildings: the Peveril, looking out across the square of the same name to the sea terminal, and the Villiers, named after Governor Loch's wife, Elizabeth Villiers, standing as the southern terminator of Loch Promenade. Both have now vanished, to be replaced with office buildings. Further along, the impressive ranks of Victorian hotels and guest-houses survive to a large extent, at least as regards their façades, although there have been amalgamations, some changes of use, and a few have undergone the process of 'demolish-and-rebuild'.

The Villiers was the work of the Stockport architect W. J. Rennison, who then went on to design most of the other hotels in the row. The Sefton, which displays his characteristic trademark of Gothic-style turrets, still stands, along with most of his others. To the north, Harris Promenade provides a break from the unrelieved ranks of hotels, with the intrusion of Frank Matcham's magnificent Gaiety Theatre and the Villa Marina. Both have benefited from recent refurbishment to restore them to first-rate venues for entertainment and artistic performance, the latter standing on the site of the original Villa Marina, the house leased from Samuel Harris by the newly arrived Governor Pigott in 1830. The latest refurbishment of 'the Villa' has included the establishment of the new Broadway Cinema, one of the town's two remaining picture-houses.

Descending to the sea-front between the Harris and Central promenades is the second main thoroughfare linking the lower and upper parts of the town. 'Broadway' must have been an apt enough description at the time of its construction but, for today's traffic conditions, its width is not over-generous. It rises to the north-west, changing its name to Ballaquayle Road to remind us of the farm long-since overwhelmed by the burgeoning town, and meets up with the original route from Lower Douglas – Woodbourne Road. The construction of Broadway allowed

Reminders of Cunningham's Camp: (above) the lower entrance in Switzerland Road, at the foot of the now-derelict lift; (below) the castellated folly at the upper level now stands on the edge of the modern Summerhill Business Park

the further spread of hotel and guest-house accommodation up behind the promenade, as well as the branching of more residential roads to right and left.

Back on the sea-front beyond Broadway, the Castle Mona, built as the stately
home of the fourth Duke of Atholl in 1804 but a hotel since 1832, still looks out
across Central Promenade to the bay. Its Arran sandstone has stood the test of
time well in a sometimes harsh maritime environment, and its reception rooms
retain much of the elegance one would expect from its origins. Further along, the
former Palace Hotel and Casino is now the Hilton Hotel and Casino, and the old
Palace Lido has been partly demolished and the remainder converted into the
Palace Cinema. On the cliff-top above, the handsome Falcon Cliff, built as a
private house in 1836 and later a hotel, now accommodates offices.

Central Promenade continues north as Queen's Promenade and, on the left,
Switzerland Road zigzags up the cliff (no through road for vehicles) to Victoria
Road, passing on the way the rather fine crenellated gate-house which gave
access to the lift that took patrons up to Cunningham's Camp. On the flat area
above, the former camping ground now houses the modern office buildings of the
Summerhill Business Park. But, out at the seaward end of the site, enveloped on
three sides by luxuriant vegetation, stands a miniature castle – similar in style to
the gate-house – on which campers could stand to take in the panoramic view
over the bay. The vegetation shuts out the view today. The little building also
provided sufficient space (but only just) for a three-berth accommodation unit. It
and the gate-house are the only visible reminders of the first holiday camp in the
British Isles.

Up at the north end of Queen's Promenade in the 1830s, some elegant houses
were being built along Strathallan Crescent, most to be occupied by 'stranger-
residents' and 'half-pay officers' released from the army after the Napoleonic
wars. Most of the dwellings are still there, a notable exception being Derby Castle,
originally a spacious family residence, then opened as a ballroom in 1877 and later
altered and extended. It was demolished in 1964 to make way for the ill-fated
Summerland sports and leisure complex. The site was still known as Derby Castle
long after the building had gone.

Summerland was completed in 1970, and was regarded as one of the most
progressive facilities of its kind. Its destruction by fire in August 1973, resulting in
fifty deaths and many injuries, was a devastating blow to the island's prestige and
self-confidence. Regardless of the initial cause of the fire, its effects were grossly
exacerbated by the properties of the plastic roof covering, which softened under
the influence of heat, and dropped in searing, molten globules onto the people
beneath. A former colleague of mine and his friend, realizing that they could not
get out of the flaming building, retreated into the toilets, sat under a wash-basin
after blocking its overflow and turning on the taps, and let the water flow over

them as the fire raged above them. Such presence of mind saved their lives. As so often happens after such incidents, fire and building regulations were revised, not only in the Isle of Man, but also in the United Kingdom. (We learn far more from our disasters than we ever do from our triumphs.) Summerland was rebuilt, but it was always a stark, unattractive building in reinforced concrete which steadily deteriorated, with its rusting steel reinforcement increasingly visible on the outside as its concrete cover flaked away. The building was demolished in 2006 and the future use of the site has yet to be determined.

The third, and later, main thoroughfare to Upper Douglas runs from Quarterbridge, a mile west of the old town which clustered around North Quay, striking through the modern (twentieth-century) suburbs of Ballabrooie and Tromode. The three main routes through the upper town coalesce at the cross-roads beside St Ninian's Church, where Bray Hill levels onto Glencrutchery Road, which then continues past the TT grandstand and forms the main road into Onchan.

By the beginning of the nineteenth century, Douglas had spread up as far as Athol Street, named after the fourth Duke of Atholl, and linking Prospect Hill with Peel Road. Its elegant Georgian buildings were originally the dwellings of merchants and other wealthy incumbents but, as the town and its commercial activities grew, Athol Street became the town's business centre. Today, it accommodates many of the island's advocates' offices, and its buildings form an amalgam of the original and modern development. The old Court House – having been made redundant by the modern premises at Deemsters' Walk, adjoining Government Buildings on Buck's Road – is at last under redevelopment after standing for some years in a dilapidated state. The building was used as Tynwald chambers from the 1860s, until the present Tynwald building was completed in 1894; it then served as the rolls office (and was the children's prison at one time) before becoming the capital's court house. Several of the former residential streets nearby have had their buildings converted into offices. In the days when there were several independent Manx newspapers (only thirty years ago), their offices were to be found along Hill Street and Ridgeway Street; today, the sole newspaper publisher is housed in modern premises on Peel Road.

Many of the developments in nineteenth-century Douglas benefited from funding from the town's greatest benefactor, Henry Bloom Noble. He was born in Westmorland in 1816 and arrived in the Isle of Man in 1835, owning – it is said – only the one pair of patched breeches that he stood in. He found employment until he was twenty-six, then set up his own businesses in wines and spirits, timber and property, becoming exceedingly rich in the process. His fortune was further enhanced by substantial investments in Manx companies, including the Steam Packet Company, the Douglas Gas Light Company, the Laxey mines and the Isle of Man Bank. In 1888, he funded the establishment of the original Noble's Hospital, the building on Crellin's Hill which now houses the Manx Museum. When he died in 1903, Noble's huge estate – administered by the trustees of the Henry Bloom Noble Trust – was divided among beneficiaries in the Isle of Man and north-west England. Principal results in the island were the second Noble's Hospital (on Westmoreland Road), St Ninian's Church, the Villa Marina, the Douglas Children's Home and the Ramsey Cottage Hospital. The Henry Bloom Noble Trust is still in being, its donation of £750,000 in 2006 funding the construction of the new children's hospice, adjoining the Isle of Man Hospice, in Braddan. This is the second such hospice (replacing the old one in Kensington Road) and stands in the grounds of the new Noble's Hospital, this one being the third to bear his name, and the first to stand outside the town of Douglas. The children's hospice is named Rebecca House, after Noble's wife, who encouraged him in his charitable funding but predeceased him by fifteen years.

Returning finally to the place where the story of Douglas first began – the harbour – the scene has changed beyond all recognition. Outside the rising sill which retains the waters of the modern yacht-haven, the bulk of commercial seaborne traffic entering the port today comprises the passenger and freight ferry services and the tankers bringing supplies of fuel-oils and liquid petroleum gas.

ISLE OF MAN NEWSPAPERS

Nordic contacts still: the Norwegian Royal yacht, Norge, *in Douglas harbour*

Fishing activity is a mere shadow of what it once was. Meanwhile, out in the bay, it is a common sight to see ocean-going vessels bound to or from Liverpool, at anchor, as they wait to pick up Mersey pilots or to put them ashore.

ONCHAN

Prior to the election of the first town commissioners for Douglas in 1860 and town boundaries being established, Douglas possessed no discrete administrative identity at all; most of it was still a part of the parish of Onchan. The exception was the small part of the town located south of the Douglas River, which was in the parish of Braddan. The Douglas Town Act of 1860 brought definitive identity to the town and separated it, once and for all, from the bordering parishes.

In administrative terms, the Village District of Onchan was divided off from the remainder of the parish in 1895 (for reasons explained in Chapter 6) but the two were recombined in 1986. The old village (known as late as 1845 as *Kiondroghad*, 'bridge-end') developed around the parish church of Kirk Conchan, which commemorates the Gaelic version of St Christopher. For some reason, Conchan was depicted in the Celtic Church as a dog-headed man, and the porch of the present parish church contains some cross-slabs from the early Christian period, bearing carvings of dog-headed figures. The present church was built on the site of an earlier one in 1833 and (for some reason) dedicated to St Peter. Within it, we find further work by architect Baillie Scott: the pulpit and altar rails are his, as is the church hall in Royal Avenue. The parish contains eight *treen* names, all but one of which are of Scandinavian origin.

The earlier parish church was the setting for the marriage, in 1781, of William Bligh (later to gain fame as captain of HMS *Bounty*) to Elizabeth Betham, daughter of the first British customs officer appointed to the island after the Revestment of 1765. Two other prominent characters in the 1787 mutiny on the *Bounty* had Manx connections. The renowned Fletcher Christian, leader of the revolt, is often stated to have been Manx-born. He was undoubtedly related to the Christians of Milntown, but his father was Charles Christian, of Brigham, in Cumberland, who was the third son of John Christian, of Milntown.

The other character featuring in the mutiny was certainly Manx-born; Peter Heywood, son of Deemster Heywood, of the Nunnery, Douglas, was born on 6 June 1773, and was only fourteen years old at the time of the mutiny. After Bligh and the nineteen crew-members who remained loyal to him had been set adrift, Heywood and some of the others who did not wish to go on were set ashore in Tahiti, whence Christian and the rest, together with some Polynesian women, sailed on to Pitcairn in search of a South-Sea sanctuary. At Pitcairn, they scuttled the *Bounty*, thereby ensuring (almost literally) that they had burned their boat[s] and there was no way back. Christian was murdered in a disagreement some years later.

The unfortunate character in the *Bounty* saga was Peter Heywood. In 1791, he and thirteen others were eventually tracked down on Tahiti by HMS *Pandora*. Although *Pandora* was wrecked on the way home, Heywood arrived in England the following year, was put on trial for complicity in the mutiny, and was condemned to death, despite having been confined below decks while the mutiny was in progress. He was subsequently reprieved, pardoned and allowed to re-enter the navy, in which he rose to achieve his own command. After leaving the navy, and in poor health, he lived out the rest of his life in London.

In the past, there was always clear, green, open space between the Douglas town conurbation and the built-up village of Onchan but, over the years – especially since the 1960s – the two have crept inexorably closer. As Douglas has spread to the north, Onchan village has spread in all directions – especially east and westward – until today in the area between Cronk-ny-Mona and Signpost Corner, the 'green belt' between the two is little more than the width of Hillberry Road. The largest area of open space remaining between the two is that forming the grounds of Government House.

The first dwelling to be encountered on entering Onchan along Governor's Road, Government House was the original Bemahague, at one time home of the Betham family, whence came the bride of William Bligh. It was still called Bemahague in 1863, when Henry Loch obtained a lease on it and became the first governor to live there. The old name shows another interesting combination of Norse and Gaelic influence: the first element stems from the Scandinavian *by* ('farm') but, instead of being suffixed to the name in the usual Scandinavian style (e.g., as in *Crosby*), it has been prefixed, presumably by a Gaelic-speaking popu-lace. The second element is probably from the Gaelic surname *Macthaidhg*, which in modern form has become *Keig*. There are similar examples in the eastern part of the parish: Begoade, meaning either 'priest's farm' or 'Goddi's farm', and Bibaloe, 'farm of the grassy bank ford', but, in each of these cases, although the name is wholly Scandinavian, the *by* element (i.e. *Be* or *Bi*) has still become prefixed. The 'grassy bank ford' was probably at or near the site of the present bridge over the Groudle River, at the bottom of White Bridge Hill, on the A2 to Laxey.

In the centre of the village today, on the site of the old mill-pond to the north of St Peter's Church, the Manx Wildlife Trust has established a nature trail and wetland reserve known as Curragh Kiondroghad ('bridge-end marsh'), thus preserving the old name of the village. In recent times, the built-up village –

constrained against the northern boundary of Douglas – has been unable to resist the pressures to expand in all other directions. In the north, it is tight up against the southern broogh of Molly Quirk's Glen, which conducts the Ballacottier River eastward to its confluence with the Groudle and its outfall to the sea. To the west, the growth of the Birch Hill estate has taken it out to Cronk-ny-Mona, whilst the eastward spread has crept out onto Onchan Head, until brought up short against the open acres of Howstrake, where spread the high-lying greens of the King Edward Bay golf course. Viewing that headland from the south today, it is difficult to avoid the conclusion that Onchan Head is one of those places where man should never have built.

Taken as a whole, the parish of Onchan is one of marked contrasts. From the dense urban concentrations of the expanded village, it opens out northward and westward, across lowland farms and on to the higher slopes, bounded in the west by the East Baldwin River and in the east by the Groudle. To the north, it extends onto the uplands to either side of the TT mountain road, and reaches almost as far as Windy Corner. Since the recombination of the former village and parish districts in 1986, it has been known – in administrative terms – as 'the Local Government District of Onchan'; its local authority is the Onchan District Commission and, for the past thirty years at least, its population has been second only to that of Douglas.

BRADDAN

The parish of Braddan and its church have had a variety of name-forms over the centuries: Bradarn (in 1231), Bradan (1291), Brandan (1550–1), Bradan/Bradon (1648), Brandin/Brendin (1700–10), Braddan (1704) and Brendin/Vraddan (1708). Such a profusion of names has not made it easy for historians to identify the intended dedication. One certainty is that there is no record of a Celtic saint named Braddan. The general consensus of scholarly opinion is that the dedicatee is the Scottish saint, Brendan, who has himself borne a number of different spellings at various times.

There are two parish churches – the old and the 'new' (built 1871–6) – standing on opposite sides of the junction of the short B27 Saddlestone (or Saddle) Road with the A1 Peel Road. The Saddlestone Road takes its name from the saddle-shaped stone projecting from the boundary wall about halfway along; it has certain 'fertility' associations. The old church, standing on the south side of the junction, was repaired and extended over the years. The above reference to the year 1291 records the holding of a synod there in that year. By 1737, the

Kirk Braddan: (above) the old and (below) the 'new'

congregation had already outgrown the church, and a gallery was built over the west end to accommodate the overspill, with access by an external flight of steps. (There is a similar feature at Kirk Maughold.)

By 1773, the congregation had again outgrown the church, which was in such a poor state of repair that partial demolition and rebuilding was the only recourse. The result was the 'old' church which stands today. The tower appears to have been built the following year, judging by the red bricks set into its east wall and arranged to form '1774'. At the east end of the roof is a fine granite finial (possibly twelfth century) bearing a sculpted depiction of the crucifixion. The south wall carries a sundial bearing an inscription of the three legs and the quotation in Manx: *Ta ny laghyn ain myr scaa* – 'Our days are as a shadow', which must have been drawn from the biblical line (in I Chronicles: 29, 15): 'Our days on the earth are as a shadow, and there is none abiding'.

The old church houses the parish's collection of Norse crosses (and some Celtic), which were moved from the churchyard into the church some years ago. The outstanding example from the Celtic tradition is the ninth- or tenth-century wheel-headed slab (similar to that at Old Kirk Lonan), whose upper vertical limb of the cross depicts two crouching beasts whose gaping jaws frame a human face – possibly a reference to Daniel in the lions' den.

There are two particularly interesting cross-slabs from the Norse period of the late tenth or early eleventh century – interesting because, instead of the usual rectangular slabs of that period, each takes the form of a tapered pillar, surmounted by a pierced ring cross-head (although the head of the second is missing). The first, complete with cross-head, is Thorleif Hnakki's cross. The two sides and one edge are finely carved with Scandinavian-style dragons, and the remaining edge carries the customary runic inscription: 'Thorleif Hnakki erected this cross to the memory of Fiac his son, brother's son to Hafr'. The inscription continues under the ring of the cross-head with the single word *Ihsus* ('Jesus'). It is notable that Fiac's father and uncle both had Norse names, whilst the deceased himself bore a Celtic one, presumably the influence of a Celtic mother. The second example, Odd's cross, consists of the tapering pillar only, with similar dragon carvings. The incomplete inscription along one edge reads: 'Odd raised this cross to the memory of Frakki his father, but Thor ...'.

The churchyard holds a number of interesting headstones. That commemorating Captain Edward Quayle (died 1862), second commodore of the Isle of Man Steam Packet Company's fleet, carries a carving of the company's steamship *Douglas*, which, after being sold, was converted as a gunboat for the Confederacy in the American Civil War. A tall obelisk of Arran sandstone marks the grave of Lord Henry Murray, son of John, fourth Duke of Atholl, and is of the same stone as that used in the building of the duke's home at Castle Mona. The old churchyard is also the final resting place of the Rev. Robert Brown, father of the island's national poet, T. E. Brown; Henry Hutchinson, whose sister married the poet William Wordsworth; and others whose stones are marked with the simple inscription: 'Cholera 1832'. Then there is the grave of Samuel Ally, who was born into slavery on the island of St Helena, where Colonel Mark Wilks was Governor at the time of Napoleon's imprisonment there. Wilks had purchased the Kirby estate, adjoining the church lands, prior to taking up the appointment. He returned home in 1816, bringing Samuel Ally with him, but the lad died in 1822, aged only eighteen. Flowers are still placed on his grave today.

By the mid-1850s, the church was again too small for its congregation. On one Sunday in 1856, when the Lord Bishop was preparing to take morning service, it was discovered that not only was the church filled to overflowing, but so was the churchyard. As the congregation continued to grow, the summer services were held in the field opposite, adjacent to where the 'new' church now stands. In 1869, it was decided that there was no alternative but to build the new church; this has stood – tall and elegant – ever since its completion in 1876, and the old church is still retained. The marble floor in the modern church is by Baillie Scott. The traditional open-air services on summer Sunday mornings continued, and the Isle of Man Railway Company established a halt on its Douglas–Peel line. Those were the days when up to 20,000 people would turn up for morning service, but that tradition has not entirely vanished, although it has undergone a change of venue. Since 1984, an open-air service has been held at the TT Grandstand on 'Mad Sunday' morning, led by the vicar of St Ninian's and with musical accompaniment by the band of the Salvation Army.

The main residential part of the parish lies less than a mile away, straddling the A1 Peel road at Union Mills, where the railway once passed beneath the main road, and the River Dhoo still does. As described in the previous chapter, the site of the now-vanished mills, which gave the place its name, today accommodates a number of light industrial units. Situated beside the north bank of the river, the old name of the village was *Mwyllin Doo Aah* (or *Doway*), 'Mill of the [river] Doo ford'. A modern trading estate is situated at Snugborough, on the eastern edge of the village. There is also local-authority housing at Snugborough, and more up the hill at Strang, near to the new Noble's Hospital and the new Isle of Man Hospice, both of which replaced the older premises in Douglas. The parish pound, where straying animals were impounded until claimed by their owners, still stands beside Strang Road.

A mile to the east of Union Mills, we find housing from a bygone age, which is still in use. Cronkbourne village is one of the few places in Man (apart from the mining areas) where housing for industrial workers was provided by their employers. The workers in this case were employed at Moore's Tromode Works,

Cronkbourne village

producing sailcloth, sackcloth and a range of household materials. Their products were in demand far and wide, the sailcloth being supplied for use on Brunel's SS *Great Britain*, on which sails were used as an auxiliary measure to reduce the consumption of coal. The forty-two cottages of Cronkbourne village were set out in two parallel rows, one alongside the Ballafletcher Road, and the other further back, the two being separated by a large rectangular green which sprouted five blocks of privies. The cottages are now owned and used as local-authority housing by the Braddan Parish Commissioners, the sanitary and other arrangements having been modernized.

Moore's factory was on the other side of the road – and the other side of the River Glass – where the Tromode Industrial Estate now is. According to the 1851 census, William Moore was employing a total of about eighty workers, of whom thirty were Irish, probably skilled recruits from the Irish linen trade. Ten years later, the total workforce had risen to 150. Power was derived from an overshot waterwheel constructed of iron, 19 feet (5.8m) in diameter and 9 feet (2.7m) wide. For times of low river-flow, a steam engine of 16-inch (406mm) bore and 3-foot (914mm) stroke was there as a standby.

Employees were required to be at their work from 6 a.m. until 7 p.m. Monday to Friday, but finished at 5 p.m. on Saturdays, and they were allowed thirty-five minutes for breakfast and forty-five minutes for dinner. They were expected to attend church at least once every Sunday and to take their children with them. There was a long list of rules and regulations, with fines for infringement. Workers were permitted five visits to the lavatory daily; each visit exceeding three minutes brought a fine of a halfpenny. Bathing in the river or the mill's reservoir or playing any games on the Sabbath brought a maximum fine of sixpence (2½p), and the use of profane, indecent or abusive language or behaviour entailed a fine of up to a shilling (5p). The works closed in 1905 and the site was taken over by a laundry, which is still there today.

About a mile to the north of Tromode, the name *Abbeylands* appears, a place which today lies just beyond the River Glass, in the parish of Onchan, but the Abbeylands of old were widespread across the two parishes, and were in the holding of the Abbot of Rushen. In Onchan, they extended north and east to include the quarterlands of Ballamenagh, Balliargey, Strenaby, Ballacoyne, Sulby (not the Lezayre one), Ballacreetch and Ballachrink, all places to be found on the map today. In Braddan, they lay to the south, taking in the quarterlands of the Nunnery, Kewaigue (both now parts of Douglas), Ballaslig and Ballacreggan, near Keristal. The Onchan Abbeylands of today are road-linked to Strang by the A22, which crosses the parish boundary at Sir George's Bridge, named after Sir George Drinkwater, of Kirby House, who part-funded its construction in 1836, having become disenchanted with having to negotiate the earlier ford. (There are Drinkwaters in the churchyard of Old Kirk Braddan.)

On the map, the parish of Braddan has an irregular 'hour-glass' shape. In the south-east, it is bounded by the Douglas town boundary and the coast as far south as Port Soderick. From there, its western boundary begins by following the course of the Crogga River. The waist of the hour-glass, barely half a mile wide, is constrained between the parallel valleys of the East and West Baldwin rivers. Beyond the upper bowl, a still narrower neck extends the parish to its northern extremity at Druidale and the headwaters of the Sulby reservoir. The northern half of the parish is sparsely populated and, taken together with the highlands of the neighbouring parishes of Marown, Michael, Lezayre and Lonan, provides the finest hill-walking country in Man.

Up in the narrow waist of the Braddan 'hour-glass', Algare was the birth-place of the Manx grammarian and lexicographer, John Kelly, in 1750. His part in translating the Bible into Manx and his compilation which became the standard Manx dictionary have been described in Chapter 9, but there is a further twist to his story. During the course of his translation of the Old Testament, he had to take his manuscript by sea to Whitehaven. The ship transporting him was wrecked, and the young Kelly had perforce to swim. It is said that he held his text above his head, clear of the water, for five hours, thereby saving his translation of the Old Testament books from Deuteronomy to Job for the printer.

Also part of the Algare estate was Cronk Keeill Abban, the hill above St Luke's Church, where a Tynwald assembly was held in 1429. St Luke's itself was built as a chapel of ease for Kirk Braddan, serving as a place of worship for those parishioners remote from the main parish church. A second chapel of ease was built at Oak Hill, in the south of the parish, but this is now a private house. Just over the hill from Algare, in the West Baldwin Valley, lies the Ard Whallin outdoor pursuits centre, run by the Department of Education. The present name of the site would suggest the translation 'whelp's height' but, on the manorial roll of 1643, the name was *Awhellan*, which J. J. Kneen suggests as coming from the Manx *Aah whallian*, 'whelp's ford', the original farm taking its name from a ford crossing the River Glass nearby.

MAROWN

The traveller following the A1 highway towards Peel will enter the parish of Marown on crossing the Trollaby stream, on the west side of Union Mills, and will remain in it until passing below the southern shoulder of Greeba Mountain and the massed trunks of the King's Forest, otherwise known as the Greeba Plantation. The fact that this is the only one of the island's seventeen parishes without a coastline has fostered the lasting conviction that it was once a part of its southern neighbour, Santon. Such a unity would have formed a long, narrow parish, rather like the neighbouring Braddan. There are two considerations which lend support to this belief. First, there is no record of any watch-keeping in Marown under the system of watch and ward. This would, in any event, have been pointless; the very purpose of watch and ward was to keep a look-out for the approach of a sea-borne enemy. Secondly, the parish boundary which separates Marown from Santon also splits the ancient treen of Sanrebreck, and this is the only place in the isle where a treen is divided between two parishes. Thus, it would appear that the division occurred after the ancient land divisions were established, and either early in the Norse period or even earlier.

The parish and its church were dedicated to the Celtic saint, Ma Ronan, *ma* being the Celtic word for 'saint'. In Latin, his name was rendered as *Runius*, and the old parish church is still known as St Runius's, or simply as Marown Old Church. The old church stands on the route of the Millennium Way, on the crest of the ridge just over half a mile south of the crossroads at Crosby, and has been restored to a far better condition than was its lot some years ago. It is again used for occasional services, and still illuminated by oil. Like most of the other old parish churches, it was probably raised on the site of an early keeill. Part of the foundation of an earlier structure remains visible outside the east gable of the present building. An internal gallery, similar to that at Old Kirk Braddan, was removed during alterations in 1850 but the external flight of steps is still there. Out in the churchyard, the Lace family memorial provides a good depiction of the art-nouveau style of Archibald Knox.

As the main centres of population in the parish became concentrated along the A1 Peel–Douglas road, the old church was no longer central to its congregation, and the modern church was built at Glen Vine in 1853. The primary school (the old one standing just down the hill from the old church) followed suit and occupies modern premises in the same village. The two main concentrations of population in the parish, at Crosby and Glen Vine, have continued to grow and almost join up alongside the A1, each of them extending modern residential developments up the hill on the north side of the road.

The emptier parts of the parish extend southward to take in the hamlet at the Braaid and the Eairy reservoir, and in its northern extremity narrowing to an apex on the col between Colden and Lhargee Ruy. Half a mile east of the Braaid cross-roads, in a field on the north side of the A24 Foxdale–Douglas road, may be found the important archaeological site sometimes known as the Braaid Circle. Within the fenced-off area, are the clear outlines of a Celtic roundhouse of the early Christian era (or possibly somewhat later) and two Norse-type rectangular buildings from around AD1000. In one of the latter, the two long walls are straight and parallel; in the other, they are bowed outwards. In both cases, there are no traces of gable walls, which – in traditional Scandinavian fashion – would have been of timber and turf.

Back on the A1 Peel road, as we head for the western end of the parish, we pass the roofless ruin of St Trinian's Chapel, which was originally St Ninian's. As explained in Chapter 9, its roofless state is all the work of the *buggane*, the legendary Manx giant who persistently refused to allow the roofers' work to remain intact. The chapel and extensive lands round about formed part of the ancient Barony of St Ninian's and was in the holding of the Prior of Whithorn, in Galloway. In the centre and west of the parish, there was also a wide spread of lands of the Bishop's Barony, held by the Bishop of Sodor and Man.

CHAPTER TWELVE

Castletown and the South

The four southern parishes of Santon, Malew, Arbory and Rushen together enclose the most populous region of the island outside Douglas. Surrounding, as they do, the old capital of Castletown, plus Port St Mary, Port Erin and the smaller – but growing – urban concentrations of Ballasalla, Ballabeg and Colby, they present a combined population in excess of 14,000 people (at the 2001 census). Despite some growth in employment in the south over the years, the majority of the working population are commuters travelling to and from Douglas.

We continue our tour in a clockwise direction, beginning with the second half of the ancient Marown/Santon parish.

SANTON

Having been separated from its northern portion at some time in the past, Santon is left as the smallest of the island's parishes, with an area of some 4,250 acres (1,720ha). Its coastline extends from Port Soderick to the mouth of the Santon Burn. It is bounded in the west by the course of that burn and in the east by the Crogga River. Its northern extent takes it almost up to the Braaid, severing (as noted earlier) the ancient treen of Sanrebreck in the process.

The parish and its church were dedicated to the Celtic saint Sanctan, and *Kirk Santan* was the name from earliest times. In the seventeenth and eighteenth centuries, it was erroneously identified with St Ann. The final change to *Santon* came in more recent times. St Sanctan's traditional dedication date was 9 May, and here we find another example of the popular reluctance to accept the correction brought about by the introduction of the Gregorian Calendar in 1752. In that year, when all dates were brought forward by eleven days, in order to correct for the accumulated error in the earlier Julian Calendar, Santan's patronal fair-day was moved back eleven days to the 20th, thereby negating the intended correction. In another parish, it made even less sense when they did the same to Midsummer Day. (And this was not just confined to the Isle of Man.)

The Santon coastline provides exhilarating walking country, with five visible sites of promontory forts, at least two of which – Cronk ny Merriu and Cass-ny-Hawin – show signs of Celtic Iron-Age occupation and later reoccupation during the Norse period. And – a sight of a different hue – close behind the coast at Meary Veg, sits (not too obtrusively) the sewage-treatment plant which is the final stage – in operational terms – of the IRIS all-island sewage-disposal scheme. In constructional terms, the system currently serves approximately two-thirds of the island's population. In the days of Watch and Ward, the parish's night watch was held at Port Grenaugh, with the day watch a mile or so to the north-east, on the summit of Knockalaughan. In 1511, the holder of the land around this hill was one William McClaghlen; the treen took its name from an ancestor of his, named Lochlainn, and so it became 'Lochlainn's hill'.

The parish church stands remote from most of its population, located just off the south side of the A25 Old Castletown Road and above the western brooch of Glen Grenaugh. Its earliest vicar is recorded in 1291. It was rebuilt in the 1720s and renovated in 1774. Standing in the churchyard, a huge tombstone commemorates the prominent Cosnahan family, from which came many members of the Manx clergy, and five of them are buried there, with their wives. Preserved inside the church is a stone bearing the Latin inscription: *AVIT – MONOMENT*, 'the monument of [or to?] Avitus'. It was found in the churchyard and dates from the fifth or sixth century AD; its history is completely unknown. It is the only Roman relic (if, indeed, it is such) to be found in the island, and by no means proves a Roman presence, despite the claim of an eighteenth-century vicar of Kirk Michael (see Chapter 14).

The main concentration of the parish's sparse population is in the village of Newtown, which straddles the A5 New Castletown Road. Less than a mile to the north-east, Mount Murray was once the home of Lord Henry Murray, son of the fourth Duke of Atholl, and has been developed to form a country hotel, golf course and residential estate in somewhat controversial circumstances on a site originally approved for holiday accommodation. In 2006, Channel 4's 'Time Team' excavated a known keeill site on the Mount Murray golf course and uncovered not only the eleventh-century keeill, but also an extensive burial ground dating back to five centuries earlier. On the south side of Newtown, Brown Cow Hill takes its name from the former Brown Cow Inn (closed in 1933) which still stands in the guise of a private house.

At the 2001 census, the population of Santon amounted to just 580 persons, from which one readily perceives that, if the land of the parish were to be divided equally between its inhabitants, every man, woman and child would be entitled to more than 7 acres (2.8ha).

MALEW

Malew is the second-largest parish in the isle. Its coastline is not extensive, running from the mouth of the Santon Burn in the east, taking in Langness and most of Castletown Bay, and continuing for a mile to the west of Scarlett Point, as far as the insignificant indentation of Poyllvaaish Bay. But it is split into two portions by the coastal frontage of the old capital, which faces out onto Castletown Bay on either side of its harbour entrance. The parish's eastern boundary is defined by the course of the Santon Burn and, in the south-west, a similar role is performed by the Dumb River, a sluggish little watercourse which reaches the sea at Poyllvaaish. Furthermore, the intersection of the town boundary of Castletown with the Dumb River ensures that a small portion of Malew parish (less than a square mile) lies detached from the rest of it. Nonetheless, this detached portion remains under the jurisdiction of the Malew Parish Commissioners, whose offices are in Ballasalla. In its northern extent, the parish boundary encloses the northern slopes of South Barrule and Stoney Mountain, but excludes the village of Foxdale.

There was some early uncertainty concerning the dedication of this parish and its church, brought about by confusion in ancient records between the Irish saint Lua (*Ma Lua*) and the French saint Lupus. The old Malew fair-day was held on 25 July, which coincides with that of St Lua, so that is generally taken to settle the matter. The parish church stands beside the A3 St John's–Castletown road at Church Bends, 300 yards south of Cross Four Ways, where the A7 crosses it. The church originally followed the traditional Manx style of a plain, rectangular building, but a north transept was added in the 1780s. The nave dates from the twelfth century, i.e. probably earlier than the present Castle Rushen. A sundial on the south wall of the church carries a Manx Gaelic inscription giving another variation of that quotation from I Chronicles, which we first encountered at Old Kirk Braddan: *Ta nyn traa er y thalloo agh scadoo*, 'Our time on the earth is but a shadow'.

The church contains a silver paten from around 1525, bearing the Latin inscription: *Sancte Lupe ora pro nobis*, 'St Lupus, pray for us', thereby perpetuating the confusion of the two saints. A heavily weathered Scandinavian cross-slab depicts the well-known scene from the Sigurd saga, in which Sigurd is seen sucking his fingers while roasting the dragon's heart on a spit. (A much

better-preserved example of this scene is to be found on a cross-slab at
Andreas.) The church is also the final resting place of William Christian, alias
Illiam Dhone (Manx patriot or traitor? – the question examined in Chapter 5),
who was executed by firing squad at Hango Hill on 2 January 1663. An entry in
the parish register relates that he was buried the following day beneath the
chancel of Kirk Malew. For more than 300 years, there was no dedicated
memorial to Christian, until the Manx Heritage Foundation agreed to fund a

The bust of William Christian in Kirk Malew

bronze bust by the Manx sculptor Bryan Kneale, to be installed in the church. It was unveiled by its creator and dedicated by the Lord Bishop of Sodor and Man, the Rt Rev. Graeme Knowles, on 2 January 2006 – the 343rd anniversary of Christian's death.

In times past, great swathes of this parish (much of the best agricultural soils) formed the abbey lands, in the holding of the abbots of Rushen. William Christian was steward of the abbey lands in 1640. The Abbey of St Mary of Rushen was established in 1134, on land granted by Olaf I on the west bank of the Silver Burn at Ballasalla. It was never on as grand a scale as such abbeys as Rievaulx and Whitby. In 1540, Rushen was one of the last monastic houses to fall to Henry VIII's dissolution. When Edward Stanley, third Earl of Derby, was appointed by Henry to act as liquidator, the abbey, its contents and extensive holdings of land were either purchased for himself or sold off to others. Thereafter, the abbey buildings rapidly deteriorated, as shown in a drawing of the ruins, dated 1660.

In the 1670s, the abbey site was bought by Deemster Moore, who used stone from the ruins to build himself a fine dwelling, Rushen Abbey House, at the northern end of the site. This became a school in the early nineteenth century, a hotel in the 1860s and a public house which lasted into the 1980s but has remained empty ever since. The site of the abbey itself, having been cleared of a large proportion of its buildings, has seen a variety of uses: market garden, jam factory, pleasure garden with restaurant and dance floor, horticultural nursery. For a time, in these various guises, it was a tourist attraction but then declined, along with the numbers of tourists.

Early excavations of the site in 1914 and 1926 revealed a number of burials, some of which were thought to be of Norse kings of Man and the Isles, including the last of the line, Magnus, who died at Castle Rushen in 1265. Then, in 1998, the property was acquired by Manx National Heritage and, after clearing the site of its accumulated clutter of modern buildings, a more continuous series of excavations was set in train. This continues through each summer season today.

The buildings that remain standing above ground level are of undressed local limestone; they display the sparse ruin of the church, of cruciform layout and with no sign of a central tower, but the north transept possessed a tower, which still stands. Other survivals include small parts of the south transept and of the western end of the nave, the infirmary, columbarium and remains of the abbot's house. The early excavations had revealed the foundations of a smaller church on the site, along with those of the chapter house and parlour. The more recent programme of MNH-sponsored works has incorporated the development of indoor exhibitions, including a scale model of the abbey as it was at the height of its glory, and other displays giving an indication of life within the abbey. All of this is an integral part of MNH's 'Story of Man'.

A short distance upstream from the abbey, stands what must surely be the most handsome reminder of the monks' handiwork: the fourteenth-century Monks' Bridge (Manx *Crossag*, 'little crossing'), the only known medieval bridge in Man. Precisely one metre (3 feet 3 inches) wide and thus built only for pack-horse and pedestrian use, this crossing over the Silver Burn gave access to the monks' pack-horse trail to the north. At the height of the abbey's power and influence, its abbot held such an expanse of Manx lands that he received almost half of the island's total tithes. And, in order to achieve access to the various tracts of abbey land, it is likely that the monks themselves were responsible for establishing and maintaining many of the island's old pack-horse roads.

Ballasalla (Manx 'Farm of the sally [or willow]') has long-since ceased to be a farm and grown into a village, spread across and around the busy junction from which the A7 departs westward towards Port Erin, leaving the A5 Douglas–Castletown road to continue south. Ballasalla is the main centre of Malew's population, with both public- and private-sector housing, supplemented by the hamlets of Derbyhaven and St Mark's. To the south of Ballasalla and east of the A5, the land is occupied by the Balthane industrial estate, the Isle of Man Freeport and Ronaldsway airport. On the west side of the A5 are more industrial concerns, including the long-established Ronaldsway Aircraft Company, manu-facturing aircraft ejection seats. Ronaldsway airport now entirely covers the land that was once Ronaldsway Farm, presented to William Christian by his father in 1643 and accepted by him under the Lord's newly imposed lease – a tenure for three lives – instead of the traditional Manx 'tenure of the straw', and gaining the Lord's trust in so doing. It was this trust which the Derbys considered to be betrayed by Christian's actions during the English Civil War, and for which he paid with his life.

The coastline of Malew is a fascinating geological mix which has been described in Chapters 1 and 10. The hamlet of Derbyhaven, sheltered deep in the nook of its eponymous bay, was known as Ronaldsway prior to 1725; then the Derbys changed it to Derbyhaven. It was their port, which eventually became a bustling fishing harbour, but other ports gained favour, and the old kippering houses along the Langness road still stand testament to the local industry's demise. In the days of Watch and Ward, the day watch was kept on the insignifi-cant summit of the Brogh, a 150-foot (45m) hillock rising between the A12 road and the Turkeyland quarry. As darkness fell, the men of the night watch would take to their shore-side stations at Ronaldsway and Scarlett.

A glance at the map shows how the A12 from Ballasalla comes to a dead-end at the north-east boundary of Ronaldsway airport, only to resume its progress beyond the opposite boundary and continue through Derbyhaven to Castletown. This loop-road is cut by the seaward thrust of the airport's main runway, which is now being extended further – not to permit the handling of larger aircraft, but to accommodate the longer run-off areas now required under international safety regulations for civil aviation.

One feature which Malew shares with its western neighbour, Arbory, is the motor-cycle road-racing circuit known variously as the Southern 100 Course or the Billown Circuit. Racing is held there in June, as part of the TT meeting, and again in July for the Southern Hundred races. The starting grid and finish line are situated on the Castletown by-pass, on the northern edge of the town. The irregular quadrilateral course is ridden in a clockwise direction, so that its four main corners are taken as right-handers, the first two, at Ballakeighen and Ballabeg, being in Arbory, the third at Cross Four Ways, by the Billown limestone quarry, leading the riders through Church Bends and on to the final corner which returns them to the Castletown by-pass. Being a road circuit, the course is littered with such hazards as stone walls, electricity poles and other solid features, but, being a relatively short circuit of some 4¼ miles, it is perhaps not surprising that its safety record is far superior to that of the TT course.

Approximately midway between the third and fourth corners of the Billown Circuit stands the stately home and country estate of Great Meadow, which is the venue for the Southern Agricultural Society's annual show in July. The history of agricultural societies and shows in the Isle of Man is a fascinating one but (sadly) it would take too much space to relate it here. It must suffice to say that the first Manks [sic] Agricultural Society held shows in the early 1800s. The subsequent story was one of successive short-lived societies, of conflict (sometimes physical) between North and South, and which often evolved into a conflict of the classes. The older of the two present societies was formed as the Isle of Man Agricultural Society in 1858, and became the Royal Manx Agricultural Society, with the assent of King George VI, in 1951. But southern farmers still felt left out of things and set up their own organization. Although four shows had been held in Castletown in the late nineteenth century, the first southern show of the modern era was held at Billown in 1914. Due to the intervention of the First World War, the second show did not take place until 1920. Apart from the years of the Second World War and 2001 (due to precautions against the foot-and-mouth epidemic which never reached the island), the Southern Agricultural Society's show has been held annually ever since. And relations between the two societies today are entirely harmonious.

Until 1985, the House of Keys constituency of Rushen was defined by the boundaries of the sheading of Rushen, and comprised the parishes of Malew, Arbory and Rushen, together with the villages of Port Erin and Port St Mary. However, in the revision of constituency boundaries in that year, Malew was extracted from the constituency of Rushen and combined with its eastern neighbour to form the new constituency of Malew and Santon, returning one member to the Keys.

Before leaving Malew, it may be prudent to warn of the potential consequences of failing to observe an old Manx custom when entering or leaving the parish (and the former abbey lands) by way of the A5 Douglas–Castletown road. One and a half miles south-west of Newtown, the road is carried over a tributary of the Santon Burn by a white-walled crossing known as the Fairy Bridge. It is a legendary place of assembly of the 'li'l folk'; they usually remain out of sight, although they have been known to appear to an observer who has downed a few drinks on his way home. Nevertheless, it has become customary, when crossing the bridge, to voice a greeting to the 'li'l folk', or at least to raise a hand in salute. Many years ago, my wife received a very painful reminder of the consequences of not doing so. She never ignored them again.

CASTLETOWN

It is said that Castletown has never forgiven Douglas for usurping its role as the capital of Man. The various branches of the administration were transferred north in stages through the course of the 1860s, and the process was complete by 1869. As early as 1511, the Manorial Roll records the town's name in the English form – Castletown. The old Manx name was *Balley Cashtal*. Whether the former was an English translation from the Manx, or vice versa, is debatable, but the translation *from* the Manx is perhaps the more likely. Speakers of Manx Gaelic today still use the Manx form of the name.

It is a compact little town, as a glance at its boundaries on the map quickly shows. Despite a moderate amount of modern development, no part of the built-up town is more than three-quarters of a mile from the harbour and castle where it all started. It is the smallest of the four towns, and even has a smaller population than the village of Port Erin. At its heart (although not at its geometrical centre) is the well-preserved medieval fortress, still standing guard over harbour and town.

Castle Rushen is widely regarded as the best-preserved fortress of the medieval period in the British Isles. There is no record to indicate the date of its construction. It is almost certain that Godred Crovan and his descendants would have maintained a fortress there for the defence of the south, but it would have been of timber construction and vanished without trace. The earliest parts of the present building are thought to date from the second half of the twelfth century. The first record relating to the present castle appears in *Chronicon*, which records the death of the last Norse king, Magnus, there in 1265 and his burial at Rushen Abbey.

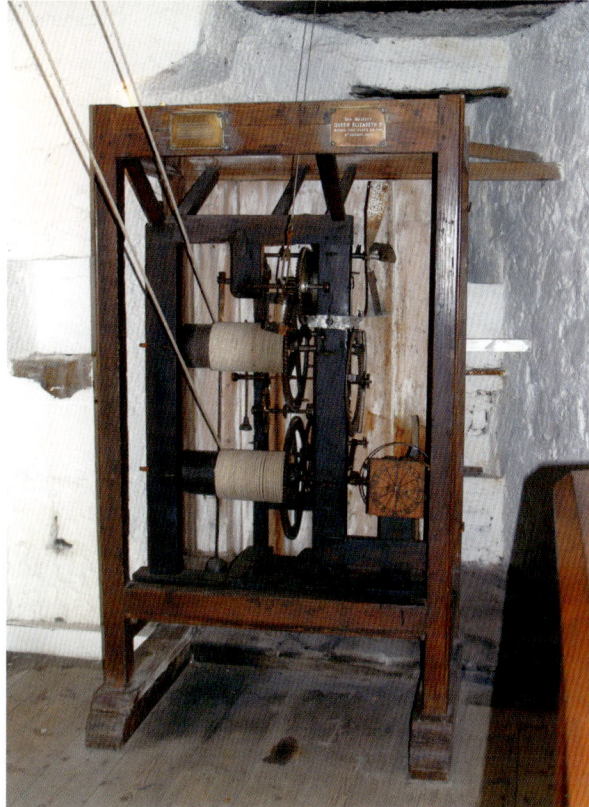

(above) Castle Rushen, with its one-fingered clock, and (right) its mechanism in the clock room

The earliest stone-built Viking fort was probably confined to the present inner keep, this and later additions being of the local limestone, mainly from the quarry at Scarlett. It would have been this much smaller fort that was attacked and left a ruin by Robert Bruce in 1313. Soon after Edward III came to the throne of England, he granted the kingship of Man to William de Montacute, first Earl of Salisbury, in 1333. Being familiar with the Norman style of castle architecture, William set about enlarging Castle Rushen in the same fashion. He built an enlarged keep which enclosed the original Viking fort, and raised an octagonal curtain wall, complete with outer gatehouse, to surround the whole thing and form a far more formidable fortress. Thus, although the Normans never attempted to conquer Man, its principal fortress evolved to display a distinct Norman influence, with marked similarities to (although on a much smaller scale than) such castle keeps as that at Caernarvon. In particular, the stonework above windows and doorways is supported by Caernarvon arches. The only entry was by way of the outer gatehouse, across the drawbridge, through two portcullises and the inner gatehouse into the keep. Above the space between the two portcullises, there were (and are) three murderholes, through which boiling oil and molten lead could be poured onto the heads of enemies who managed to penetrate that far.

The keep of Castle Rushen has towers on its east, south and west sides, the gatehouse rising on the north. The former oratory chapel on the third floor of the south tower now houses the mechanism of the famous single-handed clock, said to have been given by Elizabeth I in 1597; her monogram appears on the external face. As the pendulum escapement mechanism was not invented until the mid-seventeenth century, the present mechanism must have been a later replacement and has been dated to around 1720–40. The clock strikes on a bell given by James Stanley, tenth Earl of Derby, in 1729. The fourth floor of the tower is the roof, from which there are broad views all round – on a clear day, to the Mountains of Mourne in the west, to the Cumbrian fells in the east, and to Anglesey and the hills of Snowdonia in the south. Local wags will tell you that, if you can see the surrounding lands, it will soon be raining; if you cannot see them, it *is* raining. Just inside the outer gatehouse stands the Derby House, built by Henry, the fifth Earl, in 1582–3, because he could not stand living within the gloom of the castle's interior. On the opposite side of the path leading to the drawbridge stands the ruin of the oratory chapel which he built to avoid having to climb to the third floor of the south tower to worship.

Castle Rushen was, at various times, the residence of the Lord of Man, or the Governor, or sometimes of the two of them simultaneously, from the time of James ('the Great Stanley'), seventh Earl of Derby, onwards. Governors continued to live there until the early nineteenth century, when the drift away from Rushen began. Governor Ready (1832–45) arrived to find insufficient accommodation for him in the castle precincts and took out a lease on Lorne House, in the town. His successor, Charles Hope (1845–60), took over the lease but, on Hope's departure, Francis Pigott obtained a lease on Marine Lodge, in Douglas, and the deed was done. In addition, of course, the castle was required to house the garrison, so the place must have been rather crowded at times.

The castle served as the island's prison from the sixteenth century onwards, and its walls have held countless prisoners, including several notables. In addition to William Christian in 1662, there was Bishop Wilson, imprisoned there in 1772, when Church and State found themselves at loggerheads – not for the first time – over the powers of the Church courts, and nine weeks were to pass before he was released. Then, in 1864, James Brown, editor of *The Isle of Man Times*, was imprisoned for publishing an article which was critical of the Keys. He was held in a room which the Official Guide to the castle now identifies as 'Milady's Bedroom'. Sounds interesting but methinks they were probably not there simultaneously.

Castle Rushen remained in use as the island's prison until 1891, and the Derby House is still in use today as the southern courthouse and registry of births, deaths and marriages, and is the location for the swearing-in of lieutenant governors. Within the keep, the banqueting hall and other chambers are decked out with tableaux and sound effects to illustrate life in the castle in the days of the Derbys.

In its early days, the castle had a more intimate association with the harbour it was guarding than it has today. In those times, prior to the building of the present harbour-side road, the water at high tide lapped directly against the foot of the castle mound. The castle's association with the old town was (and is) also intimate. Buildings of local stone, crowding in along narrow streets, have grown as an organic whole around the fortress which gave it birth. The houses cluster tightly round the ramparts of the castle, as if to protect it against all comers now that its days of protecting them are over. Further west, the older parts of the town spread along Arbory Street, Malew Street (both now pedestrianized) and the Crofts, the latter displaying dwellings on a grander scale, where the town's wealthier residents once lived – and probably do so still.

At the foot of the castle's glacis and overlooked by its south tower, the Market Square (more of an oblong than a square) reaches out to the south-east. Otherwise known as the Parade, the square is a further reminder of Castletown's former role as a garrison town. In the centre, stands the tall Doric column of the Smelt Memorial, commemorating a popular lieutenant governor of the nineteenth century (1805–32). He was actually the last lieutenant governor to hold that post while its title defined the post-holder as the *deputy* governor. The overall governor in Smelt's day was John Murray, fourth Duke of Atholl, and their

Castletown: the Smelt Memorial dominates the Parade, with the former
St Mary's Church at the far end

working relationship was not a wholly congenial one. Following the days of
Murray and Smelt, each successive lieutenant governor has been *de facto*
governor, which latter title then lapsed from use.

At the far end of the Parade, stands a building which was the old garrison
church of St Mary's. Not all that long ago, it stood grim and abandoned and under
threat of demolition. It and the Smelt Memorial stood glowering at each other
along the length of the Parade, rather like two contentious gunmen in a scene
from a Western at high noon. Ultimately, the threat of demolition faded and St
Mary's was converted for office use. The replacement church, St Mary's on the
Harbour, is the result of a conversion of the former Sunday-school building which
was originally the town's school, opened on Queen Victoria's coronation day in
1838. The nearby Old Grammar School, a small building which formed part of the
old St Mary's Chapel and which stood at the east end of the old garrison church,
is now a schoolroom museum in the custody of Manx National Heritage.

Almost opposite the present entrance to Castle Rushen, the old House of Keys
is maintained as another MNH museum. The building was completed in 1709, at
a cost of £83 5s 6½d (£83.28), and was used as the Keys' debating chamber for the
next 160 years. Under the guardianship of MNH, a refurbishment was undertaken

to install furniture and fittings as near as possible to the original, and the building was opened to the public in 2001. Sound and video displays enable visitors to participate and vote in re-enactments of proceedings. Needless to say, the number of participants at any one time is limited to twenty-four.

Standing adjacent to the old Keys' building are the police station and the 'Gluepot'. The former is a fine example of the art-nouveau form of architect Baillie Scott. The 'Gluepot' is officially the *Castle Arms*, given its nick-name – so it is said – by the women of the town, who complained that their menfolk spent so much time in the place that they must be glued to it.

The buildings on the opposite side of the Parade to the Castle include a number from the eighteenth and nineteenth centuries. Among them are the *George Hotel* and Balcony House, once the home of Captain John Quilliam RN, who gained a measure of fame at the Battle of Trafalgar. Quilliam was born in Marown, the son of a farmer, but ran away to sea. He first came to the attention of Admiral Lord Nelson at the Battle of Copenhagen in 1801, where he was a lieutenant on HMS *Amazon*. The ship had come under such ferocious fire that all officers superior to Quilliam were slain and he was left in command. At some stage in the proceedings, Nelson boarded the vessel and, not being received on deck, called out to enquire who was in charge, to which a voice from a lower deck

The Old House of Keys, Castletown

replied: 'I am.' Nelson then enquired of the unseen officer: 'How are you getting on below?' to which came the reply, in a strong Manx accent: 'Augh, middlin'!' Amused and impressed by the Manxman's coolness under fire, Nelson promoted him to first lieutenant on the admiral's flagship, HMS *Victory*. At one stage of the Battle of Trafalgar in 1805, *Victory*'s wheel was shot to pieces, and Quilliam caused emergency steering gear to be rigged, which entailed steering from the gun-deck. Quilliam himself then steered the vessel, in alternate spells with the ship's master, seemingly unwilling to delegate the task to a helmsman until he was sure that his jury-rig would work as intended. He was subsequently promoted to captain.

After Trafalgar, Quilliam was ashore for a time. In 1807, he was appointed to membership of the House of Keys (those were the days before public elections) but he was back at sea the following year, although he did not resign his membership of the Keys until 1810. On his return to sea, he held a number of commands before retiring and returning to the island in 1815, apparently in a position of some wealth. He lived at the White House, in Kirk Michael, for a time and then purchased the estate of Ballakeighen, in Arbory, resuming his member-ship of the Keys in 1817. He played a leading role in the Tynwald enquiry into the state of the herring fishery in 1827 and initiated the scheme for the construction of the breakwater at Derbyhaven. He died in 1829 and was buried in the church-yard of Kirk Arbory.

On the north side of Castletown harbour, a tall, gaunt building holds further reminders of past affairs nautical. Bridge House was the home of generations of the Quayle family, from which came a succession of lawyers, bankers and busi-nessmen. It is George Quayle (1751–1835) who is most remembered today, however. In 1777, he joined the first regiment of the Royal Manx Fencibles (the Manx militia) and rose to the rank of captain. He later raised a corps of the Manx Yeomanry, which he commanded in the years of the Napoleonic Wars. He gained membership of the House of Keys in 1784 and that continued until his death. In association with his brother, Mark, he founded the first Isle of Man Bank, in Castletown, in 1802 but the venture ran into difficulties and closed sixteen years later, when Quayle sold his properties, including the Barony of St Trinian's, in Marown, in order to redeem the bank's notes.

But it is for something quite different that George Quayle is remembered today. The family home of Bridge House had an adjoining outhouse which had been fitted out as a boat-house for Quayle's boat, the *Peggy*. She was clinker-built and schooner-rigged, 26 feet 5 inches (8m) long, 7 feet 8 inches (2.3m) in beam, with a draft of 4 feet (1.2m) and displacing 6½ tons. She was constructed on a keel of elm, with planking of pine on frames of oak. Built in about 1790, she was commissioned by the British Admiralty in 1793, armed with eight small cannon and used to patrol the surrounding areas of the Irish Sea. Those were troubled times, when French privateers were busy harrying shipping between Belfast and the English ports. On returning to harbour, the *Peggy* would be hauled up the slipway inside the boat-house. Following George Quayle's death, the exit was bricked up and the *Peggy* was left high, dry and half-forgotten at the top of her slipway. When Bridge House was put up for sale in 1951, the boat-house was presented to the Manx Museum and is now preserved by MNH as a nautical museum, complete with its prize possession – the *Peggy*.

Out on the eastern edge of town, hemmed in by its playing fields on one side and the airport on the other, stand the elegant buildings of King William's College, built of local limestone to the design of John Welch, who was also responsible for the Smelt Memorial, the Tower of Refuge and several of the island's churches. The story of the school's founding has been told in Chapter 6. It was Governor Smelt who persuaded Bishop Ward to make use of the money which had been accumulating in Bishop Barrow's trust fund for 140 years to build a school, and the laying of the foundation stone was one of Smelt's last official acts. The school was built – and later developed – to form a group of buildings enclosing two courts, of which King's Court commemorates the visit of King George VI and Queen Elizabeth in 1945. The dining hall, the Barrovian Hall, perpetuates the name of the school's founder. The list of distinguished 'old boys' includes such notables as the Very Rev. Frederic Farrar (1831–1903), Dean of Canterbury 1895–1903 and a prolific author, Field Marshal Sir George White VC (1835–1912), defender of Ladysmith in the Boer War, Professor Sir William Bragg (1890–1971), Nobel laureate for physics (shared with his father) in 1915, and the Manx national poet, T. E. Brown.

King William's was a boys' school from the outset. A smaller public school for girls, the Buchan School, was founded from the benefaction of Laura, Lady Buchan, eldest daughter of Colonel Mark Wilks (the same who was Governor of St Helena at the time of Napoleon Bonaparte's imprisonment there) and later married to General Sir John Buchan. As the young Laura Wilks, she was with her parents on St Helena and met Bonaparte, who was – by all accounts – quite taken with her. In later life, following her father's death, Lady Buchan succeeded to the Wilks estate, including properties at Kirby and Castleward, in Braddan, whence came the means to found the Buchan School at Westhill, where the school and its playing fields lie hemmed in between old Castletown and its modern western suburb. In recent years, King William's and the Buchan have amalgamated and now operate as a single co-educational establishment. Although it is a public school, a number of scholarships are available each year, funded by the Department of Education.

Directly in front of the King William's College grounds and on the very edge of Castletown Bay, the ragged ruin of the Derbys' summerhouse stands on the site of William Christian's execution in 1663. The date of the building is uncertain but there is record of its existence in 1689. Much of the building, and the mound on which it stands, had fallen to the sea by the time the present sea-wall was built. The present emaciated remnant leans drunkenly, as if yearning to lie down, but is prevented from doing so by the unrelenting support of a steel prop.

Despite the growth of modern urban development and of commercial activity in and around the town, Castletown remains the smallest of the island's four towns. When one wanders through the old parts, it is not difficult to imagine the street scene of three centuries ago. In only three decades, however, the harbour-side activity has changed. The coastal trade of the recent past has gone, and even the regular arrivals of containerized freight from the small Lancashire harbour of Glasson have migrated north to Ramsey. Today, Castletown's harbour provides a peaceful haven for the recreational sailor, and there are few other activities to disturb its serenity. One of the few, however, takes the idiosyncratic form of the World Tin Bath Championships – staged in July – in which hordes of competitors line up to race across the harbour in a variety of bathing receptacles of yesteryear. There are no qualifying standards to be met but a sense of balance is a useful attribute.

Castletown harbour

ARBORY

The parish of Arbory is only slightly larger in area (227 acres, or 92ha, larger) than the island's smallest parish of Santon, but its population is almost three times as large. Its coastline is less than a mile in extent, facing out onto Bay ny Carrickey and terminating at each end in the outfall of a minor stream, one descending to the shore at Poyllvaaish, and the other flowing out at Strandhall. Its western boundary, which separates it from the parish of Rushen, is peculiar, with the ancient treen of Kentraugh (part of Rushen) jutting eastward into the south-west corner of Arbory, as if a conquest of some prehistoric conflict. From north to south, Arbory extends for some five miles, stretching north to within a few paces of the crossroads at the Round Table.

The parish's dedication to *two* saints – Caebre of Coleraine and Columba – is unusual and goes back a long way. The earliest record is contained in a papal bull of 1153, in which the parish is identified as *Terra Sancti Carebrie* but, in a further bull of 1231, it became *Terra Sti Columbae herbery vocatem*. From then on, the name changed from the one to the other and back again. In 1798, it was *Chairbrae* or *Colum Killey*, and the dual dedication has persisted to the present day, with the parish taking the name of Cairbre (later Kirk Carbery which, by attraction, became Kirk Arbory), whilst the church became St Columba's. The annual parish fair (before the introduction of the Gregorian calendar) was held on *Laa Colum Killey*, St Columba's Day, 9 June, but here again the calendar correction was not acknowledged and the fair-day was simply put back eleven days to the 20th on the new-style calendar. Like all of the other parish fairs, *Laa Columb Killey* lapsed in the nineteenth century but, unlike the others, was revived in the early twentieth century and is now held annually.

The parish church stands in the village of Ballabeg; it was built in 1759, on the site of an earlier one, in the traditional rectangular form with a simple bell turret at its west end. Around the mid-twentieth century, the turret was replaced with a squat, square tower which has generally been viewed with disfavour ever since. The earliest record of a vicar is from 1291. The churchyard contains the grave of Captain John Quilliam RN, Manx hero of the battles of Copenhagen and Trafalgar. Inside the church, a beam in the gallery commemorates the Manx lexicographer, Archibald Cregeen (1774–1841), who was born at Colby. Unaware of the work of John Kelly in the same field, Cregeen spent twenty years collecting material for his Manx dictionary, which was published in 1838. Although Kelly's work existed in manuscript form at that time, it was not published until 1866, fifty-seven years after his death.

The main centres of population in Arbory are the villages of Ballabeg and

Colby, which almost conjoin along the A7 Ballasalla–Port Erin road. The Manx name *Ballabeg* for the original farm in this area might have been taken as denoting a 'little farm' but, as the holder of the land in 1511 was one William Begson, it is more likely that it was 'Begson's farm' at that time. Today, it is the village that perpetuates the name of the old quarterland.

A similar situation exists at Colby, except that the original name was Norse rather than Manx. *Kollabyr* would have denoted that it was 'Kolli's farm'. In 1703, there were two similarly named farms in this treen, one larger than the other; hence Colby Mooar and Colby Beg. Here again, the name is preserved in that of the present village. Further along the A7, west of Colby village and on the parish boundary with Rushen, we find Colby Level. The 'Level' derives from the level adit which was driven into the hill on the north side of the road to access the lead mine at Ballacorkish (over the boundary in Rushen), the ores from which were sent for smelting at Gansey and Derbyhaven.

Further east on the same hillside, lies the ruin of *Keeill Catreeney*, 'Catherine's church', and *Chibbyr Catreeney*, 'Catherine's well'. St Catherine's feast-day, *Laa'l Catreeney*, was observed in Arbory on 6 December (on the old calendar) and, across the whole of the Southside, this was the day on which land that was due for a change of occupier had to be taken into possession. In the Northside, the corresponding arrangement was staged on St Andrew's feast-day, *Laa'l Andreays*. A. W. Moore [60] quotes the following curious verse which was recited at the Arbory fair:

Kiark Catreeney marroo,	Catherine's hen is dead,
Gow uss y kione,	Take thou the head,
As goyms ny cassyn,	And I shall take the feet,
As ver mayd ee fo'n thalloo.	And we'll put her under the ground.

Its origin is unknown. If anyone became drunk at the fair, he was said to have 'plucked a feather from the hen'.

In Ballabeg may be found the sole surviving remnant of the Franciscan Friary of Bemaken, now standing as one of the buildings on Friary Farm and once used for many years as a cattle shed. It stands on the site of an earlier Christian establishment, on land in the treen of Bemaken, granted by William de Montacute II, Earl of Salisbury and Lord of Man. It was established in 1373 and, together with Rushen Abbey and the Nunnery at Douglas, was one of the last monastic houses to fall to Henry VIII's *Act of Dissolution* of 1539. The remaining building can be seen from the road, 250 yards north of the junction of the A7 with the A28 to Ballabeg station.

The earliest Celtic inhabitants of Man to erect stone memorials to their dead embellished them with inscriptions in the ogham alphabet. Some 300 such stones

Parville, Ballabeg: Deemster Parr's house as it looks today

have been discovered in the British Isles, six of them in Man, of which two were found in Arbory. Both have incomplete inscriptions: the first translates as 'OF CUNAMALGUS SON OF ...', with the second yielding only 'OF MAQLEOG ...'. The latter is particularly interesting as possibly the earliest 'written' example of 'MAQ' (later 'Mac') to denote 'son of', indicating (i) that the deceased was the son of Leog, and (ii) the origin of the modern Manx name of Clague. The stones are now in the Manx Museum.

A short distance north of Friary Farm, just beyond the right-angle bend in the A7 (heading west), the elegant mansion house of Parville stands back from the road. The house (or an earlier version of it) was standing there as long ago as 1587, when it was in the holding of Deemster John Parr; hence this was 'Parr's villa'. The *ville* element was the Latin (and later Norman) equivalent of the Irish *baile*, Manx *balley* and Scandinavian *byr*. The appearance of the house belies its age, although it has doubtless been worked on over the centuries.

For such a small parish, the terrain of Arbory is remarkably varied, from the fertile coastal plain which it shares with its two neighbouring parishes, rising northward into the southern highlands between South Barrule and Cronk ny Arrey Laa. The only one of Arbory's ancient treens to abut on the parish's diminutive coastline is Balladoole. The estate of that name has been the ancestral home

Bay ny Carrickey, seen from Poyllvaaish

of the Stevenson (earlier 'Stephenson') family for many generations – already long-established by the time of its first mention in the Manorial Roll of 1511. The earliest record of a Manx officer in the British Army relates to Major Richard Stevenson (died 1683), of Balladoole, who married Isabel, daughter of Deemster John Christian, of Milntown. Their eldest son, John (c 1655–1737), is the family member who is best remembered in the isle today.

John Stevenson must have been a member of the Keys prior to 1704, since he is recorded as being Speaker of the House in that year. He was also a member of the Imperial parliament; his constituency is not known but he must have been well-connected 'across the water' in order to gain the seat. In the island, Stevenson is remembered for his part in representing the continuing Manx griev-ances over the question of land-tenure. The situation at that time was complicated by its arising contemporaneously with a renewal of the conflict between Church and State, and the former adopted a sympathetic view of the land-holders' complaints. The *Act of Settlement* of 1704 was supposed to settle the question, but some considerable time was to pass before all of its promised measures were implemented. In 1719, Stevenson, as Speaker, was deputed by the Keys to approach the Lord of Man (James Stanley, tenth Earl of Derby) with their appeal for justice. The result was that Stevenson was arrested, convicted on a criminal charge and imprisoned in Castle Rushen. He was soon released but, in 1722, he was imprisoned again for assisting Bishop Wilson in suppressing the publication of a book promoting the principles of free-thinking. In 1727, he was facing trouble again, accused of improper behaviour towards the Governor at a mustering of the Arbory militia. But there seems to have been a sparsity of evidence and he was discharged. The last ten years of his life are a blank but his efforts in promoting Manx rights and liberties were lauded by three writers of those times. Bishop Wilson described him as 'The Father of his Country', and Burke's *Landed Gentry* told of how he 'devoted himself to the religious and civil welfare of his country'. And in Keble's *Life of Bishop Wilson*, he was 'an unflinching champion of popular rights and liberties'.

The inclusion of John Stevenson in Burke's *Landed Gentry* and a study of the ancient histories of such families as the Stevensons of Balladoole and the Christians of Milntown illustrate how the Manx landed gentry of those times maintained their status by making 'good' marriages into other Manx families of similar status, or into the British aristocracy. The mother of Major Richard Stevenson's grandson (also Richard, 1716–85) was the former Isabel Senhouse, of Nether Hall, Cumberland, and his uncle by marriage was Richard Boyle, Viscount Shannon. His brother, John, was a colonel in the guards and owner of Ashley Park, in Surrey, which he inherited from his first cousin, the Countess of Middlesex. The histories of other prominent Manx families show similar features. Thus, from the absence of an established Manx aristocracy, it does not follow that there was an absence of a Manx class structure.

Sloping gently up behind the shore at Balladoole, Chapel Hill rises to a rounded summit of 90–100 feet (30m) and contains a host of archaeological features from various periods, which were excavated by German-born Dr Gerhard Bersu in 1945. Encircling the summit is a roughly oval-shaped rampart, extending to approximately 100 yards by 60 yards and enclosing the various sites located across the hill-top. Worked flints and other finds have yielded evidence of successive occupations through the ages, from the Mesolithic period, through the Bronze and Iron Ages and into the Viking period. At the western end of the enclosure, the low walls of *Keeill Vael* (St Michael's Chapel) remain clearly visible. Thought to date from the eleventh century, it probably marks the site of an earlier keeill. At the opposite end of the enclosure, an oval of stones marks the outline of a pagan Viking ship-burial of the late ninth or early tenth century, directly over-lying pre-existing Christian graves of about the same period. The various features of the Chapel Hill site were described in Chapters 3 and 4. The day watch for the parish of Arbory was kept on its summit, the night watch mustering closer to the shore at Poyllvaaish.

On the west side of Colby village, the course of the Colby River may be followed northward through Colby Glen (maintained by the DAFF as a Manx National Glen), heading parallel with the A27 Round Table road. Higher up, the leafy aspects of the glen give way to open, gorse-clad slopes, where the river takes on the role of boundary between Arbory and the neighbouring parish of Rushen. The parish boundary meets the A36 Foxdale road on the eastern flank of Cronk ny Arrey Laa – some 1,200 feet (350m) above the Balladoole shore – before heading north-eastward to the Round Table. There are broad views across the south of the isle from the upper reaches of Arbory.

RUSHEN

Rushen is one of two Manx parishes which share their names with the sheadings of which they form a part (the other being Michael). Rushen is also one of two parishes whose churches were dedicated to Christ or the Holy Trinity (the other being Lezayre). A document from 1408 identifies the church as *Ecclesia Sancti Trinitatis inter prata*, 'the Church of the Holy Trinity between the meadows', and the Manorial Roll of 1511 names the parish as *Parochia Sti Trinitatis in Rushen*. A century later, it had become 'Kirke Christ of Russhen'. The modern rendering of 'Kirk Christ Rushen' was in place by 1703 and, as the name of the parish, remained in use until the early years of the twentieth century. The church is still often referred to in that fashion but the parish today is usually 'Rushen'.

The name itself has always been something of an enigma. It may have derived from the pre-Norse word *ros* (diminutive form *roisen*), which could denote a wood or a peninsula. If the latter, it could have recognized the parish as forming the south-west peninsula of the island. A Russian connotation from the Norse period in Man has also been suggested. The Swedish Vikings had settled extensive areas of Russia and ruled some of its cities as early as the ninth century. In the Scandinavian languages today, anyone or anything Russian is *Russ*. In the sheading of Rushen, and especially along the coast of the parish, Scandinavian place-names are ubiquitous: the Stacks, Fleshwick, Kitterland, the Calf, Rarick, Perwick, Fistard, Strandhall; all betray the familiarity of the Norsemen with the coast of Rushen and its landing-places. In the absence of further clues, the name remains a mystery.

In the early years of public elections, the constituencies for House of Keys elections coincided with the ancient land divisions of the six sheadings (plus those of the four towns) and, to a large extent, they do so still. But, over the years, there have been changes to constituency boundaries to allow for variations in local populations. From ancient times, the sheading of Rushen has comprised the three parishes of Malew, Arbory and Rushen, including the villages of Port Erin and Port St Mary. In 1985, however, the parish of Malew was withdrawn from the *parliamentary* constituency of Rushen to form the new constituency of Malew and Santon.

In terms of *local* government administration (in which Port Erin and Port St Mary are separate entities), the parish of Rushen is divided into three portions. The administrative boundaries of the two villages conjoin across the island's south-west peninsula to cut off the main (northern) portion of the parish from the detached portion to the south. The second dividing feature is embodied by the waters of Calf Sound, beyond which lies the third portion of the parish – the Calf of Man.

Ignoring the Calf for the moment, the parish is bounded to the west and south by the sea, to the east by the boundary with Arbory as previously described, and in the north along a line which runs from north-east to south-west across the northern slopes of Cronk ny Arrey Laa and down to the coast in the vicinity of Lag ny Keeilley, 'the hollow of the chapel', which lies beyond the parish boundary, in Patrick. The length of the parish along its major axis (south-west to north-east) is approximately 7 miles, and its area (including the two villages and the 616 acres (250ha) of the Calf) is 7,456 acres (3017ha).

Outside the two villages, the main centres of population are in the expanding modern estates of Ballafesson and Ballakillowey, both sitting at the foot of the long southern slope which descends from the 997-foot (301m) crest of Lhiattee ny Beinnee. The highest point in the parish, the summit of Cronk ny Arrey Laa, stands up at its northern extremity, 1,433 feet (437m) above the western shore. Its name ('hill of the day watch') identifies its role in the days of Watch and Ward. Its situation at the northern end of the parish necessitated additional day-watch points, which were established on Bradda Head and the Carnanes. The night watch was kept down by the shore at Port Erin.

The name of Cronk ny Arrey Laa has been another point of confusion in the past, due to inconsistencies in spelling. It has often been rendered as Cronk ny *Irree* Laa, 'hill of the day *rise* [i.e. dawn]', and the folk-story attached to it held that fishermen at work on the waters below would wait for a lightening of the sky above the hill before hauling in their nets. It is a story which has all the appearance of being a tall one, but it may – possibly – hark back to an old superstition. The summit of Cronk ny Arrey Laa holds an interesting pre-Celtic archaeological site which has been described in Chapter 3. From the steeply shelving slopes of the Cronk, the magnificent coastal scenery of Rushen stretches away southward, beyond Port Erin Bay, round the tip of the south-west peninsula, then eastward until it declines into the low coast around Bay ny Carrickey. All of it is accessible to the pedestrian, being part of the *Raad ny Foillan* (see Chapter 10).

Kirk Christ Rushen, with its octagonal bell-turret

The parish church, Kirk Christ Rushen, is located 500 yards north of the Four Roads roundabout, Port St Mary, beside the junction of the A29 and B46 roads. The earliest record of a vicar is from 1408 but the church was rebuilt in 1869. The churchyard contains the grave of William Milner, a generous benefactor to the village of Port Erin, and the graves of the twenty-nine victims of the wreck of the brig *Lily* on Kitterland, in Calf Sound, in 1852. (More on Milner and the wreck of the *Lily* later.)

Although the built-up areas of the two villages do not quite link up across the narrow neck of the south-west peninsula, their actual district boundaries *do*, thereby severing the largest part of the administrative parish of Rushen from the remainder to the south. The conjoined northern boundaries of Port Erin and Port St Mary run across the peninsula by a somewhat devious route from the north side of Bradda Head, near Creg Harlot (no, not what you might suppose, but deriving from 'Sherlock's Rock', after a former land-holder), to Rhenwhyllan, at the west end of Bay ny Carrickey. The southern boundaries of the two villages cut across from Kione ny Garee, 'end of the thicket', on the south side of Port Erin Bay, to Glenchass and Perwick Bay. Glenchass was the home of Ned Maddrell, the last of the old native Manx speakers, who died in 1974 at the age of 97.

The detached portion of Rushen is enclosed by the same spectacular coast and, at its extremity, faces out across Calf Sound to the final, offshore fragment of the parish – the Calf. The onshore portion contains two historic sites of outstanding interest, the first on Meayll (or Mull) Hill overlooking the second at Cregneash. Just below the summit of Meayll Hill, lies the megalithic chambered tomb known as the Meayll Circle, which has six pairs of burial chambers arranged in a circle, with a passage leading radially inwards to the junction of each pair. The formation is unique in the British Isles and has been dated to the Neolithic period, around 2000BC. The interred remains had been cremated prior to burial. Much of the tomb's covering has been plundered during the intervening ages, its stones probably being taken to serve other purposes.

A short distance down the hill to the south-east are the remains of the ancient village of which the circle was probably the burial ground. The old Manx name for the place was *Lag-ny-boirray*, 'the hollow of botheration', and urns found there were similar to those found in the graves. (See also Chapter 3.)

Further down to the south-east, and almost in the centre of this detached piece of Rushen parish, is Cregneash, the last of the old-style Manx villages, its traditional grouping of low, thatched cottages and the adjoining farm carefully maintained by Manx National Heritage (and described in Chapter 9). In the centre of the village, Harry Kelly's Cottage perpetuates the name of one of the last of the old-time Manx-speaking crofter-fishermen. He died in 1934; he and the rest of his breed are now gone from the scene. The name of the village originates from the Norse *Krokeness*, 'crooked ness', probably applied first to the nearby contorted promontory which forms Spanish Head and Black Head, but later applied to the village itself. The modern spelling stems from its Gaelicization to *Creg n'Eash*, which gives the puzzling translation 'rock of age'. Standing beside the A31 road from Port St Mary to Calf Sound, the church of St Peter was built in 1878 as a chapel of ease for Kirk Christ Rushen.

The hamlet of Cregneash nestles in the col between Meayll Hill and Cronk ny Arrey ('hill of the watch'), the 'Cronk' being just 5 metres lower than the 'Hill'. The hill of the watch today still maintains a watch of sorts, by means of the radio-navigation beacon maintained by the Civil Aviation Authority. Below the summit, to the south and west, lies a stretch of coast which must be the most spectacular in the whole of Man's magnificent south-west frontier with the sea, its cliffs rising to 400 feet (120m) above the inaccessible shore of Bay Stacka. This name shows a blend of linguistic origins; the old Manx name was *Baie yn Stackey*, the 'bay of the stack', and the Norse *stakkr* referring to the detached pillar of the Sugar Loaf at the east end of the bay.

Immediately to the west of the Sugar Loaf lies the heavily faulted cliff-top area of the Chasms, where deep fissures slice down through a 300-foot (90m) wall of Cambrian grit to the shore. It is a place where pedestrians should tread with care, and in the middle of it we find the simple stone circle known locally as Cronk Karran. Much smaller and plainer than the formation on Meayll Hill, most of its stones were also raided for other purposes once its roof covering had collapsed and rotted away, leaving only the lowest ring of stones to delineate the circle.

The physical features of this amazing coast and its wildlife have been described in Chapter 10. This rugged promontory, which forms the island's far south-west, is often referred to as the Meayll (or Mull) Peninsula, adopting the name of its highest hill. Regardless of whether we continue along the coastal foot-path to reach the end of dry land, or backtrack to Cregneash and follow the A31 from there, we eventually find ourselves on the brink of Calf Sound, where the modern restaurant and visitors' centre offers panoramic views over the often turbulent waters to the Calf of Man. Unless one has a boat of one's own, the only way to reach the Calf is to invest in a boat-trip from Port Erin or Port St Mary. Therefore, I propose to leave our visit to that final detached piece of Rushen parish until we have been to those two places.

PORT ST MARY

Port St Mary is the epitome of the small, timeless Manx harbour-town, although (like Port Erin) it is officially a village, administered by its publicly elected village commissioners. It is a most picturesque place; if comparisons had to be invoked with similar small ports elsewhere, it would have to be with such West-Country villages as Clovelly and St Ives. When viewed from the sea, or from the outer end of the breakwater, its grey-stone houses, set along narrow streets and byways, climb in apparently random fashion onto the slopes which rise behind the harbour.

The old Manx name of the village, *Purt le Moirrey*, derived from the ancient church of St Mary, which once stood beside the shore of Chapel Bay. The modern name is the English translation. The sheltered inner harbour is enclosed on its seaward side by the Harbour Pier, which was built in 1827. This was followed some sixty years later by the outer breakwater, named the Alfred Pier, after a son of Queen Victoria, Alfred, Duke of Edinburgh, who laid the foundation stone. The Isle of Man Yacht Club has its headquarters beside the harbour, and the port's two lifeboats – one an inshore inflatable and the other an all-weather, deep-water vessel – are kept permanently afloat between the two piers. The present church of St Mary stands beside Bay View Road, overlooking Chapel Bay from the west.

The coastal frontage of the village is pleasantly varied. Up at the north end, the

Contrasting moods in Port St Mary: (above) the sun shines on Chapel Bay; (below) fishing boats shelter inside the Alfred Pier as storm waves crash against the outside

ISLE OF MAN NEWSPAPERS

residential suburb of Gansey looks out across Bay ny Carrickey. Its foreshore is rocky – of Manx slate – and hereabouts stands a house containing the studio once occupied by the artist Frank Swinnerton (died 1905). The house has a sundial (dated 1885) bearing yet another version of that quotation from I Chronicles, like those we have seen at Old Kirk Braddan and Kirk Malew. This one reads: *Ta ny laghyn er y thalloo shoh myr scaddoo*, 'The days on this earth are as a shadow'. Frank Swinnerton was also involved in the excavation of the Neolithic burial site which was uncovered during construction of the Alfred Pier in the 1880s, and his drawings of the site were considered outstanding.

Chapel Bay is the only part of the village's sea frontage which provides a sandy beach and safe bathing. The sheltered bay is backed by twin promenades – one below and in front of the other – and, behind the upper promenade, stands the old *Bay Queen Hotel* which, in its former guise as the *Ballaqueeney*, was a main centre of the Rushen internment camp during the Second World War. It presents a sorry sight today; after a number of planning proposals have come to nought, the place has stood empty for many years. The area around Chapel Bay has been the village's principal location for holiday accommodation but it has never developed in this direction to anything approaching the same extent as Port Erin – and perhaps therein lies part of its charm.

On the west side of Chapel Bay, where the sand gives way to rock once more, the lower promenade continues as an elevated walkway, close above the craggy foreshore and curving south towards the harbour. The inner harbour today is a haven for all manner of recreational sailing boats, but recent proposals to develop a yachting marina have elicited the usual response from objectors. Fishing-boat activity in the port is a mere shadow of what once was, the few boats that still operate here berthing on the inside of the Alfred Pier.

On the south side of the harbour, Kallow Point juts seaward to form the southern terminator of Port St Mary Bay. The point is rocky but it exhibits a further change of rock, for we are back – albeit briefly – with the Carboniferous limestone. The fault-line which marks the end of the limestone and the return of the Manx slates has slanted out beneath the waters of the bay from the Black Rocks, at Glentraugh, to graze Kallow Point and mark it as the most westerly visible exposure of the limestone in Man. The lime kiln which stands beside the grey waterside ledges reminds us of its former industrial exploitation. Westward beyond the point, its resurgence is soon past and the slates reign supreme. Lying back behind a string of waterfront houses, the nine-hole golf course maintains a green open space on the west side of the village, and its club-house restaurant is a favourite eating place with members and non-members alike. But the adjacent residential estate has spread west to the brink of Glenchass, confronting the hamlet of Fistard on the far side.

Most of Port St Mary was part of the ancient treen of Fistard, from the Norse *Fiskagardr*, meaning 'fish garth' or 'enclosure'. Indeed, the old Manx name, recorded in the manorial roll of 1511, was *Fyshgarth*, which makes it even clearer. In the cliffs above Perwick Bay, the strata of the slates twist and contort in weird fashion and, in places, one can see traces of the wave-cut platform notched into the cliffs at times when sea levels were higher than today's. The former *Perwick Bay Hotel* – once a pleasant venue for a meal and a drink – is now residential accommodation.

PORT ERIN

Much of the ancient treen of Edremony is now occupied by the village of Port Erin. The treen-name (implying a place between two marshes or turburies) was recorded as the above in 1511, but by 1643 it had become Rowany. Both names are now encapsulated in modern housing estates, and the latter name is also enshrined in the title of the local golf club and the eighteen-hole municipal course on the north side of the village. The derivation of the name of the village itself is far from clear. It was recorded in 1595 as *Port Earn*, and in 1712 as *Port Iron*; it has been suggested that it came from the Manx *Purt Chiarn* or *Purt Yiarn*, which may be translated as 'Lord's port' or 'Iron port', but the relevance of either is all rather hazy.

The deep rectangular indentation of Port Erin Bay provides superb shelter for the small harbour on its southern side. Protected from the north by the rocky out-thrust of Bradda Head and from the south by the steeply rising hill of the Darrag, it is exposed only to the direct westerlies. An attempt was made in 1864 to provide the bay with complete protection by building a breakwater out from the foot of the southern headland. A strong supporter of the scheme was Port Erin's generous benefactor, William Milner, the Liverpool safe-maker. But the breakwater was damaged in a storm four years later and completely wrecked in 1884. Its line of tumbled concrete blocks still provides some measure of protection from the fury of winter's westerlies. The small harbour today shelters behind the short limestone structure of the Raglan Pier, which was opened by the unpopular Governor, Lord Raglan, in 1916. The local lifeboat station was established in 1883. Overlooking this scene from the north side of the bay is Milner's Tower, erected in 1871 high up on Bradda Head in recognition of the philanthropist's charities in aid of the poor of Port Erin and of his efforts for the benefit of Manx fishermen. Appropriately, the tower is in the shape of a key to one of his safes.

Port Erin: the shore and upper promenade

If the approach to Port Erin is made by the direct route from Cregneash, it will be by way of the narrow minor road crossing the western flank of Meayll Hill, descending the steep slope of the Darrag ('oak tree') road into the southern outskirts of the village, with the whole of the bay spread out to view. Despite the modern decline in the holiday trade, Port Erin is the one place outside Douglas to have maintained its tradition in that sphere of activity, especially in the field of family holidays. Behind and above the attractive, old-style cottages that line the sandy shore at the inner end of the bay, ranks of traditional sea-view hotels gaze out across the upper promenade. But one should beware of the gulls, particularly when walking the promenade with food in hand, for it may not remain in hand for as long as you intended. To supplement the usual range of seaside activities, the Erin Arts Centre promotes events in music and the arts, including international competitions, throughout the year.

Close behind the promenade, Port Erin's red-brick railway station stands at the southern terminus of the only surviving line of the Isle of Man Steam Railway. The line was completed in 1874 and its story has been told in Chapter 7; it is now operated by the Department of Tourism and Leisure. The line was opened with high hopes of healthy freight and passenger traffic emanating from the expanded harbour facilities to be developed in the bay, but all such hopes were dashed with the destruction of the breakwater. The line operates today mainly as a tourist attraction. The present railway museum at the station was opened in 1975.

At the south-west extremity of the bay, overlooking the wreck of Milner's breakwater, is the site of a more recent loss to Port Erin's infrastructure. The world-renowned Port Erin Marine Laboratory, an out-station of Liverpool University, closed in 2006. It was opened in 1892 by the Liverpool Marine Biological Committee, an independent group led by Professor Sir William Herdman FRS, who established the fish hatchery there in 1902. The association with Liverpool University began in 1919. Over the years, the laboratory did much work to research and maintain fish and crustacean stocks in Manx waters and the Irish Sea generally, and provided advice on marine fisheries, pollution and conservation, both to the Manx government and internationally. In addition, the establishment had its educational role; at any one time, there could be more than a hundred people (staff and students) working there, most of whom lived in and formed part of the local community. The laboratory's last director, Dr Andrew Brand, arrived to complete his PhD in 1966 and stayed on for the next forty years. For many years, the laboratory had been part-funded by the DAFF, and therein lay the ultimate obstacle to the future. The existence of the Manx funding had enabled the establishment to obtain additional funds from the UK government and the European Union. By 2004, agreement could not be reached on the apportionment of future Manx funding, and Liverpool University announced that the laboratory would close. Two years later, an admirable institution with an international reputation for marine research and education – its research data and former students spread across the world – was lost.

After such a dissatisfying tale, perhaps it is understandable if we now seek solace in the solitude of the Calf of Man. Port Erin's harbour is the most likely place to find a boat-trip heading south.

THE CALF AND OTHER ROCKS

At its nearest, the Calf of Man lies a mere 500 yards from the south-west tip of the main island. The gap between – Calf Sound – sees strong tidal currents twice a day in each direction, and the flow is split by two rock formations which stud the stream, the larger and nearer to the main island being Kitterland, and the smaller being the Thousla rock. Their names perpetuate the Norse influence in this part of Man. Kitterland takes its name from the Scandinavian *Kidja-eyland*, 'kids' island'; it seems to fit into the terminological scheme of things: the Calf (from the Norse *kalfr*) implies a young animal lying beside a larger one. Furthermore, Kitterland is smaller than the Calf, and a kid is smaller than a calf; there seems to be a sense of scale bound up in the Norse toponymy here. Kitterland is grass-capped and it is said that a small flock of sheep used to be grazed there in the summer months, but the birds and seals have it to themselves nowadays.

The Thousla's name may derive from the Scandinavian *Usley*, meaning 'fire island'. Being the smaller and lower of the two formations, it arguably poses the greater threat to boats attempting to pass through the Sound, and so it is conceivable that a fire was kept burning on it. Today, it supports a permanent beacon to warn of the danger. If the old Norse name had become Gaelicized at some time in the past, it would most likely have taken the form *Yn t-Usley*, which certainly points the way to the present appellation.

Both rocks have taken their toll of shipping in the past. On 27 December 1852, the brig *Lily*, outward bound from Liverpool to West Africa, was swept into Calf Sound by a southerly gale and wrecked on Kitterland. Survivors from the crew were rescued the following day and, when conditions had subsided, a gang of thirty men was put aboard the wreck to salvage her cargo. As they worked, and in circumstances that will never be known, a gunpowder store on the ship ignited; the *Lily*, her cargo and all bar one of the salvage gang were consumed in the explosion. The remains of the twenty-nine victims are buried in Rushen churchyard, and a memorial to them stands on the cliff-top below the visitors' centre at the Sound, overlooking the scene of the tragedy.

There is an interesting – if scarcely believable – sequel to the wreck of the *Lily*. One of the 'trophies' wrested from the wreck was a brass ring, said to be used for shackling a slave. (The brig had been bound for the west coast of Africa to load slaves for trans-shipment.) The ring was subsequently kept suspended from the mantelpiece of a cottage in Cregneash. On Christmas Day 1952, just two days short of the hundredth anniversary of the wreck, the ring was seen to be swinging violently back and forth for no apparent reason. The relic was promptly taken down and thenceforth kept in a place where it was no longer free to swing.

Also located on the cliff-top overlooking the Sound is a stone cross commemorating the rescue of the French crew of the *Jeanne St Charles*, which was wrecked on the Thousla rock in 1858. In perilous conditions, five local men rowed out to the wreck to bring the stranded seamen to safety. In recognition of their courage, each of the five was awarded a medal of honour by the Emperor Napoleon III, and the French government paid for the cross to be erected on the Thousla. It was later transferred to the tip of the main island, which is where it stands today.

Beyond these two rocky hazards to navigation, lies the dominant mass of the Calf. A first sight of it, when travelling down the A31 from Cregneash, is quite impressive, but rather more arresting is the first view obtained from the coastal footpath from Port St Mary, when, on breasting the rise to cross Spanish Head, the whole of the islet's east elevation is open to view, with clear daylight showing through the wave-cut 'eye' of the Burroo rock at its southern extremity. However, if we actually wish to go there, then we must start from one of the southern harbours. Most visitors to Man never get as far as the Calf (not many Manx folk do, for that matter) but the islet has its own unique fascination.

Our boat from Port Erin will give Kitterland and the Thousla a wide berth in order to land us safely at Cow Harbour, at the northern end of the Calf. The landing gets its name from the fact that, back in the days when the Calf was farmed, livestock were landed and taken off there, the sheep being trans-shipped by boat, and the cattle being swum across at slack water – always provided that conditions were calm enough.

The Calf of Man is a 616-acre (250ha) islet of slate rising to a maximum elevation of 421 feet (128m). Its patchy capping of glacial drift contains a high proportion of transported boulders, and some of the gravel deposits have been worked at various times for building and track-mending. The Calf has an intermittent record of habitation going back well over a thousand years. The *Crucifixion Stone*, discovered when the ruin of an early Christian keeill was being demolished in 1773, has been dated to the eighth century. This incomplete, handsomely carved slab, depicting Christ on the cross with the spear-bearer at his side, now resides in the Manx Museum. There is evidence of occupation and fortification of the Calf during the Norse period. In historical times, the earliest record of the islet's name is contained in the Manorial Roll for 1511, which gives it as 'Le Calf', the first element being the Norman definite article. The Gaelic rendering of the name was *Yn Cholloo*; the strait of water between the Calf and Kitterland was *Keyllys Mooar*, the 'great sound', and the narrower strait between Kitterland and the main island was *Keyllys Beg*, the 'little sound'.

In 1511, the Calf was held by the Stevensons of Balladoole, Arbory, but, in 1648, James Stanley, seventh Earl of Derby, requisitioned it, with the intention of installing a garrison there as a defence against the parliamentary forces. By way of recompense, he granted the family an allowance of 500 'sea-parrots' (puffins?) per annum.

By virtue of its limited size, the population of the Calf was always small. They must have formed a tight-knit, self-sufficient little community, often isolated from the parent isle by winter's storms. Sometimes it was just one man, a religious recluse or an eccentric scholar such as Thomas Bushell (a friend of Francis Bacon's), who claimed to have spent three years there from 1621, living on a diet of puffin, rabbit and spring-water. But Bushell's 'puffins' were probably Manx shearwaters (*Puffinus puffinus*), a bird so named because the first specimens identified as belonging to a distinct species were taken from the Calf in 1676. Bushell

(1594–1674) was a scholar of Balliol College, Oxford, of scientific bent – particularly towards mining – and claimed to have discovered various minerals on the Calf. After his solitary sojourn there, he returned to London, became a favourite of Charles I and, after surviving the Commonwealth, was equally in favour with Charles II. At the southern extremity of the Calf, a man-made feature on the summit of the Burroo stack (most probably a Norse defensive structure) has become known as 'Bushell's Grave' but, since Bushell died in London, it is more than likely that he was buried there.

There were thousands of shearwaters on the Calf in those days. From the period of Norse rule onwards, they were valued as a source of food, and there was an annual harvest of birds and eggs, with many of the birds being pickled and stored for winter use. There is record that, in 1712, two men collected 256 dozen 'puffins', and this was thought to have been an average cull. Assuming that, for sustainability of the population, the annual harvest is unlikely to have exceeded a quarter of the young birds approaching full growth, Larch Garrad [28] has suggested that a population of 10,000 breeding pairs would not be an unrealistic estimate. The collapse in the shearwater population came – so far as we can tell – not from over-cropping, but as the result of a plague of rats following a shipwreck. By 1811, the harvesting of shearwaters had ceased, apparently because their numbers had decreased to such an extent that the arduous task was no longer worthwhile. The rats were finally brought under control in the 1960s, and the shearwaters began nesting again, but their numbers have never regained the levels that appear to have been sustained in the distant past.

In 1776, John Quayle, who was Clerk of the Rolls at the time, owned the Calf and shipped out a number of red deer and grouse, intending to establish their populations for shooting. But neither became established; the deer do not seem to have survived, and the grouse probably flew back to the larger isle whence they had come. Even some of the deer were known to brave the waters of the Sound, seemingly attracted by the greener acres on the other side. The Calf was also productive as a rabbit warren, providing food for the garrison, as the old accounts of Castle Rushen testify.

The Calf was farmed more or less continuously from the late eighteenth century until the late 1950s. There were thirty people living there in 1851. One farmer later in that century constructed a stone-built mill-house overlooking the Puddle (the bay at the southern end of the islet), supplied from a mill-pond a short distance above. Much of the land that was overlain with glacial till was enclosed within walls of local stone and used for crops or grazing, but much of it has now been reclaimed by the bracken and heather.

The Commissioners for Northern Lights began their works on the Calf in the early nineteenth century. The two lighthouses above the Stack (on the islet's

The Calf of Man: (above) Robert Stevenson's two lighthouses; (below) Stevenson's lower light gazes out to the tower on the Chicken Rock

western extremity) became operational in 1818. Both were designed by Robert Stevenson, two lights being necessary to assist shipping in navigating past the unmarked Chicken Rock, five-eighths of a mile offshore to the south-west. Duty keepers lived in houses adjoining the light-towers. These lights were made redundant in 1875 by the completion of the tower on the Chicken Rock itself, the construction of which – so susceptible to the weather, and with work on the rock impossible around high tide – had occupied the preceding six years. The tower was formed of Dalbeattie granite, each ring of stones being cut, fitted and numbered in Port St Mary before being shipped out to the rock. Houses for the accommodation of the keepers' families were built in Port St Mary some twelve years after the completion of the light.

The Chicken Rock is said to owe its name to the frequent sightings of storm petrels ('Mother Carey's chickens') in its vicinity. The rock is often referred to simply as 'the Chickens' and is the southernmost outlier of the Manx group. Its lighthouse was severely damaged in 1960 by a fire which compelled its three keepers to abandon the tower and take to the dubious safety of the reef. Their distress flares were seen in Cregneash, and they were taken off (in very difficult conditions) by the Port Erin and Port St Mary lifeboats. The tower has remained unmanned ever since, initially emitting an automatic light at reduced power and with its original function taken over by the last in the series of Manx lighthouses, which materialized after the lighthouse builders returned to the Calf in 1966. Two years later, the third lighthouse on the islet became operational. It stands between the two abandoned towers of the nineteenth century and stabbed out a beam of two million candlepower which was visible for 23 miles. But its design is utterly out of keeping with the sturdy grace of Stevenson's twin towers and with the beauty of its surroundings. However, in June 2007, the Commissioners for Northern Lights announced that the Chicken Rock light had been upgraded to 21 nautical miles, thus making the Calf light redundant. Ownership of the building has reverted to the landowner, i.e. Manx National Heritage.

The last private owner of the Calf of Man, a Mr F. J. Dickens, died in 1937 and bequeathed the property to the National Trust for England and Wales, with the intention that it should be a bird sanctuary and observatory. Following the formation of the Manx National Trust in 1951, the Calf was administered by that body as tenant of the English trust, until the formation of MNH in 1986, since when ownership has passed to MNH. The Calf is now managed solely as a bird observatory and is manned for approximately nine months of the year. The main farm buildings, near the centre of the islet, are maintained as its headquarters, with living accommodation for its wardens (usually up to three) and limited hostel facilities for staying visitors. Weather and tide permitting, summer day visitors may be landed at Cow Harbour at the end of the boat-trip from Port Erin or Port St Mary.

Calf Sound and Spanish Head from the Calf

As we roam these lonely acres of the Calf today, it is hard not to feel a creeping nostalgia at the passing of the old populations and the old ways of life. Such feelings are engendered by the sights of their deteriorating and ruinous buildings. Stevenson's light-towers still appear basically sound, but the keepers' houses are roofless ruins, as are the few in other parts of the islet, and some are just shapeless heaps of stone. There is a long-disused silage tower, the quarry from which came the building stone, a gravel pit which provided aggregate for building and hardcore for track-mending. Down in the south, the mill building is ruinous but its pond is still in evidence. Signs of old cultivation are still to be found, particularly in the form of lazy beds. All of these things serve to remind us of a way of life which has left this place for ever; so simple and uncomplicated, so close to nature, so romantic – romantic, that is, to those of us who did not have to endure it.

CHAPTER THIRTEEN

Peel and the West

The parishes of Patrick and German, including the area now occupied by the town of Peel, constituted the ancient sheading of Glenfaba. The origin of the name is unknown; it is most probably a relic of the non-Aryan folk who preceded the arrival of the Celts. Such names are found throughout the British Isles; we have no knowledge of their language, and so further conjecture over the name is pointless. It first appears in print in a papal bull of 1231, which refers to *Terra de Glenfaba*. Other early records sometimes referred to 'Glanfaba'. The pronunciation of the second element was usually rendered as either 'farba' or

Lag ny Keeilley, the most remote keeill site in the island

'fairba', but there is a long-standing modern tendency to make it 'faeba'. All three versions are heard today.

In parliamentary terms, the old sheading is now divided into two constituencies, the town of Peel electing one member to the House of Keys, and the constituency of Glenfaba (comprising the two parishes outside the town's boundaries) also sending one member.

PATRICK

Continuing on our clockwise way around the isle, Patrick is the next parish on our journey. As this was one of two Manx parishes dedicated to St Patrick (the other being Jurby), two devices were used in the past to identify this one. In 1231, we find *Ecclesia Sancti Patricii de Insula*, 'St Patrick's Church of the island', the island presumably being St Patrick's Isle, for that is where the old church stood. By 1595, it had become 'Kirk Patrick of the Peel', the peel, or *pile* (Manx *peeley*) being the fortress on St Patrick's Isle.

The parish is bounded on the west by the sea, in the south and east by the parishes of Rushen, Arbory, Malew and Marown (all described earlier), and in the north by the parish of German, the boundary with which is encountered in the midst of the Archallagan Plantation. From there, the boundary runs generally north-westward to St John's (leaving most of that village in German) and follows the course of the River Neb (more or less closely) until brought to a halt by the Peel town boundary on the west bank of the river, opposite the power station. The final run of the town's boundary is westward across Peel Hill to the sea, thereby claiming the northernmost half-mile of the ridge for the town.

The original parish church of Patrick on St Patrick's Isle shared that site with the old Kirk German. Later, after the two parishes had shared the same isle for who-knows-how-many years, they actually shared the same church, when St Peter's was built beside the market square in Peel. That situation lasted until 1714, when a parish church was erected on the present site in Patrick village, one mile south of Peel. This was replaced with the present building in 1881. A small remnant of the old church still stands in the churchyard.

This parish of some 10,000 acres (4,000ha) is quite sparsely populated (1,305 according to the 2001 census), the main centres of population being in the villages of Dalby, Glenmaye, Patrick and Higher and Lower Foxdale. On the map, the parish tapers down to its southern extremity on the coast, 2 miles south of Niarbyl – just far enough south to enclose the remote little archaeological site at Lag ny Keeilley, 'hollow of the chapel'. Situated low down on the seaward slopes of Cronk ny Arrey Laa, it sits in possibly the loneliest spot imaginable, but looking out over superb coastal panoramas. It is approachable only on foot, and any normal pedestrian is restricted to the footpath which leaves the A27 coast road to Peel at the Kerroodhoo Plantation, crossing the MNH property at Eary Cushlin and slanting down the steep western flank of the Cronk. (The path of the Raad ny Foillan is crossed *en route*.) To the left of the path on the way down, Chibbyr y vashtee, the 'well of the baptism', is passed just before reaching the keeill. The low outline of this ancient chapel, with its adjoining priest's cell, sits on an isolated level patch amid these great, sweeping slopes. A number of lintel-graves and early Celtic cross-slabs were uncovered in a burial ground adjoining the keeill's enclosure.

From this southern tip of Patrick, the parish's coastline sweeps majestically northward for almost 7 miles to its abutment against the town boundary of Peel, on the northern slope of the eponymous hill. On the way, it encompasses two significant features. After the first 2 miles, the treacherous flagstone reef of Niarbyl juts into the sea. This feature is often referred to as 'the Niarbyl' but this is a mistake, as the original Manx name was *Ny Arbyl*, meaning 'the tail'; hence the English prefix 'the' to the present name is redundant. (But I still think it looks more like a rhino's horn.)

The little bay cradled in the southern lee of the reef was once the haven of a local herring fishery, but is no more. The brace of thatched cottages beside the shore are now maintained by MNH in a spot which has become a favoured location for film-makers. The nearby wooden bungalow was a holiday haunt of the well-known music-hall artist, Florrie Forde, who played the summer seasons in Douglas from 1900 to 1937 (there is a bar named after her in the refurbished Villa Marina, in Douglas). A short distance above the shore, the Niarbyl café and visitors' centre are now in the custody of MNH.

Half a mile north-east, along the minor road from the A27, the hamlet of Dalby (from the Norse *Dalbyr*, 'dale farm') sits astride the main road to Peel. The church of St James stands here, built in 1839 to serve the south of the parish, counterbalancing the location of the parish church of the Holy Trinity, up in the north. St James's – like St Luke's at East Baldwin – was designed by John Welch and was a favourite of the Poet Laureate, John Betjeman. High up on the hillside on the east side of the road, is the site of Doarlish Cashen ('Cashen's gap'), a smallholding where, in the 1930s, the story of 'the Dalby Spook' was woven. The holding at that time was farmed by James Irving, who lived there with his wife and young daughter. In 1931, so it is said, the Irvings began hearing animal noises from behind panelling and in the attic of their cottage (not an unusual occurrence when living in the country). The thirteen-year-old Voirrey Irving then claimed that this mongoose-like creature had revealed itself and become her pet. The animal could talk and sing in several languages – but not Manx – and announced that his name was Gef, born in India in 1852 (suggesting unusual longevity for a mongoose). Gef wandered far and wide around the locality, spying on the neighbours and bringing his 'skeet' back to the Irvings. The story should have ended there, consigned to oblivion as the fanciful imaginings of an adolescent only-child – and it might have been so, had the tale not come to the attention of Harry Price.

Harry Price was an English writer and self-proclaimed expert on paranormal phenomena. He made a lucrative living by writing of all manner of unexplained happenings and selling the stories to any newspapers or magazines that would take them. He was alerted to the 'Dalby Spook' story when a Peel woman wrote to him about it in 1935. Price travelled to the island to research the story but never saw Gef. Nevertheless, once he had written his story, he sold it to newspapers around the world. English newspaper editors sent their own reporters to cover the story. The *News Chronicle* printed a supposed picture of the creature, and Rex Lambert, editor of the BBC publication, *The Listener*, felt compelled to take libel proceedings when he found his reputation being besmirched because of his coverage of the story. Price and Lambert collaborated on a book of the events at Doarlish Cashen; *The Haunting of Cashen's Gap* was published in 1936. The Irvings left the farm in 1937 and nothing more was ever heard of Gef but, ten years later, the next owner of the land claimed to have snared and killed a strange-looking animal (although another account claims that he shot it). And that is where the story ends.

However, earlier in that century, there had been other strange occurrences in the hills above Dalby, recounted by Samuel Norris in his memoirs, *Manx Memories and Movements*, published in 1938. These came to be known as the 'Dalby Outrages' and occurred over several years in the early 1900s; they were restricted to one farm and involved the killing or maiming of livestock. Fires also occurred, including one when detectives brought from England to investigate were actually concealed on the premises. The farm's domestic water came from a well, the top access of which was kept locked, and the only key was in the possession of the farmer. When the water was found to be contaminated, the well was opened up to reveal the decaying carcase of a sheep. The events were never explained, and life on the farm only returned to normality after the owner – broken in mind and body – sold up and left. Samuel Norris, businessman and reformer-member of the House of Keys, was always a reliable chronicler of his times. So, dear reader, you may perceive that strange happenings occur in the hills above Dalby. Perhaps we should move on.

The second significant feature on the Patrick coast is Glen Maye, which forms the mouth of the long, curving cleft in the southern hills sweeping down from remote Glen Rushen. The hamlet of Glenmaye is less than 2 miles north of Dalby. The six quarterland farms that lie between – Ballahutchin, Ballelby, Ballaquane, Ballnalargy, Cronk Mooar and Ballachrink – were all held at one time by the Barony of Bangor and Sabal, in the north of Ireland. This holding seems to have remained in being at least into the late eighteenth century, and possibly later. In the fifteenth century, the abbots of the barony found themselves at odds with the Lord of Man, as we shall see when we get to Kirk Michael.

Patrick village lies another 1½ miles to the north. In the churchyard is the grave of Sir George Moore of Ballamore (1709–87), who was elected Speaker of the House of Keys from 1763 to 1780. He represented the Keys in their attempts to obtain better terms for the island after the Revestment of 1765, and it was largely due to his efforts that the proposal to annex the island to Cumberland never came to fruition. More recent burials are accommodated in the 'new' churchyard of 1879. Among them is the grave of an unknown man whose body was washed up on the west coast in the early twentieth century. Florrie Forde – entertaining the holiday crowds in Douglas at the time and occupying her bungalow at Niarbyl in between – felt moved to arrange the unknown's funeral, and to pay for it. The simple inscription on the white marble surround reads: 'Some mother's son'.

Patrick churchyard was also the resting-place of some 200 internees from the nearby Knockaloe camp during the First World War, and of some British servicemen who died while on duty at the camp. In 1962, sixty-nine graves (most containing more than one coffin) were opened up to enable the bodies – all of German or Austrian civilians – to be re-interred in the German War Cemetery at Cannock Chase, in Staffordshire, so that the graves could be more easily visited by relatives. Only two German burials were left undisturbed, these being of two German Jews whose families objected to their reburial at Cannock Chase. Their headstones stand near those of seven Turkish Muslim internees who also died at the camp.

The entrance to Knockaloe Mooar is in Patrick village, 100 yards north of the junction of the A30 with the A27. The use of the farm as an internment camp in the First World War – during which it had been transformed into an establishment of twenty-three hutted compounds, each capable of holding more than 1,000 internees – left it in no fit state to perform its original function after the conflict was over. In 1923, the Manx government, aided by a £20,000 legacy from the Henry Bloom Noble Trust, purchased the property and embarked on its conversion to a 346-acre (140ha) experimental farm, which occupied the next seven years. From that time on, for more than seventy years, Knockaloe operated in that capacity, providing advice to Manx farmers, with demonstrations of crops and farming techniques, and an artificial insemination service for cattle and pigs, as well as producing seed and livestock for sale to farmers and for the domestic food market. The director of the farm doubled as the Government's agricultural adviser. During the Second World War, recruits to the Manx Women's Land Army (the island's equivalent of the Women's Land Army (WLA) in Britain) were trained here, and those experienced entrants without need for training were placed directly into mobile squads based at Knockaloe and Lezayre Lodge (since destroyed by fire but rebuilt). With many of the younger men away on war service, the women worked alongside the remaining men on farms wherever they were needed, until the Manx WLA was disbanded in 1946.

After the war, Knockaloe resumed its peacetime activities and continued to develop. But, through the 1990s, the political will seemed to falter. In 2005, it was announced that Knockaloe would close. It was the story of Port Erin's marine biological laboratory all over again. At the time of writing, the future use of Knockaloe Mooar is unknown – at least to the public.

Abutting Knockaloe Mooar to the north is the neighbouring farm of Knockaloe Beg, once the home of Thomas Corrin, who was responsible for building the landmark tower on the highest point of his property, usually referred to as Corrin's Hill. The northern portion of the same hill – inside the town's boundary – is known as Peel Hill. The day watches for the parishes of Patrick and German were kept on this summit. The night watch for German was mustered down on the Peel waterfront, whilst it is likely that night watches in Patrick would be posted by the waterside at Glen Maye and Niarbyl.

Thomas Corrin was born in 1769 and built his tower in 1806. His father had purchased Knockaloe Beg in 1740. Thomas erected the tower after the death of his wife in 1806. Their two children had also died early. As noted earlier, the staunch Nonconformist wished their bodies – and his own – to be interred in the small enclosure beside the tower. The tombstones standing there today proclaim their presence on this hilltop, but various stories prevail. Some claim that the bodies were never moved from Patrick churchyard, others that they were re-interred in some secret place. It is true that the Church initially refused to allow interment in unconsecrated ground, but it later relented. The tombstones now stand in the shadow of the tower and – in the absence of any hard evidence to the contrary – that is good enough for me.

Thomas Corrin eventually remarried and had three more children, of whom only one, Robert (born 1824), survived. He was a successful farmer, businessman and entrepreneur. He became involved in the Peel fishing industry and assembled a fleet of Peel-built vessels. From the profits, he purchased Knockaloe Mooar; the family moved into Peel (a house in Shore Road, now the *Raglan Hotel*) and the two farms (Mooar and Beg) were rented out, the rents being invested to acquire more property. A canny Manxman! Robert died in 1899, leaving a trust fund in excess of £100,000 – more than £2 million in today's money. His wife and six surviving children (none of whom married) administered the fund for the benefit of the poor and needy in Peel and the surrounding district. The almshouses for 'respectable widows and spinsters' still stand at Glenfaba Bridge. A gift of land and payment of building costs resulted in a new vicarage in Albany Road, Peel. Benefactions continued to be made through the wills of the last family members, including sums for the building of the Corrin Hall, the Peel town hall and a 'cottage hospital in Peel'. The latter eventually took the form of the Corrin Memorial Home, providing residential accommodation for the elderly, which was opened in 1956. Robert Corrin and his family were, perhaps, the Henry Bloom Nobles of Peel.

The habitable parts of Patrick are effectively split into two by the lonely spine of hills which runs south-west from above the central valley at St John's, over Slieau Whallian and Dalby Mountain to Cronk ny Arrey Laa. The spine itself is interrupted only by the steep-sided cleft of Glen Rushen and Glen Mooar, halfway along the ridge. The only significant population in the eastern half of the parish is also split between the twin villages of Higher and Lower Foxdale. They get their name from the Scandinavian *forsdalr*, 'waterfall dale', after the fall on the west side of the road at Lower Foxdale. The adjacent farm takes its Manx name, Ballanass, 'farm of the waterfall', from the same feature.

At the height of the Manx mining industry, in the second half of the nineteenth century, the mines around Foxdale and above Glen Rushen transformed this erstwhile peaceful area into a hive of industrial activity. Many of the buildings remain, now in ruinous condition, and heaps of spoil – the 'deads' – are still to be seen, although much of the material around Foxdale was removed during the Second World War to provide hardcore beneath roads and runways. With the demise of the island's mines, there was a large-scale exodus of the men who had worked in them, many seeking places where they could use their hard-won skills in other parts of the world, to remain within the ranks of the renowned 'hard-rock men'. Their departure and the loss of the industry left the two Foxdales – for many years – in a rather down-at-heel condition. In more recent times, there has been a modicum of modern development in the area, involving the building of new houses, a modern primary school at Higher Foxdale and the establishment of an industrial estate, bringing opportunities for employment.

The eastern extremity of Patrick lies near the centre of the Archallagan Plantation. Approximately one-fifth of the conifer woodland lies within the parish, the remainder being in German and Marown. The proposal to dispose of ash residue from the island's refuse incinerator at a purpose-made landfill site in the plantation resulted in much controversy.

PEEL

There are, to my mind, three centres of habitation in Man which preserve the old medieval pattern of Manx townscape. In enumerating only three, I exclude

Cregneash because (a) it is too small to exhibit a townscape, and (b) its ancient pattern of human habitat is preserved by somewhat artificial means – and, by that, I do not mean to imply criticism. But each of the three I have in mind retains the old pattern of medieval structure at its heart, whilst moving on to function in the twenty-first century. Thus, if Castletown is the archetypal medieval fortress-town, and Port St Mary exemplifies the old-style Manx fishing village, it is Peel that epitomizes the somewhat larger harbour-town from times past. Its older buildings are of the warm-hued local sandstone – houses, shops and warehouses crowding in along a hotchpotch of narrow streets which is utterly confusing to the visiting motorist, whose plight was amusingly summed up by Stenning in 1958: the promenade 'is entered at each end by reasonably broad roads starting from nowhere in particular, while the roads running up through the old houses must be accepted in faith. The motorist will eventually come out somewhere if he drives with care.' He also complained that many of the streets were too narrow for two-way traffic, but many of them are one-way today and are the better for it.

In Stenning's day, Peel was the island's principal fishing port, with Scottish and Irish boats arriving each summer to vie with the Manx vessels in the herring fishing. The harbour was a hive of activity, as were the kippering houses, but the action is much depleted today. One would be hard-pressed to decide which *is* the

Peel: the inner harbour

principal fishing port today; there are probably as many boats operating out of Ramsey as out of Peel. Peel kippers are still produced by the traditional method – oak-smoked and with no artificial dyes – but the herring for the process are often brought in from elsewhere. Conversely, the local shellfish industry flourishes.

Unlike Castletown, the town and castle of Peel have always stood aloof from one another, on either side of the River Neb. This was inevitable: St Patrick's Isle was the obvious location for a fortification to stand guard over the approach to the haven in the river-mouth, and the lower land with gentler contours on the other side was the obvious place for a town to grow. The earliest historical records relate to the military fortifications and ecclesiastical buildings on St Patrick's Isle. The earliest mention of a name is given as the Norse *Holmtun*, 'island town', and was probably used concurrently with its Manx equivalent, *Purt ny hinshey*, 'port of the island'. By 1655, the Norse-based version had changed from Holmetowne to Peeletowne, from the *peele* or *pile* (fortress) on the other side of the river. By the beginning of the eighteenth century, the 'towne' had been dropped and the residual 'Peele' soon evolved into 'Peel'.

The earliest historical record relating to Peel refers to the arrival of the Norwegian king, Magnus Barefoot, in 1098. Following the death of Godred Crovan three years earlier, Magnus journeyed south to assert his sovereignty over the *Sudreyjar,* the 'Southern Isles', of which Man was the most southerly. He erected his *peel* on St Patrick's Isle; the timber-built structure was still standing in 1260 but there is no trace of it now.

Dating from at least a century before Magnus's *peel* are the stone-built ruin of St Patrick's Church and the adjacent Round Tower. The church was of the traditional Manx pattern: plain, rectangular, with a ratio of length to breadth of about three to one. The east gable – of later date – still stands; the west gable had a belfry for two bells but this was blown down in the nineteenth century. The round tower stands close by the west end of the church. Built of sandstone from Creg Malin, at the opposite end of the bay, it stands some 50 feet (15m) high

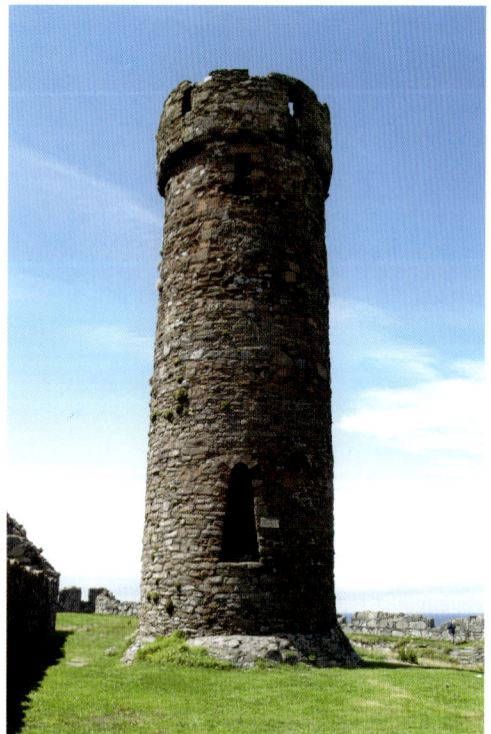

The Round Tower on St Patrick's Isle

and 45 feet (13.5m) in circumference, with the sill of its door opening set 7 feet (2.1m) above the ground. It is similar to the round towers of Ireland, where there are twenty-four such structures, but only four are known elsewhere, and just the one in the Isle of Man. An early drawing shows the tower with a conical roof, which was a common feature, but this has long-since vanished from the tower on St Patrick's Isle. Such towers were built to provide protection from the Viking raiders of the late eighth century onwards. Whenever danger threatened, the clerics would withdraw into the tower, taking the church valuables with them, haul up the ladder, secure the door and sit it out for the duration.

The roofless ruin of St German's Cathedral stands on the south-eastern corner of the castle enclosure, with its east end actually built in to the castle wall. It was built in the reign of Olaf II (1226–37), who appointed Simon of Argyll to be Bishop of Sodor in 1227. He was consecrated at Nidaros (Trondheim) and, on arrival in Man, set about enlarging the small church of St German, which would eventually become the cathedral. It is cruciform in plan, 114 feet (35m) long, 68 feet (21m) across the transepts, and with a squat, square tower over the crossing. Its walling is of random-rubble construction in Manx slate, with arch and window mouldings in red sandstone, some of which may have come from Ulster (Olaf's sister, Affreca, was patroness of Grey Abbey, in County Down, and there are said to be similarities between the two buildings).

Below the chancel of the cathedral is the most dismal of crypts, which shows no sign of ever having been used for church purposes but is known to have been in use for centuries as the Bishop's prison. Lacking even the most basic facilities, such as drainage or water – save for that which percolates from the rock at the top of the sloping floor and spills down to the lower end – the only light enters via a single lancet window 5 feet (1.5m) high and 6 inches (15cm) wide. All manner of felons convicted by the episcopal court – adulterers and fornicators, drunkards and brawlers, profaners of the Sabbath, those suspected of witchcraft, hardened offenders as well as members of the peaceable and harmless Quaker community – were herded in here and held until such time as they asked for pardon and performed their penances. Conditions must have been so grim that only the most hardened transgressor would risk returning. The use of the crypt as a prison ended in 1780.

Bishop Simon died in 1247, in the twenty-first year of his episcopacy, and was buried beneath the chancel of his cathedral. In 1871, in the course of repairs, his embalmed body was discovered, together with the skeleton of his dog. The remains were re-interred in an arched recess in the north wall, and a commemorative tablet records the fact. But the most amusing dedication in the cathedral relates to Bishop Samuel Rutter, who was the last of the island's bishops to be buried there. By all accounts, he was a lively and amiable character, a writer of elegant verse – including (it is said) the best drinking song in the Manx language – and the composer of his own epitaph in Latin which, in translation, reads: 'In this house, shared with my brothers the worms, in hope of a resurrection unto life, lie I Sam, by Divine grace Bishop of this Island. Stop, reader: look and smile at the palace of a bishop. Died 30 May 1662.'

By the time of Bishop Rutter's death, the cathedral was already in such a ruinous state that, when he was interred in the centre of the crossing, at the base of the tower, the tower itself was open to the sky. When the good Bishop Wilson arrived in 1698, the chancel had been repaired and the nave re-roofed, but the roof of the transept was in ruins. By 1710, the roof of the nave had again collapsed, and Wilson gave the lead from it to cover the new church in Patrick. In 1730, when relations between Church and State were not at their best, the Bishop was complaining that Governor Horton had taken some of the cathedral roof for use at Castle Rushen and, soon after, that the Governor had moved more components from the roof for use on his own stables. The roof of the chancel was made good in time for the installation of Bishop Hildesley in 1755 but, by 1772, the chancel had 'gone completely to ruin'. The last bishop to be installed in St German's was Claudius Crigan, in 1785. The last remaining roof timbers were blown down in 1824; things had then gone too far to be put right. In the late 1870s, Bishop Rowley Hill entertained thoughts of restoration, but the task was too daunting and the money subscribed was diverted to the building of the new church of St Peter, in the Market Place in Peel, completed in 1884.

Whilst all this ecclesiastical activity had been going on, through the course of the previous six centuries or so, the castle was also being developed. During the thirteenth and fourteenth centuries, the island suffered successive attacks by Scots, English, Irish and French interlopers, and Peel did not escape their attentions. In the time of Sir William de Montacute II as Lord of Man (1344–92), a stone-built gate-house and curtain wall replaced Magnus Barefoot's timber pile. Sir William le Scrope purchased the lordship from Montacute in 1392 and, four years later, wishing to extend the fortifications, received papal permission to build a castle on 'Patrykys holm, near and belonging to the church of Sodor'. The papal approval was conditional on le Scrope also repairing the cathedral. This he did, leaving the two buildings standing imposingly together above the harbour.

The building material for the castle works was the local Creg Malin sandstone. In the time of the Stanleys, in the late fifteenth century, le Scrope's red curtain wall was extended westward by building the 'green curtain' of slate quarried from the seaward side of the wall. This effectively completed the enclosure of the entire islet to keep out the Scots. Halfway along the western wall, Fenella's Tower stands above a sally-port, famous as the scene of Fenella's leap into the boat of her lover, Julian Peveril, in Sir Walter Scott's novel, *Peveril of the Peak*.

The castle's gate-house is the scene of a well-known tale of the super-natural, the story of the *Moddey Dhoo*, the 'black dog', the climax to which was supposed to have occurred in or about 1660. The guard-room is situated just inside the entrance to the castle. The apparition, taking the form of a large, black, shaggy spaniel, haunted the chambers of the castle, especially the guard-room, which he would approach along a nearby passage. Each evening, he would enter the guard-room and stretch out in front of the fire. The soldiers of the guard – at first alarmed by the visitation – grew accustomed to its presence but continued to regard it with awe, and none would be left alone with it. At nightfall, it was customary for the gate-keeper, having locked the gates, to deliver the keys to the Captain's house, which was beyond the cathedral, to the north. But he always ensured that he was accompanied by a colleague. One such night, a drunken soldier declared that he would deliver the keys to the Captain and he hoped that the *moddey* would follow him, so that he could discover whether the creature was dog or devil – and so he did. Some time after their departure, a great noise was heard outside but none in the guard-room would venture outside to investigate. Eventually, the man returned, suddenly very sober and quite unable to speak. He never spoke again and died three days later. The narrator of the tale stated that: 'by the distortion of his limbs and features, it might be guessed that he died in agonies more than is common in a natural death'. The *Moddey Dhoo* was never seen again and, thereafter, no-one dared use the passageway that he used to haunt; it was sealed up and another way made. The story was collected by George Waldron and recounted in his A *Description of the Isle of Man* (1731).

Although one of the buildings within the curtain wall has been identified as a barracks, there would scarcely have been space to accommodate the whole garrison, which had a permanent complement of eighty in 1660, and this could always be reinforced by detachments from the parish militias. Off-duty soldiers of the garrison would have been housed on the other side of the river; hence the presence of Barrack Lane in the old town of Peel.

In modern times, the castle grounds have been subjected to several archaeological excavations, the most extensive of which were carried out by a team from Liverpool University, in a series of summer-season investigations through the 1980s, in an area on the north side of the cathedral. These uncovered an extensive burial ground and evidence of occupation from the Mesolithic period through to the establishment of a Celtic monastic community. Numerous burials were discovered, from around AD500 to the late fourteenth century, the most striking being that of a tenth-century woman who was dubbed 'the pagan lady'. She had been buried with all the tools of the housewife's trade – a pestle and mortar, knives, shears, a cooking spit and a fine glass-bead necklace – and bearing all the signs of a high-class burial in the Norse style prior to their conversion to Christianity.

By an ironic coincidence of timing, the many exciting finds of genuine archaeological interest unearthed by the Liverpool University team on St Patrick's Isle
seemed destined, for a time, to be overshadowed by the sensational claims (sensational*ist* and fanciful would be more accurate) made by an American academic at
the end of 1986. Dr Norma Goodrich visited the Isle of Man and various places in
the United Kingdom to promote her newly published book, *King Arthur*. From her
study of medieval manuscripts, Dr Goodrich had concluded that 'King Arthur'
had conquered the Isle of Man and chose St Patrick's Isle as the site of the
legendary 'Castle of the Holy Grail', which became the headquarters of the
'Knights of the Round Table'. Furthermore, 'King Arthur' established his treasury
and built a 'magnificent palace' where Peel now stands. He and 'Queen Guinevere'
were buried on St Patrick's Isle but their bodies might have been moved before
the Vikings came. 'Lancelot' lived on the Isle of Man for fifteen years and … well,
you get the picture. I present the names of the various characters above in
inverted commas because none of them has ever been proved to have existed and
all are almost certainly more mythical than historical.

Some of the newspapers loved it. The (now defunct) *Peel City Guardian* gave
it multi-page coverage in several of its editions, others followed, and even the
UK's *Daily Telegraph* covered the story – but with a sensible degree of scepticism.
Local opinion was divided between those who wished to maintain the distinction
between fact and unsubstantiated legend and those who felt that – true or false –
the story should be plugged for all it was worth in aid of a failing tourist industry.
Why let the facts get in the way of a good story? And why should Glastonbury and
Tintagel have it all?

One of the critics (guilty!) pointed out that Arthur and 'King Arthur' were two
entirely different characters. Arthur was a Dark-Age Celtic warlord who
attempted to hold back the westward expansion of the Anglo-Saxon English in
the late fifth or early sixth century, and about whom very little is known, apart
from his name and a few very hazy details of a couple of battles he may have
fought. We do not know the names of his wife (or even that he had one) or of his
family or comrades in arms. 'King Arthur', on the other hand, together with
'Queen Guinevere', 'Lancelot' and the 'Knights of the Round Table' are the stuff of
legend, the fictional creation of *medieval* writers (Geoffrey of Monmouth *et al*)
who lived seven centuries or more after the real Arthur's death. The debate
dragged on. Writer and broadcaster Bill Grundy came over to the island to seek
out the story – a self-confessed sceptic but willing to be convinced. His report in
the *Daily Telegraph* ended with the commendably restrained conclusion: 'All sorts
of archaeological remains have been found in and around the castle. None of them
has proved Dr Goodrich's findings, so, disappointed, I went home.' More than
twenty years on, all is silence.

Before 1750, St Patrick's Isle was a true island, although it was possible to wade across the shallows from the west side of the river mouth at low water and in calm weather. Sir George Moore was responsible for the construction of the causeway across the divide, and this was widened in 1880, when the West Quay was built. In more recent times – up to about thirty years ago – pedestrians could cross the river-mouth by the small ferry which was rowed across between the town's East Quay and the base of the steps below the castle gate-house. At low tide, a slatted footway was stretched out so that pedestrians could cross the mud unsoiled. But, with the growth in car ownership, people preferred to drive round by the road-bridge at the top end of the harbour, and the ferry operation became uneconomic. Today, not far from the old ferry location, a permanent footbridge (opening to permit harbour traffic) is in place, together with a water-retention scheme for the inner harbour, similar to that installed at Douglas. There are plans to develop the inner harbour as a yacht marina.

Although Peel has experienced much modern residential expansion to the south and east, the old town still exhibits much of its ancient character, with its network of narrow streets and lanes hemmed in by buildings of Creg Malin sandstone from a bygone age. In the north-west corner of the town, enclosed by the convergence of Shore Road with East Quay, Castle Street points directly towards the fortress which gave it its name, and to the point on the quay from which soldiers of the garrison were ferried across to the castle steps. On the west side of the market place, only the clock tower and east gable of St Peter's Church now remain; the graveyard has been cleared to form public open space, with the old headstones relocated around its periphery. Once the new parish church for Patrick had been completed in 1714, St Peter's retained that role for the parish of German until the new Kirk German, beside Derby Road in Peel, was commissioned in 1884.

On completion of the new Kirk German, there was a proposal that it should become the cathedral of the diocese. Indeed, its appearance does suggest that it was designed with such an aim in mind. It does not display the usual plain, rectangular form of the traditional Manx parish church. It is built in the Gothic style, of cruciform plan with transepts, and the arches of its nave are similar in style to those of the old cathedral. However, that aim – if such it was – was not to be fulfilled at the time and, in later years, there would be some jockeying for position among Manx clergy and laity, with varying opinions as to where a new cathedral should be.

In the interim, with the old cathedral on St Patrick's Isle now unusable, the chapel of St Nicholas, adjoining the Bishop's mansion house at Bishopscourt, in Michael, came to be regarded as the 'pro-cathedral' of the diocese. However, in 1974, the newly installed bishop, Vernon Nicholls, refused to live at Bishopscourt

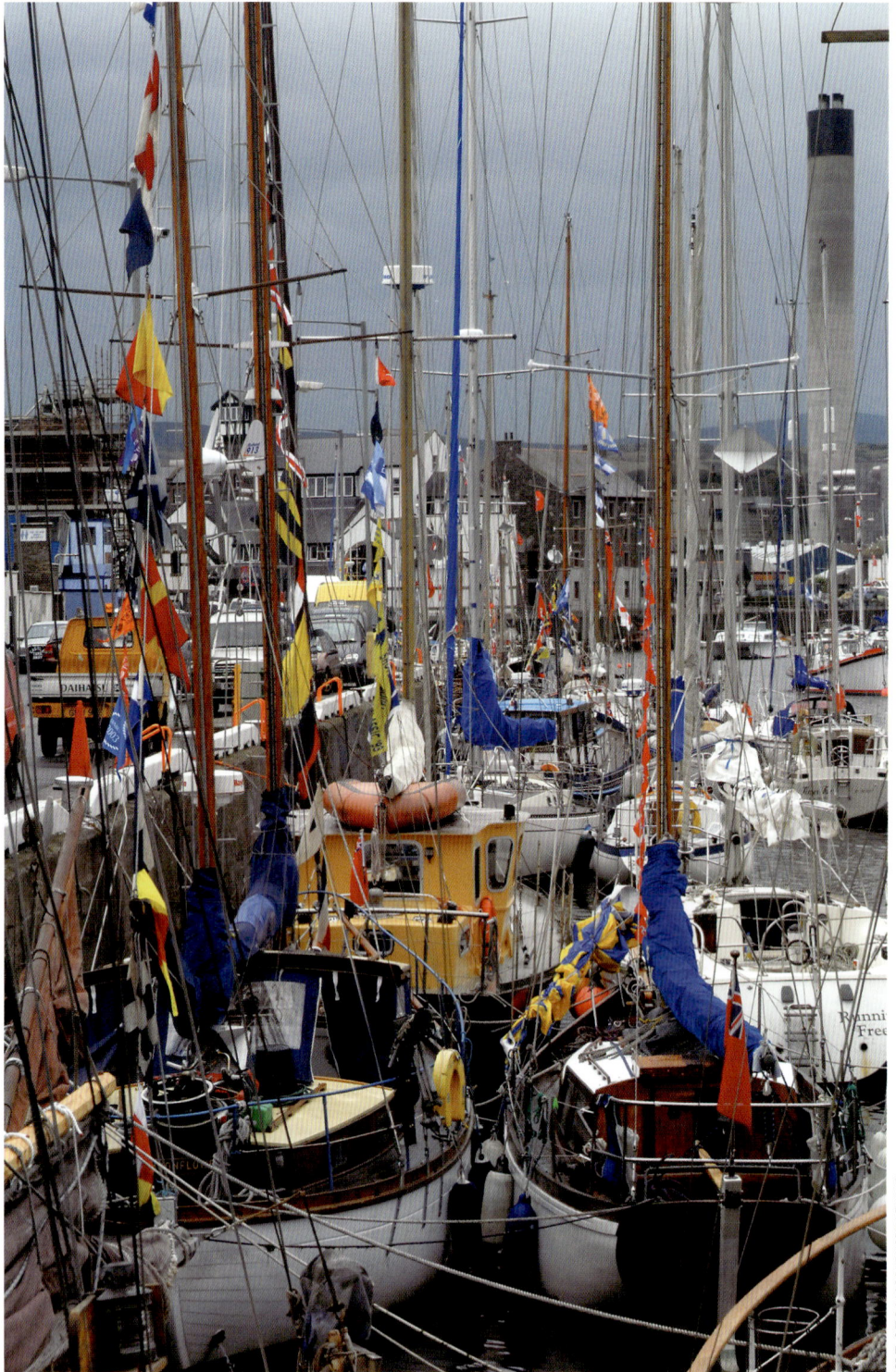

The Traditional Boat Rally, Peel

because of the size and condition of the place, and it was subsequently sold into private ownership by the Manx government. The chapel's status as the pro-cathedral then became untenable and, in 1980, Kirk German in Peel did indeed become the cathedral-church of the diocese, in addition to its being the parish church of German.

Further along Derby Road (to the east) stand the buildings and playing fields of the Peel Clothworkers' School, the primary school which is a lasting memorial to another of the town's favourite sons, Philip Christian (died 1652), who made his fortune in London, formed the Clothworkers' Company, and – not forgetting the town of his birth – left endowments for the establishment of a school, initially known as Christian's School. After a later annuity was received from the Clothworkers' Company, the school became known by its present name. It no longer occupies its earlier buildings, although they still exist in other use. Having spent the whole of his adult life away from the island, it is unlikely that, were it not for his bequests to the town, he would ever be remembered in Peel today. Down on the A1 Douglas Road, just outside the town boundary, the modern Queen Elizabeth II High School was completed in 1979 and officially opened by Her Majesty the Queen the following year, when she presided at the annual Tynwald ceremony at St John's.

Back in the old town, in Station Place, the former station building of the Isle of Man Railway now accommodates the House of Mannanan, the heritage centre and out-station of the Manx Museum which was described in Chapter 9. This attraction, and others, still draws visitors to the town during the season, although 'the season' throughout the isle is no longer what it was.

Every July, Peel jumps back 1,200 years in time to stage the annual Viking Festival, re-enacting the first Viking raid on the island, some time around the start of the ninth century. Replica Viking longships (which lie moored in the river for the rest of the year) are taken out to restage that first landing on the sandy shore of the bay. The 'Vikings' wade ashore from their ships, each raider adorned in a rather fanciful horned helmet (no authentic Viking helmet with horns has ever been found). They storm across the beach, pausing only to carry off local maidens who appear somewhat less reluctant than they might have been 1,200 years ago. The longships are also crewed through a series of races off the shore.

The Viking Festival was started in 1961. A more recent innovation in the Peel nautical scene is the Traditional Boat Rally, in which an impressive fleet of old sailing boats, and replicas, assemble for a social gathering and a day of racing. Started in 1991, the rally occupies a weekend in late July. The completion of the water-retention scheme in the harbour has found favour with visiting sailors, and has seemingly brought increasing numbers to the event. Elsewhere in the isle (apart from Douglas), proposals for water-retention schemes and marinas seem to bring little but objections. Meanwhile, over on St Patrick's Isle, as noted in Chapter 9, there is always Shakespeare in the Castle.

GERMAN

From the boundaries of Peel and Patrick, the parish of German stretches north-eastward for just over 4 miles, bounded on the north-west by the sea, and in the south-east by the parish of Marown and a small part of Braddan. In the north-east, its border with Michael strikes a somewhat irregular line, following a succession of watercourses from the coastal glen of Glion Shellan, half a mile north-east of Lady Port and the Devil's Elbow (the 180-degree hairpin on the A4 coast-road), and heading generally south-eastward until it comes up against the Braddan boundary at the head of Glion Gill. In doing so, it encloses the Skerrisdale farmsteads, the TT landmark of Cronk-y-Voddy and the headwaters of the River Neb/Rhenass.

German is in a unique position among the Manx parishes, being the only one having its parish church located in a neighbouring town – through the sequence of events described earlier. Of course, in the days prior to the formal establishment of the administrative town districts in the late nineteenth century, most of the land now occupied by the town of Peel was an integral part of the parish of German. The dedication of the parish and its church almost certainly relates to the Irish saint, German (which would have been pronounced with a hard 'G'), although there has been some confusion clouding the issue for at least 800 years. The confusion arose over the similarly named cleric of the Roman Church, St Germain of Auxerre, and, from as early as 1231, when Bishop Simon received a papal bull from Gregory IX, the suspicion has persisted that the Vatican was attempting to displace the early Irish saint from the dedication, in favour of the Roman one. St Germain's dedication date was 30 July but, in Man, there are early records of the patronal fair being held on St German's Day, 13 July (24 July after the adoption of the Gregorian calendar in 1752). The rendering 'Germain' sometimes crops up today, and is referred to as an 'alternative' spelling. It is perhaps time that someone stated unequivocally that St Germain was not at all germane to the dedication of the ancient Kirk German.

Having arrived in German on this journey around the island, we have now entered the first of the more sparsely populated northern parishes. The only significant centre of population in German is down on the southern boundary of the parish, at St John's. And here we meet another point of uniqueness, in German, for, not only does its parish church double as the cathedral-church of the diocese of Sodor and Man, but the church at the heart of the village of St John's – the Royal Chapel of St John – is the national church of the Isle of Man. It plays a unique role in the annual Tynwald assembly, and its dedication is to St John the Baptist. The dedication is thought to have some connection with the Hospitallers or Knights of St John of Jerusalem. There were two days in the old Manx calendar that were dedicated to hospitals, one being *Laa'l Spitlhin Souree*, the 'summer festival day of hospitals', on 18 May, and the other, *Laa'l Spitlhin Geuree*, the 'winter festival day of hospitals', on 18 November. On each occasion, a court and fair were held at St John's. (There also seems to have been some sort of hospital connection preserved in one of the street-names in Peel: *Boilley Spittal*, 'place of the hospital'.)

As the national church, the Royal Chapel of St John plays an integral part in the proceedings of Tynwald Day, on or about 5 July. Prior to the start of proceedings on Tynwald Hill, a service is held in the Royal Chapel, following which the dignitaries process to their places on the hill. The proceedings on the hill have been described in Chapter 9. At the end of the outdoor agenda, the procession returns to the Royal Chapel, where the members of Tynwald assemble to consider any business remaining. In this, the church is unique for two reasons: it is (to the best of my knowledge) the only Christian church in which a parliament assembles to conduct business, and which contains an unconsecrated area of seating for the parliamentary members, to accommodate the presence of any who are non-Christian. The National War Memorial stands adjacent to the Royal Chapel.

Immediately to the east of the church, the Tynwald National Park and Arboretum was established to mark the millennium of Tynwald in 1979. An attractive combination of informal parkland, gardens and pond, it contains a variety of tree species donated by nations world-wide, and planted by such dignitaries as King Olav of Norway, two presidents of Iceland and three successive governors of Man – Sir John Paul, Sir Nigel Cecil and Sir Laurence New – as well as the Commonwealth Parliamentary Association and various business groups. The wet area supports a burgeoning population of aquatic birdlife.

The Arboretum and Tynwald fair-field lie sandwiched between the A1 Peel–Douglas road and the almost parallel A20 Poortown road. Also sandwiched in there is the Tynwald Mill Centre, where the refurbished buildings of the former woollen mill house a wide variety of arts and crafts businesses. In an area where a succession of mills had exploited the energy-source of the River Neb, the last (electrically powered) mill was built in about 1920.

On the west side of Tynwald Hill, the narrow by-road which leads north from the A1 to the A20 was widened in the mid-nineteenth century, cutting through a hitherto unknown early Bronze-Age cist burial. The exposure is still visible in the roadside hedge. On reaching the Poortown road (where the motorist must turn right or left), straight ahead lies an unsurfaced track which ascends northward and, in less than a mile, joins the narrow Staarvey road, which then climbs again to 'ride the ridge' north-eastward. This is the Bishop's Road, the southern end of which we met earlier, where it crosses the Monks' Bridge in Ballasalla. Not only did this bridle-road provide the means by which the abbots of Rushen could travel to their abbey-lands in other parts of the isle, it also gave the Bishop a direct route to the abbey, with Tynwald Hill conveniently *en route*, from his mansion house at Bishopscourt.

Beyond the parish boundary and into Michael, the way reverts again to an unsurfaced track as it descends into Glen Mooar (passing the keeill-site of Cabbal Pheric ('Patrick's Chapel') and Spooyt Vane ('white spout') waterfall in the glen), then joins the modern A4 highway at Berk, on the southern outskirts of Kirk Michael and 2 miles short of Bishopscourt. A quieter way for today's pedestrian to cover those 2 miles is to take to the former railway line, to the point where, in more recent times, the Bishop had his own platform for joining and leaving the train.

From the heights of the Bishop's Road (although it never climbs above the 600-foot (180m) contour), it is possible to see much of the remainder of the parish of German. To the east (although so low as to be hidden beneath the shoulder of the hill), the TT course, having twisted and turned its way from Ballacraine and through Glen Helen, climbs steeply up Creg Willey's Hill before levelling out along the Cronk-y-Voddy straight, ready for the plunge down Barregarrow Hill and into Kirk Michael. And above Glen Helen, the empty slopes of Greeba Mountain, Slieau Ruy and Beary Mountain lead the eye round to the equally empty hills of Michael.

To the west, the Lhergy road – another narrow thoroughfare which heads north from the A20 – meets the A4 Kirk Michael coast-road at Knocksharry. Sometimes called the Knocksharry road, but more commonly 'the Switchback', it runs almost rod-straight for much of its length. Its more commonly used name arises from the pronounced 'roller-coaster' nature of its contours, which some-times entice the more adventurous motorist to travel at a speed which is somewhat in excess of prudent, bearing in mind that the troughs between the crests are such that the driver on this single-track road is frequently unaware of oncoming traffic.

On following the Switchback northward, with broad views over the coastal lowlands to the west, one first passes the Giant's Grave at Kew (one of several giants' graves in Man), and then the Giant's Fingers at Lhergydhoo. The former (Manx *Lhiabbee ny Foawr*) is a group of sandstone boulders which marks the site of a Neolithic chambered cairn, similar to those at Cashtal yn Ard and King Orry's Grave. The Giant's Fingers (Manx *Meir ny Foawr*) are a group of large quartz boulders (seven of them), foreign erratics caught up in the bottom layers of glacier ice and stranded there in the last big thaw. Their arrangement suggests that they were used to form the basis of a megalithic burial mound; they are visible for miles from the west and south-west. Myth and legend still abound concerning their presence there, tales of giants and the throwing of stones (i.e. huge boulders), and of the misfortunes befalling those who try to move them.

Down on the coast, one of the few points with public access to the shore in German is Gob y Deigan, 'point of the dagon'. A dagon was a particular type of Peel fishing-smack, and it is possible that the point gained its name from a wreck which occurred there. By this stage of our journey, the sandstone of Peel has been left behind and we are back with the Manx slates, finely brecciated to form crush conglomerate intersected by dykes of greenstone. There is an interesting system of caves nearby, accessible only at low tide, and many standing rocks on the shore have been worn into top-heavy 'mushroom' shapes by centuries of wave action. The shore here is reached by public footpath from Lynague, near the junction of the A4 with the narrow Ballabooie road from the Cronk-y-Voddy crossroads. There are two other secluded little sandy/shingly coves accessible from the A4, both a mile or so south of Gob y Deigan: White Strand (Manx *Straie Vane*) and Cain's Strand.

Resuming our journey to the north, whether by A3 or A4 (from Ballacraine or Peel, respectively), both roads roll onward and eventually converge at Kirk Michael, in the next sheading.

CHAPTER FOURTEEN

The Rural North-West

And so we arrive at the second of the island's sheadings to take its name from one of its constituent parishes. The sheading of Michael comprises the parishes of Michael, Ballaugh and Jurby. In terms of parliamentary constituencies, it is the only one of the island's ancient sheadings to have remained unaltered as a House of Keys constituency throughout the years of public franchise since 1866. All other sheading-constituencies have seen changes, either through the switching of parishes between constituencies (e.g. Marown from Middle to Glenfaba and then back again, and the formation of Onchan and Malew & Santon as separate constituencies) or by the formation of the town constituencies from their former sheadings. The sheading of Michael now votes one member into the House of Keys, although, in earlier times, it did return two.

PARISH OF MICHAEL

The parish of Michael is configured in very similar fashion to its southern neighbour, German. It is bounded in the north-west by the sea, in the south-west by German, to the south-east by Braddan and a small part of Lezayre, and to the north-east by the boundary with Ballaugh. The latter boundary meets that of Lezayre beneath the impounded waters of the Sulby reservoir, then wanders vaguely north-westward across the hills of Michael and Ballaugh until it finds the head of Bishopscourt Glen. It descends, following (almost) the course of the Bishopscourt stream, under the A3 Ramsey road, whence the stream flows sluggishly through the flatlands beyond. Then, just as the stream turns south-west to flow through Glen Trunk to the shore, the parish boundary turns away north, eventually to reach the coast on the north side of Orrisdale Head.

The parish, like its northern neighbour, is divided between a fertile coastal plain to the west and the rising hill-country to the east, where free-ranging sheep

496

partake of the rough-grazing, and various species of wildlife roam and flit more or less unhindered. The extent of the coastal strip in Michael is rather less than that of Ballaugh, where the northern plain broadens out towards the north.

In Michael, at least, there has never been any confusion or doubt over the dedication of the parish and its church. As early as the year 1240, *Chronicon* is referring to *Ecclesia Sancti Michaelis*, giving clear recognition to the Archangel Michael. The name 'Kirk Michael' appears in a Manx statute of 1422, after the Norse *kirk* had become established in the Manx vocabulary. Today, the parish is known as 'Michael' and 'Kirk Michael' is reserved for the village. From 1905 until 1989, when (for reasons explained in Chapter 6) the village district was in being as a separate administrative entity, it also was known as 'Michael' but the whole of the parish has reverted to a single local government district (Michael), and the non-administrative village is Kirk Michael.

Kirk Michael is the only significant centre of population in the parish. At the 1986 census (which was the last before the recombination of village and parish), it had a population of only 576, and was always the smallest of the island's five administrative villages. The old village was strung out along Main Road (the A3), north and south from St Michael's Church, with a western branch along Station Road. More modern residential estates have broadened the village to east and

The lych-gate at Kirk Michael

west, but mostly westward. Such developments, combined with a steady eastward retreat of the cliff-line through coastal erosion, have brought increasing calls for a protection scheme for the half-mile of coast between Glen Wyllin and Glen Balleira, the two glens which descend to the shore from the village.

St Michael's Church stands in the centre of the village. Its impressive lych-gate was built to protect the island's largest collection of Norse cross-slabs from the worst of the weather, but they were moved inside the church years ago. It is here that we come across the tenth-century slab carved by Gaut Björnson, whose runic inscription boastfully proclaims that 'Gaut made this and all in Maun'. A second slab bearing his name is displayed in Kirk Andreas, but other sculptors later developed his style of intricate, interlaced decoration to form a Gaut-led 'school' in the monumental art. Other notable cross-slabs in the Michael collection are the massive tenth/eleventh-century Joalf's Cross, standing almost 7 feet (2.1m) clear of the ground, and the handsome, early eleventh-century Dragon Cross. But, for me, the most intriguing piece in the whole collection is the so-called 'Crucifixion' slab from the late tenth or early eleventh century. It does, indeed, bear a superficial resemblance to the Calf Crucifixion Stone, unearthed on the Calf of Man in the eighteenth century. But, whereas the Calf stone depicts Christ firmly fixed to the cross with broad-headed nails, and with the spear-bearer poised to pierce His

Bishopscourt, former residence of Bishops of Sodor and Man

side, the figure on the Michael slab has no such nails, and appears to be stepping down from the cross (and is there a hint of a gesture – a nonchalant shrug of the shoulders – as He does so?), whilst the upper limb of the cross is flanked by a winged angel and a cock proclaiming the *Resurrection*. This is no mere crucifixion.

The church itself is of no great architectural or historical interest, having been built in 1835. It replaced the earlier church which had served the parish since the twelfth century and a small remnant of which still stands in the churchyard. Nearby are the graves of five of the island's bishops: the good and popular Bishop Wilson (who led the diocese for fifty-seven years), his immediate successor Mark Hildesley, then George Mason, Claudius Crigan and Leonard Thornton-Duesbery.

From the time of Bishop Simon (enthroned 1229), a long line of bishops resided at Bishopscourt, just over a mile north of Kirk Michael, until Bishop Vernon Nicholls refused to live there in 1974. In its original form, the dwelling stood as a fortress – a square peel-tower surrounded by a moat. Parts of the tower, commonly but erroneously known as 'King Orry's Tower', form the oldest portion of the present building, and the line of the moat can still be seen in the grounds. Over the centuries, the building developed into a fortified mansion. By the time of Bishop Wilson's arrival in 1698, the place was in a sad state of disrepair, and he set about its restoration and the laying-out of the grounds. This involved much planting, including his 'twelve apostles' – lime trees – of which one, dubbed 'the Judas tree', rejected all nurture, and wilted and died. The present mansion and grounds are largely Bishop Wilson's creation, although there are later additions. The chapel, adjoining the north end of the dwelling, was erected by Bishop Crigan (replacing an earlier one) and extended by Bishop Powys into its present form in 1858.

Following the final decline of the old St German's Cathedral into ruination, the Bishopscourt chapel (with the unusual dedication to St Nicholas) was adopted as the 'pro-cathedral' of the diocese. Occasional services were held there and it contained accommodation for the ceremonial presence of the bishop and the stalls of the chapter. Access to the chapel was internally, from the ground floor of the tower, where an ante-room was the official meeting-place of the Manx Convocation. When Bishopscourt was sold into private ownership, continued use of the chapel for these purposes obviously became untenable, and cathedral status was transferred to the parish church of St German, in Peel. By the time of Bishop Nicholls's refusal to live at Bishopscourt in 1974, parts of the dwelling had again deteriorated into a damp and unsatisfactory condition. A succession of private owners has restored and maintained the building as a fine and comfortable mansion. Interestingly, the parish boundary passes through the building; the dwelling is situated in Michael, the chapel in Ballaugh.

On the opposite side of the road, the boundary between the two parishes follows the course of Bishopscourt Glen – but it does so hesitantly, stepping from side to side of the stream as it goes. Just inside the entrance to the glen, a large mound bears a tablet commemorating a naval skirmish between British and French vessels, off this north-west coast of the island in 1760. The battle was watched from the cliff-top by Bishop Hildesley, as the British flotilla under Captain John Eliot in HMS *Aeolus* routed the French, who were commanded by Francois Thurot in the *Belle Ile*. The *Belle Ile* was wrecked in the fray, and some of its timbers came ashore below Bishopscourt, whereupon the Bishop had them set up on the mound in his glen and named it 'Mount Aeolus'. A brace of cannon was also installed there but these were stolen in the 1980s and never recovered. The body of Francois Thurot was cast up on the coast of Wigtownshire and was buried in the churchyard at Kirkmaiden, beside the shore of Luce Bay. He is still remembered in Man today; some of the timbers from his ship are said to have been used in the construction of a dwelling in Bride. Erected in 1809, it is still known as Thurot Cottage.

The farmland round about Bishopscourt, almost equally spread between the two parishes, was part of the Bishop's Barony, known today as the Bishop's Demesne. The Bishop's glen itself is nicely maintained by the DAFF as a Manx National Glen. Half a mile further along the A3 (in Ballaugh parish), a watery depression in a roadside field, known as the Bishop's Dub, originated as a post-glacial kettle-hole, formed by the melting of ice beneath a covering layer of glacial debris. Today, it is a very shallow pond, the lateral extent of which varies greatly with the seasons; in a prolonged summer drought, it may dry up completely.

The bishop also had his own gibbet. By the Confirmation Charter of the Bishopric of Man, granted by Thomas Stanley III, second Earl of Derby, in 1502, the bishops had 'the power of imprisoning and of releasing the imprisoned, and of the gibbet on their own lands'. The site of the gibbet is still known as Cronk y Crogher, the 'hill of the hangman'. The 'hill' is, in fact, no more than a slight mound hidden behind the hedge opposite the junction of the Orrisdale road with the A3, on the northern outskirts of Kirk Michael village.

Back in the centre of the village, the *Mitre Hotel* is reputed to be the island's oldest inn, having been catering for the needs of Michael folk and wayfarers since 1786. It is the epitome of the old coaching inn, and it is easy to imagine its broad forecourt hosting a gathering of horse-drawn coaches and farmers' carts, in place of the current ranks of modern cars. There is record from 1880 of the daily stage-coach service which made a scheduled stop at the *Mitre*.

To the rear of the pub is a field that was once the Michaelmas Fair Field. The Michaelmas Fair was one of the two great national fairs (the other, of course, being the midsummer gathering at St John's). This was the fair at which farm

Kirk Michael fire station, the former railway station

workers were hired for the coming year. Each worker taken on received a shilling (5p) from his new master, from which point the bargain was regarded as binding. The fair was held on the feast-day of St Michael, 29 September on the old calendar but, after 1752, 10 October was adopted. Here again, when the calendar was corrected by advancing all dates forward by eleven days, the correction was immediately negated by moving such feast-days back by the same amount. The last Michaelmas Fair was held in 1940.

The proximity of the Bishop's residence at Bishopscourt also accounted for the fact that a village as small as Kirk Michael possessed its own courthouse. Although no courts have been held in the village since the early 1950s, the building still stands, a rectangular, crenallated edifice bordering the south side of the *Mitre Hotel*'s forecourt. It dates from 1835, replacing an earlier one of 1766, and is now privately owned.

The railway reached Kirk Michael in 1879 and closed in 1965. The station buildings still stand beside Station Road – in the guise of the local fire station – and the portion of track between Glen Wyllin and Rhencullen now forms part of the *Raad ny Foillan*. Back on Main Road, opposite the Isle of Man Bank, two adjoining dwellings now known as Railway House and Railway Cottage were once the *Railway Hotel*. Since the 1920s this former public house has been two private ones.

Back in the days of the railway, after the Manx Northern Railway was amalgamated with the Isle of Man Company's system in 1904, the latter company developed the lower portion of Glen Wyllin, on the southern edge of the village, as a pleasure park, equipped with amusements, a boating lake and easy access to the beach. In its heyday, it was a venue to which both summer visitors and Manx folk flocked on the steam trains, which disgorged their passengers at the village station, and the trippers would file along the 300 yards of footpath beside the track to reach their destination. But the age of the car brought the demise of the railway and, during a period in private ownership, Glen Wyllin subsided into dereliction. However, it was acquired by the then Isle of Man Forestry Board in 1979 and is now maintained by the DAFF as a Manx National Glen. Approximately half of it is leased by the Michael District Commissioners and operated as a camp site, a purpose for which its sheltered location makes it admirably suited. But its northern skyline has been ruined by modern development along the crest of the *broogh*.

Yet there is another side to Glen Wyllin. The section described above, descending seaward from the A4 Peel road, is maintained for the purposes of amenity and leisure. On the east side of the road, the glen cleaves upward towards the hills, its stream flowing through the middle of a secluded residential hamlet. Here stands one of the two water-driven corn mills which gave Glen Wyllin ('mill glen') its name. The one which stands here among the cottages was much the older, listed in the earliest complete manorial roll of 1511–15. Its site is readily identified today by *Mill House*; the mill building stands beside the dwelling, and its leat follows the east side of the narrow, unsurfaced road which climbs into the upper section of the glen, known there as Cooil Dharry ('oak nook'). The second mill, Corjeag's Mill, stood down near the seaward end of Shore Road, where the sea encroached nearer, year by year, until the building was taken down in 1978, before it could fall over the edge. Shore Road now comes to an abrupt end at the cliff-top.

On the north side of the stream in Glen Wyllin hamlet, a brewery was operating in former times, just one of many small breweries that existed in the island in those days. But the growth of the large commercial breweries in the nineteenth century brought their day to its close.

'Glen Wyllin' is a relatively modern name for the glen. For well over two centuries before 1766, it was 'Bordall' or 'Borodall', from the Norse *Borgardalr*, meaning 'fort dale'. In the days of Watch and Ward, the night watch for the parish was kept down by the shore, at the mouth of the glen. It is highly likely that night-watches were also mustered at Glen Mooar, Glen Balleira and Glen Trunk – all convenient places for insurgents to come ashore.

Near the north end of Kirk Michael village, standing back from the road in a picturesque expanse of parkland, the Whitehouse mansion has been associated with several worthies of Manx history. A property of that name is recorded in the diocesan register for 1688. In 1815, it became the home of Captain John Quilliam, of Trafalgar fame, although it seems that he never owned the place; he died there in 1829. The property was purchased in 1889 by Joseph Mylchreest (1837–96), who became known as 'the diamond king'. Having started his working life as a carpenter in Peel, he went off to seek his fortune in many countries around the world. He tried prospecting for gold in Australia but was more successful in discovering diamonds in South Africa, where he actually made his fortune by selling out to the de Beers company for (what was then) an enormous sum.

Mylchreest returned to his native isle in 1888, acquired the Whitehouse estate, and set about reconstructing and enlarging the house. He also made good use of his wealth for charitable purposes and for the improvement of agriculture. He died, relatively young, in 1896. On the opposite side of the road, stands another large house (though not of mansion proportions) – Whiteholm – built for Mylchreest's daughter, Ada, who was a singer of some repute in the 1930s.

A few yards further north, the stone-built row of Whitehouse Cottages stands beside the main road, backing onto the Whitehouse lands. Although now privately owned, the cottages were originally built to house the labourers who worked the farmlands of the Whitehouse estate. At the 1861 census, there were twenty-six men employed there, which indicates a substantial farm in Manx terms.

The traveller approaching Kirk Michael from the south, along the A3 section of the TT course, will, about half a mile short of the village, pass a small hill on the right which is now known as Cronk Urleigh but was earlier called *Reneurling*. The meaning of the name has rather dubiously been given as 'hill of the eagle' or (from its similarity with an Irish place-name) 'hill of the slaughter'. It is extremely doubtful that eagles ever nested here and, if the second translation is correct, it must relate to an event all knowledge of which is now lost to us. One fanciful attribution to the eagle was given by the Rev. John Crellin, in his *Description of Kirk Michael in the Year 1774*, in which he described a tradition among his parishioners relating that the Romans of Julius Caesar visited the island and raised their eagle standard on this hill. However, although the Romans of the day were well aware of the island's existence, Caesar's own account of his brief incursion into southern Britain in 54BC shows that he came no further north than what is now Essex or Hertfordshire. Perhaps those eighteenth-century Michael folk were confused by the presence on the isle of another Julius Caesar – a scholar of the old Castletown Grammar School; there is a wall plaque in Kirk Malew commemorating him as 'a Vertuous Youth, esteemed for his Academick Learning'. He died in 1739, at the age of twenty-three.

An event which certainly did occur on this hill in Michael happened in 1422, when 'The Court of all the Tennants and Commons of Man, holden at Kirk Michaell, [assembled] upon the Hill of Reneurling', this according to an account in Mills's *Manx Statutes* (c 1832). This was an assembly of the national Tynwald, presided over by Sir John Stanley II, the second of the Stanley Lords of Man and the first to visit the isle. The purpose of the gathering was to proclaim some of the earliest Manx statutes, following a period of unrest. At an earlier assembly in the same year, the newly appointed governor, John Walton, had been driven from the hill while holding a court of justice there, by dissidents who planned to kill him. He and his party were forced to take refuge in the parish church. At the second assembly, under Sir John Stanley, the miscreants were arraigned before the court and condemned to death.

It was at this Tynwald that Sir John Stanley required eight clerics, namely the Bishop of Man, the Abbott of Rushen, the Prior of Douglas, the priors of Whithorn in Galloway and St Bede in Copeland, and the abbots of Furness, Bangor and Sabal, all being the holders of ecclesiastical lands in Man, to attend the gathering and declare fealty to the Lord of Man. The last five (those from outside the isle) failed to turn up, and it was decided by the deemsters that, unless they presented themselves within forty days, their lands in Man would be forfeit and would pass into the Lord's holding. It is presumed that the two abbots from the north of Ireland, at least, did attend within the specified time, for the holdings of the Barony of Bangor and Sabal continued in being for many years thereafter.

Kirk Michael is the only sizeable village on the whole of the 30 miles of coast which curves a lonely path northward from Peel, round the Point of Ayre, then south to Ramsey. With the village as its centre of population, the parish of Michael spreads out to north, east and south, being constrained in the west by the sea. Anyone approaching the parish from the south along the TT course will come to the Cronk-y-Voddy crossroads, where the tendency is to drive straight on. If, however, the right turn is taken and the narrow by-road is followed into the hills, one eventually arrives at Little London. And if you then search expectantly for some microcosm of the British capital city, there may be mild surprise at finding no more than a handful of scattered cottages and a couple of farms. Mains water did not arrive until a few years ago.

The original name was *Gliontan*, meaning 'little glen', which is precisely what it is; it is joined here by the wild and lonely Glion Gill ('Gill's glen'), which slices down from the slopes of Colden. In later times, when the meaning of the diminutive *tan* had been lost, an additional diminutive in Manx was tagged on as a suffix, giving *Gliontan veg*. Later still, when the English language was beginning to replace the Manx, the Gaelic suffix was replaced with the English prefix; hence

Little Gliontan, and the similarity between it and the present name tells the rest of the story.

Following the Little London road on to the north brings us to its junction with the B10 Brandywell road and, if we turn east and follow it for a couple of miles, we come to the *actual* Brandywell, *not* the landmark on the mountain section of the TT course which has usurped the name. Brandywell Cottage stands beside the junction of the B10 and the minor Druidale road, and the well (now enclosed with brick walling and capped with a concrete slab) stands beside the B10, just a few yards further east. It was sometimes known as the 'Branding Well'. This was a site where, at the time of the annual round-up of hill-sheep, shepherds would gather to brand their flocks. The story also goes that, as an adjunct to this gathering, enterprising individuals would appear and retail hot punch to all who desired it. Hence, the brandy and the branding went hand in hand. The old Manx name for the well was *Chibbyr y phunch*, 'the well of the punch'. At the same time as the branding, the male lambs were castrated, and all of this went on under the northern slope of *Slieau Maggle*, the 'mountain of the testicles'. Accordingly, an alternative Manx name for the well was *Chibbyr slieau ny maggle*.

It is sometimes said that Brandywell Cottage is the most isolated dwelling in Man, but there is another cottage, within 1½ miles of this spot, which is surely

Looking east from Slieau Dhoo, Snaefell rises beyond the Sulby reservoir

more deserving of that accolade. If, from Brandywell, we venture along the narrow
road which descends along the west flank of Druidale, at Montpelier we pass that
other cottage – probably without ever knowing it is there. It stands down by the
edge of a plantation, at the end of an unmade track leading eastward off this
narrow ribbon of tarmac. Now, in the depth of a hard winter, that really *is* isolated.

The Druidale road rolls on to the north; after dropping down to the little tributary glen at Montpelier (which cradles some lovely and varied woodland), it
crosses the old ford (which is now bridged) and climbs out onto open moorland,
where an ancient lime kiln stands up on the western slope (it must have been one
hell of a haul to get blocks of stone up here). Beyond the parish boundary, this
narrow strip of road swings west and descends into Ballaugh Glen.

But, before that final descent, the views to the east are fine and broad, across
the waters of the Sulby reservoir to the brooding summit of Snaefell and the lofty
ridge to North Barrule. To the west, the view is shut off by the ridge of three peaks,
from Sartfell (Norse: 'dark mountain') to Slieau Dhoo (Manx: 'dark mountain'),
with Slieau Freoaghane (Manx: 'bilberry mountain') standing between. But once
out of the car and onto that ridge, the western aspect is clear, across the coastal
strip and Kirk Michael village to the long and lonely curve of the north-west coast.
These hills of Michael are ideal walking country and, if the pedestrian wishes to
extend his outing into neighbouring Ballaugh, or further into Lezayre – well, there
is a complete absence of border controls.

The coast is equally inviting. If arriving from the south by the A4 coast-road, the
first access to the shore is by way of Glen Mooar, by which stage the nature of the
coast is already on the change. A mile to the south, the hard-rock coastline of the
pre-glacial island has begun its slant away from the present shore, heading initially
north-east towards Ballaugh village, and leaving us with a coastal plain of soft,
glacial till which grows steadily wider as we travel north. Its seaward edge is, for
the most part, a steadily eroding cliff-line formed of a base-layer of boulder clay,
topped with strata of post-glacial sands and flood-gravels. And on top of it all lie
several feet of blown sand which has been whipped up from the shore by the
prevailing westerlies and deposited on the lands behind the cliff-top. As noted in
Chapter 2, the distance between each of the pair of bordering escarpments in the
lower reaches of Glen Mooar and Glen Wyllin gives impressive sign of the magnitudes of the flows descending these watercourses during the final post-glacial thaw.

Kirk Michael village has two access points to the coast; in addition to Glen
Wyllin on its southern edge, Glen Balleira descends to the shore from nearer the
centre of the village. *Balleira* is another of those composite names, with the Gaelic
balla prefixing the Norse *leira*, denoting the 'farm of the muddy river'. As we
continue coastwise to the north, the last glen in the parish of Michael is Glen
Trunk, which conveys the trickle of the Bishopscourt stream to the shore below

A deserted shore in Michael

Orrisdale. This was one of the locations where ships delivering limestone from the Castletown area would bring up at high tide, dump their cargoes into the shallows, and leave them to be carted away at low water. The Orrisdale lime kiln is a short distance up the glen.

The cliffs line out to the north and north-east, beyond Orrisdale Head, into Ballaugh and on towards Jurby, with a tide-line of plastic from a score of ships' galleys stretched along their feet (with milk cartons plainly declaring their Irish origins). The eroded cliffs still occasionally surrender their secrets from past millennia. The latest – a set of antlers from a giant deer which roamed the island upwards of 10,000 years ago – was unearthed from the cliff-face in 2005. The waters close off-shore are part of the annual migration route of the basking shark, the world's second-largest fish – second only to the whale-shark. Up to 250 sightings a year are reported in Manx waters, where they were first classified as a protected species. It is a unique experience – engendering a strangely comradely feeling – to find oneself swimming off this shore when the surrounding water is studded with their protruding dorsal fins. But, although their gaping mouths are of awesome proportions, they eat only plankton and krill, and so pose no threat to the human swimmer.

This is a lonely shore; perhaps one might see the occasional pedestrian walking the dog, but where are the children? Where are the nation's youth? Often, when strolling these deserted strands, my mind goes back to those musings of T. E. Brown in *Braddan Vicarage*: 'I wonder if in that far isle,/ Some child is growing now, like me/ …' And later:

> I wonder if to him the heath-clad mountain
> With crimson pigment fills the sensuous cells;
> If like full bubbles from an emerald fountain
> Gorse-bloom luxuriant wells;
> If God with trenchant forms the insolent lushness quells.

And later again:

> I wonder if some day he, chance-conducted,
> Attains the vantage of the utmost height,
> And, by his own discovery instructed,
> Sees grassy plain and cottage white,
> Each human sign and pledge that feeds him with delight.

If, by some freak of longevity, Brown were still living today, he could not fail to notice that few children are growing now as he did. I wonder: might he respond along the following lines?

> Off-shore from these eroded cliffs of clay,
> Great leviathans plough their foaming tracks;
> Towering, glowering walls of steel splay
> The marching ranks of waves where sailing smacks
> In our youth trawled the deep beyond the bay.
> On shore, the sands once pock-marked with our tracks,
> Cliffs we scaled, braving tumbling boulder clay,
> Stand pristine and deserted at our backs.
> Parents forbid such fraught pursuits today,
> And youth stays home, the internet to crack,
> TV to watch, computer games to play,
> Shielded from spuming waves and tides and wrack.
> No more daring today – oh, feet of clay –
> Than these faltering walls that fringe this bay.

BALLAUGH

If entry into the parish of Ballaugh is made by walking along the shore from Michael (which, admittedly, is not the usual route of entry), the first point at which we may leave the shore to explore the hinterland is The Cronk, where the Ballaugh stream makes its exit to the sea. The advantage of making this our point of entry is that it brings us directly to where the cottages of the old village (more of a hamlet, really) stand grouped around the old parish church of St Mary de Ballaugh. If the tide is too high to permit the trek along the beach, the same destination can be reached by following the narrow byways of the Orrisdale and Bollyn roads, which run near-parallel courses with the coast.

The parish and its church were dedicated to the Virgin Mary and identified in Pope Gregory IX's bull of 1231 as *Ecclesia Sanctae Mariae Ballaughe*. By 1648, Blundell, in his *History of the Isle of Man*, records 'Kirk Mary Ballaugh', whereas Feltham, in his *Tour Through the Isle of Mann* in 1798, spells it as 'Ballaff', possibly because that was (and is still) the manner of its pronunciation. But, on paper, the Manx 'gh' form has persisted. The old Gaelic name of *Balley ny loghey*, 'homestead

The ancient Kirk Mary de Ballaugh

of the lake', reflected the position of the settlement beside the shore of the *Dufloch*, the 'dark lake' which formed part of the Curragh area, which still – sponge-like – held much of the melt-water from the late-glacial thaw.

The parish is bounded in the west by the sea, to the south by Michael, and to east and north by Lezayre and Jurby. The boundary with Lezayre, starting beneath the waters of the Sulby reservoir, zigzags generally northward, following the ridge of the hills to Gob y Volley, descending to cross the TT course at Quarry Bends, and on through the mire of the Curragh. In the northern part of the Curragh, it encounters Jurby, whereupon it heads west to join the Killane River in its course to the sea.

The old church of St Mary stands as a particularly charming example of the traditional Manx parish church: small, plain and rectangular, but with external adornments which make it rather more interesting than the island norm. The arch above its open porch is built in the round, Norman style, and above it rises a tall, dome-capped bell-turret surmounted by a wind-vane. At each of the four external corners, a quoin in the same local stone rises to eaves height, to be topped with a slender, tapering pinnacle, all of which lends a touch of ornateness to a basically simple form. But perhaps the most immediately striking feature as one enters the churchyard from the A10 coast-road to Bride is the pair of drunkenly leaning gate-pillars – tall and square, each topped with a pyramidal witch's cap. They lean secretively towards each other like two ancient crones exchanging a juicy piece of gossip after morning service. From the evidence of old photographs and drawings, it would appear that they have been like that for very many years.

Inside the church, is the only ancient cross-slab to be found in the parish. A particularly interesting piece, possibly carved by Gaut Björnson or a later disciple of his school, this round-headed cross-slab was, according to its runic inscription, raised by Olaf Liotulfson to the memory of Ulf, his son. Local interest arises from the name *Liotulfson*; once the Norse suffix *son* was displaced by the Gaelic prefix *mac*, the result formed the root of the present Manx name Corlett; McCurleots and Corletts have held land in Ballaugh for countless generations. The church's ancient stone font bears the Manx inscription: *Ta un Chiarn, un Credjue, un Vashtey, un Jee as Ayr jeh ooilley*, 'There is one Lord, one Faith, one Baptism, one God and Father of all'.

Services are still held in Ballaugh Old Church but, as the modern village continued to grow around the A3 Ramsey road, 1½ miles inland, the old church was neither close enough to, nor large enough for, the expanding population. The 'new' parish church was completed in 1832. By the early nineteenth century, the population of the parish had grown to almost 1,500, and the arrival of the railway in 1879 gave additional impetus to the growth of the modern village. It is ironic that the present population of the parish is little more than half of its nineteenth-century peak, as the drift to the towns has continued to deplete the numbers of country-dwellers.

The ancient hamlet and the modern village are connected by the A10 which, having paralleled the coast from the north, turns inland at the Cronk to meet the A3 at the TT landmark of Ballaugh Bridge. Roughly halfway along, the former triangular village green sits beside the road at the Dollagh, where the parish fair was held on the feast-day of the Assumption of the Virgin Mary, 15 August until the change in the calendar, but moved to the 26th thereafter. 'Dollagh' is the modern form of *Dufloch*; hereabouts was the shoreline of that 'dark lake' which gave Ballaugh its name.

The Ballaugh stream, which crosses the foreshore at the Cronk, runs a parallel course with the road between the village and the Cronk, having passed beneath the TT course at Ballaugh Bridge. It begins life high up at the head of lonely Glen Dhoo, more than 2 miles to the south of Ballaugh village. In its final mile before passing under the bridge, it closely follows the line of the minor road which drops into Ballaugh Glen after crossing the hills from Brandywell.

A mile north-east of Ballaugh village, we are on the verge of that fascinating area of watery mire which is the Curragh. Its extent is much reduced from what it

A byway in the Curragh

once was. In the north of the island, this was the main receptacle for the melt-water rushing down from the hills during the late-glacial thaw. Once deposited onto the flat lands of the northern plain, the flood had no immediate way out – only by way of three long and tortuous watercourses: the Killane to the west, the Lhen to the north, and the Sulby to the east. It is doubtless the presence of the Sulby – the island's largest river – that has caused the Curragh's eastern fringes (which once extended well into Lezayre) to shrink back to a far greater extent than occurred in the north and west. The area continues to be subject to the drying-out processes today, both by the (now much slower) natural mechanisms and through improved drainage.

The relatively 'untamed' Curragh is now contained within a rectangle enclosed by four roads: the A3 as far as Sulby crossroads, the A14 to Sandygate, the A13 to the Cronk, and the B9 completing the circuit on the A3 at Ballacrye. The northern half of the rectangle is crossed by a few narrow byways – most of them surfaced, some sprouting a central strip of grass – which meander and twist through this wilderness of willow carr and scrub. Occasionally, one passes an isolated dwelling sitting in wondrous seclusion. You may even encounter a place called Lough Dhoo (that 'dark lake' again).

Much of the southern half of the rectangle is now occupied by the government-owned Curraghs Wildlife Park and the neighbouring nature reserve of the Manx Wildlife Trust at Close Sartfield. The Wildlife Park combines the twin aims of maintaining the natural wetland environment of the Curragh and for providing areas for exhibiting animal species from various parts of the world where climatic conditions do not differ too greatly from those of the Manx environment. The 'inmates' generally seem contented but, now and again, one will decide to seek pastures new. The pelican which flew to Scotland in 2006 was not the first to do so, and in 2003 one spent a couple of weeks in Ramsey (it probably made a nice break). And I am not unique in having encountered a wallaby loping along a road some miles outside the park. The Close Sartfield reserve is famous for its rampant displays of orchids in early June and for its adoption as a winter roosting site for the largest gathering of hen harriers in Europe.

The natural habitat of the Curragh is a combination of bog and marshy grass-land, supporting growths of birch woodland and willow scrub. It is an area in which the wanderer not familiar with the terrain could find himself lost and (liter-ally) in deep water. In the park and reserve areas, the visitor is guided through the wetter regions along a series of board-walks. The Curragh is internationally recognized as an outstanding example of a maintained wetland habitat, but there is potential for conflict. In the past, the drainage of lands bordering the Curragh for the improvement of agriculture has resulted in a lowering of the water table.

Also, it is inescapable that the slow, millennia-long process of natural drying-out continues, but this is accelerated by drainage improvements in the surrounding lands. In recognizing this, the DAFF has set aside a small annual fund to encourage neighbouring farmers and landowners to develop wetlands and hay meadows around the reserved areas, to restore the natural habitat and retard the drying process.

Outside the village and the Curragh, the parish of Ballaugh is largely agricultural, though extending southward into the hills. The Celtic roundhouse site of Cashtal Lajer stands out on the hill to the east of the village. From the TT landmark bridge, Ballaugh Glen heads south for a mile before transmuting into remote Glen Dhoo ('dark glen') and striking up into the hill country. Its seclusion seems enhanced by the flanking plantations, and a nature reserve of the Manx Wildlife Trust is located near its head. Up on the slopes to east and west, hill tracks lead across to the Druidale road and to the paths in the Michael hills to the south. But, here too, there is conflict. Inevitably – or so it seems today – the tracks are under increasing pressure from the off-road motoring fraternity, and there are sections which become so rutted that walkers and horse-riders have difficulty in traversing them.

The Carlane Mill seeks protection behind a wall of rubble

The Ballaugh coastline is relatively short – a little under 2 miles. Its northern terminator is the meagre outfall of the Killane River, where the old Carlane mill building – now modernized and extended as a dwelling – sits perilously close to the cliff-edge, behind a wall of rock and concrete rubble which, though providing protection in the short term, merely accentuates the continuing erosion on either side. 'Killane' and 'Carlane' are thought to be variations of the old Norse *Kjarrland*, meaning 'brushwood land', which would have been their description of the low woodland growth covering much of the Curragh. When one considers the number of Scandinavian personal and place names in the parish, intermingled with the Gaelic, it is surprising that only one Norse cross-slab (and not a single Celtic one) has ever been discovered here. Perhaps this reflects the extent to which the parish was still waterlogged and not amenable to settlement in those far-off times.

JURBY

The landward extent of the parish of Jurby is almost completely enclosed by the Killane River in the south and the Lhen in the east, the coastline completing a near-triangle. The two rivers today remain the only effective means of drainage from the Curragh, now that its eastern region has shrunk back sufficiently to remove it from any significant influence of the Sulby. As both rivers originate in the Curragh, and in very close proximity, they can be said to have a common source, though flowing from it in opposite directions. Although the contours of the land on either side of the Lhen suggest that it has always followed a course similar to the present one, various works to improve the flow by straightening have been carried out over the centuries. Possibly as a consequence of this, the watercourse is hardly ever referred to as a river, but always as the Lhen Trench, or just the Lhen. Beyond it, lie the parish of Andreas and a small part of Lezayre. It is probable that, in the latter stages of the last glaciation, when the glacier was melting back to the north and any northern exit from the Lhen was still blocked with ice, the flow of melt-water in the channel was in the reverse (southerly) direction and the only outlet for the flood was by way of the Killane.

The name of the parish may have come from the Scandinavian *Dyrabyr*, the 'homestead of the animals'. Jurby is the second of the Manx parishes to be dedicated to St Patrick. A record from 1291 has it as *Ecclesia Sancti Patricii de Dureby* and, in 1648, Blundell identifies Kirk Patrick of Jorby. The parish church and its churchyard (probably in common with those of most other Manx parishes) stand on an ancient pagan burial ground, and relatively modern graves now crowd in on an artificial mound which may mark a pagan burial of the Viking age.

The Jurby shore: a coastal defence measure lies like a crumpled toy

In its porch, St Patrick's at Jurby has on display an interesting number of Norse cross-slabs, and some Celtic ones, in marked contrast to the solitary example held in St Mary's at Ballaugh. One of the Norse slabs depicts a scene from the Sigurd saga of Scandinavian mythology (one of several slabs in the island to do so), in which Sigurd slays the dragon Fafni. In a panel beneath, Sigurd is seen roasting three slices of Fafni's heart, using his sword as a spit. On another cross-slab, Heimdall, the janitor of the gods, is shown blowing his massive horn to summon them to Ragnarök, to the last great conflict that will bring Valhalla and all things to an end, as predicted in Norse mythology. This legend forms part of the story told in Wagner's *Ring* cycle of operas.

The east end of St Patrick's churchyard is devoted to the graves of airmen who died while flying from RAF Jurby during the Second World War. They range in age from eighteen-year-olds from Britain and the Commonwealth to Polish veterans, some well into their forties. Many died in training accidents before they could enter the fray but, victims of war none the less, they rest within sight of the field from which they flew.

Although St Patrick's stands a quarter of a mile behind the eroding cliffs of Jurby Head, its tower already shows signs of distress, having developed a marked lean to seaward in the past several years. Along the base of the cliff, some years ago, an attempt was made to protect a coastal property from erosion by placing an orderly array of stone-filled gabion baskets along the cliff-foot. But, with the passage of time, the sand on which the barrier stood was scoured out by the sea, and the structure began to lean and tumble to seaward. Today, its disordered remains lie crumpled and useless like a child's discarded toy, and the cliff continues to retreat behind it as if it had never been there.

Less than a mile south of the church, Ballateare is the site of the Viking burial mound excavated by Dr Gerhard Bursu in 1946, revealing the coffin burial of a man, together with the skeleton of a young woman, the back of whose skull had been removed with a blow from a sharp instrument. The ground beneath and around the mound yielded evidence of an extensive cemetery from the Neolithic period. All of this evidence, together with the number of Celtic and Norse crosses on display in the church, strengthens the conclusion that the parish of Jurby was far more suitable for human settlement in those times than was the neighbouring Ballaugh.

Most of the development in Jurby since the Second World War has been concentrated around the old RAF airfield. Following its use as an officer-cadet training unit after the war, the RAF vacated the site in 1966. After its transfer to the Manx government, the former married quarters formed the basis of the Bretney and Threshold housing estates, and the collection of hangars and huts on the north side of the airfield became an industrial estate for small businesses. Thus was the village of Jurby born, and it developed to become the main centre of population in the parish. In addition to the public house, which has been there since RAF days, shopping facilities and a modern primary school have been added. The DLGE has a plan for further residential development, involving more than 100 new houses. On the west side of the airfield, the island's new prison, completed in 2007, replaced the old Victorian institution in Douglas.

Although the airfield is no longer used as such (except by a handful of light aircraft), its runways and perimeter track are in regular use for motor-cycle racing, as is the triangle of public roads known as the Jurby South Road Circuit. This comprises the A13 from Ballaugh Cronk, the B5 Ballavarran road to Jurby West, with the A10 coast-road completing the triangle. These roads are, of course, closed to normal traffic when racing is in progress.

In this journey round the island, Jurby is the first parish which does not extend into the hill country. Together with Andreas and Bride, it sits squarely and exclusively in the northern plain. Along its coastline, Jurby's cliffs continue north-eastward in much the same fashion as Ballaugh's. A base-layer of dense boulder clay is surmounted by strata of sand and silt which are also heavily compounded with clay. The latter impedes the outward seepage of groundwater from the land, resulting in increasing pressure behind the cliff-face. Eventually, the pressure of groundwater becomes sufficient for it to burst free, often bringing a cliff-fall with it. Before that happens, the cliff-face glistens as the sunlight reflects off the meagre film of water that is able to seep through.

On the north side of Jurby Head, the summit of Cronk ny Arrey Lhaa, another 'hill of the day watch', rises close behind the cliff-top. But the Jurby coast also brings a change. Beyond Sartfield, where the Jurby sewer pipe runs into the sea (until connected to the IRIS system – if it ever is), the coast curves round into the north-east, turning its face away from the full brunt of the prevailing south-westerlies. A broadening band of sand dunes stretches along the foot of the cliffs. Years ago, walkers were able to follow a sequence of pleasant, narrow paths through the marram here; today, those paths have been transformed into a broad and ugly, rutted race-track. The parish boundary meets the sea on the south side of the Lhen, the outfall of which tumbles across the foreshore and waits to be forded by any who would proceed further.

CHAPTER FIFTEEN

Ramsey and the North

Out in the rural north-west, the subject of our previous chapter, there seems to be no general consensus among the folk who live there as to which is 'our town'. If you reside in Michael or Ballaugh, it is perceived to be, in Manx terms, 'an awful long way' to go to town, whether 'town' be Ramsey or Peel. However, we have now reached the stage in our journey where there is no such dilemma: up in the far north, the phrase 'going to town' implies a trip to the 'capital of the north', and it is to Ramsey that our wanderings through the sheading of Ayre will eventually bring us. But, for the moment, let us continue on our clockwise journey.

The name of the sheading is derived from the Norse *eyrr*, a 'gravel bank', which is an apt description of the low coast around the Point of Ayre and of the extensive area of raised beach behind it, which we know today as the Ayres. The area seems to have been widely settled by the Norsemen; of the thirty-four treen-names, nineteen are Scandinavian and fifteen Gaelic. The ancient sheading consisted of the parishes of Andreas, Bride and Lezayre, including much of what is now Ramsey. As regards parliamentary elections today, the constituency of Ayre, comprising the three parishes, returns one member to the Keys, whilst the town constituency of Ramsey returns two.

ANDREAS

The parish of Andreas and its church are dedicated to the Scottish St Andrew. Diocesan records for 1640 and 1700 relate to *Ecclesia Parochialis Sancti Andreæ*, but, in between – in 1648 – Blundell describes 'Kirk Andrew or Andres'. By the early years of our own era, it had become 'Kirk Andreas', and today the parish is simply 'Andreas'. It is bounded in the north by the sea and in the west by its boundary with Jurby, following the line of the Lhen Trench south into the northern fringes of the Curragh. From there, the boundary with Lezayre parallels the south side of the A13 as far as Closelake (the site of the short-lived Hall Caine Airport), before wandering off to the north-east and into the centre of the hamlet of Regaby, where the boundary with Bride is encountered. Thus, this tiny hamlet is divided between the three parishes. The boundary with Bride then extends northward, crossing the glacial moraine of the Bride Hills and running out to the Ayres coast 1 mile east of Rue Point.

The parish is largely agricultural, with its main centre of population in Andreas village, sitting in the middle of the parish, where the A19 (from the west) and the A9 (from the east) meet the A17 Sulby–Bride road. The northern section of the latter road, between Andreas and Bride, is known as 'the Burma Road', possibly a name first applied by airmen who were trained at nearby RAF Andreas before being sent to fight the war in the Far East. It skirts the north side of the airfield, replacing the old road which ran through the middle of the airfield site. The disused airfield still sits within a mile of the village, and must have been uncomfortably close to the Bride Hills. It is now the site of a small industrial estate and its runways and taxiways were for some years used for motor-cycle racing. It is still used by light aircraft (especially micro-lights) and the local gliding club. The proximity of the airfield to the village resulted in the tower of St Andrew's Church being lowered to little more than half its original height, to reduce the hazard to low-flying aircraft.

The tower of St Andrew's is unique in the island in standing detached from the main body of the church. Like St Patrick's at Jurby, a portion of the church-yard is devoted to the graves of servicemen who were killed while flying from Andreas in the Second World War. Here again, their ages range from those still in their teens to others of more advanced years who were not compelled to serve in the armed forces at all. Inside the church, two windows are dedicated to airmen who were trained at the Andreas gunnery school and subsequently lost their lives on active service. On the green outside the churchyard, the prominent war memo-rial commemorates Andreas parishioners who died in the two world wars.

On first entering St Andrew's, one is immediately aware of its fine collection of Norse crosses, superbly displayed in a screened-off ante-chamber at the entrance to the nave. Several of the pieces take us back to the legends of Norse mythology. In one well-preserved example (No. 121), we find a replay of the Sigurd scene we saw at St Patrick's, in Jurby, but in much sharper relief. Sigurd is shown roasting three slices of the dragon's heart over the flames, while sucking his fingers which have been scalded by the hot blood; his horse watches the proceedings over his shoulder. The reverse side of the slab shows a later scene from the legend. Sigurd has been slain by his foster-brother, Gunnar, for posses-sion of the gold which had been guarded by the dragon, Fafni, but the gold bears a curse for anyone who possesses it. Gunnar is depicted, hands bound together, being bitten to death in the snake pit.

A particularly arresting specimen in the Andreas collection is the tenth-century Thorwald's Cross which, on one side, displays a striking scene from Ragnarök, the last great battle of Norse pagan mythology. In it, Odin (identified by the ever-present raven on his shoulder) wields his sword ineffectually as Fenris, the wolf, proceeds to devour his leg, and then – presumably – the rest of him. The world of the pagan gods is in terminal decline, as predicted in the mythology. On the reverse side of the slab, a belted figure is shown brandishing a book, a cross

Thorwald's Cross, Kirk Andreas

and a fish (an early symbol of Christianity), while trampling a serpent underfoot. The significance of the two scenes in juxtaposition seems clear: the pagan gods are dead and Christ reigns supreme.

Andreas village has grown considerably during the past half-century, with the development of several modern housing estates. The only other (small) concentrations of population in the parish are at Regaby, on the eastern edge of the parish and St Jude's, in the south. St Jude's Church was built as a chapel of ease for St Andrew's in 1841. The building next door, now a private dwelling, was the original school; its nearby successor – also now redundant – is occupied by *Yn Cheshaght Ghailckagh*, the Manx Gaelic Society, and is known as *Thie ny Gaelgey*, the 'house of the Gaels'. A short distance to the north, the Kerroogarroo fort, dating from the time of the English Civil War, sits in the middle of a field off the A17 St Jude's–Andreas road. An imposing rectangular earthwork with the bastions at the four corners and a surrounding moat (now dry), it was erected about 1645, on the orders of Sir James Stanley, seventh Earl of Derby.

Up in the north of the parish, an artificial mound marking the site of a Viking ship-burial sits on the summit of Knock-e-Dooney, a low hill on the west-running ridge of the Bride Hills. Excavated in 1927, the mound stands close behind the cliff of the old post-glacial coastline which rises behind the raised beach of the Ayres. The day and night watches for the parish of Andreas were held on this hill.

Down on the present-day coast, from the mouth of the Lhen the shoreline continues to curve away from direct confrontation with the prevailing south-west-erly weather. As a consequence, rates of erosion are markedly lower than those further south, and the line of dunes which had developed along the northern half of the Jurby shore march on into Andreas. Over much of the Ayres coast, the process of erosion is reversed into one of accretion, as a storm-beach of shingle continues to be cast up along this northernmost frontier of Man. This is a mecha-nism which has been in progress ever since the end of the last ice age. Once the land (including the undersea land) had been relieved of its vast overburden of ice, the zone which would become the Ayres was free to rise above sea level, and the wave-driven process of ridge-building began. Ridge after ridge, stepping out to the north, led to the Vikings' description of the *eyrr*, the gravel bank. Those ridges – the troughs between filled with accumulations of blown sand – are still there, under the heath which covers much of the area today. The situation is illustrated even more plainly as we continue along the shore beyond Blue Point. The ancient cliff-line, which has been close beside us since we crossed the Lhen, has suddenly deviated inland, almost due east, and continues in that direction, along the foot of the Bride Hills, leaving the Ayres as a low, triangular tract which broadens out as we continue east into Bride.

BRIDE

If we continue along the Ayres coast, we enter the parish of Bride approximately 1 mile east of Rue Point, by which stage the old cliff-line is standing all of 1 mile inland. Apart from the minor matter of geography, any difference between the Andreas Ayres and the Bride Ayres is insignificant. The humpy heath spreads into the widening triangle between the Bride Hills and the sea. Along its western section, the dunes are still building, as sand is blown up from the shore and retained among the spreading growths of spiky marram. And wild orchids spring up in the midst of it all. Out in the eastern zone, the sand is largely replaced with shingle, and high banks of it are thrown up by winter's gales to form the great modern storm-beach which enfolds the island's northern extremity. In summer, nesting terns will dive-bomb walkers who stray too close to their nesting sites among the pebbles. And even here, on this uncompromising stony shore, plants such as the yellow-horned poppy, English stonecrop, sheep's-bit and thyme thrust out from between the pebbles and, as leaf-fall and rot provide a source of humus, growths of grass, heather and gorse follow – diverse forms of plant-life all reaching out to claim that which the sea has rejected. To repeat a phrase which I used earlier, this is life in the making. In the Ballaghennie area, Manx National

Heritage has two holdings of land, and the Manx Wildlife Trust has a visitor centre and nature trail which tell the story of this fascinating area.

There is, after all, one rather marked difference between the Ayres of Bride and the land further west, and that is the presence of industrial man. Close behind the Point of Ayre, those age-old deposits of gravel and sand have been extracted for many years for use in the construction industry. In view of the strong interest in the natural history of this heather-clad wilderness, it might be thought that the rattling machinery of the extraction and screening plant would not make a very good neighbour. But the industrial activity is restricted to closely confined areas, where wildlife seems remarkably tolerant of the noise, and there are few human neighbours to be offended – except for the residents of Bride village, through which the lorries have to pass.

For many years also, some of the worked-out pits have been used as landfill sites for refuse disposal but, with the commissioning of the island's refuse incinerator, this activity has now ceased. When the excavators move on to a new area, discarded holes in the ground may become flooded and overgrown and provide new habitats, unplanned nature reserves in a half-forgotten flatland of heather and gorse.

Kirk Bride

At the Point of Ayre itself, Robert Stevenson's red-banded lighthouse stands in splendid isolation at the end of the road from Bride village. The light is now fully automatic and the former keepers' houses have been sold off into private ownership. On the east side of the Point is the site of the early drillings for coal, which resulted in the discovery of salt in the Triassic marls beneath the glacial drift. Dissolved in water, the resulting brine was pumped to the surface and piped along the shore to the evaporating pans in Ramsey. Sections of the pipe are sometimes visible when they are uncovered by wave action. The undertaking was a commercial failure because imported salt was cheaper.

A mile and a half down the coast from the Point, the cliffs begin to rise again at Phurt, formerly known as Port Cranstal, but there is no trace of a harbour – or even an inlet – today. The night watch for the parish of Bride was kept here, with the day watch being assembled on the summit of Cronk ny Arrey Laa, the highest point on the cliffs to the south. A mile behind the coast at Phurt, Lough Cranstal is the shrunken, marshy remnant of a once much larger lake from the post-glacial age.

The A16 road from the Point of Ayre meets the A10 coast-road in the centre of the small village of Bride, watched over by the parish church, which is dedicated to St Bridget, who was Abbess of Kildare. The parish is, of course, the island's most northerly. Bounded in the west by Andreas, and to north and east by the sea, its encirclement is completed by the boundary with Lezayre, which intersects the coast on the south side of the Dog Mills and extends westward to Regaby. The Manorial Roll of 1515 has two references of interest: one to the parish, which it identifies as *Parochia Scti Brigide*, and the second to the name of a treen, *Kyrkebryde*, at the southern end of which the church itself stands. By 1722, the diocesan commission book was showing that the parish itself had become 'Kirk Bride'.

The present church was built around 1870, replacing an earlier one, and is one of several Manx churches designed by Ewan Christian, who was architect to the Church Commissioners. It has several pleasing features which distinguish it from the plain, rectangular, Manx norm. For a start, it is high, particularly in the tower, which is tall and square and topped with a slender, pyramidal cap, and with fine dressed-stone quoins cornering its dark slate walling, with warm, red sandstone framing its window and door openings. The tower, furthermore, is offset, abutting the south side of the west end of the nave. The east end is not gabled, but has a semicircular apse with a half-conical roof blending into the main ridged covering over the nave. The interior has an attractive barrelled ceiling and contains a few ancient artefacts of some interest. Part of a slate altar-front from the eighth or ninth century was found on the site of an ancient keeill at Ballavarkish, almost a mile east of the church. The *keeill* itself was dedicated to St Mark (*Ballavarkish* is

'Mark's Farm') and has long-since disappeared – probably over the cliff. Norse mythology surfaces again on the late tenth-century Thor Cross, on which – in separate panels – Thor is shown attacking a dragon, slaying the giant Ragnir and engaged in fishing, using a serpent as bait. (Those old Norse mythologers must have told some terrific fishermen's tales.) On the Druian Cross, a runic inscription reads: 'Druian son of Dufkal raised this cross to the memory of Cathmaol his wife'. This is of particular local interest because of the existence of the nearby quarter-land of Glen Truan (cf 'Druian'). It is also thought possible that the name of the Ballacowle quarterland (adjoining the churchyard) and the local surname Cowle may be derived from Cathmaol. Of somewhat later date (possibly twelfth-century), the 'Adam and Eve' stone depicts two figures standing on either side of a tree which may have been intended as the biblical Tree of Knowledge. Out in the churchyard, a gravestone commemorates a local man, John Cowle, who served on HMS *Temeraire* at the Battle of Trafalgar in 1805, and died fifty-eight years later at the age of seventy-seven. John Lace was also there, on HMS *Victory*, and lost an arm – so it is said – to the same shot that killed Nelson.

Back on the coast, this eastern frontier of Bride has almost run its course. On the shore below the summit of Cronk ny Arrey Laa, Shellag Point ('seal-creek point'), displays no sign of either creek or point, just a 250-foot (75m) wall of sand and clay which marks the abrupt eastern termination of the Bride Hills. Erosion along this north-eastern coast – although occurring at a much lower rate than that which consumes the cliffs from Michael to Jurby – has removed all evidence of the origin of such a name. To the south, the cliffs decline and stand a mere 33 feet (10m) high as we reach the parish boundary at the Dog Mills. I must admit that, when I first became aware of the name of this place, I had a mental picture of a team of dogs being set to work on a treadmill to grind the corn. In reality, the old Manx name was *Mwyllin ny moddey*, 'the mill of the dogs'; i.e. there was a stan-dard water mill at a place where there were also dogs. Further south, lies the parish of Lezayre.

LEZAYRE

Lezayre is a parish of some contradiction in such a small maritime island. Extending to more than 16,000 acres (6,500ha), it is the largest parish in Man, yet has the island's shortest coastline (except for Marown, which has no coast at all). Stretching barely 1 mile to the south, its coast is merely the last shrinking vestige of the Bride coast, with nothing to distinguish between the two; simply a low, declining cliff of silt and clay being slowly eroded by the sea. And it is the sea,

Lough Mallow, Lezayre: no sign of a lake today

together with the town of Ramsey, which forms the parish's eastern boundary. In the north, it is bounded by Bride, Andreas and Jurby, in the west by Ballaugh and Michael, in the south by Braddan, and in the south-east by Lonan and Maughold. In the latter sector, the parish boundary follows the line of the ridge from North Barrule to Mullagh Ouyr, thus following the old line of division between the Northside and the Southside, and leaving the island's highest summit wholly in Lezayre.

Having declared earlier that there are two Manx sheadings each of which has taken the name of one of its constituent parishes, it is perhaps timely to admit that there is a third sheading which – while not possessing the identical name of one of its parishes – does have a name which shared a common derivation with that of a parish. The sheading is Ayre and the parish Lezayre. The parish and its church were dedicated to the Holy Trinity, and later specifically to Christ. The earliest reference is found in Gregory IX's papal bull of 1231, which identifies *Ecclesia Sancti Trinitatis in Leayre*. In his journal of 1648, Blundell recorded 'Kirk Christ of Ayre' but, by 1710, the diocesan register was giving the final element as 'Lezayre'. By the early twentieth century, both parish and church had become Kirk Christ Lezayre, and the church is still such today. Thus, since the *le* or *lez* is the old Norman definite article, it will be seen that the names of the parish and sheading – though not identical – have been closely linked throughout their recorded history.

This large parish is one of contrasting landscapes, and was even more so in the past, when the boggy mire of the Lezayre Curragh and the broad waters of Lough Mallow lay spread across much of the north of the parish. A large area of land to the south of the Curragh was held by the monks of Mirescogh, the monastery situated on an island in the mire, the location of which is now completely lost to us. Most of the Lezayre Curragh has dried out over the centuries, either by natural process or through drainage works, and that which has not been taken in for agriculture is left as *garey* – rough, uncultivated land, one stage drier than a curragh. But the locations of some former islands are left to us in their place-names: *Close yn Ellan*, 'enclosure of the island', and *Ellanbane*, 'white island'. As recently as 1703, the water of Lough Mallow – and the fishing rights – were being let, but this feature, too, has vanished from the landscape, although the name is preserved in that of the farm beside the junction of the Garey Road and the A13, on the western outskirts of Ramsey.

The present parish church, Kirk Christ Lezayre, was built in the 1830s by Bishop

Kirk Christ Lezayre

Ward, replacing one built by Bishop Wilson in 1704. It stands, appropriately, at Churchtown, in the cusp of the B17 loop-road, which gathers the houses of this small village to traffic-free tranquillity on the south side of the A3 Sulby–Ramsey road. It sits beneath the shoulder of Sky Hill, scene of the historic victory of Godred Crovan's Norsemen over the Manx in 1079. The day watch for the parish was kept on this hill, with the night watch down by the shore at the Vollan, at the north end of Ramsey. The parish's main centre of population is at Sulby, 2 miles to the west, and a chapel of ease, St Stephen's, was built there in 1839.

Inside Kirk Christ Lezayre, a brass plaque gives details of the Christian family of Milntown (a mile along the road towards Ramsey), which must have produced more prominent men in history than any other Manx family. The house, which was the family home for 400 years, stands back from the A3 Lezayre Road, in wooded grounds beside the junction with the B16 Glen Auldyn road. This was a wide-ranging family, with branches in other parts of the island and in the north-west of England. The family name derived from the Old Norse *Kristin*, or *Crystyn*; in Man, it soon acquired the Gaelic prefix *mac* but, by the mid-seventeenth century, the prefix had been discarded and the remainder had evolved into 'Christian'. One of the first Milntown Christians to come to prominence was Deemster Ewan Christian (1579–1656). He came to the attention of James Stanley, seventh Earl of Derby (*Yn Stanlagh Mooar*), and was made a deemster at the age of twenty-six, holding the office until his death, fifty-one years later.

During his dealings on the island, 'the Great Stanley' made some astute observations on the family, writing in his diary: 'There be many of the Christians in this country – but they have made themselves chief here ... by policy they are crept into the principal places of power; and they be seated round about the country, and in the heart of it; they are matched with the best families; have the best livings [farms]; and must not be neglected'.

Three other Christians were to cause the Earl trouble during the years of the English Civil War. Captain Edward Christian (*c* 1600–61), from the Maughold branch of the family, returned to the isle in 1627, after an early career at sea, having amassed a fortune with the East India Company. He came to the attention of the Earl, who made him Captain of the Troops, but he later fell foul of the Earl when the latter attempted to change the system of Manx land tenure to the English feudal system. After Christian incited rebellion among the Manx in 1642–3, he was imprisoned in Peel Castle. Released when the forces of the Parliament took possession of the isle in 1651, he promptly began plotting against the new Lord, Fairfax. He was committed again to Peel Castle in 1660, died there the following year and was buried at Kirk Maughold.

The second troublesome Christian was William (1608–63), a younger son of the Deemster of Milntown. He first appears in Manx records as Steward of the

Abbey Lands and a member of the Keys in 1643. He it was who would become known to the Manx as *Illiam Dhone*. He worked his way into the seventh Earl's favour and was left in effective charge while the Earl was in England, fighting for the King. William's island exploits during the English Civil War, and his fate following the Restoration of the Monarchy, have (together with those of Captain Edward) been covered in some detail in Chapter 5.

But there was a third Christian thorn in James Stanley's side, and that was another William. As the holder of land at Knockrushen, Malew, this William Christian would have been a near-neighbour of Illiam Dhone's at Ronaldsway. Like his better-known namesake, William of Knockrushen at some time held the office of the Lord's Receiver (effectively his land agent). His name first appears in the records for 1642, when residents of Castletown petitioned the Governor to impose controls on his activities, for reasons which – expressed in the archaic language of the day – are not at all clear (to me, at least). In 1644, he was confined to Castle Rushen on suspicion of incitement to revolt against the Earl. Although acquitted of the charge, he remained in the castle for some months. There is no doubt that he was one of the leaders of the 1651 rising and, during the reign of the Commonwealth, was a member of the House of Keys. He seems to have died some time in 1651–2, before the Lordship of Man was restored to the Stanleys, and so escaped the retribution of the eighth Earl of Derby. Thus, that early assessment of the Christians by the seventh Earl proved to be astutely accurate.

A later descendant of the Milntown Christians (though not Manx-born) was, of course, Fletcher Christian, leader of the *Bounty* mutineers in 1787, whose lineage has been described in Chapter 11. Another Christian of Manx descent who rose to prominence in less turbulent times was the leading nineteenth-century architect, Ewan Christian, who designed the National Portrait Gallery in London, as well as a number of churches in Britain and Man, where he was architect to the Church Commissioners.

But the Christians and Milntown parted company many years ago. In more recent times, the house has been a girls' school, a hotel, and then a private residence – finally of Sir Clive Edwards, who bequeathed the estate to the Manx nation. It is now administered by the Milntown Trust, which is planning to open the house and grounds to the public.

Lezayre seems to have had a propensity for throwing up famous sons. Halfway along the A13 between Churchtown and Sulby Bridge, the B14 *Bayr ny Hayrey* strikes off northward across the former curragh. This was part of the old road which led from the foot of the northern hills, through the Lezayre Curragh, and thence across the Ayre to the island's northern extremity; hence its name – the 'Road of the Ayre'. However, we need travel no more than a couple of hundred yards along it before coming into sight of the farmhouse and buildings of Ellanbane, former home of the Standish family.

The Standishes were originally landowners of Standish Hall, in Lancashire, from whence a branch of the family arrived in Man and settled at Ellanbane around the beginning of the sixteenth century. The famous scion of the family was Myles Standish (1586–1656), the military leader of the *Mayflower* settlers who sailed to the land which they would call 'New England' in 1620. Myles may, or may not, have been born at Ellanbane; from the evidence that exists, it seems more likely that the two sisters – Rose and Barbara Standish – both of whom he would in course of time marry, were born there, and that he and they were cousins. In his *Manx Worthies*, A. W. Moore considers it probable that John Standish, who was a member of the House of Keys in 1593, was Rose and Barbara's father. A William Standish of Ellanbane (perhaps John's son and the girls' brother) was a member of the Keys from 1629 to 1656. He was certainly involved in the 1651 rising against the Stanleys, and was one of the party which negotiated the terms of the island's surrender to Colonel Duckenfield's parliamentary forces. As a further twist in the tale, between 1661 and 1665, another John Standish, probably William's son, was also an MHK and was one of those involved in the trial of Illiam Dhone for treason.

As regards Myles Standish himself, he was a military man who was involved in the war of independence in Holland, at the end of which he made the acquaintance of some of the English emigrants at Leyden. He is said to have visited the Isle of Man about 1618 and to have married Rose there (although marriage records in the isle do not go back that far). Returning with Rose to Holland, Standish was elected military leader of the emigrants and sailed with them from England in the autumn of 1620. But their settlement at New Plymouth was soon ravaged by the privations and sickness of their first North American winter. Rose was one of the first to succumb, and was dead before the coming of spring. In 1623, her sister Barbara sailed for New England in the ship *Ann*, and she and Myles were married soon after her arrival. They had six children and were together for thirty years.

In his will, Myles Standish listed all of the lands which he regarded as his rightful inheritance and which he wished to bequeath to his son, Alexander, these being six properties in England, in addition to the Manx holdings. The will claimed that these lands had been 'surreptitiously detained' from Myles by the action of his grandfather, but this may be explained by the fact that his grandfather, having heard nothing of him since his crossing of the Atlantic, left the properties to his grandson, William, Myles's nephew. Alexander, in his will of 1702, also laid claim to the estates but it would appear that he never did gain possession. It is interesting that the earliest document relating to these lands is signed by a Standish who styled himself *Johannem Standishe de Insula de Mane*.

The village of Sulby stretches along the mile-long Sulby Straight of the TT course, with arms branching out to north and south where the A14 crosses the course and the *Sulby Glen Hotel* stands sentinel over the junction. The village lies at the foot of Sulby Glen, the southern section of the A14 having descended the full length of the valley from the mountain section of the TT course at the Bungalow. A short distance before reaching the main road, a byroad (the B8) shoots off to the right and passes through the Claddagh, a 'water-meadow land' on the banks of the Sulby River. (A *claddagh* is one stage drier than a *garey*, which, in turn, is one stage drier than a *curragh*.) The Sulby Claddagh is said to be the island's only patch of common land; all other land in Man is either in the ownership of someone or in the custody of some body. This particular claddagh (pronounced to rhyme with 'barrack') is maintained by the DAFF as an amenity area and a site for informal camping.

Overlooking the Claddagh from the east is the dramatic, twin-summited hump of Cronk Sumark, which is supposed to have been the site of the traditional witches' dance. All of the Manx witches would assemble here and (according to Stenning) entice young unmarried women to join them 'in a lewd Bacchanal dance', forming a ring around the hill, but the practice has now died out – I think. Somewhere along the way, the popular myth has grown up claiming that the

Cronk Sumark rises abve the Sulby River and the Claddagh

English translation of this hill-name is 'Primrose Hill'. In fact, it derives from a combination of the Gaelic *cronk* (for 'hill') and the Norse *skammhryggr*, meaning a 'short ridge'; i.e. a short-ridged hill. In the 1703 Manorial Roll, it was Knock Shemerick, which was closer to the Norse original.

Halfway along the Sulby Straight, Staward Farm has been the site of the Royal Manx Agricultural Society's two-day show in August for many years. Fewer people than ever work in agriculture today, but the shows still attract wide interest, though numbers attending will probably never again approach the 1947 record, in excess of 12,000; that was a year when local attendances were swollen by a post-war resurgence in visitor numbers. The present lease allowing the annual use of the show-field is due to expire in 2010, and it appears that it will not be renewed. It has been suggested that the show could be transferred to the DAFF's farm-site at Knockaloe but the question remains open.

In and around Sulby, folk-memories still abound concerning Arthur Caley, otherwise known as the Sulby Giant or the Manx Giant. Those locals harbouring the memories do not always agree, and when those memories have been passed by word of mouth down the generations, the result is always a dubious source of historical fact. However, it would appear that Arthur Caley was born in 1824, one of a large family living in a small cottage, a mile from the Sulby crossroads. By the age of twenty-two, he stood 7 feet 8 inches (2.3m) tall, and would eventually reach 7 feet 11 inches (2.4m) and 620 pounds (281kg) in weight. He left the island in 1851 and was soon being exhibited as a giant in shows in London, and later in Paris, where he was reported to have died in 1853. But this may have been a ruse to collect the £2,000 from his life-insurance policy, for he next turned up in the United States, being shown in the famous Barnum and Bailey Circus. He was then appearing as Colonel Ruth (or Routh) Goshen (or Goshun) (the spelling on the bill-boards varied), and was styled as 'the Palestine Giant'. Caley, or someone close to him, sent a photograph of him to the family in the Isle of Man, and they were in no doubt that the big man in the picture was Arthur. He died in retirement in New Jersey in 1889. The Manx Museum has several exhibits relating to him.

Running south from the Sulby crossroads, the magnificent water-cut valley of Sulby Glen strikes upward into the highest reaches of the island's hill-country, cradling the tarmac of the A14 and the waters of the Sulby River as it goes. In spring, the floor of the glen is carpeted with massed bluebells. To the west, it is flanked by Mount Karrin and the Michael hills, to the east by Slieau Managh and Snaefell, and blocked off at its top end by the line-up of Beinn-y-Phott, Carraghan and Slieau Maggle, with the impounded waters of the Sulby reservoir nestling tranquilly below. Pedestrians desirous of a traffic-free route into the hills may go by way of Narradale or Glen Auldyn or by several routes between. Superb hill-walking is to be had in these northern highlands of Man, and the slopes that

Sulby Glen in summer

encircle the upper reaches of Sulby Glen are littered with ancient cairns, hut circles and shielings. A few of these, above the small reservoir at Block Eary, have been excavated and were probably used as temporary dwellings during the summer months, when livestock was brought onto the upper slopes for grazing. The only datable object found was a coin from the reign of King Stephen, c 1140, but it is likely that these sites were in use in much earlier times.

RAMSEY

'The Capital of the North' or 'Royal Ramsey' (ever since Prince Albert came ashore in 1847 and climbed to the top of the hill where the Albert Tower now stands), the town of Ramsey lies astride the mouth of the Sulby River, sandwiched between the two parishes, of which it once formed part. The northern part of the boundary between the parishes of Lezayre and Maughold follows the line of a minor stream known today as the Lickney but formerly as the Strooan ny Craue. After flowing through the Ramsey golf course, the stream disappears under the town and emerges from the mouth of a tunnel beneath West Quay, where its waters are discharged into the harbour, there to join the much larger flow of the Sulby River. It is the older name of the Lickney which gives the clue to the origin of the town's name. 'Lickney' comes from the Manx *Leaghyrnee*, a 'rushy place', but the older *Strooan ny Craue* denotes a 'stream of the wild garlic', and it must be significant that the Norse *Ramsá* has the same meaning. In Norway today, such names as Ramsdal, Ramsland, Ramsnes and Ramsvik are quite frequently encountered, all of them redolent of wild garlic.

In times past, North Ramsey (north of the Sulby River) was in the parish of Lezayre, and South Ramsey was in Maughold. A chapel of ease for Kirk Maughold was built early on at Ballure; standing on the site of an ancient keeill, it was rebuilt for the first (recorded) time in 1640. It was restored in 1850 and dedicated to St Catherine, but its congregation had already outgrown it. St Paul's Church was built in 1822, facing out onto a lake adjoining the south side of the harbour. The lake was filled in thirteen years later and is now the Market Place. The old chapel at Ballure lay unused for many years but has since been converted into a dwelling. It is reputed to be the oldest surviving building in the town. The night watch for the parish of Maughold was kept at Ballure, which was the most northerly treen

The inner harbour at Ramsey

in the parish. As in South Ramsey, so in the north, a chapel of ease for Kirk Christ Lezayre was built. The foundation stone for St Olave's Church was laid in 1861 but it required another nine years to see its completion.

Before 1755, there was no bridge linking the two parts of the town. It would have been possible to ford the river at the inner end of the harbour at low tide, but it would have been a very muddy process. The favoured fording point seems to have been at Gardener's Lane, where the present footbridge enables pedestrians to cross, but the ford itself is rather deep for modern road vehicles. A short distance further upstream, stepping stones permitted a foot-crossing at low tide.

The original stone bridge at the upper end of the harbour was built in 1755 and was widened in 1840. Halfway down the harbour, the iron swing-bridge was opened in 1892 to provide more direct access from South Ramsey to the new developments on the *Mooragh* ('waste-land by the sea') in the north. The original sand dunes and marsh were cleared and the area converted into the Mooragh Park, with gardens and leisure facilities centred on a sea-water boating lake. An impressive line of hotels sprang up along the Mooragh Promenade to attract the new breed of Victorian middle-class visitor that was reaching the island. Who could have foretold then that, less than fifty years on, the visitors would be 'enemy aliens', and the promenade and its buildings would be transformed into an internment camp? But prior to all these modern developments, it was amid the dunes and marsh of the original Mooragh that the Isle of Man Cabbage, *Rhinchosinapsis monensis*, was first recorded by the famed biologist John Ray in 1662. A line of low sand dunes persists today along the seaward side of the promenade.

Throughout recorded history, Ramsey has been a landing-place for kings, warlords and sundry others. In earliest times, such landings had perforce to be made either on the open beach or in an exposed river-mouth. The haven in the river-mouth began to emerge as a protected harbour with the construction of the two piers. The South Pier was built in 1790 and extended in 1874–6. The North Pier followed in stages between 1842 and 1868. Much of the earlier construction, consisting of dry-set vertical slabs, is still visible. There has been a lifeboat stationed at Ramsey since 1829 but, because of the tidal nature of the harbour, it is housed on South Promenade and launched from the beach outside the South Pier.

On the landward side of the swing-bridge, the inner harbour branches off northward, as if intent on linking up with the Mooragh Lake. The two bodies of water lie along the old course of the Sulby River, with only the embankment which carries North Shore Road standing between them. But there is, indeed, a connection between the two, since a gated sluice passes beneath the roadway, enabling the lake to be drained into the harbour at low tide for cleaning and maintenance, and to be refilled from the harbour at high tide. Proposals to develop the inner harbour into a gated marina, enabling yachts to remain afloat at all states of the tide, continue to resurface from time to time, and continue to raise the same chorus of objections.

The mouth of the inner harbour is flanked by the swing-bridge on the east side and the shipyard on the west. The shipyard opened in 1832 and maintained an impressive record of shipbuilding through much of the nineteenth century, among its output being four three-masted barques – the *Erato, Euridica, Euterpe* and *Ramsey*. The most famous of these is the third-named, built of iron and later renamed the *Star of India*; she is said to be the oldest ship still afloat, and is preserved in the maritime museum in San Diego. The *Ramsey* is reputed to have been the first oil tanker ever built.

By the turn of the century, the demand was for larger ships, and the Ramsey shipyard – constrained by the shallow, tidal harbour in which it had to operate – was in terminal trouble. After its closure, the site was taken over by the Manx Salt & Alkali Company for evaporating the brine that was piped down from the Point of Ayre. But, as noted earlier, this enterprise failed in the face of cheaper imports from elsewhere. By the 1960s, the shipyard was again in business, for the building, refitting and overhaul of smaller vessels, and remained open through the rest of the twentieth century – but often with the aid of government subsidy. Threatened with closure, the yard was subject to a management buyout in 2003, and survives. The site and buildings are owned by the Department of Trade & Industry and leased to Booth W. Kelly (2003) Ltd, thus preserving the old name of the yard.

Ramsey's harbour continues as a fishing port, on a par with the level of activity remaining in Peel. But it is as a commercial port that Ramsey stands out – in Manx terms – today. The port of Douglas has the ferry traffic and the imports of fuel oil, and Peel also has the latter, but, for general commercial cargoes, Ramsey is the port of entry. The Isle of Man Steam Packet Company has long-since left the port, and the old insular coastal trade has gone with it. But two companies, the Ramsey Steamship Company and Mezeron Ltd, continue to ply their trades, the latter bringing regular shipments of general cargo from Belfast and Glasson Dock, and the former carrying bulk cargoes from ports around the Irish Sea.

Less than half a mile south of the harbour mouth, the iron structure of the Queen's Pier strides out 2,150 feet (655m) towards England, today an enduring symbol of shame on successive Manx governments. The pier was opened in 1886 to provide berthing for vessels to discharge passengers at all states of the tide. A narrow-gauge (3-foot, or 914mm) railway was installed along its length, its train initially hauled by man-power but later by a petrol-driven locomotive. The docking of vessels against the pier ceased in 1970, and it was closed to everyone else in 1991 on safety grounds. The structure is supposed to be in the care of the Department of Transport, but the use of the term 'care' is questionable. A few years ago, notice was served on the DoT by the DLGE (one government department serving notice on

Barrack Lane, one of the few surviving remnants of old South Ramsey

another), requiring minimal work to be carried out to make the structure safe, and 'minimal' *was* the work carried out. The pier is supposed to be protected as a listed structure and, if it had been in the custody of a private owner, far more stringent measures would have been brought against that owner long ago. But there has been little but procrastination. Up to the end of May 2006, the Manx government had received fifteen reports on the condition of the pier in the space of thirteen years. In that time, £124,287 had been spent, of which just £38,986 was expenditure on the structure itself; the remainder had been spent on reports. In the meantime, suspicion had been growing among the population at large that decision-makers harbour the hope that, if the decision can be postponed for long enough, the problem will go away – or, at least, that it will fall down and be beyond repair. And perhaps that is still the awaited outcome.

On the north side of the Queen's Pier, some remnants of eighteenth-century coastal defence works are still visible. In 1630, in response to storm damage to the town south of the river-mouth, a loose-stone barrier was placed along the shore as protection. This was known as the Ramsey Fence. In 1744, the Fence was breached and a number of houses swept away. Several jetties were subsequently built, projecting seaward from the Fence, and the remains of one of these can still be seen beside the pier. The eventual construction of the Queen's Promenade solved the problem for good.

The first railway link to the town was completed by the Manx Northern Railway in 1878, its primary purpose being to transport ores from the Foxdale mines for shipping out through the port. In this, the line was never a commercial success, and its potential for passenger traffic by the long, west-coast route was ruined by the arrival of the Manx Electric Railway in 1899, using the direct east-coast route from Douglas. The site of the MNR's station, in Station Road, is now occupied by the modern premises of the Ramsey Bakery. The original MER station building has also gone, its replacement being rather more functional than decorative, and incorporating a small visitor centre which houses the locomotive that used to run along the Queen's Pier.

In the drastic redevelopment of the 1960s, much of old South Ramsey was cleared to make way for modern building. A small sample of what was there remains in the quadrilateral pattern of streets and alleys – Mona Street, Neptune Street and Barrack Lane – sandwiched between East Quay and South Promenade. Mona Street has buildings dating from 1755, and Barrack Lane gained its name from the garrison that was stationed there in 1793 and was housed in a long warehouse which was later converted into the present terrace of tiny cottages. Overlooking the harbour from East Quay, the Old Custom House received a contingent of nine British customs men after the Revestment of 1765 brought the Isle of Man under direct British control, which spelt the end of the smuggling trade.

On Waterloo Road, Mysore Cottages (a short terrace of them) stand as a reminder of Sir Mark Cubbon (1775–1861), who was the highly regarded Commissioner of Mysore at the time of the Indian Mutiny, during which, Mysore remained perfectly calm under his administration. He resigned his post in 1861 due to ill health and died at Suez within a month of leaving India. His body was brought back to his native isle and interred at Kirk Maughold, where his father had been vicar. His sister, Elizabeth Cubbon, purchased the land at Waterloo Road, and the cottages were erected in his memory in 1865. Built as almshouses for elderly ladies, they are now private dwellings.

Two other Manx worthies are commemorated in Ramsey. In Parliament Street, a building named Kermode House stands on the site of an earlier house which was the birthplace of the renowned Manx antiquarian, P. M. C. Kermode (1855–1932), first director of the Manx Museum. He, too, is buried at Kirk

Former almshouses: Mysore Cottages, Ramsey

Maughold. A plaque recording his birth and achievements was rescued from the old house and now adorns the present building.

The other notable acknowledgement (also marked with a plaque) relates to the Manx 'national poet', T. E. Brown (1830–97), who spent the last four years of his retirement at *Glan y Don,* at the seaward end of Windsor Road, overlooking the Mooragh Park. But he died while on a return visit to Clifton College, Bristol, where he had taught for almost thirty years, and is buried there beside his wife and son, Braddan.

Near the junction of the A13 Jurby Road with Bowring Road (the main road out of town to the north), stands an elderly persons' residential home called Beaconsfield Towers. It stands back from the road, at the end of its driveway, but a glance at its form – incorporating a wide, truncated tower – gives the clue to its name. It was known in the past as the Old Windmill, or Monk's Mill, and was one of the island's few windmills. It was built as a corn-mill in 1840 by John Monk, and, from 1871, when steam power was also installed, it became the Ramsey Steam and Wind Mills. The sight of its broad, surviving stump gives an indication of the scale of the original.

Off the opposite side of Bowring Road is the scene of another government-

Motor sport at Ramsey in the annual Lhergy Frissell Hill Climb

induced controversy which has been raging in the north of the island for several years; this one is the Ramsey and District Cottage Hospital. It was opened in 1907, funded by the Henry Bloom Noble Trust, and originally contained ten beds and two cots. With the aid of a further contribution from the trustees of another bene-factor, Pierre Baume, an endowment fund was set up to meet future costs. After the Second World War, the hospital was one of three which remained opera-tionally independent, but with public funding. It was not until the passing of an Act of 1963 that all of the island's hospitals became fully integrated into the Manx National Health Service. Over the years, a voluntary League of Friends of the hospital has raised many thousands of pounds for new equipment. Thus it has come about that the people of Ramsey and the north have developed strong feel-ings of affinity towards 'their' hospital.

Prior to 2003, the hospital was a fully operational unit, with its own accident and emergency and X-ray departments and its own operating theatre, the latter two having been provided by charity. The facility operated twenty-four hours a day, seven days a week. Today, patient admissions are not accepted at night or at weekends, and the suspicion has grown that, with the completion of the new Noble's Hospital in Braddan, the DHSS would be content to see the Ramsey facility run down, or even closed. The department has repeatedly denied this – but the service is, notwithstanding, less comprehensive than it was. And, four years after Tynwald resolved to reintroduce 24-hour service, it has still not happened. The outcome is awaited amid an atmosphere of resentment and suspicion.

Moving to lighter matters, *Yn Chruinnaght*, the annual Celtic festival of music and dance, was held in Ramsey for many years but, for a combination of reasons, including a growing shortage of accommodation, the 2006 festival, though based in Ramsey, had some of its events staged in other places. For the 2007 festival – the thirtieth anniversary of the gathering – the focus was moved to Peel, to coincide with the traditional boat weekend held there in July, in the hope that the two events would complement one another and enhance the overall festival atmosphere in the west-coast port. It is too early to say whether the change is permanent.

Before leaving Ramsey, let us take a short journey beyond the town's northern boundary to find a half-forgotten relic of the Cold War. Along the A10 coast-road, half a mile beyond the *Grand Island Hotel*, a gate on the right-hand side provides access to a narrow field, on the edge of the cliff. Inside the gate, is a low, grass-and-bramble-covered mound, with an access hatch and ventilation shafts poking through the top of it. This was the Royal Observer Corps's observation post M3

Reminder of the Cold War: Royal Observer Corps observation post M3, near Ramsey

(originally Q3), from where reports of damage and readings of radioactive fall-out were to be transmitted to regional centres in the event of an attack from behind the Iron Curtain. There were four such posts in the island: Q1 in Douglas, Q2 in Peel, Q3 in Ramsey and Q4 in Castletown. They became operational in the early 1960s and the designations were changed from Q to M in 1968. Long ago, I saw the inside of one such post; my main recollection is of a bunker that was small and damp and smelt of must. And I am aware that training briefings and the like at M3 were, whenever feasible, carried out in the more convivial surroundings of the *Grand Island Hotel*. Fortunately, the Soviet Union disintegrated before the threat materialized.

CHAPTER SIXTEEN

Laxey and the North-East

As we enter the final stage of our journey round the Isle of Man, we come to the sheading of Garff which, since 1796, has comprised the two parishes of Maughold and Lonan. Prior to that year, the parish of Onchan was also included. The sheading as presently constituted is identical with the parliamentary constituency of Garff, which returns one member to the House of Keys.

We have already noted examples of a sheading taking the name of one of its constituent parishes. There are also cases where a sheading has taken the name of a much smaller land division within it – specifically that of a treen. Garff appears to be one such; Middle is another. In the case of Garff, the starting point seems to be the treen known as *Grauff* in 1511 and *Grawe* today, in the parish of Lonan. This comes from the Scandinavian *Gröf* (plural *Grafir*), meaning a 'pit' or 'ravine'. The treen in question is bounded by Glen Roy and Laxey Glen, both of which could be termed ravines. The name of Glen Roy itself could have come from the same derivation. The straight translation of its modern Manx name is 'red glen', but it is quite feasible that the Norse would know it as *Grödal*, 'ravine dale', which became Gaelicized to *Glengrawe* and the second 'g' eventually being dropped. Place-names containing the element *gröf* or *grafir*, or derivations of them, are widespread in the Hebrides, the Orkneys, Shetland and Iceland, all places which came under Scandinavian domination. And J. J. Kneen has pointed out that the treen-names in the old sheading of Garff (including Onchan) were five-sixths Norse and only one-sixth Gaelic.

The main centre of population in Garff is the village of Laxey, which sits midway down the coast of Lonan, with a smaller concentration at Baldrine (rhyming with 'line'), 1½ miles further south. In terms of local government administration, Laxey is one of the three remaining Village Districts (Port St Mary and Port Erin being the others), administered by Village Commissioners.

MAUGHOLD

Maughold is the northernmost of the two parishes of Garff, and is largely agri-
cultural, with a scattering of minor population centres at Port Lewaigue, Port e
Vullen, Ballajora, Cornaa, Glen Mona and the Dhoon. But the population in total
is only 941 (in 2001). The parish is bounded in the north and west by the town of
Ramsey and the parish of Lezayre, as described earlier, and in the east by the sea.
Its boundary in the south is that with the parish of Lonan, which is encountered
in the west on the hillside just below the A18 mountain road at the Black Hut.
From there, the line meanders east and south-east, following the ridge linking the
summits of Slieau Lhean, Slieau Ouyr and Slieau Ruy, before running out to the
coast above Bulgham Bay.

As described in Chapter 3, Kirk Maughold was the most important monastic
centre in the early history of the Christian Church in Man. The present parish
church is one of the oldest in the isle and probably stands on the site of an earlier
keeill. The sites of four other keeills in the churchyard are known. The church and
its churchyard were examined in detail by the Manx antiquarian and first director
of the Manx Museum, P. M. C. Kermode, who is buried here. The whole of the
eastern boundary of the churchyard (the side nearest the sea) was protected by a
substantial earthen embankment which sloped outward into a moat, an arrangement reminiscent of early Irish monasteries. The summit of Maughold Head,
which rises above the churchyard to the east, was similarly fortified.

The parish and its church were dedicated to the Celtic saint Maughold, or
Machud (down the centuries, his name was sometimes spelt with an 'l', some-
times not). In Pope Gregory IX's bull of 1231, the identification is to *Ecclesia
Scti Maughaldi* and, more than a century later, *Chronicon* has *Ecclesia Scti
Machutus*. Ancient Irish manuscripts, as well as insular Manx records (admittedly of a later date), suggest that the Celtic Church was well established in
Man in the fifth century. The story of Maughold's expulsion from Ireland and
arrival in Man is told in *The Book of Armagh*. Maughold, or Machud, or
McCuill, was a native of Ulster and had lived a most dissolute life, culminating
in a foul murder. He was brought before St Patrick, who decreed that the
miscreant's fate should be left to God's mercy. Maughold was set adrift in a
coracle formed from a single ox-hide (a pretty small coracle), and eventually
came ashore at the foot of the headland which has since borne his name. He
was assisted ashore by two pious men, Conindri and Romuil, who had arrived
in Man earlier and had been preaching the Word to the islanders. They
completed the repentant Maughold's conversion, and he is said to have taken
the bishopric after them. St Maughold's Well, on the seaward face of the head-

land, is reputed to mark the spot where Maughold fell to his knees on arrival to give thanks for his deliverance.

But the extent to which such ancient accounts as this relate to historical fact is always difficult to assess in the absence of corroborating evidence. The stories are told in such fascinating – even fanciful – detail that one cannot but harbour feelings of doubt. When Maughold is consigned to the coracle on the Irish shore, he is locked in chains and the key is cast into the water by St Patrick. Maughold is to remain in chains until the Almighty sees fit to deliver the key to him, and Maughold acquiesces in this. In Man, on the eve of the day on which Maughold is to receive holy orders, a cook delivers to him an object he has retrieved from the gut of a fish he is about to cook – it is the key. So, the events may have been as related, or...? But perhaps one doubts too readily. *The Book of Armagh* also tells of the arrival of St Bridget in Man to found the Nunnery at Douglas, and of her installation as its first abbess by Bishop McCuill.

In his *Folklore of the Isle of Man*, A. W. Moore considered legends such as those surrounding St Maughold to be 'pious stories invented by monks and priests for the edification of simple-minded laymen' and believed they could probably be regarded as – at least – semi-historical. Some accounts record that Maughold (or Machutus, or McCuill) became Bishop in Man in 498 and that, on his death, he was buried in the grounds of his monastery at Kirk Maughold. Subsequently, the land immediately to the east of the churchyard was known as Staff Land and was held on free tenure by the holder of the neighbouring Ballaterson, 'farm of the crosier', in return for his keeping the crosier, or staff, of St Maughold in safe custody. The staff has long since disappeared but the place-names serve to remind us of the story. The Staff Land eventually came into the possession of the Christian family but it is not known how this came about.

The present church exhibits the traditional pattern of Manx parish churches: a simple rectangular plan-form without transepts. An open turret above the west door supports a single bell, and an external flight of steps provides access to the gallery which accommodates the organ and choir. Much of the older work in the

The grave of Sir Hall Caine, Kirk Maughold

structure, some dating from around the eleventh century, is plain to see, particularly in the arch mouldings to the porch and windows. The original churchyard – approaching 4 acres (1.6ha) in extent and said to be the largest in the isle – is full to capacity, and the modern cemetery extension is 200 yards down the road.

If the bones of St Maughold do, indeed, lie beneath the turf of his old churchyard, we shall doubtless remain in ignorance of their location. But there are interments of later times whose sites are clearly identified. Edward Christian lies here, having died in the dungeon of Peel Castle in 1661. A farm whose lands adjoin those of Ballaterson is Crowville, purchased in the early 1800s by Ramsey-born Hugh Crow, a retired sea-captain and one-

The fourteenth-century Maughold Cross, seen before it was moved inside the church

time slave-trader. In 1817, he moved to Liverpool, where he spent his remaining years but, on his death in 1829, his body was brought back for burial at Kirk Maughold. Some small slabs of slate commemorate unnamed victims of cholera in 1833. Other notable graves include those of Sir Mark Cubbon, Commissioner of Mysore for twenty-six years, John Swynnerton, the sculptor who died in 1910, and the novelist, Sir Hall Caine (died 1931), whose tall, dark stone obelisk, designed by Archibald Knox, is impossible to miss. Then there is the aforementioned P. M. C. Kermode, who died in 1932 and is accompanied by his sister, Josephine, who was known as the poet 'Cushag'; and Sir Charles Kerruish (died 2003), who was one of the outstanding Manx politicians of the post-war period, a member of the House of Keys from 1946, who became Speaker in 1962 and then President of Tynwald from 1990 until his retirement in 2000.

In the south-east corner of the churchyard is a memorial to four American fighter pilots of the RAF's 133 (Eagle) Squadron, who were killed when their aircraft crashed on farmland at Ballafayle and Ballaskeig on 8 October 1941. Fifteen Hurricane fighter aircraft had taken off from RAF Sealand, near Chester, that day to fly to Northern Ireland, and were due to refuel in the Isle of Man on the way. Some landed at Jurby, others at Andreas. Of the remaining four, one was seen to be on fire before crashing into a field, and the others were heard flying above the cloud, first from east to west, then west to east, as if unsure of their positions. They then (apparently) attempted to get under the lowering cloud, with fatal results. One of the locals who ran to the scene of the crashes in the forlorn hope of being able to render assistance was a young Charles Kerruish, who had yet to make his entry into Manx politics. The four who lost their lives were among the many who crossed the Atlantic to join the RAF before their own country officially joined the war. The Eagle Squadrons were formed to accommodate them; 133 Squadron was the third such squadron to be formed.

Kirk Maughold's collection of ancient crosses, which includes almost a third of the island's pre-Norse specimens, is assembled in the cross-house beside the church. The magnificent medieval Maughold Cross, which stood outside until 1989, is now housed in the church, protected from the ravages of the weather. Carved in the fourteenth century from an 8-foot (2.4m) pillar of St Bees sandstone, it is generally held as presenting one of the two earliest examples of the three legs of Man, the other being on the haft of the Manx sword of state.

The summit of Maughold Head rises some 300 yards east of the parish church. From the cliff-top beyond, its eastern face descends precipitously to a secluded little cove at Traie Curn, 'shore of the cairns', overlooked by the lighthouse (now

Traie Curn, at the foot of Maughold Head

fully automated) which marks the island's eastern extremity. This is the place where (tradition has it), during the Kingdom of Man and the Isles, the eight members of the Keys representing the 'Out Isles' (the Hebrides) would land each year to attend the midsummer gathering of Tynwald. Welcomed ashore by the sixteen Keys of Man – who had already made the perilous descent of the cliff – the twenty-four would make the equally perilous ascent from the shore to begin the journey to Tynwald Hill. The old Manx name for Traie Curn was *Purt ny Kiare as Feed*, 'port of the four and twenty', and their route from the shore to the cliff-top – their 'road' – was the *Raad ny Kiare as Feed*. But, once again, the question: why would anyone choose such a hazardous start to a journey when there existed so many more benign landing sites – to the north of the headland, there lay Ramsey, Port Lewaigue and Port e Vullen; to the south, Dhyrnane, Port Mooar, Port Cornaa and Dhoon Bay. And why did they need to land so far north anyway? It remains a puzzle. Through the ages of Watch and Ward, day watches were kept on Maughold Head and Slieau Lewaigue.

The parish of Maughold is a haven of rural calm. The A18 – the mountain section of the TT course – runs on the far side of the ridge that extends from North Barrule to Clagh Ouyr, and the only highway passing through the parish which could be described as 'busy' is the A2 Ramsey–Laxey–Douglas road. It generally follows the contours that divide the lower, greener coastal landscapes from the higher slopes that rise to the west. The MER also runs through it, in its first few northern miles taking a more devious course, as it seeks out somewhat easier contours and calls at the several hamlets on the way.

Apart from the A2, the only other A-road wending its way through Maughold parish is the A15 Maughold loop-road which, having reached Maughold village from the north, strikes south to parallel the MER route for a while, before rejoining the A2 at the Hibernian, where there was once a public house of that name. The minor road which strikes off to the north here follows the line of the old pack-horse trail into Ramsey. The A15 also provides access to the very narrow by-road which climbs steeply up from Ballajora to reach Rhullick ny Quakeryn, the Quakers' burial ground, then drops into Cornaa village before climbing again to the Neolithic chambered cairn at Cashtal yn Ard, the 'castle of the height'. Both sites lie in peaceful seclusion amid glorious surroundings.

The coastal fringe of the parish has some superb scenery, especially in Ballaglass Glen, Glen Mona, Cornaa and Dhoon Glen, the last-named being short and steep and magnificent, with its waterfalls and great slabs of Lonan flagstone slanting steeply up from the shore at the bottom. To the west of the A2, there are several tracks leading into the uplands between North Barrule and Slieau Ouyr, where the two ridges of hills cradle the long valley of the

Cornaa stream. The name stems from the Norse *Kverná* ('mill water') and relates to the horizontal water-wheel which the Scandinavians introduced into Man and the Hebrides. The name of the neighbouring treen, Cardle, comes from the same root. The hamlet of Corrany, on the A2, has yet another variant of the same name.

In the upper reaches of the Cornaa valley, there is a system of deep, water-cut gulleys known as the *Breids*. In the stream below them is a pool called *Lhing Berree Dhone*, 'Brown Berree's Pool', the name recalling the exploits of a renowned Maughold witch who got up to all manner of mischief hereabouts and is the subject of an old Manx ballad. But there is an annoying lack of detail in the narrative, particularly when she is consigned to the gallows but, in some unexplained manner, escapes the final act. Thus:

> She went to the gallows,
> But she found favour there,
> And came back to Mullagh Ouyr
> Leading home a goat.

There are tales of Berree and her coven disappearing inside North Barrule, and of their shrieks reverberating into the night. So, if you do venture up there, just make sure that you get down again before nightfall.

LAXEY AND LONAN

The parish of Lonan is thought to have been named after an Irish saint of that name; the only problem has been that there were no fewer than eight of them bearing the name. J. J. Kneen considered that the most likely candidate was Lonan MacLaisre, who is recorded in the *Martyrology of Donegal*, so perhaps we should be content to follow the Manx scholar's instinct. The old parish church (Old Kirk Lonan), however, is dedicated to St Adamnan of Iona. It stands in splendid isolation about a mile south of Baldrine, on the seaward side of the narrow byway which runs north from Groudle and formed part of the old drove road between Douglas and Ramsey. It may have stood roughly central in the lowland region of the parish, but the population was so dispersed that the church stood close to no-one in particular. Dating, perhaps, from the twelfth century, it probably stands on the site of an earlier keeill, harking back to the time when there might have been a dozen small keeills dotted across the parish – one in every treen. A foundation from an earlier date is known to lie beneath it.

Old Kirk Lonan

The parish is bounded in the north by Maughold and Lezayre, in the west by Braddan and Onchan, and in the east by the sea, its coastline stretching from Bulgham Bay to Groudle. Of the parish's twelve treens, all have Scandinavian names. Old Kirk Lonan continued to serve the parish until 1733, by which time dissatisfaction with its location was rife, and the construction of a replacement was commenced, but there is some doubt as to its location. The present parish church of All Saints, on the southern outskirts of Laxey, was completed in 1837 but the instruction to demolish St Adamnan's was never carried out. Instead, when Canon John Quine was Vicar of Lonan in the 1890s, he saw to the restoration of the eastern half of the building, resulting in a tiny chapel where occasional services are still held today and the illumination is still by oil lamps. Entry to the restored half is via the roofless western portion. Out in the churchyard, an impressive wheel-headed cross-slab of the ninth or tenth century stands in a plain socket of stone in what may well be its original location. Carved with tightly interlaced Celtic designs, it is very similar in style to a slab in the collection at Old Kirk Braddan. The remainder of the Lonan collection is gathered in a shelter in the southern corner of the churchyard. Christ Church, in the centre of Laxey, was built in the 1850s, largely with the labour of mineworkers.

Although the village of Laxey has its own local government identity, administered by its own village commissioners and quite distinct from the administration
of the surrounding parish, it has always seemed (to me, at least) that the story of
the village is inextricably bound up with that of the parish. Certainly, the mining
industry of the nineteenth and early twentieth centuries, centred on the village
and its immediate surroundings, cast its influence – and the shadow of its spoil
heaps (the 'deads') – across much of the northern part of the parish and into
neighbouring Maughold.

The name of the village comes from the Norse *Laxá*, meaning 'salmon river'.
The night watch for the parish of Lonan was kept here, at the mouth of the Laxey
River. But the rise of the mining industry and the run-off from the washing tables
being discharged into the river soon put paid to the Laxey's days as a salmon river.
In the heyday of the industry, the mine workings radiated out from Laxey and
Agneash, along the valleys of the Glen Roy, Laxey and Cornaa rivers. An account
of the industry has been given in Chapter 7. Following the closure of the mines,
the affected rivers slowly recovered. At the start of the Second World War, much
of the spoil still heaped in the middle of Laxey was removed, to be used as hardcore in the construction of airfield runways. The site of the washing floors, which

The wheel from the Snaefell Mine now turns in the Valley Gardens, Laxey

received the ores from the Glen Mooar workings, has been transformed into the pleasant Valley Gardens. The ore was brought down to the village by narrow-gauge (19-inch, or 483mm) railway, hauled by two small locomotives known as *Ant* and *Bee*; they were sold for scrap in 1935 but were retrieved and now haul passengers at weekends in the summer along a section of track between the former washing floors and the adit of the mine.

There are other reminders still of the mining days in Laxey. The most famous, of course, is the great Laxey Wheel, otherwise known as the 'Lady Isabella', after Lady Isabella Hope, wife of the Lieutenant Governor of the day. The boundary of the Village District of Laxey advances just far enough up the valley to enclose the wheel within it. It was designed by a Manxman, Robert Casement, with the assistance of an outside expert named Bowden who spent a year on site, advising on it (a fact which often goes unremarked in Manx circles). Originally designed to drive the pumps which removed water from the mine workings, the wheel now turns for the benefit of sightseers only. And the sights to be seen are extensive from the top platform, reached by a spiral stair around the outside of the tower through which water is gravity-fed onto the wheel. A short length of the adit which gave access to the Glen Mooar workings (up towards Agneash) has also been opened up to visitors, and gives a fascinating glimpse of the working conditions of those times. Inside, the track along which the *Ant* and *Bee* hauled their cargoes is still *in situ*.

Since 2006, Laxey has been the custodian of a second water-wheel from the area's mining history, although not in its original location. This one is the wheel from the Snaefell mines, at the head of the Laxey Valley, just below the A18 mountain road at the Verandah. Fifty feet (15m) in diameter (as compared with the Lady Isabella's 72 feet 6 inches, or 22m), it was constructed in 1865 and continued turning until 1908, by which time the mines themselves were approaching the end of their working lives. The wheel was dismantled and left the island for use in the Cornish china-clay workings. By the 1950s, it had fallen into disuse and it lay in pieces for many years. In 2003, the Laxey Mines Research Group traced the wheel, arranged for its return to the island and undertook its reassembly and restoration. It would have been both impracticable and pointless to reinstall it in its original location, where few people would have seen it, and so it now sits in its masonry casing beside the river in the Valley Gardens, the site of the old washing floors.

At the southern end of 'Ham and Egg Terrace' (proper name Dumbell's Terrace), where the MER's Ramsey and Snaefell lines diverge, a statue of a miner stands to commemorate the Snaefell Mine disaster of 1897, in which twenty men were asphyxiated in a build-up of carbon monoxide. The name 'Ham and Egg

The Mines Tavern, *Laxey, once the home of the Captain of Mines*

Terrace' originated from the number of eating places there during the mining era; today there is just one. On the opposite side of the main road, much of the old Mines Yard is occupied by the MER station, and the former house of the captain of mines is now the *Mines Tavern*. The main road itself, crossing the river in the upper part of the village, did not exist before 1855. Before that, the only road through Laxey plunged (as it plunges still) down Minorca Hill from the north, crossing the river behind the harbour before climbing steeply out on the other side.

Laxey is a much quieter place today. The largest industrial concern in the village is the island's only flour mill (now government-owned), which stands adjacent to the attractive, DAFF-maintained Laxey Glen Gardens. Both the Laxey Glen Mills and the Gardens seem oddly misnamed, since they both sit at the bottom end of Glen Roy, rather than in Laxey Glen itself. The handsome, stone-faced building on the south side of the harbour was the mining company's warehouse. After several years as a pipe-making factory, and several more of disuse, the building is now owned by a manufacturer of heavy mining equipment as a base for its international purchasing operation. On the north side of the river, the Laxey Woollen Mill, established in 1881, is still in operation.

Returning to the old pack-horse route through the village, Minorca Hill (the

B1 road) rises steeply on the north side of the village and crosses the modern A2 coast-road, whereupon it becomes the B11 and continues north, passing the tiny hamlet of Ballaragh and rejoining the A2 at the Dhoon. Shortly after crossing the A2, the old road cuts through the site of the Neolithic chambered tomb which has been saddled with the misnomer 'King Orry's Grave' for many years. The western half of the site was previously situated in a private garden but was acquired by Manx National Heritage in 1999 and is now open to view. The site has been described in Chapter 3.

On crossing the Laxey village boundary and passing onto the hills of north Lonan, we come to one of the scenes of conflict between two groups of country-goers: walkers and horse-riders on the one hand, and off-road vehicle users – mainly motor-cyclists – on the other. Heated debate arises spasmodically in the correspondence columns of the Manx press, with each side branding the other as selfish. There should be no problem concerning those tracks designated as public footpaths, but there is; vehicle drivers and riders who use them do so illegally. A further problem arises on the relatively large number of unsurfaced tracks that are designated as 'byways open to all traffic'. As the numbers of motor vehicles using them (quite legally) increase, the surfaces become more eroded and deeply rutted and, in wet weather, the ruts fill with water. Consequently, the tracks become more hazardous for walkers and horse-riders and, in the end, such byways are no longer open to *all* traffic. These tracks, which were formed in the age of the horse, when today's vehicles were unheard of, are, in many cases, no longer fit for the horses they were created for. Meanwhile, successive Manx governments (in the form of the DoT) have made it clear that they have no plans either to control the vehicle-users or to maintain the tracks. *There* lies the problem, and the arguments continue to rage.

Let us head south into calmer climes. The southern half of Lonan parish takes on a softer, lowland mien, and there are fewer hill-tracks to suffer the same problem. But, like Maughold to the north, Lonan witnessed its own tragedy in the Second World War, and there is a memorial to this in the parish churchyard. It was on the afternoon of 14 July 1944 that a Handley Page Halifax bomber of 433 (Canadian) Squadron took off from RAF Leeming, in Yorkshire, on a training flight which would take it on a westward course to Douglas, where a course adjustment would be made. As it approached the island, the aircraft was already in trouble. It headed along the coast as far as Laxey, then turned inland before returning from the west. By this time, it was on fire and small parts were begin-ning to detach from it over Laxey. Then a wing containing fuel tanks and an engine descended on a bungalow at Pinfold Hill, before the fuselage and crew came to earth at Lower Grawe Farm. Wreckage was strewn from Gretch Veg, on the north side of the valley, to the rocks along the shore of Laxey Bay. The crew of

seven perished; six Canadians were interred at Kirk Andreas, and the seventh –
the only RAF man on board – was taken for burial in his native Yorkshire. In the
bungalow at Pinfold Hill, a three-year-old boy was with his mother and grand-
parents when it was hit by the wreckage and the ruptured fuel tanks caused a
rapid spread of fire. The occupants were taken to the military hospital in Onchan,
where the child died the following morning, the only civilian fatality in the incident.

Delving back some 200 years further in history, we find a man who may well
have been Lonan's best-known son – perhaps surprisingly so, since he left the
island when young and never returned to it. He was Captain Henry Skillicorne
(1678–1763), a merchant seaman whose story is told in an extraordinarily long and
detailed epitaph in the old parish church at Cheltenham:

> … born at Kirk Lonan in the Isle of Man in 1678, taught by Dr Wilson, … justly
> called the good Bishop of that Island. When young he went to sea [sailing out
> of Bristol] … quitting the sea after 40 Years' Service, [he and his wife] … in 1738
> came to live upon their Estate in this Town [Cheltenham], where he gave his
> mind to increase the Knowledge and extend the Use of Cheltenham Spa, which
> became his Property. He found the Old Spring open and exposed to the
> Weather. He made the Well there as it now is, made the Walks, and planted the
> Trees of the Upper and Lower Parades, And by Conduct ingenuous & Manners
> attentive, … brought this most salutary Water to just estimation & extensive
> Use … by the greatest Persons of the Age, … that the Present Most Gracious
> Majesty King GEORGE The Third, With His Most Amiable Queen CHAR-
> LOTTE … visited it. … Captain SKILLICORNE was buried the 18th of October
> 1763 with his Son HENRY, … at the West Door on the Inside of this Church …

That is not the half of the praises sung in his epitaph. From it, we gather that he
was practically the founder of Cheltenham as a spa-town. But, although he spent
most of his life away from the isle, it would appear that he never forgot his native
parish, for he donated a considerable sum towards the building of the new parish
church in 1733.

Down in the south of the parish, Lonan meets its end on the banks of the
Groudle River. Beyond lies Onchan and, beyond that, the island's capital town of
Douglas, which is where we started. Thus we come to the end of our circumambulation of this fascinating island, which offers such a unique variety of features
in both the natural and the built environments.

Epilogue

Anyone returning to the Isle of Man today from a grave entered a century or more ago would, at first sight, scarcely recognize the place. Certainly with regard to the built environment, the constitutional position and its standing in the world, the island has changed beyond all recognition. The development of new industrial and commercial activities has brought the inevitable requirement for an expanded workforce and the associated expansion of housing development. Although the brunt of modern house-building has been borne by Douglas and Onchan, it has also made its mark on the other three towns – Castletown, Peel and Ramsey – and the three administrative villages of Laxey, Port Erin and Port St Mary. Its influence has also spread westward along the central valley, through the smaller villages of Union Mills, Glen Vine and St John's. Indeed, there are few of the old centres of population that have not seen their bounds set wider, from Andreas and a clutch of others in the north to Ballasalla, Colby and others in the south. And these developments have resulted in the inevitable increases in traffic on the island's roads, which are especially apparent at peak times of commuter travel.

Some may lament the changes which have been wrought by the island's advance into the modern world, but there is another side to the coin, and that relates to much-reduced levels of unemployment and sustained growth in the island's economy and the prosperity of its people. The conditions which had to be endured in the 1950s have gone from the scene: times when men employed in the Manx tourist industry during the summer had to leave the island to find employment on the farms of Lincolnshire and East Anglia through the winter. Today, the much-reduced Manx tourist industry could not even employ them through the summer, and the much-mechanized agricultural industry over the water would no longer need them in the winter. Thus, it is fortunate indeed that the modern industrial and commercial opportunities have arisen to provide constant, year-round employment in the island.

But, away from the centres of population and industry and commerce, there is still much in the open countryside with which the returnee would be familiar.

Admittedly, modern agricultural practices have wrought some changes in lowland landscapes, but these have been relatively minor – certainly nothing to compare with those which have swept countless acres in the adjacent islands. And, beyond the mountain wall or hedge, the upland slopes remain much as they have ever been, apart from the addition of a few forest plantations, and there is an abundance of unspoilt open countryside still remaining, over which one may wander freely. Out there, the island's natural beauty stands undimmed. The Manx hill-country and much of the coastal landscapes remain as havens of peace and tranquillity, ready to engender feelings of comfort and stability in times of political and social change. And, out there in the open country, there are things to be found, features to be seen, that others before you have failed to find or see. So, dear reader, go forth and seek out those wonders of Man that others may have missed, and – above all – savour the freedom of that sweet mountain air which has nurtured and sustained countless generations of Manx folk and incomers, of whom I have been privileged to be one.

The sun sets behind Bradda Head

ISLE OF MAN NEWSPAPERS

Some Manx Place-names

A few personal names are included where pronunciation is not obvious.

Name	Parish	Derivation
Agneash	Lonan	Norse *Eggjarnes*, 'edge ness'
Andreas	Andreas	St Andrew
Arbory	Arbory	Irish saint, Cairbre
Archallagan	Patrick	Gaelic *Ard-tealchan*, 'the little height'. (First element pronounced 'arch')
Auldyn (Glen)	Lezayre	Norse *Alptardalr*, 'swan's glen'
Ayre	Sheading	Norse *eyrr*, 'a gravel bank'
Baldrine	Lonan	Gaelic *Balley drine*, 'farm of the blackthorn'. (Pronounced to rhyme with 'line')
Baldwin	Braddan	Norse *Boldalr*, 'homestead dale'
Ballabeg	Arbory	Gaelic *Ballabegson*, 'Begson's farm'. Ballabeg also occurs in other parishes, probably derived from 'little farm'
Ballacraine	German	Gaelic, 'Craine's farm'
Balladoole	Arbory	Gaelic, a farm, possibly by a 'black stream' or relating to an extinct surname, O'Doole
Ballafayle	Maughold	Gaelic, 'Fayle's farm'
Ballakilley	many	Gaelic, 'farm of the church'. Farms of this name were once owned by the Church. (Pronounced as 'killya')
Ballamodha	Malew	Gaelic *Balley Moddey*, 'farm of the dogs'
Ballaqueeney	Rushen	Gaelic, 'Queeney's farm'
Ballaugh	Ballaugh	Gaelic *Balley ny loghey*, 'farm of the lake'. (Pronounced to rhyme with 'laugh')
Ballure	Maughold	Gaelic *Balley euar*, 'yew-tree farm'
Barregarrow	Michael	Gaelic *Bayr garroo*, 'rough road'. (Pronounced 'Begarrow')
Barrule (North and South)	Maughold/ Lezayre/Malew	Norse *Vördufjall*, 'ward fell, hill or mountain', recalling the era of Watch and Ward

Name	Parish	Derivation
Billown	Malew	Norse/Gaelic *Bylodinn*, 'Lodinn's farm'
Braaid	Marown	Gaelic *Breid*, 'gorge', 'glen' or 'sheltered vale'
Bradda	Rushen	Either Middle English *Bradhou*, 'broad headland' or Norse *Bratthaugr*, 'steep headland'
Braddan	Braddan	St Brendan
Bride	Bride	St Bridget
Calf [of Man]	Rushen	Norse *Kâlfr*, 'calf', a small animal or island lying beside a larger one
Cardle	Maughold	Norse *Kvernardalr*, 'mill dale'
Cashtal yn Ard	Maughold	Gaelic, 'castle of the height'
Cass ny Hawin	Santon	Gaelic, 'the foot of the river'
Chibbyr Vaghal	Maughold	Gaelic, '[St] Maughold's well'
Claddagh	several	Gaelic, 'river-meadow or water-meadow', to rhyme with 'barrack'
Clagh Vane	Malew	Gaelic, 'white stone', one of many *claghs*
Colby	Arbory	Norse *Kollabyr*, 'Kolli's farm'
Cooil	Braddan	Gaelic, 'nook', one of many Cooils or Cooills
Cornaa	Maughold	Norse *Kverná*, 'mill water'
Cronk ny Arrey Laa	several	Gaelic, 'hill of the day watch'
Cronk ny Merriu	Santon	Gaelic, 'hill of the dead'
Cronk Sumark	Lezayre	Norse *Skammhryggr*, 'short ridge', with Gaelic *Cronk*
Cronk Urleigh	Michael	Gaelic, possibly 'hill of the slaughter'
Cronk-y-Voddy	German	Gaelic, 'hill of the dog'
Crosby	Marown	Norse *Krossbyr*, 'cross village' or 'homestead'
Curragh	several	Gaelic, 'marsh' or 'mire', to rhyme with 'ruck'
Dalby	Patrick	Norse *Dalbyr*, 'the farmstead in the dale'
Dhoon	Maughold	Gaelic *Doon*, 'fort'
Douglas	town	Gaelic *Dubhghlais*, 'dark stream'
Dreemskerry	Maughold	Gaelic, possibly 'Skarry's ridge'
Dreswick	Malew	Norse *Drangsvik*, 'rock creek'. (Pronounced without the 'w')
Droghadfayle	Rushen	Gaelic, 'Fayle's bridge'
Eairy	Marown	Gaelic, 'shieling' or 'summer settlement'
Ellanbane	Lezayre	Gaelic, 'white island', one of several *ellans* now surrounded by dry land
Faaie ny Cabbal	Ballaugh	Gaelic, 'flat' or 'green of the chapel'
Fistard	Rushen	Norse *Fiskagardr*, 'fish garth' or 'enclosure'
Foxdale	Patrick	Norse *Forsdalr*, 'dale of the waterfall'
Gansey	Rushen	Norse, 'magic isle' or 'bay'
Garey	several	Gaelic *Garee*, rough uncultivated land beside a river or stream
Garff	Sheading	Norse *Gröf*, 'ravine'

Name	Parish	Derivation
Garwick	Lonan	Norse *Gjarvik*, 'cave creek'
German	German	St German
Glen Chass	Rushen	Gaelic *Glion shast*, 'sedge glen'
Glen Darragh	Marown	Gaelic, 'oak glen'
Glenfaba	Sheading	Gaelic, possibly from an earlier form of 'Neb' (the river)
Glen Maye	Patrick	Gaelic *Glion muigh*, 'yellow glen'
Glen Mooar	several	Gaelic 'great glen'
Glen Roy	Lonan	Possibly from Gaelicized Norse *Glen Grawe*, 'ravine glen'
Glentramman	Lezayre	Gaelic, 'glen of the elder-tree'
Glen Wyllin	Michael	Gaelic, 'mill of the glen'
Glion Gill	Michael	Gaelic, 'Gill's glen'
Gob ny Rona	Maughold	Gaelic, 'point of the seal'
Greeba	German	Norse *gnipa*, 'a peak'
Grenaby	Bride	Norse *Graenbyr*, 'green farm'
Groudle	Onchan	Norse *Krappdalr*, 'narrow glen'
Hango Hill	Malew	Norse *Hangahóll*, 'hill of hanging'
Howstrake	Onchan	Norse *Höfudstradkr*, 'headland track'
Injebreck	Braddan	Norse *Ingabrekka*, 'Inga's slope'
Jurby	Jurby	Possibly Norse *Dyrabyr*, 'farmstead of the animals'
Keeill Vael	several	Gaelic, '[St] Michael's Church'
Kennaugh	personal	Pronounced 'Kenyuck'
Kentraugh	Rushen	Gaelic, 'shore end'. (To rhyme with 'raw')
Kerroogarroo	Andreas	Gaelic, 'rough quarterland'
Killane (River)	Jurby	Norse *Kjarrland*, 'brushwood land'
Killey	personal	Pronounced 'Kilya'
Kionedroghad	several	Gaelic, 'bridge end'
Kirby	Braddan	Norse *Kirkubyr*, 'church farmstead'
Kitterland	Rushen	Probably Norse *Kidja-eyland*, 'kid's island'
Knockaloe	Patrick	Gaelic, 'Allowe's hill'. (Pronounced with stress on the 'a')
Lag ny Keeilley	Patrick	Gaelic, 'hollow of the church'
Langness	Malew	Norse or Old English, 'long ness'
Laxey	Lonan	Norse *Laxá*, 'salmon river'
Lezayre	Lezayre	Norman/Norse *le Ayre*, 'the ayre', or 'gravel bank'
Lhen	Andreas	Probably remnant of Norse *Kjarrland*, 'brushwood land'
Lhergydoo	German	Gaelic, 'black slope'
Lynague	German	Norse *Lyngvik*, 'ling' or 'heather creek'. (Pronounced 'Linyugh')
Malew	Malew	St Lua or, in Gaelic, *Ma Lua*
Marown	Marown	St Ronan, or *Ma Ronan*

Name	Parish	Derivation
Maughold	Maughold	St Maughold
Michael	Michael	St Michael the Archangel
Middle	Sheading	Probably from Norse *Middalr*, 'mid-dale'
Mooragh	Ramsey	Gaelic, 'waste-land by the sea'
Mull Hill	Rushen	Gaelic *Meayl*, 'bald' or 'bare [hill]'
Narradale	Lezayre	Gaelic *yn* + Norse *Ergdalr*, 'the shieling dale'
Niarbyl	Patrick	Gaelic *Yn Arbyl*, 'the tail [of rocks]'
Onchan	Onchan	St Conchan
Orrisdale	Michael	Norse *Orrastadr*, possibly 'Orri's estate'
Patrick	Patrick	St Patrick
Peel	town	Probably borrowed English *pile*, 'fortress'
Perwick	Rushen	Gaelic/Norse *Portvik*, 'harbour-creek'
Poortown	German	Said to be named after a member of the de la Poer family
Port Erin	Rushen	Gaelic *Purt Chiarn*, 'lord's port', or *Purt Yiarn*, 'iron port'
Port St Mary	Rushen	English translation from the Gaelic *Purt le Moirrey*
Port Soderick	Braddan	Second element Norse *Sudrvik*, 'south creek'
Port Soldrick	Santon	Second element Norse *Solvik*, 'sun creek'
Poyll Breinn	Malew	Gaelic, 'stinking pool'
Poyllvaaish	Arbory	Gaelic, 'pool of death'
Qualtrough	personal	To rhyme with 'low'
Ramsey	town	Norse *Ramsá*, 'wild-garlic river'
Regaby	Andreas	Norse *Hryggarbyr*, 'ridge farmstead'
Rhencullen	Michael	Gaelic, 'holly ridge'
Rhullick ny Quakeryn	Maughold	Gaelic, 'cemetary of the Quakers'
Ronague	Arbory	Gaelic *Eairy Shynnagh*, 'the shieling of foxes'
Ronaldsway	Malew	Norse *Rögnaldsvad*, 'Ronald's path'
Round Table	Arbory	English translation of Gaelic *Boayrd runt*, a tumulus which has given its name to the nearby crossroads
Rushen	Rushen	Pre-Norse, possibly referring to a wood or peninsula
Sandygate	Jurby	Second element from Norse *gata*, 'road'
Santon	Santon	St Sanctan
Sartfell	Michael	Norse *Svartfjall*, 'black mountain'
Scarlett	Malew	Norse *Skarfakluft*, 'cormorant's cleft'
Sky Hill	Lezayre	Norse *Skogarfjall*, 'wooded hill'
Slieau Dhoo	Michael	Gaelic, 'black mountain'
Slieau Freoghane	Michael	Gaelic, 'bilberry mountain', pronounced 'farrane'
Slieau Whallian	Patrick	Gaelic *Slieau Aleyn*, 'Aleyn's mountain'
Sloc	Rushen	Gaelic, 'pit' or 'hollow'

Name	Parish	Derivation
Smeale	Andreas	Norse *Smidabol*, 'homestead of the smiths'
Snaefell	Lezayre	Norse *Snaefjall*, 'snow mountain'
Staarvey	German	Gaelic, a 'rough, shallow ford'
Sulby	Lezayre	Norse *Solabyr*, 'Soli's farmstead'
Tholt-e-Will	Lezayre	Gaelic *Tolta yn woaillee*, 'hill of the cattle fold'
Traie Curn	Maughold	Gaelic, 'shore of the cairns', one of many *traies*
Trollaby	Marown	Norse *Trolla-byr*, either 'farm of the trolls' or 'Trolli's farm'
Tromode	Douglas	Norse *Thrumsoddr*, 'Thrumr's place'
Tynwald Hill	German	First element is Norse *Thingvöllr*, 'assembly field'

Kings, Lords and Governors of Man

Date	King/Lord of Man	Date	Governor
			(From 1832, the Governor's role has been styled as 'Lieutenant Governor')
1079	Godred I (Crovan)		
1095	Lagman		
1096	Donald		
1099	Sigurd		
1113	Olaf I		
1153	Godred II		
1158	Somerled		
1187	Reginald I		
1226	Olaf II		
1237	Harald I		
1249	Reginald II		
1249	Harald II (Godredson)		
1250	Ivar the Usurper		
1252	Magnus		
1265	Magnus died		
1266	Alexander III of Scotland		
1284	Margaret of Scotland	1285	Richard de Burgh
1290	Edward I	1290	William de Huntercombe
		1293	John Balliol
1298	Edward II	?1310	Anthony de Beck
		1311	Piers Gaveston
1313	Thomas Randolph (Scottish suzerainty)	1312	Henry de Bello Monte
1333	William de Montacute I		
1344	William de Montacute II		
1392	William le Scrope (by purchase)		
1399	Henry Percy, Earl of Northumberland (gift of Henry IV)		

Date	King/Lord of Man	Date	Governor
1405	Sir John Stanley I	1405	Michael Blundell
1414	Sir John Stanley II	1417	John Litherland
		1422	John Walton
1432	Thomas Stanley I (First Baron)	1428	Henry Byron
1460	Thomas Stanley II (First Earl of Derby)	1496	Peter Dutton
		1497	Henry Radcliffe
1504	Thomas Stanley III (Second Earl)	1508	Ralph Rushton
		1511	Sir John Ireland
		1518	John Fazakerley
1521	Edward Stanley (Third Earl)	1521	Thomas Danport
		1527	Henry Stanley
		1532	John Ffleming
		1536	George Stanley
		1545	William Stanley
		1552	Henry Stanley
1572	Henry Stanley (Fourth Earl)	1576	John Harmer
		1580	Richard Sherburne
		1580	John Meyrick (also Bishop)
1593	Ferdinando (Fifth Earl)	1593	The Hon. William Stanley
1594	Elizabeth I	1594	Ranulph Stanley
		1595	Sir Thomas Gerard
		1596	Piers Legh
1603	James I	1599	Cuthbert Gerard
1607	Henry, Earl of Northampton and	1600	Robert Molyneux
	Robert, Earl of Salisbury as joint	1609	John Ireland
	Administrators		
1610	William Stanley, Sixth Earl of Derby	1623	Sir Frederick Liege
	and Countess Elizabeth jointly	1626	Edward Holmewood
1627	James Stanley (Seventh Earl)	1627	Sir Charles Gerard
		1639	Ffoulkes Hunckes
		1640	John Greenhalghe
		1651	Sir Philip Musgrave
1651	The Commonwealth	1651	Colonel Robert Duckenfield
1652	Lord Fairfax	1652	Matthew Cadwell
		1656	William Christian
		1659	James Chaloner
1660	Charles Stanley (Eighth Earl)	1660	Roger Nowell
		1664	Isaac Barrow (also Bishop)
1672	William Stanley II (Ninth Earl)	1673	Henry Nowell
		1677	Henry Stanley
		1678	Robert Heywood
		1690	Roger Kenyon
		1693	William Sacheverell

Date	King/Lord of Man	Date	Governor
		1696	Nicholas Sankey
		1701	James Cranstown
1702	James Stanley II (Tenth Earl)	1703	Robert Mawdesley
		1713	The Hon. Charles Z. Stanley
		1718	Alexander Horne
		1723	John Lloyd
		1725	Thomas Horton
1736	James, Second Duke of Atholl	1736	James Murray
		1744	Patrick Lindesay
		1751	Basil Cochrane
1764	Charlotte, Duchess, and John, Third Duke of Atholl, conjointly	1761	John Wood
1765	George III (The Act of Revestment)	1777	Edward Smith
		1793	John, Fourth Duke of Atholl
		1805	Colonel Cornelius Smelt
1820	George IV		
1830	William IV	1832	Colonel John Ready
1837	Victoria	1845	The Hon. Charles Hope
		1860	Francis Stainsby-Conant-Pigott
		1863	Henry Brougham Loch
		1882	Spencer Walpole
		1893	Sir Joseph Ridgeway
		1895	Lord Henniker
1900	Edward VII	1902	Lord Raglan
1912	George V	1918	Sir William Fry
		1925	Sir Claude Hill
		1931	Sir Montagu Butler
1936	Edward VIII		
1936	George VI	1937	Vice-Admiral Earl Granville
		1945	Air Vice-Marshal Sir Geoffrey Bromet
1952	Elizabeth II	1952	Sir Ambrose Flux Dundas
		1959	Sir Ronald Garvey
		1966	Sir Peter Stallard
		1974	Sir John Paul
		1980	Sir Nigel Cecil
		1985	Sir Laurence New
		1990	Sir Laurence Jones
		1995	Sir Timothy Daunt
		2000	Air Marshal Ian MacFadyen
		2005	Vice-Admiral Sir Paul Haddocks

APPENDIX C

Bishops of Man

Date	Incumbent	Date	Incumbent
?447	Germanus ?	1483	Richard Oldon
?474	Romulus ?	1487	Huan Blackleach
?498	Machutus (Maughold) ?	1503	Hugh Hesketh
1025	Brandon	1523	John Hounden
1070	Rulwer	1546	Henry Mann
1079	Hammond (Manx)	?1555	Thomas Stanley
1125	Walter de Coventry	1568	(Vacant)
1135	Wimond	1569	John Salesbury
1150	John of Seez	1576	John Meyrick (also Governor)
1154	Gamaliel of Peterborough	1599	George Lloyd
1158	Christian of Bangor	1604	John Phillips
1164	Michael (Manx)	1633	William Foster
1204	Nicholas of Argyll	1634	Richard Parr
1217	Reginald	1644	(Vacant)
1225	John	1661	Samuel Rutter
1229	Simon of Argyll	1663	Isaac Barrow
1248	Lawrence	1671	Henry Bridgman
1249	(Vacant)	1682	John Lake
1253	Richard of St Andrews	1684	Baptisa Levinz
1266	(Vacant)	1693	(Vacant)
1275	Mark of Galloway	1698	Thomas Wilson
1305	Alan of Galloway	1755	Mark Hildesley
1321	Gilbert McLellan	1773	Richard Richmond
1329	Bernard de Linton	1780	George Mason
1334	Thomas of Dunkeld	1784	Claudius Crigan
1348	William Russell	1814	George Murray
1374	John Donkan (Manx)	1827	William Ward
1392	John Sprotton	1838	James Bowstead
1410	Richard Payl	1840	Henry Pepys
1429	Richard Pully	1841	Thomas Vowler Short
1433	John Burghersh	1847	Walter Augustus Shirley
1435	John Seyr	1847	Robert John Eden
1455	Thomas Burton	1854	Horatio Powys
1458	Thomas Kirkham	1877	Rowley Hill

Date	Incumbent	Date	Incumbent
1887	John W. Bardesley	1943	J. Ralph S. Taylor
1892	Norman D. J. Straton	1955	Benjamin Pollard
1907	Thomas W. Drury	1966	G. Eric Gordon
1911	James Denton-Thompson	1974	Vernon S. Nicholls
1925	Charles Leonard Thornton-Duesbery	1983	Arthur H. Attwell
		1989	Noel D. Jones
1928	William Stanton-Jones	2003	Graeme P. Knowles

Bibliography

1 Bawden, T. A., Garrad, L. S., Qualtrough, J. K., and Scatchard, W. J., *The Industrial Archaeology of the Isle of Man* (David & Charles, 1972)

2 Belchem, John (ed.), *A New History of the Isle of Man, Vol V: The Modern Period, 1830–1999* (Liverpool University Press, 2000)

3 Bersu, G., *A Promontory Fort on the Shore of Ramsey Bay, Isle of Man* (Antiquarian Journal, 1949)

4 Bersu, G., *Three Iron-Age Round Houses in the Isle of Man* (Manx Museum & National Trust, 1977)

5 Bersu, G., and Wilson, D. M., *Three Viking Graves in the Isle of Man* (Society of Medieval Archaeology Monograph Series 1, 1966)

6 Birch, J. W., *The Isle of Man: A Study in Economic Geography* (University of Bristol, 1964)

7 Boulton, G. S., Jones, A. S., Clayton, K. M., and Kenning, M. J., 'A British Ice-Sheet Model and Patterns of Glacial Erosion and Deposition in Britain', in F. W. Shotton (ed), *British Quaternary Studies* (Oxford University Press, 1977)

8 Brown, T. E., *The Collected Poems* (Macmillan, 1900, reprinted Manx Museum & National Trust, 1976)

9 Bruce, J. R., Megaw, B. R. S., and Megaw, E. M., 'A Neolithic Site at Ronaldsway, Isle of Man' (*Proceedings of the Prehistoric Society*, 1947)

10 Caine, Sir Thomas Henry Hall, *The Little Manx Nation* (Appleton, 1892)

11 Chappell, Connery, *Island of Barbed Wire* (Hale, 1984)

12 Chetham Society, Publications, Vols lxi, lxvi, lxvii, lxx

13 Commissioners' Report, *Commission of Enquiry for the Isle of Man*, 1792

14 Craine, David, *Tynwald: Symbol of an Ancient Kingdom* (Printing Committee of Tynwald, 1961, revised 1976)

15 Cubbon, A. M., 'Clay Head Cooking Place Sites: the Excavation of a Group of Cairns' (*Proceedings, Isle of Man Natural History and Antiquarian Society*, 1964. Additional notes on dating, 1972–4)

16 Cubbon, A. M., *The Art of the Manx Crosses* (Manx Museum & National Trust, 1971)

17 Cubbon, A. M., 'The Ice Age in the Isle of Man' (*Proceedings, Isle of Man Natural History and Antiquarian Society*, 1957)

18 Cubbon, W., *Island Heritage* (Manchester, 1952)

19 Dackombe, R. V., and Thomas, G. S. P., *Field Guide to the Quaternary of the Isle of Man* (Quaternary Research Association, Cambridge, 1985)

20 Dackombe, R., 'Solid Geology', in V. Robinson and D. McCarroll (eds), *The Isle of Man: Celebrating a Sense of Place*, (Liverpool University Press, 1990)

21 Davey, P., 'Bronze-Age Metalwork from the Isle of Man', in P. Davey (ed.) *Man and Environment in the Isle of Man* (British Archaeological Reports, Oxford, 1978)

22 Dickson, C. A., Dickson, J. H. P., and Mitchell, G. F., 'The Late Weichselian Flora of the Isle of Man' (*Philosophical Transactions of the Royal Society of London*, 1970)

23 Dyson, John, *Business in Great Waters: The Story of British Fishermen* (Angus & Robertson, 1977)

24 Edge, P. W., *Manx Public Law* (Isle of Man Law Society, 1997)

25 Evans, J. G., *The Environment of Early Man in the British Isles* (Elek, 1975)

26 Forbes, E., *Malacologia Monensis* (Edinburgh, 1838)

27 Garrad, L. S., 'Evidence for the History of the Vertebrate Fauna of the Isle of Man', in P. Davey (ed.), *Man and the Environment in the Isle of Man* (British Archaeological Reports, Oxford, 1978)

28 Garrad, L. S., *The Naturalist in the Isle of Man* (David & Charles, 1972)

29 Gell, James (ed.), *An Abstract of the Laws, Customs and Ordinances of the Isle of Man* (Attorney-General of the Isle of Man, 1867)

30 Gelling, P. S., 'A Norse Homestead near Doarlish Cashen' (*Medieval Archaeology*, 1970)

31 Gelling, P. S., 'Close ny Chollagh, an Iron-Age Fort at Scarlett, Isle of Man' (*Proceedings, Prehistoric Society*, 1958)

32 Gelling, P. S., 'Excavation of a Promontory Fort at Cass ny Hawin, Malew, Isle of Man' (*Proceedings, Isle of Man Natural History and Antiquarian Society*, 1957)

33 Gelling, P. S., 'Excavation of a Promontory Fort at Port Grenaugh, Santon, Isle of Man (*Proceedings, Isle of Man Natural History and Antiquarian Society*, 1952)

34 Gelling, P. S., 'Medieval Shielings in the Isle of Man' (*Medieval Archaeology*, 1962–3)

35 Gill, J. F. (ed.), *Statutes of the Isle of Man* (London, 1883)

36 Gill, W. H., *Manx National Song Book* (Boosey, 1896, reprinted Shearwater Press, Onchan, 1979)

37 Hafström, G., 'Atlantic and Baltic Earldoms' (*Proceedings of the Sixth Viking Congress*, ed. P. G. Foote and D. Strömbäck, London, 1971)

38 Joachim, K., *Late Glacial Coleopteron Assemblages from the West Coast of the Isle of Man* (University of Birmingham, unpublished doctoral thesis, 1978)

39 Johnson, Paul, *A History of Christianity* (Weidenfeld & Nicolson, 1976)

40 Jolliffe, I. P., *An Investigation into Coastal Erosion Problems in the Isle of Man: Causes, Effects and Remedial Strategies* (Report to the Isle of Man Harbour Board, 1981)

41 Kermode, David G., *Offshore Island Politics: The Constitutional and Political Development of the Isle of Man in the Twentieth Century* (University of Liverpool, 2001)

42 Kermode, P. M. C., 'Knock y Doonee' (*Proceedings, Isle of Man Natural History and Antiquarian Society*, 1930)

43 Kermode, P. M. C., *Manx Crosses* (London, 1907)

44 Kinvig, R. H., *The Isle of Man: A Social, Cultural and Political History* (Liverpool University Press, 1975)

45 Kneen, J. J., *The Place-Names of the Isle of Man* (Yn Cheshaght Ghailckagh, 1925, reprinted 1973)

46 Lamplugh, G. W., *The Geology of the Isle of Man* (Memoir of the Geological Survey of Great Britain, 1903)

47 Loyn, H. R., *The Vikings in Britain* (Batsford, 1977)

48 Manx Civil Records *Libri Scaccarii*, (Exchequer books, containing judgments on breaches of penal statutes, appeals from the Spiritual Court, etc)

49 Manx Society, *A Short Treatise of the Isle of Man* (Manx Society, Vol. 10, Douglas, 1864)

50 Manx Society, *Illiam Dhone and the Manx Rebellion* (Manx Society, Vol. 26, Douglas, 1877)

51 Manx Society, *Stanley Legislation of Man* (Manx Society, Vol. 3, Douglas, 1860)

52 Marstrander, C. J. S. 'Det Norske Landnåm på Man' (*Norsk Tidsskrift for Sprogvidenskap*, Oslo, 1932, contains English summary)

53 McCarroll, D., Garrad, L. S., and Dackombe, R., 'Lateglacial and Postglacial Environmental History', in V. Robinson and D. McCarroll (eds), *The Isle of Man: Celebrating a Sense of Place* (Liverpool University Press, 1990)

54 McCarroll, D., 'The Quaternary Ice-Age in the Isle of Man: A Historical Perspective', in V. Robinson and D. McCarroll (eds), *The Isle of Man: Celebrating a Sense of Place*, (Liverpool University Press, 1990)

55 Megaw, B. R. S., 'The Monastery of St Maughold' (*Proceedings, Isle of Man Natural History and Antiquarian Society*, 1950)

56 Mitchell, G. F., *The Pleistocene History of the Irish Sea* (Advancement of Science, 1960)

57 Moore, A. W., *A History of the Isle of Man* (Unwin, 1900, reprinted Manx Museum and National Trust, 1977)

58 Moore, A. W., *Manx Ballads and Music* (Broadbent, Douglas, 1896)

59 Moore, A. W., *Manx Worthies* (Broadbent, Douglas, 1901, reprinted Manx Museum & National Trust, 1971)

60 Moore, A. W., *The Folk-Lore of the Isle of Man* (Broadbent, Douglas, 1891, reprinted Llanerch Publishers, Felinfach, 1994)

61 Norris, Samuel, *Manx Memories and Movements* (1938, revised 1941, reprinted Manx Heritage Foundation, 1994)

62 P. A. International Management Consultants, *An Economic Appreciation of the Isle of Man* (P. A., London, 1971)

63 P. A. International Management Consultants, *Economic Survey of the Isle of Man* (P. A., London, 1975)

64 P. A. International Management Consultants, *Review of the Isle of Man – UK Common Purse Agreement* (P. A., London, 1976)

65 Page, R. I., 'The Manx Rune-Stone', in C. Fell, P. Foote, J. Graham-Campbell and R. Thomson (eds), *The Viking Age in the Isle of Man* (University College, London, 1983)

66 Pennington, W., *The History of British Vegetation* (Unibooks, London, 1969)

67 Quilliam, Leslie, *A Gazetteer of the Isle of Man* (Cashtal Books, 2004)

68 Robinson, V., and McCarroll, D. (eds), *The Isle of Man: Celebrating a Sense of Place* (Liverpool University Press, 1990)

69 Savage, Anne (trans.), *The Anglo-Saxon Chronicles* (Heinemann, 1982)

70 Seacome, J., *The History of the House of Stanley* (Seacombe, 1821)

71 Solly, Mark, *Government and Law in the Isle of Man* (Parallel Books, Castletown, 1994)

72 Stenning, E. H., *Portrait of the Isle of Man* (Hale, 1958, revised 1978)

73 Thrower, L. B., *Manx Agriculture 1945-2000: A Review of the June Census* (Centre for Manx Studies, University of Liverpool, 2002)

74 Waldron, George, *A Description of the Isle of Man* (Manx Society, 1731)

75 Walpole, Spencer, *The Land of Home Rule* (London, 1893)

76 Williams ab Ithel, J. (ed.), *Annales Cambriae* (London Rolls Series, 1860)

Index

Page numbers in *italics* refer to illustrations